Lecture Notes in Computer Science 14654

Founding Editors

Gerhard Goos
Juris Hartmanis

The series Lecture Notes in Computer Science (LNCS), including its subseries Lecture Notes in Artificial Intelligence (LNAI) and Lecture Notes in Bioinformatics (LNBI), has established itself as a medium for the publication of new developments in computer science and information technology research, teaching, and education.

LNCS enjoys close cooperation with the computer science R & D community, the series counts many renowned academics among its volume editors and paper authors, and collaborates with prestigious societies. Its mission is to serve this international community by providing an invaluable service, mainly focused on the publication of conference and workshop proceedings and postproceedings. LNCS commenced publication in 1973.

Marc Joye · Gregor Leander
Editors

Advances in Cryptology – EUROCRYPT 2024

43rd Annual International Conference on the Theory
and Applications of Cryptographic Techniques
Zurich, Switzerland, May 26–30, 2024
Proceedings, Part IV

 Springer

Editors
Marc Joye 🔟
Zama
Paris, France

Gregor Leander 🔟
Ruhr University Bochum
Bochum, Germany

ISSN 0302-9743   ISSN 1611-3349 (electronic)
Lecture Notes in Computer Science
ISBN 978-3-031-58736-8   ISBN 978-3-031-58737-5 (eBook)
https://doi.org/10.1007/978-3-031-58737-5

This Springer imprint is published by the registered company Springer Nature Switzerland AG
The registered company address is: Gewerbestrasse 11, 6330 Cham, Switzerland

Paper in this product is recyclable.

Preface

EUROCRYPT 2024 is the 43rd Annual International Conference on the Theory and Applications of Cryptographic Techniques. It was held in Zurich, Switzerland, during May 26-30, 2024. EUROCRYPT is an annual conference organized by the International Association for Cryptologic Research (IACR).

EUROCRYPT 2024 received 501 submissions, out of which 469 formally went to the review process. Every submission was assigned in a double blind way to three program committee members and, in some cases, one or two extra reviewers were added. The IACR version of the HotCRP software was used for the whole review process. In total, 1436 reviews were produced and 5200+ comments were made during the whole process. After a first round, 290 papers were pre-selected by the program committee to enter the second round. These remaining papers were offered a rebuttal to answer questions and requests for clarification from the reviewers. After several weeks of subsequent discussions, the committee ultimately selected 105 papers for acceptance.

The program committee was made up of 110 top cryptography researchers, all expert in their respective fields. For some papers, external sub-referees were appointed by the committee members. We warmly thank all the committee members and their sub-referees for the hard work in the peer review and their active participation in the discussions. We greatly benefited from the help of the area chairs: Shweta Agrawal for "Public Key Primitives with Advanced Functionalities", Serge Fehr for "Theoretical Foundations", Pierre-Alain Fouque for "Secure and Efficient Implementation, Cryptographic Engineering, and Real-World Cryptography", María Naya-Plasencia for "Symmetric Cryptology", Claudio Orlandi for "Multi-Party Computation and Zero-Knowledge", and Daniel Wichs for "Classic Public Key Cryptography". They each led the discussions and the paper selection in their respective area. The previous program chairs for IACR flagship conferences were also very helpful; in particular, we are grateful to Carmit Hazay and Martijn Stam for sharing their experience with EUROCRYPT 2023.

The IACR aims to support open and reproducible research within the field of cryptography. For the first time for a flagship conference, authors of accepted papers were invited to submit artifacts associated with their papers, such as software or datasets, for review, in a collaborative process between authors and the artifact review committee. We thank Martin Albrecht for having accepted to chair the artifact committee.

Three papers were awarded this year. The Best Paper Awards went to Pierrick Dartois, Antonin Leroux, Damien Robert and Benjamin Wesolowski for their paper "SQIsignHD: New Dimensions in Cryptography" and to Itai Dinur for his paper "Tight Indistinguishability Bounds for the XOR of Independent Random Permutations by Fourier Analysis". The Early-Career Best Paper Award was given to Maria Corte-Real Santos, Jonathan Komada Eriksen, Michael Meyer, and Krijn Reijnders for their paper "AprèsSQI: Extra Fast Verification for SQIsign Using Extension-Field Signing".

In addition to the contributed papers, EUROCRYPT 2024 featured two invited talks: "Cryptography in the Wild" by Kenny Paterson and "An Attack Became a Tool: Isogeny-based Cryptography 2.0" by Wouter Castryck. The conference also included a panel discussion on the future of publications; the panel was moderated by Anne Canteaut. The traditional rump session featuring short and entertaining presentations was held on Wednesday 29th.

Several people were key to the success of the conference. Our two general chairs, Julia Hesse and Thyla van der Merwe, did a fantastic job with the overall organization of EUROCRYPT 2024. Kevin McCurley ensured everything went smoothly with the review software and in the collection of the final papers. The conference relied on sponsors to help ensure student participation and reduce costs. We gratefully acknowledge the financial support of (in alphabetical order): Apple, AWS, CASA, City of Zürich, Concordium, Cosmian, Ethereum Foundation, Fair Math, Google, Huawei, IBM, Input/Output, NTT Research, SandboxAQ, Swiss National Science Foundation, Starkware, TII, Zama, and ZISC.

May 2024   Marc Joye
                                                                        Gregor Leander

Organization

General Co-chairs

Thyla van der Merwe   Google, Switzerland
Julia Hesse   IBM Research Zurich, Switzerland

Program Co-chairs

Marc Joye   Zama, France
Gregor Leander   Ruhr-University Bochum, Germany

Area Chairs

Shweta Agrawal   IIT Madras, India
Serge Fehr   CWI Amsterdam and Leiden University,
     The Netherlands
Pierre-Alain Fouque   Université de Rennes, CNRS and Inria, France
María Naya-Plasencia   Inria, France
Claudio Orlandi   Aarhus University, Denmark
Daniel Wichs   Northeastern University and NTT Research, USA

Program Committee

Martin R. Albrecht   King's College London and SandboxAQ, UK
Diego F. Aranha   Aarhus University, Denmark
Nuttapong Attrapadung   AIST, Japan
Christof Beierle   RUB, Germany
Sonia Belaïd   CryptoExperts, France
Tim Beyne   KU Leuven, Belgium
Olivier Blazy   Ecole Polytechnique, France
Jeremiah Blocki   Purdue University, USA
Alexandra Boldyreva   Georgia Tech University, USA
Xavier Bonnetain   Inria, France
Jonathan Bootle   IBM Research Europe – Zurich, Switzerland
Christina Boura   University of Versailles, France

Zvika Brakerski   Weizmann Institute of Science, Israel
Chris Brzuska   Aalto University, Finland
Christian Cachin   University of Bern, Switzerland
Anne Canteaut   Inria, France
Dario Catalano   University of Catania, Italy
Chen-Mou Cheng   BTQ Technologies Corp, Canada
Jung Hee Cheon   Seoul National University/CryptoLab, Korea
Alessandro Chiesa   EPFL, Switzerland
Chitchanok Chuengsatiansup   University of Melbourne, Australia
Jean-Sébastien Coron   University of Luxembourg, Luxembourg
Henry Corrigan-Gibbs   MIT, USA
Craig Costello   Microsoft Research, USA
Elizabeth Crites   Web3 Foundation, Switzerland
Bernardo David   IT University of Copenhagen, Denmark
Gabrielle De Micheli   UC San Diego, USA
Patrick Derbez   Université Rennes, CNRS and IRISA, France
Jack Doerner   Technion, Israel
Nico Döttling   Cispa Helmholtz Center, Germany
Maria Eichlseder   TU Graz, Austria
Daniel Escudero   J.P. Morgan AI Research & J.P. Morgan
                               AlgoCRYPT CoE, USA
Thomas Espitau   PQShield, France
Andre Esser   Technology Innovation Institute,
                               United Arab Emirates
Dario Fiore   IMDEA Software Institute, Spain
Marc Fischlin   TU Darmstadt, Germany
Chaya Ganesh   IISc, India
Juan A. Garay   Texas A&M University, USA
Sanjam Garg   UC Berkeley, USA
Pierrick Gaudry   CNRS Nancy, France
Romain Gay   IBM Research Europe – Zurich, Switzerland
Niv Gilboa   Ben-Gurion University, Israel
Louis Goubin   Versailles University, France
Robert Granger   University of Surrey, UK
Lorenzo Grassi   RUB, Germany
Vincent Grosso   CNRS and Université Jean Monnet Saint-Etienne,
                               France
Jens Groth   Nexus, Switzerland
David Heath   University of Illinois Urbana-Champaign, USA
Akinori Hosoyamada   NTT Social Informatics Laboratories, Japan
Xiaolu Hou   Slovak University of Technology, Slovakia
Tibor Jager   University of Wuppertal, Germany

Stanislaw Jarecki	UC Irvine, USA
Jérémy Jean	ANSSI, France
Bhavana Kanukurthi	Indian Institute of Science, India
Shuichi Katsumata	PQShield LTD, UK, and AIST, Japan
Ilan Komargodski	Hebrew University of Jerusalem and NTT Research, Israel
Yashvanth Kondi	Aarhus University, Denmark
Venkata Koppula	IIT Delhi, India
Fabien Laguillaumie	Université de Montpellier, LIRMM, France
Wei-Kai Lin	University of Virginia, USA
Jiahui Liu	The University of Texas at Austin, USA
Chen-Da Liu-Zhang	HSLU and Web3 Foundation, Switzerland
Mark Manulis	Universität der Bundeswehr, Munich, Germany
Bart Mennink	Radboud University, The Netherlands
Pratyay Mukherjee	Supra Research, USA
Ruben Niederhagen	Academia Sinica, Taiwan, and University of Southern Denmark, Denmark
Svetla Nikova	KU Leuven, Belgium, and University of Bergen, Norway
Ryo Nishimaki	NTT Social Informatics Laboratories, Japan
Anca Nitulescu	Protocol Labs, France
Ariel Nof	Bar Ilan University, Israel
Kaisa Nyberg	Aalto University, Finland
Jiaxin Pan	University of Kassel, Germany and NTNU, Norway
Omer Paneth	Tel Aviv University, Israel
Arpita Patra	Indian Institute of Science, India
Duong Hieu Phan	Telecom Paris, France
Raphael C.-W. Phan	Monash University, Malaysia
Stjepan Picek	Radboud University, The Netherlands
Thomas Pornin	NCC Group, Canada
Manoj Prabhakaran	IIT Bombay, India
Carla Ràfols	Universitat Pompeu Fabra, Spain
Divya Ravi	Aarhus University, Denmark
Doreen Riepel	UC San Diego, USA
Matthieu Rivain	CryptoExperts, France
Mélissa Rossi	ANSSI, France
Adeline Roux-Langlois	CNRS, GREYC, France
Andy Rupp	University of Luxembourg, Luxembourg, and KASTEL SRL, Germany
Alessandra Scafuro	NC State University, USA
Peter Scholl	Aarhus University, Denmark

André Schrottenloher	Inria, Université de Rennes, IRISA, France
Peter Schwabe	MPI-SP, Germany, and Radboud University, The Netherlands
Yannick Seurin	Ledger, France
Mark Simkin	Ethereum Foundation, Denmark
Pratik Soni	University of Utah, USA
Akshayaram Srinivasan	University of Toronto, Canada
Damien Stehlé	CryptoLab, France
Siwei Sun	Chinese Academy of Sciences, China
Berk Sunar	Worcester Polytechnic Institute, USA
Yosuke Todo	NTT Social Informatics Laboratories, Japan
Junichi Tomida	NTT Social Informatics Laboratories, Japan
Serge Vaudenay	EPFL, Switzerland
Frederik Vercauteren	KU Leuven, Belgium
Ivan Visconti	University of Salerno, Italy
David Wu	UT Austin, USA
Mark Zhandry	NTT Research, USA

External Reviewers

Marius A. Aardal
Aysajan Abdin
Ittai Abraham
Damiano Abram
Hamza Abusalah
Anasuya Acharya
Léo Ackermann
Amit Agarwal
Ahmet Agirtas
Prabhanjan Ananth
Yoshinoro Aono
Ananya Appan
Nicolas Aragon
Arasu Arun
Gennaro Avitabile
Renas Bacho
Youngjin Bae
David Balbas
Marshall Ball
Fabio Banfi
Zhenzhen Bao
Manuel Barbosa

Augustin Bariant
Cruz Barnum
Khashayar Barooti
James Bartusek
Balthazar Bauer
Amit Behera
Shalev Ben-David
Shany Ben-David
Omri Ben-Eliezer
Loris Bergerat
Ward Beullens
Varsha Bhat
Ritam Bhaumik
Kaartik Bhushan
Alexander Bienstock
Alexander Block
Erica Blum
Jan Bobolz
Nicolas Bon
Charlotte Bonte
Carl Bootland
Joppe Bos

Katharina Boudgoust
Alexandre Bouez
Clemence Bouvier
Cyril Bouvier
Pedro Branco
Nicholas Brandt
Lennart Braun
Alessio Caminata
Matteo Campanelli
Sébastien Canard
Kevin Carrier
Ignacio Cascudo
Gaëtan Cassiers
Guilhem Castagnos
Wouter Castryck
Pierre-Louis Cayrel
André Chailloux
Debasmita Chakraborty
Hubert Chan
Anirudh Chandramouli
Rahul Chatterjee
Rohit Chatterjee
Mingjie Chen
Yanlin Chen
Yilei Chen
Yu Long Chen
Jesús-Javier Chi-Domínguez
Ilaria Chillotti
Hyeongmin Choe
Wonseok Choi
Wutichai Chongchitmate
Arka Ra Choudhuri
Hao Chung
Kai-Min Chung
Michele Ciampi
Sebastian Clermont
Benoît Cogliati
Daniel Collins
Brice Colombier
Sandro Coretti
Alain Couvreur
Daniele Cozzo
Wei Dai
Quang Dao
Debajyoti Das

Sourav Das
Pratish Datta
Emma Dauterman
Gareth T. Davies
Leo de Castro
Thomas De Cnudde
Paola de Perthuis
Giovanni Deligios
Cyprien Delpech de Saint Guilhem
Rafael del Pino
Amit Deo
Julien Devevey
Siemen Dhooghe
Zijing Di
Emanuele Di Giandomenico
Christoph Dobraunig
Rafael Dowsley
Leo Ducas
Jesko Dujmovic
Betül Durak
Avijit Dutta
Christoph Egger
Martin Ekera
Felix Engelmann
Simon Erfurth
Reo Eriguchi
Jonathan Komada Eriksen
Hülya Evkan
Thibauld Feneuil
Giacomo Fenzi
Rex Fernando
Valerie Fetzer
Rune Fiedler
Ben Fisch
Matthias Fitzi
Nils Fleischhacker
Pouyan Forghani
Boris Fouotsa
Cody Freitag
Sapir Freizeit
Daniele Friolo
Paul Frixons
Margot Funk
Phillip Gajland
Daniel Gardham

Rachit Garg
Francois Garillot
Gayathri Garimella
John Gaspoz
Robin Geelen
Paul Gerhart
Diana Ghinea
Satrajit Ghosh
Ashrujit Ghoshol
Emanuele Giunta
Kristian Gjøsteen
Aarushi Goel
Evangelos Gkoumas
Eli Goldin
Rishab Goyal
Adam Groce
Ziyi Guan
Zichen Gui
Antonio Guimaraes
Felix Günther
Kanav Gupta
Nirupam Gupta
Kamil Doruk Gur
Hosein Hadipour
Mohammad Hajiabadi
Ghaith Hammouri
Guillaume Hanrot
Keisuke Hara
Patrick Harasser
Dominik Hartmann
Keitaro Hashimoto
Rachelle Heim
Nadia Heninger
Alexandra Henzinger
Julius Hermelink
Julia Hesse
Hans Heum
Shuichi Hirahara
Taiga Hiroka
Marc Houben
James Hsin-Yu Chiang
Kai Hu
Yungcong Hu
Tao Huang
Zhenyu Huang

Loïs Huguenin-Dumittan
James Hulett
Atsunori Ichikawa
Akiko Inoue
Tetsu Iwata
Joseph Jaeger
Jonas Janneck
Dirmanto Jap
Samuel Jaques
Ruta Jawale
Corentin Jeudy
Ashwin Jha
Dan Jones
Philipp Jovanovic
Bernhard Jungk
Fatih Kaleoglu
Chethan Kamath
Jiayi Kang
Minsik Kang
Julia Kastner
Hannah Keller
Qiao Kexin
Mustafa Khairallah
Dmitry Khovratovich
Ryo Kikuchi
Jiseung Kim
Elena Kirshanova
Fuyuki Kitagawa
Michael Klooß
Christian Knabenhans
Lisa Kohl
Sebastian Kolby
Dimitris Kolonelos
Chelsea Komlo
Anders Konring
Nishat Koti
Mukul Kulkarni
Protik Kumar Paul
Simran Kumari
Norman Lahr
Russell W. F. Lai
Baptiste Lambin
Oleksandra Lapiha
Eysa Lee
Joohee Lee

Jooyoung Lee
Seunghoon Lee
Ryan Lehmkuhl
Tancrède Lepoint
Matthieu Lequesne
Andrea Lesavourey
Baiyu Li
Shun Li
Xingjian Li
Zengpeng Li
Xiao Liang
Chuanwei Lin
Fuchun Lin
Yao-Ting Lin
Fukang Liu
Peiyuan Liu
Qipeng Liu
Patrick Longa
Julian Loss
Paul Lou
George Lu
Steve Lu
Zhenghao Lu
Reinhard Lüftenegger
Vadim Lyubashevsky
Fermi Ma
Varun Madathil
Christian Majenz
Giulio Malavolta
Mary Maller
Nathan Manohar
Mario Marhuenda Beltrán
Ange Martinelli
Elisaweta Masserova
Takahiro Matsuda
Christian Matt
Noam Mazor
Pierrick Méaux
Jeremias Mechler
Jonas Meers
Willi Meier
Kelsey Melissaris
Nikolas Melissaris
Michael Meyer
Pierre Meyer

Charles Meyer-Hilfiger
Peihan Miao
Chohong Min
Brice Minaud
Kazuhiko Minematsu
Tomoyuki Morimae
Hiraku Morita
Mahnush Movahedi
Anne Mueller
Michael Naehrig
Marcel Nageler
Vineet Nair
Yusuke Naito
Varun Narayanan
Hugo Nartz
Shafik Nassar
Patrick Neumann
Lucien K. L. Ng
Ruth Ng
Dinh Duy Nguyen
Jérôme Nguyen
Khoa Nguyen
Ky Nguyen
Ngoc Khanh Nguyen
Phong Nguyen
Phuong Hoa Nguyen
Thi Thu Quyen Nguyen
Viet-Sang Nguyen
Georgio Nicolas
Guilhem Niot
Julian Nowakowski
Koji Nuida
Sabine Oechsner
Kazuma Ohara
Olya Ohrimenko
Jean-Baptiste Orfila
Astrid Ottenhues
Rasmus Pagh
Arghya Pal
Tapas Pal
Mahak Pancholi
Omkant Pandey
Lorenz Panny
Jai Hyun Park
Nikitas Paslis

Alain Passelègue
Rutvik Patel
Shravani Patil
Sikhar Patranabis
Robi Pedersen
Alice Pellet-Mary
Hilder V. L. Pereira
Guilherme Perin
Léo Perrin
Thomas Peters
Richard Petri
Krzysztof Pietrzak
Benny Pinkas
Guru-Vamsi Policharla
Eamonn Postlethwaite
Thomas Prest
Ludo Pulles
Kirthivaasan Puniamurthy
Luowen Qian
Kexin Qiao
Xianrui Qin
Willy Quach
Rahul Rachuri
Rajeev Raghunath
Ahmadreza Rahimi
Markus Raiber
Justin Raizes
Bhavish Raj Gopal
Sailaja Rajanala
Hugues Randriam
Rishabh Ranjan
Shahram Rasoolzadeh
Christian Rechberger
Michael Reichle
Krijn Reijnders
Jean-René Reinhard
Bhaskar Roberts
Andrei Romashchenko
Maxime Roméas
Franck Rondepierre
Schuyler Rosefield
Mike Rosulek
Dragos Rotaru
Yann Rotella
Lior Rotem

Lawrence Roy
Ittai Rubinstein
Luigi Russo
Keegan Ryan
Sayandeep Saha
Yusuke Sakai
Matteo Salvino
Simona Samardjiska
Olga Sanina
Antonio Sanso
Giacomo Santato
Paolo Santini
Maria Corte-Real Santos
Roozbeh Sarenche
Pratik Sarkar
Yu Sasaki
Rahul Satish
Sarah Scheffler
Dominique Schröder
Jacob Schuldt
Mark Schultz-Wu
Gregor Seiler
Sruthi Sekar
Nicolas Sendrier
Akash Shah
Laura Shea
Yixin Shen
Yu Shen
Omri Shmueli
Ferdinand Sibleyras
Janno Siim
Tjerand Silde
Jaspal Singh
Nitin Singh
Rohit Sinha
Luisa Siniscalchi
Naomi Sirkin
Daniel Slamanig
Daniel Smith-Tone
Yifan Song
Yongsoo Song
Eduardo Soria-Vazquez
Nick Spooner
Mahesh Sreekumar Rajasree
Sriram Sridhar

Srivatsan Sridhar
Lukas Stennes
Gilad Stern
Marc Stöttinger
Bing Sun
Ling Sun
Ajith Suresh
Elias Suvanto
Jakub Szefer
Akira Takahashi
Abdullah Talayhan
Abdul Rahman Taleb
Suprita Talnikar
Tianxin Tang
Samuel Tap
Stefano Tessaro
Jean-Pierre Tillich
Ivan Tjuawinata
Patrick Towa
Kazunari Tozawa
Bénédikt Tran
Daniel Tschudi
Yiannis Tselekounis
Ida Tucker
Nirvan Tyagi
LaKyah Tyner
Rei Ueno
Gilles Van Assche
Wessel Van Woerden
Nikhil Vanjani
Marloes Venema
Michiel Verbauwhede
Javier Verbel
Tanner Verber
Damien Vergnaud
Fernando Virdia
Damian Vizár
Benedikt Wagner
Roman Walch
Julian Wälde

Alexandre Wallet
Chenghong Wang
Mingyuan Wang
Qingju Wang
Xunhua Wang
Yuyu Wang
Alice Wanner
Fiona Weber
Christian Weinert
Weiqiangg Wen
Chenkai Weng
Ivy K. Y. Woo
Lichao Wu
Keita Xagawa
Aayush Yadav
Anshu Yadav
Saikumar Yadugiri
Shota Yamada
Takashi Yamakawa
Hailun Yan
Yibin Yang
Kevin Yeo
Eylon Yogev
Yang Yu
Chen Yuan
Mohammad Zaheri
Gabriel Zaid
Riccardo Zanotto
Arantxa Zapico
Maryam Zarezadeh
Greg Zaverucha
Marcin Zawada
Runzhi Zeng
Tina Zhang
Yinuo Zhang
Yupeng Zhang
Yuxi Zheng
Mingxun Zhou
Chenzhi Zhu

Contents – Part IV

Theoretical Foundations (II/II)

The NISQ Complexity of Collision Finding

Yassine Hamoudi[1]([✉])[iD], Qipeng Liu[2][iD], and Makrand Sinha[3][iD]

[1] Université de Bordeaux, CNRS, LaBRI, Talence, France
ys.hamoudi@gmail.com
[2] University of California at San Diego, La Jolla, USA
[3] University of Illinois, Urbana-Champaign, Champaign, USA
msinha@illinois.edu

Abstract. Collision-resistant hashing, a fundamental primitive in modern cryptography, ensures that there is no efficient way to find distinct inputs that produce the same hash value. This property underpins the security of various cryptographic applications, making it crucial to understand its complexity. The complexity of this problem is well-understood in the classical setting and $\Theta(N^{1/2})$ queries are needed to find a collision. However, the advent of quantum computing has introduced new challenges since quantum adversaries—equipped with the power of quantum queries—can find collisions much more efficiently. Brassard, Høyer and Tapp [15] and Aaronson and Shi [3] established that full-scale quantum adversaries require $\Theta(N^{1/3})$ queries to find a collision, prompting a need for longer hash outputs, which impacts efficiency in terms of the key lengths needed for security.

This paper explores the implications of quantum attacks in the Noisy-Intermediate Scale Quantum (NISQ) era. In this work, we investigate three different models for NISQ algorithms and achieve *tight bounds for all of them*:

1. A hybrid algorithm making adaptive quantum or classical queries but with a limited quantum query budget, or
2. A quantum algorithm with access to a noisy oracle, subject to a dephasing or depolarizing channel, or
3. A hybrid algorithm with an upper bound on its maximum quantum depth; *i.e.* a classical algorithm aided by low-depth quantum circuits.

In fact, our results handle all regimes between NISQ and full-scale quantum computers. Previously, only results for the preimage search problem were known for these models (by Sun and Zheng [50], Rosmanis [45,46], Chen, Cotler, Huang and Li [17]) while nothing was known about the collision finding problem.

Along with our main results, we develop an information-theoretic framework for recording query transcripts of quantum-classical algorithms. The main feature of this framework is that it allows us to record queries in two incompatible bases—classical queries in the standard basis and quantum queries in the Fourier basis—consistently. We call the framework the *hybrid compressed oracle* as it naturally interpolates between the classical way of recording queries and the compressed oracle

The full version of the paper is accessible at [30].

© International Association for Cryptologic Research 2024
M. Joye and G. Leander (Eds.): EUROCRYPT 2024, LNCS 14654, pp. 3–32, 2024.
https://doi.org/10.1007/978-3-031-58737-5_1

framework of Zhandry for recording quantum queries. We demonstrate its applicability by giving simpler proofs of the optimal lower bounds for NISQ preimage search and by showing optimal lower bounds for NISQ collision finding.

Keywords: Query complexity · Collision finding · Preimage search · NISQ

1   Introduction

In modern cryptography, collision-resistant hashing stands as a cornerstone, providing countless cryptographic protocols and systems. Collision resistance refers to the intractability of recovering two distinct inputs that produce the same hash value. Collision resistance is crucial to establishing the security of many cryptographic applications, including digital signatures [37], Merkle trees [41], zero-knowledge proofs/arguments [10], and many more. Thus, understanding collision resistance (or the complexity of collision finding) is particularly important to understand the security of these cryptographic applications.

The so-called generic attacks or black-box query model has received a lot of attention in understanding the security of various cryptographic primitives. In this model, when working with hash functions, an algorithm can only take advantage of the input-output behavior of the function, but does not have access to its actual implementation or other side-information. This approach not only provides simpler proof techniques, but indeed effectively encapsulates real-world attack scenarios. Classically, the complexity of collision finding in the black-box model is well understood. For instance, when employing an ideal hash function, denoted as $F : [M] \to [N]$, the best possible attack needs to make $\Omega(\sqrt{N})$ queries to the hash function to find a collision pair with high probability[1], aligning with the upper bound implied by the Birthday problem. In practical applications, it is imperative that adversaries with limited resources, typically no more than 2^{128} units of computational time, are unable to find a collision. This requirement necessitates a minimum output length of at least 256 bits. As an illustrative example, the latest addition to the Secure Hash Algorithm family of standards, SHA3-256, as released by NIST, frequently finds use in such applications.

The emergence of quantum computing requires us to significantly reevaluate existing cryptography since quantum adversaries can be much more powerful. In the quantum black-box model, *quantum queries*, i.e. the ability to access in superposition the values of a black-box function [16] is treated as a fundamental resource. This idealized input model gave rise to the early quantum algorithms by Deutsch and Jozsa [26], Simon [49] (paving the way for Shor's factoring algorithm [48]), and Bernstein and Vazirani [12].

For collision finding, how should we set the output length such that the hash function is still collision resistant even against quantum adversaries? Brassard,

---

[1] We remark that for typical applications the parameter M satisfies $M = \Omega(N)$.

Høyer and Tapp [15] and Aaronson and Shi [3] proved that in the quantum black-box model, $\Theta(N^{1/3})$ queries are both sufficient and necessary for finding a collision. This suggests that to maintain the same level of security (i.e., secure against quantum algorithms that run in time 2^{128}), the output length of the hash function needs to be extended to $3 \times 128 = 384$. Consequently, this adjustment in output length has affected storage requirements and the overall efficiency of various cryptographic protocols. However, as we are in the noisy-intermediate scale quantum (NISQ) era, quantum computation is noisy and quantum memory is short-lived, we ask the following question:

Should we sacrifice efficiency for potential quantum attacks, especially in the NISQ era?

The question above has a natural motivation stemming from practice. In particular, various constraints on near-term quantum hardware often necessitate the use of classical processing in addition to quantum operations. For instance, in certain scenarios, it might not be feasible that superposition queries could be made to the entire input, or the cost of making such queries might be prohibitive. Furthermore, the depth of possible quantum computation in near-term devices is also limited since the decoherence effects accumulate, thus additional classical processing is warranted to fully utilize the capabilities of such devices.

Motivated by the above considerations, in this paper, we investigate the limitations of NISQ algorithms for collision finding, as well as introduce a general technique/framework for proving lower bounds in the NISQ era. Using the new framework, along with the lower bounds for collision finding, we also give simpler and unified proofs of several results on preimage finding by Sun and Zheng [50], Rosmanis [45,46], and Chen, Cotler, Huang and Li [17].

1.1 Contributions

We first present our contributions on the limitations of NISQ collision finding.

Collision Finding (Sect. 4). The problem is to find a pair of elements $x \neq y \in [M]$ that evaluate to the same value $F(x) = F(y)$, given a uniformly random function $F : [M] \rightarrow [N]$. Classically, a tight bound $\Theta(c^2/N)$ for the optimal success probability is easily proved for this problem, where c is the number of classical queries. When a full-scale quantum computer with q quantum queries is available, one can use the so-called BHT algorithm [15] to find a collision pair with probability $O\left(q^3/N\right)$ (assuming $M = \Omega\left(N^{2/3}\right)$). However, this algorithm requires q quantum queries, meaning no noise or upper bounds on quantum depth were considered for implementing the algorithm, leaving the potential quantum speed-up elusive in the NISQ era. Towards resolving this issue, we propose three different models for NISQ algorithms and show tight bounds for each of these models.

Model 1. Bounded Quantum Queries. In this model, we consider a quantum algorithm that only has limited access to its quantum capabilities: namely, an upper bound on the number of quantum queries, denoted by q. Additionally, the algorithm can make (potentially significantly more) c classical queries. This model is closely related to "d-QC model" discussed in the line of work [9,18,24,32], where d quantum queries are interleaved with classical queries. Rosmanis [45] proved a tight bound for preimage search in this model, and posed an open question on collision finding. We answer this question below:

Theorem 5, First Bullet. The optimal success probability of an algorithm making q quantum and c classical queries for solving the Collision Finding problem is $\Theta\left((c^2 + cq^2 + q^3)/N\right)$. There is a matching hybrid algorithm that achieves asymptotically the same success probability.

Our bound is tight when $M = \Omega\left(N^{2/3}\right)$ because of the following variant of the BHT algorithm: the first $c + \lceil q/2 \rceil$ queries are classical[2] and are used to collect distinct $(x, F(x))$ pairs. If there is a collision among these values the algorithm terminates. Otherwise, the remaining $\lfloor q/2 \rfloor$ quantum queries are used to run Grover's search on the rest of F, where an element x is marked if its image $F(x)$ occurs among the collected pairs. This algorithm stops working for small domains of size $M = O\left(N^{2/3}\right)$, as is the case for the BHT algorithm. In fact, we conjecture that the optimal bound is $\Theta\left((c^2 + q^3)/N\right)$ when $M = \Theta\left(\sqrt{N}\right)$ (which is the regime of the Element Distinctness problem). We also note that $M > N$ is safe to assume for most cryptographic applications.

Model 2. Noisy Quantum Queries. In the second model, we consider noisy quantum machines, whose only noise comes from quantum queries to the hash function. More explicitly, we assume each quantum query to the hash function is affected by a dephasing noise $b \in (0, 1]$: with probability $1 - b$, it is a quantum query; otherwise (with probability b), it is a classical query. We ignore all other noises in this model and only pose constraints on oracle queries.

Theorem 5, Second Bullet. The optimal success probability of an algorithm making t noisy queries with dephasing noise $b \in [\frac{1}{t}, 1]$ for solving the Collision Finding problem is $\Theta\left(t^2/(bN)\right)$. There is a matching hybrid algorithm that achieves asymptotically the same success probability.

In the above theorem statement, we only consider $b \geq \frac{1}{t}$, as when b is sufficiently small, t noisy queries are already very likely to be all quantum. Our bound is tight when $M = \Omega\left(N^{2/3}\right)$ due to the following variant of the BHT algorithm. First, make $t/2$ classical queries to collect distinct $(x, F(x))$ pairs (note that a noisy query can be made purely classical by simply measuring both the input and output registers). Next, run bt independent instances of Grover's search, each using $1/(2b)$ noisy queries, and try to find a collision within the collected pairs. As there are only $1/(2b)$ noisy queries, each instance is a purely quantum algorithm with high probability. Thus, each instance succeeds with probability $\Omega\left(1/(2b)^2 \cdot t/(2N)\right) = \Omega\left(t/(b^2N)\right)$. Consequently, this algorithm succeeds with probability $\Omega\left(bt \cdot t/(b^2N)\right) = \Omega\left(t^2/(bN)\right)$.

---

[2] The first $\lceil q/2 \rceil$ quantum queries are also used to make classical queries.

Model 3. Bounded Quantum Depth. In this model, we consider a quantum algorithm that is almost classical, but has access to quantum helper subroutines that
have bounded depth d. In other words, the collection of algorithms in this model
can be modeled as $\mathsf{BPP}^{\mathsf{QNC}_d}$. This model captures a significant NISQ scenario
where we have access to arbitrary polynomial-time randomized classical algorithms, but all usable quantum machines are vulnerable to noise and completely
collapse after a certain period of time. This model is the "d-CQ model" discussed
in the line of work [9,18,24,32].

Theorem 5, Third Bullet. The optimal success probability of an algorithm
making t quantum queries with bounded depth $d \leq t$ for solving the Collision
Finding problem is $\Theta\left(dt^2/N\right)$. There is a matching algorithm that achieves
asymptotically the same success probability.

The tightness of the bound follows from a similar algorithm to the one in
model 2 when $b = 1/d$.

Our results are proven using a new information-theoretic framework that we
call the hybrid compressed oracle. We next provide a high-level description of
this framework. A more detailed overview is given in the full version of the paper.

Hybrid Compressed Oracle (Sect. 3). The main technical contribution of this
work is a new information-theoretic lower-bound framework, called the *hybrid
compressed oracle*, for analyzing the success probability of hybrid algorithms
that perform a mix of quantum and classical queries. As the name suggests, our
framework is an extension of the compressed oracle technique of Zhandry [52].
This part of our work broadly fits under the long-term goal in complexity
theory to develop general lower-bound techniques that characterize the *tradeoffs* between the number of queries and other computational resources. For
instance, prior works have studied the interplay between quantum queries and
memory space [8,31,38], circuit depth [9,18,19,24,32,50], parallel computation [7,14,21,28,36,51], proof size [1,2,47], advice size [22,23,29,33,42], among
others. These results are often tailored to the problems at hand and do not
provide general lower-bound frameworks however.

Our hybrid lower-bound framework departs from a recent method introduced
by Zhandry [52], called the *compressed oracle*, that quantizes the classical *lazy
sampling* technique. The classical variant of the method records a *query transcript* representing the knowledge gained by an algorithm (the "attacker") on
the input and on an intuitive level uses it to argue that the algorithm does not
record enough information via these queries to succeed. However, the recording
of quantum queries is a blurry task to define due to the no-cloning theorem and
the superposition input access. Some important features of Zhandry's solution to
these problems are the construction of a quantum query transcript in the Fourier
domain, and the ability for the attacker to erase the transcript (for instance, by
running its algorithm in reverse).

We first extend Zhandry's construction to support recording both classical and quantum queries. This is not as easy as it may seem since it requires

merging two ways of recording on distinct bases (the standard and the Fourier basis). Our solution relies on replacing the original classical and quantum query operators with two "recording query operators" (Sect. 3.1) that maintain a consistent classical-quantum query transcript throughout the execution of the algorithm (Proposition 4). In the extreme cases where all the queries are classical or quantum, our framework recovers the classical lazy sampling and the quantum compressed oracle techniques, respectively. Moreover, as in previous work, our hybrid recording perfectly simulates the behavior of the original algorithm (Proposition 3).

We then further extend our framework to record *mixtures* of the classical and quantum oracles. Such mixtures capture the model where a quantum query can collapse into a classical one because of dephasing noise. We handle this setting by interpolating between the two types of recording that happen when the query is purely classical or quantum. Our simulation is again indistinguishable from the viewpoint of the algorithm. Furthermore, we demonstrate a close connection between a mixture that puts probability $b \in (0, 1]$ on the classical oracle and the model where the quantum depth is bounded by $1/b$. The latter amounts to a complete collapse of the quantum memory after every $1/b$ quantum queries. We show that, when replacing each quantum query with the aforementioned mixture and removing the depth constraint, the success probability of the algorithm is barely changed. Hence, the depth-bounded model can be analyzed in our framework using the appropriate interpolation parameter.

Apart from proving NISQ lower bounds for collision finding, we also demonstrate the applicability of our framework by proving NISQ lower bounds for preimage search in all three models. These lower bounds were previously shown by [17,45,46,50] and we are able to give unified and simplified proofs of these results. Please refer to the full version for these results.

1.2   Related Work

Query Complexity Lower Bounds. There are two main systematic techniques for proving lower bounds in quantum query complexity: the polynomial [11] and the adversary [6] methods. A different information-theoretic method, called the compressed oracle technique, was recently introduced by Zhandry [52]. This method is useful in proving lower bounds for search problems when the superposition queries are made to a *uniformly random* function, a setting that is often used to model various cryptographic scenarios, and is commonly called *the random oracle model* in the cryptography literature. The compressed oracle technique has led to new and simpler lower bounds for certain search problems (e.g. [31,39,44]) and security proofs in post-quantum cryptography (e.g. [5,13,20,25,34,40]).

While the classical counterparts of these methods are often easy to manipulate, it is generally unknown how to adapt them to the hybrid setting. Indeed, the only prior works concerning the hybrid quantum-classical query model, that we are aware of, use ad-hoc methods that are tailor-made for the specific problem being studied.

Lower Bounds for Hybrid and NISQ Algorithms. As mentioned before, in a recent work, Rosmanis [45] characterized the optimal success probability of solving the preimage search problem, although not in the random oracle model. The proof techniques are specific to the search problem and inspired by a lower bound for Grover's search with quantum faulty oracles by Regev and Schiff [43].

Another related line of work [9,18,19,24,32] proves lower bounds for hybrid algorithms in the so-called "d-QC model" where d quantum queries are interleaved with polynomially (in the number of input qubits) many classical queries. This model is akin to small-depth *measurement-based quantum computation,* where measurement outcomes are classically processed to select subsequent quantum gates and is encompassed by our hybrid quantum-classical query model when the number of quantum queries is bounded by d. This model is captured by the first hybrid model with a bound on the number of quantum queries. The aforementioned works show that certain carefully constructed variants of Glued-Trees and Simons problems require a large quantum depth. For the preimage search problem, Sun and Zheng [50], Chen, Cotler, Huang and Li [17] and Rosmanis [46] also considered the case of hybrid algorithms that make noisy queries or have bounded depth, as mentioned above.

In post-quantum cryptography, several works [4,35] studied the post-quantum security of the Even-Mansour and FX constructions when the attacker has quantum access to the underlying block cipher and classical access to the keyed primitive. These results are based on new "reprogramming" lemmas for analyzing the advantage of distinguishing between two oracles that differ in some specific way. Additionally, [35] introduced a variant of the compressed oracle for recording both classical and quantum queries *in the Fourier domain.* It allows the authors to argue that, for a variant of the FX construction, the classical and quantum queries can be (approximately) treated as acting on disjoint domains. This method does not seem generalizable to the proof of more general hybrid results.

2   Hybrid Random Oracle Model

Below we define a computational model that captures hybrid algorithms that make both classical and quantum queries to a random function (which we also refer to as a random oracle for consistency with the compressed oracle framework). We also note that our model captures the QC model [18], a generalized model for measurement-based quantum computation, as a special case.[3]

Memory. The memory of an algorithm accessing an oracle $D : [M] \rightarrow [N]$ is made of three quantum registers defined as follows:

---

[3] In the QC model, there are $2q$ rounds of computation where in the even numbered rounds, c/q classical queries are made, and in the odd numbered round, one quantum query is made followed by a (possibly partial) measurement. The measurements can be deferred till the end using ancilla qubits.

- Index register $\mathcal{X}$ holding $x \in [M]$.
- Phase register $\mathcal{P}$ holding $p \in [N]$.
- Workspace register $\mathcal{W}$ holding $w \in \{0,1\}^*$ (the size of the register may increase during the computation as we allow appending new qubits to it).

We represent a basis state in the corresponding Hilbert space as $|x, p, w\rangle_\mathcal{A}$, where $\mathcal{A} = \mathcal{XPW}$ is a shorthand for the registers on which the algorithm operates. The initial state of the memory is the all-zero basis state $|0, 0, 0\rangle_\mathcal{A}$.

Quantum Phase Oracle. We define the quantum oracle $\mathcal{O}_0^D$ as the unitary operator acting on the memory of the algorithm as follows.

$$\mathcal{O}_0^D : |x, p, w\rangle_\mathcal{A} \mapsto \omega_N^{pD(x)} |x, p, w\rangle_\mathcal{A} \quad \text{where} \quad \omega_N = e^{\frac{2i\pi}{N}}.$$

Note that this oracle returns the value $D(x)$ in the phase but it is equivalent to the standard oracle that maps $|x, p, w\rangle_\mathcal{A}$ to $|x, p \oplus D(x), w\rangle_\mathcal{A}$ up to a unitary transformation.

Classical Oracle. A classical oracle query is defined as a query to the standard oracle that maps $|x, p, w\rangle_\mathcal{A}$ to $|x, p \oplus D(x), w\rangle_\mathcal{A}$ followed by a measurement on the index register $\mathcal{X}$ and phase register $\mathcal{P}$. Since we are working with phase oracles for convenience, we define them in the following way, equivalent to the above up to a unitary transformation.

We add a *history* register $\mathcal{H} = \mathcal{H}_1 \cdots \mathcal{H}_t$ where the c-th subregister $\mathcal{H}_c$ is used to purify the c-th classical query (there are at most t queries in total) and stores a value in $([M] \times [N]) \cup \{\star\}$. The initial state of that register is $|\star, \ldots, \star\rangle_\mathcal{H}$. The classical oracle $\mathcal{O}_1^D$ is defined as the unitary operator acting as follows

$$\mathcal{O}_1^D : \qquad |x, p, w\rangle_\mathcal{A} |(x_1, y_1), \ldots, (x_c, y_c), \star, \ldots, \star\rangle_\mathcal{H}$$

$$\mapsto \omega_N^{pD(x)} |x, p, w\rangle_\mathcal{A} |(x_1, y_1), \ldots, (x_c, y_c), (x, D(x)), \star, \ldots, \star\rangle_\mathcal{H}.$$

Since we only care about a bounded number of t queries, the above oracle can easily be made a unitary. For convenience, we denote the list $((x_1, y_1), \ldots, (x_c, y_c), \star, \ldots, \star)$ by H and we say $x \in H$ if and only if there exists $1 \leq i \leq c$ such that $x_i = x$. We use the following shorthand for appending a new pair (x, y) to H.

Definition 1 ($H_{x \leftarrow y}$). *Given a history* $H = ((x_1, y_1), \ldots, (x_c, y_c), \star, \ldots, \star)$ *with at least one star entry, we define*

$$H_{x \leftarrow y} = ((x_1, y_1), \ldots, (x_c, y_c), (x, y), \star, \ldots, \star)$$

where the leftmost star has been replaced with (x, y).

Sometimes, we will identify the above list with a function $H : [M] \to [N] \cup \{\star\}$ if there are no ambiguous pairs, i.e. no pairs of the form (x, y) and (x, y') where $y \neq y'$. We also let $\mathcal{H}$ denote the set of all possible histories H.

Hybrid Oracle. We extend the above definitions by allowing for probabilistic choices between the two oracles. This is represented by a channel that applies the quantum oracle $\mathcal{O}_0^D$ with probability $1 - b$, for some $b \in [0, 1]$, and applies the classical oracle $\mathcal{O}_1^D$ otherwise. Additionally, we assume that the algorithm is provided with a query type bit (or "flag") indicating which oracle has been applied. We represent this operation by an isometry $\mathcal{O}_b^D$ acting as

$$\mathcal{O}_b^D \; : \qquad |x, p, w\rangle_\mathcal{A} |H\rangle_\mathcal{H}$$

$$\mapsto \omega_N^{pD(x)} |x, p\rangle_{\mathcal{XP}} \left(\sqrt{1 - b} \cdot |w0\rangle_\mathcal{W} |H\rangle_\mathcal{H} + \sqrt{b} \cdot |w1\rangle_\mathcal{H} |H_{x \leftarrow D(x)}\rangle_\mathcal{H} \right).$$

where the bit appended to the workspace w indicates the nature of the oracle. We recover the quantum and classical oracles when $b = 0$ and $b = 1$ respectively (ignoring the query type bit). We will use $b \notin \{0, 1\}$ in the analysis of noisy and bounded-depth quantum algorithms.

Hybrid Algorithm. An algorithm with t queries is defined as a sequence $U_0, \ldots, U_t$ of unitary transformations acting on the memory register $\mathcal{A}$ and a list of real numbers $b(1), \ldots, b(t) \in [0, 1]$ that specifies which interpolation parameter is used at each query. The state $|\psi_t^D\rangle$ of the algorithm after t queries is

$$|\psi_t^D\rangle = U_t \, \mathcal{O}_{b(t)}^D \, U_{t-1} \cdots U_1 \, \mathcal{O}_{b(1)}^D \, U_0 \left(|0\rangle_\mathcal{A} |\star, \ldots, \star\rangle_\mathcal{H} \right). \tag{2.1}$$

The function D is chosen uniformly at random from the set $\{D : [M] \to [N]\}$. We model that by adding another purification register (the *database*) $\mathcal{D} = \mathcal{D}_0 \ldots \mathcal{D}_{M-1}$ where each subregister $\mathcal{D}_x$ for $x \in [M]$ holds a value $D(x) \in [N]$ and we define the following joint state,

$$|\psi_t\rangle = \frac{1}{N^{M/2}} \sum_{D \in [N]^M} |\psi_t^D\rangle_{\mathcal{AH}} \otimes |D\rangle_\mathcal{D} = U_t \, \mathcal{O}_{b(t)} \, U_{t-1} \cdots U_1 \, \mathcal{O}_{b(1)} \, U_0 |\psi_0\rangle, \tag{2.2}$$

where $\mathcal{O}_b := \sum_D \mathcal{O}_b^D \otimes |D\rangle\langle D|_\mathcal{D}$ and $|\psi_0\rangle := |0\rangle_\mathcal{A} \otimes |\star, \cdots, \star\rangle_\mathcal{H} \otimes \frac{1}{N^{M/2}} \sum_D |D\rangle_\mathcal{D}$.

Output. The output of a hybrid algorithm is obtained by performing a computational basis measurement on the final state $|\psi_t\rangle$ where we measure a designated part of the workspace register $\mathcal{W}$. Since in this paper the output is always a tuple $(x_1, \ldots, x_k) \in [M]^k$ with $k \leq 2$, by making k extra classical queries, we may assume that all the indices $x_1, \ldots, x_k$ are in the history register at the end.

2.1   Models for NISQ Algorithms

We describe the three models of NISQ quantum query complexity than can be analyzed in our framework of hybrid algorithms and state some of their properties.

Model 1. Bounded Quantum Queries and Adaptiveness. We first consider the case of algorithms that make only two types of queries: quantum queries and classical queries (i.e. $b \in \{0, 1\}$). Here, one can consider two types of algorithms: static or adaptive. A "static" algorithm fixes the order of which type of queries to make before it interacts with the oracle. An "adaptive" algorithm adaptively chooses the query type for each individual query, as long as the total number of quantum (and classical) queries is unchanged.

Below, we present a theorem, as a special case of [27, Theorem 1], showing that any hybrid algorithm can be assumed to be static without loss of generality.

Theorem 1. *In the hybrid random oracle model, for any adaptive hybrid quantum algorithm making at most q quantum queries and c classical, there exists a static hybrid algorithm making at most $2q$ quantum queries and $2c$ classical queries such that their outputs are always identical.*

Given the above theorem, we will only consider lower bounds for static algorithms in the rest of the paper.

Before we move on, we give some intuition on why Theorem 1 holds. For fixed c, q, there exists a sequence $b^* = b_1^* b_2^* \cdots b_{2c+2q}^* \in \{0, 1\}^{2c+2q}$ with exactly $2c$ elements being 1, such that every $b = b_1, \cdots, b_{c+q} \in \{0, 1\}^{c+q}$ is a subsequence of b^*. This was proved in [27, Lemma 1]; we ignore the proof and refer interested readers to [27] for full details. Assuming the statement about the existence of such a sequence is true, a static hybrid algorithm just picks the fixed sequence b^* and every time it makes the next query, it checks if the current query type in b^* is equal to the next query type in b. If yes, it makes the query; otherwise, it makes a junk query (for example, regardless of the query type, querying on input 0 classically and discarding both the input and output). This strategy results in identical behavior of the static hybrid algorithm and any adaptive hybrid algorithm.

Model 2. Noisy Quantum Queries. We next consider the case of algorithms that have access to a noisy quantum oracle with noise level $b \in [0, 1]$. We define this model using the mixed state representation ρ of the memory of an algorithm (over the registers $\mathcal{XPW}$) and the channel $\mathcal{N}_{\mathcal{XP}}$ that dephases the index and phase registers (i.e. $\mathcal{N}_{\mathcal{XP}}(\rho) = \sum_{x,p} (|x, p\rangle\langle x, p| \otimes \mathbb{I}_{\mathcal{W}}) \rho (|x, p\rangle\langle x, p| \otimes \mathbb{I}_{\mathcal{W}}))$. The noisy oracle is represented by the channel

$$\mathcal{N}_b^D : \rho \mapsto (1 - b) \cdot \mathcal{O}_0^D \rho \mathcal{O}_0^D \otimes |0\rangle\langle 0| + b \cdot \mathcal{N}_{\mathcal{XP}} \left(\mathcal{O}_0^D \rho \mathcal{O}_0^D \right) \otimes |1\rangle\langle 1|. \qquad (2.3)$$

This channel dephases the query registers after each quantum query with probability $b \in [0, 1]$ and appends a "noise flag" qubit indicating whether the dephasing occurred. The state of the algorithm after t queries is defined recursively as $\rho_0^D = |0, 0, 0\rangle\langle 0, 0, 0|$ and $\rho_t^D = U_t \mathcal{N}_b^D(\rho_{t-1}^D) U_t^\dagger$ where U_t is the unitary operator applied by the algorithm after the t-th query. One can observe that the hybrid oracle $\mathcal{O}_b^D$ is a purification of the noise channel $\mathcal{N}_b^D$, where the environment is enacted by the history register $\mathcal{H}$.

Fact 2. *Let $|\psi_t^D\rangle$ be the state defined in Eq. (2.1) for a given sequence of unitaries $U_0, \ldots, U_t$ and hybrid oracles $\mathcal{O}_{b(1)}^D, \ldots, \mathcal{O}_{b(t)}^D$. Let ρ_t^D be the state obtained by applying the same sequence of unitaries and replacing each oracle $\mathcal{O}_{b(i)}^D$ with $\mathcal{N}_{b(i)}^D$. Then, $\rho_t^D = \mathrm{Tr}_{\mathcal{H}}(|\psi_t^D\rangle\langle\psi_t^D|)$.*

This fact implies that the complexity of solving any problem using noisy quantum oracles is captured by the above model of hybrid algorithms. We will use this connection to derive the complexity of the preimage search and collision finding problems with noisy oracles.

Notice that our model is particularly versatile for proving hardness results (as is the goal in the present paper). Indeed, it can simulate algorithms that do not have access to the noise flag (just ignore the flag), algorithms that are subject to depolarizing noise (measure the flag qubit and depolarize the state on purpose when it is 1) and algorithms whose entire memory is subject to noise. Hence, our lower bounds apply to these models as well.

Model 3. Bounded Quantum Depth. Finally, we consider the model of bounded-depth quantum computation where the entire system decoheres periodically. Given a depth parameter d, this amounts to applying the channel $\mathcal{N}_{\mathcal{XPW}}$ that dephases all the memory (i.e. $\mathcal{N}_{\mathcal{XPW}}(\rho) = \sum_{x,p,w} |x,p,w\rangle\langle x,p,w|\rho|x,p,w\rangle\langle x,p,w|$) every d queries. The state of the algorithm can again be defined recursively as $\rho_0^D = |0,0,0\rangle\langle 0,0,0|$, $\rho_t^D = U_t \mathcal{N}_{\mathcal{XPW}} \left(\mathcal{O}_0^D \rho_{t-1}^D \mathcal{O}_0^D \right) U_t^\dagger$ if t is a multiple of d, and $\rho_t^D = U_t \mathcal{O}_0^D \rho_{t-1}^D \mathcal{O}_0^D U_t^\dagger$ otherwise. This captures the scenario where a classical computer has access to a quantum computer of depth d and performs t queries in total, which is also known as the d-CQ scheme [18, 24].

We show that any d-depth algorithm can be simulated by an unbounded-depth algorithm that uses the hybrid oracle $\mathcal{O}_{1/d}$ without increasing the query complexity significantly. Intuitively, the interpolation parameter $1/d$ is sufficiently small so that d calls to the hybrid oracle will behave almost as d calls to the quantum oracle.

Proposition 1. *Fix any d-depth algorithm that makes t quantum queries in total. Then, there exists an algorithm in the hybrid model that makes at most $2t$ queries in expectation to the oracle $\mathcal{O}_{1/d}$ and outputs the same outcome as the bounded-depth algorithm.*

Proof. It is sufficient to explain how to simulate a sequence of d quantum queries using at most $2d$ queries in expectation to the hybrid oracle $\mathcal{O}_{1/d}$. The proposition follows by applying this simulation to the $\lceil t/d \rceil$ sequences of queries occurring between the applications of the channel $\mathcal{N}_{\mathcal{XPW}}$ in the bounded-depth model.

Consider an algorithm making d queries to a quantum oracle $\mathcal{O}_0^D$. Suppose that we instead use the hybrid oracle $\mathcal{O}_{1/d}^D$ and measure after each query whether the query type bit is 0 – indicating that the query is quantum. If it is not 0, we restart the simulation (the initial memory is classical, hence it can be cloned to restart as many times as needed). The algorithm stops once it obtains a sequence of d consecutive 0 (which will perfectly simulate the bounded-depth algorithm). Since each query is quantum with probability $1 - 1/d$, the expected number of calls to $\mathcal{O}_{1/d}^D$ corresponds to the number of coin flips needed to get d consecutive heads when a coin has probability $1 - 1/d$ of coming up heads. This is equal to $((1 - 1/d)^{-d} - 1)d \leq 2d$. □

We can easily modify the above algorithm to make exactly $4t$ queries to $\mathcal{O}_{1/d}$ and succeeds in doing the simulation with probability at least $1/2$. This leads to the following corollary for deriving lower bounds in the depth-bounded model.

Corollary 1. *Let $\sigma(t, b)$ denote the optimal success probability for solving a given problem using t queries to the oracle $\mathcal{O}_b$ where $b \in (0, 1]$. Then, the optimal success probability for solving the same problem using t quantum queries in the bounded-depth model with depth $d = \lceil 1/b \rceil$ is at most $2\sigma(4t, b)$.*

While this reduction may not be tight in general, we show in this paper that it provides optimal bounds (up to constant factors) for the preimage search and collision finding problems.

3   Hybrid Compressed Oracle

In this section, we define the hybrid compressed oracle framework and prove some of its main properties. We also describe general results for constructing and analyzing progress measures in this framework.

3.1   Construction

We start by defining the compressed encoding of the database that will be compatible with the history register. For this, we first augment the alphabet used for the database register such that $\mathcal{D}_x$ can now hold $D(x) \in \{\perp\} \cup [N]$ and with the convention that $\omega_N^{pD(x)} = 1$ if $D(x) = \perp$. The initial state of the database is defined to be $|\perp, \ldots, \perp\rangle_\mathcal{D}$. We also augment the alphabet of the history register so it can also store tuples of the form $(x, \perp)$ where $x \in [M]$. We say that $x \in H$ if there is a tuple of the form $(x, y) \in H$ where $y \in \{\perp\} \cup [N]$. Note that if there are no ambiguous pairs in the list, we can identify H as a function mapping $[M]$ to $\{\perp, \star\} \cup [N]$ with the extended alphabet (we will prove in Proposition 4 that such a property always holds in practice).

Next, we define the uncompression operator S. Let $|\hat{p}\rangle_{\mathcal{D}_x} = \frac{1}{\sqrt{N}} \sum_{y \in [N]} \omega_N^{py} |y\rangle$ for $p = 0, \ldots, N - 1$, denote the Fourier basis states and let S_x be the unitary operator acting on $\mathcal{D}_x$ such that

$$S_x : \begin{cases} |\perp\rangle_{\mathcal{D}_x} \longmapsto |\hat{0}\rangle_{\mathcal{D}_x} \\ |\hat{0}\rangle_{\mathcal{D}_x} \longmapsto |\perp\rangle_{\mathcal{D}_x} \\ |\hat{p}\rangle_{\mathcal{D}_x} \longmapsto |\hat{p}\rangle_{\mathcal{D}_x} \quad \text{for } p = 1, \ldots, N - 1. \end{cases}$$

Note that S_x is unitary and Hermitian. We now define a controlled unitary $S_{x,H}$ acting on $\mathcal{D}_x$:

$$S_{x,H} = \begin{cases} \mathbb{I} & \text{if } x \in H \\ S_x & \text{otherwise.} \end{cases} \tag{3.1}$$

Define the Hermitian unitary operator S acting on $\mathcal{AHD}$ such that:

$$S = \sum_{x \in [M], H \in \mathcal{H}} |x\rangle\langle x|_{\mathcal{X}} \otimes \mathbb{I}_{\mathcal{PW}} \otimes |H\rangle\langle H|_{\mathcal{H}} \otimes \left(\mathbb{I}_{\mathcal{D}_0 \ldots \mathcal{D}_{x-1}} \otimes S_{x,H} \otimes \mathbb{I}_{\mathcal{D}_{x+1} \ldots \mathcal{D}_{M-1}} \right).$$

The hybrid compressed oracle $\mathcal{R}_b$ is defined as follows,

$$\mathcal{R}_b = S\mathcal{O}_b S \quad \text{where} \quad \mathcal{O}_b = \sum_{D \in (\{\perp\} \cup [N])^M} \mathcal{O}_b^D \otimes |D\rangle\langle D|_{\mathcal{D}},$$

for $b \in [0,1]$. The idea behind these definitions is that, for any basis state $|x, p, w\rangle_{\mathcal{A}} |H, D\rangle_{\mathcal{HD}}$:

- If the queried input satisfies $x \in H$, it means that x has been queried classically before; then we stop (un)compressing $\mathcal{D}_x$, and it behaves like a regular phase oracle on input x.
- Otherwise $x \notin H$, then $\mathcal{D}_x$ is simulated as a compressed oracle.

In particular, note that the quantum compressed oracle $\mathcal{R}_0$ only acts on the register $\mathcal{H}$ as control. We provide an alternative definition to $\mathcal{R}_0$ and $\mathcal{R}_1$ in Sect. 3.3 that makes these observations more formal. Finally, the joint state $|\phi_t\rangle$ of the algorithm and the oracle after t queries in the compressed oracle model is defined as

$$|\phi_t\rangle = U_t \, \mathcal{R}_{b(t)} \, U_{t-1} \cdots U_1 \, \mathcal{R}_{b(1)} \, U_0 \left(|0\rangle_{\mathcal{A}} |\star, \ldots, \star\rangle_{\mathcal{H}} |\perp, \ldots, \perp\rangle_{\mathcal{D}} \right). \tag{3.2}$$

Following Eq. (3.2), we define the initial state $|\phi_0\rangle = |0\rangle_{\mathcal{A}} \otimes |\star, \cdots, \star\rangle_{\mathcal{H}} \otimes |\perp, \ldots, \perp\rangle_{\mathcal{D}}$.

3.2 Structural Properties

Indistinguishability. We show that the compression and uncompression operations behave as intended. For this, we will need some auxiliary definitions and lemmas. Let us define the unitary operator S_{all} that applies $S_{x,H}$ on every $\mathcal{D}_x$:

$$S_{\text{all}} = \sum_{H \in \mathcal{H}} \mathbb{I}_{\mathcal{XPW}} \otimes |H\rangle\langle H|_{\mathcal{H}} \otimes (S_{0,H} \otimes S_{2,H} \otimes \cdots \otimes S_{M-1,H}).$$

In other words, we uncompress every entry of $\mathcal{D}$ (that is not in H) instead of only $\mathcal{D}_x$. Observe that $S_{\text{all}}|\phi_0\rangle = |\psi_0\rangle$. We also have the following proposition:

Proposition 2. $\mathcal{R}_b = S\mathcal{O}_b S = S_{\text{all}}\mathcal{O}_b S_{\text{all}}$ *for all* $b \in [0,1]$.

Proof. This is because for $|x, p, w\rangle_\mathcal{A}$, the oracle $\mathcal{O}_b$ acts as identity on the registers $\mathcal{D}_{<x}$ and $\mathcal{D}_{>x}$. Therefore, for every $x' \neq x$, we have that $S_{x'}$ in the left multiplication with S_{all} cancels with $S_{x'}$ in the right multiplication with S_{all}. $\square$

The next proposition shows that $|\phi_t\rangle$ in the compressed oracle framework can be viewed as a compressed encoding of the state $|\psi_t\rangle$.

Proposition 3 (Indistinguishability). *The states $|\psi_t\rangle$ from (2.2) and $|\phi_t\rangle$ from (3.2) satisfy $S_{\mathsf{all}}|\phi_t\rangle = |\psi_t\rangle$. In particular, the two states are identical when we trace out the database register.*

Proof. Using (3.2), the left-hand side is equal to

$$
\begin{aligned}
S_{\mathsf{all}} |\phi_t\rangle &= S_{\mathsf{all}} U_t \, \mathcal{R}_{b(t)} \, U_{t-1} \cdots U_1 \, \mathcal{R}_{b(1)} \, U_0 \, |\phi_0\rangle \\
&= S_{\mathsf{all}} U_t \, (S_{\mathsf{all}}\mathcal{O}_{b(t)} S_{\mathsf{all}}) \, U_{t-1} \cdots U_1 \, (S_{\mathsf{all}}\mathcal{O}_{b(1)} S_{\mathsf{all}}) \, U_0 \, |\phi_0\rangle \\
&= (S_{\mathsf{all}} \, S_{\mathsf{all}}) \, U_t \, \mathcal{O}_{b(t)} (S_{\mathsf{all}} \, S_{\mathsf{all}}) \, U_{t-1} \cdots U_1 \, \mathcal{O}_{b(1)} \, U_0 \, S_{\mathsf{all}} \, |\phi_0\rangle \\
&= U_t \, \mathcal{O}_{b(t)} \, U_{t-1} \cdots U_1 \, \mathcal{O}_{b(1)} \, U_0 \, |\psi_0\rangle \\
&= |\psi_t\rangle.
\end{aligned}
$$

The second line follows from Proposition 2. The third line is true because U_i only operates on $\mathcal{A}$ and commutes with S_{all} (which only operates on $\mathcal{HD}$). Finally, the last line uses that S_{all} is Hermitian, unitary and satisfies $S_{\mathsf{all}}|\phi_0\rangle = |\psi_0\rangle$. $\square$

Consistency. We aim at characterizing what basis states can be in the support of $|\phi_t\rangle$. We introduce the following vector space $\mathbb{H}_t$ spanned by *consistent states*.

Definition 2 (History-Database Consistent State). *Given an integer t, we say that (H, D) is a* history-database t-consistent pair *it has the following properties:*

1. *(DATABASE SIZE) The database satisfies $D(x) \neq \perp$ for at most t different values of x.*
2. *(HISTORY SIZE) The history is of the form $H = ((x_1, y_1), \ldots, (x_c, y_c), \star, \ldots, \star)$ where $x_1, \ldots, x_c \in [M]$ and $y_1, \ldots, y_c \in \{\perp\} \cup [N]$ for some $c \leq t$.*
3. *(UNIQUENESS) We can identify the history with a function $H : [M] \to \{\star, \perp\} \cup [N]$ where $H(x_j) = y_j$ for all $j \in \{1, 2, \cdots c\}$ (meaning no two pairs in the history can differ on the second coordinate only) and $H(x) = \star$ for $x \notin \{x_1, \ldots, x_c\}$.*
4. *(EQUALITY) The database coincides with the history on non-$\star$ values, meaning that $H(x) \neq \star$ implies $D(x) = H(x)$.*

We let $\mathbb{H}_t$ denote the vector space spanned by all basis state $|x, p, w\rangle_\mathcal{A}|H, D\rangle_{\mathcal{HD}}$ where (H, D) is history-database t-consistent. We say that a basis state is history-database consistent *if it is in $\mathbb{H}_t$ for some integer t.*

The reader may wonder why we allow the history register to contain $(x, \perp)$ in the above definition since such a case shall not occur in $|\psi_t\rangle$ and $|\phi_t\rangle$ because of Proposition 3. This is only to provide more flexibility in further analysis. We now prove that $|\phi_t\rangle$ is supported over consistent basis states only.

Proposition 4 (Consistency). *Any state $|\phi_t\rangle$ obtained after t queries in the compressed oracle model satisfies $|\phi_t\rangle \in \mathbb{H}_t$.*

Proof. We check the four properties stated in Definition 2. The first property follows from the fact that each query can increase the number of non-$\perp$ entries in D by at most 1. For the second and third properties, we note that they hold for $|\psi_t\rangle$ and, by Proposition 3, the states $|\psi_t\rangle$ and $|\phi_t\rangle$ have the same reduced density matrix over $\mathcal{H}$. Finally, the fourth property holds for $|\psi_t\rangle$ since $H(x) \neq \star$ implies that $D(x) = H(x)$. By Proposition 3 and Eq. (3.1), for any x such that $H(x) \neq \star$, the unitary S_{all} acts like an identity on $\mathcal{D}_x$. Therefore, the same holds for $|\phi_t\rangle$ as well. $\square$

Because of the above proposition, it suffices to only consider history-database consistent basis states while analyzing any algorithm and we shall tacitly assume that this is the case in any of the proofs that follow.

3.3   Sampling and Resampling

In this section, we prove that the compressed oracle follows a similar behavior as the classical lazy-sampling strategy, namely the sampling of each input coordinate is delayed until it gets queried. There are some crucial differences yet, due to the reversibility of quantum computation. In particular, a coordinate can get "resampled" to a different value with a small probability.

In the rest of the paper, we abbreviate the root of unity $\omega_N = e^{\frac{2i\pi}{N}}$ as ω. We also adopt the following notation to modify one entry of a database (we recall that for a history H the notation $H_{x \leftarrow y}$ is used for appending (x, y) to the list).

Definition 3 ($D_{x \leftarrow y}$). *Let $(x, y) \in [M] \times (\{\perp\} \cup [N])$. Given $D : [M] \to \{\perp\} \cup [N]$, we define the database $D_{x \leftarrow y}$ over the same domain as D by*

$$D_{x \leftarrow y}(x') = \begin{cases} y & \text{if } x' = x, \\ D(x') & \text{if } x' \neq x. \end{cases}$$

The next lemmas describe what happens to the history and database when making a quantum or classical query. Among all the cases described below, the most interesting one is when the query is made at an index x that is in the database but not in the history (i.e. $D(x) \neq \perp$ and $H(x) = \star$): up to a small resampling error, the database remains unchanged apart from an added phase.

Lemma 1 (Quantum Query $\mathcal{R}_0$). *Let $|x, p, w\rangle|H, D\rangle$ be a history-database consistent basis state. Then, $\mathcal{R}_0$ maps this state to $|x, p, w0\rangle|H\rangle|\varphi\rangle$ where the state $|\varphi\rangle$ of the database register is*

$\cdot\ \omega^{pD(x)}|D\rangle$ (if $H(x) \neq \star$ or $p = 0$)

$\cdot\ \displaystyle\sum_{y\in[N]} \frac{\omega^{py}}{\sqrt{N}}|D_{x\leftarrow y}\rangle$ (if $H(x) = \star$, $D(x) = \bot$, $p \neq 0$)

$\cdot\ \omega^{pD(x)}|D\rangle + \dfrac{\omega^{pD(x)}}{\sqrt{N}}|D_{x\leftarrow\bot}\rangle + \displaystyle\sum_{y\in[N]} \frac{1 - \omega^{pD(x)} - \omega^{py}}{N}|D_{x\leftarrow y}\rangle$

(if $H(x) = \star$, $D(x) \neq \bot$, $p \neq 0$)

Lemma 2 (Classical Query $\mathcal{R}_1$). *Let $|x, p, w\rangle|H, D\rangle$ be a history-database consistent basis state. Then, $\mathcal{R}_1$ maps this state to $|x, p, w1\rangle|\varphi\rangle$ where the state $|\varphi\rangle$ of the history-database registers is*

$\cdot\ \omega^{pD(x)}|H_{x\leftarrow D(x)}, D\rangle$ (if $H(x) \neq \star$)

$\cdot\ \displaystyle\sum_{y\in[N]} \frac{\omega^{py}}{\sqrt{N}}|H_{x\leftarrow y}, D_{x\leftarrow y}\rangle$ (if $H(x) = \star$, $D(x) = \bot$)

$\cdot\ \omega^{pD(x)}|H_{x\leftarrow D(x)}, D\rangle + \dfrac{1}{\sqrt{N}}|H_{x\leftarrow\bot}, D_{x\leftarrow\bot}\rangle - \displaystyle\sum_{y\in[N]} \frac{\omega^{py}}{N}|H_{x\leftarrow y}, D_{x\leftarrow y}\rangle$

(if $H(x) = \star$, $D(x) \neq \bot$)

In the above lemmas, when x is not in the history but is in the database, after making a quantum or classical query, most likely $D(x)$ remains unchanged (corresponding to the $|D\rangle$ term), but there is a small probability that $D(x)$ gets removed (corresponding to the $|D_{x\leftarrow\bot}\rangle$ term) or resampled (corresponding to a superposition of $|D_{x\leftarrow y}\rangle$ over y). We call the first term "unchanged term" (the database does not get updated), the second term "removed term" (the outcome on x gets removed) and the last one "resampled term" in both items above. The proofs can be found in the full version.

3.4   Progress Measures

All progress measures studied in this paper will be expressed in terms of the norm of the projection onto basis states satisfying certain predicates.

Definition 4 (Basis-State Predicate). *Consider a predicate function P : $(x, p, w, H, D) \mapsto \{\text{FALSE}, \text{TRUE}\}$ over all basis states $|x, p, w\rangle_{\mathcal{A}}|H, D\rangle_{\mathcal{HD}}$. We define the projection*

$$\Pi_{\mathrm{P}} = \sum_{(x,p,w,H,D)\in\mathrm{P}^{-1}(\text{TRUE})} |x, p, w, H, D\rangle\langle x, p, w, H, D|$$

over all basis states satisfying P. *We let* $\overline{\mathrm{P}}$ *denote the* negation *of* P *and, given two predicates* P_1 *and* P_2, *we let* $\mathrm{P}_1 \cdot \mathrm{P}_2$ *denote their conjunction and* $\mathrm{P}_1 + \mathrm{P}_2$ *denote their disjunction.*

Fact 3. *Let* P_1 *and* P_2 *be two basis-state predicates. Then, the projections* Π_{P_1} *and* Π_{P_2} *are commuting operators. We have* $\Pi_{\overline{P_1}} = \mathbb{I} - \Pi_{P_1}$, $\Pi_{P_1 \cdot P_2} = \Pi_{P_1} \Pi_{P_2}$ *and* $\Pi_{P_1 + P_2} = \Pi_{P_1} + \Pi_{P_2} - \Pi_{P_1} \Pi_{P_2}$. *Moreover,* $P_1 \Rightarrow P_2$ *if and only if* $\Pi_{P_1} \preceq \Pi_{P_2}$, *where* $\preceq$ *is the Loewner order.*

Most of the predicates considered in this paper will in fact depend only on the values of H and D (a few predicates will also depend on the query index x).

We define the following general notions of progress measure and overlap.

Definition 5 (Progress Measure and Progress Overlap). *Given a state* $|\phi\rangle$, *a real* $b \in [0,1]$ *and a projector* Π *over* $\mathcal{AHD}$, *we define*

$$\Delta_b(\Pi, |\phi\rangle) = \|\Pi \mathcal{R}_b |\phi\rangle\|^2 - \|\Pi |\phi\rangle\|^2 \quad \text{and} \quad \Gamma_b(\Pi, |\phi\rangle) = \frac{\|\Pi \mathcal{R}_b (\mathbb{I} - \Pi) |\phi\rangle\|^2}{\|(\mathbb{I} - \Pi) |\phi\rangle\|^2},$$

with the convention that $\Gamma_b(\Pi, |\phi\rangle) = 0$ *if* $\|(\mathbb{I} - \Pi) |\phi\rangle\| = 0$.

The quantity $\Delta_b(\Pi, |\phi\rangle) \in [-1, 1]$ represents the increase in norm of the projection onto Π after applying a hybrid query $\mathcal{R}_b$. These will be used as a measure of progress later in the proofs.

The quantity $\Gamma_b(\Pi, |\phi\rangle) \in [0, 1]$ tracks the amplitude that moves after making a query from a subspace to its orthogonal complement. In particular, if $\Gamma_b(\Pi, |\phi\rangle) \leq \gamma$, then we have that $\|\Pi \mathcal{R}_b (\mathbb{I} - \Pi) |\phi\rangle\|^2 \leq \gamma \|(\mathbb{I} - \Pi) |\phi\rangle\|^2$. In this paper, we only consider projectors Π_P for some predicates P. In such cases, we can equivalently write

$$\Gamma_b(\Pi_P, |\phi\rangle) = \frac{\|\Pi_P \mathcal{R}_b \Pi_{\overline{P}} |\phi\rangle\|^2}{\|\Pi_{\overline{P}} |\phi\rangle\|^2}.$$

Next, we give two general lemmas that bound how much increase a single classical or quantum query can have towards a target history–database pair. These lemmas will apply when the predicate satisfies the following definition, which is similar to the notion of "database property" introduced in [20,21]. One difference in our definition is that we need to take the classical history into account.

Definition 6 (History-Database Predicate). *Let* P : $(H, D) \mapsto$ {FALSE, TRUE} *be a predicate function over all history-database pairs. We say that it is a* history-database predicate *if for every true-pair* $(H, D) \in$ $P^{-1}(\text{TRUE})$,

- *(CONSISTENT) The pair* (H, D) *is history-database consistent (see Definition 2).*
- *(HISTORY INVARIANT) For every list* H' *such that* (H', D) *is history-database consistent, if* $H(x') = H'(x')$ *for all* $x' \in [M]$ *then* $(H', D) \in P^{-1}(\text{TRUE})$.
- *(DATABASE MONOTONE) For every database* D' *that is obtained by replacing a* $\perp$ *in* D *with another value (i.e.* $D = D'_{x' \leftarrow \perp}$ *for some* $x' \in [M]$), *we have* $(H, D') \in P^{-1}(\text{TRUE})$.

By extension, we say that P : $(x, p, w, H, D) \mapsto$ {FALSE, TRUE} *is a history-database predicate if it does not depend on* (x, p, w) *and its restriction to* (H, D) *satisfies the above properties.*

The next lemmas bound the progress overlap Γ_0 (resp. Γ_1) in terms of the probability γ that a history-database predicate becomes true when a new uniformly random value y is added to the database (resp. database and history). We first provide the lemma for quantum queries, which follows the ideas used in previous work, starting from [52]. Then we state the lemma for classical queries, which is new, but the core argument in the proof is similar. These results encompass most, although not all (see Lemma 8), of the progress overlap bounds needed in subsequent applications. The proofs can be found in the full version.

Lemma 3 (Progress Overlap, Quantum Query). *Let* P *be a history-database predicate,* t *be an integer and* $\gamma \in [0, 1]$ *be a real parameter. Suppose that, for every false-state* $(H, D) \in P^{-1}(\text{FALSE}) \cap \mathbb{H}_t$ *where* $D(x) = \bot$, *the probability to make the predicate true by replacing* $D(x)$ *with a random value* y *is at most*

$$\Pr_{y \leftarrow [N]} \left[(H, D_{x \leftarrow y}) \in P^{-1}(\text{TRUE}) \right] \leq \gamma. \tag{3.3}$$

Then, the quantum progress overlap is at most $\Gamma_0(\Pi_P, |\phi\rangle) \leq 10\gamma$ *for all* $|\phi\rangle \in \mathbb{H}_t$.

The adaptation of the above lemma to the classical query case requires making one extra assumption stated in Eq. (3.5) below. This condition rules out predicates that can become true by simply copying a value from the database to the history.

Lemma 4 (Progress Overlap, Classical Query). *Let* P *be a history-database predicate,* t *be an integer and* $\gamma \in [0, 1]$ *be a real parameter. Suppose that, for every false-state* $(H, D) \in P^{-1}(\text{FALSE}) \cap \mathbb{H}_t$ *where* $D(x) = \bot$, *the probability to make the predicate true by replacing* $H(x)$ *and* $D(x)$ *with the same random value* y *is at most*

$$\Pr_{y \leftarrow [N]} \left[(H_{x \leftarrow y}, D_{x \leftarrow y}) \in P^{-1}(\text{TRUE}) \right] \leq \gamma. \tag{3.4}$$

Assume further that, for every false-state $(H, D) \in P^{-1}(\text{FALSE})$, *the predicate does not become true when* $(x, D(x))$ *is appended to the history, i.e.*

$$(H, D) \in P^{-1}(\text{FALSE}) \quad \Rightarrow \quad (H_{x \leftarrow D(x)}, D) \in P^{-1}(\text{FALSE}). \tag{3.5}$$

Then, the classical progress overlap is at most $\Gamma_1(\Pi_P, |\phi\rangle) \leq 2\gamma$ *for all* $|\phi\rangle \in \mathbb{H}_t$.

Note that γ will often depend on the maximum number t of values contained in the database and in the history. Moreover, if Lemmas 3 and 4 hold with parameters γ_0 and γ_1 respectively, then the progress interpolates as $\Gamma_b(\Pi_P, |\phi\rangle) \leq 10(1 - b)\gamma_0 + 2b\gamma_1$.

Finally, we state some simple facts that will be used frequently throughout the paper.

Fact 4. *Let $|\phi\rangle, |\phi'\rangle$ be two states defined over the registers $\mathcal{AHD}$. Let U be a unitary operator over $\mathcal{A}$. Let Π, Π' be two projectors over $\mathcal{AHD}$. Then,*

- *(Monotonicity) If $\Pi \preceq \Pi'$ then $\Pi \cdot \Pi' = \Pi' \cdot \Pi = \Pi$.*
- *(Commutativity) If $\Pi = \mathbb{I}_{\mathcal{A}} \otimes \Pi_{\mathcal{HD}}$ for some projector $\Pi_{\mathcal{HD}}$ then $\|\Pi U |\phi\rangle\| = \|\Pi |\phi\rangle\|$.*
- *(Sub-multiplicativity) $\|\Pi |\phi\rangle\| \le \||\phi\rangle\|$.*

4   Collision Finding

In this section, we prove our main theorem on hybrid collision-finding algorithms:

Theorem 5. *The success probability of finding a colliding pair, in a uniformly random function $D : [M] \to [N]$, is at most*

- *(Model 1.) $O\left(\frac{c^2 + cq^2 + q^3}{N}\right)$ using q quantum queries and c classical queries,*
- *(Model 2.) $O\left(\frac{t^2}{bN}\right)$ using t queries to the hybrid oracle $\mathcal{O}_b$ where $1/t \le b \le 1$,*
- *(Model 3.) $O\left(\frac{dt^2}{N}\right)$ using t quantum queries with bounded-depth $1 \le d \le t$.*

The section is organized as follows. The progress measures needed for the proof of the above theorem are introduced in Sect. 4.1. The main part of the proof is contained in Sect. 4.2. It uses some auxiliary lemmas whose demonstrations are deferred to Sects. 4.3 and 4.4.

4.1   Progress Measure

We define three types of collision pairs that can be recorded by a hybrid compressed oracle.

Definition 7 (Collision Type). *Given a pair (H, D) that is history-database consistent, we say that it contains a collision if there exist two values $x_1 \ne x_2$ such that $D(x_1) = D(x_2) \ne \bot$. Additionally, if $x_1, x_2 \notin H$ the collision is said to be* quantum, *if $x_1, x_2 \in H$ it is said to be* classical *and if $x_1 \notin H$, $x_2 \in H$ it is said to be* hybrid.

We now give a series of predicates that characterize what types of collisions have been recorded in a basis state. Later on, we will combine these predicates together to define the measures of progress needed in our proofs.

Definition 8. *The following predicates evaluate a basis state $|x, p, w, H, D\rangle$ to* TRUE *if and only if it is history-database consistent (see Definition 2) and satisfies the next conditions:*

- *Q, H, C: there is respectively at least one quantum, one hybrid or one classical collision contained in (H, D).*
- *XQ: the predicate Q holds and the query index x is contained in every quantum collision.*

- XH: *the predicate* H *holds* and *the query index is contained in every hybrid collision* and *the query index is not in the history.*
- $\overline{\text{X}}$Q *(resp.* $\overline{\text{X}}$H*): the predicate* Q *(resp.* H*) holds, but not* XQ *(resp.* XH*).*

Note that XQ $+ \overline{\text{X}}$Q $=$ Q and XH $+ \overline{\text{X}}$H $=$ H. Furthermore, the predicate $\overline{\text{X}}$Q is equivalent to the existence of a quantum collision not containing the query index. The last four predicates are the only ones that depend on the value x contained in the index register. The other predicates depend only on the history-database (H, D).

We will combine the above predicates into the potential

$$\Psi(|\phi\rangle) = \|\Pi_{\text{c}}|\phi\rangle\|^2 + 3\|\Pi_{\text{H}\cdot\overline{\text{c}}}|\phi\rangle\|^2 + 7\|\Pi_{\text{Q}\cdot\overline{\text{H}}\cdot\overline{\text{c}}}|\phi\rangle\|^2$$

that allows for bounding the probability $\|\Pi_{\text{Q+H+c}}|\phi\rangle\|^2 = \|\Pi_{\text{c}}|\phi\rangle\|^2 + \|\Pi_{\text{H}\cdot\overline{\text{c}}}|\phi\rangle\|^2 + \|\Pi_{\text{Q}\cdot\overline{\text{H}}\cdot\overline{\text{c}}}|\phi\rangle\|^2$ of recording any type of collision.

4.2   Main Result

We now turn to the proof of Theorem 5, delaying auxiliary lemmas to later sections. First, it is simple to argue that, for a t-query algorithm computing a state $|\phi_t\rangle$ in the hybrid compressed oracle model, the probability $\|\Pi_{\text{Q+H+c}}|\phi_t\rangle\|^2$ of recording any type of collision is an upper bound on the success probability. Since a direct bound on this quantity is difficult to obtain, we instead analyze the three predicates c, H $\cdot \overline{\text{c}}$, Q $\cdot \overline{\text{H}} \cdot \overline{\text{c}}$ separately, and later combine them into a bound on the potential $\Psi(|\phi_t\rangle)$.

We first show that performing a quantum query incurs the following progress increases.

Lemma 5 (Progress Measure, Quantum Query). *Given an integer t and a state $|\phi\rangle \in \mathbb{H}_t$ with norm at most 1, the progress caused by one quantum query on $|\phi\rangle$ are at most,*

$$\Delta_0(\Pi_{\text{c}}, |\phi\rangle) = 0,$$

$$\Delta_0(\Pi_{\text{H}\cdot\overline{\text{c}}}, |\phi\rangle) \leq 2\sqrt{\frac{10t}{N}}\|\Pi_{\text{XH}\cdot\overline{\text{c}}}|\phi\rangle\| + \frac{10t}{N},$$

$$\Delta_0(\Pi_{\text{Q}\cdot\overline{\text{H}}\cdot\overline{\text{c}}}, |\phi\rangle) \leq \sqrt{\frac{8t}{N}}\|\Pi_{\text{XH}\cdot\overline{\text{c}}}|\phi\rangle\| + 2\sqrt{\frac{20t}{N}}\|\Pi_{\text{XQ}\cdot\overline{\text{H}}\cdot\overline{\text{c}}}|\phi\rangle\| + \frac{20t}{N}.$$

Recall that, by Definition 5, the quantity $\Delta_0(\Pi_{\text{P}}, |\phi\rangle) \in [-1, 1]$ for a predicate P represents the progress increase $\Delta_0(\Pi_{\text{P}}, |\phi\rangle) = \|\Pi_{\text{P}}\mathcal{R}_0|\phi\rangle\|^2 - \|\Pi_{\text{P}}|\phi\rangle\|^2$ when doing a quantum query. Hence, the first equality reflects the fact that a quantum query cannot create or destroy a classical collision. The second inequality is based on the observation that, when adding a random value to the database, the probability that it creates a hybrid collision is at most t/N since it must collide with one of the at most t values contained in the history. The third inequality is slightly more involved since it must also take into account the case of *removing* a hybrid collision from the history-database.

We next look at the progress increase when the query is classical.

Lemma 6 (Progress Measure, Classical Query). *Given an integer t and a state $|\phi\rangle \in \mathbb{H}_t$ with norm at most 1, the progress caused by one classical query on $|\phi\rangle$ are at most,*

$$\Delta_1(\Pi_{\mathrm{C}}, |\phi\rangle) \le 2\|\Pi_{\mathrm{XH}\cdot\overline{\mathrm{C}}}|\phi\rangle\|^2 + \delta_1 + \frac{4t}{N},$$

$$\Delta_1(\Pi_{\mathrm{H}\cdot\overline{\mathrm{C}}}, |\phi\rangle) \le -\|\Pi_{\mathrm{XH}\cdot\overline{\mathrm{C}}}|\phi\rangle\|^2 + 2\|\Pi_{\mathrm{XQ}\cdot\overline{\mathrm{H}}\cdot\overline{\mathrm{C}}}|\phi\rangle\|^2 - \delta_1 + 2\delta_2 + \frac{12t}{N},$$

$$\Delta_1(\Pi_{\mathrm{Q}\cdot\overline{\mathrm{H}}\cdot\overline{\mathrm{C}}}, |\phi\rangle) \le \sqrt{\frac{2t}{N}}\|\Pi_{\mathrm{XH}\cdot\overline{\mathrm{C}}}|\phi\rangle\| - \|\Pi_{\mathrm{XQ}\cdot\overline{\mathrm{H}}\cdot\overline{\mathrm{C}}}|\phi\rangle\|^2 - \delta_2$$

where $\delta_1 = \|\Pi_{\mathrm{C}}\mathcal{R}_1\Pi_{\overline{\mathrm{XH}}\cdot\overline{\mathrm{C}}}|\phi\rangle\|^2$ and $\delta_2 = \|\Pi_{\mathrm{H}\cdot\overline{\mathrm{C}}}\mathcal{R}_1\Pi_{\overline{\mathrm{XQ}}\cdot\overline{\mathrm{H}}\cdot\overline{\mathrm{C}}}|\phi\rangle\|^2$.

The negative terms on the right-hand side represent the amount of progress transferred by one classical query between different progress measures. Note that, as a simple case, if an algorithm makes only classical queries then there can be no hybrid or quantum collision, hence $\|\Pi_{\mathrm{XH}\cdot\overline{\mathrm{C}}}|\phi_t\rangle\| = \|\Pi_{\mathrm{XQ}\cdot\overline{\mathrm{H}}\cdot\overline{\mathrm{C}}}|\phi_t\rangle\| = 0$ and the above inequalities simplify to $\Delta_1(\Pi_{\mathrm{C}}, |\phi_t\rangle) = \|\Pi_{\mathrm{C}}\mathcal{R}_1|\phi_t\rangle\|^2 - \|\Pi_{\mathrm{C}}|\phi_t\rangle\|^2 \le 4t/N$. Thus, we recover the birthday bound $\|\Pi_{\mathrm{C}}|\phi_t\rangle\|^2 = O\left(t^2/N\right)$ after t classical queries.

We now combine the two lemmas to bound the potential increase under applying the hybrid compressed oracle $\mathcal{R}_b$.

Proposition 5. *Given an integer t and a state $|\phi\rangle \in \mathbb{H}_t$ with norm at most 1, upon applying the hybrid compressed oracle $\mathcal{R}_b$, the potential increases by at most*

$$\Psi(\mathcal{R}_b|\phi\rangle) \le \Psi(|\phi\rangle) + \min\left(81\sqrt{\frac{t \cdot \Psi(|\phi\rangle)}{N}}, \frac{1641t}{bN}\right) + \frac{170t}{N} \qquad (4.1)$$

for all $b \in [0, 1]$.

Proof. We start by proving

$$\Psi(\mathcal{R}_b|\phi\rangle) \le \Psi(|\phi\rangle) - b\|\Pi_{\mathrm{XH}\cdot\overline{\mathrm{C}}+\mathrm{XQ}\cdot\overline{\mathrm{H}}\cdot\overline{\mathrm{C}}}|\phi\rangle\|^2 + 81\sqrt{\frac{t}{N}}\|\Pi_{\mathrm{XH}\cdot\overline{\mathrm{C}}+\mathrm{XQ}\cdot\overline{\mathrm{H}}\cdot\overline{\mathrm{C}}}|\phi\rangle\| + \frac{170t}{N} \tag{4.2}$$

for all $b \in [0, 1]$. By combining Lemmas 5 and 6 with the fact that

$$\Psi(\mathcal{R}_b|\phi\rangle) = (1 - b)\Psi(\mathcal{R}_0|\phi\rangle) + b\Psi(\mathcal{R}_1|\phi\rangle)$$
$$= \Psi(|\phi\rangle) + \Delta_b(\Pi_{\mathrm{C}}, |\phi\rangle) + 3\Delta_b(\Pi_{\mathrm{H}\cdot\overline{\mathrm{C}}}, |\phi\rangle) + 7\Delta_b(\Pi_{\mathrm{Q}\cdot\overline{\mathrm{H}}\cdot\overline{\mathrm{C}}}, |\phi\rangle),$$

we have that

$$\Psi(\mathcal{R}_b|\phi\rangle) \le \Psi(|\phi\rangle) - b(\|\Pi_{\mathrm{XH}\cdot\overline{\mathrm{C}}}|\phi\rangle\|^2 + \|\Pi_{\mathrm{XQ}\cdot\overline{\mathrm{H}}\cdot\overline{\mathrm{C}}}|\phi\rangle\|^2)$$
$$+ 40\sqrt{\frac{t}{N}}\|\Pi_{\mathrm{XH}\cdot\overline{\mathrm{C}}}|\phi\rangle\| + 70\sqrt{\frac{t}{N}}\|\Pi_{\mathrm{XQ}\cdot\overline{\mathrm{H}}\cdot\overline{\mathrm{C}}}|\phi\rangle\| + \frac{170t}{N}.$$

Equation (4.2) follows by observing that

$$\|\Pi_{\mathsf{XH}\cdot\overline{\mathsf{C}}}|\phi\rangle\|^2 + \|\Pi_{\mathsf{XQ}\cdot\overline{\mathsf{H}}\cdot\overline{\mathsf{C}}}|\phi\rangle\|^2 = \|\Pi_{\mathsf{XH}\cdot\overline{\mathsf{C}}+\mathsf{XQ}\cdot\overline{\mathsf{H}}\cdot\overline{\mathsf{C}}}|\phi\rangle\|^2, \text{ and}$$

$$40\|\Pi_{\mathsf{XH}\cdot\overline{\mathsf{C}}}|\phi\rangle\| + 70\|\Pi_{\mathsf{XQ}\cdot\overline{\mathsf{H}}\cdot\overline{\mathsf{C}}}|\phi\rangle\| \le \sqrt{40^2 + 70^2}\|\Pi_{\mathsf{XH}\cdot\overline{\mathsf{C}}+\mathsf{XQ}\cdot\overline{\mathsf{H}}\cdot\overline{\mathsf{C}}}|\phi\rangle\|,$$

where the last inequality follows from Cauchy–Schwarz.

Finally, the proposition is derived from Eq. (4.2) and the fact that

$$-b\|\Pi_{\mathsf{XH}\cdot\overline{\mathsf{C}}+\mathsf{XQ}\cdot\overline{\mathsf{H}}\cdot\overline{\mathsf{C}}}|\phi\rangle\|^2 + 81\sqrt{\frac{t}{N}}\|\Pi_{\mathsf{XH}\cdot\overline{\mathsf{C}}+\mathsf{XQ}\cdot\overline{\mathsf{H}}\cdot\overline{\mathsf{C}}}|\phi\rangle\|$$

$$\le \min\left\{81\sqrt{\frac{t}{N}}\|\Pi_{\mathsf{XH}\cdot\overline{\mathsf{C}}+\mathsf{XQ}\cdot\overline{\mathsf{H}}\cdot\overline{\mathsf{C}}}|\phi\rangle\|, \frac{1641t}{bN}\right\}$$

$$\le \min\left\{81\sqrt{\frac{t}{N}}\cdot\Psi\left(|\phi\rangle\right), \frac{1641t}{bN}\right\}$$

since the polynomial $-bZ^2 + 81\sqrt{\frac{t}{N}}Z$ is maximized at $Z = 81\sqrt{\frac{t}{4b^2N}}$. □

Finally, we can prove our main theorem by tuning the interpolation coefficient b.

Proof of Theorem 5. We first consider the case of hybrid algorithms that only make classical or quantum queries (model 1). We want to upper bound the probability that an algorithm outputs a collision pair after $t = c + q$ queries, of which c are classical and q are quantum. Fix any such algorithm and let $|\phi_t\rangle$ denote its state as defined in Eq. (3.2). We can always assume, at the cost of doing two extra classical queries, that the output is contained in the history register. Hence, the success probability of the algorithm is upper bounded by the probability $\|\Pi_{\mathsf{C}}|\phi_t\rangle\|^2$ of having recorded a classical collision. We now prove the upper bound $\|\Pi_{\mathsf{C}}|\phi_t\rangle\|^2 = O((c^2 + cq^2 + q^3)/N)$ that matches our theorem. For that, we consider the potential after t queries defined as

$$\Psi_t := \|\Pi_{\mathsf{C}}|\phi_t\rangle\|^2 + 3\|\Pi_{\mathsf{H}\cdot\overline{\mathsf{C}}}|\phi_t\rangle\|^2 + 7\|\Pi_{\mathsf{Q}\cdot\overline{\mathsf{H}}\cdot\overline{\mathsf{C}}}|\phi_t\rangle\|^2.$$

Our proof is by induction on t. Initially, $\Psi_0 = 0$ since the history and database registers of $|\phi_0\rangle$ are empty by definition. By Proposition 5, at each query, the potential increases by at most,

$$\Psi_t \le \begin{cases} \left(\sqrt{\Psi_{t-1}} + 41\sqrt{\frac{t-1}{N}}\right)^2 & \text{if the } t\text{-th query is quantum } (b = 0), \\ \Psi_{t-1} + \frac{1811(t-1)}{N} & \text{if the } t\text{-th query is classical } (b = 1). \end{cases}$$

The maximum increase permitted by the above two inequalities is achieved when all the classical queries are performed first. Thus, we conclude that

$$\Psi_{c+q} = O\left(c\cdot\frac{c+q}{N} + q^2\cdot\frac{c+q}{N}\right) = O\left(\frac{c^2 + cq^2 + q^3}{N}\right).$$

We now study the case of algorithms that make t queries to the same hybrid oracle $\mathcal{O}_b$ where $b > 0$ (model 2). By using the same definition of Ψ_t as above, together with Proposition 5, we obtain that

$$\Psi_t = O\left(\frac{t^2}{bN}\right)$$

since each query increases the potential by at most $O\left(t/(bN)\right)$.

Finally, the case of bounded-depth algorithms (model 3) follows by the result in model 2 and Corollary 1. □

4.3   Progress Overlap Lemmas

In this section, we prove several simple lemmas that upper bound the progress overlap when making one classical or quantum query. Roughly speaking, these quantities correspond to the probability of recording new collisions in the history-database register when a new coordinate of the input is revealed by a query.

We first give a central fact that will be used throughout the next sections. It describes certain subspaces that remain orthogonal after applying one (classical or quantum) query to them.

Fact 6. *The following linear maps are equal to zero over the subspace $\mathbb{H}_t$ of consistent states:*

$$\Pi_{\overline{C}}\mathcal{R}_0\Pi_{C}, \;\; \Pi_C\mathcal{R}_0\Pi_{\overline{C}}, \;\; \Pi_{Q\cdot H}\mathcal{R}_0\Pi_{\overline{Q}\cdot\overline{H}}, \;\; \Pi_{\overline{H}}\mathcal{R}_0\Pi_{\overline{X}H}$$

and

$$\Pi_{\overline{C}}\mathcal{R}_1\Pi_C, \;\; \Pi_Q\mathcal{R}_1\Pi_{\overline{Q}}, \;\; \Pi_{\overline{Q}}\mathcal{R}_1\Pi_{\overline{X}Q}, \;\; \Pi_{\overline{H}}\mathcal{R}_1\Pi_{\overline{X}H}\,.$$

For any states $|\phi_1\rangle, |\phi_2\rangle \in \mathbb{H}_t$ and basis-state predicate P, the following vectors are orthogonal:

$$\Pi_P\mathcal{R}_b\Pi_{\overline{X}Q}|\phi_1\rangle \perp \mathcal{R}_b(\Pi_{\overline{Q}} + \Pi_{XQ})|\phi_2\rangle \quad \text{and} \quad \Pi_P\mathcal{R}_b\Pi_{\overline{X}H}|\phi_1\rangle \perp \mathcal{R}_b(\Pi_{\overline{H}} + \Pi_{XH})|\phi_2\rangle.$$

for $b \in \{0,1\}$.

Proof. The statement follows by simple applications of Lemmas 1 and 2.

We detail the proof of the equality $\Pi_Q\mathcal{R}_1\Pi_{\overline{Q}} = 0$. Consider any basis state $|x, p, w, H, D\rangle \in \mathrm{supp}\,(\Pi_{\overline{Q}})$. By Lemma 2, every history-database (H', D') contained in the support of the post-query state $\mathcal{R}_1|x, p, w, H, D\rangle$ must be identical to (H, D) except possibly on the value x. Furthermore, since x must be in the history after the classical query (i.e. $H'(x) \neq \star$) it cannot contribute to any quantum collision in (H', D'). Thus, no quantum collision can be contained in (H', D').

We sketch the proof of $\Pi_P\mathcal{R}_1\Pi_{\overline{X}H}|\phi_1\rangle \perp \mathcal{R}_1\Pi_{\overline{H}}|\phi_2\rangle$. Every basis state in the support of $\mathcal{R}_1\Pi_{\overline{X}H}|\phi_1\rangle$ has a hybrid collision that does not contain the query index. On the other hand, none of the basis states in the support of $\mathcal{R}_1\Pi_{\overline{H}}|\phi_2\rangle$ satisfy this property since the only possible hybrid collisions must contain the index on which $\mathcal{R}_1$ is queried. Hence, $\mathcal{R}_1\Pi_{\overline{X}H}|\phi_1\rangle \perp \mathcal{R}_1\Pi_{\overline{H}}|\phi_2\rangle$. Finally, applying Π_P does not change the orthogonality property since it can only remove basis states from the support of these states. □

We now analyze the effect of quantum and classical queries on the progress overlaps $\Gamma_0(\Pi, |\phi\rangle), \Gamma_1(\Pi, |\phi\rangle) \in [0, 1]$ for different projectors Π. Recall that, by Definition 5, these numbers give the relative amplitude that moves from the support of $\mathbb{I} - \Pi$ to the support of Π after making a query, i.e. $\Gamma_b(\Pi, |\phi\rangle) = \|\Pi \mathcal{R}_b(\mathbb{I} - \Pi)|\phi\rangle\|^2 / \|(\mathbb{I} - \Pi)|\phi\rangle\|^2$. Notice that Fact 6 already shows that $\Gamma_0(\Pi_C, |\phi\rangle) = \Gamma_0(\Pi_{\overline{C}}, |\phi\rangle) = \Gamma_1(\Pi_{\overline{C}}, |\phi\rangle) = 0$.

Lemma 7. *Given an integer t and a state $|\phi\rangle \in \mathbb{H}_t$, the progress overlap caused by one quantum query on $|\phi\rangle$ are at most,*

$$\Gamma_0(\Pi_Q, |\phi\rangle) \leq \frac{10t}{N}, \quad (4.3) \qquad \Gamma_0(\Pi_{Q+H}, |\phi\rangle) \leq \frac{10t}{N}, \quad (4.4)$$

$$\Gamma_0(\Pi_H, |\phi\rangle) \leq \frac{10t}{N}, \quad (4.5)$$

and the progress overlap caused by one classical query on $|\phi\rangle$ are,

$$\Gamma_1(\Pi_Q, |\phi\rangle) = 0, \quad (4.6) \qquad \Gamma_1(\Pi_{Q+H}, |\phi\rangle) \leq \frac{2t}{N}. \quad (4.7)$$

Proof. The inequalities for quantum queries follow from Lemma 3 as Q, Q + H and H are history-database predicates (Definition 6) with the γ parameters being t/N. Similarly, for classical queries, the two inequalities follow from Lemma 4 with the γ parameters being 0 and t/N respectively. $\square$

Finally, we give four inequalities that do not follow from Lemmas 3 and 4. Equations (4.8) and (4.10) below upper bound the progress made towards *removing* all hybrid and classical collisions from the history-database, which is not a database monotone property (see Definition 6). The purpose of Eq. (4.9) is to upper bound the probability that a classical query transfers the query index x from one hybrid collision to a *different* hybrid collision. Finally, Eq. (4.11) overcomes the fact that the predicate H + C does not satisfy the condition stated in Eq. (3.5).

Lemma 8. *Given an integer t and a state $|\phi\rangle \in \mathbb{H}_t$, we have*

$$\Gamma_0(\Pi_{\overline{H+C}}, |\phi\rangle) \leq \frac{10t}{N}, \quad (4.8) \qquad \|\Pi_H \mathcal{R}_1 \Pi_{XH} |\phi\rangle\|^2 \leq \frac{t}{N} \cdot \|\Pi_{XH} |\phi\rangle\|^2, \quad (4.9)$$

$$\Gamma_1(\Pi_{\overline{H+C}}, |\phi\rangle) \leq \frac{2t}{N}, \quad (4.10) \qquad \|\Pi_C \mathcal{R}_1 \Pi_{\overline{H+C}} |\phi\rangle\|^2 \leq \frac{2t}{N} \cdot \|\Pi_{\overline{H+C}} |\phi\rangle\|^2. \quad (4.11)$$

The proofs of these equations use similar ideas to those of Lemmas 3 and 4. They are deferred to the full version.

4.4 Progress Increase Lemmas

In this section, we analyze the progress measures for: (1) finding a classical collision, (2) finding a hybrid collision but no classical ones and (3) finding quantum collisions only. We start with the case of quantum queries.

Lemma 5 (Progress Measure, Quantum Query). Given an integer t and a state $|\phi\rangle \in \mathbb{H}_t$ with norm at most 1, the progress caused by one quantum query on $|\phi\rangle$ satisfies

$$\Delta_0(\Pi_{\mathrm{c}}, |\phi\rangle) = 0, \tag{4.12}$$

$$\Delta_0(\Pi_{\mathrm{H}\cdot\overline{\mathrm{c}}}, |\phi\rangle) \leq 2\sqrt{\frac{10t}{N}}\|\Pi_{\mathrm{xH}\cdot\overline{\mathrm{c}}}|\phi\rangle\| + \frac{10t}{N}, \tag{4.13}$$

$$\Delta_0(\Pi_{\mathrm{Q}\cdot\overline{\mathrm{H}}\cdot\overline{\mathrm{c}}}, |\phi\rangle) \leq \sqrt{\frac{8t}{N}}\|\Pi_{\mathrm{xH}\cdot\overline{\mathrm{c}}}|\phi\rangle\| + 2\sqrt{\frac{20t}{N}}\|\Pi_{\mathrm{xQ}\cdot\overline{\mathrm{H}}\cdot\overline{\mathrm{c}}}|\phi\rangle\| + \frac{20t}{N}. \tag{4.14}$$

Proof of Eq. (4.12). We have $\|\Pi_{\mathrm{c}}\mathcal{R}_0|\phi\rangle\|^2 = \|\Pi_{\mathrm{c}}\mathcal{R}_0\Pi_{\mathrm{c}}|\phi\rangle\|^2 = \|\Pi_{\mathrm{c}}|\phi\rangle\|^2$ since $\mathbb{I} = \Pi_{\mathrm{c}} + \Pi_{\overline{\mathrm{c}}}$ and $\Pi_{\mathrm{c}}\mathcal{R}_0\Pi_{\overline{\mathrm{c}}} = \Pi_{\overline{\mathrm{c}}}\mathcal{R}_0\Pi_{\mathrm{c}} = 0$ by Fact 6. □

Proof of Eq. (4.13). We decompose the identity operator as $\mathbb{I} = \Pi_{\overline{\mathrm{x}}\mathrm{H}\cdot\overline{\mathrm{c}}} + \Pi_{\mathrm{xH}\cdot\overline{\mathrm{c}}} + \Pi_{\overline{\mathrm{H}}\cdot\overline{\mathrm{c}}} + \Pi_{\mathrm{c}}$. By Fact 6, $\Pi_{\mathrm{H}\cdot\overline{\mathrm{c}}}\mathcal{R}_0\Pi_{\mathrm{c}} = 0$ and the states $\Pi_{\mathrm{H}\cdot\overline{\mathrm{c}}}\mathcal{R}_0\Pi_{\overline{\mathrm{x}}\mathrm{H}\cdot\overline{\mathrm{c}}}|\phi\rangle = \Pi_{\mathrm{H}\cdot\overline{\mathrm{c}}}\mathcal{R}_0\Pi_{\overline{\mathrm{x}}\mathrm{H}}\Pi_{\overline{\mathrm{c}}}|\phi\rangle$ and $\Pi_{\mathrm{H}\cdot\overline{\mathrm{c}}}\mathcal{R}_0(\Pi_{\mathrm{xH}\cdot\overline{\mathrm{c}}} + \Pi_{\overline{\mathrm{H}}\cdot\overline{\mathrm{c}}})|\phi\rangle = \Pi_{\mathrm{H}\cdot\overline{\mathrm{c}}}\mathcal{R}_0(\Pi_{\mathrm{xH}} + \Pi_{\overline{\mathrm{H}}})\Pi_{\overline{\mathrm{c}}}|\phi\rangle$ are orthogonal. Therefore,

$$\|\Pi_{\mathrm{H}\cdot\overline{\mathrm{c}}}\mathcal{R}_0|\phi\rangle\|^2 = \|\Pi_{\mathrm{H}\cdot\overline{\mathrm{c}}}\mathcal{R}_0(\Pi_{\overline{\mathrm{x}}\mathrm{H}\cdot\overline{\mathrm{c}}} + \Pi_{\mathrm{xH}\cdot\overline{\mathrm{c}}} + \Pi_{\overline{\mathrm{H}}\cdot\overline{\mathrm{c}}} + \Pi_{\mathrm{c}})|\phi\rangle\|^2$$
$$= \|\Pi_{\mathrm{H}\cdot\overline{\mathrm{c}}}\mathcal{R}_0\Pi_{\overline{\mathrm{x}}\mathrm{H}\cdot\overline{\mathrm{c}}}|\phi\rangle\|^2 + \|\Pi_{\mathrm{H}\cdot\overline{\mathrm{c}}}\mathcal{R}_0(\Pi_{\mathrm{xH}\cdot\overline{\mathrm{c}}} + \Pi_{\overline{\mathrm{H}}\cdot\overline{\mathrm{c}}})|\phi\rangle\|^2$$
$$\leq \|\Pi_{\overline{\mathrm{x}}\mathrm{H}\cdot\overline{\mathrm{c}}}|\phi\rangle\|^2 + (\|\Pi_{\mathrm{xH}\cdot\overline{\mathrm{c}}}|\phi\rangle\| + \|\Pi_{\mathrm{H}}\mathcal{R}_0\Pi_{\overline{\mathrm{H}}}|\phi\rangle\|)^2$$
$$= \|\Pi_{\mathrm{H}\cdot\overline{\mathrm{c}}}|\phi\rangle\|^2 + 2\|\Pi_{\mathrm{xH}\cdot\overline{\mathrm{c}}}|\phi\rangle\| \cdot \|\Pi_{\mathrm{H}}\mathcal{R}_0\Pi_{\overline{\mathrm{H}}}|\phi\rangle\| + \|\Pi_{\mathrm{H}}\mathcal{R}_0\Pi_{\overline{\mathrm{H}}}|\phi\rangle\|^2$$

where the third line uses the triangle inequality, and the last line uses that $\|\Pi_{\mathrm{H}\cdot\overline{\mathrm{c}}}|\phi\rangle\|^2 = \|\Pi_{\overline{\mathrm{x}}\mathrm{H}\cdot\overline{\mathrm{c}}}|\phi\rangle\|^2 + \|\Pi_{\mathrm{xH}\cdot\overline{\mathrm{c}}}|\phi\rangle\|^2$. Finally, $\|\Pi_{\mathrm{H}}\mathcal{R}_0\Pi_{\overline{\mathrm{H}}}|\phi\rangle\|^2 \leq 10t/N$ by Eq. (4.5). □

Proof of Eq. (4.14). We use the decomposition $\mathbb{I} = \Pi_{\overline{\mathrm{Q}}\cdot\overline{\mathrm{H}}\cdot\overline{\mathrm{c}}} + \Pi_{\overline{\mathrm{x}}\mathrm{Q}\cdot\overline{\mathrm{H}}\cdot\overline{\mathrm{c}}} + \Pi_{\mathrm{xQ}\cdot\overline{\mathrm{H}}\cdot\overline{\mathrm{c}}} + \Pi_{\mathrm{xH}\cdot\overline{\mathrm{c}}} + \Pi_{\overline{\mathrm{x}}\mathrm{H}\cdot\overline{\mathrm{c}}} + \Pi_{\mathrm{c}}$. By Fact 6, $\Pi_{\mathrm{Q}\cdot\overline{\mathrm{H}}\cdot\overline{\mathrm{c}}}\mathcal{R}_0(\Pi_{\overline{\mathrm{x}}\mathrm{H}\cdot\overline{\mathrm{c}}} + \Pi_{\mathrm{c}}) = 0$ and the states $\Pi_{\mathrm{Q}\cdot\overline{\mathrm{H}}\cdot\overline{\mathrm{c}}}\mathcal{R}_0\Pi_{\overline{\mathrm{x}}\mathrm{Q}\cdot\overline{\mathrm{H}}\cdot\overline{\mathrm{c}}}|\phi\rangle$ and $\Pi_{\mathrm{Q}\cdot\overline{\mathrm{H}}\cdot\overline{\mathrm{c}}}\mathcal{R}_0(\Pi_{\overline{\mathrm{Q}}\cdot\overline{\mathrm{H}}\cdot\overline{\mathrm{c}}} + \Pi_{\mathrm{xQ}\cdot\overline{\mathrm{H}}\cdot\overline{\mathrm{c}}})|\phi\rangle$ are orthogonal. Therefore,

$$\|\Pi_{\mathrm{Q}\cdot\overline{\mathrm{H}}\cdot\overline{\mathrm{c}}}\mathcal{R}_0|\phi\rangle\|^2$$
$$= \|\Pi_{\mathrm{Q}\cdot\overline{\mathrm{H}}\cdot\overline{\mathrm{c}}}\mathcal{R}_0(\Pi_{\overline{\mathrm{Q}}\cdot\overline{\mathrm{H}}\cdot\overline{\mathrm{c}}} + \Pi_{\overline{\mathrm{x}}\mathrm{Q}\cdot\overline{\mathrm{H}}\cdot\overline{\mathrm{c}}} + \Pi_{\mathrm{xQ}\cdot\overline{\mathrm{H}}\cdot\overline{\mathrm{c}}} + \Pi_{\mathrm{xH}\cdot\overline{\mathrm{c}}} + \Pi_{\overline{\mathrm{x}}\mathrm{H}\cdot\overline{\mathrm{c}}} + \Pi_{\mathrm{c}})|\phi\rangle\|^2$$
$$\leq \|\Pi_{\mathrm{Q}\cdot\overline{\mathrm{H}}\cdot\overline{\mathrm{c}}}\mathcal{R}_0\Pi_{\overline{\mathrm{x}}\mathrm{Q}\cdot\overline{\mathrm{H}}\cdot\overline{\mathrm{c}}}|\phi\rangle\|^2 + \|\Pi_{\mathrm{Q}\cdot\overline{\mathrm{H}}\cdot\overline{\mathrm{c}}}\mathcal{R}_0(\Pi_{\overline{\mathrm{Q}}\cdot\overline{\mathrm{H}}\cdot\overline{\mathrm{c}}} + \Pi_{\mathrm{xQ}\cdot\overline{\mathrm{H}}\cdot\overline{\mathrm{c}}})|\phi\rangle\|^2$$
$$\quad + 3\|\Pi_{\mathrm{Q}\cdot\overline{\mathrm{H}}\cdot\overline{\mathrm{c}}}\mathcal{R}_0\Pi_{\mathrm{xH}\cdot\overline{\mathrm{c}}}|\phi\rangle\|$$
$$\leq \|\Pi_{\overline{\mathrm{x}}\mathrm{Q}\cdot\overline{\mathrm{H}}\cdot\overline{\mathrm{c}}}|\phi\rangle\|^2 + (\|\Pi_{\mathrm{Q}}\mathcal{R}_0\Pi_{\overline{\mathrm{Q}}}|\phi\rangle\| + \|\Pi_{\mathrm{xQ}\cdot\overline{\mathrm{H}}\cdot\overline{\mathrm{c}}}|\phi\rangle\|)^2 + 3\|\Pi_{\overline{\mathrm{H}}}\mathcal{R}_0\Pi_{\mathrm{xH}\cdot\overline{\mathrm{c}}}|\phi\rangle\|$$
$$= \|\Pi_{\mathrm{Q}\cdot\overline{\mathrm{H}}\cdot\overline{\mathrm{c}}}|\phi\rangle\|^2 + 2\|\Pi_{\mathrm{xQ}\cdot\overline{\mathrm{H}}\cdot\overline{\mathrm{c}}}|\phi\rangle\| \cdot \|\Pi_{\mathrm{Q}}\mathcal{R}_0\Pi_{\overline{\mathrm{Q}}}|\phi\rangle\| + \|\Pi_{\mathrm{Q}}\mathcal{R}_0\Pi_{\overline{\mathrm{Q}}}|\phi\rangle\|^2$$
$$\quad + 3\|\Pi_{\overline{\mathrm{H}}}\mathcal{R}_0\Pi_{\mathrm{xH}\cdot\overline{\mathrm{c}}}|\phi\rangle\|$$

where the second line uses the identity $\|a+b\|^2 \leq \|a\|^2 + 3\|b\|$ when $\|a\|, \|b\| \leq 1$, the third line uses the triangle inequality and the last line uses that $\|\Pi_{Q\cdot\overline{H}\cdot\overline{c}}|\phi\rangle\|^2 = \|\Pi_{\overline{x}Q\cdot\overline{H}\cdot\overline{c}}|\phi\rangle\|^2 + \|\Pi_{xQ\cdot\overline{H}\cdot\overline{c}}|\phi\rangle\|$. Finally, $\|\Pi_Q\mathcal{R}_0\Pi_{\overline{Q}}|\phi\rangle\|^2 \leq 10t/N$ by Eq. (4.3) and $\|\Pi_{\overline{H}}\mathcal{R}_0\Pi_{xH\cdot\overline{c}}|\phi\rangle\|^2 \leq (10t/N)\|\Pi_{xH\cdot\overline{c}}|\phi\rangle\|^2$ by Eq. (4.8). $\qquad \square$

We now analyze the case of classical queries.

Lemma 6 (Progress Measure, Classical Query). Given an integer t and a state $|\phi\rangle \in \mathbb{H}_t$ with norm at most 1, the progress caused by one classical query on $|\phi\rangle$ are at most,

$$\Delta_1(\Pi_c, |\phi\rangle) \leq 2\|\Pi_{xH\cdot\overline{c}}|\phi\rangle\|^2 + \delta_1 + \frac{4t}{N}, \tag{4.15}$$

$$\Delta_1(\Pi_{H\cdot\overline{c}}, |\phi\rangle) \leq -\|\Pi_{xH\cdot\overline{c}}|\phi\rangle\|^2 + 2\|\Pi_{xQ\cdot\overline{H}\cdot\overline{c}}|\phi\rangle\|^2 - \delta_1 + 2\delta_2 + \frac{12t}{N}, \tag{4.16}$$

$$\Delta_1(\Pi_{Q\cdot\overline{H}\cdot\overline{c}}, |\phi\rangle) \leq \sqrt{\frac{2t}{N}}\|\Pi_{xH\cdot\overline{c}}|\phi\rangle\| - \|\Pi_{xQ\cdot\overline{H}\cdot\overline{c}}|\phi\rangle\|^2 - \delta_2 \tag{4.17}$$

where $\delta_1 = \|\Pi_c\mathcal{R}_1\Pi_{\overline{x}H\cdot\overline{c}}|\phi\rangle\|^2$ and $\delta_2 = \|\Pi_{H\cdot\overline{c}}\mathcal{R}_1\Pi_{\overline{x}Q\cdot\overline{H}\cdot\overline{c}}|\phi\rangle\|^2$.

Proof of Eq. (4.15). We use the decomposition $\mathbb{I} = \Pi_c + \Pi_{xH\cdot\overline{c}} + \Pi_{\overline{x}H\cdot\overline{c}} + \Pi_{\overline{H}\cdot\overline{c}}$. By Fact 6, the states $\Pi_c\mathcal{R}_1\Pi_c|\phi\rangle$, $\Pi_c\mathcal{R}_1\Pi_{\overline{x}H\cdot\overline{c}}|\phi\rangle$ and $\Pi_c\mathcal{R}_1(\Pi_{xH\cdot\overline{c}} + \Pi_{\overline{H}\cdot\overline{c}})|\phi\rangle$ are orthogonal. Therefore,

$$\begin{aligned}
\|\Pi_c\mathcal{R}_1|\phi\rangle\|^2 &= \|\Pi_c\mathcal{R}_1(\Pi_c + \Pi_{xH\cdot\overline{c}} + \Pi_{\overline{x}H\cdot\overline{c}} + \Pi_{\overline{H}\cdot\overline{c}})\|^2 \\
&= \|\Pi_c\mathcal{R}_1\Pi_c\|^2 + \|\Pi_c\mathcal{R}_1\Pi_{\overline{x}H\cdot\overline{c}}\|^2 + \|\Pi_c\mathcal{R}_1(\Pi_{xH\cdot\overline{c}} + \Pi_{\overline{H}\cdot\overline{c}})|\phi\rangle\|^2 \\
&\leq \|\Pi_c\|^2 + \|\Pi_c\mathcal{R}_1\Pi_{\overline{x}H\cdot\overline{c}}\|^2 + 2\|\Pi_{xH\cdot\overline{c}}|\phi\rangle\|^2 + 2\|\Pi_c\mathcal{R}_1\Pi_{\overline{H}\cdot\overline{c}}|\phi\rangle\|^2
\end{aligned}$$

where the last line uses the identity $\|a+b\|^2 \leq 2\|a\|^2 + 2\|b\|^2$. Finally, by Eq. (4.11), $\|\Pi_c\mathcal{R}_1\Pi_{\overline{H}\cdot\overline{c}}|\phi\rangle\|^2 \leq 2t/N$. $\qquad \square$

Proof of Eq. (4.16). We use the decomposition $\mathbb{I} = \Pi_c + \Pi_{\overline{x}H\cdot\overline{c}} + \Pi_{xH\cdot\overline{c}} + \Pi_{\overline{H}\cdot\overline{c}}$. By Fact 6, $\Pi_{H\cdot\overline{c}}\mathcal{R}_1\Pi_c = 0$ and $\Pi_{H\cdot\overline{c}}\mathcal{R}_1\Pi_{\overline{x}H\cdot\overline{c}}|\phi\rangle$ and $\Pi_{H\cdot\overline{c}}\mathcal{R}_1(\Pi_{xH\cdot\overline{c}} + \Pi_{\overline{H}\cdot\overline{c}})|\phi\rangle$ are orthogonal. Therefore,

$$\begin{aligned}
&\|\Pi_{H\cdot\overline{c}}\mathcal{R}_1|\phi\rangle\|^2 \\
&= \|\Pi_{H\cdot\overline{c}}\mathcal{R}_1\Pi_{\overline{x}H\cdot\overline{c}}\|^2 + \|\Pi_{H\cdot\overline{c}}\mathcal{R}_1(\Pi_{xH\cdot\overline{c}} + \Pi_{\overline{H}\cdot\overline{c}})|\phi\rangle\|^2 \\
&= \|\Pi_{H\cdot\overline{c}}\|^2 - \|\Pi_{xH\cdot\overline{c}}\|^2 - \|\Pi_c\mathcal{R}_1\Pi_{\overline{x}H\cdot\overline{c}}\|^2 + \|\Pi_{H\cdot\overline{c}}\mathcal{R}_1(\Pi_{xH\cdot\overline{c}} + \Pi_{\overline{H}\cdot\overline{c}})|\phi\rangle\|^2
\end{aligned}$$

where the second line uses that $\|\Pi_{H\cdot\overline{c}}\|^2 - \|\Pi_{xH\cdot\overline{c}}\|^2 - \|\Pi_c\mathcal{R}_1\Pi_{\overline{x}H\cdot\overline{c}}\|^2 = \|\Pi_{\overline{x}H\cdot\overline{c}}\|^2 - \|\Pi_c\mathcal{R}_1\Pi_{\overline{x}H\cdot\overline{c}}\|^2 = \|\Pi_{\overline{c}}\mathcal{R}_1\Pi_{\overline{x}H\cdot\overline{c}}\|^2 = \|\Pi_{H\cdot\overline{c}}\mathcal{R}_1\Pi_{\overline{x}H\cdot\overline{c}}\|^2$ since $\Pi_{\overline{H}\cdot\overline{c}}\mathcal{R}_1\Pi_{\overline{x}H\cdot\overline{c}} = 0$ by Fact 6. It remains to bound $\|\Pi_{H\cdot\overline{c}}\mathcal{R}_1(\Pi_{xH\cdot\overline{c}} + \Pi_{\overline{H}\cdot\overline{c}})|\phi\rangle\|^2$. We further decompose $\Pi_{\overline{H}\cdot\overline{c}}$ into $\Pi_{\overline{H}\cdot\overline{c}} = \Pi_{xQ\cdot\overline{H}\cdot\overline{c}} + \Pi_{\overline{x}Q\cdot\overline{H}\cdot\overline{c}} + \Pi_{\overline{Q}\cdot\overline{H}\cdot\overline{c}}$ and observe that $\Pi_{H\cdot\overline{c}}\mathcal{R}_1\Pi_{xQ\cdot\overline{H}\cdot\overline{c}}|\phi\rangle$ and $\Pi_{H\cdot\overline{c}}\mathcal{R}_1\Pi_{\overline{x}Q\cdot\overline{H}\cdot\overline{c}}|\phi\rangle$ are orthogonal by Fact 6. Hence,

$$\|\Pi_{\mathsf{H}\cdot\overline{\mathsf{c}}}\mathcal{R}_1(\Pi_{\mathsf{xH}\cdot\overline{\mathsf{c}}} + \Pi_{\overline{\mathsf{H}}\cdot\overline{\mathsf{c}}})|\phi\rangle\|^2$$
$$\leq 2\|\Pi_{\mathsf{H}\cdot\overline{\mathsf{c}}}\mathcal{R}_1(\Pi_{\mathsf{xQ}\cdot\overline{\mathsf{H}}\cdot\overline{\mathsf{c}}} + \Pi_{\overline{\mathsf{x}}\mathsf{Q}\cdot\overline{\mathsf{H}}\cdot\overline{\mathsf{c}}})|\phi\rangle\|^2 + 2\|\Pi_{\mathsf{H}\cdot\overline{\mathsf{c}}}\mathcal{R}_1(\Pi_{\mathsf{xH}\cdot\overline{\mathsf{c}}} + \Pi_{\overline{\mathsf{Q}}\cdot\overline{\mathsf{H}}\cdot\overline{\mathsf{c}}})|\phi\rangle\|^2$$
$$= 2\|\Pi_{\mathsf{H}\cdot\overline{\mathsf{c}}}\mathcal{R}_1\Pi_{\mathsf{xQ}\cdot\overline{\mathsf{H}}\cdot\overline{\mathsf{c}}}|\phi\rangle\|^2 + 2\|\Pi_{\mathsf{H}\cdot\overline{\mathsf{c}}}\mathcal{R}_1\Pi_{\overline{\mathsf{x}}\mathsf{Q}\cdot\overline{\mathsf{H}}\cdot\overline{\mathsf{c}}}|\phi\rangle\|^2$$
$$+ 2\|\Pi_{\mathsf{H}\cdot\overline{\mathsf{c}}}\mathcal{R}_1(\Pi_{\mathsf{xH}\cdot\overline{\mathsf{c}}} + \Pi_{\overline{\mathsf{Q}}\cdot\overline{\mathsf{H}}\cdot\overline{\mathsf{c}}})|\phi\rangle\|^2$$
$$\leq 2\|\Pi_{\mathsf{xQ}\cdot\overline{\mathsf{H}}\cdot\overline{\mathsf{c}}}|\phi\rangle\|^2 + 2\|\Pi_{\mathsf{H}\cdot\overline{\mathsf{c}}}\mathcal{R}_1\Pi_{\overline{\mathsf{x}}\mathsf{Q}\cdot\overline{\mathsf{H}}\cdot\overline{\mathsf{c}}}|\phi\rangle\|^2 + \frac{12t}{N}$$

where the last line uses the triangle inequality and Eqs. (4.7) and (4.9) on $\|\Pi_{\mathsf{H}\cdot\overline{\mathsf{c}}}\mathcal{R}_1(\Pi_{\mathsf{xH}\cdot\overline{\mathsf{c}}} + \Pi_{\overline{\mathsf{Q}}\cdot\overline{\mathsf{H}}\cdot\overline{\mathsf{c}}})|\phi\rangle\|^2 \leq (\|\Pi_{\mathsf{H}\cdot\overline{\mathsf{c}}}\mathcal{R}_1\Pi_{\mathsf{xH}\cdot\overline{\mathsf{c}}}|\phi\rangle\| + \|\Pi_{\mathsf{H}\cdot\overline{\mathsf{c}}}\mathcal{R}_1\Pi_{\overline{\mathsf{Q}}\cdot\overline{\mathsf{H}}\cdot\overline{\mathsf{c}}})|\phi\rangle\|)^2 \leq (1+\sqrt{2})^2 t/N$. □

Proof of Eq. (4.17). We use the decomposition $\mathbb{I} = \Pi_{\overline{\mathsf{Q}}\cdot\overline{\mathsf{H}}\cdot\overline{\mathsf{c}}} + \Pi_{\overline{\mathsf{x}}\mathsf{Q}\cdot\overline{\mathsf{H}}\cdot\overline{\mathsf{c}}} + \Pi_{\mathsf{xQ}\cdot\overline{\mathsf{H}}\cdot\overline{\mathsf{c}}} + \Pi_{\overline{\mathsf{x}}\mathsf{H}\cdot\overline{\mathsf{c}}} + \Pi_{\mathsf{xH}\cdot\overline{\mathsf{c}}} + \Pi_{\mathsf{c}}$. By Fact 6, $\Pi_{\mathsf{Q}\cdot\overline{\mathsf{H}}\cdot\overline{\mathsf{c}}}\mathcal{R}_1(\Pi_{\overline{\mathsf{Q}}\cdot\overline{\mathsf{H}}\cdot\overline{\mathsf{c}}} + \Pi_{\mathsf{xQ}\cdot\overline{\mathsf{H}}\cdot\overline{\mathsf{c}}} + \Pi_{\overline{\mathsf{x}}\mathsf{H}\cdot\overline{\mathsf{c}}} + \Pi_{\mathsf{c}}) = 0$. Therefore,

$$\|\Pi_{\mathsf{Q}\cdot\overline{\mathsf{H}}\cdot\overline{\mathsf{c}}}\mathcal{R}_1|\phi\rangle\|^2 = \|\Pi_{\mathsf{Q}\cdot\overline{\mathsf{H}}\cdot\overline{\mathsf{c}}}\mathcal{R}_1(\Pi_{\overline{\mathsf{x}}\mathsf{Q}\cdot\overline{\mathsf{H}}\cdot\overline{\mathsf{c}}} + \Pi_{\mathsf{xH}\cdot\overline{\mathsf{c}}})|\phi\rangle\|^2$$
$$\leq \|\Pi_{\mathsf{Q}\cdot\overline{\mathsf{H}}\cdot\overline{\mathsf{c}}}\mathcal{R}_1\Pi_{\overline{\mathsf{x}}\mathsf{Q}\cdot\overline{\mathsf{H}}\cdot\overline{\mathsf{c}}}|\phi\rangle\|^2 + 3\|\Pi_{\mathsf{Q}\cdot\overline{\mathsf{H}}\cdot\overline{\mathsf{c}}}\mathcal{R}_1\Pi_{\mathsf{xH}\cdot\overline{\mathsf{c}}}|\phi\rangle\|$$
$$\leq \|\Pi_{\mathsf{Q}\cdot\overline{\mathsf{H}}\cdot\overline{\mathsf{c}}}|\phi\rangle\|^2 - \|\Pi_{\mathsf{xQ}\cdot\overline{\mathsf{H}}\cdot\overline{\mathsf{c}}}|\phi\rangle\|^2 - \|\Pi_{\mathsf{H}\cdot\overline{\mathsf{c}}}\mathcal{R}_1\Pi_{\overline{\mathsf{x}}\mathsf{Q}\cdot\overline{\mathsf{H}}\cdot\overline{\mathsf{c}}}|\phi\rangle\|^2$$
$$+ 3\|\Pi_{\mathsf{Q}\cdot\overline{\mathsf{H}}\cdot\overline{\mathsf{c}}}\mathcal{R}_1\Pi_{\mathsf{xH}\cdot\overline{\mathsf{c}}}|\phi\rangle\|$$

where the last line uses $\|\Pi_{\mathsf{Q}\cdot\overline{\mathsf{H}}\cdot\overline{\mathsf{c}}}\mathcal{R}_1\Pi_{\overline{\mathsf{x}}\mathsf{Q}\cdot\overline{\mathsf{H}}\cdot\overline{\mathsf{c}}}|\phi\rangle\|^2 \leq \|(\Pi_{\overline{\mathsf{H}}\cdot\overline{\mathsf{c}}} + \Pi_{\mathsf{c}})\mathcal{R}_1\Pi_{\overline{\mathsf{x}}\mathsf{Q}\cdot\overline{\mathsf{H}}\cdot\overline{\mathsf{c}}}|\phi\rangle\|^2 = \|\Pi_{\mathsf{Q}\cdot\overline{\mathsf{H}}\cdot\overline{\mathsf{c}}}|\phi\rangle\|^2 - \|\Pi_{\mathsf{xQ}\cdot\overline{\mathsf{H}}\cdot\overline{\mathsf{c}}}|\phi\rangle\|^2 - \|\Pi_{\mathsf{H}\cdot\overline{\mathsf{c}}}\mathcal{R}_1\Pi_{\overline{\mathsf{x}}\mathsf{Q}\cdot\overline{\mathsf{H}}\cdot\overline{\mathsf{c}}}|\phi\rangle\|^2$. Finally, by Eq. (4.10), $\|\Pi_{\mathsf{Q}\cdot\overline{\mathsf{H}}\cdot\overline{\mathsf{c}}}\mathcal{R}_1\Pi_{\mathsf{xH}\cdot\overline{\mathsf{c}}}|\phi\rangle\|^2 \leq (2t/N)\|\Pi_{\mathsf{xH}\cdot\overline{\mathsf{c}}}|\phi\rangle\|^2$. □

Acknowledgements. The authors would like to thank Ansis Rosmanis for fruitful discussions and for sharing a draft of his work on noisy oracles [46]. The authors are also grateful to the anonymous referees for their valuable comments and suggestions which helped to improve the paper. Part of this work was supported by the Simons Institute through Simons-Berkeley Postdoctoral Fellowships.

References

1. Aaronson, S.: Impossibility of succinct quantum proofs for collision-freeness. Quantum Information & Computation **12**(1-2), 21—28 (2012). https://doi.org/10.26421/QIC12.1-2-3
2. Aaronson, S., Kothari, R., Kretschmer, W., Thaler, J.: Quantum lower bounds for approximate counting via Laurent polynomials. In: Proceedings of the 35th Computational Complexity Conference (CCC) (2020). https://doi.org/10.4230/LIPIcs.CCC.2020.7
3. Aaronson, S., Shi, Y.: Quantum lower bounds for the collision and the element distinctness problems. J. ACM **51**(4), 595–605 (2004). https://doi.org/10.1145/1008731.1008735
4. Alagic, G., Bai, C., Katz, J., Majenz, C.: Post-quantum security of the Even-Mansour cipher. In: Proceedings of the 41st International Conference on the Theory and Applications of Cryptographic Techniques (EUROCRYPT). pp. 458–487 (2022). https://doi.org/10.1007/978-3-031-07082-2_17

5. Alagic, G., Majenz, C., Russell, A., Song, F.: Quantum-access-secure message authentication via blind-unforgeability. In: Proceedings of the 39th International Conference on the Theory and Applications of Cryptographic Techniques (EURO-CRYPT). pp. 788–817 (2020). https://doi.org/10.1007/978-3-030-45727-3_27

6. Ambainis, A.: Quantum lower bounds by quantum arguments. J. Comput. Syst. Sci. **64**(4), 750–767 (2002). https://doi.org/10.1006/jcss.2002.1826

7. Ambainis, A., Hamburg, M., Unruh, D.: Quantum security proofs using semi-classical oracles. In: Proceedings of the 39th International Cryptology Conference (CRYPTO), pp. 269–295 (2019). https://doi.org/10.1007/978-3-030-26951-7_10

8. Ambainis, A., Špalek, R., de Wolf, R.: A new quantum lower bound method, with applications to direct product theorems and time-space tradeoffs. Algorithmica **55**(3), 422–461 (2009). https://doi.org/10.1007/s00453-007-9022-9

9. Arora, A.S., Gheorghiu, A., Singh, U.: Oracle separations of hybrid quantum-classical circuits (2022). https://doi.org/10.48550/arXiv.2201.01904, arXiv:2201.01904 [quant-ph]

10. Barak, B., Goldreich, O.: Universal arguments and their applications. SIAM J. Comput. **38**(5), 1661–1694 (2009). https://doi.org/10.1137/070709244

11. Beals, R., Buhrman, H., Cleve, R., Mosca, M., de Wolf, R.: Quantum lower bounds by polynomials. J. ACM **48**(4), 778–797 (2001). https://doi.org/10.1145/502090.502097

12. Bernstein, E., Vazirani, U.V.: Quantum complexity theory. SIAM J. Comput. **26**(5), 1411–1473 (1997). https://doi.org/10.1137/S0097539796300921

13. Bindel, N., Hamburg, M., Hövelmanns, K., Hülsing, A., Persichetti, E.: Tighter proofs of CCA security in the quantum random oracle model. In: Proceedings of the 17th Conference on Theory of Cryptography (TCC), pp. 61–90 (2019). https://doi.org/10.1007/978-3-030-36033-7_3

14. Blocki, J., Lee, S., Zhou, S.: On the security of proofs of sequential work in a post-quantum world. In: Proceedings of the 2nd Conference on Information-Theoretic Cryptography (ITC), pp. 22:1–22:27 (2021). https://doi.org/10.4230/LIPIcs.ITC.2021.22

15. Brassard, G., Høyer, P., Tapp, A.: Quantum cryptanalysis of hash and claw-free functions. In: Proceedings of the 3rd Latin American Symposium on Theoretical Informatics (LATIN), pp. 163–169 (1998). https://doi.org/10.1007/bfb0054319

16. Buhrman, H., de Wolf, R.: Complexity measures and decision tree complexity: a survey. Theoret. Comput. Sci. **288**(1), 21–43 (2002). https://doi.org/10.1016/S0304-3975(01)00144-X

17. Chen, S., Cotler, J., Huang, H.Y., Li, J.: The complexity of NISQ. Nature Commun. **14**(1), 6001 (2023). https://doi.org/10.1038/s41467-023-41217-6

18. Chia, N.H., Chung, K.M., Lai, C.Y.: On the need for large quantum depth. J. ACM **70**(1) (2023). https://doi.org/10.1145/3570637

19. Chia, N.H., Hung, S.H.: Classical verification of quantum depth (2022). https://doi.org/10.48550/arXiv.2205.04656, arXiv:2205.04656 [quant-ph]

20. Chiesa, A., Manohar, P., Spooner, N.: Succinct arguments in the quantum random oracle model. In: Proceedings of the 17th Conference on Theory of Cryptography (TCC), pp. 1–29 (2019). https://doi.org/10.1007/978-3-030-36033-7_1

21. Chung, K.M., Fehr, S., Huang, Y.H., Liao, T.N.: On the compressed-oracle technique, and post-quantum security of proofs of sequential work. In: Proceedings of the 40th International Conference on the Theory and Applications of Cryptographic Techniques (EUROCRYPT), pp. 598–629 (2021). https://doi.org/10.1007/978-3-030-77886-6_21

22. Chung, K.M., Guo, S., Liu, Q., Qian, L.: Tight quantum time-space tradeoffs for function inversion. In: Proceedings of the 61st Symposium on Foundations of Computer Science (FOCS), pp. 673–684 (2020). https://doi.org/10.1109/FOCS46700.2020.00068

23. Chung, K.M., Liao, T.N., Qian, L.: Lower bounds for function inversion with quantum advice. In: Proceedings of the 1st Conference on Information-Theoretic Cryptography (ITC), pp. 8:1–8:15 (2020). https://doi.org/10.4230/LIPIcs.ITC.2020.8

24. Coudron, M., Menda, S.: Computations with greater quantum depth are strictly more powerful (relative to an oracle). In: Proceedings of the 52nd Symposium on Theory of Computing (STOC), pp. 889—901 (2020). https://doi.org/10.1145/3357713.3384269

25. Czajkowski, J., Majenz, C., Schaffner, C., Zur, S.: Quantum lazy sampling and game-playing proofs for quantum indifferentiability (2019). https://doi.org/10.48550/arXiv.1904.11477. arXiv:1904.11477 [quant-ph]

26. Deutsch, D., Jozsa, R.: Rapid solution of problems by quantum computation. Proc. R. Soc. Lond. Ser. A **439**(1907), 553–558 (1992). https://doi.org/10.1098/rspa.1992.0167

27. Don, J., Fehr, S., Huang, Y.H.: Adaptive versus static multi-oracle algorithms, and quantum security of a split-key PRF. In: Proceedings of the 20th Conference on Theory of Cryptography (TCC), pp. 33–51 (2022). https://doi.org/10.1007/978-3-031-22318-1_2

28. Grover, L.K., Radhakrishnan, J.: Quantum search for multiple items using parallel queries (2004). https://doi.org/10.48550/arXiv.quant-ph/0407217, arXiv:quant-ph/0407217

29. Guo, S., Li, Q., Liu, Q., Zhang, J.: Unifying presampling via concentration bounds. In: Proceedings of the 19th Conference on Theory of Cryptography (TCC), pp. 177–208 (2021). https://doi.org/10.1007/978-3-030-90459-3_7

30. Hamoudi, Y., Liu, Q., Sinha, M.: The NISQ complexity of collision finding (2024). https://doi.org/10.48550/ARXIV.2211.12954, arXiv:2211.12954 [quant-ph]

31. Hamoudi, Y., Magniez, F.: Quantum time-space tradeoff for finding multiple collision pairs. ACM Trans. Comput. Theory **15**(1-2) (2023). https://doi.org/10.1145/3589986

32. Hasegawa, A., Gall, F.L.: An optimal oracle separation of classical and quantum hybrid schemes. In: Proceedings of the 33rd International Symposium on Algorithms and Computation (ISAAC), pp. 6:1–6:14 (2022). https://doi.org/10.4230/LIPIcs.ISAAC.2022.6

33. Hhan, M., Xagawa, K., Yamakawa, T.: Quantum random oracle model with auxiliary input. In: Proceedings of the 25th International Conference on the Theory and Applications of Cryptology and Information Security (ASIACRYPT), pp. 584–614 (2019). https://doi.org/10.1007/978-3-030-34578-5_21

34. Hosoyamada, A., Iwata, T.: 4-round Luby-Rackoff construction is a qPRP. In: Proceedings of the 25th International Conference on the Theory and Applications of Cryptology and Information Security (ASIACRYPT), pp. 145–174 (2019). https://doi.org/10.1007/978-3-030-34578-5_6

35. Jaeger, J., Song, F., Tessaro, S.: Quantum key-length extension. In: Proceedings of the 19th Conference on Theory of Cryptography (TCC), pp. 209–239 (2021). https://doi.org/10.1007/978-3-030-90459-3_8

36. Jeffery, S., Magniez, F., de Wolf, R.: Optimal parallel quantum query algorithms. Algorithmica **79**(2), 509–529 (2017). https://doi.org/10.1007/s00453-016-0206-z

37. Katz, J., Lindell, Y.: Introduction to Modern Cryptography: Principles and Protocols. Chapman & Hall/CRC, 1st edn. (2007). https://doi.org/10.1201/9781420010756

38. Klauck, H., Špalek, R., de Wolf, R.: Quantum and classical strong direct product theorems and optimal time-space tradeoffs. SIAM J. Comput. **36**(5), 1472–1493 (2007). https://doi.org/10.1137/05063235X

39. Liu, Q., Zhandry, M.: On finding quantum multi-collisions. In: Proceedings of the 38th International Conference on the Theory and Applications of Cryptographic Techniques (EUROCRYPT), pp. 189–218 (2019). https://doi.org/10.1007/978-3-030-17659-4_7

40. Liu, Q., Zhandry, M.: Revisiting post-quantum Fiat-Shamir. In: Proceedings of the 39th International Cryptology Conference (CRYPTO), pp. 326–355 (2019). https://doi.org/10.1007/978-3-030-26951-7_12

41. Merkle, R.C.: A certified digital signature. In: Proceedings of the 9th International Conference on the Theory and Applications of Cryptology (CRYPTO), pp. 347–363 (1989). https://doi.org/10.1007/0-387-34805-0_21

42. Nayebi, A., Aaronson, S., Belovs, A., Trevisan, L.: Quantum lower bound for inverting a permutation with advice. Quantum Inform. Comput. **15**(11&12), 901–913 (2015). https://doi.org/10.26421/QIC15.11-12-1

43. Regev, O., Schiff, L.: Impossibility of a quantum speed-up with a faulty oracle. In: Proceedings of the 35th International Colloquium on Automata, Languages, and Programming (ICALP), pp. 773—781 (2008). https://doi.org/10.1007/978-3-540-70575-8_63

44. Rosmanis, A.: Tight bounds for inverting permutations via compressed oracle arguments (2021). https://doi.org/10.48550/arXiv.2103.08975. arXiv:2103.08975 [quant-ph]

45. Rosmanis, A.: Hybrid quantum-classical search algorithms (2022). https://doi.org/10.48550/arXiv.2202.11443, arXiv:2202.11443 [quant-ph]d

46. Rosmanis, A.: Quantum search with noisy oracle (2023). https://doi.org/10.48550/ARXIV.2309.14944, arXiv:2309.14944 [quant-ph]

47. Sherstov, A.A., Thaler, J.: Vanishing-error approximate degree and QMA complexity. Chicago J. Theor. Comput. Sci. **2023**(3) (2023). https://doi.org/10.4086/cjtcs.2023.003

48. Shor, P.W.: Polynomial-time algorithms for prime factorization and discrete logarithms on a quantum computer. SIAM J. Comput. **26**(5), 1484–1509 (1997). https://doi.org/10.1137/S0097539795293172

49. Simon, D.R.: On the power of quantum computation. SIAM J. Comput. **26**(5), 1474–1483 (1997). https://doi.org/10.1137/S0097539796298637

50. Sun, X., Zheng, Y.: Hybrid decision trees: Longer quantum time is strictly more powerful (2019). https://doi.org/10.48550/arXiv.1911.13091. arXiv:1911.13091 [cs.CC]

51. Zalka, C.: Grover's quantum searching algorithm is optimal. Phys. Rev. A **60**, 2746–2751 (1999). https://doi.org/10.1103/PhysRevA.60.2746

52. Zhandry, M.: How to record quantum queries, and applications to quantum indifferentiability. In: Proceedings of the 39th International Cryptology Conference (CRYPTO), pp. 239–268 (2019). https://doi.org/10.1007/978-3-030-26951-7_9

Non-malleable Codes with Optimal Rate for Poly-Size Circuits

Marshall Ball[1][(⊠)], Ronen Shaltiel[2], and Jad Silbak[3]

[1] New York University, New York, USA
marshall.ball@cs.nyu.edu
[2] University of Haifa, Haifa, Israel
ronen@cs.haifa.ac.il
[3] Northeastern University, Boston, USA

Abstract. We give an explicit construction of non-malleable codes with rate $1 - o(1)$ for the tampering class of poly-size circuits. This rate is optimal, and improves upon the previous explicit construction of Ball, Dachman-Soled and Loss [9] which achieves a rate smaller than $\frac{1}{n}$. Our codes are based on the same hardness assumption used by Ball, Dachman-Soled and Loss, namely, that there exists a problem in $E = DTIME(2^{O(n)})$ that requires nondeterministic circuits of size $2^{\Omega(n)}$. This is a standard complexity theoretic assumption that was used in many papers in complexity theory and cryptography, and can be viewed as a scaled, nonuniform version of the widely believed assumption that $EXP \not\subseteq NP$. Our result is incomparable to that of Ball, Dachman-Soled and Loss, as we only achieve computational (rather than statistical) security. Non-malleable codes with Computational security (with lower error than what we get) were obtained by [12,26] under strong cryptographic assumptions. We show that our approach can potentially yield statistical security if certain explicit constructions of pseudorandom objects can be improved.

By composing our new non-malleable codes with standard (information theoretic) error-correcting codes (that recover from a p fraction of errors) we achieve the *best of both worlds*. Namely, we achieve explicit codes that recover from a p-fraction of errors and have the same rate as the best known explicit information theoretic codes, while *also* being non-malleable for poly-size circuits.

Moreover, if we restrict our attention to errors that are introduced by poly-size circuits, we can achieve best of both worlds codes with rate $1 - H(p)$. This is superior to the rate achieved by standard (information theoretic) error-correcting codes, and this result is obtained by composing our new non-malleable codes with the recent codes of Shaltiel and Silbak [55].

Our technique combines ideas from non-malleable codes and pseudorandomness. We show how to take a low rate "small set non-malleable code (this is a variant of non-malleable codes with a different notion of security that was introduced by Shaltiel and Silbak [54]) and compile it into a (standard) high-rate non-malleable code. Using small set

© International Association for Cryptologic Research 2024
M. Joye and G. Leander (Eds.): EUROCRYPT 2024, LNCS 14654, pp. 33–54, 2024.
https://doi.org/10.1007/978-3-031-58737-5_2

non-malleable codes (as well as seed-extending PRGs) bypasses difficulties that arise when analysing standard non-malleable codes, and allows us to use a simple construction.

1 Introduction

1.1 Error Correcting Codes and Non-malleable Codes

Standard Error-Correcting Codes. Coding theory studies message transmission in noisy channels. The objective is to design an error-correcting code (namely, a pair (Enc, Dec) of encoding and decoding algorithms) that correct from a specified number of errors. Error correction relies on adding redundancy to the message, and the code's rate is the ratio between the length of a message and the length of its encoding. The major goals of coding theory are to design codes with the largest possible rate for a specified number of errors and achieve this with explicit constructions (namely, with poly-time encoding and decoding algorithms).

Non-malleable Codes. Non-malleable codes, introduced by Dziembowski, Pietrzak, and Wichs [29], consider a more extreme scenario where there is no a-priori restriction on the number of bits that the channel may alter. Such a channel might choose to erase the encoded message and replace it with a different string. Obviously, in this case, one cannot expect the decoding algorithm to recover the original message. Instead, it is required that encoding and decoding satisfy the following:

- Recovery from no errors. If the channel does not alter the encoded message, then decoding produces the original message.
- Non-malleability. If the channel alters the encoded message, then the decoded message is either the original or unrelated to the original message.

The definition of non-malleable codes also includes two modifications over the standard coding scenario:

- It is impossible to handle all channels, and so, a non-malleable code is defined against a specific family $\mathcal{C}$ of channels (a.k.a "tampering functions").
- The encoding algorithm Enc is allowed to be randomized.

This leads to the following definition by [29] (which is stated informally below).

Definition 1 (non-malleable codes [29], informal). *A randomized encoding function* Enc : $\{0,1\}^{Rn} \to \{0,1\}^n$ *and a deterministic decoding function* Dec : $\{0,1\}^n \to \{0,1\}^{Rn} \cup \{\bot\}$ *form a rate R, non-malleable code against a class $\mathcal{C}$ of tampering functions, if for every $m \in \{0,1\}^{Rn}$, Dec(Enc(m)) = m, and for* every $C : \{0,1\}^n \rightarrow \{0,1\}^n$ in $\mathcal{C}$, there exists a distribution D_C over $\{0,1\}^{Rn} \cup \{same, \bot\}$, such that for every $m \in \{0,1\}^{Rn}$, the experiment

$$Tamper_C(m) = \left\{ \begin{array}{c} z \leftarrow Enc(m), v \leftarrow C(z), \bar{m} \leftarrow Dec(v) \\ Output\ \bar{m}. \end{array} \right\}$$

is indistinguishable from the following experiment

$$Simulated_C(m) = \left\{ \begin{array}{c} \bar{m} \leftarrow D_C \\ Output\ m\ if\ \bar{m} = same,\ and\ \bar{m}\ otherwise. \end{array} \right\}$$

Note that in the simulated experiment, the distribution D_C does not depend on m, and this is the sense in which "$\bar{m}$ is unrelated to m".

Since the seminal work of Dziembowski, Pietrzak and Wichs [29], various different classes of tampering functions were considered in the literature. Loosely speaking, these can be split into "tampering functions with limited information," such as bit-wise tampering [25,29], split-state tampering [1–4,20,30,45–47,49], interleaved tampering [22]; and "tampering functions with restricted computational power," such as local tampering [13,15,35], AC^0 tampering [11,14,15,21], low degree polynomial tampering [10,21], streaming tampering [14], and polynomial size circuit tampering [9,12,26]. This paper belongs to the latter category, and considers the family of tampering functions implemented by circuits of fixed polynomial size.

Non-malleable Codes for Poly-size Circuits.

Dziembowski, Pietrzak and Wichs, [29] showed (by a probabilistic argument) that there exist non-malleable codes against poly-size circuits (in fact, against any "small" class of tampering functions). Later work by Faust et al. [31], and Cheraghchi and Guruswami [24], improved the probabilistic analysis and showed that there exist non-malleable codes against poly-size channel with rate $1 - o(1)$.

It is easy to see that the decoding function Dec of a non-malleable code against circuits of size n^c, cannot be computed by circuits of size n^c. This implies that in an explicit construction of non-malleable codes against size n^c circuit, we must allow the decoding algorithm to run in a polynomial time that is larger than n^c, and furthermore, that such an explicit construction implies circuit lower bounds (which are referred to as hardness assumptions).[1]

Ball, Dachman-Soled and Loss [9] gave an explicit construction of non-malleable codes for poly-size circuits (based on a hardness assumption). They showed that for every constant $c > 1$, there is a pair of algorithms (Enc, Dec) that run in time poly(n^c), and form a non-malleable code against circuits of size n^c. The rate achieved by this construction is $\frac{1}{n^{\Theta(1)}}$ which is quite small.

---

[1] Cheraghchi and Guruswamui [24] and Faust et al. [31] considered an intermediate notion of explicitness where the encoding and decoding algorithms also receive a uniformly chosen string of length poly(n^c) (which is chosen and published, once and for all, in a pre-processing stage) and the non-malleability is guaranteed w.h.p. over this random choice. This is termed a "Monte-Carlo construction" in coding theory, and a "construction in the CRS model" in cryptography.

Hardness Assumptions Against Nondeterministic Circuits. This construction relies on a standard hardness assumption from complexity theory: Namely, the assumption that E is hard for exponential size nondeterministic circuits. This assumption loosely says that there is a problem in E = DTIME($2^{O(n)}$) that cannot be computed by nondeterministic circuits of size $2^{\Omega(n)}$. The assumption that E is hard for exponential size (deterministic) circuits was used by the celebrated work of Impagliazzo and Wigderson [39] to imply that BPP = P. The stronger assumption that E is hard for exponential size nondeterministic circuits was introduced for implying that AM = NP, and used in many papers in complexity theory and cryptography [6,7,9,17,18,23,27,28,32,37,38,43,50,56–58,60]. This assumption can be viewed as a scaled, nonuniform version of the assumption: EXP $\not\subseteq$ NP.

Other (nearly) explicit constructions of non-malleable codes for poly-size circuits were given by Ball, Dachman-Soled, Kulkarni, Lin, and Malkin [12] as well as by Dachman-Soled, Komargodski and Pass [26]. These constructions follow a template laid out in [14] (whose codes, in contrast, were mostly in the common random string model) and rely on a variety of very strong cryptographic assumptions, particularly assumptions that are not known how to provably instantiate outside of the random oracle model.[2] Rate was not the focus of these works, and accordingly the codes achieve rate that is just $\frac{1}{n^{\Theta(1)}}$.[3]

1.2 Our Results: Non-malleable Codes with Optimal Rate

In this paper we give an explicit construction of non-malleable codes for poly-size circuits that achieve optimal rate of $R = 1 - o(1)$, under the same hardness assumption used by Ball, Dachman-Soled and Loss [9].

Theorem 1 (Non-malleable codes with rate $1 - o(1)$, informal). *If E is hard for exponential size nondeterministic circuits, then for every constant c, there is a non-malleable code (Enc, Dec) against circuits of size n^c, with rate $R = 1 - o(1)$. Furthermore, Enc and Dec can be computed in time $\mathrm{poly}(n^c)$.*

Theorem 1 is stated in a more formal way in the full version of this paper [8].

---

[2] [12] relies on plain model P-certificates (with uniform soundness) among other assumptions and [26] relies on keyless multi-collision resistant hash functions. Neither of these assumptions are known how to provably instantiate from standard cryptographic assumptions, which is why we refer to the codes as "nearly explicit." Note that [12] also relies on the same hardness assumption made in this work and [9] ([26] uses a strong assumption about the hardness of repeated squaring in place of this hardness assumption).

[3] The conclusions of [9] and [26] are incomparable as the former achieves security with statistical indistinguishability, and the latter achieves only computational indistinguishability, but the latter achieves indistinguishability with a negligible advantage, whereas the former only achieves indistinguishability with an arbitrary fixed inverse polynomial advantage.

Improving the Rate of Non-malleable Codes. In order to prove Theorem 1 we show how to improve the rate of a variant of non-malleable codes (called "small set non-malleable code"), and obtain (standard) non-malleable codes with rate $1 - o(1)$.[4]

More specifically, Shaltiel and Silbak [54] defined a notion called "small set non-malleable codes" (which is closely related to a notion of "bounded non-malleable codes" introduced by Faust et al. [31]). Loosely speaking, this notion of small-set non-malleability (which is incomparable to the standard notion of non-malleability) requires that for every tampering function C, there exists a small set H of messages, such that when C gets to corrupt the encoding of a uniformly chosen message m, it is unlikely that the decoding will produce a message that is neither in H, nor the original message m. (See the definition in the full version [8] for a precise formulation).

Loosely speaking, in small set non-malleability we are interested in the *variety* of outcomes a tampering function can effectively produce in the tampering experiment in which a uniform message is encoded. Note that a poly-size tampering circuit is *nonuniform*, and can be hardwired with a polynomial size set of messages and their codewords. This enables the tampering circuit to lead the decoding to produce any one of these small set of messages. Intuitively, for a small-set non-malleable code there is no markedly better approach than to implement this behavior. We remark that this security guarantee seems incomparable to the standard definition of non-malleable codes.[5]

Shaltiel and Silbak [55] showed how to convert the aforementioned non-malleable codes of [9] into small set non-malleable codes (with the same parameters, and under the same hardness assumption). The result reported in Theorem 1 follows by applying our new "rate improvement technique" to the small set non-malleable codes of [55]. In Sect. 1.3 we elaborate on the ideas that are used in this "rate improvement", and explain how we use the security guarantee of

---

[4] We note that non-malleable code rate compilers for other tampering classes have been constructed in the past. Loosely speaking, these compilers as well as our own follow a similar framework akin to key-encapsulation mechanisms. However, they all differ dramatically in both construction and analysis. We refer the reader to Sect. 1.4 for more details.

[5] Loosely speaking, small-set non-malleable codes give a weaker form of non-malleability (called "bounded non-malleability in [31]) as they allow the tampering function to correlate the original message with the choice of which message in H is being decoded. On the other hand, the security definition in small-set non-malleable codes implies that the tampering function cannot produce an encoding of a uniform and independent random message (as this would allow it to break small-set non-malleability). This is in contrast to standard non-malleability which does not seem to rule out that the tampering function can compute the encoding (as demonstrated by Dachman-Soled, Komargodski and Pass [26]). Another difference, is that the security definition of non-malleable codes rules out tampering functions that can compute the decoding algorithm, whereas small-set non-malleable codes do not. See discussion in [54].

small-set non-malleable codes, and why the security of (standard) non-malleable codes does not seem to suffice.

Comparison of Theorem 1 with Previous Work. The non-malleable codes of Theorem 1 achieve rate $1 - o(1)$, but with a weaker security guarantee than that of [9]. We only achieve computational indistinguishability in Definition 1, whereas [9] achieves statistical indistinguishability. Additionally, like [9], we only achieve a distinguishing advantage that is an arbitrary fixed inverse polynomial, rather than negligible (as is the case in [12,26], which achieves negligible computational indistinguishability under very strong cryptographic assumptions). There are known barriers to achieving negligible (statistical) indistinguishability from nondeterministic hardness assumptions (like the one we use) via black-box reductions [9].[6]

Towards Achieving Statistical Indistinguishability. While we do not obtain statistical indistinguishability in Theorem 1, our technique can potentially yield statistical indistinguishability (and the same security guarantee as in [9]) if the parameters of certain "hard to sample functions" (HTS) that were introduced and constructed by Shaltiel and Silbak [55] could be improved.

More specifically, Shaltiel and Silbak [55] defined a notion called "HTS" which is a function that is "hard to sample on distributions with sufficient min-entropy" (a precise definition of an HTS can be found in the full version of this paper [8]). Loosely speaking, an HTS is a function f, such that for every size n^c circuit A that samples some distribution over pairs (X, Y), there exists a small set H of inputs, such that the probability that $Y = f(X)$ and $X \notin H$, is small. This notion is similar in spirit to the aforementioned notion of small set non-malleable codes: A *nonuniform* poly-size sampling circuit A may be hardwired with a polynomial size set H of inputs x, together with their output $f(x)$. This enables such a circuit to sample a distribution $(X, f(X))$ where X has small support. Intuitively, there is no markedly better approach to sample a distribution of the form $(X, f(X))$, than to implement this behavior, and a poly-size circuit cannot sample a distribution $(X, f(X))$ where X has min-entropy significantly larger than $\log |H|$.

Shaltiel and Silbak [55] gave explicit constructions of HTS (under the assumption that E is hard for exponential size nondeterministic circuits). (In fact, the aforementioned construction of small set non-malleable codes of [55] is achieved by composing the non-malleable codes of [9] with a suitable HTS). The HTS constructions of [55] rely on components from pseudorandomness, and specifically on "high error seeded dispersers" [62]. The min-entropy threshold of known explicit constructions of such dispersers [16,62] are quantitatively inferior compared to the parameters that can be achieved by a probabilistic argument, and

---

[6] The barriers of [9] generalize barriers on black-box constructions of negligible error Nisan-Wigderson style PRGs from nondeterministic hardness assumptions [6,33]. As our "rate improvement" relies on Nisan-Wigderson style PRGs (see Sect. 1.3 for an overview) these barriers also apply to our rate improvement technique.

this makes some of the HTS constructions of [55] have sets size that is small, but still larger than a polynomial.

Our next result states that if the bound on the size of small sets in the HTS construction of [55] can be improved, then we can achieve statistical indistinguishability in our Theorem 1.

Theorem 2 (Statistical indistinguishability assuming improved parameters for HTS, informal). *If (under the hardness assumption) there is an explicit HTS* $f : \{0,1\}^n \to \{0,1\}^{o(n)}$ *against poly-size circuits, with polynomial set size, then Theorem 1 holds with statistical indistinguishability.*

By a standard application of the probabilistic method, a random function f, is w.h.p. an HTS with these parameters. Moreover, a future improvement in the parameters of explicit constructions of high error seeded dispersers will give an HTS with parameters that are sufficient to apply Theorem 2 and achieve statistical indistinguishability in Theorem 1.

A formal statement of Theorem 2 and an explanation of this direction appear in the full version of this paper [8]. In Sect. 1.3 we explain how an HTS with improved quantitative parameters can be used to convert our non-malleable codes into ones with a statistical security guarantee.

Best of both Worlds: Composing Non-malleable Codes with Codes that Correct from Errors. It is natural to try and combine non-malleable codes with codes that correct from errors, aiming to get the best of both worlds. More specifically, given a parameter $0 \le p < \frac{1}{4}$ (measuring the specified fraction of errors we need to recover from) we would like to obtain codes with the following properties:

- Recovery from a p-fraction of errors. If the channel does not alter more than a p-fraction of the encoded message, then decoding produces the original message.
- Non-malleability. If the channel alters more than a p-fraction of the encoded message, then the decoded message is either the original or unrelated to the original message.

A natural way to construct such codes is by composition. Namely, to encode a message m, we first encode it by a non-malleable code Enc_{nm}, and then encode $\text{Enc}_{nm}(m)$, by a code Enc_p that is designed to recover from a p-fraction of errors. In order to argue that this composition is non-malleable, we need that in addition to the tampering function, the encoding and decoding algorithms $(\text{Enc}_p, \text{Dec}_p)$ are also in the class $\mathcal{C}$. We are considering the case where $\mathcal{C}$ is the class of poly-size circuits, and so, can use any *explicit* construction of codes that are designed to recover from p errors.

When composing two codes $\text{Enc}_{nm}, \text{Enc}_p$, the rate of the composed code is the product of the two rates. As by Theorem 1 we now have non-malleable codes with rate $1 - o(1)$, applying this composition, we can get codes that are both non-malleable and recover from a p-fraction of errors, at the *same rate* of the best explicit codes that recover from a p-fraction of errors. In particular, we get the following corollary (which is stated more formally in the full version of this paper [8]).

Corollary 1 (Codes that are best of both worlds, informal). *Let $R_{\text{explicit}}(p)$ denote the best rate for which there are explicit codes that recover from a p fraction of errors. If E is hard for exponential size nondeterministic circuits, then for every $0 \leq p < \frac{1}{4}$, and every constant c, there is a non-malleable code (Enc, Dec) against circuits of size n^c, with rate R approaching $R_{\text{explicit}}(p)$, that recovers from a p-fraction of errors. Furthermore, Enc and Dec can be computed in time $\text{poly}(n^c)$.*

Let $R_{\text{best}}(p)$ denote the best rate for which there are codes that recover from a p-fraction of errors (without the explicitness requirement). Obviously, $R_{\text{explicit}}(p) \leq R_{\text{best}(p)}$. Determining these rates is a notoriously difficult long-standing major open problem of coding theory. It is known that $1 - H(2p) \leq R_{\text{best}}(p) < 1 - H(p)$. (The left inequality is the Gilbert-Varshamov bound, and the right inequality is a consequence of the Elias-Bassalygo bound). The best known explicit codes are inferior to the Gilbert-Varshamov bound, and have $R_{\text{explicit}}(p) < 1 - H(2p)$. (Recently, there has been progress on explicit codes with rate that is close to the Gilbert-Varshamov bound for p approaching $\frac{1}{4}$ [19,40,59]).

Codes Against Poly-size Circuits with Rate that is Superior to that of Coding Theory. In our scenario, we are already assuming that channels are poly-size circuits, and that encoding maps are randomized. For this scenario, there are recent explicit constructions by Shaltiel and Silbak [55] of codes that recover from a p-fraction of errors (w.h.p) and have rate $R(p) = 1 - H(p)$. That is, these codes have rate $R(p)$ that is superior to $R_{\text{best}}(p)$ (let alone $R_{\text{explicit}}(p)$). These constructions rely on the same hardness assumption used in Theorem 1, and by applying composition with these codes, we obtain the following corollary.

Corollary 2 (Codes that are best of both worlds, with rate $R = 1 - H(p)$, informal) *If E is hard for exponential size nondeterministic circuits, then for every $0 \leq p < \frac{1}{4}$, and every constant c, there is a non-malleable code (Enc, Dec) against circuits of size n^c, with rate R approaching $1 - H(p)$, such that for every message $m \in \{0,1\}^{Rn}$, and every size n^c circuit C that alters at most a p-fraction of the bits of $\text{Enc}(m)$, with high probability over the randomness of Enc it holds that $\text{Dec}(\text{Enc}(m)) = m$. Furthermore, Enc and Dec can be computed in time $\text{poly}(n^c)$.*

It is instructive to compare Corollary 1 to Corollary 2. As we have explained above, the latter achieves codes with rate $1 - H(p)$ that is superior to $R_{\text{best}}(p)$, and thus also to $R_{\text{explicit}}(p)$ (that is achieved by the former). In fact, the rate of $R(p) = 1 - H(p)$ achieved in [55], and inherited in Corollary 2, matches the capacity of codes for Shannon's binary symmetric channel.

However, the former gives a stronger guarantee of recovering from a p-fraction of errors in the sense that decoding is guaranteed to produce the original message with probability one, whenever the channel does not alter more than a p-fraction of the encoded message (and this holds also for tampering functions that are not computationally bounded). In contrast, Corollary 2 achieves a weaker guarantee, correct decoding is only guaranteed with high probability (say probability $1-\frac{1}{n^c}$), and only in the case that the tampering function is a size n^c circuit). These weaker decoding guarantees are inherited from the codes of Shaltiel and Silbak [55], and are in some sense unavoidable, see [55] for a discussion.

Perspective. It is our view that as the scenario of non-malleable codes already assumes that tampering functions are computationally bounded, and already incorporates an error parameter in the security definition, the weaker decoding guarantee of Corollary 2 (which only holds against channels that are poly-size circuits) is quite natural in this scenario, and allows achieving rate that is superior to the best possible rate of standard error correcting codes.

1.3   Overview of the Technique

In this section, we give an overview of the main ideas that we use. For this purpose, we will allow ourselves to be informal, and not entirely precise. The later technical sections do not build on the content of this section, and the reader can skip to the technical section if they wish.

Improving the Rate of Non-malleable Codes for Poly-size Circuits. As explained in the previous section, in order to prove Theorem 1 we will try to take a non-malleable code Enc$'$ that does not have good rate, and "compile" it into new non-malleable code Enc with rate $1 - o(1)$. Our initial plan is to apply this transformation on the non-malleable codes of [9], but as we will explain later in Sect. 1.3, it will turn out that we need Enc$'$ to have a different variant of non-malleability.

A Naive Attempt Using PRGs. Let us start with the following naive attempt (that we will refine later on), which will nonetheless be instructive. In order to construct a non-malleable code Enc with block length n and message length k, we will take $k' \ll k$, and a PRG $G : \{0,1\}^{k'} \to \{0,1\}^k$. We will also require and a non-malleable code Enc$'$: $\{0,1\}^{k'} \to \{0,1\}^{n'}$ (that may have bad rate, say $n' = \text{poly}(k')$). By choosing the stretch of G to be sufficiently large, we can arrange that $n' = o(k)$. In order to encode a message $m \in \{0,1\}^k$, we will choose a uniform seed $S \leftarrow \{0,1\}^{k'}$ and define:

$$\text{Enc}(m) = m \oplus G(S), \text{Enc}'(S).$$

That is, we mask m with $G(S)$ (here, G will be a PRG that fools the tampering function C, which is a poly-size circuit) and append Enc$'(S)$.

The decoding algorithm Dec (of the constructed code) will apply the decoding algorithm Dec$'$ (of the initial code) on the second block, to obtain some seed $\bar{S}$, and complete the decoding, by computing $G(\bar{S})$, and xoring it with the first block to produce the decoded message $\bar{m}$. More formally:

$$\bar{m} = \text{Dec}(V1, V2) = V_1 \oplus G(\bar{S}) = V_1 \oplus G(\text{Dec}'(V_2)).$$

The advantage of this naive approach is that the rate of the constructed code Enc is indeed

$$\frac{k}{n} = \frac{k}{k+n'} = \frac{k}{k+o(k)} = 1 - o(1).$$

A Simple Attack that We Ignore for Now. Note that a poly-size circuit $C : \{0,1\}^n \to \{0,1\}^n$ can easily attack this construction by simply ignoring the second block, and xoring the first block with some fixed value $v \in \{0,1\}^k$. As C does not alter the second block, the decoding $\text{Dec}'(\text{Enc}'(S))$ will produce $\bar{S} = S$, which gives that:

$$\bar{m} = \text{Dec}(C(\text{Enc}(m)) = ((m \oplus G(S)) \oplus v) \oplus G(\bar{S}) = m \oplus G(S) \oplus G(S) \oplus v = m \oplus v,$$

This attack completely breaks non-malleability as $\bar{m} = m \oplus v$ is related to m. We ignore this attack for now. This is because using a MAC, it is not difficult to modify the construction to handle this simple attack (which does not alter the second block). We will deal with this concern later in Sect. 1.3. It is more problematic to handle attacks that alter the second block, and handling these kinds of attacks is the main problem that we contend with in this paper.

How Do We Plan to Use the Non-malleability of Enc$'$**?** Let us focus on attacks that only modify the second block. When preparing the second block, we have encoded S with the non-malleable code Enc$'$. It is instructive to ask what would happen if when preparing the second block, we did not encode S, and instead sent S "in the clear". This would have allowed C to replace S with some $\psi(S)$ (for a function ψ that is computable by a small circuit). Note that we have no non-malleability guarantee for the PRG G, and as far as we know, it may be the case that there exists a fixed $v \in \{0,1\}^k$, such that for every $S \in \{0,1\}^{k'}$, $G(S) \oplus G(\psi(S)) = v.$[7]

If this happens then a tampering circuit C that by ignores the first block, and applying ψ on the second block, leads the decoding algorithm Dec to decode to

$$\bar{m} = m \oplus G(S) \oplus G(\psi(S)) = m \oplus v,$$

---

[7] It is easy to construct a PRG G with this property, given an arbitrary PRG G'. More specifically, given a PRG G', we construct a PRG G where the seed of G has one additional bit. If this bit is zero, we output the output of G on the first part of the seed, and if not, we xor the output of G with the fixed string v. It is easy to check that this is a PRG that satisfies $G(S) \oplus G(\psi(S)) = v$, for the function ψ that flips the additional bit of the seed S.

and once again we have that $\bar{m} = m \oplus v$ and this attack completely break non-malleability. We will refer to this attack as *the ψ-attack*.

In the ψ-attack, C was able to arrange that the "decoded seed" $\bar{S}$ is $\psi(S)$ that is *correlated* with S. Intuitively, encoding S by the non-malleable code Enc$'$ is supposed to guarantee that the decoded seed $\bar{S}$ is *not correlated* with S, and rule out the ψ-attack. More formally, we will want to argue that having encoded S with a non-malleable code we have that if $\bar{S} \neq S$ then:

1. $\bar{S}$ is independent of S, which will be used to argue that:
2. $G(S) \oplus G(\bar{S})$ is pseudorandom (as xoring the pseudorandom string $G(S)$ with the independent string $G(\bar{S})$ yields a pseudorandom string).

If we can do this, this will mean that an attack that only modifies the second block, leads the decoding to decode to:

$$\bar{m} = (m \oplus G(S)) \oplus G(\bar{S}) = m \oplus (G(S) \oplus G(\bar{S})),$$

which is a pseudorandom distribution that "masks out" m. This intuitively implies that $\bar{m}$ is unrelated to m (as required).

Difficulties in Implementing the Plan Above. In the intuition above, we did not take into account that when the tampering circuit C tampers the second block of Enc(m) (which is the string Enc$'(m)$) it also receives the first block of Enc(m) (which is the string $m \oplus G(S)$). This in particular means that when C tries to break the non-malleability of Enc$'$, it receives additional information about S that the definition of non-malleability does not account for.

As far as we know, it may be the case that G and Enc$'$ are related in a way that makes it possible for a size n^c circuit C, that sees both $m \oplus G(S)$ and Enc$'(S)$ to lead the decoding Dec$'$ to decode to $\bar{S} = \psi(S)$ which *is* correlated with S.[8] Even worse, such a C can break non-malleability of Enc by implementing the ψ-attack described above.

Summing up, it seems that encoding S by a non-malleable code Enc$'$, does not have the desired effect, and does not rule out the ψ-attack.

Using Seed-Extending PRGs. Can we argue that seeing the first block (that is seeing $m \oplus G(S)$) (in addition to the second block Enc(S)) does not help a circuit C to lead Dec$'$ to decode to a string $\bar{S}$ that is correlated with S?

It turns out that we can achieve such behavior if we require that the PRG G is *seed-extending*. A seed extending PRG is a PRG G that remains secure even when its seed is revealed to the distinguisher. More formally, if the function $G'(x) = G(x), x$ is also a PRG. Before explaining why this is the case, let us discuss the notion of seed-extending PRGs.

---

[8] For example, it does not seem that we can rule out the case that a prefix of $G(S)$ is a string Enc$'(\psi(S))$ where ψ is a OWF. In such a case (and assume for simplicity that m starts with a prefix of zeros) a small circuit C can lead the Dec$'$ to output $\psi(S)$, by simply replacing the second block with a prefix of the first block.

Seed-Extending PRGs. Seed-extending PRGs exist only in a scenario where the intended class of distinguisher cannot run the PRG. In particular, cryptographic PRGs (which fool distinguishers that can run the PRG) cannot be seed-extending. In contrast, known constructions of Nisan-Wigderson style PRGs [39,51,56] are seed-extending, and these can be instantiated using the hardness assumption that E is hard for exponential size deterministic circuits (that we are already assuming).[9]

Why Seed Extending PRGs Help. We now explain how seed-extending PRGs bypass the problem above. This argument is inspired by a related approach that was used by Shaltiel and Silbak [55] in their construction of codes that recover from errors induced by poly-size channels.

We will require that in addition to the circuit C, the seed-extending PRG G, also fools $\mathrm{Enc}', \mathrm{Dec}'$ (and this can be achieved as $\mathrm{Enc}', \mathrm{Dec}'$ indeed run in fixed polynomial time). For a seed extending PRG, we have that:

$$(G(S), S) \equiv_c (U_k, S).$$

Using the fact that G fools Enc', we conclude that:

$$(G(S), \mathrm{Enc}'(S)) \equiv_c (U_k, \mathrm{Enc}'(S)).$$

As we have required that G also fools C and Dec', this means that even after applying the tampering function C, and then applying Dec' on the second block, to obtain $\bar{S}$, we have that the triplet $(G(S), S, \bar{S})$ (obtained in the left hand side) is computationally indistinguishable from the triplet $(G(S), S, \tilde{S})$ (obtained in the right hand side). (Here, $\tilde{S}$ is the string obtained when applying Dec' in the experiment on the right hand side, where $G(S)$ is replaced with U_k.)

In the right hand side we have that S and $\tilde{S}$ are independent. This is because in the experiment on the right hand side, the additional string that C sees is U_k (rather than $G(S)$), and as C could have sampled this string on its own, it does not help C to break the non-malleability of Enc'. We can therefore use the non-malleability of Enc', and conclude that S and $\tilde{S}$ are independent.

From the indistinguishability of the left hand side and the right hand side, we can now conclude that S and $\bar{S}$ are computationally indistinguishable from being independent.

Summing up this discussion, using seed-extending PRGs, we are able to obtain a weakened version of item (1) in our plan above. While we can't show

---

[9] Another drawback of seed-extending PRGs, is that their error is not negligible, but rather an arbitrary fixed inverse polynomial. It is known that black-box proofs cannot achieve such PRGs that run in poly-time and have a negligible error, under standard hardness assumptions [6,33]. There are also extensions of these negative results, that rule out certain black-box constructions of non-malleable codes with negligible error, from the assumption that E is hard for exponential size nondeterministic circuits [9]. This is (one of the) reasons why [9] (as well as our Theorem 1) do not obtain non-malleable code with negligible distinguishing advantage.

that if $\bar{S} \neq S$, then $\bar{S}$ is *statistically independent* from S (as in the original item (1)), we can show that if $\bar{S} \neq S$, then $\bar{S}$ and S are *computationally indistinguishable* from being independent.

Unfortunately, this weaker conclusion is not sufficient to imply item (2) in our plan above. Specifically, we cannot argue that $G(S) \oplus G(\bar{S})$ is pseudorandom. This is because such a conclusion requires the distinguisher to the PRG G, to compute $G(\bar{S})$ given $\bar{S}$, and as we have already observed, because G is seed-extending, distinguishers for G cannot run G.

While this doesn't succeed, we note that we would have been able to argue that $G(S) \oplus G(\bar{S})$ is pseudorandom, if we could guarantee that $\bar{S}$ is either S or a *fixed* string $\bar{s}$. In that case, the fixed string $\bar{s}$ (as well as the fixed string $G(\bar{s})$) could be hardwired to the distinguisher, and we would be able to argue that $G(S) \oplus G(\bar{s})$ is pseudorandom.

Replacing Non-malleable Codes with Small Set Non-malleable Codes. Fortunately, the notion of "small-set non-malleable codes" (abbreviated as SS-non-malleable codes) described in the introduction, essentially allows us to assume that $\bar{S}$ is a fixed string, and implement our plan.

More specifically, if we take Enc$'$ to be an SS-non-malleable code, then the security guarantee of SS-non-malleable codes gives that for every tampering circuit C, there exists a small set $H \subseteq \{0, 1\}^{k'}$, such that it is unlikely that C will lead the Dec$'$ to decode to a string $\bar{S}$ that is neither in H, nor the original seed S.

For the sake of intuition, note that if H was of size one, this would exactly say that $\bar{S}$ is either S or a fixed string. While we cannot expect H to be of size one, the SS-non-malleable codes of [55] achieve H with a polynomial size. By setting G to fool circuits that are sufficiently larger than the size of H, we can allow a distinguisher for G to be hardwired with all the pairs $(s, G(s))$ for $s \in H$. This suffices to implement the plan outlined above, and show that in our construction, either $\bar{S} = S$ or $G(S) \oplus G(\bar{S})$ is pseudorandom.

Summing up, by refining our naive attempt, taking G to be a seed-extending PRG, and Enc$'$ to be an SS-non-malleable code, we are able to circumvent the ψ-attack.

The Final Construction of Enc. We now turn our attention to the simple attack (that we outlined in Sect. 1.3) and modify the construction of Enc so that it also bypasses the simple attack. This will be done as follows:

In addition to the PRG G and the SS-non-malleable code Enc$'$, we will also use a pairwise independent family of hash functions mapping n bits to k' bits. In order to encode a message $m \in \{0, 1\}^k$, we will choose a two uniform seeds $S_{\mathrm{PRG}}, S_{\mathrm{Hash}} \leftarrow \{0, 1\}^{k'}$. We define $S = (S_{\mathrm{PRG}}, S_{\mathrm{Hash}})$, $K = G(S_{\mathrm{Hash}})$, and set $T = h_K(m)$. That is, we use $K = G(S_{\mathrm{Hash}})$ as a "key" to choose a function h_K from the pairwise independent hash family, and set $T = h_K(m)$. Finally, we encode m by:

$$\mathrm{Enc}(m) = m \oplus G(S_{\mathrm{PRG}}), \mathrm{Enc}'((S, T)).$$

The decoding algorithm Dec proceeds as before, namely, Dec will apply the decoding algorithm Dec' (of the SS-non-malleable code) on the second block, to obtain some string $(\bar{S}, \bar{T})$. It will then compute $G(\bar{S}_{\text{PRG}})$, and xor it with the first block to produce a candidate message $\bar{m}$. At this point, Dec will compute $\bar{K} = G(\bar{S}_{\text{Hash}})$, and check whether $h_{\bar{K}}(\bar{m}) = \bar{T}$. If this is the case, Dec will output $\bar{m}$, and otherwise Dec will fail.

Circumventing the Simple Attack. The addition of the hash function is done in order to circumvent the simple attack described in Sect. 1.3. Recall that in that simple attack the tampering function does not alter the second block, and only alters the first block. In this refined construction, we will be able to argue that it is unlikely that Dec will produce a message $\bar{m}$ (rather than failing) on this simple attack.

Here is a rough sketch of this argument. Let C be a tampering circuit. Recall that G is a seed extending PRG that fools both C and Dec'. If C implements the simple attack, we are willing to reveal m, S and T to C (and note that this reveals all the randomness of Enc as well as the message m). However, because G is seed-extending, S_{Hash} is (computationally) independent of $K = G(S_{\text{Hash}})$, which intuitively means that even after we revealed S_{Hash}, C does not have information on the key K used to choose the hash function. By a standard application of pairwise independence, this can be used to argue that C cannot find a message $\bar{m} \neq m$, on which $h_K(\bar{m}) = h_K(m)$, and so, Dec will fail w.h.p., and the simple attack cannot make Dec output a message $\bar{m}$ (let alone one that is related to m).

We remark that here, we once again benefited from the fact that G is a seed-extending PRG. Specifically, this allowed us to reveal the seed S_{Hash}, and still maintain that $K = G(S_{\text{Hash}})$ is "secret".

A Sketch of the Non-malleability Proof. So far, we have only explained how our construction avoids very specific attacks. In this section, we will give a sketch of the non-malleability proof. The high level idea is to compare two experiments: The first experiment is the "real experiment" in which the encoding Enc, tampering function C, and decoding Dec run as designed. The second is an "imagined experiment" in which the strings $G(S_{\text{PRG}})$, and $G(S_{\text{Hash}})$ are replaced by uniform strings.

A Simplifying Assumption. Let's assume for simplicity that the pseudorandomness of G implies that these two experiments are computationally indistinguishable. Note that this does not directly follow from the fact that G is a PRG, because Dec (which is applied in the two experiments) needs to run G as part of the decoding, and as G is seed-extending, it cannot fool adversaries that run G.

An important observation is that the imagined experiment can be carried out *without* knowing m. This follows because in this experiment, in the encoding phase, the first block of Enc(m) is $m \oplus U_k$ (which is independent of m). Furthermore, in the imagined experiment, the pair (S, T) is a uniformly distributed string (that is independent of m). Therefore, one can sample it, *without* knowing m.[10]

The fact that the imagined experiment can be carried out without knowing m, allows us to get a simulator for the non-malleable code. Loosely speaking, this simulator will sample from the imagined experiment, and we will use the computational indistinguishability of the real experiment and the imagined experiment to argue the correctness of the simulator. We remark that this description hides many details.

Justifying the Simplifying Assumption Using SS-Non-malleability. While the computational indistinguishability of the real experiment and the imagined experiment does not follow from the pseudorandomness of G. We are able to show that it does follow, by also using the SS-non-malleability of Enc'. This argument is similar in flavor to the argument that we explained in Sect. 1.3.

Loosely speaking, the idea is that using SS-non-malleability (as well as the fact that G is a seed-extending PRG, and the ideas explained in Sects. 1.3 and 1.3) we can show that in the imagined experiment, for every tampering function C, there exists a small set H of seeds, such that it is unlikely that C can lead Dec' to output a seed $\bar{S}$ which is neither in H, nor the original S. As in Sect. 1.3, we can set the PRG G to fool distinguishers of size slightly larger than $|H|$. This will allow us to argue that the two experiments are computationally indistinguishable.

Recall that previously, we could not argue that the real experiment and the imagined experiment are computationally indistinguishable, because in both experiments a potential distinguisher needed to compute G, and is therefore "too large" to be fooled by G.

However, as it is unlikely that an $\bar{S} \notin H$ would come up, it is now sufficient to fool a distinguisher that is hardwired with the triplet $s, G(s_{\text{PRG}}), G(s_{\text{Hash}})$ for every $s \in H$. (As this allows the distinguisher to run G on all inputs that are likely to come up in the experiment).

We can indeed set G so that it fools such distinguishers, and this allows us to argue that the real experiment and the imagined experiment are computationally indistinguishable.

While we are hiding some details here, this argument is similar in spirit to our explanation of how to handle the ψ-attack. In particular, it critically relies on the fact that G is seed-extending, and that Enc' is SS-non-malleable.[11]

---

[10] Note that here we crucially use that when preparing the key K for the hash function, we applied a seed-extending PRG G, and took $K = G(S_{\text{Hash}})$ (rather than $K = S_{\text{Hash}}$). In the former case, when we replace $G(S_{\text{Hash}})$ with U_k, we obtain a key K that is independent of S_{Hash}, and this is why we get that (S, T) is uniformly distributed. Had we used the more natural choice of $K = S_{\text{Hash}}$, then the pair $S_{\text{Hash}}, h_{S_{\text{Hash}}(m)}$ contains information about m, and we can't sample such a pair without knowing m.

[11] Curiously, our simulator is non-black box in the following manner: It is not sufficient for our simulator to receive black-box access to the tampering circuit C, and it also requires to be hardwired with the set H (associated with C, by SS-non-malleability) as well as the triplet $s, G(s_{\text{PRG}}), G(s_{\text{Hash}})$ for every $s \in H$.

Achieving Statistical Indistinguishability with a Suitable HTS. The construction that we have outlined in the previous sections only achieves computational indistinguishability. In this section, we explain the direction stated in Theorem 2 which shows that we can get a code with statistical indistinguishability if we have a suitable HTS.

More specifically, given an HTS $f : \{0,1\}^k \to \{0,1\}^{o(k)}$ (as promised in Theorem 2) we will modify the code (Enc, Dec) of Theorem 1 as follows: To encode a message m, we will apply Enc on the string $(m, f(m))$. (Note that as $|f(m)| = o(|m|)$ this only slightly reduces the rate of the initial code). Having made this change, when decoding, we expect to get a pair of the form $(X, f(X))$, and decoding will fail if this is not the case.

Recall that an HTS is a function that is hard to sample, and we plan to apply the HTS against the simulator of (Enc, Dec). The transformation described above applies to any non-malleable codes with the following property: For every tampering circuit C of size n^c, there is a simulator Sim_C that is a circuit of size $n^{c_{\text{Sim}}}$ that produces a distribution D_C (as required in Definition 1) where computational indistinguishability holds against distinguishers that are circuits of size $n^{c'}$ (for a constant c' that is sufficiently larger than c, c_{Sim}). The code construction of Theorem 1 has this property.

The security definition of the HTS (when applied against circuits of size $n^{c_{\text{Sim}}}$) guarantees that for every circuit C of size n^c, the HTS f is secure against Sim_C. This formally means that there exists a small set H (that depends on C) such that Sim_C is unlikely to sample a pair (X, Y) such that $X \notin H$, and $Y = f(X)$.

This implies that the distribution D_C (sampled by Sim_C) is statistically close to having small support. We can set the parameters so that this support is much smaller than $n^{c'}$. By the definition of non-malleability, we get that D_C cannot be distinguished from $\text{Tamper}_C(m)$ by circuits of size $n^{c'}$.

However, when a distribution has support size $n^{c'}$, any statistical test can be implemented by a circuit of size roughly $n^{c'}$. This means that statistical indistinguishability immediately follows from computational indistinguishability.

Shaltiel and Silbak [55] constructed an HTS from the hardness assumption that we are already assuming. However, their construction does not achieve a set size that is sufficiently small for our purposes, for a function $f : \{0,1\}^n \to \{0,1\}^{o(n)}$.

We remark that the set size in the construction of [55] would be sufficiently small for our purposes, if the parameters of explicit constructions of high-error seeded dispersers are improved. See [55] for details.

1.4   Other Rate Compilers for Non-Malleable Codes

Our work is not the first to consider rate optimizing compilers for non-malleable codes. All of these compilers, including the one in this paper, share a similar structure that mimics "hybrid" encryption paradigm: in each compiler some form of a low rate non-malleable code (NMC) is combined with some form of symmetric key "authenticated encryption." That said, despite the high level similarity the specific instantiations of each primitive vary widely, and each setting requires overcoming very different analytical challenges.

The rate compiler in this paper instantiates high-rate "authenticated encryption" by hiding the message with a (non-cryptographic) seed-extending PRG and applying a information-theoretic MAC with a pseudorandom key. Moreover, low-rate the non-malleable code used is not an NMC for polynomial tampering, but instead a small-set NMC. As seen in Sect. 1.3, these choices were made to deal with challenges specific to the setting of tampering by polynomial-size circuits.

In contrast to this work, all other compilers are for settings where the tampering must obey some kind of locality constraint: the tampering function corresponding to any particular tampered output bit only has access to partial information about the original codeword.

Local Tampering. Perhaps the first rate compiler was introduced by [5] who showed how to compile a polynomial rate non-malleable code for the family of 1-local tampering functions (where each output bit depends on at most one input bit) to a rate 1 non-malleable code for the same class. In this compiler "authenticated encryption" is instantiated by encoding the message in a high rate error-correcting threshold secret-sharing scheme, flipping a few bits, and writing down the indices changed. This scheme is obviously highly tailored to this very restricted tampering setting, yet nonetheless, the analysis is quite delicate.

Later [35] techniques from the compiler of [5] as well as techniques used by [13] to construct non-malleable codes for local tampering to achieve rate 1 non-malleable codes for $c \lg n$-local functions where $c < 1$ (i.e. tampering functions where each bit depends on the output). This work did not compile non-malleable codes for local functions directly, but instead compiled codes for a tampering class (called "leaky input-output local" tampering) which was a class considered in [13] in order to build NMC for local functions.

Computationally Bounded Split-State Tampering. After [5]'s initial compiler, [1] showed how to compile a polynomial rate NMC for split-state tampering (which remains secure special leakage resilient properties, a so-called *augmented* split-state NMC) to a rate 1 NMC for computational split-state tampering. Computational split-state tampering is split-state tampering (where the left half of the codeword must be tampered independently of the right half) which is additionally restricted to be computable in polynomial time.[12] Note that without this additional computational restriction rate 1/2 is the best possible [24].

Their compiler simply encoded the key to a high rate authenticated encryption scheme with using a split-state NMC, then the ciphertext is simply appended to one of the NMC codeword halves. To handle the fact that the tampering function can jointly tamper the ciphertext text (which depends on the secret key) with half of the codeword, augmented non-malleability was introduced.

---

[12] In contrast, to the tampering model considered in this work the polynomial time bound need not be fixed a priori. However, in the model considered here each tampered codeword bit may depend on all the bits of the original codeword.

Split-State Tampering. A sequence of works [3,4,34,41,42] used rate compilers to improve the rate of NMCs for split-state tampering and t-state tampering (where the codeword is broken into $t > 2$ blocks which are tampered independently).

[41] showed how to compile a low rate split-state NMC to a rate 1/3 4-state NMC. [34,42] later showed reduce the states in the resulting code to 3. Finally, [3] showed how to reduce the states in the resulting code to just 2, yielding a rate 1/3 split-state NMC, which is currently the best known rate of any explicit NMC in this setting. There are slight differences between these compilers but they largely follow the template established in [41]: a seeded extractor is used to build a high rate leakage-resilient encoding scheme which is then tagged using an information theoretic MAC, then the (short) seed for the leakage resilient encoding scheme and the key for the information theoretic MAC are encoded using a low-rate split-state NMC. The analysis critically relies on the independence between the states (making the template work for just 2 tampering states is particularly subtle).

1.5   Organization of This Paper

Due to space limitations this document is only an extended abstract. The reader is referred to the full version of this paper [8] that contains precise definitions and proofs.

Acknowledgement. We are grateful to Banny Applebaum and Iftach Haitner for helpful discussions.

Disclosure of Interests.   Ronen Shaltiel was supported by ISF grants 1006/23 and 1628/17.

Jad Silbak is funded by the Khoury College Distinguished Postdoctoral Fellowship. Part of this work was done while the author was at Tel Aviv University and was supported by ISF grants 666/19 and 2805/21 and by the European Union (ERC, NFITSC, 101097959). Views and opinions expressed are however those of the author(s) only and do not necessarily reflect those of the European Union or the European Research Council. Neither the European Union nor the granting authority can be held responsible for them.

References

1. Aggarwal, D., Agrawal, S., Gupta, D., Maji, H.K., Pandey, O., Prabhakaran, M.: Optimal computational split-state non-malleable codes. In: Kushilevitz, E., Malkin, T. (eds.) TCC 2016-A, Part II. LNCS, vol. 9563, pp. 393–417. Springer, Heidelberg (2016). https://doi.org/10.1007/978-3-662-49099-0_15
2. Aggarwal, D., Dodis, Y., Lovett, S.: Non-malleable codes from additive combinatorics. In: Shmoys, D.B. (ed.) Symposium on Theory of Computing, STOC 2014, New York, NY, USA, 31 May–03 June 2014, pp. 774–783. ACM (2014). https://doi.org/10.1145/2591796.2591804

3. Aggarwal, D., Kanukurthi, B., Obbattu, S.L.B., Obremski, M., Sekar, S.: Rate one-third non-malleable codes. In: Leonardi, S., Gupta, A. (eds.) STOC 2022: 54th Annual ACM SIGACT Symposium on Theory of Computing, Rome, Italy, 20–24 June 2022, pp. 1364–1377. ACM (2022).https://doi.org/10.1145/3519935.3519972

4. Aggarwal, D., Obremski, M.: A constant rate non-malleable code in the split-state model. In: Irani, S. (ed.) 61st IEEE Annual Symposium on Foundations of Computer Science, FOCS 2020, Durham, NC, USA, 16–19 November 2020, pp. 1285–1294. IEEE (2020).https://doi.org/10.1109/FOCS46700.2020.00122

5. Agrawal, S., Gupta, D., Maji, H.K., Pandey, O., Prabhakaran, M.: A rate-optimizing compiler for non-malleable codes against bit-wise tampering and permutations. In: Dodis, Y., Nielsen, J.B. (eds.) TCC 2015, Part I. LNCS, vol. 9014, pp. 375–397. Springer, Heidelberg (2015). https://doi.org/10.1007/978-3-662-46494-6_16

6. Applebaum, B., Artemenko, S., Shaltiel, R., Yang, G.: Incompressible functions, relative-error extractors, and the power of nondeterministic reductions. In: 30th Conference on Computational Complexity, pp. 582–600 (2015).https://doi.org/10.4230/LIPIcs.CCC.2015.582

7. Artemenko, S., Impagliazzo, R., Kabanets, V., Shaltiel, R.: Pseudorandomness when the odds are against you. In: 31st Conference on Computational Complexity, CCC, vol. 50, pp. 9:1–9:35 (2016).https://doi.org/10.4230/LIPIcs.CCC.2016.9

8. Bal, M., Shaltiel, R., Silbak, J.: Non-malleable codes with optimal rate for poly-size circuits. Electronic Colloquium Comput. Complex. (ECCC) (2024). https://eccc.weizmann.ac.il/report/2023/167/

9. Ball, M., Dachman-Soled, D., Loss, J.: (Nondeterministic) hardness vs. non-malleability. In: Dodis, Y., Shrimpton, T. (eds.) CRYPTO 2022. LNCS, vol. 13507, pp. 148–177. Springer, Heidelberg (2022). https://doi.org/10.1007/978-3-031-15802-5_6

10. Ball, M., Chattopadhyay, E., Liao, J., Malkin, T., Tan, L.: Non-malleability against polynomial tampering. In: Micciancio, D., Ristenpart, T. (eds.) CRYPTO 2020, Part III. LNCS, vol. 12172, pp. 97–126. Springer, Heidelberg (2020). https://doi.org/10.1007/978-3-030-56877-1_4

11. Ball, M., Dachman-Soled, D., Guo, S., Malkin, T., Tan, L.: Non-malleable codes for small-depth circuits. In: Thorup, M. (ed.) 59th IEEE Annual Symposium on Foundations of Computer Science, FOCS 2018, Paris, France, 7–9 October 2018, pp. 826–837. IEEE Computer Society (2018). https://doi.org/10.1109/FOCS.2018.00083

12. Ball, M., Dachman-Soled, D., Kulkarni, M., Lin, H., Malkin, T.: Non-malleable codes against bounded polynomial time tampering. In: Ishai, Y., Rijmen, V. (eds.) EUROCRYPT 2019, Part I. LNCS, vol. 11476, pp. 501–530. Springer, Heidelberg (2019). https://doi.org/10.1007/978-3-030-17653-2_17

13. Ball, M., Dachman-Soled, D., Kulkarni, M., Malkin, T.: Non-malleable codes for bounded depth, bounded fan-in circuits. In: Fischlin, M., Coron, J. (eds.) EUROCRYPT 2016, Part II. LNCS, vol. 9666, pp. 881–908. Springer, Heidelberg (2016). https://doi.org/10.1007/978-3-662-49896-5_31

14. Ball, M., Dachman-Soled, D., Kulkarni, M., Malkin, T.: Non-malleable codes from average-case hardness: $AC0$, decision trees, and streaming space-bounded tampering. In: Nielsen, J.B., Rijmen, V. (eds.) EUROCRYPT 2018, Part III. LNCS, vol. 10822, pp. 618–650. Springer, Heidelberg (2018). https://doi.org/10.1007/978-3-319-78372-7_20

15. Ball, M., Guo, S., Wichs, D.: Non-malleable codes for decision trees. In: Boldyreva, A., Micciancio, D. (eds.) CRYPTO 2019, Part I. LNCS, vol. 11692, pp. 413–434. Springer, Heidelberg (2019). https://doi.org/10.1007/978-3-030-26948-7_15

16. Barak, B., Kindler, G., Shaltiel, R., Sudakov, B., Wigderson, A.: Simulating independence: new constructions of condensers, ramsey graphs, dispersers, and extractors. J. ACM **57**(4), 1–52 (2010)

17. Barak, B., Ong, S.J., Vadhan, S.P.: Derandomization in cryptography. SIAM J. Comput. **37**(2), 380–400 (2007)

18. Bitansky, N., Vaikuntanathan, V.: A note on perfect correctness by derandomization. In: Coron, J.S., Nielsen, J. (eds.) EUROCRYPT 2017. LNCS, vol. 10211, pp. 592–606. Springer, Heidelberg (2017). https://doi.org/10.1007/978-3-319-56614-6_20

19. Blanc, G., Doron, D.: New near-linear time decodable codes closer to the GV bound. Electron. Colloquium Comput. Complex. **TR22-027** (2022). https://eccc.weizmann.ac.il/report/2022/027

20. Chattopadhyay, E., Goyal, V., Li, X.: Non-malleable extractors and codes, with their many tampered extensions. In: Wichs, D., Mansour, Y. (eds.) Proceedings of the 48th Annual ACM SIGACT Symposium on Theory of Computing, STOC 2016, Cambridge, MA, USA, 18–21 June 2016, pp. 285–298. ACM (2016).https://doi.org/10.1145/2897518.2897547

21. Chattopadhyay, E., Li, X.: Non-malleable codes and extractors for small-depth circuits, and affine functions. In: Hatami, H., McKenzie, P., King, V. (eds.) Proceedings of the 49th Annual ACM SIGACT Symposium on Theory of Computing, STOC 2017, Montreal, QC, Canada, 19–23 June 2017, pp. 1171–1184. ACM (2017). https://doi.org/10.1145/3055399.3055483

22. Chattopadhyay, E., Li, X.: Non-malleable codes, extractors and secret sharing for interleaved tampering and composition of tampering. In: Pass, R., Pietrzak, K. (eds.) TCC 2020, Part III. LNCS, vol. 12552, pp. 584–613. Springer, Heidelberg (2020). https://doi.org/10.1007/978-3-030-64381-2_21

23. Chen, L., Tell, R.: When arthur has neither random coins nor time to spare: superfast derandomization of proof systems. Electron. Colloquium Comput. Complex. **TR22-057** (2022). https://eccc.weizmann.ac.il/report/2022/057

24. Cheraghchi, M., Guruswami, V.: Capacity of non-malleable codes. IEEE Trans. Inf. Theory **62**(3), 1097–1118 (2016)

25. Cheraghchi, M., Guruswami, V.: Non-malleable coding against bit-wise and split-state tampering. In: Lindell, Y. (ed.) TCC 2014. LNCS, vol. 8349, pp. 440–464. Springer, Heidelberg (2014). https://doi.org/10.1007/978-3-642-54242-8_19

26. Dachman-Soled, D., Komargodski, I., Pass, R.: Non-malleable codes for bounded parallel-time tampering. In: Malkin, T., Peikert, C. (eds.) CRYPTO 2021, vol. 12827, pp. 535–565. Springer, Heidelberg (2021). https://doi.org/10.1007/978-3-030-84252-9_18

27. Doron, D., Moshkovitz, D., Oh, J., Zuckerman, D.: Nearly optimal pseudorandomness from hardness. J. ACM **69**(6), 43:1–43:55 (2022). https://doi.org/10.1145/3555307

28. Drucker, A.: Nondeterministic direct product reductions and the success probability of SAT solvers. In: 54th Annual IEEE Symposium on Foundations of Computer Science, FOCS, pp. 736–745 (2013). https://doi.org/10.1109/FOCS.2013.84. http://doi.ieeecomputersociety.org/10.1109/FOCS.2013.84

29. Dziembowski, S., Pietrzak, K., Wichs, D.: Non-malleable codes. J. ACM **65**(4), 20:1–20:32 (2018). https://doi.org/10.1145/3178432

30. Dziembowski, S., Kazana, T., Obremski, M.: Non-malleable codes from two-source extractors. In: Canetti, R., Garay, J.A. (eds.) CRYPTO 2013, Part II. LNCS, vol. 8043, pp. 239–257. Springer, Heidelberg (2013). https://doi.org/10.1007/978-3-642-40084-1_14
31. Faust, S., Mukherjee, P., Venturi, D., Wichs, D.: Efficient non-malleable codes and key derivation for poly-size tampering circuits. IEEE Trans. Inf. Theory **62**(12), 7179–7194 (2016)
32. Goldreich, O., Wigderson, A.: Derandomization that is rarely wrong from short advice that is typically good. In: APPROX-RANDOM, pp. 209–223 (2002)
33. Grinberg, A., Shaltiel, R., Viola, E.: Indistinguishability by adaptive procedures with advice, and lower bounds on hardness amplification proofs. In: 59th IEEE Annual Symposium on Foundations of Computer Science, pp. 956–966 (2018). https://doi.org/10.1109/FOCS.2018.00094
34. Gupta, D., Maji, H.K., Wang, M.: Constant-rate non-malleable codes in the split-state model. IACR Cryptol. ePrint Arch. p. 1048 (2017). http://eprint.iacr.org/2017/1048
35. Gupta, D., Maji, H.K., Wang, M.: Explicit rate-1 non-malleable codes for local tampering. In: Boldyreva, A., Micciancio, D. (eds.) CRYPTO 2019, Part I. Lncd, vol. 11692, pp. 435–466. Springer, Heidelberg (2019). https://doi.org/10.1007/978-3-030-26948-7_16
36. Guruswami, V., Smith, A.: Optimal rate code constructions for computationally simple channels. J. ACM (JACM) **63**(4), 35 (2016)
37. Gutfreund, D., Shaltiel, R., Ta-Shma, A.: Uniform hardness versus randomness tradeoffs for arthur-merlin games. Comput. Complex. **12**(3–4), 85–130 (2003)
38. Hubáček, P., Naor, M., Yogev, E.: The journey from NP to TFNP hardness. In: 8th Innovations in Theoretical Computer Science Conference, ITCS, vol. 67, pp. 60:1–60:21 (2017). https://doi.org/10.4230/LIPIcs.ITCS.2017.60
39. Impagliazzo, R., Wigderson, A.: $P = BPP$ if E requires exponential circuits: derandomizing the XOR lemma. In: STOC, pp. 220–229 (1997)
40. Jeronimo, F.G., Srivastava, S., Tulsiani, M.: Near-linear time decoding of ta-shma's codes via splittable regularity. In: STOC '21: 53rd Annual ACM SIGACT Symposium on Theory of Computing, pp. 1527–1536 (2021). https://doi.org/10.1145/3406325.3451126
41. Kanukurthi, B., Obbattu, S.L.B., Sekar, S.: Four-state non-malleable codes with explicit constant rate. In: Kalai, Y., Reyzin, L. (eds.) TCC 2017, Part II. LNCS, vol. 10678, pp. 344–375. Springer, Heidelberg (2017). https://doi.org/10.1007/978-3-319-70503-3_11
42. Kanukurthi, B., Obbattu, S.L.B., Sekar, S.: Non-malleable randomness encoders and their applications. In: Nielsen, J.B., Rijmen, V. (eds.) EUROCRYPT 2018, Part III. LNCS, vol. 10822, pp. 589–617. Springer, Heidelberg (2018). https://doi.org/10.1007/978-3-319-78372-7_19
43. Klivans, A., van Melkebeek, D.: Graph nonisomorphism has subexponential size proofs unless the polynomial-time hierarchy collapses. SIAM J. Comput. **31**(5), 1501–1526 (2002)
44. Kopparty, S., Shaltiel, R., Silbak, J.: Quasilinear time list-decodable codes for space bounded channels. In: To Appear in the 60th Annual Symposium on Foundations of Computer Science (FOCS) (2019)
45. Li, X.: Improved non-malleable extractors, non-malleable codes and independent source extractors. In: Hatami, H., McKenzie, P., King, V. (eds.) Proceedings of the 49th Annual ACM SIGACT Symposium on Theory of Computing, STOC 2017, Montreal, QC, Canada, 19–23 June 2017, pp. 1144–1156. ACM (2017).https://doi.org/10.1145/3055399.3055486

46. Li, X.: Non-malleable extractors and non-malleable codes: partially optimal constructions. In: Shpilka, A. (ed.) 34th Computational Complexity Conference, CCC 2019, New Brunswick, NJ, USA, 18–20 July 2019, LIPIcs, vol. 137, pp. 28:1–28:49. Schloss Dagstuhl - Leibniz-Zentrum für Informatik (2019). https://doi.org/10.4230/LIPIcs.CCC.2019.28

47. Li, X.: Two source extractors for asymptotically optimal entropy, and (many) more. Electron. Colloquium Comput. Complex. **TR23-023** (2023). https://eccc.weizmann.ac.il/report/2023/023

48. Lipton, R.J.: A new approach to information theory. In: 11th Annual Symposium on Theoretical Aspects of Computer Science, pp. 699–708 (1994). https://doi.org/10.1007/3-540-57785-8_183

49. Liu, F., Lysyanskaya, A.: Tamper and leakage resilience in the split-state model. In: Safavi-Naini, R., Canetti, R. (eds.) CRYPTO 2012. LNCS, vol. 7417, pp. 517–532. Springer, Heidelberg (2012). https://doi.org/10.1007/978-3-642-32009-5_30

50. Miltersen, P.B., Vinodchandran, N.V.: Derandomizing arthur-merlin games using hitting sets. Comput. Complex. **14**(3), 256–279 (2005)

51. Nisan, N., Wigderson, A.: Hardness vs. randomness. JCSS: J. Comput. Syst. Sci. **49** (1994)

52. Shaltiel, R., Silbak, J.: Explicit list-decodable codes with optimal rate for computationally bounded channels. Comput. Complex. **30**(1), 3 (2021). https://doi.org/10.1007/s00037-020-00203-w

53. Shaltiel, R., Silbak, J.: Explicit uniquely decodable codes for space bounded channels that achieve list-decoding capacity. In: STOC '21: 53rd Annual ACM SIGACT Symposium on Theory of Computing, pp. 1516–1526 (2021). https://doi.org/10.1145/3406325.3451048

54. Shaltiel, R., Silbak, J.: Error correcting codes that achieve BSC capacity against channels that are poly-size circuits. In: 63rd IEEE Annual Symposium on Foundations of Computer Science, FOCS, pp. 13–23 (2022).https://doi.org/10.1109/FOCS54457.2022.00009

55. Shaltiel, R., Silbak, J.: Explicit codes for poly-size circuits and functions that are hard to sample on low entropy distributions. Electronic Colloquium Comput. Complex. (ECCC) (149) (2023)

56. Shaltiel, R., Umans, C.: Simple extractors for all min-entropies and a new pseudorandom generator. J. ACM **52**(2), 172–216 (2005). http://doi.acm.org/10.1145/1059513.1059516

57. Shaltiel, R., Umans, C.: Pseudorandomness for approximate counting and sampling. Comput. Complex. **15**(4), 298–341 (2006)

58. Shaltiel, R., Umans, C.: Low-end uniform hardness versus randomness tradeoffs for am. SIAM J. Comput. **39**(3), 1006–1037 (2009)

59. Ta-Shma, A.: Explicit, almost optimal, epsilon-balanced codes. In: Proceedings of the 49th Annual ACM SIGACT Symposium on Theory of Computing, STOC, pp. 238–251 (2017). https://doi.org/10.1145/3055399.3055408

60. Trevisan, L., Vadhan, S.P.: Extracting randomness from samplable distributions. In: 41st Annual Symposium on Foundations of Computer Science, pp. 32–42 (2000)

61. Viola, E.: The complexity of distributions. SIAM J. Comput. **41**(1), 191–218 (2012)

62. Zuckerman, D.: Linear degree extractors and the inapproximability of max clique and chromatic number. Theory Comput. **3**(1), 103–128 (2007). https://doi.org/10.4086/toc.2007.v003a006

Approximate Lower Bound Arguments

Pyrros Chaidos[1,4], Aggelos Kiayias[2,5], Leonid Reyzin[3],
and Anatoliy Zinovyev[3(✉)]

[1] National and Kapodistrian University of Athens, Athens, Greece
[2] University of Edinburgh, Edinburgh, UK
[3] Boston University, Boston, USA
tolik@bu.edu
[4] IOG, Athens, Greece
[5] IOG, Edinburgh, UK

Abstract. Suppose a prover, in possession of a large body of valuable evidence, wants to quickly convince a verifier by presenting only a small portion of the evidence.

We define an Approximate Lower Bound Argument, or ALBA, which allows the prover to do just that: to succinctly prove knowledge of a large number of elements satisfying a predicate (or, more generally, elements of a sufficient total weight when a predicate is generalized to a weight function). The argument is approximate because there is a small gap between what the prover actually knows and what the verifier is convinced the prover knows. This gap enables very efficient schemes.

We present noninteractive constructions of ALBA in the random oracle and Uniform Random String models and show that our proof sizes are nearly optimal. We also show how our constructions can be made particularly communication-efficient when the evidence is distributed among multiple provers working together, which is of practical importance when ALBA is applied to a decentralized setting.

We demonstrate two very different applications of ALBAs: for large-scale decentralized signatures and for achieving universal composability in general-purpose succinct proof systems (SNARKs).

1 Introduction

Suppose a prover is in possession of a large body of valuable evidence that is individually verifiable. The evidence is so voluminous that presenting and verifying all of it is very expensive. Instead, the prover wants to convince a verifier by presenting only a small portion of the evidence.

More formally, let R be a predicate. We explore succinct arguments of knowledge for a prover who knows a set S_p of values that satisfy R such that $|S_p| \geq n_p$ and wants to convince a verifier that $|S_p| > n_f$, where n_f is somewhat smaller than n_p. Because $n_f < n_p$, the verifier obtains a lower bound approximation to the actual cardinality of S_p; hence we call this primitive an *Approximate Lower Bound Argument* or ALBA.

L. Reyzin—Work done while visiting the Blockchain Technology Lab at the University of Edinburgh.

M. Joye and G. Leander (Eds.): EUROCRYPT 2024, LNCS 14654, pp. 55–84, 2024.
https://doi.org/10.1007/978-3-031-58737-5_3

This problem has a long history. In 1983, in order to prove that $\mathrm{BPP} \subseteq \mathrm{RP}^{\mathrm{NP}}$, Sipser and Gács [Sip83, Section V, Corollary to Theorem 6] showed a simple two-round interactive protocol for proving a lower bound on the size of the set S of accepting random strings. Their construction is based on hash collisions: the verifier chooses some number of universal hash functions $h_1, \ldots, h_m$ [CW79] and the prover shows s, s' such that $s \neq s'$ and $h_i(s) = h_i(s')$ for some $i \in \{1, \ldots, m\}$. If S is small (of size at most n_{f}), then such hash collisions are very unlikely to exist, and if S is big (of size at least n_{p}), then they must exist by the pigeonhole principle. In 1986, Goldwasser and Sipser [GS86, Section 4.1] used a slightly different approach, based on the existence of inverses rather than collisions, for proving that public coins suffice for interactive proofs (we provide more details in the full version of our paper [CKRZ23]). To the best of our knowledge, the term "approximate lower bound" in the context of proof systems appears first in Babai's work [Bab85, Section 5.2].

In designing ALBAs, we will aim to minimize communication and computational complexity; these metrics improve as the "gap" $n_{\mathrm{p}}/n_{\mathrm{f}}$ increases. The proof size and verifier time in classical techniques above are far from optimal. While this does not affect the classical applications of ALBAs (such as in proving that any IP language can be decided by an Arthur-Merlin protocol, where the gap can be a large constant and the prover has exponential time), as we will see it does become a pressing concern in modern applications of ALBAs.

1.1   Our Setting

The prover and verifier have access to a predicate R and the prover needs to show some elements of S_{p} to the verifier so it is convinced that the prover possesses more than n_{f} elements that pass R. The goal is to find some property that is unlikely to hold for small sets S_{f} of size n_{f}, likely to hold for large sets S_{p} of size n_{p}, and can be shown with just a few elements.

Generalization to Weighted Sets. We generalize a predicate R that determines validity of set elements, and consider instead a weight function W that takes a set element and outputs its nonnegative integer weight. In that context we wish to explore succinct arguments of knowledge that convince a verifier that the prover knows a set S that satisfies a lower bound $\sum_{s \in S} W(s) > n_{\mathrm{f}}$. When W is $\{0, 1\}$-valued, we are in the setting of a predicate, and we call this case "unweighted."

We emphasize that R or W are used in a black-box way in our protocols. Thus, our protocols can be used in settings when these functions do not have a known specification—for example, they may be evaluated by human judges who weigh evidence or via some complex MPC protocol that uses secret inputs.

Setup and Interaction Models. Our main focus is on building ALBA protocols that are succinct Non-Interactive Random Oracle Proofs of Knowledge or NIROPK (see Sect. 2 for the definition). If the prover is successful in convincing the verifier, then the knowledge extractor can obtain a set of total weight exceeding n_{f} by simply observing the random oracle queries; in other words, the protocol is straight-line extractable in the nonprogrammable random oracle model. Our security is information-theoretic as long as the predicate R (or the weight function W) is independent of the random oracle; by the standard technique of adding a commitment to R (or W) to every random oracle query, we obtain computational security even if this function is adaptively chosen to depend on the oracle.

We also show simple modifications of our protocols that replace random oracles with pseudorandom functions (PRFs). By simply publishing the PRF seed as a shared random string, we obtain a non-interactive proof of knowledge in the Uniform Random String (URS) model, in which extractor works by reprogramming the URS. Alternatively, we can obtain a two-round public coin proof of knowledge by having the verifier send the PRF seed (we would then use rewinding for extraction). Protocols in these two models are non-adaptively secure—i.e., they require that the predicate R is independent of the URS or the verifier's first message.

Decentralized Setting. The set S_p may be distributed among many parties. For instance, in a blockchain setting it could be the case that multiple contributing peers hold signatures on a block of transactions and they wish to collectively advance a protocol which approves that block. To capture such settings, we introduce decentralized ALBAs: in such a scheme, the provers diffuse messages via a peer to peer network, and an aggregator (who may be one of the provers themselves) collects the messages and produces the proof. Note that not all provers may decide to transmit a message. In addition to the complexity considerations of regular ALBAs, in the decentralized setting we also wish to minimize the total communication complexity in the prover interaction phase as well as the computational complexity of the aggregator.

1.2   Our Results

Our goal is to design protocols that give the prover a short, carefully chosen, sequence of elements from S_p. We show how to do this with near optimal efficiency.

Let λ be the parameter that controls soundness and completeness: the honest prover (who possesses a set of weight n_p) will fail with probability $2^{-\lambda}$ and the dishonest prover (who possesses a set of weight at most n_f) will succeed with, say, also probability $2^{-\lambda}$. Let u be the length of the sequence the prover sends.

The unweighted case. We first show an unweighted ALBA in which the prover sends only

$$u = \frac{\lambda + \log \lambda}{\log \frac{n_\mathrm{p}}{n_\mathrm{f}}} \tag{1}$$

elements of S_p. Moreover, we show that this number is essentially tight, by proving that at least

$$u = \frac{\lambda}{\log \frac{n_\mathrm{p}}{n_\mathrm{f}}}$$

elements of S_p are necessary. (Note that all formulas in this section omit small additive constants for simplicity; the exact formulas are given in subsequent sections.)

Such a protocol is relatively easy to build in the random oracle model if one disregards the running time of the prover: just ask the prover to brute force a sequence of u elements of S_p on which the random oracle gives a sufficiently rare output. Calibrate the probability ε of this output so that $\varepsilon \cdot n_f^u \leq 2^{-\lambda}$ for soundness, but $(1 - \varepsilon)^{n_p^u} \leq 2^{-\lambda}$ for completeness. A bit of algebra shows that $u = \frac{\lambda + \log \lambda}{\log \frac{n_p}{n_f}}$ suffices to satisfy both soundness and completeness constraints, so the proof is short.[1] However, in this scheme, the prover has to do an exhaustive search of $1/\varepsilon$ sequences of length u, and thus the running time is exponential.

It follows that the main technical challenge is in finding a scheme that maintains the short proof while allowing the prover to find one quickly. In other words, the prover needs to be able to find a sequence of u elements with some special rare property (that is likely to occur among n_p elements but not among n_f elements), without looking through all sequences. We do so in Sect. 3 by demonstrating the *Telescope* construction.

Its core idea is to find a sequence of values that itself and also all its prefixes satisfy a suitable condition determined by a hash function (and modeled as a random oracle). This *prefix invariant* property enables the prover to sieve through the possible sequences efficiently expanding gradually the candidate sequence as in an unfolding telescope. We augment this basic technique further via parallel self composition to match the proof length of the exhaustive search scheme. The resulting prover time (as measured in the number of random oracle queries) is dropped from exponential to $O(n_p \cdot \lambda^2)$. We then show how to drop further the prover complexity to $O(n_p + \lambda^2)$ by prehashing all elements and expressing the prefix invariant property as a hash collision. We also establish that our constructions are essentially optimal in terms of proof size by proving a lower bound in the number of elements than must be communicated by any ALBA scheme that satisfies the extractability requirements of Definition 4.

Weights and Decentralized Provers. In the case where all elements have an integer weight, the straightforward way to design a weighted scheme is to give each set element a multiplicity equal to its weight and apply the algorithms we described above. However, the prover's running time becomes linear in the input's total weight n_p which could be in the order of 2^{64} (number of coins in popular cryptocurrencies). A way to solve this problem is to select (with the help of the random oracle) a reasonably-sized subset of the resulting multiset by sampling, for each weighted element, a binomial distribution in accordance with its weight. Given this precomputation, we can then proceed with the Telescope construction as above and with only a (poly)logarithmic penalty due to the weights. We detail this technique in Sect. 5.

Turning our attention to the decentralized setting we present two constructions. In the first one, each party performs a private random-oracle-based coin flip to decide whether to share her value. The aggregator produces a proof by

---

[1]   Let $\varepsilon = 2^{-\lambda} n_f^{-u}$ to satisfy soundness. Then $(1 - \varepsilon)^{n_p^u} < \exp(-2^{-\lambda} n_f^{-u})^{n_p^u} = \exp(-2^{-\lambda}(n_p/n_f)^u)$ is needed for completeness, so it suffices to have $\exp(-2^{-\lambda}(n_p/n_f)^u) \leq 2^{-\lambda}$, i.e., $2^{-\lambda}(n_p/n_f)^u \cdot \log e \geq \lambda$, i.e. $(n_p/n_f)^u \geq 2^\lambda \cdot \lambda / \log e$. Taking logarithm gives the desired result.

concatenating a number of the resulting values equal to a set threshold. In the second construction, we combine the above idea with the Telescope construction letting the aggregator do a bit more work; this results in essentially optimal proof size with total communication complexity $O(\lambda^3)$, or proof size an additive term $\sqrt{\lambda}$ larger than optimal and total communication complexity $O(\lambda^2)$.

1.3   Applications

Beyond the classical applications of ALBAs in complexity theory described earlier [CW79, Sip83, Bab85, GS86], there are further applications of the primitive in cryptography.

Weighted Multisignatures and Compact Certificates. In a multisignature scheme, a signature is accepted if sufficiently many parties have signed the message (depending on the flavor, the signature may reveal with certainty, fully hide, or reveal partially who the signers are). In consensus protocols and blockchain applications, schemes that accommodate large numbers of parties have been put to use in the context of certifying the state of the ledger. In a "proof-of-stake" setting, each party is assigned a weight (corresponding to its stake), and the verifier needs to be assured that parties with sufficient stake have signed a message.

Most existing approaches to building large-scale multisignatures exploit properties of particular signatures or algebraic structures. For example, the recent results of Das et al. and Garg et al. [GJM+23, DCX+23] are based on bilinear pairings and require a structured setup.

In contrast, our work relies *only* on random oracles, making it compatible with any complexity assumption used for the underlying signature scheme, including ones that are post-quantum secure. Expectedly, the black box nature of our construction with respect to the underlying signature results in longer proofs (they can be shortened using succinct proof systems, as we discuss in Sect. 1.4).

In more detail, in order to apply an ALBA scheme to the problem of multisignatures, we treat individual signatures as set elements. The underlying signature scheme needs to be *unique*: it should be impossible (or computationally infeasible) to come up with two different signatures for the same message and public key. Otherwise, it is easy to come up with a set of sufficient total weight by producing multiple signatures for just a few keys[2]. Alternatively, if the knowledge extractor is allowed to rewind (need not be straight-line), one can use an arbitrary (not necessarily unique) signature scheme as follows: treat the public keys as set elements and for every selected public key in the ALBA proof, add its signature. Using an ALBA with decentralized provers is particularly suited to the blockchain setting as signatures will be collected from all participants.

A closely related approach is compact certificates by Micali et al. [MRV+21] who also treat the underlying signature scheme as a black box. In more detail, their construction collects all individual signatures in a Merkle tree, and selects

---

[2] The verifier could check that all public keys are distinct, but since the proof contains just a small subset of the signatures, a malicious prover could try many signatures, or "grind," until it finds a proof that satisfies this check.

a subset of signatures to reveal via lottery (that can be instantiated via the Fiat-Shamir transform [BR93]). Compared to compact certificates, our Telescope scheme obviates the need for the Merkle tree and hence shaves off a multiplicative logarithmic factor in the certificate length. It is also not susceptible to grinding while in compact certificates the adversary can try different signatures to include in the Merkle tree, and unlike compact certificates that rely inherently on the random oracle, our scheme can be instantiated in the CRS/URS model. Finally, our decentralized prover constructions drastically reduce communication. On the other hand, compact certificates cleverly tie the lottery to public keys rather than signatures and support an arbitrary signature scheme (not necessarily unique) while still providing straight-line knowledge extraction.

Reducing communication complexity was also the focus of Chaidos and Kiayias in Mithril, a weighted threshold multisignature, [CK21], that also uses unique signatures and random-oracle-based selection. In our terminology, Mithril applies a decentralized ALBA scheme to unique signatures (possibly followed by compactification via succinct proof systems, as discussed in Sect. 1.4). In comparison to Mithril, our decentralized prover construction achieves significantly smaller proof sizes (when comparing with the simple concatenation version of [CK21]) at the cost of higher communication. In Sect. 4.1 we present a simple lottery that is asymptotically similar to Mithril with concatenation proofs, and offer a comparison in Sect. 8.

Straight-Line Witness Extraction for SNARKs. Ganesh et al. [GKO+23] addressed the problem of universal composability [Can00] for witness-succinct non-interactive arguments of knowledge. Universal composability requires the ability to extract the witness without rewinding the prover. However, since the proof is witness-succinct (i.e., shorter than the witness), the extractor must look elsewhere to obtain the witness. Building on the ideas of Pass [Pas03] and Fischlin [Fis05], Ganesh et al. proposed the following approach: the prover represents the witness as a polynomial of some degree d, uses a polynomial commitment scheme to commit to it, and then makes multiple random oracle queries on evaluations of this polynomial (together with proofs that the evaluations are correct with respect to the commitment) until it obtains some rare output of the random oracle (much like the Bitcoin proof of work). The prover repeats this process many times, and includes in the proof only the queries that result in the rare outputs. The verifier can be assured that the prover made more than d queries with high probability, because otherwise it would not be able to obtain sufficiently many rare outputs. Thus, the knowledge extractor can reconstruct the witness via polynomial interpolation by simply observing the prover's random oracle queries.

We observe that this approach really involves the prover trying to convince the verifier that the size of the set of random oracle queries is greater than d. This approach is just an ALBA protocol, but not a particularly efficient one. Applying our scheme instead of the one custom-built by Ganesh et al. results in less work for the prover. To get a proof of size $u \leq \lambda$, the protocol of Ganesh et al. requires the prover to compute $d \cdot u \cdot 2^{\lambda/u}$ polynomial evaluations and decommitment proofs,[3]whereas our Telescope construction from Sect. 3 requires only $d \cdot \lambda^{1/u} \cdot 2^{\lambda/u}$ of those.[4] Thus, our approach speeds up this part of prover's work by a factor of about u (which is close to the security parameter λ).

1.4   Relation to General-Purpose Witness-Succinct Proofs

In cases where the weight function can be realized by a program, one can use general-purpose witness-succinct proofs to tackle the construction of ALBA schemes via utilizing SNARKs [Gro16, GWC19].

These general purpose tools, however, are quite expensive, especially for the prover. First, the proving time can become impractical when the number of set elements in the witness is large. Second, given that the weight function W must be encoded as a circuit, the proving cost also depends heavily on the complexity of W. Moreover, W cannot always be specified as a circuit, but is evaluated by a more complex process—via a secure multi-party computation protocol or a human judge weighing the strength of the evidence.

On the other hand, these tools can give very short, even constant-size, proofs. To get the best of both worlds—prover efficiency and constant-size proofs— one can combine an ALBA proof with a witness-succinct proof of knowledge of the ALBA proof. This is indeed the approach proposed by Chaidos and Kiayias [CK21]: it first reduces witness size n_f to u by using very fast random-oracle-based techniques, and then has the prover prove u (instead of n_f) weight computations. We can also apply this technique to our constructions, something that can result in a constant size proof with a computationally efficient prover. And given that our constructions can work in the CRS model, one can avoid heuristically instantiating the random oracle inside a circuit.

2   Definitions

Below we present a definition of ALBA inspired by the non-interactive random oracle proof of knowledge (NIROPK) [BCS16] with straight-line extraction. To introduce arbitrary weights, we use a weight oracle $W : \{0,1\}^* \rightarrow \mathbb{N} \cup \{0\}$ and denote for a set S, $W(S) = \sum_{s \in S} W(s)$.

Definition 1. *The triple* (Prove, Verify, Extract) *is a* $(\lambda_{sec}, \lambda_{rel}, n_p, n_f)$-*NIROPK ALBA scheme if and only if*

- Prove^{H,W} *is a probabilistic program that has access to the random oracle H and a weight oracle W;*
- Verify^{H,W} *is a program that has access to the random oracle H and a weight oracle W;*

---

[3] This value follows from the formula $\lambda = r(b - \log d)$ in the "Succinctness" paragraph of [GKO+23, Section 3.1]. Note that r is u in our notation, and the expected number of random oracle queries by the prover is $r \cdot 2^b$. Solving the formula for b, we get $2^b = d2^{\lambda/r}$.

[4] This value is obtained by setting $n_f = d$ and solving (1) for n_p.

- $\mathsf{Extract}^{H,W,\mathcal{A}}$ is a probabilistic program that has access to the random oracle H, a weight oracle W and an adversary program $\mathcal{A}$;
- completeness: for all weight oracles W and all S_p such that $W(S_p) \geq n_p$, $\Pr[\mathsf{Verify}^{H,W}(\mathsf{Prove}^{H,W}(S_p)) = 1] \geq 1 - 2^{-\lambda_{rel}}$;
- proof of knowledge: consider the following experiment $ExtractExp(\mathcal{A}^{H,W}, W)$:

  $S_f \leftarrow \mathsf{Extract}^{H,W,\mathcal{A}}()$;
  output 1 iff $W(S_f) > n_f$;

  we require that for all weight oracles W and all probabilistic oracle access programs $\mathcal{A}^{H,W}$,

$$\Pr[ExtractExp(\mathcal{A}, W) = 1] \geq \Pr\left[\mathsf{Verify}^{H,W}\left(\mathcal{A}^{H,W}()\right) = 1\right] - 2^{-\lambda_{sec}};$$

  moreover, $\mathsf{Extract}^{H,W,\mathcal{A}}()$ is only allowed to run $\mathcal{A}^{H,W}$ once with the real H and W and only observes the transcript with its oracles (straight-line extraction property), $\mathsf{Extract}$ runs in time polynomial in the size of this transcript.

As presented, this definition is non-adaptive; i.e., it does not allow W to depend on H; adaptivity can be added if it is possible to commit to W; see Sect. 6 for further discussion.

The above formulation of ALBAs captures the setting where a prover has the entire set S_p in its possession. We will also be interested in ALBAs where the prover is *decentralized*—by this we refer to a setting where a number of prover entities, each one possessing an element $s \in S_p$ wish to act in coordination towards convincing the verifier. We now define a decentralized ALBA.

Definition 2. *The quadruple* (Prove, Aggregate, Verify, Extract) *is a* $(\lambda_{sec}, \lambda_{rel}, n_p, n_f)$*-decentralized NIROPK ALBA scheme if and only if*

- $\mathsf{Prove}^{H,W}$ is a probabilistic program that has access to the random oracle H and a weight oracle W;
- $\mathsf{Aggregate}^{H,W}$ is a probabilistic program that has access to the random oracle H and a weight oracle W;
- $\mathsf{Verify}^{H,W}$ is a program that has access to the random oracle H and a weight oracle W;
- $\mathsf{Extract}^{H,W,\mathcal{A}}$ is a probabilistic program that has access to the random oracle H, a weight oracle W and an adversary program $\mathcal{A}$;
- completeness: consider the following experiment $CompExp(S_p, W)$:

  $S := \emptyset$;
  for $s \in S_p$ **do**
  $\quad m \leftarrow \mathsf{Prove}^{H,W}(s)$;
  $\quad$ **if** $m \neq \varepsilon$ **then**   ▷ *if m is not empty string*
  $\quad\quad S := S \cup \{m\}$;
  $\pi \leftarrow \mathsf{Aggregate}^{H,W}(S)$;
  $r \leftarrow \mathsf{Verify}^{H,W}(\pi)$;
  return r;

we require that for all weight oracles W and all S_p such that $W(S_p) \geq n_p$,
$$\Pr[CompExp(S_p, W) = 1] \geq 1 - 2^{-\lambda_{rel}};$$
– *proof of knowledge: consider the following experiment $ExtractExp(\mathcal{A}^{H,W}, W)$:*

    $S_f \leftarrow \mathsf{Extract}^{H,W,\mathcal{A}}();$

    ***output** 1 iff $W(S_f) > n_f$;*

we require that for all weight oracles W and all probabilistic oracle access programs $\mathcal{A}^{H,W}$,

$$\Pr[ExtractExp(\mathcal{A}, W) = 1] \geq \Pr\left[\mathsf{Verify}^{H,W}\left(\mathcal{A}^{H,W}()\right) = 1\right] - 2^{-\lambda_{sec}};$$

moreover, $\mathsf{Extract}^{H,W,\mathcal{A}}()$ is only allowed to run $\mathcal{A}^{H,W}$ once with the real H and W and only observes the transcript with its oracles (straight-line extraction property), $\mathsf{Extract}$ runs in time polynomial in the size of this transcript.

In this model, we would like to minimize not only the proof size, but also the amount of communication characterized by the size of S in CompExp. Note that the above definition can be extended to multiple rounds of communication, but this is not something we explore in this work—all our decentralized constructions are "1-round."

Finally, we present a proof of knowledge ALBA definition in the CRS model. Unlike for NIROPK, the knowledge extractor here is allowed to rewind the adversary $\mathcal{A}$ and is given it as regular input. Note that the definition crucially requires the CRS to be independent of W; see Sect. 7 for further discussion.

Definition 3. (Prove, Verify, Extract, GenCRS) *is a $(\lambda_{sec}, \lambda_{rel}, n_p, n_f)$-CRS proof of knowledge ALBA scheme if and only if*

– Prove^W *is a probabilistic program;*
– Verify^W *is a program having access to a weight oracle W;*
– $\mathsf{Extract}^W$ *is a probabilistic program having access to a weight oracle W;*
– GenCRS *is a probabilistic program;*
– *completeness: consider the following experiment $CompExp(W, S_p)$:*

    $crs \leftarrow \mathsf{GenCRS}();$

    $\pi \leftarrow \mathsf{Prove}(crs, S_p);$

    $r \leftarrow \mathsf{Verify}^W(crs, \pi);$

    return r;

we require that for all weight oracles W and all S_p such that $W(S_p) \geq n_p$,
$$\Pr[CompExp(W, S_p) = 1] \geq 1 - 2^{-\lambda_{rel}};$$
– *proof of knowledge: consider the following experiment $SoundExp(\mathcal{A}^W, W)$:*

    $crs \leftarrow \mathsf{GenCRS}();$

    $\pi \leftarrow \mathcal{A}^W(crs);$

    $r \leftarrow \mathsf{Verify}^W(crs, \pi);$

    return r;

we require that for all weight oracles W and all probabilistic oracle access programs $\mathcal{A}^W$, if $\mathcal{A}$ runs in time T and $\varepsilon = \Pr[SoundExp(\mathcal{A}^W, W) = 1] - 2^{-\lambda_{sec}} > 0$, then $S_f \leftarrow \mathsf{Extract}^W(\mathcal{A})$ runs in expected time $poly(T, 1/\varepsilon)$ and $\Pr\left[W(S_f) > n_f\right] = 1$.

3   Telescope ALBA

In this section we present two ALBA schemes in sequence. We start with a less efficient but simpler construction to illustrate the main idea. We then proceed to optimize the scheme's efficiency.

For both constructions, we will assume we have three random oracles H_0, H_1, and H_2 having particular output distributions. We explain how to implement these using a single random oracle which outputs binary strings in the full version [CKRZ23] of this work. Further, we initially restrict weights to be either 0 or 1, and generalize to integers in Sect. 5. Finally, we postpone showing the proof of knowledge property and instead consider a simpler notion of soundness: given n_f elements fixed in advance, what is the probability that a valid proof exists containing only those elements? Sect. 6 will then show how a knowledge extractor can be constructed.

3.1   Basic Construction

The main idea is as follows. Let d, u and q be parameters. The prover first considers all pairs consisting of an integer in $[d]$ and one of the elements of S_p and selects each of the $n_p d$ pairs with probability $1/n_p$. In expectation he will have d pairs selected. Now these pairs are treated as single units and they are paired with each element of S_p, resulting in triples that are selected again with probability $1/n_p$. This process is repeated u times ending with, in expectation, d tuples consisting of one integer in $[d]$ and u set elements. Now, each of the tuples is selected with probability q and any selected tuple will be a valid proof.

More formally, let H_1 and H_2 be random functions returning 1 with probability $1/n_p$ and q respectively, and returning 0 otherwise. Any tuple $(t, s_1, ..., s_u)$ such that

- $1 \le t \le d$;
- for all $1 \le i \le u$, $H_1(t, s_1, ..., s_i) = 1$;
- $H_2(t, s_1, ..., s_u) = 1$;

is a valid proof (see Sect. 3.3 how to implement H_1 efficiently). Define the program Verify accordingly.

Intuitively, this works because the honest prover maintains d tuples in expectation at each stage, while the malicious prover's tuples decrease n_p/n_f times with each stage. However, to implement and analyze the prover algorithm, it will be convenient to represent all tuples $(t, s_1, ..., s_i)$, where $1 \le t \le d$, $0 \le i \le u$ and $s_1, ..., s_i \in S_p$, as d trees of height u with $\{(1), ..., (d)\}$ being the roots of the trees and $\{(t, s_1, ..., s_u)\}_{1 \leq t \leq d, s_1, ..., s_u \in S_p}$ being the leaves. To implement Prove, simply run depth first search (DFS) to find a "valid" path from a root to a leaf.

We will now analyze soundness of this construction. As mentioned above, the soundness error is defined to be the probability that a valid proof exists containing only elements from a fixed set S_f of size n_f.

Theorem 1. *Let*

$$u \geq \frac{\lambda_{sec} + \log(qd)}{\log \frac{n_p}{n_f}}.$$

Then soundness error is $\leq 2^{-\lambda_{sec}}$.

Proof. We analyze soundness error, denoted by S, using simple union bound.

$$S \leq \left(\frac{1}{n_p}\right)^u \cdot q \cdot d \cdot n_f^u = \left(\frac{n_f}{n_p}\right)^u \cdot qd.$$

Then

$$-\log S \geq -\left(u \log \frac{n_f}{n_p} + \log(qd)\right) = u \log \frac{n_p}{n_f} - \log(qd) \geq \lambda_{sec}.$$

We now analyze completeness.

Theorem 2. *Let*

$$d \geq \frac{2u\lambda_{rel}}{\log e}; q = \frac{2\lambda_{rel}}{d \log e}.$$

Then completeness error is $\leq 2^{-\lambda_{rel}}$ *and the probability that there exists a valid proof with a particular integer t is at least* $q - (u+1) \cdot \frac{q^2}{2}$.

Proof. Completeness can be described using the following recursive formula. For $0 \leq k \leq u$, let $f(k)$ be the probability that when fixing a prefix of an integer in $[d]$ and $u - k$ elements $t, s_1, ..., s_{u-k}$, there is no suffix of honest player's elements that works, meaning there is no $s_{u-k+1}, ..., s_u \in S_p$ such that for all $u - k + 1 \leq i \leq u$, $H_1(t, s_1, ..., s_i) = 1$, and $H_2(t, s_1, ..., s_u) = 1$. Then one can see that

- $f(0) = 1 - q$;
- for $0 \leq k < u$, $f(k+1) = \left((1 - \frac{1}{n_p}) + \frac{1}{n_p} \cdot f(k)\right)^{n_p}$;
- the probability that there does not exist a valid proof with a particular integer t is $f(u)$;
- the probability that the algorithm fails in the honest case is $\left(f(u)\right)^d$.

This recursive formula can be approximated:

$$f(k+1) = \left(1 + \frac{1}{n_p}(f(k) - 1)\right)^{n_p} \leq \left(e^{\frac{1}{n_p}(f(k)-1)}\right)^{n_p} = e^{f(k)-1}. \qquad (2)$$

It is convenient to look at the negative logarithm of this expression; we will prove by induction that $-\ln f(k) \geq q - k \cdot \frac{q^2}{2}$.

Basic case: $-\ln f(0) = -\ln(1-q) \geq -\ln(e^{-q}) = q$.

Inductive step: by Eq. 2,

$$-\ln f(k+1) \geq 1 - f(k) \geq 1 - e^{-\left(q - k \cdot \frac{q^2}{2}\right)}[\geq]$$

Using the values for d and q, one can see that $k \cdot \frac{q^2}{2} \leq u \cdot \frac{q^2}{2} \leq q$, then

$$[\geq]1 - \left(1 - \left(q - k \cdot \frac{q^2}{2}\right) + \frac{\left(q - k \cdot \frac{q^2}{2}\right)^2}{2}\right) \geq$$

$$\left(q - k \cdot \frac{q^2}{2}\right) - \frac{q^2}{2} = q - (k+1) \cdot \frac{q^2}{2}.$$

Hence, $-\ln f(u) \geq q - u \cdot \frac{q^2}{2}$ and the probability that the honest prover fails is $(f(u))^d \leq \exp\left(-(q - u \cdot \frac{q^2}{2})d\right)$. Using the values for d and q, one can see that this is at most $2^{-\lambda_{rel}}$. Additionally, the probability that there exists a valid proof with a particular integer t is

$$1 - f(u) \geq e^{-\left(q - u \cdot \frac{q^2}{2}\right)} \geq$$

$$1 - \left(1 - \left(q - u \cdot \frac{q^2}{2}\right) + \frac{(q - u \cdot \frac{q^2}{2})^2}{2}\right) \geq q - (u+1) \cdot \frac{q^2}{2}.$$

$\square$

Corollary 1. *Let*

$$u \geq \frac{\lambda_{sec} + \log \lambda_{rel} + 1 - \log \log e}{\log \frac{n_p}{n_f}}; d \geq \frac{2u\lambda_{rel}}{\log e}; q = \frac{2\lambda_{rel}}{d \log e}.$$

Then soundness error is $\leq 2^{-\lambda_{sec}}$ *and completeness error is* $\leq 2^{-\lambda_{rel}}$.

It is worth noting that the constant in d, and thus algorithm's running time, can be reduced. We show how to do this in the full version. Although the scheme still remains less efficient than the improved construction in Sect. 3.2, the optimizations can potentially be transferred over; we leave that for future work.

Running Time. In this section we analyze the prover's running time.

Assume S_p is a set with cardinality n_p. As mentioned above, all tuples $(j, s_1, ..., s_i)$ can be represented as d trees. We would like to analyze the number of "accessible" vertices in these trees. Let the indicator random variable

$$A_{j,s_1,...,s_i} = \begin{cases} 1 & \text{if for all } 1 \leq r \leq i, H_1(j, s_1, ..., s_r) = 1 \\ 0 & \text{otherwise.} \end{cases}$$

If $A_{j,s_1,\ldots,s_i} = 1$ we say the vertex $(j, s_1, \ldots, s_i)$ is accessible.

Let us first prove that the expected number of accessible vertices in a single tree at a particular height is 1.

Theorem 3. *For any j and $0 \le i \le u$,*

$$\mathbb{E}\left[\sum_{s_1,\ldots,s_i \in S_p} A_{j,s_1,\ldots,s_i} \right] = 1.$$

We present the proof in the full version [CKRZ23] of this work.

Assuming the prover runs DFS, Theorem 2 gives a bound on the expected number of evaluated trees. And by the above theorem, the algorithm invokes H_1 $n_p u$ times and H_2 once in expectation per tree. Thus, the expected total number of hash evaluations shall be the product of the expected number of evaluated trees and $(n_p u + 1)$. This, however, needs a more careful proof.

Theorem 4. *The expected number of hash evaluations is at most*

$$\left(q - (u + 1) \cdot \frac{q^2}{2} \right)^{-1} (n_p u + 1)$$

We present the proof in the full version [CKRZ23] of this work.

Taking parameter values from Corollary 1 and letting $\lambda = \lambda_{\mathrm{sec}} = \lambda_{\mathrm{rel}}$, we thus obtain an expected number of hash evaluations of $O(n_p \cdot \lambda^2)$.

We might also wish to have a tighter bound on the running time or on the number of accessible vertices to argue that an adversary cannot exploit an imperfect hash function or a PRF by making too many queries. Below we present a Chernoff style bound on the number of accessible non-root vertices in all d trees

$$Z = \sum_{\substack{1 \le j \le d, \\ 1 \le i \le u, \\ s_1,\ldots,s_i \in S_p}} A_{j,s_1,\ldots,s_i}.$$

Note that $\mathbb{E}[Z] = du$.

Theorem 5.

$$\Pr[Z \ge (1 + \delta)du] \le \exp\left(-\frac{\delta^2}{4(1+\delta)} \cdot \frac{d}{u} \right).$$

We present the proof in the full version [CKRZ23] of this work.

Taking parameter values from Corollary 1 and letting $\lambda = \lambda_{\mathrm{sec}} = \lambda_{\mathrm{rel}}$, we thus conclude that the algorithm does $O(n_p \cdot \lambda^3)$ hash evaluations with overwhelming probability.

3.2   Construction with Prehashing

The basic scheme described above has proving expected time $O(n_\mathrm{p} \cdot \lambda^2)$ and verification time $O(\lambda)$ if we let $\lambda = \lambda_{\mathrm{sec}} = \lambda_{\mathrm{rel}}$. The modification described in this section has proving expected time $O(n_\mathrm{p} + \lambda^2)$ and verification time is unchanged.

The improvement is inspired by balls-and-bins collisions. Whereas in the previous scheme for every tuple we tried each of n_p possible extensions, here we hash tuples to a uniform value in $[n_\mathrm{p}]$ and hash individual set elements to a uniform value in $[n_\mathrm{p}]$, and consider a valid extension to be such that the tuple and the extension both hash to the same value. More formally, we have random functions H_0 and H_1 producing a uniformly random value in $[n_\mathrm{p}]$ and hash function H_2 returning 1 with probability q and 0 otherwise, and consider a tuple $(t, s_1, ..., s_u)$ a valid proof if and only if

- $1 \leq t \leq d$;
- for all $1 \leq i \leq u$, $H_1(t, s_1, ..., s_{i-1}) = H_0(s_i)$;
- $H_2(t, s_1, ..., s_u) = 1$;

(see Sect. 3.3 how to implement H_1 efficiently). Define the Verify program accordingly.

As before, we have d valid tuples in expectation at each stage but by precomputing $H_0(\cdot)$ (balls to bins) we avoid trying all n_p extensions for a tuple. The analysis of completeness, however, is more complicated. Before, we assumed in the recursive formula that failure events for each element extension are all independent. Here, it is not true: the fact that one extension eventually succeeds can tell that the balls-to-bins are well distributed. Indeed, if each bin gets exactly one ball, then there will always be a tuple that succeeds except maybe for the requirement that $H_2(\cdot) = 1$. However, if all balls land in one bin, then the success probability is smaller. To get rid of this dependency, we can however fix the balls-to-bins arrangement. Then such events become independent again.

The proof has two parts: the first one says that if the arrangement of the balls is "nice", then with high probability the honest player succeeds. The second part proves that we get a "nice" distribution of balls with high probability. The "nice" property itself is artificial, but one can notice that if the number of bins of size s is exactly the expected number of bins of size s if the size of each bin is a Poisson random variable with mean 1, then the analysis of completeness becomes very similar to that of the previous scheme. By using Poisson approximation and Chernoff like analysis, we can show that the property we care about does hold with high probability. We need, however, assume that the number of set elements n_p is large enough (on the order of λ^3). Alternatively, we can generate multiple balls per set element.

We first analyze soundness. As mentioned previosly, we define soundness error to be the probability that a valid proof can be constructed using elements S_f with $|S_\mathrm{f}| = n_\mathrm{f}$ (simple soundness).

Theorem 6. *Let*

$$u \geq \frac{\lambda_{sec} + \log(qd)}{\log \frac{n_p}{n_f}}.$$

Then soundness error is $\leq 2^{-\lambda_{sec}}$.

We present the proof in the full version [CKRZ23] of this work.

Theorem 7. *Assume*

$$d \geq \frac{16u(\lambda_{rel} + \log 3)}{\log e}; q = \frac{2(\lambda_{rel} + \log 3)}{d \log e}; n_p \geq \frac{d^2 \log e}{9(\lambda_{rel} + \log 3)}. \tag{3}$$

Then completeness error is $\leq 2^{-\lambda_{rel}}$.

We present the proof in the full version [CKRZ23] of this work.

Corollary 2. *Assume*

$$u \geq \frac{\lambda_{sec} + \log(\lambda_{rel} + \log 3) + 1 - \log \log e}{\log \frac{n_p}{n_f}}; d \geq \frac{16u(\lambda_{rel} + \log 3)}{\log e};$$

$$q = \frac{2(\lambda_{rel} + \log 3)}{d \log e}; n_p \geq \frac{d^2 \log e}{8(\lambda_{rel} + \log 3)}.$$

Then soundness is $\leq 2^{-\lambda_{sec}}$ *and completeness error is* $\leq 2^{-\lambda_{rel}}$.

It is worth noting that the $n_p \geq \Omega(\lambda^3)$ requirement can be removed as follows. Instead of doing Chernoff like analysis, that requires large n_p, one can utilize Markov's inequality to show that the "nice" arrangement of balls into bins happens with moderate probability, e.g. $\frac{3}{4}$, to achieve a scheme with completeness $\frac{1}{2}$. Such a scheme can then be amplified to achieve arbitrary λ_{rel} by setting $\lambda_{sec} := \lambda_{sec} + \log \lambda_{rel}$ and having the verifier accept any one of λ_{rel} independent proofs. As a result, the expected running time is no longer $\Omega(\lambda^3)$ but $O(n_p + \lambda^2)$, but we need to apply H_0 to all elements twice in expectation as opposed to exactly once. Hence, for large n_p it still makes sense to use the algorithm as described at the beginning of the section. The Markov analysis can be found in the full version [CKRZ23] of this paper.

Running Time. In this section we analyze the prover's running time. Assume S_p is a set with cardinality n_p. As described in Sect. 3.1, all tuples $(j, s_1, ..., s_i)$ can be represented as d trees of height u. We would like to analyze the number of "accessible" vertices in these trees. Let the indicator random variable

$$A_{j,s_1,...,s_i} = \begin{cases} 1 & \text{if for all } 1 \leq r \leq i, H_1(j, s_1, ..., s_{r-1}) = H_0(s_r) \\ 0 & \text{otherwise.} \end{cases}$$

If $A_{j,s_1,...,s_i} = 1$ we say the vertex $(j, s_1, ..., s_i)$ is accessible.

Similarly to Sect. 3.1, one can prove that the expected number of accessible vertices in a single tree at a particular height is 1. This holds independently of the value of H_0!

Theorem 8. *For any j and $0 \leq i \leq u$,*

$$\mathbb{E}\left[\sum_{s_1,\ldots,s_i \in S_p} A_{j,s_1,\ldots,s_i} \middle| H_0 \right] = 1.$$

We will now analyze the expected running time of the prover. The hash function H_0 is invoked exactly n_p times, so we will only upper bound the expected number of invocations of H_1 and H_2.

Theorem 9. *The expected number of invocations of H_1 and H_2 is at most*

$$\frac{u+1}{1 - e^{-q+4uq^2}} + 2e^{-\frac{9}{4}n_p q^2} \cdot d(u+1).$$

We present the proof in the full version [CKRZ23] of this work.

Taking parameter values from Corollary 2 and letting $\lambda = \lambda_{\text{sec}} = \lambda_{\text{rel}}$, we thus get expected number of evaluations of H_1 and H_2 $O(\lambda^2)$. This is dominated by n_p invocations of H_0 since n_p is assumed to be $\Omega(\lambda^3)$.

Below we also present a tight bound on the number of accessible non-root vertices in all d trees

$$Z = \sum_{\substack{1 \leq j \leq d, \\ 1 \leq i \leq u, \\ s_1,\ldots,s_i \in S_p}} A_{j,s_1,\ldots,s_i}.$$

Note that $\mathbb{E}[Z] = du$.

Theorem 10. *Let*

$$\lambda > 0; \quad \lambda' = \frac{\lambda+2}{\log e}; \quad n_p \geq \frac{u^2 \lambda'}{2};$$

$$u! \cdot \frac{u - e^{\frac{1}{3u}}}{u^3} \geq 72e^{-\frac{2}{3}} \cdot 2^\lambda; \quad \delta = e^{1+\sqrt{\frac{18u^2\lambda'}{n_p}}}\left(\frac{3u\lambda'}{d} + 1\right).$$

Then

$$\Pr[Z \geq \delta du] \leq 2^{-\lambda}.$$

We present the proof in the full version [CKRZ23] of this work.

Taking parameter values from Corollary 2 and letting $\lambda = \lambda_{\text{sec}} = \lambda_{\text{rel}}$, we thus conclude that the prover algorithm evaluates H_1 and H_2 $O(\lambda^3)$ times with overwhelming probability.

3.3 Implementing Random Oracles with Long Inputs

We describe our protocols assuming a random oracle H_1 that can accommodate inputs of any length, which, in particular, implies independence of outputs for inputs of different lengths. However, to have an accurate accounting for running times, one has to charge for the cost of running a random oracle in proportion to the input length. Because the Telescope construction runs $H_1(j)$, $H_1(j, s_1)$, $H_1(j, s_1, s_2)$, $H_1(j, s_1, s_2 \ldots, s_u)$, the cost of just one u-tuple is quadratic in u. To reduce this cost to linear (thus saving a factor of u in running time), we will implement $H_1(j, s_1, \ldots, s_{i+1})$ to reuse most of the computation of $H_1(j, s_1, \ldots, s_i)$. The most natural way to do so is to slightly modify the Merkle-Damgård construction: use a two-input random oracle f ("compression function") with a sufficiently long output and a function g that maps the range of f to the distribution needed by H_1. We present the details of implementing g in the full version of this work. Inductively define $H_1'(j, s_1, \ldots, s_{i+1}) = f(H_1'(j, s_1, \ldots, s_i), s_{i+1})$ and let $H_1(x) = g(H_1'(x))$.

While not indifferentiable from a random oracle (see Coron et al. [CDMP05] for similar constructions that are), this construction suffices for our soundness and extractability arguments, because those arguments need independence only for a single chain (they handle multiple different chains by the union bound). Neither length extension attacks nor collisions are important. Completeness suffers very slightly by the probability of f-collisions, which can be made negligible by making the output of f large enough and using the bound on the number of queries made by the honest prover (Theorems 5 and 10).

3.4   Optimality of the Certificate Size

In this section, we show that the number of set elements u included in a proof is essentially optimal for our constructions. Because our construction works for a black-box weight function that formally is implemented via an oracle (and in reality may be implemented by MPC, a human judge, etc.), the verifier must query the weight function on some values; else the verifier has no knowledge of whether any values in the prover's possession have any weight.

Thus, for the sake of proving optimality, we consider only protocols that make this part of verification explicit. We define an algorithm Read (see the definition below) that takes a proof and returns set elements; these set elements must have been in the prover's possession. We bound the proof size in terms of the number of set elements returned by Read, showing that if it is too small, the protocol cannot be secure. We also note that the following definition can be used for upper bound results too, as demonstrated in Sect. 7 for the CRS model.

Definition 4. (Prove, Read, Verify) *is a* $(\lambda_{sec}, \lambda_{rel}, n_p, n_f)$-*ALBA scheme if and only if*

- Prove^H *is a probabilistic random oracle access program;*
- Verify^H *is a random oracle access program;*
- Read *is a program;*
- *completeness: consider the following experiment* $CompExp(S_p)$:

   $\pi \leftarrow \text{Prove}^H(S_p)$;

   ***output** 1 iff* $\text{Read}(\pi) \subseteq S_p$ *and* $\text{Verify}^H(\pi) = 1$;

   we require that for all sets S_p *with size* $\geq n_p$, $\Pr[CompExp(S_p) = 1] \geq 1 - 2^{-\lambda_{rel}}$.

– *soundness: consider the following experiment SoundExp(S_f):*

   output 1 *iff* $\exists \pi$, Read$(\pi) \subseteq S_f \wedge$ Verify$^H(\pi) = 1$;
   we require that for all sets S_f with size $\leq n_f$, Pr$[SoundExp(S_f) = 1] \leq 2^{-\lambda_{sec}}$;

We now prove a lower bound for a scheme satisfying this definition.

Theorem 11. *Assume $\lambda_{rel} \geq 1$, define $\alpha = \frac{\lambda_{sec}-3}{\log(n_p/n_f)}$, assume $n_f \geq 3\alpha^2$, let S_p be an arbitrary set of size n_p, and let* (Prove, Read, Verify) *be a $(\lambda_{sec}, \lambda_{rel}, n_p, n_f)$-ALBA scheme. Then*

$$\Pr\left[\left|\mathsf{Read}(\mathsf{Prove}^H(S_p))\right| > \alpha\right] \geq \frac{1}{4}.$$

We present the proof in the full version [CKRZ23] of this work.

4   ALBAs with Decentralized Prover

In the previous section we assumed the ALBA prover has all the set elements at hand. In many applications however, such as threshold signatures, this is not the case. The set elements may be spread across numerous parties who will then jointly compute a proof. A trivial solution is to use a centralized protocol, by designating one of the parties as the lead prover and have all other parties communicate their set elements to that party. However, this incurs a communication cost equal to the size of the set, which we would rather avoid.

In this section we present protocols where the various parties holding set elements start out by performing computations locally and only conditionally communicate their elements to a designated prover or aggregator. Whilst our constructions we present in this section still use weights of 0 or 1, they can be generalized to integer weights as explained in Sect. 5. Finally, as in Sect. 3, instead of proof of knowledge we consider a simpler notion of soundness: the probability that a valid proof exists containing only elements from set S_f of size n_f. Section 6 demonstrates how to do knowledge extraction.

4.1   Simple Lottery Construction

The simple lottery scheme is parametrized by the expected number of network participants μ. Let H be a random oracle that outputs 1 with probability $p = \frac{\mu}{n_p}$ and 0 otherwise. Each set element s is sent to the aggregator over the network if and only if $H(s) = 1$. Now let $r_s, r_c > 1$ such that $r_s r_c = \frac{n_p}{n_f}$ and set $u = r_s \cdot pn_f$ (or equivalently $u = \frac{pn_p}{r_c}$). The aggregator needs to collect and concatenate u set elements and the verifier accepts if it receives u values that each hash to 1.

Lemma 1. *Assuming*

$$u \geq \frac{\lambda_{sec} \cdot \ln 2}{\ln r_s - 1 + \frac{1}{r_s}},$$

soundness error of the scheme is $\leq 2^{-\lambda_{sec}}$.

We present the proof in the full version [CKRZ23] of this work.

Lemma 2. *Assuming*

$$u \geq \frac{\lambda_{rel} \cdot \ln 2}{r_c - 1 - \ln r_c},$$

completeness error of the scheme is $\leq 2^{-\lambda_{rel}}$.

We present the proof in the full version [CKRZ23] of this work. Thus, to minimize u, we need to minimize

$$\max \left\{ \frac{\lambda_{\mathrm{sec}} \cdot \ln 2}{\ln r_s - 1 + \frac{1}{r_s}}, \frac{\lambda_{\mathrm{rel}} \cdot \ln 2}{r_c - 1 - \ln r_c} \right\}.$$

Noting that the first term is decreasing with respect to r_s and the second term is decreasing with respect to r_c, the minimum is achieved when the two terms are equal. If $\lambda_{\mathrm{sec}} = \lambda_{\mathrm{rel}} = \lambda$, then setting $r_c = \frac{n_p}{n_p - n_f} \cdot \ln \frac{n_p}{n_f}$ and $r_s = \frac{n_p - n_f}{n_f} \cdot \frac{1}{\ln \frac{n_p}{n_f}}$ gives the smallest u.

We note the interesting fact that choosing r_s and r_c that minimize u also minimizes μ. Since $\mu = p n_p = u r_c$, we have

$$\mu \geq \max \left\{ \frac{\lambda_{\mathrm{sec}} \cdot \ln 2}{\ln r_s - 1 + \frac{1}{r_s}} \cdot r_c, \frac{\lambda_{\mathrm{rel}} \cdot \ln 2}{r_c - 1 - \ln r_c} \cdot r_c \right\}.$$

The first term is decreasing with respect to r_s since r_c is, and it can be seen that the second term is decreasing with respect to r_c. Hence, μ is minimized when the two terms are equal which is the same as the condition for minimizing u.

4.2 Decentralized Telescope

The next logical step to minimize the size of the proof is to run a smarter aggregator, Telescope, and calculate an appropriate increase to the security and reliability parameters. While combining a simple lottery with an ALBA aggregator is a generic technique, the generic analysis requires one to calculate two lottery tail bounds: one for soundness and one for completeness. By using Telescope for the aggregator, we benefit from omitting the soundness tail bounds from analysis; this section has all details.

As previously, we have parameter μ and select each element to be transmitted over the network with probability μ/n_p. After receiving enough elements selected by the simple lottery, the aggregator runs the algorithm from Sect. 3.2. Note that it assumes that the number of set elements is large enough, see a bound on n_p in Theorem 7. Since μ can be much smaller than said bound, we artificially increase the number of set elements by producing k sub-elements for each element, for an appropriate k. This is a purely technical hindrance that goes away in the full version [CKRZ23] of this paper which describes an ALBA scheme without this requirement.

We employ threshold analysis here: calculate the number of set elements selected by the simple lottery such that 1) this number is achievable with probability $1 - \frac{1}{4} \cdot 2^{-\lambda_{\text{rel}}}$ and 2) the Telescope aggregator will produce a valid certificate with probability $1 - \frac{3}{4} \cdot 2^{-\lambda_{\text{rel}}}$.

For all $1 \leq i \leq n_{\text{p}}$, let X_i be 1 if and only if element s_i is selected and 0 otherwise. Let $X = \sum_{i=1}^{n_{\text{p}}} X_i$; then $\mathbb{E}[X] = \mu$. Assume $\rho \in \mathbb{N}$ satisfies $\Pr[X \geq \rho] \geq 1 - 2^{-\lambda_{\text{rel}} - 2}$. Reducing the honest-malicious gap from $\frac{n_{\text{p}}}{n_{\text{f}}}$ to $\frac{\rho}{\frac{\mu}{n_{\text{p}}} \cdot n_{\text{f}}} = \frac{n_{\text{p}}}{n_{\text{f}}} \cdot \frac{\rho}{\mu}$ results in increasing the certificate size to

$$\frac{\lambda_{\text{sec}} + \log(\lambda_{\text{rel}} + 2) + 1 + \log e - \log\log e}{\log \frac{n_{\text{p}}}{n_{\text{f}}} + \log \frac{\rho}{\mu}}$$

(we have $\lambda_{\text{sec}} + \log(\lambda_{\text{rel}} + 2) + 1 + \log e - \log\log e$ instead of $\lambda_{\text{sec}} + \log(\lambda_{\text{rel}} + \log 3) + 1 - \log\log e$ in Theorem 2 because we instantiate it with $\lambda_{\text{sec}} := \lambda_{\text{sec}} + \log e$ and $\lambda_{\text{rel}} := \lambda_{\text{rel}} + \log \frac{4}{3}$ for technical reasons).

One can think of the gap $\frac{\rho n_{\text{p}}}{\mu n_{\text{f}}}$ as $\frac{(1-\delta) n_{\text{p}}}{n_{\text{f}}}$ if we set $\rho = (1 - \delta)\mu$. Note that we only decrease n_{p} in the $\frac{n_{\text{p}}}{n_{\text{f}}}$ gap. n_{f} remains the same since the union bound argument for soundness still works, but with some modifications. Particularly, it requires μ to be on the order of u^2. If we wanted to decrease μ even further, we could improve the proof below or employ a two-sided threshold analysis as well.

Let Lottery $: \{0,1\}^* \rightarrow \{0,1\}$ be an oracle returning 1 with probability $\frac{\mu}{n_{\text{p}}}$ and assume $H = (H_0, H_1, H_2, \text{Lottery})$ where H_0, H_1, H_2 are as defined in Sect. 3.2. Also let $A.\text{Prove}^H$, $A.\text{Verify}^H$ be as in Sect. 3.2 and define the following.

---

procedure $B.\text{Prove}^H(s)$
  if $\text{Lottery}(s) = 1$ **then**
    return s;
  else
    return empty string;

procedure $B.\text{Aggregate}^H(S)$
  return $A.\text{Prove}^H(S)$;
procedure $B.\text{Verify}^H(\pi)$
  parse $(t, s_1, ..., s_u) = \pi$;
  return 1 iff $A.\text{Verify}^H(\pi) = 1 \wedge$
    $\forall 1 \leq i \leq u, \text{Lottery}(s_i) = 1$;

Theorem 12. *Assume*

$$k \geq \frac{d^2 \log e}{9\rho(\lambda_{rel} + 2)}$$

and instantiate the algorithm in Sect. 3.2 with $d \geq \frac{16u(\lambda_{rel}+2)}{\log e}$, $q := \frac{2(\lambda_{rel}+2)}{d \log e}$, and $n_p := k\rho$. Then completeness error is $\leq 2^{-\lambda_{rel}}$.

Proof. As assumed above, the simple lottery chooses at least ρ set elements with probability at least $1 - 2^{-\lambda_{\text{rel}} - 2}$. Given this event, by Theorem 7, the algorithm outputs a valid certificate with probability at least $1 - 2^{-\lambda_{\text{rel}} - \log \frac{4}{3}}$. Therefore, completeness error is $\leq 2^{-\lambda_{\text{rel}}}$. □

We now calculate soundness error defined as the probability that a valid proof can be constructed using elements S_{f} with $|S_{\text{f}}| = n_{\text{f}}$.

Theorem 13. *Assume*

$$\mu \geq \frac{n_p u^2}{n_f}; \qquad \frac{\rho n_p}{\mu n_f} > 1;$$

$$u \geq \frac{\lambda_{sec} + \log(\lambda_{rel} + 2) + 1 + \log e - \log \log e}{\log \frac{n_p}{n_f} + \log \frac{\rho}{\mu}}.$$

Then soundness error is $\leq 2^{-\lambda_{sec}}$.

We present the proof in the full version [CKRZ23] of this work. Theorem 12 and 13 give

Corollary 3. *Assume*

$$\mu \geq \frac{n_p u^2}{n_f}; \qquad \frac{\rho n_p}{\mu n_f} > 1; \qquad k \geq \frac{d^2 \log e}{9\rho(\lambda_{rel} + 2)};$$

$$u \geq \frac{\lambda_{sec} + \log(\lambda_{rel} + 2) + 1 + \log e - \log \log e}{\log \frac{n_p}{n_f} + \log \frac{\rho}{\mu}}$$

and instantiate the algorithm in Sect. 3.2 with $u := u$, $d \geq \frac{16u(\lambda_{rel}+2)}{\log e}$, $q := \frac{2(\lambda_{rel}+2)}{d \log e}$, *and* $n_p := k\rho$. *Then soundness error is* $\leq 2^{-\lambda_{sec}}$ *and completeness error is* $\leq 2^{-\lambda_{rel}}$.

Using this, we can see how big μ needs to be if we increase $u \log \frac{n_p}{n_f}$ only by some amount C. To calculate a suitable ρ, we just use a Chernoff bound: $\Pr[X \leq (1 - \delta)\mu] \leq e^{-\frac{\mu\delta^2}{2}}$. Setting this to $2^{-\lambda_{rel}-2}$, we get $\delta = \sqrt{\frac{2(\lambda_{rel}+2)}{\mu \log e}}$. We now set $\rho = \lceil (1 - \delta)\mu \rceil$.

Corollary 4. *Assume*

$$C > 0; \quad u \geq \frac{\lambda_{sec} + \log(\lambda_{rel} + 2) + 1 + \log e - \log \log e + C}{\log \frac{n_p}{n_f}}; \quad k \geq \frac{d^2 \log e}{9\rho(\lambda_{rel} + 2)};$$

$$\mu \geq \max\left\{ \frac{8(\lambda_{rel} + 2)}{\log e}, \frac{n_p u^2}{n_f}, \frac{9u^2(\lambda_{rel} + 2) \log e}{2C^2} \right\}; \mu > \frac{2(\lambda_{rel} + 2)}{\left(1 - \frac{n_f}{n_p}\right)^2 \log e};$$

and instantiate the algorithm in Sect. 3.2 just like in corollary 3. Then soundness error is $\leq 2^{-\lambda_{sec}}$ *and completeness error is* $\leq 2^{-\lambda_{rel}}$.

We present the proof in the full version [CKRZ23] of this work.

Thus, if we let $\lambda = \lambda_{sec} = \lambda_{rel}$ and let u only be a constant larger than optimal, we have $\mu = O(\lambda^3)$ as well as the time complexity of the centralized algorithm also $O(\lambda^3)$. Moreover, μ is proportional to $\frac{1}{C^2}$. We note, however, that setting $\lambda_{rel} := 1$ and $\lambda_{sec} := \lambda_{sec} + \log \lambda_{rel}$ and amplifying the completeness via parallel repetitions as mentioned in Sect. 3.2 lets us reduce the expected communication complexity to $O(\lambda^2)$. However, it requires some network engineering to avoid redundant communication, specifically delaying repetitions until the previous ones have certainly failed.

In the full version [CKRZ23], we also present a different corollary showing what u needs to be in terms of μ.

4.3   Optimality of the Certificate Size - Communication Tradeoff

We can attempt to find a lower bound for the tradeoff between the certificate size u and μ. For this purpose, we use the following definition.

Definition 5. (Prove, Read, Verify) *is a* $(\lambda_{sec}, \lambda_{rel}, n_p, n_f, \mu)$-*lottery based ALBA scheme if and only if*

- Prove^H *is a probabilistic random oracle access program;*
- Verify^H *is a random oracle access program;*
- Read *is a program;*
- *if L is a random function such that for all x, $\Pr[L(x) = 1] = \frac{\mu}{n_p}$ and we define $Lottery(S) = \{x \in S : L(x) = 1\}$, then*
    - *completeness: consider the following experiment $CompExp(S_p)$:*

        $\pi \leftarrow$ Prove$^H(Lottery(S_p))$;
        output 1 *iff* Read$(\pi) \subseteq Lottery(S_p)$ *and* Verify$^H(\pi) = 1$;

        we require that for all sets S_p with size $\geq n_p$, $\Pr[CompExp(S_p) = 1] \geq 1 - 2^{-\lambda_{rel}}$.
    - *soundness: consider the following experiment $SoundExp(S_f)$:*

        output 1 *iff* $\exists \pi$, Read$(\pi) \subseteq Lottery(S_f) \wedge$ Verify$^H(\pi) = 1$;

        we require that for all sets S_f with size $\leq n_f$, $\Pr[SoundExp(S_f) = 1] \leq 2^{-\lambda_{sec}}$;

The following theorem presents our lower bound.

Theorem 14. *Assume ρ satisfies* $\Pr\left[B(n_p, \frac{\mu}{n_p}) \leq \rho\right] \geq 2^{-\lambda_{rel}+1}$ *where $B(n,p)$ is a binomial random variable with n experiments each with probability of success p. Also assume*

$$\frac{\rho n_p}{\mu n_f} > 1; \quad \mu \geq \frac{3u^2 n_p \log e}{2n_f}; \quad n_f \geq \rho,$$

let S_p be an arbitrary set of size n_p and let (Prove, Read, Verify) *be a* $(\lambda_{sec}, \lambda_{rel}, n_p, n_f, \mu)$-*lottery based ALBA scheme such that*

$$\Pr\left[\left|\text{Read}(\text{Prove}^H(Lottery(S_p)))\right| \leq u\right] = 1.$$

Then

$$u > \frac{\lambda_{sec} - 4}{\log \frac{n_p}{n_f} + \log \frac{\rho}{\mu}}.$$

We present the proof in the full version [CKRZ23] of this work.

Using this, we can establish a lower bound similar to the upper bound Corollary 4.

Corollary 5. *Let* $C > 0$, *define*

$$\alpha = \frac{\lambda_{sec} - 4 + C}{\log \frac{n_p}{n_f}}; u = \lfloor \alpha \rfloor$$

and assume

$$\max\left\{\frac{4}{\lambda_{rel}}, \frac{\lambda_{rel}}{(1 - \frac{n_f}{n_p})^2}, \frac{3u^2 n_p \log e}{2n_f}\right\} \leq \mu \leq \min\left\{\frac{\alpha^2 \lambda_{rel} \log^2 e}{4C^2}, \frac{(\frac{4}{e})^{\lambda_{rel}}}{4e^{10}}\right\};$$

$$n_f \geq 2\mu.$$

Let S_p *be an arbitrary set of size* n_p *and let* (Prove, Read, Verify) *be a* $(\lambda_{sec}, \lambda_{rel}, n_p, n_f, \mu)$-*lottery based ALBA scheme. Then*

$$\Pr\left[\left|\mathsf{Read}(\mathsf{Prove}^H(Lottery(S_p)))\right| > \alpha\right] > 0.$$

We present the proof in the full version [CKRZ23] of this work.

Alternatively, in the full version we also present a corollary showing a lower bound on the certificate size as of function of μ.

5 Adding Weights

We will assume, without loss of generality, that the weight function W outputs integers. A naive way to handle weights other than 0 and 1 is to interpret each set element s as $W(s)$ elements $(s, 1), \ldots, (s, W(s))$ and apply schemes designed for the unweighted case to (s, i) pairs. Unfortunately, this approach makes the prover running time linear in the total weight which could be in the order of 2^{64}.

Fortunately, any lottery-based scheme in which the number of lottery winners is independent of n_p (or at most polylogarithmic in n_p) is amenable to a more efficient solution (and the Telescope scheme in Sect. 3 can be turned into a lottery-based scheme first using Sect. 4.2). We simply view $(s, 1), \ldots, (s, W(s))$ pairs as $W(s)$ different lottery participants. For efficiency, instead of having each of them play the lottery individually with probability p, we sample the number of winners from the binomial distribution $\mathrm{Binom}(W(s), p)$ (similar to the sortition algorithm used in Algorand [GHM+17]). We do so because it does not matter which i values win—what matters is only the number of winners. If the binomial sampling returns k, then $(s, 1), \ldots, (s, k)$ are considered winners. This does not increase the complexity compared to the unweighted-lottery-based scheme, except for binomial sampling rather than lottery applied to each element.

Using Corollary 4 with $\lambda_{sec} := \lambda_{sec} + \log \lambda_{rel}$, $\lambda_{rel} := 1$ and $C := 1$, we achieve a weighted $(\lambda_{sec}, \lambda_{rel}, n_p, n_f)$-ALBA scheme with proof size

$$\frac{\lambda_{sec} + \log \lambda_{rel} + 2 + \log 3 + \log e - \log \log e}{\log \frac{n_p}{n_f}}$$

and expected prover running time $O(n + \lambda_{sec}^2)$, where n is the number of weighted elements in the input.

6 Knowledge Extraction for NIROPK

In this section we show how Definitions 1 and 2 can be realized. While Sects. 3 and 4 provide intuitive constructions with clean combinatorial analysis, they have a missing piece — a knowledge extractor. As we will see, the simple soundness proven there does not immediately imply proof of knowledge, and more reasoning is needed. We also remind that the knowledge extractor must be straightline; i.e., rewinding of the prover is not allowed but observing its queries to the oracles is. Here we describe the full NIROPK scheme including its knowledge extactor for the case of the basic Telescope construction from Sect. 3.1 while other Telescope constructions can be made NIROPK in a similar fashion. For $H = (H_1, H_2)$, define

---

procedure Prove$^{H,W}(S_p)$
  run DFS as described in
  Section 3.1
procedure Verify$^{H,W}(\pi)$
  parse $(t, s_1, ..., s_u) = \pi$
  return 1 iff

  $- 1 \leq t \leq d;$
  $- \forall 1 \leq i \leq u,$
    $H_1(t, s_1, ..., s_i) = 1;$
  $- H_2(t, s_1, ..., s_u) = 1;$
  $- \forall 1 \leq i \leq u, W(s_i) = 1$

procedure Extract$^{H,W,\mathcal{A}}$
  function $A_1^{H,W}$
    $\pi \leftarrow \mathcal{A}^{H,W}();$
    $v \leftarrow \text{Verify}^{H,W}(\pi);$
    return π;
  run $\mathcal{A}_1^{H,W}()$ and observe its oracles transcript τ;
  $S_f := \emptyset;$
  for x queried to H_1 or H_2 in τ **do**
    if $W(x) = 1$ **then**
      add x to S_f;
  return S_f.

Theorem 15. *Define parameters as in Theorem 1. Then algorithms* Verify^{H,W} *with* Extract$^{H,W,\mathcal{A}}$ *satisfy the proof of knowledge property of Definition 1.*

Proof. The extractor succeeds whenever $\mathcal{A}$ succeeds, unless $\mathcal{A}$ succeeds after querying fewer than n_f elements of S, which happens with probability at most $2^{-\lambda_{sec}}$ by the following lemma. Thus, the proof of knowledge property follows by the union bound.

We present the proof in the full version [CKRZ23] of this work.

The following lemma resembles the simple soundness result in Theorem 1, but unfortunately is harder to prove. Whereas the proof of Theorem 1 is a simple application of union bound, the fact that the adversary can choose what weight-1 elements to query adaptively based on past RO responses makes the "vanilla" union bound argument inapplicable. Fortunately, there exists a way around this problem.

Lemma 3. *Define parameters as in Theorem 1 and let E be the event that a valid proof can be made from the first n_f (or less) weight-1 elements that $\mathcal{A}_1^{H,W}$ queries to H. Then $\Pr[E] \leq 2^{-\lambda_{sec}}$.*

We present the proof in the full version [CKRZ23] of this work.

Combining the proof of knowledge property with completeness proven in Sect. 3.1, we now state the main result of this section.

Corollary 6. *Using parameters from Corollary 1,* (Prove, Verify, Extract) *is a* $(\lambda_{sec}, \lambda_{rel}, n_p, n_f)$*-NIROPK ALBA scheme.*

In summary, we achieve information-theoretic but non-adaptive security; i.e., additional computational power does not help the adversary avoid knowledge extraction but he is not allowed to choose the predicate/weight function based on the random oracle. Adaptive security can be achieved the traditional way: rerandomize the random oracle by including a commitment to the weight function as additional input to the random oracle. However, the security downgrades to computational: assuming that adversary makes at most 2^q RO queries, we need to increase ALBA's λ_{sec} parameter by q.

7 Replacing the Random Oracle with PRF

In this section we show how to remove the need for the random oracle and instantiate our scheme in the Common Reference String model (or alternatively, the Uniform Random String model). This is a novel feature of our scheme in comparison to compact certificates which inherently rely on the random oracle because of Fiat-Shamir. We utilize a PRF for the hash function H with the CRS being a random PRF key (or alternatively, uniformly random bits sufficient to generate one). We note that although the PRF is only secure against computationally bounded distinguishers, our ALBA scheme retains information-theoretic security.

Assume (GenKey, F) is a PRF such that for any oracle access program $\mathcal{A}^O$ with running time bounded by T,

$$\left| \Pr\left[\mathcal{A}^H() = 1\right] - \Pr\left[\mathcal{A}^{F(\mathsf{GenKey}(),\cdot)}() = 1\right] \right| \leq \varepsilon_{\mathrm{prf}}(T). \tag{4}$$

We will assume the unweighted case, but the following can extended to support weights as well. Combining the improved Telescope construction from Sect. 3.2 with the tight bound on the number of accessible vertices (Theorem 10) and instantiating the scheme with the standard (binary) random oracle (the latter is described in the full version) one can build a Telescope scheme such that for some $B \in O(\lambda^3)$,

- the honest prover's DFS visits at most B vertices and outputs a valid proof with probability $\geq 1 - 2^{-\lambda}$;
- there exists a valid proof containing elements from S_f or the number of accessible vertices exceeds B with probability $\leq 2^{-\lambda}$.

Implement $\mathsf{Prove}^H(S_p)$ as the standard DFS that visits at most B vertices and define $\mathsf{Verify}^H(\pi)$ in a natural way. We show an ALBA scheme under Definition 4 where the random oracle is replaced with CRS. Below is the new definition and a Telescope construction for it.

Definition 6. (Prove, Read, Verify, GenCRS) *is a* $(\lambda_{sec}, \lambda_{rel}, n_p, n_f)$-*CRS ALBA scheme if and only if*

- Prove *is a probabilistic program;*
- Verify *is a program;*
- Read *is a program;*
- GenCRS *is a probabilistic program;*
- *completeness: consider the following experiment* $CompExp(S_p)$:
  we require that for all sets S_p *with size* $\geq n_p$, $\Pr[CompExp(S_p) = 1] \geq 1 - 2^{-\lambda_{rel}}$.
- *soundness: consider the following experiment* $SoundExp(S_f)$:

  $crs \leftarrow$ GenCRS();
  output 1 *iff* $\exists \pi$, Read(π) $\subseteq S_f \wedge$ Verify(crs, π) $= 1$;
  we require that for all sets S_f *with size* $\leq n_f$, $\Pr[SoundExp(S_f) = 1] \leq 2^{-\lambda_{sec}}$;

---

procedure R.Prove(crs, S_p)	procedure R.Read(π)
$\pi \leftarrow$ Prove$^{F(crs,\cdot)}(S_p)$;	parse $(t, s_1, ..., s_u) = \pi$;
return π;	return $\{s_1, ..., s_u\}$;
procedure R.Verify(crs, π)	procedure R.GenCRS
$r \leftarrow$ Verify$^{F(crs,\cdot)}(\pi)$;	$k \leftarrow$ GenKey();
return r;	return k;

Theorem 16. R *is a* $(\lambda'_{sec}, \lambda'_{rel}, n_p, n_f)$-*CRS ALBA scheme where* $\lambda'_{sec} = \lambda'_{rel} = -\log\left(2^{-\lambda} + \varepsilon_{prf}(O(n_p + \lambda^3))\right)$.

Proof. Completeness follows from the fact that Prove's running time is bounded by $O(n_p + B) = O(n_p + \lambda^3)$ steps and that Prove$^H(S_p)$, when instantiated with the random oracle H, finds a valid proof with probability $\geq 1 - 2^{-\lambda}$. Acting as a PRF distinguisher, we conclude that Prove$^{F(GenKey(),\cdot)}$ outputs a valid proof with probability $\geq 1 - 2^{-\lambda} - \varepsilon_{prf}(O(n_p + \lambda^3))$.

To prove soundness, we can observe whether a DFS on set S_f finds a valid proof or does not terminate after visiting B vertices. In the random oracle case, one or both happen with probability $\leq 2^{-\lambda}$, so in the PRF case it is $\leq 2^{-\lambda} + \varepsilon_{prf}(O(n_p + \lambda^3))$. But the probability that there *exists* a valid proof in the PRF case cannot be larger. □

We present the complete version of the proof in the full version [CKRZ23] of this work.

7.1   Knowledge Extraction For Definition 6/4

In this section we show how to generically convert an ALBA scheme under Definition 6 to a proof of knowledge scheme under Definition 3. We still assume the unweighted scenario $(W : \{0,1\}^* \to \{0,1\})$ but the following can be generalized to add weights. Sometimes it will be convenient to treat W as a set: $\{s : W(s) = 1\}$.

Let $X = (X.\text{Prove}, X.\text{Read}, X.\text{Verify}, X.\text{GenCRS})$ be a $(\lambda_{\text{sec}}, \lambda_{\text{rel}}, n_\text{p}, n_\text{f})$-CRS ALBA scheme (as in Definition 6) and define $Y = (Y.\text{Prove}, Y.\text{Verify}, Y.\text{Extract}, Y.\text{GenCRS})$ as follows.

procedure $Y.\text{GenCRS}$	procedure $Y.\text{Extract}^W(\mathcal{A})$
return $X.\text{GenCRS}()$;	$S_\text{f} := \emptyset$;
procedure $Y.\text{Prove}^W(\text{crs}, S_\text{p})$	while $\lvert S_\text{f} \rvert \leq n_\text{f}$ do
return $X.\text{Prove}(\text{crs}, S_\text{p} \cap W)$;	$\text{crs} \leftarrow X.\text{GenCRS}()$;
procedure $Y.\text{Verify}^W(\text{crs}, \pi)$	$\pi \leftarrow \mathcal{A}^W(\text{crs})$;
$S := X.\text{Read}(\pi)$;	$S := X.\text{Read}(\pi)$;
return 1 iff $S \subseteq W \wedge$	$S_\text{f} := S_\text{f} \cup (S \cap W)$;
$X.\text{Verify}(\text{crs}, \pi) = 1$;	return S_f;

Theorem 17. Y is $(\lambda_{sec}, \lambda_{rel}, n_p, n_f)$-CRS proof of knowledge ALBA scheme.

Proof. It is easy to see that Y satisfies the completeness property. We are left to prove the proof of knowledge property.

First, notice that $Y.\text{Extract}$ can only output a set S_f such that $S_\text{f} \subseteq W$ and $\lvert S_\text{f} \rvert > n_\text{f}$. Now examine a single loop iteration in $Y.\text{Extract}$. We know that $\varepsilon = \Pr\left[Y.\text{Verify}^W(\text{crs}, \pi) = 1\right] - 2^{-\lambda_{\text{sec}}} > 0$ and $Y.\text{Verify}^W(\text{crs}, \pi) = 1$ implies that $S \subseteq W$ and $X.\text{Verify}(\text{crs}, \pi) = 1$. So,

$$2^{-\lambda_{\text{sec}}} + \varepsilon = \Pr[Y.\text{Verify}^W(\text{crs}, \pi) = 1] \leq \Pr[S \subseteq W \wedge X.\text{Verify}(\text{crs}, \pi) = 1].$$

At the same time, since $\lvert S_\text{f} \rvert \leq n_\text{f}$, by the soundness of X (considering the experiment $\text{SoundExp}(S_\text{f})$ from Definition 6), $\Pr[S \subseteq S_\text{f} \wedge X.\text{Verify}(\text{crs}, \pi) = 1] \leq 2^{-\lambda_{\text{sec}}}$. Therefore,

$$\varepsilon = (2^{-\lambda_{\text{sec}}} + \varepsilon) - 2^{-\lambda_{\text{sec}}} \leq$$
$$\Pr[S \subseteq W \wedge X.\text{Verify}(\text{crs}, \pi) = 1] - \Pr[S \subseteq S_\text{f} \wedge X.\text{Verify}(\text{crs}, \pi) = 1] \leq$$
$$\Pr[(S \subseteq W \wedge X.\text{Verify}(\text{crs}, \pi) = 1) \wedge \neg(S \subseteq S_\text{f} \wedge X.\text{Verify}(\text{crs}, \pi) = 1)] =$$
$$\Pr[S \subseteq W \wedge S \not\subseteq S_\text{f} \wedge X.\text{Verify}(\text{crs}, \pi) = 1] \leq$$
$$\Pr[S \subseteq W \wedge S \not\subseteq S_\text{f}] \leq$$
$$\Pr[\exists x \in (S \cap W) \setminus S_\text{f}].$$

So, a single iteration of the loop adds at least one new element of W to S_f with probability at least ε. Therefore, in expectation, the loop runs for at most $(n_\text{f} + 1) \cdot \frac{1}{\varepsilon}$ iterations. Then it is easy to see that $Y.\text{Extract}$ runs in expected time $\text{poly}(T, 1/\varepsilon)$ (treating n_f as constant). $\square$

In summary, we achieve information-theoretic but non-adaptive security; i.e., additional computational power does not help the adversary avoid knowledge

n_p/n_f	60/40		66/33		80/20	
ALBA Protocol	Size	Comms	Size	Comms	Size	Comms
GS [GS86]	82944σ		16384σ		3237σ	
C. Cert. [MRV$^+$21] (2^{80})	$356\sigma + 356\eta$		$208\sigma + 208\eta$		$104\sigma + 104\eta$	
C. Cert. [MRV$^+$21] (2^{128})	$438\sigma + 438\eta$		$256\sigma + 256\eta$		$128\sigma + 128\eta$	
Telescope, no weights (Sect. 3)	232σ		136σ		68σ	
Telescope, weights (Sect. 4.2,5)	239σ		140σ		70σ	
Simple Lottery (Sect. 4.1)	4157σ	5058σ	1428σ	1981σ	364σ	675σ
Simple Lottery ($\lambda_{rel} = 64$)	3060σ	3591σ	1069σ	1395σ	283σ	466σ
Dec. Telescope (Sect. 4.2)	262σ	114264σ	151σ	49929σ	74σ	23104σ

Fig. 1. Certificate sizes and expected communication cost, expressed in revealed/sent set elements (σ) and, in the case of [MRV+21], secondary reveals of the same elements in the form of Merkle Tree paths (η). The parameters $\lambda_{sec}, \lambda_{rel}$ are set to 128 unless otherwise indicated.

extraction but he is not allowed to choose the predicate/weight function based on the CRS. Even then, this can be useful; one example is applications where PRF seed is chosen by a randomness beacon after the statement to be proven is already decided. As a last resort, adaptive security can be achieved by rerandomizing the PRF using the random oracle: let the CRS be the output of the random oracle on the description of the weight function. This can be beneficial to instantiating ALBA purely in the random oracle model, for example, when the knowledge of an ALBA proof is proven by a SNARK. In that case, calculating the CRS outside of the SNARK circuit and using PRF inside the circuit lets one avoid heuristically instantiating RO in the circuit.

8   Performance Comparisons

In terms of prover computation, the Simple Lottery scheme requires negligible effort from the aggregator (apart from verifying membership and eligibility of the received set elements). Compact certificates require the prover to build a commitment to the set of received set items in the form of a Merkle tree, requiring $O(n)$ hash evaluations, where n is the number of weighted elements in prover's input. Telescope in turn requires $O(n + \lambda^2)$ hashes in expectation and Goldwasser-Sipser requires $O(n_p \cdot \lambda)$ hashes.

In terms of number of revealed elements, compact certificates need to reveal at least $\frac{\lambda_{sec}}{\log(n_p/n_f)}$ set elements (denoted by σ) but they additionally need to reveal the Merkle tree path of each element (denoted by η) with regards to the commitment constructed by the prover. The Simple Lottery scheme only reveals set elements and the number of reveals has the same, linear dependency on λ_{sec}, but has a more complex (and more costly) dependency on (n_p/n_f). Telescope combines the best of both worlds, as it only needs to reveal close to $\frac{\lambda_{sec}}{\log(n_p/n_f)}$ set elements and the integer t with no need for secondary openings. Goldwasser-Sipser requires $8\lambda \cdot (n_p/n_f)^4 \cdot (n_p/n_f - 1)^{-4}$ reveals.

In Fig. 1 we compare proof sizes and communication costs of our constructions with those of existing protocols: compact certificates [MRV+21] and the

Goldwasser-Sipser [GS86] scheme. Our analysis of the simple lottery scheme of Sect. 4.1 is also applicable to Mithril [CK21] as the combinatorics are very similar. Compact certificates have computational security and we provide proof sizes secure against adversaries making 2^{80} and 2^{128} queries; Telescope, on the other hand, has information-theoretic security and smaller number of revealed elements, but becomes computationally secure with number of revealed elements similar to compact certificates when the adversary is allowed to choose the weight function.

We consider communication costs only where they are meaningful, i.e. in decentralized schemes. We note that these costs may be significantly lower in the case of weighted sets where the same element may appear multiple times with different indices. For compact certificates, we derive values using the formula from [MRV+21]. For the simple lottery we use direct calculation, slightly improving on the bounds of Sect. 4.1, for Goldwasser-Sipser we use the analysis performed in the full version, and for Telescope and Decentralized Telescope we use the bounds from Corollaries 2 and 5. For the weighted Telescope scheme we use the formula in Sect. 5.

Acknowledgement. We are grateful to Mahak Pancholi and Akira Takahashi for discussion about UC SNARKs. This material is based upon work supported in part by a gift from Input Output - IOG and by DARPA under Agreements No. HR00112020021 and HR00112020023. Any opinions, findings and conclusions or recommendations expressed in this material are those of the author(s) and do not necessarily reflect the views of the United States Government or DARPA.

References

[Bab85] Babai, L.: Trading group theory for randomness. In: 17th ACM STOC, pp. 421–429. ACM Press, May 1985

[BCS16] Ben-Sasson, E., Chiesa, A., Spooner, N.: Interactive oracle proofs. In: Hirt, M., Smith, A. (eds.) TCC 2016. LNCS, vol. 9986, pp. 31–60. Springer, Heidelberg (2016). https://doi.org/10.1007/978-3-662-53644-5_2

[BR93] Bellare, M., Rogaway, P.: Random oracles are practical: a paradigm for designing efficient protocols. In: Denning, D.E., Pyle, R., Ganesan, R., Sandhu, R.S., Ashby, V. (eds.) ACM CCS 1993, pp. 62–73. ACM Press (1993)

[Can00] Canetti, R.: Security and composition of multiparty cryptographic protocols. J. Cryptol. **13**(1), 143–202 (2000)

[CDMP05] Coron, J.-S., Dodis, Y., Malinaud, C., Puniya, P.: Merkle-Damgård revisited: how to construct a hash function. In: Shoup, V. (ed.) CRYPTO 2005. LNCS, vol. 3621, pp. 430–448. Springer, Heidelberg (2005)

[CK21] Chaidos, P., Kiayias, A.: Mithril: stake-based threshold multisignatures. Cryptology ePrint Archive, Report 2021/916 (2021). https://eprint.iacr.org/2021/916

[CKRZ23] Chaidos, P., Kiayias, A., Reyzin, L., Zinovyev, A.: Approximate lower bound arguments. Cryptology ePrint Archive, Paper 2023/1655 (2023). https://eprint.iacr.org/2023/1655

[CW79] Carter, L., Wegman, M.N.: Universal classes of hash functions. J. Comput. Syst. Sci. **18**(2), 143–154 (1979)

[DCX+23] Das, S., Camacho, P., Xiang, Z., Nieto, J., Bunz, B., Ren, L.: Threshold signatures from inner product argument: succinct, weighted, and multi-threshold. Cryptology ePrint Archive, Paper 2023/598 (2023). https://eprint.iacr.org/2023/598

[Fis05] Fischlin, M.: Communication-efficient non-interactive proofs of knowledge with online extractors. In: Shoup, V. (ed.) CRYPTO 2005. LNCS, vol. 3621, pp. 152–168. Springer, Heidelberg (2005)

[GHM+17] Gilad, Y., Hemo, R., Micali, S., Vlachos, G., Zeldovich, N.: Algorand: scaling byzantine agreements for cryptocurrencies. In: Proceedings of the 26th Symposium on Operating Systems Principles, pp. 51–68 (2017)

[GJM+23] Garg, S., Jain, A., Mukherjee, P., Sinha, R., Wang, M., Zhang, Y.: hints: threshold signatures with silent setup. Cryptology ePrint Archive, Paper 2023/567 (2023). https://eprint.iacr.org/2023/567

[GKO+23] Ganesh, C., Kondi, Y., Orlandi, C., Pancholi, M., Takahashi, A., Tschudi, D.: Witness-succinct universally-composable SNARKs. In: Hazay, C., Stam, M. (eds.) EUROCRYPT 2023, Part II. LNCS, vol. 14005, pp. 315–346. Springer, Heidelberg (2023). https://doi.org/10.1007/978-3-031-30617-4_11

[Gro16] Groth, J.: On the size of pairing-based non-interactive arguments. In: Fischlin, M., Coron, J.-S. (eds.) EUROCRYPT 2016, Part II. LNCS, vol. 9666, pp. 305–326. Springer, Heidelberg (2016). https://doi.org/10.1007/978-3-662-49896-5_11

[GS86] Goldwasser, S., Sipser, M.: Private coins versus public coins in interactive proof systems. In: 18th ACM STOC, pp. 59–68. ACM Press (1986)

[GWC19] Gabizon, A., Williamson, Z.J., Ciobotaru, O.: PLONK: permutations over lagrange-bases for oecumenical noninteractive arguments of knowledge. Cryptology ePrint Archive, Report 2019/953 (2019). https://eprint.iacr.org/2019/953

[MRV+21] Micali, S., Reyzin, L., Vlachos, G., Wahby, R.S., Zeldovich, N.: Compact certificates of collective knowledge. In: 2021 IEEE Symposium on Security and Privacy, pp. 626–641. IEEE Computer Society Press (2021)

[Pas03] Pass, R.: On deniability in the common reference string and random oracle model. In: Boneh, D. (ed.) CRYPTO 2003. LNCS, vol. 2729, pp. 316–337. Springer, Heidelberg (2003)

[Sip83] Sipser, M.: A complexity theoretic approach to randomness. In: 15th ACM STOC, pp. 330–335. ACM Press (1983)

Software with Certified Deletion

James Bartusek[1], Vipul Goyal[2,3]([✉]), Dakshita Khurana[4], Giulio Malavolta[5,6], Justin Raizes[2], and Bhaskar Roberts[1]

[1] UC Berkeley, Berkeley, CA, USA
`bhaskarr@eecs.berkeley.edu`
[2] CMU, Pittsburgh, PA, USA
`vipul@cmu.edu, jraizes@andrew.cmu.edu`
[3] NTT Research, Sunnyvale, CA, USA
[4] UIUC, Champaign, IL, USA
`dakshita@illinois.edu`
[5] Bocconi University, Milan, Italy
[6] Max Planck Institute for Security and Privacy, Bochum, Germany

Abstract. Is it possible to prove the deletion of a computer program after having executed it? While this task is clearly impossible using classical information alone, the laws of quantum mechanics may admit a solution to this problem. In this work, we propose a new approach to answer this question, using quantum information. In the *interactive* settings, we present the first fully-secure solution for blind delegation with certified deletion, assuming post-quantum hardness of the learning with errors (LWE) problem. In the *non-interactive* settings, we propose a construction of obfuscation with certified deletion, assuming post-quantum iO and one-way functions.

Our main technical contribution is a new deletion theorem for subspace coset states [Vidick and Zhang, EUROCRYPT'21, Coladangelo et al., CRYPTO'21], which enables a generic compiler that adds the certified deletion guarantee to a variety of cryptographic primitives. In addition to our main result, this allows us to obtain a host of new primitives, such as functional encryption with certified deletion and secure software leasing for an interesting class of programs. In fact, we are able for the first time to achieve a *stronger notion of* secure software leasing, where even a *dishonest* evaluator cannot evaluate the program after returning it.

1 Introduction

Consider the following scenario: Alice is a software developer who has written a program that she would like to sell, in order to get financially rewarded for her effort. Bob is interested in using Alice's software, but only for a limited amount of time. Can Alice temporarily lease her software to Bob, without the risk of him pirating the program?

Ideally, we would like to design a protocol where Alice can lease her software to Bob and start charging him for a subscription fee. Once Bob is done using the

M. Joye and G. Leander (Eds.): EUROCRYPT 2024, LNCS 14654, pp. 85–111, 2024.
https://doi.org/10.1007/978-3-031-58737-5_4

software, he can produce a *deletion certificate* which guarantees that he deleted his local copy of the program. At this point, Alice can rest assured that Bob is no longer in possession of the software, and she can stop charging him. In case of a dispute, the deletion certificate will unequivocally determine which of the two parties misbehaved.

If we consider only classical information, then it is easy to see that no protocol can satisfy the security notion sketched above: Whatever information Alice sent to Bob, he can always create a perfect copy of it, thus continuing using the program even after producing the deletion certificate. In fact, nothing prevents Bob from pirating copies of Alice's program. On the other hand, the same argument does not hold if we consider quantum information, since the no-cloning theorem [42] postulates that there does not exist a general algorithm to create perfect copies of quantum states. Indeed, recent works on quantum copy protection [1] and secure software leasing [8,18,33] propose using quantum information to solve similar problems. Unfortunately, all of the existing definitions are subject to strong impossibility results [5,8] and the aforementioned works either attain heuristic constructions in idealized models, or focus on restricted classes of programs. At present, the problem of general-purpose software with certified deletion is wide open (even with quantum information).

To better understand the challenge of constructing software with certified deletion, let us make more concrete the desiderata for such protocol. To cover the full spectrum of software with certified deletion, in this work we consider and formalize two complementary settings.

Interactive Settings: Blind Delegation with Certified Deletion. In the interactive settings, Alice is assisting Bob to evaluate the program, i.e., to compute the output of the software on some input, via an exchange of messages. This allows Alice to control exactly how many inputs Bob has queried to the software, so she can charge him accordingly.

It is well-known that *fully-homomorphic encryption* [26] provides the ability to delegate a computation to an untrusted server, while revealing nothing about the computation itself. However, an FHE ciphertext is a classical string that information-theoretically contains Alice's software, and the only thing preventing recovery of this data is the conjectured hardness of a mathematical problem. If this problem becomes easy to solve in the future due to computational or scientific advances, or if Alice's secret key is leaked to Bob, there is no way to prevent Bob from recovering the underlying plaintext.

To mitigate this risk, we want Alice to be able to request Bob to delete their data at the end of the protocol, in such a way that, if Bob produces a valid certificate, then Alice is guaranteed that Bob has deleted the software *information theoretically*. This notion is known as *blind delegation with certified deletion*[1] [12,17,35]. However, existing proposals are actually insecure against

---

[1] In the standard notion of blind delegation, Alice delegates the computation of a hidden input on a public function to Bob. Alice is then assumed to receive the output. However, this is easily seen to be equivalent to the version where the function is also

a malicious Bob, who may deviate from the description of the protocol in an attempt to learn the Alice's software (more details on this later).

Non-interactive Settings: Obfuscation with Certified Deletion. In the non-interactive settings, Alice ships a copy of the software to Bob, who can evaluate it freely on as many inputs as he wants. After some amount of time, Bob wants to produce a certificate of deletion that convinces Alice that, from that moment on, her software has been deleted information-theoretically. In other words, we want to encode a computer program into a quantum state that preserves its functionality, while enabling an evaluator to information-theoretically delete the underlying program.

We refer to this notion as *obfuscation with certified deletion*. Although a-priori it is not clear that this notion has anything to do with program obfuscation, we argue that the two are in fact intimately connected. After all, if Bob was able to learn Alice's software from its description, then there would really be no way to erase Bob's knowledge after the fact.

Limitations of Existing Approaches to Certified Deletion. Despite much recent progress designing cryptosystems with certified deletion [12,17,28–30,35], the above natural questions have remained unanswered. Arguably, we can trace the lack of progress back to the fact that we are missing a technique that allows for *repeated access* to partial information about the encoded data, followed by certified deletion of whatever is left. In other words, all works[2] thus far have focused on "all-or-nothing" style primitives: E.g. secret-key encryption, public-key encryption, attribute-based encryption, timed-release encryption, and commitments [12,17,28,30,38]. Even known constructions of *fully-homomorphic encryption* with certified deletion [12,35] are all-or-nothing, in the sense that security becomes compromised (as we show in this work) once we give the evaluator access to some type of decryption oracle.

1.1   Our Results

In this work, we introduce a new paradigm for secure information-theoretic deletion of data. Our main technical ingredient, that enables all of our results, is a new deletion theorem for *subspace coset states* [21,39]. Subspace coset states have previously been used for designing *uncloneable* cryptographic primitives [6,21], and we demonstrate how to use them to obtain information-theoretic deletion. Our proof technique generalizes the work of [12] to states beyond BB84

---

hidden, using universal circuits. Furthermore, we can let Bob receive the output by adding one more round.

[2] An exception to this claim is a very recent work of [29] which constructs *functional encryption* with certified deletion of ciphertexts. However, in contrast with one of the goals of this work, their scheme is only secure in the setting of bounded collusions, where there is an a-priori upper bound on the number of functional keys an adversary can request.

states. This allows us to achieve *information-theoretic* certified deletion for cryptographic primitives beyond all-or-nothing. Specifically, we obtain the following results:

- **Blind delegation.** We develop the first maliciously secure blind delegation protocol with certified deletion. Our construction is based solely on the quantum hardness of learning with errors (LWE) [36], and carefully combines subspace coset states with compact fully-homomorphic encryption (FHE) [26] and succinct non-interactive arguments (SNARGs) for P.
  We also provide the first construction of *two-message* blind delegation with certified deletion, based on post-quantum sub-exponentially secure indistinguishability obfuscation. In particular, once the client sends their encoding of x, the server can return *both* the evaluated output $f(x)$ *and* a certificate that all other information about x has been deleted without any more interaction with the client.
- **Obfuscation.** Assuming post-quantum indistinguishability obfuscation, we obtain the first construction of differing inputs obfuscation with certified deletion (di$\mathcal{O}$-CD), for a polynomial number of differing inputs. Loosely speaking, di$\mathcal{O}$-CD satisfies the standard notion of differing inputs obfuscation [10], in addition to the following certified deletion property: Let Π_0 and Π_1 two programs that differ on one input y^* (or a polynomial number of hard to find inputs), then it is hard to distinguish an obfuscation of Π_0 from an obfuscation of Π_1, *even given a differing input y^**, provided that the distinguisher outputs the deletion certificate first. Intuitively, this formalizes the guarantee that, after deleting a program, one can no longer evaluate it on any input (more discussion on this later).

We can also conceptually abstract the above results as the following (informal) theorem, in an oracle model: For any classical functionality f, one can prepare an oracle that can be queried repeatedly (polynomially many times) before being *permanently deleted*. That is, after deletion, even an unbounded number of queries to the oracle will not reveal any more information about f. This general result may be of independent interest.

To demonstrate the usefulness of our newly developed tools, we show how they enable new applications in quantum cryptography, and in some cases they allow us to make progress on important open problems:

- **Secure Software Leasing.** As an immediate corollary of differing inputs obfuscation with certified deletion, we obtain a strong notion of secure software leasing for every differing inputs circuits family. Whereas the standard notion guarantees that the *honest* evaluation procedure fails for pirated copies of software, this strong notion guarantees security against arbitrary evaluation procedures.
- **Functional encryption.** We obtain two flavors of functional encryption with certified deletion: (i) one where *ciphertexts* can be certifiably deleted, and (ii) one where *secret keys* can be certifiably deleted (also known as key revocation or secure key leasing). The former assumes a strong-enough notion of

post-quantum functional encryption (in particular, public-key multi-input FE with arity 2). The latter follows from differing inputs obfuscation with certified deletion, combined with post-quantum public-key encryption and injective one-way functions. Functional encryption with key revocation is our *only* result with a computational certified deletion guarantee. This is inherent in the primitive, as key revocation only emulates the case where a secret key was never received.

- **Public verification.** We develop a generic compiler that results in a variety of primitives with *publicly verifiable* certified deletion, assuming post-quantum indistinguishability obfuscation.

2 Technical Overview

2.1 Warm-Up Example

We illustrate the challenges and the techniques that we introduce in this work via a toy example. Namely, we will start from the, by now standard, notion of encryption with certified deletion and highlight the barriers that one encounters when trying to reveal some partial information about the plaintext. Specifically, we will try to build obfuscation with certified deletion starting from the latter.

Public-Key Encryption with Certified Deletion. We recall the basic notion of public-key encryption with certified deletion, and describe a recent construction due to [12] based on Wiesner encodings / BB84 states [14,41]. For describing these states, we use the notation $|x\rangle_\theta$, where $x \in \{0,1\}^n$ is a string of bits, and $\theta \in \{0,1\}^n$ is a string of basis choices. Let Enc be the encryption algorithm for a post-quantum public-key encryption scheme. Then to encrypt a bit b, sample $x, \theta \leftarrow \{0,1\}^n$, and release

$$|x\rangle_\theta, \mathsf{Enc}(\theta, b \oplus \bigoplus_{i:\theta_i=0} x_i).$$

To delete, measure $|x\rangle_\theta$ in the Hadamard basis to obtain a string x'. This verifies as a valid deletion certificate if $x'_i = x_i$ for all $i : \theta_i = 1$. [12] show that since Enc is semantically secure and thus hides the choice of θ, any computationally-bounded adversary that produces a valid deletion certificate must have (essentially) measured most of the qubits in the Hadamard basis, erasing enough information about $\{x_i\}_{i:\theta_i=0}$ to claim that b is now statistically hidden.

Obfuscation and Malleability. One nice property of the above scheme is that it can be decrypted classically after measuring $|x\rangle_\theta$ in the computational basis. This suggests a natural construction for obfuscation with certified deletion. First, encrypt (with certified deletion) the description of the circuit C. Then, obfuscate the classical program that does the following: given a circuit input, the secret key, and a classical measurement outcome obtained from the ciphertext encrypting C, recover the description of C, and then evaluate it on the input.

Unfortunately, such a construction *does not even satisfy indistinguishability obfuscation* (let alone any certified deletion guarantee). The issue is that the encryption scheme is clearly malleable: An adversary only has to guess a single index i where $\theta_i = 0$ in order to flip the message bit. Let's imagine an adversary that can maul the ciphertext to delete a single gate. It tries to distinguish an obfuscation of C_0 from one of C_1, where C_0 and C_1 are built from the same base circuit except that C_0 appends an identity gate and C_1 appends two consecutive NOT gates. This adversary can attempt to remove the last gate in the circuit. If this flips the output, the gate must have been C_1. This simple mauling capability therefore violates indistinguishability obfuscation (even *before* deletion). Under more sophisticated mauling attacks, it may even be possible to recover the whole circuit from the obfuscation!

Ciphertext Validity Check. A simple idea to overcome this issue is to enable the classically obfuscated program to check that the ciphertext has not been tampered with. Say the adversary provides y to the obfuscated program as the alleged measurement of $|x\rangle_\theta$. To verify that the ciphertext is intact, the program only needs to verify that $y_i = x_i$ whenever $\theta_i = 0$. This can be done using a hard-coded x and θ. Otherwise, it can output $\perp$.

Unfortunately, the encryption scheme becomes completely insecure in the presence of such a program. An adversary can learn a description of θ one bit at a time, by flipping a bit of its state $|x\rangle_\theta$ and observing whether the program returns a successful evaluation or rejects. Once it learns θ, we cannot hope for any certified deletion guarantees. Moreover, the adversary can make additional queries to learn $\{x_i\}_{i:\theta_i=0}$, and, eventually, the circuit C.

Subspace Coset States. Fortunately, there is a way to get around the problem that BB84 states are learnable in this sense. Prior work (for example, in the setting of publicly-verifiable quantum money) has switched to using entangled *subspace* states [2] and the more-general subspace coset states. A subspace coset state is defined by a subspace S of $\mathbb{F}_2^n$ and two vectors $\mathsf{v}, \mathsf{w} \in \mathbb{F}_2^n$, and is written as

$$|S_{\mathsf{v},\mathsf{w}}\rangle := \frac{1}{\sqrt{|S|}} \sum_{z \in S+\mathsf{v}} |z\rangle (-1)^{\langle z, \mathsf{w} \rangle}.$$

It is useful to think of BB84 states as a type of subspace coset state in which the subspace is spanned by the standard basis vectors $\{e_i\}_{i:\theta_i=1}$. The coset in the primal space is determined by the bits $\{x_i\}_{i:\theta_i=0}$, which are used to hide the plaintext bit b, and the coset in the dual space is determined by the bits $\{x_i\}_{i:\theta_i=1}$, which determine what constitutes a valid deletion certificate.

Thus, in an attempt to make the obfuscation scheme secure, we replace the use of BB84 states with more-general subspace coset states. To encrypt each bit b of the description of the circuit, consider a ciphertext of the form

$$|S_{\mathsf{v},\mathsf{w}}\rangle, \mathsf{Enc}(S, C \oplus \langle \mathsf{v}, \mathbf{1}\rangle),$$

where we set S to be a random $n/2$-dimensional subspace, and a valid deletion certificate is now any vector $\tilde{z} \in S^\perp + \mathsf{w}$. The decryption algorithm, on input a vector z and ciphertext ct, will decrypt ct to obtain (S, b'), compute a canonical coset representative of $S + z$, and use this resulting vector to unmask b.

Additionally, it is possible to check whether z has been tampered with by verifying that $z \in S + v$. It is even possible to publish an oracle for this consistency check, *without* leaking S and v [21]. However, proving that the consistency oracle does not compromise the certified deletion security of the encryption scheme requires new ideas, and is a main technical contribution of this work.

Noisy Consistency Check. In order to carry out this consistency check, the obfuscated program must have S and v hard-coded. Unfortunately, the obfuscation only hides S and v computationally. After deletion, an unbounded adversary could learn v and $b \oplus \langle v, \mathbf{1} \rangle$, which reveals b.

To information-theoretically protect b after deletion, we will instead sample a random superspace of S called T and hard-code the coset $T + u$ that contains $S + v$. We set $\dim(T) = 3n/4$ as a happy medium, which has two nice properties. First, since T is a negligible fraction of $\mathbb{F}_2^n$, it is hard for an adversary to find a vector in $T + u \setminus S + v$, so the consistency check will be essentially as good as using $S + v$. Second, since S is a negligible fraction of T, $T + u$ statistically hides enough information about v that $\langle v, \mathbf{1} \rangle$ is uniformly random, even given $T + u$. Therefore, the proof of certified deletion works.

It turns out that this "noisy consistency check" will be also be a crucial component in our constructions of both blind delegation and functional encryption with certified deletion.

2.2   General Compiler for Certified Deletion

Now we will present the tool that underlies all of our applications: a compiler that adds a certified deletion guarantee to a variety of cryptographic primitives.

First consider a simple template for certified deletion: to hide a bit b, we give the adversary the following state:

$$|S_{v,w}\rangle, \mathcal{Z}(S, b \oplus \langle v, \mathbf{1} \rangle),$$

where $|S_{v,w}\rangle$ is a random subspace coset state and $\mathcal{Z}$ is some side information, which may be classical. $\mathcal{Z}$ will often represent the primitive to which we are adding a certified deletion guarantee.

Note that given only the side information, b is statistically hidden because it is masked by $\langle v, \mathbf{1} \rangle$. However, the information needed to remove the mask v is stored in the computational basis of the subspace coset state. To prove deletion, an honest party measures the subspace coset state in the Hadamard basis to get a vector $\tilde{z} \in S^\perp + w$, which destroys essentially all information about v and removes b from their view. We will hope to prove that *any* strategy an (efficient) adversary uses to obtain a $\tilde{z} \in S^\perp + w$ will also statistically remove b from their view.

The recent work of [12] showed how to prove this when $\mathcal{Z}$ satisfies *semantic security* with respect to S.[3] However our applications need a much richer set

---

[3] Also they only consider the case where the quantum state is a string of BB84 states.

of choices for $\mathcal{Z}$ that do not necessarily hide S semantically. For instance, we want the ability to perform the noisy consistency check. That is: we want $\mathcal{Z}$ to output a randomized (T, u) where $S + v \subset T + u$. This is essential for our constructions of blind delegation and obfuscation with certified deletion. But $\mathcal{Z}$ would no longer hide S semantically because T reveals some basis vectors of $S^\perp$. In this case [12]'s proof falls short.

We present a compiler that supports a greater variety of choices for $\mathcal{Z}$, including the noisy consistency check. Specifically, we develop techniques to allow any choice of $\mathcal{Z}$ that satisfies a form of subspace-hiding against QPT adversaries. Morally, subspace-hiding means that an adversary cannot tell whether $\mathcal{Z}$ was testing membership in S (and $S^\perp$) or random superspaces $T \geq S$ (and $R \geq S^\perp$). We sketch our notion of subspace-hiding below:

Definition 1 (Subspace-Hiding, Informal). *Given any subspace S of dimension $n/2$ and two cosets $S + v$ and $S^\perp + w$, let $T + u$ and $R + x$ be random cosets that contain the first two: $S + v \subset T + u$ and $S^\perp + w \subset R + x$. Then, $\mathcal{Z}(S, T, u, w, b \oplus \langle v, 1 \rangle)$ is subspace-hiding if there exists a simulator $\mathcal{S}(R, T, u, x, b \oplus \langle v, 1 \rangle)$ such that*

$$\mathcal{Z}(S, T, u, w, b \oplus \langle v, 1 \rangle) \approx_c \mathcal{S}(R, T, u, x, b \oplus \langle v, 1 \rangle),$$

where $\approx_c$ denotes indistinguishability to a quantum polynomial-time adversary.

Next, we claim that if $\mathcal{Z}$ satisfies subspace-hiding (which is a notion of *computational* security), then after the deletion certificate is accepted, b is *statistically* hidden, even if the inputs to $\mathcal{Z}$ are leaked at a later point. We sketch the security claim below.

Claim (Certified Deletion Security, Informal). Let $\mathsf{EXP}(b)$ be the output of the following experiment:

1. *Challenge:* The challenger samples the following challenge and sends it to the adversary:
$$|S_{v,w}\rangle, \mathcal{Z}_\lambda(S, T, u, w, b \oplus \langle v, 1 \rangle)$$

2. *Response:* The adversary responds with a deletion certificate $\tilde{z} \in \mathbb{F}_2^n$ and an auxiliary state ρ.

3. *Outcome:* The challenger checks that
$$\tilde{z} \in S^\perp + w$$

If so, they output ρ and all the inputs to $\mathcal{Z}$; if not, they output $\perp$.

If $\mathcal{Z}$ is computationally subspace-hiding, then the statistical distance between $\mathsf{EXP}(0)$ and $\mathsf{EXP}(1)$ is negligible.

Proof Overview. First, we claim that b is statistically hidden given *only* the side information $\mathcal{Z}(S, T, u, w, b \oplus \langle v, 1 \rangle)$. Note that b is masked by $\langle v, 1 \rangle$, and although $\mathcal{Z}$ may give some information about v in the form of (T, u), there is still some randomness left in v. In more detail, we can decompose v into its deterministic and random components by defining $v_0 = v - u$. Then given (S, T, u, w), u is deterministic, and v_0 is uniformly random over $co(S) \cap T$.[4] Because v_0 is uniformly random given (S, T, u, w), the bit $\langle v, 1 \rangle$ is also uniformly random (with overwhelming probability over the choice of (S, T)).

Next, recall that the adversary's view also includes the quantum state $|S_{v,w}\rangle = |S_{u+v_0,w}\rangle$, which stores v_0 in the computational basis. Now, b is not necessarily statistically hidden given both $|S_{u+v_0,w}\rangle$ and $\mathcal{Z}(S, T, u, w, b \oplus \langle v, 1 \rangle)$. However, we will show that to prove deletion, the adversary must essentially measure $|S_{u+v_0,w}\rangle$ in the Hadamard basis, destroying all information that the state had about v_0.

To show this, instead of giving the adversary $|S_{u+v_0,w}\rangle$, we imagine giving them the following state, which stores a random $\tilde{v}_0$ in the Hadamard basis:

$$|T_{u,\tilde{v}_0+w}\rangle \quad \text{where } \tilde{v}_0 \leftarrow co(T^{\perp}) \cap S^{\perp}.$$

$|T_{u,\tilde{v}_0+w}\rangle$ is in some sense dual with $|S_{u+v_0,w}\rangle$. Both states store u in the computational basis and w in the Hadamard basis. The only difference is that $|S_{u+v_0,w}\rangle$ encodes a random v_0 in the computational basis, and instead $|T_{u,\tilde{v}_0+w}\rangle$ encodes a random $\tilde{v}_0$ in the Hadamard basis. Furthermore, the adversary's behavior will be the same no matter which of the two states we give them. Indeed, we show that for any fixed S, T, u, w, the following states σ_0 and σ_1 are equivalent:[5]

$$\sigma_0 \propto \sum_{v_0 \in co(S) \cap T} |S_{u+v_0,w}\rangle\langle S_{u+v_0,w}|$$

$$\sigma_1 \propto \sum_{\tilde{v}_0 \in co(T^{\perp}) \cap S^{\perp}} |T_{u,\tilde{v}_0+w}\rangle\langle T_{u,\tilde{v}_0+w}|$$

This can be seen as a generalization of the fact that

$$\frac{1}{2}\big(|0\rangle\langle 0| + |1\rangle\langle 1|\big) = \frac{1}{2}\big(|+\rangle\langle +| + |-\rangle\langle -|\big).$$

In other words, the state is the same whether it's a maximal mixture of computational basis eigenstates or Hadamard basis eigenstates. Establishing this claim requires new techniques which seem to be generally useful for handling subspace coset states (more detail in Sect. 2.3).

Now, we want to argue that if the adversary produces a valid deletion certificate $\tilde{z} \in S^{\perp} + w$, then given their remaining state, v_0 is statistically close to uniform. Imagine the adversary is given $|T_{u,\tilde{v}_0+w}\rangle$ and they output a valid deletion certificate $\tilde{z} \in S^{\perp} + w$ with non-negligible probability. Recall that $T^{\perp} + \tilde{v}_0 + w$ is an affine subspace of $S^{\perp} + w$, so one way to do this is to make a measurement

---

[4] $co(S)$ is a group of coset representatives of S. See Sect. 4.1 for a precise definition of $co(S)$.

[5] This is implicitly shown in the supplementary material by purifying σ_0 and σ_1 and showing that there exists a unitary acting on the purifying register that maps between the two states.

of the vector $\widetilde{v}_0 + w$ encoded in the phase, producing a vector in $T^\perp + \widetilde{v}_0 + w$. In fact, we show that since $\mathcal{Z}$ is computationally subspace-hiding for S, *any* adversary's strategy must be *statistically close* to making a measurement of $\widetilde{v}_0 + w$.[6] Then, if the adversary were instead given $|S_{u+v_0,w}\rangle$, this same measurement of the phase would destroy all information about v_0, completing the proof.

2.3   Discussion

To gain some context, it is useful to zoom out from our main theorem, and compare our proof technique with existing works. As we shall see shortly, our settings require new proof techniques and cannot be framed as a special case of existing theorems.

New Techniques for Subspace Coset States. While the previous section provides intuition, our actual proof is trickier and requires new techniques. Essentially, facts that are obvious for continuous vector spaces are sometimes false or difficult to formalize for discrete vector spaces. We develop new techniques for working with subspace cosets, and the culmination is an algorithm for *delayed preparation of subspace coset states*. Section 4 presents these results.

Our first contribution is to define a coset group $\mathsf{co}(S)$ that is isomorphic to $\mathbb{F}_2^n/S$ and that is a subspace of $\mathbb{F}_2^n$. This improves on prior work, [21], which defined a set of canonical coset representatives that was not necessarily a group. The algebraic structure of $\mathsf{co}(S)$ allows us to prove more-sophisticated claims than what was possible with [21]'s coset representatives.

Our second contribution is to develop a toolkit for proving such claims.

Our third contribution is an algorithm for delayed preparation of subspace coset states. This formalizes the intuition that the adversary's behavior is the same whether they are asked to play a game based on $|S_{u+v_0,w}\rangle$ or a game based on $|T_{u,\widetilde{v}_0+w}\rangle$. We formalize this by showing that we can purify σ_0 and σ_1 by adding a second register, and then show that there is a unitary that acts on the second register and maps the purification of σ_0 to that of σ_1. The unitary could be applied after the adversary acts on the first register, so the adversary's behavior will be the same in either case.

Why Monogamy-of-Entanglement Techniques Fail. Prior works [21,37] that dealt with subspace coset states relied on monogamy-of-entanglement (MoE) theorems, but these theorems fail to achieve the strong guarantees needed in our setting.

First, monogamy of entanglement is an information-theoretic property, and it does not necessarily hold if the adversary receives a computationally-secure encryption of the subspace S. We note that a recent work [7] does use a MoE property to establish a certified deletion property, but crucially only in the information-theoretic one-time-pad encryption setting.

---

[6] That is, we use *computational* hardness to establish a *statistical* claim, as done in [12] in the context of BB84 states.

Next, MoE claims in prior work do not seem to easily extend to rule out the possibility that Bob outputs the string x, and Charlie simultaneously outputs the parity of x with non-negligible advantage. If this were possible, then even when one player produces a valid deletion certificate, the other player might learn a bit of data with non-negligible advantage, which would violate certified deletion security.

Why Non-committing Encryption Techniques Fail. Recall that we would like to eventually prove information-theoretic deletion of a secret that is initially information-theoretically determined by the adversary's view. Prior works (e.g., [4]) used receiver non-committing encryption schemes which have an "equivocality" property, allowing one to sample the fake keys after S is revealed. These were inherently limited to proving weaker forms of security; e.g., restricted to (computational) security against key-leakage attacks. Furthermore, equivocality is hard to achieve [31] for applications such as blind delegation, which involves FHE. Another setting where an equivocality-based approach fails is differing-inputs obfuscation. The choice of whether to behave as C_0 or C_1 is "hidden" under the differing inputs. Thus, the differing inputs act as a key to decrypt S, which reveals this choice bit. However, any differing input (i.e. key) y^* is easy to check by simply evaluating the two programs C_0 and C_1 on y^*, allowing fake keys to be immediately recognized. While [12] developed methods to overcome the equivocality issue for certified deletion, they only apply their techniques to settings where the subspace S is semantically hidden.

2.4 Blind Delegation with Certified Deletion

In this section, we discuss our construction of maliciously-secure blind delegation with certified deletion.

Insecurity of Prior Protocols Against Malicious Adversaries. We first discuss why both prior protocols [12,35], while secure against semi-honest adversaries, are *insecure* against malicious adversaries.

Both of these protocols consist of four messages. First, the client encrypts their input m and sends a quantum ciphertext $|\mathsf{Enc}(m)\rangle$ to the server. Next, the server evaluates a function f to obtain a register holding a superposition over output ciphertexts $|\mathsf{Enc}(f(m))\rangle$, which is sent to the client. The client then coherently applies FHE decryption using their secret key, which allows them to recover $f(m)$ without disturbing the state, and then reverse their computation and send the undisturbed register back to the server. Finally, the server can uncompute f and recover the original ciphertext $|\mathsf{Enc}(m)\rangle$. Then, if they want, they can measure the ciphertext in a particular way to recover a certificate of deletion, which is sent to the client.

Now, consider the following attack. Suppose that the server wants to learn the first bit m_1 of m. They can easily prepare a state of the form

$$\frac{1}{\sqrt{2}}|\mathsf{Enc}(m_1)\rangle^{\mathsf{C}}|0\rangle^{\mathsf{S}} + \frac{1}{\sqrt{2}}|\mathsf{Enc}(0)\rangle^{\mathsf{C}}|1\rangle^{\mathsf{S}},$$

where $\mathsf{Enc}(0)$ is a freshly prepared encryption of 0. Then, suppose they send register C to the client in place of the second message of the protocol described above. In the case that $m_1 = 0$, the client's computation will not disturb the state, and the server will receive back the C register unharmed. But in the case when $m_1 = 1$, the client's measurement of the output *will* collapse the state. Thus, if the server unentangles register C and S, measures S in the Hadamard basis, and observes outcome $|-\rangle$, they will learn *for sure* that $m_1 = 1$, breaking privacy of the protocol.[7]

Our Solution. The attack above relies on the fact that the client always immediately applies an operation that depends on their FHE secret key sk. To prevent this attack, we must introduce a way for the client to *check* that the server is honestly following the protocol, *before* using its secret key to operate on the state.

Suppose the client's input is a single bit b, and consider our basic encryption scheme

$$|S_{\mathsf{v},\mathsf{w}}\rangle, \mathsf{Enc}(S, b \oplus \langle \mathsf{v}, 1 \rangle),$$

but where Enc is now instantiated as a fully-homomorphic encryption (FHE) scheme. We will have the server perform a classical FHE evaluation for circuit f in superposition over the vectors in $S + \mathsf{v}$, resulting in a superposition over $\mathsf{Enc}(f(b))$. Now, the client will need to perform two checks to make sure the server was behaving honestly:

- The client needs to check that the FHE evaluation in superposition was performed honestly. This can by accomplished by requesting that the server use a succinct non-interactive argument (SNARG) for P (polynomial-time computation) in superposition, and having the client verify this proof before decrypting. Moreover, SNARGs for P are known just from the LWE assumption [20], and it is straightforward to see that this SNARG remains post-quantum secure assuming the post-quantum hardness of LWE.
- The client *also* needs to check that the *input* to the server's computation is honest. This input is supposed to include any vector in $S + \mathsf{v}$. Thus, one solution is to have the client remember a description of $S + \mathsf{v}$, and also perform this check on the input before decrypting the output. However, this solution

---

[7] This attack does not contradict any claims made in [35] or [12] because neither paper claims that their protocol is maliciously-secure. In [35], the correctness and security properties are defined entirely separately. That is, it is argued that correctness of the four-message protocol holds assuming parties are honest, but *security* (and certified deletion security) is only argued *assuming that the server does not interact with the client*. Thus, the claim is essentially that *either* correctness of delegation holds, *or* privacy against a malicious server holds. But it is never claimed that both can hold simultaneously. In [12], the authors do jointly consider correctness and security of the four-message protocol. However, they only claim security against servers that are *semi-honest* during the protocol execution (and potentially malicious after, while producing the deletion certificate). Thus, the above attack is explicitly disallowed by the semi-honest assumption.

requires that the client keep the vector v around in memory, which if leaked would completely compromise certified deletion security. Instead, we use the same "noisy consistency check" as explained earlier, and have the client sample a random affine superspace $T + u$ of $S + v$, and only keep this around in memory.

This is the basic idea of our blind delegation scheme.

Remarks on the Security Definition.

- We prove simulation-based security in the "protocols with certified deletion" framework of [12]. That is, we show that our protocol securely realizes an ideal functionality that takes input (f, x) from the client, delivers *only* f to the server, and delivers the output $f(x)$ to the client. Thus, in the simulated world, the server obtain *no* information about the client's private input x. We show that conditioned on the server producing a valid deletion certificate, their final view in the ideal protocol and in the ideal world are *statistically* indistinguishable, indicating that they have information-theoretically lost all information about x.
- We show that our protocol in fact realizes a *reusable* ideal functionality, where the client can request that the server compute for them multiple functions $f_1(x), f_2(x), \ldots$ on their original encrypted data x, and security still holds.
- In the case that deletion is accepted, we also explicitly leak all of the client's secret parameters to the adversary, and still require that statistical security holds. We capture this by defining a "long-term secrets" tape sec, where after each message, the honest client is supposed to write all of the information it needs to interact in the remainder of the protocol on this tape. Conditioned on deletion being accepted, we give the adversary access to this tape.

Finally, we remark that prior to our work, maliciously-secure blind delegation with certified deletion was not known *even without reusability*, and *even without requiring information-theoretic security after deletion*.

2.5   Obfuscation with Certified Deletion

A certifiably deletable program is an encoding of a classical circuit C into a quantum state $|\widetilde{C}\rangle$ that allows for evaluation of $C(x)$ on any input x. To realize certified deletion, there should also be a procedure for measuring $|\widetilde{C}\rangle$ in a particular way that certifiably destroys information about C.

While the natural notion of virtual black-box obfuscation is impossible to achieve in general [10], several relaxed notions are plausibly achievable. We focus on the case of differing inputs obfuscation for a polynomial number of differing inputs [10], which is implied by the related notion of indistinguishability obfuscation [15]. This notion requires that for any two circuits C_0 and C_1 which differ on a polynomial number of hard-to-find inputs, an obfuscation of C_0 is indistinguishable from an obfuscation of C_1.

Our goal is thus to achieve differing inputs obfuscation with certified deletion for a polynomial number of differing inputs.[8] This is described by the following (simplified) game.

1. The challenger samples two programs C_0 and C_1 from a given distribution, where it holds that $C_0(y) = C_1(y)$, except for some y^*, that we refer to as the *differing input*. Importantly, even given the description of C_0 and C_1, it is computationally hard to find y^*.
2. The challenger flips a coin $b \leftarrow \{0,1\}$ and sends an obfuscation of C_b to the attacker.
3. At some point of the experiment, the attacker outputs the deletion certificate, which is verified by the challenger.
4. If the certificate correctly verifies, then the challenger sends y^* to the attacker.
5. The attacker outputs a guess for the bit b.

We say that an obfuscation scheme is secure if the success probability of the attacker is negligibly close to $1/2$. We note that if the attacker becomes unbounded after outputting a valid deletion certificate, then they could compute y^* themselves. Thus, we remove Step 4 in our definition for information-theoretic certified deletion.

To justify this definition, we argue that it captures the intuitive guarantees that one would expect from software with certified deletion. First, there is a sense in which software with certified deletion implies some notion of obfuscation: if one could learn the program by just looking at its code, then there would be no point in issuing a deletion certificate. Second, we want to model the fact that once the adversary has deleted the program, they can no longer evaluate it on any input. However, it is not clear how to model the information which the adversary learned before deletion, i.e., when they had a *functional* copy of the program. We have no way of "looking inside the adversary's head" to learn which inputs they evaluate, and, even worse, the attacker may not even execute the program properly. Our definition sidesteps this issue, by requiring security for inputs that are hidden even given the plain description of the program (i.e., the differing inputs). In this sense, our definition can be interpreted as saying that the deletion prevents the adversary from learning any information that was not obviously leaked from having a running copy of the program.[9]

Construction. As outlined previously, the general structure of the construction is to encrypt the circuit C under a random coset v of the subspace S. Suppose for a moment that we can simultaneously hide all bits of C with a single vector v. To use the noisy consistency check, we will sample a uniform superspace $T + \mathsf{u}$ of

---

[8] Our definition also generalizes to the case of an arbitrary number of differing inputs. However, achieving this would imply the existence of general differing inputs obfuscation, contrary to current evidence [13,24].

[9] Our definition does not prevent an adversary from evaluating the program on *easy-to-find* inputs after deletion. This is because we cannot rule out the possibility of them having already evaluated those inputs before deletion.

$S+v$. Then, we will hard-code S, T and u into a classical program $P[S, T, u, C+v]$ to be obfuscated. $P[S, T, u, C + v]$ takes as input a vector z (which should be in $S + v$) and a string x to be evaluated. It checks that $z \in T + u$, then computes the coset v of S that z belongs to, unmasks C using v, and finally computes and outputs $C(x)$. If $z \notin T + u$, it aborts. Then, the construction is

$$|S_{v,w}\rangle, \mathsf{Obf}(P[S, T, u, C + v])$$

To argue security, we would like to switch an obfuscation of C_0 to an obfuscation of C_1, and argue that this switch is *statistically* indistinguishable to an adversary that produces a successful deletion certificate. Our main theorem provides a way to obtain such statistical guarantees, but it only handles statistically hiding a single bit. Thus, we must perform a hybrid argument over the bits of the descriptions of the circuits. We cannot do this naively, since descriptions of circuits "in between" C_0 and C_1 are not guaranteed to be functionally equivalent to C_0 and C_1. Instead, we make use of the *two-slot technique* [34], and we defer details of this to the technical sections.

The above describes the main intuition and techniques that allow us to hide functionality, while still allowing for certified deletion. In the body of the paper, we also derive the following related results and applications.

Application: Strong Secure Software Leasing. Secure software leasing is defined with respect to a family of programs [8]. The adversary is given a leased program randomly chosen from this family and outputs two programs. If one of the programs is authenticated, then the other cannot be evaluated using the honest evaluation procedure.

We observe that any differing inputs program family can be securely leased by obfuscating it with certified deletion. A differing inputs program family contains pairs of programs (C_0, C_1) such that given a random pair, it is hard to find an input y^* where $C_0(y^*) \neq C_1(y^*)$. If an obfuscation of C_0 is returned to the lessor who then generates a valid deletion certificate, then the residual state cannot be used to distinguish whether the program was C_0 or C_1, even given a differing input y^*. In particular, the adversary that returned the program cannot later evaluate a pirated copy of it on y^* - otherwise they could check which program matched the output. Therefore, a leased program can be validated by attempting to delete it and checking the deletion certificate.

We emphasize that this guarantee is *stronger* than the original notion of secure software leasing, which permits the adversary to evaluate a pirated (i.e. unauthenticated) program as long as they do not use the honest evaluation procedure. In our definition, security is guaranteed even if the adversary uses an *arbitrary* evaluation procedure after returning a valid copy of the program.

Since we construct obfuscation with certified deletion for a polynomial number of differing inputs, we immediately obtain (strong) secure software leasing for differing inputs program families with a polynomial number of differing inputs. Existing impossibility results for secure software leasing [5,8] rule out secure software leasing for families containing programs which cannot be learned with black-box query access, but *can* be learned using non-black-box access to any functionally equivalent program. In contrast, a differing inputs program family contains programs which cannot be learned, even with non-black-box access to an obfuscation of the program.

Application: Functional Encryption with Key Revocation. To substantiate the usefulness of our definition, we show that our obfuscation scheme allows a simple and intuitive construction of public-key encryption, and even *functional encryption*, with key revocation. Moreover, our key revocation guarantee is *publicly-verifiable*. In key revocation, one or more secret keys are temporarily distributed to users. Later on, if the users comply with the revocation process, these keys are deleted and cannot be used to decrypt freshly generated ciphertexts [3,9].[10]

Our construction is essentially the same as the transformation from obfuscation to functional encryption given in [23], but our obfuscation scheme supports certified deletion. We describe a simplified version of their construction here. The secret key for a function f will be an obfuscated circuit that first decrypts a classical ciphertext to recover the message m, and then computes and returns $f(m)$. The encryption of m will use a standard public-key encryption scheme.

The above construction already guarantees that a key sk_f *only* reveals information about $f(m)$, by virtue of being a functional encryption scheme. The certified deletion property *additionally* ensures that, if the adversary has a key for f, but deletes it before receiving the challenge ciphertext, then he learns nothing. In fact, a straightforward reduction to the certified deletion security of the obfuscation scheme ensures that this is the case even if the adversary has access to other secret keys (security against *unbounded* collusion). We note that a similar technique allows adding publicly-verifiable key revocation to other encryption schemes, assuming iO.

3   Related Work

3.1   Prior Work

We first discuss prior works that build cryptographic schemes from subspace coset states. These states were first used by [39] in the context of proofs of quantum knowledge and by [21] to construct signature tokens (among other unclonable primitives) in the plain model. These were also used to build semi-quantum tokenized signatures [37]. Most recently, [6] used subspace coset states to construct unclonable encryption satisfying the notion of unclonable indistinguishability. We remark that, while there are clearly similarities between the notions of unclonable encryption and encryption with certified deletion, our security definitions and proofs are quite different than those in [6]. For example, [6] crucially rely on *random oracles*, while our results are all in the plain

---

[10] This property has also been referred to as secure key leasing.

model. Moreover, we achieve security definitions that promise *everlasting security* against unbounded adversaries after deletion, while [6,21,37] focuses on proving that computationally-bounded (or query-bounded) adversaries cannot perform a certain task, e.g., generating additional signatures.

Next, we mention two prior works that have considered functional encryption with certified deletion. [32] achieves a *private*-key version of functional encryption with certified deletion of secret keys. [29] achieves functional encryption where the ciphertext can be deleted and it is certified everlasting (i.e. information-theoretic certified deletion). Their construction is secure against bounded collusions, and either relies on the QROM or requires quantum certificates of deletion, and assumes public-key encryption. On the other hand, our functional encryption schemes support *public*-key encryption and are secure (in the sense of certified deletion) against an unbounded number of colluding users. We assume iO, which (up to subexponential hardness factors) is necessary, since it is implied by unbounded-collusion FE.

Finally, we remark that the blind delegation protocol of [35] is also shown to be publicly-verifiable, under the strong Gaussian-collapsing conjecture, and thus our results on blind delegation with public verification are technically incomparable. However, [35]'s conjecture involves an interactive game that has a baked in certified deletion component, wherein the adversary receives some trapdoor information conditioned on them successfully returning a pre-image of the hash function. On the other hand, indistinguishability obfuscation a priori has nothing to do with certified deletion. While post-quantum indistinguishability obfuscation is also not known from standard assumptions, this is a very active area of research with many candidates proposed over the last few years [11,16,19,22,25,40].

3.2 Concurrent and Independent Work

We will discuss three recent works [3,9,27] that construct revocable/deletable cryptographic primitives, a few of which overlap with ours. We compare the results in more detail below. At a high level, our constructions produce *publicly-verifiable, classical* deletion certificates in the plain model. The deletion certificates of [3,9,27] are all *privately* verifiable, and some of their constructions require *quantum* deletion certificates. Furthermore, our work unifies techniques using a general compiler for certified deletion based on subspace coset states. Whereas [3,27] developed different techniques for constructing, respectively, FE with certified deletion for ciphertexts and FE with key revocation, we construct both primitives from a single technique.

[27] construct functional encryption with certified deletion for *ciphertexts*. One of their main techniques is a way to verify BB84 states by individually signing them with a one-time signature. This serves a similar purpose as our use of subspace coset states. One difference is that their one-time signature approach results in privately-verifiable certificates of deletion, while our subspace coset state approach also supports public verification when combined with iO. They also construct several primitives with certified deletion that are not considered in our work: compute-and-compare obfuscation and predicate encryption.

Likewise, we construct blind delegation, CCA encryption, and (differing-inputs) obfuscation, which they do not consider.

Next, [3] construct functional encryption that supports revocation of *secret keys*. They call this notion *secure key leasing*, which is the same as key revocation, except that their "certificate of deletion" is a privately-verifiable quantum state (the key itself) whereas ours is a classical string obtained by performing a destructive measurement on the quantum key. They also show how to add secure key leasing to various encryption schemes (public-key, identity-based, attribute-based, and functional) while requiring no additional assumptions. We only consider functional encryption with secure key leasing and assume iO, which is implied by subexponentially-secure functional encryption. Our technique is generic and could also be used to add publicly-verifiable secure key leasing to other encryption schemes, at the cost of assuming iO.

Finally, [9] also study revocable cryptography, which is the same notion of secure key leasing as studied by [3]. They obtain various primitives (including psuedorandom functions, PKE, and fully-homomorphic encryption) with key revocation, from the hardness of LWE. The comparison with our work is similar to the previous paragraph: [9] achieve constructions from standard assumptions, but only support privately-verifiable quantum certificates of revocation.

4   Delayed Preparation of Coset States

Here we develop tools for working with subspace coset states that will help us prove Theorem 2, which is our main theorem. In particular, we show how to prepare a random subspace coset state but delay the choice of subspace until after the register has been given out. Similar techniques exist for BB84/Wiesner states, but it is non-trivial to extend them to subspace coset states. Along the way, we develop a framework for representing the cosets of two subspaces $S \leq T$ that maintains the algebraic structure of the quotient groups $\mathbb{F}_2^n/S$ and $\mathbb{F}_2^n/T$. We believe the techniques in this section are interesting independently of their applications to certified deletion.

4.1   Coset Representatives

Given a subspace $S \leq \mathbb{F}_2^n$, let $\mathsf{co}(S)$ be a subspace of $\mathbb{F}_2^n$ that contains exactly one vector from every coset of S.[11] Note, $\mathsf{co}(S)$ is analogous to the quotient group $\mathbb{F}_2^n/S$, whose elements are the actual cosets of S and which has the same algebraic structure as $\mathsf{co}(S)$. $\mathsf{co}(S)$ is useful for decomposing vectors since every $\mathsf{z} \in \mathbb{F}_2^n$ has a *unique* decomposition as $\mathsf{z} = \mathsf{u} + \mathsf{v}$, for some $(\mathsf{u}, \mathsf{v}) \in S \times \mathsf{co}(S)$ (Lemma 1).

It is useful intuition to imagine choosing $\mathsf{co}(S) = S^\perp$, but this is not always allowed. Because S is a subspace of $\mathbb{F}_2^n$ and not $\mathbb{R}^n$, it's possible that some coset of S contains multiple vectors from $S^\perp$ and another coset contains none.

---

[11] [21] used a different set of coset representatives, called Can_S, which is not necessarily a vector space.

For any S, there exists a valid $\mathsf{co}(S)$ (see Definition 2 and Lemma 2). Usually, there are many valid choices of $\mathsf{co}(S)$, so we pick one of them to be canonical. To avoid ambiguity, let the description of S include a basis for the following subspaces: $[S, S^\perp, \mathsf{co}(S), \mathsf{co}(S^\perp)]$. This defines the canonical choices for $\mathsf{co}(S)$ and $\mathsf{co}(S^\perp)$.

Lemma 1 shows that the definition of $\mathsf{co}(S)$ is equivalent to some useful properties. In this lemma, we refer to $\mathsf{co}(S)$ as C.

Lemma 1. *For subspaces* $S, C \leq \mathbb{F}_2^n$, *the following are equivalent:*

1. C *contains exactly one element from each coset of* S.
2. *For any* $\mathsf{z} \in \mathbb{F}_2^n$, *there is a unique pair* $(\mathsf{u}, \mathsf{v}) \in S \times C$ *such that* $\mathsf{z} = \mathsf{u} + \mathsf{v}$.
3. $\dim(C) = n - \dim(S)$ *and* $\mathsf{span}(S, C) = \mathbb{F}_2^n$.

4.2 Sampling Procedure

In this section, we give a procedure for choosing $\mathsf{co}(S)$. We actually consider a more-general problem: given two subspaces $S \leq T$, we will choose $[\mathsf{co}(S), \mathsf{co}(S^\perp), \mathsf{co}(T), \mathsf{co}(T^\perp)]$ that satisfy $\mathsf{co}(T) \leq \mathsf{co}(S)$ along with some other useful properties. In later sections, whenever we need to sample two subspaces, $S \leq T$, we will implicitly use Definition 2 to sample the associated coset representatives.

Definition 2 (Procedure to Sample Coset Representatives). *Given two subspaces* $S \leq T \leq \mathbb{F}_2^n$:

1. *Choose* n *linearly independent vectors* $\{\mathsf{z}_1, \ldots, \mathsf{z}_n\}$ *uniformly at random such that*

$$S = \mathsf{span}(\mathsf{z}_1, \ldots, \mathsf{z}_{\dim(S)})$$
$$T = \mathsf{span}(\mathsf{z}_1, \ldots, \mathsf{z}_{\dim(T)})$$

2. *Then let*

$$\mathsf{co}(S) = \mathsf{span}(\mathsf{z}_{\dim(S)+1}, \ldots, \mathsf{z}_n)$$
$$\mathsf{co}(T) = \mathsf{span}(\mathsf{z}_{\dim(T)+1}, \ldots, \mathsf{z}_n)$$
$$\mathsf{co}(S^\perp) = \mathsf{co}(S)^\perp$$
$$\mathsf{co}(T^\perp) = \mathsf{co}(T)^\perp$$

3. *Choose a fresh random basis for each subspace in* $[\mathsf{co}(S), \mathsf{co}(S^\perp), \mathsf{co}(T), \mathsf{co}(T^\perp)]$, *and output these bases. Note that the subspaces do not change in this step – just the bases used to represent them.*

The reason we choose fresh random bases for each subspace is so that someone with a description of S and $\mathsf{co}(S)$ but not T does not learn anything about T other than the fact that $S \leq T$. The original basis we chose for $\mathsf{co}(S)$ was built from the basis for T, which might leak information about T.

Lemma 2 analyzes the procedure in Definition 2 and proves that it satisfies some useful properties.

Lemma 2. *Given two subspaces $S \leq T \leq \mathbb{F}_2^n$, the procedure in Definition 2 chooses the subspaces $[\mathsf{co}(S), \mathsf{co}(S^\perp), \mathsf{co}(T), \mathsf{co}(T^\perp)]$ such that:*

1. *$\mathsf{co}(S)$ is valid: it contains exactly one element from each coset of S. The analogous statement holds for $\mathsf{co}(S^\perp), \mathsf{co}(T), \mathsf{co}(T^\perp)$.*
2. *$\mathsf{co}(T) \leq \mathsf{co}(S)$ and $\mathsf{co}(S^\perp) \leq \mathsf{co}(T^\perp)$.*
3. *$\mathsf{co}(S^\perp) = \mathsf{co}(S)^\perp$ and $\mathsf{co}(T^\perp) = \mathsf{co}(T)^\perp$.*

4.3 Delayed Preparation of Coset States

Our goal in this section is for Alice to prepare a random subspace coset state for Bob, but delay choosing the underlying subspace until after she sends the register to Bob. This technique is used in the proof of the main theorem, Theorem 2, and it uses the formalism for coset representatives that we developed above.

Let Alice be given two subspaces $S \leq T \leq \mathbb{F}_2^n$, and let the corresponding coset representatives $[\mathsf{co}(S), \mathsf{co}(S^\perp), \mathsf{co}(T), \mathsf{co}(T^\perp)]$ be sampled from the procedure in Definition 2. Next, let Alice be given cosets $\mathsf{u} \in \mathsf{co}(T)$ and $\mathsf{w} \in \mathsf{co}(S^\perp)$, which partially determine the subspace coset state that Alice will sample.

Alice will sample the subspace coset state from one of the following distributions:

- Distribution 0: Sample $|S_{\mathsf{v},\mathsf{w}}\rangle$ such that $S + \mathsf{v} \subseteq T + \mathsf{u}$, uniformly at random.
- Distribution 1: Sample $|T_{\mathsf{u},\tilde{\mathsf{v}}}\rangle$ such that $T^\perp + \tilde{\mathsf{v}} \subseteq S^\perp + \mathsf{w}$, uniformly at random.

Bob's register will eventually contain the sampled state. But there's a twist: Alice will decide which distribution to sample from *after* she sends Bob her register.

Here is one way for Alice to sample from distribution 0 or 1:

1. To sample from distribution 0, Alice prepares the following state on two n-qubit registers:

$$|\psi\rangle_0 := \frac{1}{\sqrt{|A|}} \sum_{\mathsf{v}_0 \in A} |S_{\mathsf{u}+\mathsf{v}_0,\mathsf{w}}\rangle |\mathsf{v}_0\rangle$$

where $A = \mathsf{co}(S) \cap T$. She sends the first register to Bob, and measures the second register in the computational basis.

2. To sample from distribution 1, she prepares the following state:

$$|\psi\rangle_1 := \frac{1}{\sqrt{|B|}} \sum_{\tilde{\mathsf{v}}_0 \in B} |T_{\mathsf{u},\tilde{\mathsf{v}}_0+\mathsf{w}}\rangle |\tilde{\mathsf{v}}_0\rangle$$

where $B = \mathsf{co}(T^\perp) \cap S^\perp$. She sends the first register to Bob, and measures the second register in the computational basis.

Claim. The procedure above correctly samples from distribution 0 or distribution 1.

Proof. In this procedure, we have decomposed v into its deterministic and random components, u and v_0 respectively. Every $v \in co(S)$ has a unique decomposition as $v = u + v_0$ for some $u \in co(T)$ and $v_0 \in A$ (see supplementary material). Since v_0 is sampled uniformly at random from A, v is sampled uniformly at random such that $v \in co(S)$ and $S + v \subseteq T + u$. Therefore, the procedure correctly samples from distribution 0.

A similar argument works for distribution 1. We have decomposed $\widetilde{v}$ into its deterministic and random components, w and $\widetilde{v}_0$ respectively. Every $\widetilde{v} \in co(T^{\perp})$ has a unique decomposition as $\widetilde{v} = \widetilde{v}_0 + w$ for some $\widetilde{v}_0 \in B$ and $w \in co(S^{\perp})$ (see supplementary material). Since $\widetilde{v}_0$ is sampled uniformly at random from B, $\widetilde{v}$ is sampled uniformly at random such that $\widetilde{v} \in co(T^{\perp})$ and $T^{\perp} + \widetilde{v} \subseteq S^{\perp} + w$. Therefore, the procedure correctly samples from distribution 1. □

Next, Alice can map between $|\psi\rangle_0$ and $|\psi\rangle_1$ by applying local operations to the second register. We will define a unitary U that acts on the second register and maps superpositions over to A to superpositions over B. For any $v_0 \in A$, let

$$U|v_0\rangle = \frac{1}{\sqrt{c}} \sum_{\widetilde{v}_0 \in B} |\widetilde{v}_0\rangle \cdot (-1)^{\langle v_0, \widetilde{v}_0 \rangle}$$

and for any $\widetilde{v}_0 \in B$, let

$$U^{\dagger}|\widetilde{v}_0\rangle = \frac{1}{\sqrt{c}} \sum_{v_0 \in A} |v_0\rangle \cdot (-1)^{\langle v_0, \widetilde{v}_0 \rangle}$$

where c is a normalization constant. Technically, U acts on any superposition over $\mathbb{F}_2^n$, and we define it fully in the supplementary materials. We show in the supplementary material that when U is applied to the second register of $|\psi\rangle_0$, it maps the state to $|\psi\rangle_1$.

Now we have the tools to do delayed preparation of the subspace coset state:

Delayed Preparation of a Subspace Coset State

1. Alice prepares $|\psi\rangle_0$ on two n-qubit registers. She sends the first register to Bob.
2. (a) To sample from distribution 0: Alice measures the second register in the computational basis to get a random $v_0 \leftarrow A$. The state on Bob's register collapses to $|S_{u+v_0,w}\rangle$.
   (b) Instead, to sample from distribution 1: Alice applies U to the second register, mapping $|\psi\rangle_0$ to $|\psi\rangle_1$. Then she measures the second register in the computational basis to get a random $\widetilde{v}_0 \leftarrow B$. The state on Bob's register collapses to $|T_{u,\widetilde{v}_0+w}\rangle$.

---

5 General Compiler for Certified Deletion

In this section, we present a general technique for proving certified deletion that works well with existing cryptographic primitives and enables the constructions in subsequent sections.

Consider the following simple construction. To hide a bit b, we give the adversary:

$$|S_{v,w}\rangle, b \oplus \langle v, 1 \rangle$$

where $|S_{v,w}\rangle$ is a subspace coset state, sampled uniformly at random such that $\dim(S) = n/2$, $v \in \mathsf{co}(S), w \in \mathsf{co}(S^{\perp})$. The bit b is masked by $\langle v, 1 \rangle$, and the information needed to remove the mask is stored in the subspace coset state.

To prove deletion, the adversary measures the subspace coset state in the Hadamard basis to get a vector $\tilde{z} \in S^{\perp} + w$. We'll show that if they prove deletion, then all but negligible information about v is lost. That is, even if S is leaked at a later point, b remains statistically hidden because $\langle v, 1 \rangle$ is statistically close to uniformly random.

Definition 3 below describes this scenario. We say that security holds if the output of EXP^* is statistically close between the cases where $b = 0$ and $b = 1$.

Definition 3 (Certified Deletion Game, Abstract Form). *Let b be a bit, let $\{A_\lambda\}_{\lambda \in \mathbb{N}}$ be a QPT adversary, and let $\{Z_\lambda\}_{\lambda \in \mathbb{N}}$ be a quantum or classical operation. Then let $\mathsf{EXP}^*(1^\lambda, A_\lambda, Z_\lambda, b)$ be the output of the following experiment:*

1. *Challenge: Let $n = 4\lambda$. The challenger samples a subspace S of dimension $n/2$ along with vectors $(v, w) \leftarrow \mathsf{co}(S) \times \mathsf{co}(S^{\perp})$, uniformly at random.*

   Next, they sample a subspace T uniformly at random such that $S \leq T$ and $\dim(T) = 3n/4$, using the procedure in Definition 2. Let $u \in \mathsf{co}(T)$ be the unique coset such that $S + v \subset T + u$.

   Finally, the challenger sends the adversary the following challenge:

   $$|S_{v,w}\rangle, Z_\lambda(S, T, u, w, b \oplus \langle v, 1 \rangle)$$

2. *Response: The adversary, running A_λ, responds with a deletion certificate $\tilde{z} \in \mathbb{F}_2^n$ and an auxiliary state ρ.*

3. *Outcome: The challenger checks that*

   $$\tilde{z} \in S^{\perp} + w$$

   If so, they output $(\rho, S, T, u, w, b \oplus \langle v, 1 \rangle)$; if not, they output $\perp$.

In Definition 3, Z represents the side information given to the adversary. In the simplest case, $Z = \perp$, and it's simple to prove that security holds. Note that we cannot give S, v, or w in the clear because then the adversary could learn v while also outputting a $\tilde{z} \in S^{\perp} + w$. In all of our applications, we need to give the adversary some information about (S, v, w), but we're careful to hide it. For instance, when $Z = \mathsf{Enc}(1^\lambda, S)$ for some semantically-secure encryption scheme Enc, or $Z = [\mathsf{Enc}(1^\lambda, S), i\mathcal{O}(P_{S^{\perp}+w})]$, we can prove that security holds. The latter case allows the deletion certificate to be *publicly verifiable*, assuming post-quantum $i\mathcal{O}$.

Theorem 1 (Encryption with Publicly-Verifiable Deletion). *Let Enc be a semantically secure encryption scheme, and assume post-quantum indistinguishability obfuscation ($i\mathcal{O}$). Next, for any $\lambda \in \mathbb{N}$, let*

$$Z_\lambda(S, T, u, w, b') = [\mathsf{Enc}(1^\lambda, S), i\mathcal{O}(P_{S^{\perp}+w})].$$

Then for any QPT adversary $\{\mathcal{A}_\lambda\}_{\lambda \in \mathbb{N}}$,

$$\mathsf{TD}\left(\mathsf{EXP}^*(1^\lambda, \mathcal{A}_\lambda, \mathcal{Z}_\lambda, 0), \mathsf{EXP}^*(1^\lambda, \mathcal{A}_\lambda, \mathcal{Z}_\lambda, 1)\right) = \mathrm{negl}(\lambda).$$

It is natural to wonder whether we can include $i\mathcal{O}(P_{S+v})$ in $\mathcal{Z}$, just like we included $i\mathcal{O}(P_{S^\perp + w})$. In fact, this is not allowed because $i\mathcal{O}$ only hides v computationally. If $\langle v, 1 \rangle$ is not statistically hidden, then neither is b. However, $\mathcal{Z}$ can include (T, u), which satisfy $S + v \subset T + u$, and for our applications that is good enough. The bit b remains statistically hidden because even given (S, T, u, w), $\langle v, 1 \rangle$ is uniformly random (with overwhelming probability over the choice of (S, T)).

5.1 General Theorem

The previous theorems are special cases of Theorem 2 below. We will use it in subsequent sections to prove certified deletion. Theorem 2 says that security holds in EXP^* if any information that $\mathcal{Z}$ gives the adversary about $S^\perp + w$ could also be computed from a larger random coset $R + x$ that contains $S^\perp + w$. We call this property *subspace hiding*, and it is analogous to [43]'s notion of subspace-hiding obfuscation . Below, we will precisely define the property of $\mathcal{Z}$ we need.

Definition 4 (Subspace Hiding). *Let $\mathscr{A}$ be a class of adversaries[12] . We say that a quantum operation $\{\mathcal{Z}_\lambda\}_{\lambda \in \mathbb{N}}$ is **subspace-hiding** for $\mathscr{A}$ if there exists a simulator $\{\mathcal{S}_\lambda\}_{\lambda \in \mathbb{N}}$ such that for any adversary in $\mathscr{A}$, their advantage in the following game is negligible in λ:*

1. *Let $n = 4\lambda$. The adversary chooses subspaces $S, T \leq \mathbb{F}_2^n$ such that $S \leq T, \dim(S) = n/2$, and $\dim(T) = 3n/4$, they choose vectors $u \in \mathsf{co}(T)$ and $w \in \mathsf{co}(S^\perp)$, and they choose a bit b'. Then they send these variables to the challenger.*
2. *The challenger samples R, a uniformly random superspace of $S^\perp$ of dimension $3n/4$. Let $x \in \mathsf{co}(R)$ be the unique coset such that $S^\perp + w \subset R + x$. Next, the challenger samples a bit $c \leftarrow \{0, 1\}$. If $c = 0$, they compute $\mathcal{Z}_\lambda(S, T, u, w, b')$ and send the output to the challenger. If $c = 1$, they compute $\mathcal{S}_\lambda(R, T, u, x, b')$ and send the output to the challenger.*
3. *The adversary outputs a guess $c' \in \{0, 1\}$ for c.*

The adversary's advantage is $|\Pr(c' = c) - 1/2|$.

Finally, the theorem below says that b is statistically hidden in EXP^* if $\mathcal{Z}$ is subspace-hiding.

---

[12] $\mathscr{A}$ should be closed under constant-factor increases in space and time. That is say: for any adversary $\{\mathcal{A}_\lambda\}_{\lambda \in \mathbb{N}} \in \mathscr{A}$ and any quantum adversary $\{\mathcal{B}_\lambda\}_{\lambda \in \mathbb{N}}$, if the time and space complexity of $\{\mathcal{B}_\lambda\}_{\lambda \in \mathbb{N}}$ is more than that of $\{\mathcal{A}_\lambda\}_{\lambda \in \mathbb{N}}$ by a constant factor, then $\{\mathcal{B}_\lambda\}_{\lambda \in \mathbb{N}}$ is also in $\mathscr{A}$.

Theorem 2 (General theorem). *Let* $\{\mathcal{Z}_\lambda\}_{\lambda \in \mathbb{N}}$ *be defined as it was in* EXP^*, *and let* $\mathscr{A}$ *be a class of adversaries. Next, if* $\{\mathcal{Z}_\lambda\}_{\lambda \in \mathbb{N}}$ *is subspace-hiding for* $\mathscr{A}$, *then for any adversary* $\{\mathcal{A}_\lambda\}_{\lambda \in \mathbb{N}} \in \mathscr{A}$,

$$\mathsf{TD}\left(\mathsf{EXP}^*(1^\lambda, \mathcal{A}_\lambda, \mathcal{Z}_\lambda, 0), \mathsf{EXP}^*(1^\lambda, \mathcal{A}_\lambda, \mathcal{Z}_\lambda, 1)\right) = \mathrm{negl}(\lambda)$$

Acknowledgments. We thank Sanjam Garg for collaboration and valuable contributions during the earlier stages of this research.

D.K. was supported by DARPA SIEVE, AFOSR, NSF CAREER CNS-2238718 and NSF CNS-2247727. This material is based upon work supported by the Defense Advanced Research Projects Agency through Award HR00112020024, and by the Air Force Office of Scientific Research under award number FA9550-23-1-0543.

G.M. was supported by the European Research Council through an ERC Starting Grant (Grant agreement No. 101077455, ObfusQation).

J.R was supported in part by the NSF award 1916939, DARPA SIEVE program, a gift from Ripple, a DoE NETL award, a JP Morgan Faculty Fellowship, a PNC center for financial services innovation award, and a Cylab seed funding award.

References

1. Aaronson, S.: Quantum copy-protection and quantum money. In: Proceedings of the 24th Annual IEEE Conference on Computational Complexity, CCC 2009, Paris, France, 15-18 July 2009, pages 229–242. IEEE Computer Society (2009)

2. Aaronson, S., Christiano, O.: Quantum money from hidden subspaces. In: Proceedings of the Forty-Fourth Annual ACM Symposium on Theory of Computing, STOC 2012, page 41-60. Association for Computing Machinery, New York (2012)

3. Agrawal, S., Kitagawa, F., Nishimaki, R., Yamada, S., Yamakawa, T.: Public key encryption with secure key leasing. Cryptology ePrint Archive, Paper 2023/264 / (2023). https://eprint.iacr.org/2023/264

4. Ananth, P., Kaleoglu, F.: Unclonable encryption, revisited. LNCS, pp. 299–329. Springer, Heidelberg (2021)

5. Ananth, P., Kaleoglu, F.: A note on copy-protection from random oracles. Cryptology ePrint Archive, Paper 2022/1109 (2022). https://eprint.iacr.org/2022/1109

6. Ananth, P., Kaleoglu, F., Li, X., Liu, Q., Zhandry, M.: On the feasibility of unclonable encryption, and more. In: CRYPTO (2022). https://doi.org/10.1007/978-3-031-15979-4_8

7. Ananth, P., Kaleoglu, F., Liu, O.: Cloning games: a general framework for unclonable primitives. In: Handschuh, H., Lysyanskaya, A. (eds.) Advances in Cryptology – CRYPTO 2023, pp. 66–98. Springer Nature Switzerland, Cham (2023). https://doi.org/10.1007/978-3-031-38554-4_3

8. Ananth, P., La Placa, R.L.: Secure software leasing. In: Canteaut, A., Standaert, F.-X. (eds.) EUROCRYPT 2021. LNCS, vol. 12697, pp. 501–530. Springer, Cham (2021). https://doi.org/10.1007/978-3-030-77886-6_17

9. Ananth, P., Poremba, A., Vaikuntanathan, V.: Revocable cryptography from learning with errors. Cryptology ePrint Archive, Paper 2023/325 (2023). https://eprint.iacr.org/2023/325

10. Barak, B., et al.: On the (im)possibility of obfuscating programs. J. ACM **59**(2), 6:1–6:48 (2012)

11. Bartusek, J., Guan, J., Ma, F., Zhandry, M.: Return of GGH15: provable security against zeroizing attacks. In: Beimel, A., Dziembowski, S. (eds.) TCC 2018. LNCS, vol. 11240, pp. 544–574. Springer, Cham (2018). https://doi.org/10.1007/978-3-030-03810-6_20

12. Bartusek, J., Khurana, D.: Cryptography with certified deletion. In: Handschuh, H., Lysyanskaya, A. (eds.) Advances in Cryptology – CRYPTO 2023, pp. 192–223. Springer Nature Switzerland, Cham (2023)

13. Bellare, M., Stepanovs, I., Waters, B.: New negative results on differing-inputs obfuscation. In: Fischlin, M., Coron, J.-S. (eds.) EUROCRYPT 2016. Part II, volume 9666 of LNCS, pp. 792–821. Springer, Heidelberg (2016). https://doi.org/10.1007/978-3-662-49896-5_28

14. Bennett, C.H., Brassard, G.: Quantum cryptography: public key distribution and coin tossing. In: Proceedings of the IEEE International Conference on Computers, Systems, and Signal Processing, pp. 175–179 (1984)

15. Boyle, E., Chung, K.-M., Pass, R.: On extractability obfuscation. In: Lindell, Y. (ed.) TCC 2014. LNCS, vol. 8349, pp. 52–73. Springer, Heidelberg (2014). https://doi.org/10.1007/978-3-642-54242-8_3

16. Brakerski, Z., Döttling, N., Garg, S., Malavolta, G.: Factoring and pairings are not necessary for IO: circular-secure LWE suffices. In: Bojańczyk, M., Merelli, E., Woodruff, D.P. (eds.) 49th International Colloquium on Automata, Languages, and Programming (ICALP 2022), vol. 229. Leibniz International Proceedings in Informatics (LIPIcs), Dagstuhl, Germany, pp. 28:1–28:20. Schloss Dagstuhl – Leibniz-Zentrum für Informatik (2022)

17. Broadbent, A., Islam, R.: Quantum encryption with certified deletion. In: Pass, R., Pietrzak, K. (eds.) TCC 2020. LNCS, vol. 12552, pp. 92–122. Springer, Cham (2020). https://doi.org/10.1007/978-3-030-64381-2_4

18. Broadbent, A., Jeffery, S., Lord, S., Podder, S., Sundaram, A.: Secure software leasing without assumptions. In: Nissim, K., Waters, B. (eds.) TCC 2021. LNCS, vol. 13042, pp. 90–120. Springer, Cham (2021). https://doi.org/10.1007/978-3-030-90459-3_4

19. Chen, Y., Vaikuntanathan, V., Wee, H.: GGH15 beyond permutation branching programs: proofs, attacks, and candidates. In: Shacham, H., Boldyreva, A. (eds.) CRYPTO 2018. LNCS, vol. 10992, pp. 577–607. Springer, Cham (2018). https://doi.org/10.1007/978-3-319-96881-0_20

20. Choudhuri, A.R., Jain, A., Jin, Z.: Snargs for $\mathcal{P}$ from LWE. In: 62nd IEEE Annual Symposium on Foundations of Computer Science, FOCS 2021, Denver, CO, USA, 7-10 February 2022, pp. 68–79. IEEE (2021)

21. Coladangelo, A., Liu, J., Liu, Q., Zhandry, M.: Hidden cosets and applications to unclonable cryptography. In: Malkin, T., Peikert, C. (eds.) CRYPTO 2021. LNCS, vol. 12825, pp. 556–584. Springer, Cham (2021). https://doi.org/10.1007/978-3-030-84242-0_20

22. Devadas, L., Quach, W., Vaikuntanathan, V., Wee, H., Wichs, D.: Succinct LWE sampling, random polynomials, and obfuscation. In: Nissim, K., Waters, B. (eds.) TCC 2021. LNCS, vol. 13043, pp. 256–287. Springer, Cham (2021). https://doi.org/10.1007/978-3-030-90453-1_9

23. Garg, S., Gentry, C., Halevi, S., Raykova, M., Sahai, A., Waters, B.: Candidate indistinguishability obfuscation and functional encryption for all circuits. In: 54th FOCS, pp. 40–49. IEEE Computer Society Press (October 2013)

24. Garg, S., Gentry, C., Halevi, S., Wichs, D.: On the implausibility of differing-inputs obfuscation and extractable witness encryption with auxiliary input. In:

Garay, J.A., Gennaro, R. (eds.) CRYPTO 2014. Part I, volume 8616 of LNCS, pp. 518–535. Springer, Heidelberg (2014). https://doi.org/10.1007/978-3-662-44371-2_29

25. Gay, R., Pass, R.: Indistinguishability obfuscation from circular security. In: Proceedings of the 53rd Annual ACM SIGACT Symposium on Theory of Computing, STOC 2021, pp. 736-749. Association for Computing Machinery, New York (2021)

26. Gentry, C.: Fully homomorphic encryption using ideal lattices. In: Mitzenmacher, M. (ed.) 41st ACM STOC, pp. 169–178. ACM Press (May/June 2009)

27. Hiroka, T., Kitagawa, F., Morimae, T., Nishimaki, R., Pal, T., Yamakawa, T.: Certified everlasting secure collusion-resistant functional encryption, and more. Cryptology ePrint Archive, Paper 2023/236 (2023). https://eprint.iacr.org/2023/236

28. Hiroka, T., Morimae, T., Nishimaki, R., Yamakawa, T.: Quantum encryption with certified deletion, revisited: public key, attribute-based, and classical communication. In: Tibouchi, M., Wang, H. (eds.) ASIACRYPT 2021. LNCS, vol. 13090, pp. 606–636. Springer, Cham (2021). https://doi.org/10.1007/978-3-030-92062-3_21

29. Hiroka, T., Morimae, T., Nishimaki, R., Yamakawa, T.: Certified everlasting functional encryption. CoRR, abs/ arXiv: 2207.13878 (2022)

30. Hiroka, T., Morimae, T., Nishimaki, R., Yamakawa, T.: Certified everlasting zero-knowledge proof for QMA. In: Advances in Cryptology - CRYPTO 2022 - 42nd Annual International Cryptology Conference, Santa Barbara, CA, USA (2022)

31. Katz, J., Thiruvengadam, A., Zhou, H.-S.: Feasibility and infeasibility of adaptively secure fully homomorphic encryption. In: Kurosawa, K., Hanaoka, G. (eds.) PKC 2013. LNCS, vol. 7778, pp. 14–31. Springer, Heidelberg (2013). https://doi.org/10.1007/978-3-642-36362-7_2

32. Kitagawa, F., Nishimaki, R.: Functional encryption with secure key leasing. In: Advances in Cryptology - ASIACRYPT 2022. Springer Cham (2022). https://doi.org/10.1007/978-3-031-22972-5_20

33. Kitagawa, F., Nishimaki, R., Yamakawa, T.: Secure software leasing from standard assumptions. In: Nissim, K., Waters, B. (eds.) TCC 2021. LNCS, vol. 13042, pp. 31–61. Springer, Cham (2021). https://doi.org/10.1007/978-3-030-90459-3_2

34. Naor, M., Yung, M.: Public-key cryptosystems provably secure against chosen ciphertext attacks. In: ACM Symposium on Theory of Computing (2001)

35. Poremba, A.: Quantum proofs of deletion for learning with errors. In: Kalai, Y.T. (ed.)14th Innovations in Theoretical Computer Science Conference, ITCS 2023, 10-13 January2023, vol. 251. pp. 90:1–90:14. LIPIcs, Schloss Dagstuhl - Leibniz-Zentrum für Informatik. MIT, Cambridge (2023)

36. Regev, U.: On lattices, learning with errors, random linear codes, and cryptography. In: Gabow, H.N., Fagin, R. (eds.) 37th ACM STOC, pp. 84–93. ACM Press (May 2005)

37. Shmueli, O.: Semi-quantum tokenized signatures. In: Dodis, Y., Shrimpton, T. (eds.) Advances in Cryptology - CRYPTO 2022 - 42nd Annual International Cryptology Conference, CRYPTO 2022, , Proceedings, Part I, vol. 13507. LNCS, pp. 296–319. Springer (2022). https://doi.org/10.1007/978-3-031-15802-5_11

38. Unruh, D.: Revocable quantum timed-release encryption. In: Nguyen, P.Q., Oswald, E. (eds.) EUROCRYPT 2014. LNCS, vol. 8441, pp. 129–146. Springer, Heidelberg (2014). https://doi.org/10.1007/978-3-642-55220-5_8

39. Vidick, T., Zhang, T.: Classical proofs of quantum knowledge. In: Canteaut, A., Standaert, F.-X. (eds.) EUROCRYPT 2021. LNCS, vol. 12697, pp. 630–660. Springer, Cham (2021). https://doi.org/10.1007/978-3-030-77886-6_22

40. Wee, H., Wichs, D.: Candidate obfuscation via Oblivious LWE sampling. In: Canteaut, A., Standaert, F.-X. (eds.) EUROCRYPT 2021. LNCS, vol. 12698, pp. 127–156. Springer, Cham (2021). https://doi.org/10.1007/978-3-030-77883-5_5

41. Wiesner, S.: Conjugate coding. SIGACT News **15**, 78–88 (1983)

42. Wootters, W.K., Zurek, W.H.: A single quantum cannot be cloned. Nature **299**(5886), 802–803 (1982)

43. Zhandry, M.: Quantum lightning never strikes the same state twice. In: Ishai, Y., Rijmen, V. (eds.) EUROCRYPT 2019. Part III, volume 11478 of LNCS, pp. 408–438. Springer, Heidelberg (2019). https://doi.org/10.1007/978-3-030-17659-4_14

Public-Coin, Complexity-Preserving, Succinct Arguments of Knowledge for NP from Collision-Resistance

Cody Freitag[1](✉), Omer Paneth[2], and Rafael Pass[3]

[1] Northeastern University, Boston, USA
c.freitag@northeastern.edu
[2] Tel Aviv University, Tel Aviv, Israel
omerpa@mail.tau.ac.il
[3] Tel Aviv University & Cornell Tech, Tel Aviv, Israel
rafaelp@tau.ac.il

Abstract. Succinct arguments allow a powerful (yet polynomial-time) prover to convince a weak verifier of the validity of some NP statement using very little communication. A major barrier to the deployment of such proofs is the unwieldy overhead of the prover relative to the complexity of the statement to be proved. In this work, we focus on *complexity-preserving* arguments where proving a non-deterministic time t and space s RAM computation takes time $\tilde{O}(t)$ and space $\tilde{O}(s)$.

Currently, all known complexity-preserving arguments either are private-coin, rely on non-standard assumptions, or provide only weak succinctness. In this work, we construct complexity-preserving succinct argument based solely on collision-resistant hash functions, thereby matching the classic succinct argument of Kilian (STOC '92).

1 Introduction

In an interactive proof system, a powerful prover tries to convince a weak verifier the validity of some statement over potentially many rounds of interaction. In order to be meaningful, such a protocol needs to satisfy *completeness*—an honest prover will successfully convince the verifier of a true statement—and *soundness*—a cheating prover cannot convince the verifier of a false statement (at least with high probability). Proof systems where soundness only holds with respect to computationally bounded (i.e. polynomial-time) provers are known as *arguments*. In this work, we focus on *succinct* arguments where the verifier's running time and the communication between the prover and verifier are extremely small, essentially independent of the complexity of the underlying statement.

Building upon the machinery of probabilistically checkable proofs (PCPs) [2], Kilian [58] gave the first succinct argument for NP, where soundness only relies on the existence of a collision-resistant hash function (CRH). Even though the prover in Kilian's protocol is theoretically "efficient"—the prover runs in

© International Association for Cryptologic Research 2024
M. Joye and G. Leander (Eds.): EUROCRYPT 2024, LNCS 14654, pp. 112–141, 2024.
https://doi.org/10.1007/978-3-031-58737-5_5

polynomial-time as a function of the complexity of underlying NP statement—the concrete overheads of PCPs have made such an argument system prohibitively expensive in practice. Over the last 30 years, much progress has been made on improving the overheads of PCPs (see e.g. [13,15–17,39,65]) even at the cost of additional rounds of communication (see e.g. [12,14,68,69]). Despite all of this progress, there is still a fundamental barrier to making Kilian's protocol (or similar variants) practically efficient. The issue is that the prover needs to seemingly store the entire PCP in memory, meaning the high PCP costs are not only felt in the time to compute the proof but also in the space required by the prover.

Complexity-Preserving Succinct Arguments. Motivated by the above issue, Valiant [73] proposed the notion of *complexity-preserving* succinct arguments where, in order to prove a statement with an NP verifier running in time t and space s, the prover only needs to use time $\tilde{O}(t)$ and space $\tilde{O}(s)$.[1] Notably, the prover cannot use space that depends even linearly on the time t to verify the NP relation. Complexity-preserving SNARKs can be from standard SNARKs based on the idea of recursive proof composition. Valiant [73] and, subsequently, Bitansky et al. [19] constructed complexity-preserving succinct *non-interactive* arguments of knowledge (SNARKs) for NP based on plain SNARKs for NP, via recursive proof composition. The existence of SNARKs for NP, however, is a non-falsifiable "knowledge" assumption, and there are known barriers for basing SNARKs on falsifiable assumption [46].

Towards basing complexity-preserving, succinct arguments on more standard assumptions, Bitansky and Chiesa [21] show how to construct a complexity-preserving multi-prover interactive proof (MIP), which can then be compiled into a complexity-preserving succinct interactive argument using fully homomorphic encryption (FHE). Compared to Kilian's protocol, their succinct argument has two main downsides. First, they rely on the heavier cryptographic machinery of FHE rather than only collision-resistance. Second, and more notably, their transformation results in a private-coin rather than a public-coin protocol. This means that their verifier needs to keep private state hidden from the prover in order for the protocol to maintain soundness. In contrast, the verifier in Kilian's protocol maintains no private state and simply sends public random coins for each of its messages. Public-coin protocols can be verified publicly, which is crucial for increasingly important applications of proofs in the distributed setting. Indeed, this was one of the main open questions posed in [21]:

Do there exist public-coin complexity-preserving succinct arguments for NP whose security can be based on standard cryptographic assumptions?

Some recent works provide initial indications towards a positive resolution, but they all either rely on non-standard assumptions or fall short of achieving full succinctness. Block, Holmgren, Rosen, Rothblum, and Soni [23] construct a

---

[1] For simplicity, we suppress polynomial factors in the security parameter in the introduction.

public-coin argument for NP with succinct communication in the random oracle model (ROM) assuming hardness of discrete log.[2] However, the verifier in their protocol runs in time $\tilde{O}(t)$ so the argument is not "fully" succinct.[3] Finally, an even more recent paper by Block, Holmgren, Rosen, Rothblum, and Soni [24] construct the first public-coin, complexity-preserving, *fully succinct* argument for NP in the "plain" model (i.e., without a random oracle). This construction uses $O(\log t)$ rounds of communication and relies on the assumption that a group of hidden order can be sampled using public coins—the only candidate such groups are class groups of an imaginary quadratic field, which were first suggested for cryptographic use by [37] but have seen relatively little attention as a cryptographic assumption.

Bangalore, Bhadauria, Hazay, and Venkitasubramaniam [4] construct complexity preserving arguments based only on *black-box* use of CRH, matching the assumptions for Kilian's protocol. Their protocol, however, is not fully succinct as it requires communication $\tilde{O}(t/s)$ and verifier running time $\tilde{O}(t/s + s)$. Furthermore, they demonstrate barriers for getting a fully succinct protocol in this setting.

Even when allowing for private coins, we emphasize that the protocol of [21] assumes FHE, which is a significantly stronger assumption than CRH, required for Kilian's original (non-complexity-preserving) protocol. Viewing these assumptions qualitatively through the lens of Impagliazzo's five worlds [50], FHE is a "Cryptomania" assumption compared to the substantially weaker "Minicrypt" assumption of CRH.[4] Very recent work by [38,53,66] obtain publicly verifiable complexity-preserving SNARGs from a host of other assumptions (not all known to imply FHE), but these SNARG are only for languages in P; furthermore, these assumptions are still Cryptomania assumptions. This raises the following question:

Do (even private-coin) complexity-preserving succinct arguments
for NP (or even P) exist in Minicrypt?

1.1   Our Results

We resolve both of the above open problems, showing the existence of a public-coin, complexity-preserving, succinct argument for all non-deterministic, polynomial-time RAM computation based solely on collision-resistance. Similar to [21] (as well as Kilian's protocol [58] with a suitable underlying PCP), we actually

---

[2] Even though SNARKs for NP can be built in the ROM [63], the construction of [19] makes non-black-box use of the underlying SNARK verifier, so it is not clear how to prove their construction secure in the ROM.

[3] Note that this is still non-trivial since their scheme has succinct communication.

[4] Strictly speaking, Impagliazzo defined Minicrypt as the potential world where one-way functions (and hence symmetric-key encryption) exist yet public-key encryption does not. Technically, one-way functions do not generically imply CRH in a black-box way [71]. However, CRH are still often considered to be a Minicrypt assumption and viewed as a much weaker assumption than the existence of public-key encryption.

give an *argument of knowledge* for NP. This is a stronger property that intuitively stipulates that if the prover convinces the verifier on some NP statement, it must actually "know" a corresponding witness.

Theorem 1.1 (Informal; see Theorem 4.1). *Assuming the existence of collision-resistant hash functions, there exists a public-coin, complexity preserving, succinct argument of knowledge for NP. On input statements for security parameter λ and time bound t, the protocol requires $O(\log_\lambda t)$ rounds of communication.*

We note that we require slightly super constant round complexity for our protocol to be sound for all non-deterministic (not a priori bounded) $\mathsf{poly}(\lambda)$-time computations. Specifically, for every bound c such that the RAM computation requires time λ^c on inputs of length λ, we give a protocol that uses $6c+6$ messages of communication. So, there is no fixed constant bounding the number of rounds for a protocol that handles all non-deterministic, polynomial-time computation. It is a fascinating open problem to give a protocol with a fixed constant number of rounds.

Our construction is based on recursive proof composition similar to [19,73]. However, we compose *interactive* arguments rather than SNARKs, so we are able to get a result based only on CRH. To implement our recursive proof composition, we make non-black box use of the underlying hash function. This allows us to circumvent the barrier of [4].

Applications of Our Main Theorem. We get the following applications using our construction from Theorem 1.1:

- **Zero-knowledge:** We can generically transform our protocol into one that satisfies zero-knowledge, based on the techniques of [8] adapted to the setting of public-coin, succinct arguments of knowledge. In a bit more detail, we have the prover first commit to its messages and then prove in zero-knowledge that it can open the commitments to messages that would cause the verifier to accept. Using the constant-round, public-coin, zero-knowledge protocol of [5,6] based on CRH, this results in a zero-knowledge protocol that preserves the succinctness and public-coin properties at the cost of a constant number of additional rounds. See the full version for full details.
- **Parallelizability (SPARKs):** Applying the transformation of [40] to our construction, we can construct a public-coin, complexity-preserving, succinct *parallelizable* argument of knowledge (SPARK) for NP in $\mathsf{poly}(\log t)$ rounds from collision-resistance. In a SPARK, the prover leverages $\mathsf{poly}(\log t)$ parallel processors in order run in nearly optimal parallel time $t + \mathsf{poly}(\log t)$ (with no multiplicative overhead). This construction resolves an open problem from [40] (Section 8.1).
- **Non-interactive SNARGs and SPARGs in the ROM:** Since our construction is a public-coin protocol, it can be made non-interactive via the Fiat-Shamir transform [42] by replacing the verifier's public-coin messages with a hash of the communication transcript so far. Soundness of this transformation holds for all non-deterministic polynomial-time computations in

the ROM by the analysis of [47].[5] This yields the first *non-interactive*, public-coin, complexity-preserving, succinct argument for NP based on *any* standard assumption in the ROM.[6] (Recall that previous such results either rely on non-standard assumptions [19,24], or have a linear-time verifier [23] and still rely on Cryptomania assumptions.)

Applying the transformation of [40] to our non-interactive protocol results in a non-interactive, complexity-preserving, succinct parallelizable argument (SPARG) in the ROM. The corresponding complexity-preserving construction of [40] relied on recursive composition of SNARKs à la [19], where security is not known to hold in the ROM.

– **Tighter memory-hard VDFs in the ROM:** We note that [43] construct a non-complexity-preserving, non-interactive SPARG for P from LWE, which yields generic constructions of verifiable delay functions (VDFs) from any inherently sequential function. Furthermore, if the underlying sequential function requires "large" memory usage,[7] this is preserved by the transformation, so they also get a memory-hard VDF assuming any memory-hard sequential function.[8] However, since their non-interactive SPARG is not space-preserving, their honest evaluation algorithm requires much more space than a potential adversary who does not need to compute the corresponding proof. As our non-interactive protocol is complexity-preserving, it yields a memory-hard VDF in the ROM based on CRH and any memory-hard sequential function with a much tighter memory gap for the honest and adversarial evaluations than [43].[9] Recall that the complexity-preserving, non-interactive SPARK for NP from [40] also implies a tighter memory-hard VDF, but they

---

[5] [47] proves security of Fiat-Shamir in the ROM for constant-round arguments with negligible soundness error. We can apply their analysis to our protocol since for every fixed polynomial-bound on the NP verification time, our protocol only requires a constant number of rounds.

[6] It isn't clear how to argue the resulting non-interactive protocol is an argument *of knowledge* in the ROM. In particular, Valiant [73] first showed that Micali's protocol [63] is an argument of knowledge, which requires that the CRH be extractable/implemented by a random oracle. A corresponding argument does not immediately hold in the ROM for protocols based on recursive composition.

[7] Memory-hardness can be formalized in many ways, but the application of SPARKs does not depend on the exact formulation; see [40] for further discussion on this point.

[8] Plain VDFs are useful for generating shared randomness in the distributed setting of blockchains, and memory-hardness further resists the use of energy-wasteful ASICs for this task, based on the assumption that most modern CPUs are already heavily optimized for memory accesses.

[9] We note that all current candidate constructions of memory-hard sequential functions are proven secure in the ROM, which we then have to heuristically instantiate before applying our non-interactive, complexity-preserving, SPARK. As such, we need to assume the existence of a memory-hard sequential function. It would be very interesting to directly construct an unconditionally secure memory-hard VDF in the ROM.

rely on the existence of SNARKs and there is no proof of security in the ROM.

1.2 Technical Overview

In this section, we provide a high-level overview for the main ideas underlying our construction. Throughout the overview, we will consider a fixed non-deterministic RAM computation that runs in time t and space s. Furthermore, we'll assume for simplicity that $t, s \leq 2^\lambda$ for security parameter λ, and we will suppress λ, $\log t$, and $\log s$ terms in asymptotic statements.

We proceed in three steps to motivate our full construction. First, we provide a warm-up protocol where the prover runs in time $t \cdot \mathsf{poly}(s)$ and space $\sqrt{t} \cdot \mathsf{poly}(s)$. Then, we show how to implement this idea recursively where the prover's space, verifier's running time, and communication all grow with $\mathsf{poly}(s)$. In other words, this protocol is complexity-preserving and succinct for small-space computations. Finally, we show how to use this to handle non-deterministic computations of arbitrary space, where the prover runs in time $t \cdot \mathsf{poly}(\lambda)$ and space $s \cdot \mathsf{poly}(\lambda)$.

Warm-Up: A ($\sqrt{t} \cdot \mathsf{poly}(s)$)-Space Solution. We view the RAM computation as transitioning between a sequence of size s configurations over fixed updates consisting of some polynomial $\alpha = \alpha(s)$ steps. Specifically, let M be an α-time non-deterministic function that on input a state st and witness w, outputs a new state st' of size s in time $\alpha(s)$. We consider the associated update language $\mathcal{L}_{\mathsf{Upd},\alpha}$ consisting of instances $(M, \mathsf{st}, \mathsf{st}', t)$ such that there exists a sequence of t witnesses $w_1, \ldots, w_t$ such that starting with initial state $\mathsf{st}_0 := \mathsf{st}$, computing $\mathsf{st}_j := M(\mathsf{st}_{j-1}, w_j)$ for all $j \in [t]$, results in a final state $\mathsf{st}_t = \mathsf{st}'$.

We start by recalling how Kilian's [58] 4-message succinct argument works with the setup as above. The verifier starts by sending a hash key. Next, the prover writes down a probabilistically checkable proof (PCP) for the statement that $(M, \mathsf{st}, \mathsf{st}', t) \in \mathcal{L}_{\mathsf{Upd},\alpha}$ using witnesses $w_1, \ldots, w_t$. The prover uses a hash tree [61] to commit to this PCP and sends the verifier the associated hash root, which acts as a succinct digest of the PCP. The verifier then asks the prover to open a few random locations in the PCP, with associated local opening proofs with respect to the provided hash root. The prover opens the corresponding locations in the PCP, and the verifier accepts if the PCP verifier would have accepted these responses and all of the openings are valid.

The issue with above approach is that the prover needs to store the entire PCP, which requires space $t \cdot \mathsf{poly}(s)$ even with the most efficient PCPs.[10] The use of PCPs, however, is extremely useful for reducing the necessary communication and run-time of the verifier. We want to leverage the efficiency benefits of PCPs without having to store a PCP for the entire computation. So, we observe that

---

[10] To the best of our knowledge, the most space-efficient PCP construction is due to [13], where they show how, given the size $O(t \cdot s)$ tableau of the computation, you can efficiently compute each bit of the PCP in low depth. It is a fascinating open question to construct complexity-preserving PCPs that don't require storing the entire computation tableau.

we can do this by only computing a PCP for a part of the computation instead of the full computation. Specifically, for some choice of k (assuming t is a multiple of k for simplicity), we split the computation into k sub-statements each of size t/k,

$$(M, \mathsf{st}_0, \mathsf{st}_{t/k}, t/k), \ldots, (M, \mathsf{st}_{(k-1) \cdot t/k}, \mathsf{st}_t, t/k),$$

where each st_i corresponds to the ith state when iteratively computing M using witnesses $w_1, \ldots, w_t$. The prover will then compute and commit to a PCP for each of the k sub-statements. The verifier will then send PCP queries as in Kilian's protocol to open up each PCP and accept if all such PCPs accept.

We proceed to analyze the efficiency of this warm-up protocol, starting with the space complexity of the prover. As the sub-statements are independent of each other, the prover can compute each PCP with associated hash root independently and then forget the full expensive PCP. At any point in time, the prover only needs to store a single PCP and associated hash tree for t/k steps of computation as well as k hash roots. Together, this only requires space $(k + (t/k)) \cdot \mathsf{poly}(s)$ to compute the first message. The dependence on t is minimized by setting $k = \sqrt{t}$, resulting in space complexity $\sqrt{t} \cdot \mathsf{poly}(s)$. Furthermore, note that the prover is deterministic, so whenever the prover needs to provide PCP openings in the next round for the verifier, the prover can recompute the PCP and hash tree as needed using an additional pass over the underlying witnesses.

In minimizing the space complexity of the prover above, we have actually lost the original succinctness of Kilian's protocol. Namely, as k is set larger in the above protocol, the communication and verifier efficiency suffer. The prover has to send the k intermediate statements and PCP openings corresponding to each statement, and the verifier then has to check all k PCP proofs. As such, the communication and verifier's run-time grow with $k = \sqrt{t}$ when minimizing the prover's space complexity. Additionally, if we choose k to be smaller to satisfy succinctness, the prover's space complexity grows to be essentially as large as Kilian's protocol. So, have we really gained anything?

Towards constructing a full-fledged succinct argument with a space-efficient prover, we separately tackle the issues of succinctness and prover's space complexity as follows:

- **Fixing succinctness via "commit-and-prove":** In order to reduce the communication and verifier's efficiency, we can generically use a standard "commit-and-prove" technique. Namely, instead of having the prover send messages for all k sub-protocols, the prover will hash the messages together and send a fixed size digest committing to the various messages in each round. In response to each digest sent, the verifier will send a single public-coin message that can be reused across all k statements. At the end of this "committed" interaction by the prover, the prover will use a succinct argument to prove that it "knows" a set of messages that would have convinced the verifier in all k sub-protocols. Using Kilian's protocol for this succinct argument, this adds 4 messages to the interaction while ensuring that the communication and verifier complexity are always succinct and independent of k.

- **Fixing prover's space complexity via recursion:** Using the blueprint above, the prover's space complexity grows with the complexity to prove a single sub-statement. So, we will instead use a more space-efficient protocol to prove each sub-statement rather than Kilian's—like the one we just built! This leads to a natural recursive approach to reduce the prover's space complexity at the cost of an increase in round complexity.

We next show how to apply both of these fixes simultaneously to construct a complexity-preserving succinct argument for bounded space computation.

Handling Small-Space, Non-deterministic Computation. Throughout, we let λ denote the security parameter and consider input statements of the form $(M, \mathsf{st}, \mathsf{st}', t) \in \mathcal{L}_{\mathsf{Upd},\alpha}$ as defined above where st and st' are size s states. By "small-space", we mean that $s \in \mathsf{poly}(\lambda)$ independent of t.

For every $r \geq 0$, we recursively construct a public-coin proof system (P_r, V_r) for the above update language $\mathcal{L}_{\mathsf{Upd},\alpha}$. For every r, we will maintain the following invariants on the efficiency of (P_r, V_r):

- P_r runs in time $t \cdot \mathsf{poly}(s, r)$ and space $(t/\lambda^r) \cdot \mathsf{poly}(s, r)$,
- V_r runs in time $\mathsf{poly}(s, r)$,
- and the communication is at most $\mathsf{poly}(\lambda)$ per message.

Our final protocol will then simply set $r = \log_\lambda t$, yielding a complexity-preserving protocol for bounded space computations.

For the base case of $r = 0$, (P_0, V_0) simply runs Kilian's succinct argument. We saw above that the prover runs in time and space $t \cdot \mathsf{poly}(s)$, and the verifier and communication complexity are at most polynomial in the statement size, which in this case is at most $\mathsf{poly}(s)$ since $\mathsf{st}, \mathsf{st}'$ are part of the statement. So, the required invariants hold.

In the general case of $r > 0$, we split the proof into two phases: (1) committing to sub-proofs, and (2) recursive proof merging:

- **Committing to sub-proofs:** P_r will split the computation of t steps into λ many sub-computations of t/λ steps each. Rather than directly proving each sub-computation using (P_{r-1}, V_{r-1}), P_r will instead succinctly commit to prover messages for P_{r-1} for all sub-computations in each round. Since V_{r-1} is public-coin, it maintains no private state, so it can send a single message per round that can be used across all sub-computations.
- **Recursive proof merging:** Next, the prover P_r will use Kilian's succinct argument to prove that it committed to prover messages in the previous phase that would cause V_{r-1} to accept on all λ sub-computations.

Completeness and argument of knowledge for (P_r, V_r) follow in a straightforward manner assuming (P_{r-1}, V_{r-1}) and Kilian's protocol are complete, arguments of knowledge. Briefly, to show that (P_r, V_r) is an argument of knowledge, we show how to use an extractor for Kilian's protocol to build a cheating prover for (P_{r-1}, V_{r-1}) by extracting out the committed prover messages (which will be unique and convincing assuming collision-resistance of the commitments).

Given this cheating prover, we can use the extractor for (P_{r-1}, V_{r-1}) to extract out witnesses for the sub-computations, which can simply be pieced together to form an overall witness for the full sequence of updates. So, the only assumption we rely on is collision-resistance. However, the running time of the extractor will grow exponentially with r, but for $\mathsf{poly}(\lambda)$-time computations, $r = \log_\lambda t$ will only be a constant.

Below, we briefly argue why each efficiency property holds separately:

- **Round complexity:** The round complexity of (P_r, V_r) adds a constant number of rounds over (P_{r-1}, V_{r-1}). So, in total, the protocol will consist of $O(r)$ rounds.
- **Communication complexity:** In the first phase, the prover commits to each of its messages, so its communication will be independent of r in each round. V_r needs to send the communication required for a single instance of V_{r-1}, *not* λ instances for each sub-computation. The communication in the second phase is bounded by the succinctness of Kilian's protocol, which is fixed and essentially independent of r and s. It follows that each message sent has fixed size at most $\mathsf{poly}(\lambda)$, so the total communication is at most $r \cdot \mathsf{poly}(\lambda)$.
- **Verifier efficiency:** This follows from the efficiency of Kilian's succinct argument, resulting in a verifier that runs in time polynomial in the statement size for the proof merging phase. This statement consists of proving committed messages are consistent with r digests according to the input statements of size s. It follows that the verifier will run in time $\mathsf{poly}(s, r)$.
- **Prover efficiency:** We first analyze the complexity required to commit to the sub-proofs. By assumption, P_{r-1} requires time $(t/\lambda) \cdot \mathsf{poly}(s, r)$ and space $(t/\lambda)/\lambda^{r-1} \cdot \mathsf{poly}(s, r) = (t/\lambda^r) \cdot \mathsf{poly}(s, r)$ to prove each sub-computation. So, to prove all λ sub-computations requires time $\lambda \cdot (t/\lambda) \cdot \mathsf{poly}(s, r) = t \cdot \mathsf{poly}(s, r)$. Since all sub-computations can be proved independently, the prover can erase the additional space needed for each sub-proof, so the total space doesn't grow.
  For the second phase of recursive proof merging, the prover's space grows polynomially with the time to verify all sub-computations are consistent with the committed prover messages. By succinctness of (P_{r-1}, V_{r-1}), the prover's messages are short—total size $r \cdot \mathsf{poly}(\lambda)$—and the running time of V_{r-1} is at most $\mathsf{poly}(s, r)$. So, the total time and space for the second phase is at most $\mathsf{poly}(s, r)$.
  Combining the complexity for the two phases, the total time of the prover remains $t \cdot \mathsf{poly}(s, r)$ while using space $(t/\lambda^r) \cdot \mathsf{poly}(s, r)$. We note that a little more care is required to show that the exact polynomial functions for each r don't grow too much, which we defer to the full proof.

Combining the above, this yields a complexity-preserving, succinct argument of knowledge for small-space $s \in \mathsf{poly}(\lambda)$ NP computations.

Handling Arbitrary Space, Non-deterministic Computation. To handle arbitrary space RAM computations, we follow the blueprint for RAM delegation of [54] adapted to the non-deterministic setting. Specifically, rather than proving updates to the actual space of the computation, we keep track of a hash tree for the space of the computation and prove updates hold relative to the digest for the hash tree.

Using the framework of update languages as above, we consider the update function where the state only keeps track of the hash tree digest. The witness needed to update the state provides information to: (1) prove the bit read at each step of the computation is correct with respect to the hash tree digest, and (2) if the computation step causes a write to memory, computes and proves the updated digest with respect to the new memory.

The state size for this update function is some fixed $\mathsf{poly}(\lambda)$ rather than s. So, if we use the protocol above for this, we only require $(t/\lambda^r) \cdot \mathsf{poly}(\lambda, r)$ space by the prover to run (P_r, V_r) for this update function. Furthermore, we can compute these hash tree proofs needed as the witnesses for P_r using space only $s \cdot \mathsf{poly}(\lambda)$ as opposed to $\mathsf{poly}(s)$. By setting $r = \log_\lambda t$ above, the prover's total space complexity is $s \cdot \mathsf{poly}(\lambda)$, so we get a public-coin, complexity-preserving, succinct argument of knowledge for proving general non-deterministic RAM computation in $O(\log_\lambda t)$-rounds.

1.3   Related Work on Succinct Arguments

We overview the current landscape of succinct arguments, with a focus on complexity-preserving protocols. First, we overview the main techniques for constructing succinct arguments for NP from information theoretic proofs in idealized oracle models. Second, we describe the recursive composition framework underlying constructions of complexity-preserving, succinct *non-interactive* arguments for NP from non-falsifiable assumptions. Lastly, we briefly highlight the relevant work implementing recursive composition for *deterministic* computation from falsifiable assumptions. At a very high level, we note that our main construction follows from a hybrid of the above techniques by recursively composing Kilian's succinct argument in a space-efficient way, which only relies on collision-resistant hash functions.

Information-Theoretic Compilers for Succinct Arguments for NP. Almost all constructions of succinct arguments for NP go through the following general blueprint. First, construct an information-theoretic proof with oracle access to an idealized object. Next, instantiate the oracle with a cryptographic commitment to the idealized object. Below, we overview existing constructions of succinct arguments, organized by their corresponding idealized models.

- **Probabilistically Checkable Proofs (PCPs):** PCPs (introduced for positive results in [2] and for hardness of approximation results in [41]) are non-interactive, information-theoretic proofs given oracle query access to a long proof string. Kilian [58] showed how to compile PCPs into succinct arguments by committing to the proof string using a vector commitment, which can be constructed from CRH using Merkle trees [61]. Furthermore, Micali [63] showed how to make this approach non-interactive using the Fiat-Shamir transform [42] in the ROM since the underlying protocol is public-coin.

- **Interactive Oracle Proofs (IOPs):** IOPs (independently introduced by [14] and [68]) are interactive, public-coin variants of PCPs, where in each round the prover provides oracle access to a new long string. This generalization of PCPs can result shorter and more prover-efficient proofs (see e.g. [12,69]) at the cost of extra rounds of communication. Like PCPs, IOPs can be compiled to succinct arguments using vector commitments and hence only using CRH.

  Most relevant to this work is the IOP-based complexity-preserving argument of [4], which builds off the Ligero protocol [1]. Because this protocol is based on IOPs, it only requires assuming CRH. However, their proof size is $\tilde{O}(t/s)$ and verifier runns in time $\tilde{O}(t/s + s)$, so their protocol is not fully succinct. They complement their result with a lower bound, roughly showing that this proof length is tight for complexity-preserving IOP-based protocols. Specifically, they show that any such encoding of the size $O(t)$ transcript using space s must have distance $O(s/t)$, resulting in query complexity—and hence proof length of the compiled argument—of at least $\Omega(t/s)$.

- **Linear PCPs:** Linear PCPs (introduced by [51] and further studied in [22,26, 45]) are proofs given oracle access to a linear function. [51] first shows how to convert a linear PCP into a linear multi-prover interactive proof (MIP), where the proof gives oracle access to potentially many different linear functions. They then compile this linear MIP into a (private-coin) argument using a particular multi-commitment scheme for linear functions that can be built from any additive homomorphic encryption scheme. In contrast to (plain) PCPs, the benefit of linear PCPs is that you don't need to materialize the full linear function in order to commit to it. However, their argument is not succinct since their linear PCP exponentially long, so the verifier's query must be linear in the complexity of the language. Still, their approach results in very short communication from the prover and gets around the efficiency bottleneck of using (plain) PCPs.

- **Multi-prover Interactive Proofs (MIPs):** MIPs (introduced by [9] and further studied in [21,25]) are interactive proofs with oracle access to independent, arbitrary functions that act as various provers who are not allowed to talk to each other. Bitansky and Chiesa [21] show how to compile MIPs into (private-coin) succinct arguments using succinct multi-function commitments, which can be constructed from fully homomorphic encryption. Bitansky and Chiesa use MIPs over PCPs because they can construct *complexity-preserving* MIPs where, for a time t space s non-deterministic computation, each prover can be implemented in time $\tilde{O}(t)$ and space $\tilde{O}(s)$. Then, their compiler results in a complexity-preserving succinct argument. We note that it is still a very intriguing open question to construct complexity-preserving PCPs.

- **Polynomial IOPs:** Polynomial IOPs (first formalized by [32] but implicit in previous works) generalize linear PCPs by (1) using oracles for higher degree polynomials as opposed to only linear functions and (2) allowing interaction as in IOPs. Polynomial IOPs can be compiled into arguments using polynomial commitments [57]. Constructing both polynomial IOPs and polynomial commitments have been at the forefront of practical succinct (non-interactive) argument constructions (see e.g. [11,33,44,60,70,72] for examples of polynomial IOPs and [10,23,24,27,31,32,57] for examples of polynomial commitments).

Of particular interest to this work are the complexity-preserving arguments of [23,24]. [23] construct a *publicly verifiable*, complexity-preserving, zero-knowledge argument in the ROM assuming hardness of discrete log. However, the verifier in their protocol runs in time $\tilde{O}(t)$, which is still non-trivial given their additional focus on zero knowledge and succinct communication. Building off of [23] and [24,32] construct the first public-coin, complexity-preserving, *fully succinct* argument. Their protocol requires $O(\log t)$ rounds of communication and relies on the existence of a public-coin *hidden order* group. The only candidate such groups are class groups of an imaginary quadratic field, which were first suggested for cryptographic use by [37] but have seen relatively little attention as a cryptographic assumption. Alternatively by relying on RSA groups or other private-coin hidden order groups, the protocol of [24] is only private-coin or relies on trusted setup.

Recursive Composition. Bitansky, Canetti, Chiesa, and Tromer [19]—based on the construction of incrementally verifiable computation of Valiant [73]—show how to bootstrap any (pre-processing) succinct, non-interactive, argument of knowledge [18] (SNARK) for NP into a complexity-preserving SNARK using *recursive composition*. The idea is that the prover can first use the underlying SNARK to prove that each step of the computation was performed correctly. Instead of having the verifier check each such proof, the prover will instead batch subsequent proofs together and use the same underlying SNARK to prove that it knows accepting proofs that would have caused the verifier to accept. This idea can be applied recursively until the verifier only has to check a single, succinct proof! Furthermore, the independent nature of the sub-proofs allow the prover to generate the individual proofs in pieces without blowing up its space complexity, overall resulting in a complexity-preserving SNARK.

The main downside of this approach is the fact that the existence of SNARKs is a non-falsifiable, "knowledge" assumption. Furthermore, even without the strong knowledge-soundness property, non-falsifiable assumptions are likely inherent [46]. Also, SNARKs for NP can only possibly exist with respect to restricted auxiliary-input distributions assuming indistinguishability obfuscation [20,28]. For these reasons, we focus on more standard, falsifiable assumptions in this work. In fact, our main construction can be viewed as implementing the recursive composition technique of [19] from falsifiable assumptions using interaction.

Delegation for P. In light of the inherent limitations for constructing succinct, non-interactive arguments for NP [46], there has been a long and fruitful line of work focusing on building succinct, non-interactive arguments in the common reference string model—or delegation protocols—for deterministic computation and other subclasses of NP (see e.g. [3, 29, 30, 35, 38, 48, 49, 52, 54–56, 66, 67, 74]). Of particular note, Holmgren and Rothblum [48] construct privately verifiable, complexity-preserving delegation protocols for P from the (sub-exponential) learning with errors assumption. The works of [34, 35, 49, 55, 74] construct publicly verifiable (yet not complexity-preserving) delegation protocols for P from various falsifiable assumptions. Underlying these constructions are novel techniques for implementing recursive composition from falsifiable assumptions, albeit restricted to deterministic computations. The works of [38, 53, 66] extend these works to construct incrementally verifiable computation [73] under the same assumptions, which directly yield publicly verifiable, complexity-preserving delegation protocols for P.

Comparison of Complexity-Preserving Arguments. In Table 1 below, we summarize various efficiency properties and cryptographic assumptions for existing complexity-preserving arguments for NP. For simplicity, we use $\tilde{O}(\cdot)$ notation to suppress all multiplicative $\mathsf{poly}(\lambda, |x|, \log t, \log s)$ terms. All protocols in the table have prover time $\tilde{O}(t)$ and space $\tilde{O}(s)$. We note that the various schemes may differ in the exact terms hidden in the $\tilde{O}(\cdot)$ notation, but our primary focus is on the asymptotics in terms of t and s. Finally, we note that all of the public-coin protocols can heuristically be compressed to a single message via the Fiat-Shamir transform in the random oracle model (ROM).

Table 1. Comparison of complexity-preserving arguments for non-deterministic time t and space s computation. For simplicity, we use $\tilde{O}(\cdot)$ notation to suppress all multiplicative $\mathsf{poly}(\lambda, |x|, \log t, \log s)$ terms.

Protocol	Verifier Time	Communication	Messages	Public Coin?	Assumption
[21]	$\tilde{O}(1)$	$\tilde{O}(1)$	4	No	FHE
[19,73]	$\tilde{O}(1)$	$\tilde{O}(1)$	1	Yes	SNARKs for NP
[23]	$\tilde{O}(t)$	$\tilde{O}(1)$	1	Yes	DLog + ROM
[24]	$\tilde{O}(1)$	$\tilde{O}(1)$	$O(\log t)$	Yes	Class Groups
[4]	$\tilde{O}(t/s + s)$	$\tilde{O}(t/s)$	$O(1)$	Yes	CRH
This work	$\tilde{O}(1)$	$\tilde{O}(1)$	$O(\log_\lambda t)$	Yes	CRH

2   Preliminaries

We let $\mathbb{N} = \{1, 2, 3, \dots\}$ denote the set of natural numbers, and for any $n \in \mathbb{N}$, we write $[n]$ to denote the set $[n] = \{1, \dots, n\}$. For integers $a, b \in \mathbb{Z}$ with $a \leq b$, we write $[a, b]$ to denote the set $\{a, a + 1, \dots, b\}$. For a set Σ, referred to as the *alphabet*, we denote Σ^* the set of strings consisting of 0 or more elements from Σ. We let Σ^n denote the set of n-character strings from Σ and $\Sigma^{\leq n}$ the set of string of length at most n. For a string $s \in \Sigma^*$, we let $|s|$ denote the length of s. For any string $s \in \Sigma^*$ and $i \in [|s|]$, let $s[i]$ denote the ith character of s. For $i \notin [|s|]$, we assume that $s[i]$ always returns a special character $\perp$. Unless specified otherwise, we assume that a string s is defined over the binary alphabet $\{0, 1\}$.

We write $\lambda \in \mathbb{N}$ to denote the security parameter. We say that a function $p \colon \mathbb{N} \to \mathbb{N}$ is in the set $\mathsf{poly}(\lambda)$ and is *polynomially-bounded* if there exists a constant c and an index $i \in \mathbb{N}$ such that $p(\lambda) \leq \lambda^c$ for all $\lambda \geq i$. We say that a function $\mathsf{negl} \colon \mathbb{N} \to \mathbb{R}$ is negligible if for every constant $c > 0$ there exists $i \in \mathbb{N}$ such that $\mathsf{negl}(\lambda) \leq \lambda^{-c}$ for all $\lambda \geq i$.

We use PPT to denote the acronym *probabilistic, polynomial time*. A uniform algorithm A is a RAM program with a fixed (constant-size) description length. A non-uniform algorithm A consists of a sequence of algorithms $\{A_\lambda\}_{\lambda \in \mathbb{N}}$, one for each security parameter λ; we assume for simplicity that A_λ always receives 1^λ as its first input. When the security parameter is clear from context, we may write $A(\cdot)$ instead of $A_\lambda(\cdot)$ for simplicity. A non-uniform PPT algorithm is one where the description size of A_λ as a function of λ is in $\mathsf{poly}(\lambda)$.

For a distribution X, we write $x \leftarrow X$ to denote the process of sampling a value x from the distribution X. For a set $\mathcal{X}$, we use $x \leftarrow \mathcal{X}$ to denote the process of sampling a value x from the uniform distribution over $\mathcal{X}$. We use $x = A(\cdot)$ to denote the output of a deterministic algorithm and $x \leftarrow A(\cdot)$ to denote the output of a randomized algorithm. For a randomized algorithm, we write $x = A(\cdot; r)$ to denote the deterministic output given sequential access to the random coins r. We write $x := y$ to denote the assignment of value y to x. For a distribution D, we define $\mathsf{Supp}(D)$ to denote the support of the distribution D.

RAM Computation. We model a non-deterministic RAM computation by a machine M with local word size n, and random access to a working memory string $D \in \{0, 1\}^{2^n}$ and a read-only witness. The computation of M is carried out one step at a time by a polynomial-time CPU algorithm step that takes as input a description of a program M, a RAM state rst of size $O(n)$, a bit b^{mem} read from memory, and a witness bit b^{wit}. It then outputs a tuple

$$(\mathsf{rst}_{\mathsf{new}}, i^{\mathsf{mem}}, i^{\mathsf{wrt}}, b^{\mathsf{wrt}}, i^{\mathsf{wit}}) = \mathsf{step}(M, \mathsf{rst}, b^{\mathsf{mem}}, b^{\mathsf{wit}}),$$

where $\mathsf{rst}_{\mathsf{new}}$ is the updated state, i^{mem} is the next location to read from memory, i^{wrt} is the location in memory to write next, b^{wrt} is the bit to be written, and i^{wit} is the next location to read from the witness.

We write $M^D(w)$ to denote the computation of M with working memory D and witness w. We write $M(x, w)$ to denote the computation $M^D(w)$ where D is initialized to start with an encoding of the input x followed by 0s.

The program starts with initial empty state rst_0, initial memory and witness read locations $i_0^{\mathsf{mem}} = i_0^{\mathsf{wit}} = 1$. Starting from $j = 1$, the jth execution step proceeds as follows:

1. Read the memory bit $b_{j-1}^{\mathsf{mem}} := D[i_{j-1}^{\mathsf{mem}}]$ and witness bit $b_{j-1}^{\mathsf{wit}} := w[i_{j-1}^{\mathsf{wit}}]$.
2. Compute $(\mathsf{rst}_j, i_j^{\mathsf{mem}}, i_j^{\mathsf{wrt}}, b_j^{\mathsf{wrt}}, i_j^{\mathsf{wit}}) = \mathsf{step}(M, \mathsf{rst}_{j-1}, b_{j-1}^{\mathsf{mem}}, b_{j-1}^{\mathsf{wit}})$.

3. If $i_j^{\text{wrt}} \neq \perp$, write a bit to memory $D[i_j^{\text{wrt}}] := b_j^{\text{wrt}}$.

The execution terminates when step outputs a special terminating state for rst_t, which specifies whether the computation is accepting and outputs 1 or rejecting and outputs 0. Note that we only consider machines with binary output in this work.

For a RAM computation $M^D(w)$, we define its running time t as the number of steps until M halts and its space s as the maximum index i_j^{mem} accessed. Note that the witness tape is read-only and does not count towards the space.

We say that a RAM computation $M^D(w)$ makes m passes over its witness if reads its witness from left to right at most m times. That is, $|\{j \in [t] : i_j^{\text{wit}} < i_{j-1}^{\text{wit}}\}| < m$, where t is the computation's running time.

Universal Languages. The universal relation $\mathcal{R}_{\mathcal{U}}$ is the set of instance-witness pairs $((M, x, t), w)$ where M is a RAM program with word size n such that $M(x, w)$ accepts and outputs 1 within t steps. We assume that the description of M contains its word size 1^n in unary, so $|M|$ is always at least n. We let $\mathcal{L}_{\mathcal{U}}$ be the corresponding language with relation $\mathcal{R}_{\mathcal{U}}$, which we call the universal language.

Interactive Machines. We consider interactive protocols with interactive RAM programs. To allow for communication between two interacting machines, we assume there is a specified part of a machine's memory for input from and output to another interactive machine. Once one machine halts after writing downs its output, we say that it has sent a message consisting of its output to the other machine. Given a pair of interactive RAM programs A and B, we denote by $\langle A(w), B \rangle(x)$ the random variable representing the output of B with common input x, when interacting with A with common input x and witness w, when the random tape of each machine is uniformly and independently chosen. We let $\text{View}_B(\langle A(w), B \rangle(x))$ be the random variable representing the view of B in the interaction between A and B, consisting of its inputs, random coins, and the communication it receives from A. The message complexity of the protocol is the number of distinct messages sent between A and B before B produces its final output.

2.1 Collision-Resistant Hash Functions

We give the notion of a keyed collision-resistant hash functions (CRH) that we use in this work. We emphasize that our definition below allows for arbitrary length input and produces a fixed size digest, but it is well known that this is implied by any compressing CRH with fixed input length [36,61,62].

Definition 2.1 (Collision-Resistant Hash Function). *A keyed collision-resistant hash function is given by an algorithm* Hash *with the following syntax:*

- dig = Hash(hk, x): *A deterministic algorithm that on input a hash key* hk $\in \{0,1\}^\lambda$ *and string* $x \in \{0,1\}^*$, *outputs a digest* dig $\in \{0,1\}^\lambda$.

We require that Hash *runs in polynomial-time and satisfies the following security property:*

– **Collision Resistance:** *For all non-uniform polynomial-time adversaries A, there exists a negligible function* negl *such that for all $\lambda \in \mathbb{N}$, it holds that*

$$\Pr\begin{bmatrix} \mathsf{hk} \leftarrow \{0,1\}^{\lambda} & x \neq x' \\ (x,x') \leftarrow A(\mathsf{hk}) & : \mathsf{Hash}(\mathsf{hk},x) = \mathsf{Hash}(\mathsf{hk},x') \end{bmatrix} \leq \mathsf{negl}(\lambda).$$

2.2   Hash Trees

We follow the definition of hash trees from [54] with slight modifications from [40].

Definition 2.2 (Hash Tree). *A* hash tree *is a tuple of algorithms* (KeyGen, Hash, Read, Write, VerRead, VerWrite) *with the following syntax and efficiency:*

– $\mathsf{hk} \leftarrow \mathsf{KeyGen}(1^{\lambda})$: *A randomized polynomial-time algorithm that on input the security parameter 1^{λ} outputs a hash key* hk.
– $(\mathsf{tree}, \mathsf{dig}) = \mathsf{Hash}(\mathsf{hk}, D)$: *A deterministic polynomial-time algorithm that on input a hash key* hk *and a database $D \in \{0,1\}^s$ outputs a hash tree* tree *and a string* $\mathsf{dig} \in \{0,1\}^{\lambda}$. *We require that* tree *has size at most $s \cdot \mathsf{poly}(\lambda, \log s)$.*
– $\mathsf{dig} = \mathsf{Digest}(\mathsf{hk}, D)$: *A deterministic algorithm that on input a hash key* hk *and a database $D \in \{0,1\}^s$ outputs a string* $\mathsf{dig} \in \{0,1\}^{\lambda}$. *For databases of the form $D = x \| 0^{s-|x|}$,* Digest *runs in time $(|x| + 1) \cdot \mathsf{poly}(\lambda, \log s)$.*
– $(b, \pi^{\mathsf{rd}}) = \mathsf{Read}^{\mathsf{tree}}(i^{\mathsf{rd}})$: *A read-only deterministic RAM program that accesses a database* tree *and on input an index i^{rd} outputs a bit b^{rd} and a proof π^{rd}. The program runs in time $\mathsf{poly}(\lambda, \log s)$.*
– $(\mathsf{dig}_{\mathsf{new}}, \pi^{\mathsf{wrt}}) = \mathsf{Write}^{\mathsf{tree}}(i^{\mathsf{wrt}}, b^{\mathsf{wrt}})$: *A deterministic RAM program that accesses a database* tree *and on input an index i^{wrt} and bit b^{wrt} outputs a new digest $\mathsf{dig}_{\mathsf{new}}$ and a proof π^{wrt}. The program runs in time $\mathsf{poly}(\lambda, \log s)$ and* tree *remains fixed size.*
– $b = \mathsf{VerRead}(\mathsf{dig}, i^{\mathsf{rd}}, b^{\mathsf{rd}}, \pi^{\mathsf{rd}})$: *A deterministic polynomial-time algorithm that on input a digest* dig, *an index i^{rd}, a bit b^{rd}, and a proof π^{rd} outputs a bit b.*
– $b = \mathsf{VerWrite}(\mathsf{dig}, i^{\mathsf{wrt}}, b^{\mathsf{wrt}}, \mathsf{dig}', \pi^{\mathsf{wrt}})$: *A deterministic polynomial-time algorithm that on input a digest* dig, *an index i^{wrt}, a bit b^{wrt}, a new digest dig', and a proof π^{wrt} outputs a bit b.*

We require that (KeyGen, Hash, Read, Write, VerRead, VerWrite) *satisfy the following properties:*

– **Digest Consistency:** *For every $\lambda \in \mathbb{N}$ and $D \in \{0,1\}^s$, it holds that*

$$\Pr\begin{bmatrix} \mathsf{hk} \leftarrow \mathsf{KeyGen}(1^{\lambda}) \\ (\cdot, \mathsf{dig}) = \mathsf{Hash}(\mathsf{hk}, D) : \mathsf{dig} = \mathsf{dig}' \\ \mathsf{dig}' = \mathsf{Digest}(\mathsf{hk}, D) \end{bmatrix} = 1.$$

– **Correctness of Read:** *For every $\lambda \in \mathbb{N}$, $D \in \{0,1\}^s$, $i^{rd} \in [s]$, $m \geq 0$, and sequence of pairs $(i_j, b_j) \in [s] \times b$ for $j \in [m]$, let $D' \in \{0,1\}^s$ be the database equal to D followed by updates b_j to index i_j for each $j \in [m]$. Then, it holds that*

$$\Pr\left[\begin{array}{l} \mathsf{hk} \leftarrow \mathsf{KeyGen}(1^\lambda) \\ (\mathsf{tree}, \mathsf{dig}_0) = \mathsf{Hash}(\mathsf{hk}, D) \\ \forall j \in [m], \\ \quad (\cdot, \mathsf{dig}_j) = \mathsf{Write}^{\mathsf{tree}}(i_j, b_j) \\ (b^{rd}, \pi^{rd}) = \mathsf{Read}^{\mathsf{tree}}(i^{rd}) \end{array} : \begin{array}{l} \mathsf{VerRead}(\mathsf{dig}_m, i^{rd}, b^{rd}, \pi^{rd}) = 1 \\ \wedge\, b^{rd} = D'[i^{rd}] \end{array}\right] = 1.$$

– **Correctness of Write:** *For every $\lambda \in \mathbb{N}$, $D \in \{0,1\}^s$, $i^{wrt} \in [s]$, $b^{wrt} \in \{0,1\}$, $m \geq 0$, and sequence of pairs $(i_j, b_j) \in [s] \times \{0,1\}$ for $j \in [m]$, let $D' \in \{0,1\}^s$ be the database equal to D followed by updates b_j to index i_j for each $j \in [m]$. Let D'_{new} be the database equal to D' followed by one more update b^{wrt} to index i^{wrt}. Then, it holds that*

$$\Pr\left[\begin{array}{l} \mathsf{hk} \leftarrow \mathsf{KeyGen}(1^\lambda) \\ (\mathsf{tree}, \mathsf{dig}_0) = \mathsf{Hash}(\mathsf{hk}, D) \\ \forall j \in [m], (\cdot, \mathsf{dig}_j) = \mathsf{Write}^{\mathsf{tree}}(i_j, b_j) \\ (\mathsf{dig}_{new}, \pi^{wrt}) = \mathsf{Write}^{\mathsf{tree}}(i^{wrt}, b^{wrt}) \\ (\cdot, \mathsf{dig}') = \mathsf{Hash}(\mathsf{hk}, D'_{new}) \end{array} : \begin{array}{l} \mathsf{VerWrite}(\mathsf{dig}_m, i^{wrt}, \\ \quad b^{wrt}, \mathsf{dig}_{new}, \pi^{wrt}) = 1 \\ \wedge\, \mathsf{dig}_{new} = \mathsf{dig}' \end{array}\right] = 1.$$

– **Soundness of Read:** *For every non-uniform PPT A, there exists a negligible function negl such that for all $\lambda \in \mathbb{N}$, it holds that*

$$\Pr\left[\begin{array}{l} \mathsf{hk} \leftarrow \mathsf{KeyGen}(1^\lambda) \\ (\mathsf{dig}, i, b, \pi, b', \pi') \leftarrow A(\mathsf{hk}) \end{array} : \begin{array}{l} b \neq b' \\ \wedge\, \mathsf{VerRead}(\mathsf{dig}, i, b, \pi) = 1 \\ \wedge\, \mathsf{VerRead}(\mathsf{dig}, i, b', \pi') = 1 \end{array}\right] \leq \mathsf{negl}(\lambda).$$

– **Soundness of Write:** *For every non-uniform PPT A, there exists a negligible function negl such that for all $\lambda \in \mathbb{N}$, it holds that*

$$\Pr\left[\begin{array}{l} \mathsf{hk} \leftarrow \mathsf{KeyGen}(1^\lambda) \\ (\mathsf{dig}, i, b, \mathsf{dig}_{new}, \pi, \\ \mathsf{dig}'_{new}, \pi') \leftarrow A(\mathsf{hk}) \end{array} : \begin{array}{l} \mathsf{dig}_{new} \neq \mathsf{dig}'_{new} \\ \wedge\, \mathsf{VerWrite}(\mathsf{dig}, i, b, \mathsf{dig}_{new}, \pi) = 1 \\ \wedge\, \mathsf{VerWrite}(\mathsf{dig}, i, b, \mathsf{dig}'_{new}, \pi') = 1 \end{array}\right] \leq \mathsf{negl}(\lambda).$$

Based on Merkle trees [61], we can construct hash trees that satisfy the above definition from any CRH.

Theorem 2.3 ([40,61]). *Assuming the existence of a keyed collision-resistant hash function, there exists a hash tree as per Definition 2.2.*

2.3 Arguments of Knowledge

We define arguments of knowledge for the universal language $\mathcal{L}_\mathcal{U}$. We use a definition from [40] which is equivalent to the more standard definition of [7] (see Remark 2.5). We choose to work with this definition since it is more convenient in settings involving composition (see Remark 2.6). We note that in contrast to the notion of universal arguments [6], our arguments of knowledge property only considers polynomial time computations.

Definition 2.4 (Argument of Knowledge). *A pair of interactive RAM programs (P, V) is an* argument of knowledge *for $\mathcal{R}_\mathcal{U}$ if the following hold:*

- **Prover Efficiency:** *There exists a polynomial q such that for every $\lambda \in \mathbb{N}$ and $((M, x, t), w) \in \mathcal{R}_\mathcal{U}$, the prover P on common input $(1^\lambda, (M, x, t))$ and witness w runs in time $q(\lambda, |M, x|, t)$.*
- **Completeness:** *For every $\lambda \in \mathbb{N}$ and $(y, w) \in \mathcal{R}_\mathcal{U}$, it holds that*

$$\Pr\left[\langle P(w), V\rangle(1^\lambda, y) = 1\right] = 1.$$

- **Argument of Knowledge:** *For every polynomial p, there exists a probabilistic oracle machine $\mathcal{E}$ and a polynomial q such that for every non-uniform polynomial-time prover P^*, there exists a negligible function negl such that for every $\lambda \in \mathbb{N}$, and instance $y = (M, x, t)$ such that $|M, x| \le p(\lambda)$ and $t \le p(\lambda)$, the following hold.*
  Let $V[\rho]$ denote the verifier V using randomness $\rho \in \{0, 1\}^{\ell(\lambda)}$ where $\ell(\lambda)$ is a bound on the number of random bits used by V. Then:
  1. *The expected running time of $\mathcal{E}^{P^*}(1^\lambda, y, \rho)$ is bounded by $q(\lambda)$ where the expectation is over $\rho \leftarrow \{0, 1\}^{\ell(\lambda)}$ and the random coins of $\mathcal{E}$, and oracle calls to P^* cost only a single step.*
  2. *It holds that*

$$\Pr\left[\begin{matrix} \rho \leftarrow \{0, 1\}^{\ell(\lambda)} \\ w \leftarrow \mathcal{E}^{P^*}(1^\lambda, y, \rho) \end{matrix} : \begin{matrix} (y, w) \notin \mathcal{R}_\mathcal{U} \\ \wedge \langle P^*, V[\rho]\rangle(1^\lambda, y) = 1 \end{matrix}\right] \le \mathsf{negl}(\lambda).$$

Remark 2.5 (Equivalence to definition of [7]). The "standard" definition of an argument of knowledge is due to Bellare and Goldreich [7] (BG). The BG extractor always succeeds in extracting a valid witness (in contrast to succeeding in accordance with a uniformly sampled view given by the verifier's randomness ρ) but runs in expected time $\mathsf{poly}(\lambda)/(\epsilon - \mathsf{negl}(\lambda))$ for negligible function negl where ϵ is the probability that $\langle P^*, V\rangle(1^\lambda, y) = 1$. The existence of a BG extractor implies the existence of an EFKP extractor (as defined above) and vice versa [40]. This implication from BG to EFKP is shown via the intermediate notion of witness-extended emulation from Lemma 3.1 of [59] and Lemma A.6 of [40]. To construct a BG extractor from an EFKP extractor, you first sample randomness ρ for the verifier, check if $\langle P^*, V[\rho]\rangle(1^\lambda, y)$ is accepting, run the EFKP extractor with ρ if so, and repeat if the transcript is rejecting or the extractor fails.

Remark 2.6 (On composition for the definition of [40]). A key challenge when composing arguments of knowledge is bounding the running time of the final extractor. One notion that composes well is "precise" arguments of knowledge [64] where, for any given view of the cheating prover (defined by the verifier's randomness ρ as above), the extractor's running time is a fixed polynomial in the running time of the cheating prover on that particular view. This notion, however, is quite strong and not known to hold for arguments of knowledge from standard assumptions.

In a more standard—and also achievable—argument of knowledge notion called witness-extended emulation [59], the extractor is not given a view, but instead must output a uniformly distributed view of the verifier and a corresponding witness if the verifier accepts the view. Furthermore, an extractor for witness-extended emulation only needs to run in expected polynomial time and may use rewinding. However, the view chosen by the extractor may not be consistent with the external view when used as a sub-protocol.

The argument of knowledge notion of [40] gives the extractor a uniformly sampled view and requires that the extractor run in expected polynomial-time over the choice of the view (although to compose well, this polynomial must be independent of the cheating prover's strategy). This relaxes the strict efficiency requirement of [64] since the extractor need not run in fixed polynomial time, but also (conceptually) strengthens the notion of [59] as the extractor must work for a given view rather than outputting one itself. Existentially, the definitions of [40] and [59] are equivalent however; see the above remark.

Public-Coin Protocols. We say that an argument (P, V) is public-coin—or equivalently that V is a public-coin verifier—if all of V's messages simply consist of random coins, and V maintains no other private state. Specifically, the final output of V is a function only of the protocol's transcript.

Efficiency. We consider two efficiency requirements of arguments for $\mathcal{R}_\mathcal{U}$: *succinct* and *complexity-preserving* arguments. Roughly speaking, in succinct arguments the communication complexity and verification time are logarithmic in the running time of the computation that is being proved. In complexity-preserving arguments, the time and space complexity of the honest prover are close to the complexity of the original computation. When measuring efficiency, we model the prover P and verifier V as interactive RAM programs. We formalize these notions below.

Definition 2.7 (Succinct Arguments). *Let (P, V) be an argument for $\mathcal{R}_\mathcal{U}$. We say that (P, V) is succinct if there exists a polynomial q such that for any $\lambda \in \mathbb{N}$ and $(y = (M, x, t), w) \in \mathcal{R}_\mathcal{U}$, the following always hold during the experiment $\langle P(w), V \rangle(1^\lambda, y)$:*

- *Succinct Verification: The verifier V runs in time at most $q(\lambda, |M, x|, \log t)$.*
- *Succinct Communication: The length of the transcript is at most $q(\lambda, \log |M, x|, \log t)$.*

Succinct arguments of knowledge are known based on CRH.

Theorem 2.8 ([58]). *Assuming the existence of a keyed collision-resistant hash function, there exists a 4-message, public-coin, succinct argument of knowledge for $\mathcal{R}_\mathcal{U}$.*

Definition 2.9 (Complexity-Preserving Arguments). *Let (P, V) be an argument for $\mathcal{R}_\mathcal{U}$. We say that (P, V) is complexity-preserving if there exists* *a polynomial q such that for any $\lambda \in \mathbb{N}$ and $(y = (M, x, t), w) \in \mathcal{R}_\mathcal{U}$ such that $M(x, w)$ uses space s, the prover P in the experiment $\langle P(w), V \rangle(1^\lambda, y)$ runs in time at most $t \cdot q(\lambda, |M, x|, \log t)$ and uses space at most $s \cdot q(\lambda, |M, x|, \log t)$.*

3 Arguments of Knowledge for Bounded Space Computation

As a step towards our main result, we construct an argument of knowledge for the update language in this section. In the update language, we consider a non-deterministic polynomial-time Turing machine M updating a state of size s. The language contains tuples $(M, \mathsf{st}, \mathsf{st}', t)$ such that M moves from state st to state st' via a sequence of t updates. In Sect. 4, we turn this argument for the update language into a complexity preserving succinct argument of knowledge for $\mathcal{R}_\mathcal{U}$.

Definition 3.1 (Update Language). *Let α be a polynomial. The update language $\mathcal{L}_{\mathsf{Upd},\alpha}$ with relation $\mathcal{R}_{\mathsf{Upd},\alpha}$ consists of instance-witness pairs of the form $((M, \mathsf{st}, \mathsf{st}', t), w)$ where M is an α-time non-deterministic Turing machine, st, $\mathsf{st}' \in \{0, 1\}^s$, $t \in \mathbb{N}$, and $w = (w_1, \ldots, w_t) \in \{0, 1\}^{\alpha(s) \times t}$ such that the following procedure accepts:*

- *Set $\mathsf{st}_0 = \mathsf{st}$.*
- *For $i = 1, \ldots, t$:*
  - *Emulate $M(\mathsf{st}_{i-1}, w_i)$. If M does not halt within $\alpha(s)$ steps then reject.*
  - *Obtain M's output st_i. If $|\mathsf{st}_i| \neq s$ then reject.*
- *Accept if $\mathsf{st}_t = \mathsf{st}'$ and reject otherwise.*

We construct a sequence of arguments for $\mathcal{L}_{\mathsf{Upd},\alpha}$.

Theorem 3.2. *Assume the existence of a keyed collision-resistant hash function. There exists $d \in \mathbb{N}$ such that for every polynomial α, there exists sequence of interactive RAM programs $\{(P_r, V_r)\}_{r \geq 0}$ such that the following hold:*

- **Completeness:** *For every $\lambda \in \mathbb{N}$, $r \geq 0$, and $(y, w) \in \mathcal{R}_{\mathsf{Upd},\alpha}$, it holds that*

$$\Pr\left[\langle P_r(w), V_r \rangle(1^\lambda, y) = 1\right] = 1.$$

- **Argument of Knowledge:** *For every polynomial p, there exists a probabilistic oracle machine $\mathcal{E}$ and a polynomial q such that for every non-uniform polynomial-time prover $P^\star$ and function $r = r(\lambda)$ such that $(\lambda \cdot r)^r \leq p(\lambda)$, there exists a negligible function negl such that for every $\lambda \in \mathbb{N}$, instance $y = (M, \mathsf{st}, \mathsf{st}', t)$ such that $|y|, t \leq p(\lambda)$, the following hold. Let $V_r[\rho]$ denote the verifier V_r using randomness $\rho \in \{0, 1\}^{\ell(\lambda)}$. Then:*
  1. *The expected running time of $\mathcal{E}^{P^\star}(1^\lambda, y, \rho, r)$ is bounded by $q(\lambda)$.*
  2. *It holds that*

$$\Pr\left[\begin{array}{c} \rho \leftarrow \{0, 1\}^{\ell(\lambda)} \\ w \leftarrow \mathcal{E}^{P^\star}(1^\lambda, y, \rho, r) \end{array} : \begin{array}{c} (y, w) \notin \mathcal{R}_{\mathsf{Upd},\alpha} \\ \wedge \langle P^\star, V_r[\rho] \rangle(1^\lambda, y) = 1 \end{array}\right] \leq \mathsf{negl}(\lambda).$$

- **Efficiency:** *There exists a polynomial q such that for every $\lambda \in \mathbb{N}$, $r \geq 0$, and $(y = (M, \mathsf{st}, \mathsf{st}', t), w) \in \mathcal{R}_{\mathsf{Upd}, \alpha}$ such that $|\mathsf{st}| = s$, the following efficiency properties always hold in the experiment $\langle P_r(w), V_r \rangle(1^\lambda, y)$ assuming $(\lambda \cdot |M| \cdot \alpha(s) \cdot t \cdot r)^d \leq 2^\lambda$:*

  - **Efficiently Computable:** *There exists a polynomial-time Turing machine that on input 1^r outputs the descriptions of the interactive RAM programs (P_r, V_r).*
  - **Round Complexity:** *The interaction between P_r and V_r consists of $6r + 4$ messages.*
  - **Prover Efficiency:** *The prover P_r runs in time at most $t \cdot q(\lambda, |M|, s, r)$ and space at most $(t/\lambda^r) \cdot q(\lambda, |M|, s, r)$ and makes at most 1 pass over its witness per message it sends.*
  - **Verifier Efficiency:** *The verifier V_r is public-coin and runs in time at most $q(\lambda, |M|, s, r)$.*
  - **Communication Efficiency:** *The length of each message sent by P_r or V_r is at most $q(\lambda)$.*

The full construction is provided in Sect. 3.1 with associated proofs deferred to the full version.

3.1   Construction

Let α be any polynomial. We construct a sequence of interactive RAM programs $(P_r, V_r)_{r \geq 0}$ satisfying the properties stated in Theorem 3.2.

Let $(P_{\mathsf{base}}, V_{\mathsf{base}})$ be a 4-message, public-coin, succinct argument of knowledge for $\mathcal{R}_{\mathcal{U}}$ (see Theorem 2.8). In the base case (P_0, V_0), we use $(P_{\mathsf{base}}, V_{\mathsf{base}})$ by converting an the instance $y = (M, \mathsf{st}, \mathsf{st}', t) \in \mathcal{L}_{\mathsf{Upd}, \alpha}$ to an input for $\mathcal{L}_{\mathcal{U}}$ as follows. We define M' to be the machine that takes as input $(\mathsf{st}, \mathsf{st}', t)$, sets $\mathsf{st}_0 := \mathsf{st}$, computes $\mathsf{st}_i := M(\mathsf{st}_{i-1}, w_i)$ for $i = 1, \ldots, t$, and outputs 1 if $\mathsf{st}' = \mathsf{st}_t$ and 0 otherwise. Note that M' runs in non-deterministic time $t \cdot \alpha(s)$ given witness $w \in \{0,1\}^{\alpha(s) \times t}$. The prover P_0 and verifier V_0 in the interaction $\langle P_0(w), V_0 \rangle(1^\lambda, (M, \mathsf{st}, \mathsf{st}', t))$ simply emulate $\langle P_{\mathsf{base}}(w), V_{\mathsf{base}} \rangle(1^\lambda, (M', (\mathsf{st}, \mathsf{st}', t), t \cdot \alpha(s)))$, and V_0 returns the output of V_{base}.

For $r \geq 1$, the construction of (P_r, V_r) relies on a keyed collision-resistant hash function Hash and on the protocol (P_{r-1}, V_{r-1}). At a high level, the protocol has two phases: In the first phase the prover splits the update statements into λ smaller sub-statements and proves all sub-statements in parallel using the protocol (P_r, V_r). To keep the communication from growing too much, in each round, the prover only provides a short commitment the messages of the λ parallel executions. In the second phase, the prover uses the protocol $(P_{\mathsf{base}}, V_{\mathsf{base}})$ to succinctly prove that the λ committed transcripts are all accepting.

We proceed to give a formal description of the protocol (P_r, V_r). The prover P_r and verifier V_r receive as common input a security parameter 1^λ and an instance $y = (M, \mathsf{st}, \mathsf{st}', t) \in \mathcal{L}_{\mathsf{Upd}, \alpha}$. The prover additionally receives a witness $w = (w_1, \ldots, w_t) \in \{0,1\}^{\alpha(s) \times t}$ such that $(y, w) \in \mathcal{R}_{\mathsf{Upd}, \alpha}$.

- V_r samples a hash key $\mathsf{hk} \leftarrow \{0,1\}^\lambda$ and sends it to P_r.

- Set $\tau = \lceil t/\lambda \rceil$. P_r sets $\mathsf{st}_0 := \mathsf{st}$ and for $i = 1, \ldots, t$, it computes $\mathsf{st}_i := M(\mathsf{st}_{i-1}, w_i)$. During this computation, P_r only saves the states $\mathsf{st}_0, \mathsf{st}_t$ and the $\lambda - 1$ intermediate states $\mathsf{st}_{i \cdot \tau}$ for $i \in [\lambda - 1]$. Every other state is erased as soon as the next state is computed. P_r computes $\mathsf{dig}_0 = \mathsf{Hash}(\mathsf{hk}, (\mathsf{st}_1, \ldots, \mathsf{st}_{\lambda-1}))$ and sends dig_0 to V_r.
- For $i \in [\lambda - 1]$, let $y_i = (M, \mathsf{st}_{(i-1) \cdot \tau}, \mathsf{st}_{i \cdot \tau}, \tau)$ and let $y_\lambda = (M, \mathsf{st}_{(\lambda-1) \cdot \tau}, \mathsf{st}_t, t - (\lambda - 1) \cdot \tau)$. For $i \in [\lambda - 1]$, let $\mathsf{wit}_i = (w_{(i-1) \cdot \tau + 1}, \ldots, w_{i \cdot \tau})$ and let $\mathsf{wit}_\lambda = (w_{(i-1) \cdot \tau + 1}, \ldots, w_t)$.
- For $j = 1, \ldots, 3r - 1$ corresponding to each back-and-forth round of (P_{r-1}, V_{r-1}):
  - V_r samples $\mathsf{vmsg}_j \leftarrow \{0,1\}^\ell$, where ℓ is a bound on the length of length of each messages sent by V_{r-1} on input $(1^\lambda, y_i)$. V_r sends vmsg_j to P_r.
  - For $i = 1, \ldots, \lambda$, P_r emulates P_{r-1} with input $(1^\lambda, y_i)$, witness wit_i and verifier messages $\mathsf{vmsg}_1, \ldots, \mathsf{vmsg}_j$ and obtains P_{r-1}'s next message $\mathsf{pmsg}_{j,i}$. The prover saves the message $\mathsf{pmsg}_{j,i}$ and erases the memory used to emulate P_{r-1} as soon as $\mathsf{pmsg}_{j,i}$ is computed. P_r computes $\mathsf{dig}_j = \mathsf{Hash}(\mathsf{hk}, (\mathsf{pmsg}_{j,1}, \ldots, \mathsf{pmsg}_{j,\lambda}))$ and sends dig_j to V_r.
- Let $x_{\mathsf{mrg}} = (1^\lambda, r, t, M, \mathsf{hk}, \mathsf{st}_0, \mathsf{st}_t, \vec{\mathsf{dig}}, \vec{\mathsf{vmsg}})$ for $\vec{\mathsf{dig}} = (\mathsf{dig}_0, \ldots, \mathsf{dig}_{3r-1})$ and $\vec{\mathsf{vmsg}} = (\mathsf{vmsg}_1, \ldots, \mathsf{vmsg}_{3r-1})$. Let $w_{\mathsf{mrg}} = (\vec{\mathsf{st}}, \mathsf{Pmsg})$ where $\vec{\mathsf{st}} = (\mathsf{st}_\tau, \ldots, \mathsf{st}_{(\lambda-1) \cdot \tau})$ and $\mathsf{Pmsg} = (\mathsf{pmsg}_{j,i})_{j \in [3r-1], i \in [\lambda]}$. The prover emulates P_{base} and the verifier emulates V_{base} in the interaction

$$\langle P_{\mathsf{base}}(w_{\mathsf{mrg}}), V_{\mathsf{base}} \rangle (1^\lambda, (\mathsf{Merge}, x_{\mathsf{mrg}}, t_{\mathsf{mrg}})),$$

where Merge is the non-deterministic machine of Fig. 1 and t_{mrg} is the time to compute $\mathsf{Merge}(x_{\mathsf{mrg}}, w_{\mathsf{mrg}})$. The verifier returns the output of V_{base}.

4   Complexity-Preserving Succinct Arguments of Knowledge

In this section, we build a complexity-preserving succinct argument of knowledge for $\mathcal{L}_\mathcal{U}$ using the argument for the update language given in Sect. 3. At a high level, we follow the blueprint of [19] where each step of the update language emulates one step of the RAM computation. Instead of accessing memory, the memory content is provided as part of the witness. A hash tree is used to verify memory accesses (Definition 2.2).

Theorem 4.1. *Assume the existence of a keyed collision-resistant hash function. There exists a public-coin, succinct, complexity-preserving, argument of knowledge (P, V) for $\mathcal{R}_\mathcal{U}$. On common input $(1^\lambda, (M, x, t))$, the message complexity of the protocol is at most $6 \log_\lambda t + 6$, and P makes at most $3 \log_\lambda t + 3$ passes over its witness.*

To prove the theorem, we provide a construction in Sect. 4.1 with associated proofs deferred to the full version.

Machine Merge

Inputs: A security parameter 1^λ, a recursion depth $r \in \mathbb{N}$, a number of steps $t \in \mathbb{N}$, a machine M, a hash key hk, an initial state st_0, a final state st_t, a sequence of digests $\vec{\mathsf{dig}} = (\mathsf{dig}_0, \ldots, \mathsf{dig}_{3r-2})$, and a sequence of verifier messages $\vec{\mathsf{vmsg}} = (\mathsf{vmsg}_1, \ldots, \mathsf{vmsg}_{3r-3})$.

Witness: A sequence of intermediate states $\vec{\mathsf{st}} = (\mathsf{st}_\tau, \ldots, \mathsf{st}_{(\lambda-1)\cdot\tau})$, and prover messages $\mathsf{Pmsg} = (\mathsf{pmsg}_{j,i})_{j \in [3r-2], i \in [\lambda]}$.

Verification: $\mathsf{Merge}(x_{\mathsf{mrg}} = (1^\lambda, r, t, M, \mathsf{hk}, \mathsf{st}_0, \mathsf{st}_t, \vec{\mathsf{dig}}, \vec{\mathsf{vmsg}}), w_{\mathsf{mrg}} = (\vec{\mathsf{st}}, \mathsf{Pmsg}))$ outputs 1 if all of the following checks pass:

1. $\mathsf{dig}_0 = \mathsf{Hash}(\mathsf{hk}, \vec{\mathsf{st}})$.
2. For each $j \in [3r-2]$, $\mathsf{dig}_j = \mathsf{Hash}(\mathsf{hk}, (\mathsf{pmsg}_{j,1}, \ldots, \mathsf{pmsg}_{j,\lambda}))$.
3. For each $i \in [\lambda - 1]$, V_{r-1} outputs 1 on common input $(1^\lambda, (M, \mathsf{st}_{(i-1)\cdot\tau}, \mathsf{st}_{i\cdot\tau}, \tau))$ given the transcript of message $(\mathsf{vmsg}_1, \mathsf{pmsg}_{1,i}, \ldots, \mathsf{vmsg}_{3r-1}, \mathsf{pmsg}_{3r-1,i})$. For $i = \lambda$, the above holds but for common input consisting of statement $(M, \mathsf{st}_{(\lambda-1)\cdot\tau}, \mathsf{st}_t, t - (\lambda - 1)\cdot\tau)$.

Fig. 1. The non-deterministic machine Merge used to verify the validity of all intermediate $\mathcal{L}_{\mathsf{Upd},\alpha}$ statements.

4.1 Construction

We construct a proof system (P, V) for $\mathcal{R}_\mathcal{U}$ satisfying the properties stated in Theorem 4.1. In the construction we make use of the update function UpdHT given in Fig. 2. At a high level, each call to UpdHT runs a step of M and updates a hash tree digest over the memory. Let α be the polynomial specifying the running time of UpdHT as a function of its state size. Our construction relies on a hash tree HT (see Theorem 2.3) and the arguments $(P_r, V_r)_{r \geq 0}$ for $\mathcal{L}_{\mathsf{Upd},\alpha}$ given by Theorem 3.2 with associated constant d.

The prover P and verifier V receive as common input the security parameter 1^λ and an instance $y = (M, x, t) \in \mathcal{L}_\mathcal{U}$. The prover additionally receives a witness w such that $(y, w) \in \mathcal{R}_\mathcal{U}$.

Let $|\mathsf{st}|$ denote the state size for UpdHT. We run the following protocol using security parameter $\lambda' := \max(\lambda, d \cdot \lceil \log(|\mathsf{UpdHT}| \cdot \alpha(|\mathsf{st}|) \cdot \log t) \rceil)$, which ensures that $(\lambda' \cdot |\mathsf{UpdHT}| \cdot \alpha(|\mathsf{st}|) \cdot t \cdot \log_{\lambda'} t)^d \leq 2^{\lambda'}$ as required for the efficiency properties of Theorem 3.2 to hold. Note that this will not effect the asymptotic succinctness or complexity-preserving properties of our protocol as $\lambda' \in O(\lambda + \log|M, x| + \log t)$. For simplicity, we simply write λ instead of λ' in the protocol description.

The proof system is defined as follows:

- V samples a hash key $\mathsf{hk} \leftarrow \mathsf{HT.KeyGen}(1^\lambda)$ and sends it to P.
- P computes $(\mathsf{tree}^{\mathsf{mem}}, \mathsf{dig}_0^{\mathsf{mem}}) = \mathsf{HT.Hash}(\mathsf{hk}, D)$, where D is the initial memory that starts with an encoding of x followed by 0s. V computes the same digest via $\mathsf{dig}_0^{\mathsf{mem}} = \mathsf{HT.Digest}(\mathsf{hk}, D)$. Both P and V set $\mathsf{st}_0 = (\mathsf{rst}_0, \mathsf{dig}_0^{\mathsf{mem}}, i_0^{\mathsf{mem}})$ where rst_0 is the initial RAM state and $i_0^{\mathsf{mem}} = 1$.

Update Function UpdHT

Hardcoded: The input machine M.

State: Each state consists of a RAM state rst, a memory hash tree digest dig^{mem}, and a memory index i^{mem}. An invalid state is indicated by $\perp$.

Witness: Each witness consists of a witness bit b^{wit}, a read memory bit b^{mem}, a memory read proof π^{mem}, a new memory digest $\text{dig}^{\text{mem}}_{\text{new}}$, and a write proof π^{wrt}.

Computation: The function $\text{UpdHT}(\text{st}, w)$ computes a new state st_{new} as follows:

1. Verify that $\text{st} \neq \perp$. Parse $\text{st} = (\text{rst}, \text{dig}^{\text{mem}}, i^{\text{mem}})$ and $w = (b^{\text{wit}}, b^{\text{mem}}, \pi^{\text{mem}}, \text{dig}^{\text{mem}}_{\text{new}}, \pi^{\text{wrt}})$.
2. Verify that $\text{HT.VerRead}(\text{dig}^{\text{mem}}, i^{\text{mem}}, b^{\text{mem}}, \pi^{\text{mem}}) = 1$.
3. Compute $(\text{rst}_{\text{new}}, i^{\text{mem}}_{\text{new}}, i^{\text{wrt}}, b^{\text{wrt}}, i^{\text{wit}}_{\text{new}}) = \text{step}(M, \text{rst}, b^{\text{mem}}, b^{\text{wit}})$.
4. If $i^{\text{wrt}} = \perp$, verify that $\text{dig}^{\text{mem}}_{\text{new}} = \text{dig}^{\text{mem}}$ and $\pi^{\text{wrt}} = \perp$. Otherwise, verify that $\text{HT.VerWrite}(\text{dig}^{\text{mem}}, i^{\text{wrt}}, b^{\text{wrt}}, \text{dig}^{\text{mem}}_{\text{new}}, \pi^{\text{wrt}}) = 1$.
5. If all verifications pass, output $\text{st}_{\text{new}} = (\text{rst}_{\text{new}}, \text{dig}^{\text{mem}}_{\text{new}}, i^{\text{mem}}_{\text{new}})$. Otherwise, output $\text{st}_{\text{new}} = \perp$.

Fig. 2. The update function UpdHT for proving the correctness of non-deterministic RAM computation in small state using a hash tree HT.

- For $j = 1, \ldots, t$, P computes the next state st_j and witness wit_j given the current state st_{j-1} as follows:
  1. Let $\text{st}_{j-1} = (\text{rst}_{j-1}, \text{dig}^{\text{mem}}_{j-1}, i^{\text{mem}}_{j-1})$.
  2. Compute $(b^{\text{mem}}_{j-1}, \cdot) = \text{HT.Read}^{\text{tree}^{\text{mem}}}(i^{\text{mem}}_{j-1})$.
  3. Compute $(\text{rst}_j, i^{\text{mem}}_j, i^{\text{wrt}}_j, b^{\text{wrt}}_j, i^{\text{wit}}_j) = \text{step}(M, \text{rst}_{j-1}, b^{\text{mem}}_{j-1}, w[i^{\text{wit}}_{j-1}])$.
  4. If $i^{\text{wrt}}_j = \perp$, set $\text{dig}^{\text{mem}}_j = \text{dig}^{\text{mem}}_{j-1}$ and $\pi^{\text{wrt}}_j = \perp$. Otherwise, set $(\text{dig}^{\text{mem}}_j, \cdot) = \text{HT.Write}^{\text{tree}^{\text{mem}}}(i^{\text{wrt}}_j, b^{\text{wrt}}_j)$.
  5. P saves $\text{st}_j = (\text{rst}_j, \text{dig}^{\text{mem}}_j, i^{\text{mem}}_j)$ for the next iteration and erases st_{j-1} and all other working memory aside from its inputs and tree^{mem}.

P sends st_t to V and erases all of its working memory other than its inputs.

- Let $r = \lceil \log_\lambda t \rceil$. P and V emulate P_r and V_r, respectively, in the interaction

$$\langle P_r(\text{wit}_1, \ldots, \text{wit}_t), V_r \rangle (1^\lambda, (\text{UpdHT}, \text{st}_0, \text{st}_t, t)).$$

In order to compute each of its messages, P_r makes a single pass over the witness $(\text{wit}_1, \ldots, \text{wit}_t)$. To emulate this, P computes each message for P_r as follows:

- Compute $(\text{tree}^{\text{mem}}, \text{dig}^{\text{mem}}_0) = \text{HT.Hash}(\text{hk}, D)$ and initialize $\text{st}_0 = (\text{rst}_0, \text{dig}^{\text{mem}}_0, i^{\text{mem}}_0)$.
- For $j = 1, \ldots, t$, P does the following:

1. Let $\mathsf{st}_{j-1} = (\mathsf{rst}_{j-1}, \mathsf{dig}_{j-1}^{\mathsf{mem}}, i_{j-1}^{\mathsf{mem}})$.
2. Compute $(b_{j-1}^{\mathsf{mem}}, \pi_{j-1}^{\mathsf{mem}}) = \mathsf{HT.Read}^{\mathsf{tree}^{\mathsf{mem}}}(i_{j-1}^{\mathsf{mem}})$.
3. Compute $(\mathsf{rst}_j, i_j^{\mathsf{mem}}, i_j^{\mathsf{wrt}}, b_j^{\mathsf{wrt}}, i^{\mathsf{wit}}) = \mathsf{step}(M, \mathsf{rst}_{j-1}, b_{j-1}^{\mathsf{mem}}, w[i_{j-1}^{\mathsf{wit}}])$.
4. If $i_j^{\mathsf{wrt}} = \bot$, set $\mathsf{dig}_j^{\mathsf{mem}} = \mathsf{dig}_{j-1}^{\mathsf{mem}}$ and $\pi_j^{\mathsf{wrt}} = \bot$. Otherwise, set $(\mathsf{dig}_j^{\mathsf{mem}}, \pi_j^{\mathsf{wrt}}) = \mathsf{HT.Write}^{\mathsf{tree}^{\mathsf{mem}}}(i_j^{\mathsf{wrt}}, b_j^{\mathsf{wrt}})$.
5. P saves $\mathsf{st}_j = (\mathsf{rst}_j, \mathsf{dig}_j^{\mathsf{mem}}, i_j^{\mathsf{mem}})$ and witness $\mathsf{wit}_j = (w[i_{j-1}^{\mathsf{wit}}], b_{j-1}^{\mathsf{mem}}, \pi_{j-1}^{\mathsf{mem}}, \mathsf{dig}_j^{\mathsf{mem}}, \pi_j^{\mathsf{wrt}})$ and erases st_{j-1} and all other working memory aside from its inputs and $\mathsf{tree}^{\mathsf{mem}}$.
6. P emulates P_r providing access to wit_j until P_r reads from the next witness wit_{j+1}, at which point P erases wit_j and continues in the loop in order to compute wit_{j+1}.

- Once P_r has computed its next message, P sends it to V and erases all of its working memory other than its inputs.

To emulate V_r, V simply needs to run its code given the transcript of messages from P. At the end of the emulated interaction, V outputs 1 if rst_t corresponds to an accepting state and V_r outputs 1.

Acknowledgments. Cody Freitag is supported by a Khoury College Distinguished Postdoctoral Fellowship. His work was partially done while at Cornell Tech and Boston University, and he is supported in part by the NSF Graduate Research Fellowship under Grant No. DGE-2139899, DARPA Award HR00110C0086, AFOSR Award FA9550-18-1-0267, NSF CNS-2128519, and DARPA under Agreement No. HR00112020023.

Omer Paneth is a member of the Checkpoint Institute of Information Security and is supported by an Azrieli Faculty Fellowship, Len Blavatnik and the Blavatnik Foundation and ISF grant 1789/19. Supported in part by AFOSR Award FA9550-23-1-0312. Any opinions, findings and conclusions or recommendations expressed in this material are those of the author(s) and do not necessarily reflect the views of the United States Government or AFOSR.

Rafael Pass is supported in part by AFOSR Awards FA9550-18-1-0267, FA9550-23-1-0387, FA9550-23-1-0312, ISF Grant No. 2338/23 and an Algorand Foundation award. This material is based upon work supported by DARPA under Agreement No. HR00110C0086. Any opinions, findings and conclusions or recommendations expressed in this material are those of the author(s) and do not necessarily reflect the views of the United States Government, DARPA, AFOSR or the Algorand Foundation.

References

1. Ames, S., Hazay, C., Ishai, Y., Venkitasubramaniam, M.: Ligero: lightweight sublinear arguments without a trusted setup. In: CCS, pp. 2087–2104. ACM (2017)
2. Babai, L., Fortnow, L., Levin, L.A., Szegedy, M.: Checking computations in polylogarithmic time. In: Proceedings of the 23rd Annual ACM Symposium on Theory of Computing, STOC, pp. 21–31 (1991)
3. Badrinarayanan, S., Kalai, Y.T., Khurana, D., Sahai, A., Wichs, D.: Succinct delegation for low-space non-deterministic computation. In: STOC, pp. 709–721. ACM (2018)

4. Bangalore, L., Bhadauria, R., Hazay, C., Venkitasubramaniam, M.: On black-box constructions of time and space efficient sublinear arguments from symmetric-key primitives. In: Kiltz, E., Vaikuntanathan, V. (eds.) TCC 2022. LNCS, vol. 13747, pp. 417–446. Springer, Cham (2022). https://doi.org/10.1007/978-3-031-22318-1_15

5. Barak, B.: How to go beyond the black-box simulation barrier. In: 42nd Annual Symposium on Foundations of Computer Science, FOCS, pp. 106–115 (2001)

6. Barak, B., Goldreich, O.: Universal arguments and their applications. SIAM J. Comput. **38**(5), 1661–1694 (2008)

7. Bellare, M., Goldreich, O.: On defining proofs of knowledge. In: Brickell, E.F. (ed.) CRYPTO 1992. LNCS, vol. 740, pp. 390–420. Springer, Heidelberg (1993). https://doi.org/10.1007/3-540-48071-4_28

8. Ben-Or, M., et al.: Everything provable is provable in zero-knowledge. In: Goldwasser, S. (ed.) CRYPTO 1988. LNCS, vol. 403, pp. 37–56. Springer, New York (1990). https://doi.org/10.1007/0-387-34799-2_4

9. Ben-Or, M., Goldwasser, S., Kilian, J., Wigderson, A.: Multi-prover interactive proofs: how to remove intractability assumptions. In: STOC, pp. 113–131. ACM (1988)

10. Ben-Sasson, E., Bentov, I., Horesh, Y., Riabzev, M.: Fast Reed-Solomon interactive oracle proofs of proximity. In: Chatzigiannakis, I., Kaklamanis, C., Marx, D., Sannella, D. (eds.) 45th International Colloquium on Automata, Languages, and Programming, ICALP 2018, Prague, Czech Republic, 9–13 July 2018. LIPIcs, vol. 107, pp. 14:1–14:17. Schloss Dagstuhl - Leibniz-Zentrum für Informatik (2018). https://doi.org/10.4230/LIPIcs.ICALP.2018.14

11. Ben-Sasson, E., Bentov, I., Horesh, Y., Riabzev, M.: Scalable zero knowledge with no trusted setup. In: Boldyreva, A., Micciancio, D. (eds.) CRYPTO 2019. LNCS, vol. 11694, pp. 701–732. Springer, Cham (2019). https://doi.org/10.1007/978-3-030-26954-8_23

12. Ben-Sasson, E., Chiesa, A., Gabizon, A., Riabzev, M., Spooner, N.: Interactive oracle proofs with constant rate and query complexity. In: ICALP. LIPIcs, vol. 80, pp. 40:1–40:15. Schloss Dagstuhl - Leibniz-Zentrum für Informatik (2017)

13. Ben-Sasson, E., Chiesa, A., Genkin, D., Tromer, E.: On the concrete efficiency of probabilistically-checkable proofs. In: Boneh, D., Roughgarden, T., Feigenbaum, J. (eds.) Symposium on Theory of Computing Conference, STOC 2013, Palo Alto, CA, USA, 1–4 June 2013, pp. 585–594. ACM (2013). https://doi.org/10.1145/2488608.2488681

14. Ben-Sasson, E., Chiesa, A., Spooner, N.: Interactive oracle proofs. In: Hirt, M., Smith, A. (eds.) TCC 2016. LNCS, vol. 9986, pp. 31–60. Springer, Heidelberg (2016). https://doi.org/10.1007/978-3-662-53644-5_2

15. Ben-Sasson, E., Goldreich, O., Harsha, P., Sudan, M., Vadhan, S.P.: Short PCPs verifiable in polylogarithmic time. In: 20th Annual IEEE Conference on Computational Complexity (CCC 2005), San Jose, CA, USA, 11–15 June 2005, pp. 120–134. IEEE Computer Society (2005). https://doi.org/10.1109/CCC.2005.27

16. Ben-Sasson, E., Kaplan, Y., Kopparty, S., Meir, O., Stichtenoth, H.: Constant rate PCPs for circuit-sat with sublinear query complexity. J. ACM **63**(4), 32:1–32:57 (2016)

17. Ben-Sasson, E., Sudan, M.: Short PCPs with polylog query complexity. SIAM J. Comput. **38**(2), 551–607 (2008)

18. Bitansky, N., et al.: The hunting of the SNARK. J. Cryptol. **30**(4), 989–1066 (2017)

19. Bitansky, N., Canetti, R., Chiesa, A., Tromer, E.: Recursive composition and bootstrapping for SNARKS and proof-carrying data. In: Boneh, D., Roughgarden, T., Feigenbaum, J. (eds.) Symposium on Theory of Computing Conference, STOC 2013, Palo Alto, CA, USA, 1–4 June 2013, pp. 111–120. ACM (2013). https://doi.org/10.1145/2488608.2488623

20. Bitansky, N., Canetti, R., Paneth, O., Rosen, A.: On the existence of extractable one-way functions. SIAM J. Comput. **45**(5), 1910–1952 (2016)

21. Bitansky, N., Chiesa, A.: Succinct arguments from multi-prover interactive proofs and their efficiency benefits. In: Safavi-Naini, R., Canetti, R. (eds.) CRYPTO 2012. LNCS, vol. 7417, pp. 255–272. Springer, Heidelberg (2012). https://doi.org/10.1007/978-3-642-32009-5_16

22. Bitansky, N., Chiesa, A., Ishai, Y., Paneth, O., Ostrovsky, R.: Succinct non-interactive arguments via linear interactive proofs. In: Sahai, A. (ed.) TCC 2013. LNCS, vol. 7785, pp. 315–333. Springer, Heidelberg (2013). https://doi.org/10.1007/978-3-642-36594-2_18

23. Block, A.R., Holmgren, J., Rosen, A., Rothblum, R.D., Soni, P.: Public-coin zero-knowledge arguments with (almost) minimal time and space overheads. In: Pass, R., Pietrzak, K. (eds.) TCC 2020. LNCS, vol. 12551, pp. 168–197. Springer, Cham (2020). https://doi.org/10.1007/978-3-030-64378-2_7

24. Block, A.R., Holmgren, J., Rosen, A., Rothblum, R.D., Soni, P.: Time- and space-efficient arguments from groups of unknown order. In: Malkin, T., Peikert, C. (eds.) CRYPTO 2021. LNCS, vol. 12828, pp. 123–152. Springer, Cham (2021). https://doi.org/10.1007/978-3-030-84259-8_5

25. Blumberg, A.J., Thaler, J., Vu, V., Walfish, M.: Verifiable computation using multiple provers. IACR Cryptology ePrint Archive, p. 846 (2014)

26. Boneh, D., Boyle, E., Corrigan-Gibbs, H., Gilboa, N., Ishai, Y.: Zero-knowledge proofs on secret-shared data via fully linear PCPs. In: Boldyreva, A., Micciancio, D. (eds.) CRYPTO 2019. LNCS, vol. 11694, pp. 67–97. Springer, Cham (2019). https://doi.org/10.1007/978-3-030-26954-8_3

27. Bootle, J., Cerulli, A., Chaidos, P., Groth, J., Petit, C.: Efficient zero-knowledge arguments for arithmetic circuits in the discrete log setting. In: Fischlin, M., Coron, J.-S. (eds.) EUROCRYPT 2016. LNCS, vol. 9666, pp. 327–357. Springer, Heidelberg (2016). https://doi.org/10.1007/978-3-662-49896-5_12

28. Boyle, E., Pass, R.: Limits of extractability assumptions with distributional auxiliary input. In: Iwata, T., Cheon, J.H. (eds.) ASIACRYPT 2015. LNCS, vol. 9453, pp. 236–261. Springer, Heidelberg (2015). https://doi.org/10.1007/978-3-662-48800-3_10

29. Brakerski, Z., Brodsky, M.F., Kalai, Y.T., Lombardi, A., Paneth, O.: SNARGs for monotone policy batch NP. In: Handschuh, H., Lysyanskaya, A. (eds.) CRYPTO 2023. LNCS, vol. 14082, pp. 252–283. Springer, Cham (2023). https://doi.org/10.1007/978-3-031-38545-2_9

30. Brakerski, Z., Holmgren, J., Kalai, Y.T.: Non-interactive delegation and batch NP verification from standard computational assumptions. In: STOC, pp. 474–482. ACM (2017)

31. Bünz, B., Bootle, J., Boneh, D., Poelstra, A., Wuille, P., Maxwell, G.: Bulletproofs: short proofs for confidential transactions and more. In: IEEE Symposium on Security and Privacy, pp. 315–334. IEEE Computer Society (2018)

32. Bünz, B., Fisch, B., Szepieniec, A.: Transparent SNARKs from DARK compilers. In: Canteaut, A., Ishai, Y. (eds.) EUROCRYPT 2020. LNCS, vol. 12105, pp. 677–706. Springer, Cham (2020). https://doi.org/10.1007/978-3-030-45721-1_24

33. Chiesa, A., Hu, Y., Maller, M., Mishra, P., Vesely, N., Ward, N.: Marlin: preprocessing zkSNARKs with universal and updatable SRS. In: Canteaut, A., Ishai, Y. (eds.) EUROCRYPT 2020. LNCS, vol. 12105, pp. 738–768. Springer, Cham (2020). https://doi.org/10.1007/978-3-030-45721-1_26

34. Choudhuri, A.R., Garg, S., Jain, A., Jin, Z., Zhang, J.: Correlation intractability and SNARGs from sub-exponential DDH. In: Handschuh, H., Lysyanskaya, A. (eds.) CRYPTO 2023. LNCS, vol. 14084, pp. 635–668. Springer, Cham (2023). https://doi.org/10.1007/978-3-031-38551-3_20

35. Choudhuri, A.R., Jain, A., Jin, Z.: SNARGs for P from LWE. In: 62nd IEEE Annual Symposium on Foundations of Computer Science, FOCS, pp. 68–79 (2021)

36. Damgård, I.B.: A design principle for hash functions. In: Brassard, G. (ed.) CRYPTO 1989. LNCS, vol. 435, pp. 416–427. Springer, New York (1990). https://doi.org/10.1007/0-387-34805-0_39

37. Damgård, I., Fujisaki, E.: A statistically-hiding integer commitment scheme based on groups with hidden order. In: Zheng, Y. (ed.) ASIACRYPT 2002. LNCS, vol. 2501, pp. 125–142. Springer, Heidelberg (2002). https://doi.org/10.1007/3-540-36178-2_8

38. Devadas, L., Goyal, R., Kalai, Y., Vaikuntanathan, V.: Rate-1 non-interactive arguments for batch-NP and applications. In: FOCS, pp. 1057–1068. IEEE (2022)

39. Dinur, I.: The PCP theorem by gap amplification. J. ACM 54(3), 12 (2007)

40. Ephraim, N., Freitag, C., Komargodski, I., Pass, R.: SPARKs: succinct parallelizable arguments of knowledge. In: Canteaut, A., Ishai, Y. (eds.) EUROCRYPT 2020. LNCS, vol. 12105, pp. 707–737. Springer, Cham (2020). https://doi.org/10.1007/978-3-030-45721-1_25

41. Feige, U., Goldwasser, S., Lovász, L., Safra, S., Szegedy, M.: Interactive proofs and the hardness of approximating cliques. J. ACM 43(2), 268–292 (1996)

42. Fiat, A., Shamir, A.: How to prove yourself: practical solutions to identification and signature problems. In: Odlyzko, A.M. (ed.) CRYPTO 1986. LNCS, vol. 263, pp. 186–194. Springer, Heidelberg (1987). https://doi.org/10.1007/3-540-47721-7_12

43. Freitag, C., Pass, R., Sirkin, N.: Parallelizable delegation from LWE. In: Kiltz, E., Vaikuntanathan, V. (eds.) TCC 2022. LNCS, vol. 13748, pp. 623–652. Springer, Cham (2022). https://doi.org/10.1007/978-3-031-22365-5_22

44. Gabizon, A., Williamson, Z.J., Ciobotaru, O.: PLONK: permutations over Lagrange-bases for oecumenical noninteractive arguments of knowledge. IACR Cryptology ePrint Archive, p. 953 (2019)

45. Gennaro, R., Gentry, C., Parno, B., Raykova, M.: Quadratic span programs and succinct NIZKs without PCPs. In: Johansson, T., Nguyen, P.Q. (eds.) EUROCRYPT 2013. LNCS, vol. 7881, pp. 626–645. Springer, Heidelberg (2013). https://doi.org/10.1007/978-3-642-38348-9_37

46. Gentry, C., Wichs, D.: Separating succinct non-interactive arguments from all falsifiable assumptions. In: STOC, pp. 99–108. ACM (2011)

47. Goldreich, O., Krawczyk, H.: On the composition of zero-knowledge proof systems. In: International Colloquium on Automata, Languages, and Programming, ICALP, pp. 268–282 (1990)

48. Holmgren, J., Rothblum, R.: Delegating computations with (almost) minimal time and space overhead. In: FOCS, pp. 124–135. IEEE Computer Society (2018)

49. Hulett, J., Jawale, R., Khurana, D., Srinivasan, A.: SNARGs for P from Subexponential DDH and QR. In: Dunkelman, O., Dziembowski, S. (eds.) EUROCRYPT 2022. LNCS, vol. 13276, pp. 520–549. Springer, Cham (2022). https://doi.org/10.1007/978-3-031-07085-3_18

50. Impagliazzo, R.: A personal view of average-case complexity. In: Proceedings of the Tenth Annual Structure in Complexity Theory Conference, pp. 134–147. IEEE Computer Society (1995)

51. Ishai, Y., Kushilevitz, E., Ostrovsky, R.: Efficient arguments without short PCPs. In: CCC, pp. 278–291. IEEE Computer Society (2007)

52. Jawale, R., Kalai, Y.T., Khurana, D., Zhang, R.Y.: SNARGs for bounded depth computations and PPAD hardness from sub-exponential LWE. In: STOC 2021: 53rd Annual ACM SIGACT Symposium on Theory of Computing, STOC, pp. 708–721 (2021)

53. Kalai, Y., Lombardi, A., Vaikuntanathan, V., Wichs, D.: Boosting batch arguments and RAM delegation. In: STOC, pp. 1545–1552. ACM (2023)

54. Kalai, Y., Paneth, O.: Delegating RAM computations. In: Hirt, M., Smith, A. (eds.) TCC 2016. LNCS, vol. 9986, pp. 91–118. Springer, Heidelberg (2016). https://doi.org/10.1007/978-3-662-53644-5_4

55. Kalai, Y.T., Paneth, O., Yang, L.: How to delegate computations publicly. In: STOC, pp. 1115–1124. ACM (2019)

56. Kalai, Y.T., Raz, R., Rothblum, R.D.: How to delegate computations: the power of no-signaling proofs. In: STOC, pp. 485–494. ACM (2014)

57. Kate, A., Zaverucha, G.M., Goldberg, I.: Constant-size commitments to polynomials and their applications. In: Abe, M. (ed.) ASIACRYPT 2010. LNCS, vol. 6477, pp. 177–194. Springer, Heidelberg (2010). https://doi.org/10.1007/978-3-642-17373-8_11

58. Kilian, J.: A note on efficient zero-knowledge proofs and arguments (extended abstract). In: Proceedings of the 24th Annual ACM Symposium on Theory of Computing, STOC, pp. 723–732 (1992)

59. Lindell, Y.: Parallel coin-tossing and constant-round secure two-party computation. J. Cryptol. **16**(3), 143–184 (2003)

60. Maller, M., Bowe, S., Kohlweiss, M., Meiklejohn, S.: Sonic: zero-knowledge snarks from linear-size universal and updatable structured reference strings. In: CCS, pp. 2111–2128. ACM (2019)

61. Merkle, R.C.: A digital signature based on a conventional encryption function. In: Pomerance, C. (ed.) CRYPTO 1987. LNCS, vol. 293, pp. 369–378. Springer, Heidelberg (1988). https://doi.org/10.1007/3-540-48184-2_32

62. Merkle, R.C.: A certified digital signature. In: Brassard, G. (ed.) CRYPTO 1989. LNCS, vol. 435, pp. 218–238. Springer, New York (1990). https://doi.org/10.1007/0-387-34805-0_21

63. Micali, S.: CS proofs (extended abstracts). In: 35th Annual Symposium on Foundations of Computer Science, FOCS, pp. 436–453 (1994)

64. Micali, S., Pass, R.: Local zero knowledge. In: STOC, pp. 306–315. ACM (2006)

65. Mie, T.: Short PCPPs verifiable in polylogarithmic time with O(1) queries. Ann. Math. Artif. Intell. **56**(3–4), 313–338 (2009)

66. Paneth, O., Pass, R.: Incrementally verifiable computation via rate-1 batch arguments. In: FOCS, pp. 1045–1056. IEEE (2022)

67. Paneth, O., Rothblum, G.N.: On zero-testable homomorphic encryption and publicly verifiable non-interactive arguments. In: Kalai, Y., Reyzin, L. (eds.) TCC 2017. LNCS, vol. 10678, pp. 283–315. Springer, Cham (2017). https://doi.org/10.1007/978-3-319-70503-3_9

68. Reingold, O., Rothblum, G.N., Rothblum, R.D.: Constant-round interactive proofs for delegating computation. SIAM J. Comput. **50**(3) (2021)

69. Ron-Zewi, N., Rothblum, R.D.: Local proofs approaching the witness length [extended abstract]. In: FOCS, pp. 846–857. IEEE (2020)

70. Setty, S.: Spartan: efficient and general-purpose zkSNARKs without trusted setup. In: Micciancio, D., Ristenpart, T. (eds.) CRYPTO 2020. LNCS, vol. 12172, pp. 704–737. Springer, Cham (2020). https://doi.org/10.1007/978-3-030-56877-1_25

71. Simon, D.R.: Finding collisions on a one-way street: can secure hash functions be based on general assumptions? In: Nyberg, K. (ed.) EUROCRYPT 1998. LNCS, vol. 1403, pp. 334–345. Springer, Heidelberg (1998). https://doi.org/10.1007/BFb0054137

72. Szepieniec, A., Zhang, Y.: Polynomial IOPs for linear algebra relations. In: Hanaoka, G., Shikata, J., Watanabe, Y. (eds.) PKC 2022. LNCS, vol. 13177, pp. 523–552. Springer, Cham (2022). https://doi.org/10.1007/978-3-030-97121-2_19

73. Valiant, P.: Incrementally verifiable computation or proofs of knowledge imply time/space efficiency. In: Canetti, R. (ed.) TCC 2008. LNCS, vol. 4948, pp. 1–18. Springer, Heidelberg (2008). https://doi.org/10.1007/978-3-540-78524-8_1

74. Waters, B., Wu, D.J.: Batch arguments for np and more from standard bilinear group assumptions. In: Dodis, Y., Shrimpton, T. (eds.) CRYPTO 2022. LNCS, vol. 13508, pp. 433–463. Springer, Cham (2022). https://doi.org/10.1007/978-3-031-15979-4_15

Unbiasable Verifiable Random Functions

Emanuele Giunta[1,2,3(✉)] and Alistair Stewart[1]

[1] Web3 Foundation, Zug, Switzerland
{emanuele,alistair}@web3.foundation
[2] IMDEA Software Institute, Madrid, Spain
emanuele.giunta@imdea.org
[3] Universidad Politecnica de Madrid, Madrid, Spain

Abstract. Verifiable Random Functions (VRFs) play a pivotal role in Proof of Stake (PoS) blockchain due to their applications in secret leader election protocols. However, the original definition by Goldreich, Goldwasser and Micali is by itself insufficient for such applications. The primary concern is that adversaries may craft VRF key pairs with skewed output distribution, allowing them to unfairly increase their winning chances.

To address this issue David, Gaži, Kiayias and Russel (2017/573) proposed a stronger definition in the universal composability framework, while Esgin et al. (FC '21) put forward a weaker game-based one. Their proposed notions come with some limitations though. The former appears to be too strong, being seemingly impossible to instantiate without a programmable random oracle. The latter instead is not sufficient to prove security for VRF-based secret leader election schemes.

In this work we close the above gap by proposing a new security property for VRF we call *unbiasability*. On the one hand, our notion suffices to imply fairness in VRF-based leader elections protocols. On the other hand, we provide an efficient compiler in the plain model (with no CRS) transforming any VRF into an unbiasable one under standard assumptions. Moreover, we show folklore VRF constructions in the ROM to achieve our notion without the need to program the random oracle. As a minor contribution, we also provide a generic and efficient construction of certified 1 to 1 VRFs from any VRF.

1 Introduction

Verifiable Random Functions (VRF), introduced in [MRV99], are the natural extension of pseudorandom functions to the public key setting. A secret key sk is required to perform evaluations. Any users can then verify the result given the public verification key vk and an opening proof. Since their introduction VRFs have found many applications including e-lotteries [MR02, LBM20], secure DNS [GNP+14, PWH+17], and Proof of Stake blockchain [CM16, KRDO17, DGKR17, BASV23b] for secret leader elections.

The VRF definition in [MRV99] however only applies to *honestly generated* keys and offers very limited guarantees against *adversarially generated* ones.

M. Joye and G. Leander (Eds.): EUROCRYPT 2024, LNCS 14654, pp. 142–167, 2024.
https://doi.org/10.1007/978-3-031-58737-5_6

This crucially affects VRF-based leader election protocols. In that context, the winner of an election is defined as the user with the lowest VRF output on a random public input. Therefore, being able to choose a key pair with biased outputs directly translates into unfairly higher winning chances.

This issue was first acknowledged in [DGKR17] where a stronger VRF definition was given in the Universal Composability framework [Can01]. One of the requirements in their notion is that the VRF output for any key pair must match the truly random values returned by an ideal functionality. Although this entirely prevents adversaries from skewing the output distribution, their approach comes with some controversial aspects.

First of all, their notion appears to be impossible to instantiate without access to an explicitly programmable random oracle [CDG+18]. This stems from the fact that in the security proof the simulator must program the VRF output, even with maliciously generated keys, to match the truly random output given by the ideal functionality. Note that on the contrary, VRFs are known to exist in the plain model. Secondly, due to the very high level of technical details in the original definitions of UC-VRF, it is not clear what are the exact security guarantees it implies, besides being sufficient for PoS-blockchain applications. The high level of complexity is further highlighted by subsequent revisions [BGK+18,BGQR22] proposing fixes to overlooked corner cases.

An alternative game-based definition was later proposed in [EKS+21]. Although their notion can be achieved in the plain model, it appears to be insufficient for applications for two main reasons. First of all, it does not keep adversaries from biasing some bits of the output, as we show later. Secondly, it does not prevent adversaries to maliciously create several VRF keys returning correlated outputs, also leading to attacks in VRF-based election protocols.

Given the current state of the art, we ask whether it is possible to provide a simple security notion that simultaneously can be obtained in the plain model and suffices to imply security in current applications.

Our Results. In this work we close the aforementioned foundational gap by proposing a game-based security property we call *unbiasability*. Informally, we say VRF is unbiasable if no adversary can find a set of VRF keys whose outputs on random inputs significantly bias an adversarially chosen predicate p. To provide evidence that our notion does indeed fill the above gap we

1. Prove it to imply desirable properties. In particular we show that assuming an adversary to always return correct VRF evaluations, unbiasability implies the output distribution to be computationally close to uniform on random inputs. Our notion also implies the weaker one proposed in [EKS+21].
2. Prove that folklore constructions in the ROM from a verifiable unpredictable function (VUF) satisfy our notion. This notably includes ECVRF [PWH+17] currently part of the standardization effort in [GRPV23].
3. Provide two compilers transforming any VRF into an unbiasable VRF in the plain model. Our most efficient construction only requires one VRF evaluation

and is proven secure assuming DDH and a PRF's pseudorandomness hold against adversaries with exponential-time preprocessing[1].

4. Observe it to immediately imply fairness in VRF-based leader election for PoS-blockchain application. In other words, no adversary can win any random election with probability significantly higher than prescribed.

As a minor contribution of independent interest we also construct generically a certified 1 to 1 VRF, which we call *Verifiable Random Bijection* (VRB), from any VRF. This is efficient, requiring only two VRF evaluations, and security just relies on the VRF security and hardness of the discrete logarithm problem.

Technical Overview. We now provide a more detailed overview of our definition, starting from the weaker notion introduced in [EKS+21], and later summarize the constructions we provide and study.

Defining Unbiasability. Our starting point to define a strong unbiasability property is the definition provided in [EKS+21] (Sect. 2.1). There, an adversary is asked initially to generate a verification key vk and guess the final VRF output y^*. Later, on input a random value x, the adversary is asked to provide a tuple (y, π). If π is a valid proof for y and $y = y^*$ it wins the game. According to their notion a VRF is unbiasable if any adversary cannot win with probability significantly higher than randomly guessing y.

Although we see this definition as a step in the right direction, it comes with two limitations. First of all, even if the adversary is unable to guess correctly the output consistently, it may still be able to bias some bits. Secondly, this definition fails to exclude VRFs in which several keys can be crafted to return correlated outputs, although individual values are hard to bias. Such weakness could be exploited in VRF-based leader election by several corrupted users to ensure at least one VRF value is always small enough, allowing them to win VRF-based elections unfairly more than honest users.

To circumvent such limitations, we modify their game as follows: first the adversary chooses several verification keys $vk_1, \ldots, vk_n$ and a predicate p with certain properties (which we clarify later). Next, on random inputs $x_1, \ldots, x_m$, the adversary returns a vector $\mathbf{y}$ containing the evaluation of each VRF of its choice on all provided inputs, along with evaluation proofs. Those values in $\mathbf{y}$ whose proof is incorrect are overwritten with $\bot$. Finally the adversary wins if $p(\mathbf{y})$ is true significantly more often than $p(\mathbf{z})$ for a uniformly sampled $\mathbf{z}$.

If we were to allow all predicates p, our game would have a trivial attack: simply choosing p to be 1 if and only if the given vector contains at least one erased value $\bot$ and then, once asked to evaluate the VRF, producing incorrect opening proofs. Note that we sample entries of $\mathbf{z}$ from the output space, meaning they will never be equal to $\bot$. This attack however appears to be orthogonal to

---

[1] More precisely we will only assume the preprocessing to be capable of solving the discrete logarithm problem, something that can be also achieved in quantum probabilistic polynomial time [Sho94].

the attempt of biasing the output, and rather comes from the fact adversaries can always decide not to evaluate their VRF. We therefore factor this classes of attacks out of our definition by only considering predicates in which erasing any entry of a vector $\mathbf{y}$ can never turn the output from *false* to *true*. We call those predicates *monotone*. Restricting p to be monotone essentially means that an adversary cannot gain any advantage from producing incorrect evaluations.

Constructions in the ROM. In the random oracle model we study two folklore transformation of any VUF into a VRF. The first one is defined by hashing the VUF output salted with the input and the VUF verification key. In other words an evaluation on x is defined as $\mathsf{H}(\mathsf{vk}, x, y)$ where vk is the VUF verification key and y, π the VUF output on input x. We show this to be unbiasable information theoretically when H is a Random Oracle.

In order to capture also ECVRF [PWH+17], we extend our analysis to a weaker VUF to VRF transformation in which the output is simply defined as $\mathsf{H}(y)$ with y being the VUF output. We observe that in general the resulting VRF may not be unbiasable due to corner cases in which for instance, there may be a weak verification key defining a constant function or two distinct keys defining identical functions. Nevertheless we still prove security under mild collision-resistance assumptions, which are satisfied by the VUF underlying ECVRF.

Constructions in the Plain Model. Next we provide two compilers transforming any VRF into an unbiasable VRF without relying on a CRS nor the ROM. We opt for a modular approach and describe our transformation in two steps: First we transform any VRF into one achieving a weaker notion of pseudorandomness and unbiasability, where the latter holds information theoretically. More in details the above properties are weakened as follows:

- *Pseudorandomness*: Inputs are of the form (x_0, x_1) and security holds if the VRF is never evaluated on different points with the same first entry.
- *Unbiasability*: For each verification key vk_i, the challenger asks for evaluations on a set of freshly sampled points $x_{i,1}, \ldots, x_{i,m}$, as opposed to asking evaluations for all keys on the same set of points.

We then provide a second compiler turning any VRF with the above properties into fully fledged unbiasable VRF.

Padded VRF. Focusing on VRFs which only satisfy our weaker properties greatly simplifies our problem. This is exemplified by our first construction, the *padded VRF*: given a VRF $F_{\mathsf{sk}}(\cdot)$ it is defined as

$$\overline{F}_{\mathsf{sk}}(u, v) = F_{\mathsf{sk}}(u) \oplus v.$$

Pseudorandomness holds as long as no adversary can query the same u twice. Moreover, on uniformly random inputs (u, v) the output will also be random thanks to v, no matter how skewed the distribution of $F_{\mathsf{sk}}(u)$ ends up being, which we use to show unbiasability. Note that if the VRF returns values in a group $(\mathbb{G}, +)$, the xor operator can be replaced with the group addition up to assuming $v \in \mathbb{G}$.

2 Round Feistel. Another approach to achieve this weaker notion of unbiasability unconditionally is to guarantee the resulting VRF is 1 to 1. We call such VRF a Verifiable Random Bijection and show that they satisfy unbiasability (with independently sampled points for each key) information theoretically, because bijections preserve the input distribution. In order to realize VRF with this property we observe that 2 Feistel Round [LR88] suffices. The construction is schematized in Fig. 1 assuming the VRF has output values in a group $(\mathbb{G}, +)$.

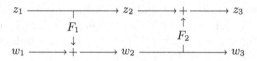

Fig. 1. 2-Feistel Rounds with $F_i(\cdot) = \mathsf{VRF.Eval}(\mathsf{sk}_i, \cdot)$ and output space a group $(\mathbb{G}, +)$.

The reason why two rounds are sufficient as opposed to three or more is that at this stage we only target the weaker pseudorandomness notion, where the VRF is never evaluated on different points with the same first entry z_1.

VRB Compiler. As warm up toward our final compiler, we start with a simpler problem: how can we improve the 2-Feistel Round construction to achieve pseudorandomness? Our approach to this problem is to compose the 2-Feistel Round scheme with a (publicly computable) function ϕ_h, i.e. obtaining $F_{\mathsf{sk}} \circ \phi_h(x)$, and then study what properties should ϕ satisfy.

First of all, we need the composed function to remain 1 to 1 for any key choice. Thus ϕ_h has to be a certified bijection[2]. For pseudorandomness instead, recall that F_{sk} achieves it as long as it is never evaluated on two different inputs with the same first component. A way to enforce this is assuming ϕ_h to be collision resistant in the first component.

The last step is finding a map satisfying the above properties. Our solution is based on a group $\mathbb{G}$ of prime order q where the discrete logarithm problem (DLP) is hard.

$$h = [a_1, a_2] \in \mathbb{G}^2 \qquad \phi_h : \mathbb{F}_q^2 \to \mathbb{G}^2 \ : \ \phi_h(x_1, x_2) = \begin{bmatrix} a_1 & a_2 \\ 1 & 0 \end{bmatrix} \cdot \begin{pmatrix} x_1 \\ x_2 \end{pmatrix}$$

where we denote $[a] = a \cdot G$, with G being the group generator. Because ϕ_h in the first component is a Pedersen commitment to $x = (x_1, x_2)$, it is collision resistant if a_1, a_2 are sampled uniformly and the DLP is hard. Conversely, even when ϕ_h is created adversarially, it suffice to check $a_2 \neq 0$ to verify that ϕ_h defines a 1 to 1 map.

---

[2] In other words, deciding whether ϕ_h is a bijection can be done in polynomial time.

Final Compiler. Our final problem is to compile any VRF $F_{\sf sk}$ with the weaker pseudorandomness and unbiasability properties defined above to a fully fledged unbiasable VRF.

As before, pseudorandomness can be achieved composing $F_{\sf sk} \circ \phi_h$ with a slightly more generalized ϕ_h defined as

$$h = ([{\bf a}], {\bf b}) \qquad \phi_h : \mathbb{F}_q^\mu \to \mathbb{G}^2 \ : \ \phi_h({\bf v}) = \left([{\bf a}^\top {\bf v}], [{\bf b}^\top {\bf v}]\right).$$

which can be publicly checked to be surjective and, for uniformly sampled ${\bf a}$, is collision resistant in the first component if DLP is hard. The technical challenge is enhancing unbiasability. Our (stronger) definition requires the output to be unbiasable even when multiple verification keys are evaluated on the same (random) input. However $F_{\sf sk}$ is guaranteed to be unbiasable only when we evaluate different verification keys on independently sampled points.

To eventually reduce security to this weaker property we need a mechanism to expand a random input x into several (random-looking) ones $x_1, \ldots, x_m$ to later evaluate the VRF with key vk_i on input x_i. A first attempt to do so is through a PRF f: we interpret the input as a PRF key k and evaluate each VRF on $f_k(\mathsf{vk})$. However the map $k \mapsto f_k(\mathsf{vk})$ may not be collision resistant and finding collisions would allow breaking pseudorandomness. Conversely, the map $k \mapsto (k, f_k(\mathsf{vk}))$ is injective, but since $F_{\sf sk} \circ \phi_h$ would also receive the PRF key as input in this case, we cannot argue that $f_k(\mathsf{vk})$ is pseudorandom anymore.

Our final solution is to provide $f_k(\mathsf{vk})$ along with a perfectly binding commitment to k (in our case, ElGamal). More specifically we will interpret a VRF input x as a tuple $({\bf r}, k, {\sf pp}, \rho)$ and define

$$\mathsf{Encode}({\bf r}, k, {\sf pp}, \rho, \mathsf{vk}) \ = \ ({\bf r}, f_k(\mathsf{vk}), {\sf pp}, \mathsf{Com}_{\sf pp}(k; \rho))$$

which, using ElGamal, is injective and does not leak any knowledge about k. The elements ${\bf r}$ are included for technical reasons, namely because in the proof of unbiasability we need ϕ_h to be a chameleon hash function [KR98] in the first output component. We finally show $F_{\sf sk} \circ \phi_h \circ \mathsf{Encode}$ to be an unbiasable VRF.

Related Work. The study of VRF, initiated by Goldreich, Goldwasser and Micali [GGM86], is an active area of research in cryptography. Several constructions have been proposed over the years based on (the list is not exhaustive) generic VUF [MRV99], identity-based KEM [ACF09], pairing groups [HW10, BMR10, HJ16, Koh19], lattices [EKS+21, ESLR22] and isogenies [Lai23].

VRF satisfying extra properties have also been introduced and studied. Most notably simulatable VRFs [CL07] where opening proofs can be simulated given a trapdoor key. Constrained VRFs [Fuc14], which allow leaking a constrained secret key to perform evaluation only over a given subset. Ring VRFs [BASV23a], which allow evaluating a VRF anonymously among a ring of users. As the original definition however, they do not imply any form of security for maliciously chosen keys. More related to our work, the notion of UC-VRF [DGKR17, BGK+18, BGQR22] and "unbiasability" in [EKS+21], both address security under maliciously chosen keys, albeit with the aforementioned limitations. Orthogonally, distributed VRF [GLOW21] prevent maliciously generated keys by producing and storing them in a distributed fashion. However, while useful for random beacons [CD17, CD20], distributed VRFs do not appear suited for applications such as leader election, where parties may dynamically join and leave, and need to evaluate the VRF frequently and privately.

Finally, the issue of adversaries generating biased VRF keys was also noted in [BGRV09] while instantiating the hidden-bit model [FLS90] from weak-VRF. The issue was however addressed as in [BY96] for the specific application, without providing a general security notion.

2   Preliminaries

2.1   Notation

λ denotes the security parameter. A function $\varepsilon(\lambda)$ is negligible if it approaches 0 faster than the inverse of any polynomial in λ. $[n] = \{1, \ldots, n\}$. Whenever unspecified, we assume all Turing machines (including security games) in this paper to take as first input 1^λ. Given a set X, $x \xleftarrow{\$} X$ means x is sampled uniformly in X. We denote a random variable x uniformly distributed in X with $x \sim U(X)$. $\Delta(x, y)$ is the statistical distance between x and y. For a Probabilistic Turing Machine $\mathcal{A}$ we write $y \xleftarrow{\$} \mathcal{A}(x)$ to denote that y is the output of $\mathcal{A}$ on input x. $\mathbb{F}_q$ is the field of integers modulo q with q a prime number. Given $\mathbf{a}, \mathbf{b} \in \mathbb{F}_q^n$, then $\mathbf{a}^\top \mathbf{b}$ is their inner product. We write groups $(\mathbb{G}, +)$ in additive notation and, in a prime order group with a canonical generator G we denote $[a] = a \cdot G$.

2.2   Preprocessing Adversaries

Many computationally hard problems are often defined in terms of interactive games, where the adversary is asked to solve a given problem efficiently. These however typically fail to capture real adversaries which may have performed an inefficient *preprocessing* before approaching the problem. A way to model such attacks is through *non-uniform* adversaries, which initially receive a polynomially bounded advice that is a *function* of the security parameter only[3]. In this section, in order to later state more fine-grained computational assumptions, we give an explicit definition for preprocessing adversary. In particular the following notion allow us to specify the computational class C of the preprocessing algorithm.

Definition 1. *Given a computational class* C, *we say an algorithm* $\mathcal{A}$ *to be* PPT *with* C *preprocessing if there exists* $(\mathcal{A}_0, \mathcal{A}_1)$ *with* $\mathcal{A}_0$ *in* C *returning a polynomially bounded output and* $\mathcal{A}_1$ PPT, *such that*

$$\mathcal{A}(1^\lambda, \mathsf{input}) = \mathcal{A}_1(1^\lambda, \mathsf{input}, \mathcal{A}_0(1^\lambda)).$$

---

[3] This means that the advice may not even be *computable* by Turing Machines.

2.3   Discrete Logarithm Problem and DDH

Given a prime order group $(\mathbb{G}, +)$ with generator G, the discrete logarithm assumption state that any PPT adversary, given xG with $x \sim U(\mathbb{F}_q)$ can retrieve x only with negligible probability. The Decisional Diffie-Hellman assumption instead, state that (G, xG, yG, xyG) is computationally indistinguishable from (G, xG, yG, zG) with $x, y, z \sim U(\mathbb{F}_q)$ for any PPT adversary.

In our constructions we will sometime base security on mildly stronger assumption, requiring that both DLP and DDH are hard even if some preprocessing occurred. More concretely, we will assume this preprocessing to occur in PPT time but with oracle access to a Discrete Logarithm solver. More formally, to make use of the Definition 1, let us call $\mathsf{PPT}^{\mathsf{DL}}$ the class of PPT algorithms $\mathcal{A}^{\mathsf{DL}}$ where for all $H \in \mathbb{G}$, $\mathsf{DL}(H) = x$ with $H = xG$.

Definition 2. *Given a group* $\mathbb{G}$ *with generator* G *we say that* DLPrep-DLP *is hard if for any* PPT *adversary with* $\mathsf{PPT}^{\mathsf{DL}}$*-preprocessing, given* $x \sim U(\mathbb{F}_q)$ *there exists a negligible* $\varepsilon(\lambda)$ *such that*

$$\mathsf{Adv}(\mathcal{A}) := \Pr\left[\mathcal{A}(1^\lambda, G, xG) \to x\right] \leq \varepsilon(\lambda).$$

Definition 3. *Given a group* $\mathcal{G}$ *with generator* g *we say that* DLPrep-DDH *is hard if for any* PPT *adversary with* $\mathsf{PPT}^{\mathsf{DL}}$*-preprocessing, given* $x, y, z \sim U(\mathbb{F}_q)$ *there exists a negligible* $\varepsilon(\lambda)$ *such that*

$$\mathsf{Adv}(\mathcal{A}) := \left|\Pr\left[\mathcal{A}(1^\lambda, xG, yG, xyG) \to 1\right] - \Pr\left[\mathcal{A}(1^\lambda, xG, yG, zG) \to 1\right]\right| \leq \varepsilon(\lambda).$$

To justify the plausibility of these assumptions we refer to [CK18] where the security of the DLP and DDH is studied in the Generic Group Model with preprocessing. Their results imply that with any polynomially bounded length advice (potentially computed in unbounded time), the DLP only loses $\log(\lambda)$ bit of security with respect to the non-preprocessing DLP. DDH with unbounded preprocessing time instead suffers a quadratic loss, or in other words, loses half of its security bits.

We remark that problems proved hard in the GGM are plausibly as hard in groups where generic attacks are also the best known so far. Furthermore, we stress that our assumptions are significantly milder as we only assume the preprocessing capable of breaking DLP (as opposed to being computationally unbounded). Finally, note that in the algebraic group model [FKL18], DLPrep-DLP and DLPrep-DDH reduces both respectively to DLP and DDH without any security loss, as the preprocessing already knows the discrete logarithm of queried group elements.

Certified Groups. As a technical detail we note that all our constructions require the group to be *certified* [HJ16]. This means that even when the group parameters are chosen adversarially, it is possible to verify it has the claimed prime order, and membership test and group additions are guaranteed to be efficient.

2.4   Pseudo Random Functions

We recall the definition of pseudo random function (PRF) [GGM86], that is a couple of algorithm $(\mathsf{PRF.Gen}, f)$, along with a key space $\mathcal{K}$ an input space $\mathcal{X}$ and an output space $\mathcal{Y}$ such that

- $k \leftarrow^{\$} \mathsf{PRF.Gen}(1^{\lambda})$ generates a secret key $k \in \mathcal{K}$
- $f : \mathcal{K} \times \mathcal{X} \rightarrow \mathcal{Y}$ is a keyed function family.

The main security property of PRFs is pseudorandomness, defined as follows (Fig. 2):

Definition 4. *A couple of* PPT *algorithms* $(\mathsf{PRF.Gen}, f)$ *is called a Pseudo Random Function if, for any* PPT *adversary there exists a negligible function* ε *such that*

$$\mathsf{Adv}(\mathcal{A}) := \left| \Pr\left[\mathsf{Exp}^{\mathsf{prf}}(\mathcal{A}) = 1 \right] - \frac{1}{2} \right| \leq \varepsilon(\lambda).$$

$\mathsf{Exp}^{\mathsf{prf}}(\mathcal{A})$	$\mathcal{O}_{\mathsf{prf}}(x)$
1 : $b \leftarrow^{\$} \{0,1\}$	1 : **If** $b = 1$:
2 : Sample $k \leftarrow^{\$} \mathsf{PRF.Gen}(1^{\lambda})$	2 : **Return** $f_k(x)$
3 : Sample $f^* \leftarrow^{\$} \{g \; : \; g : \mathcal{X} \rightarrow \mathcal{Y}\}$	3 : **Else:**
4 : Run $b' \leftarrow \mathcal{A}^{\mathcal{O}_{\mathsf{prf}}}(1^{\lambda})$	4 : **Return** $f^*(x)$
5 : **Return** $b == b'$	

Fig. 2. The pseudorandomness game with adversary $\mathcal{A}$ and PRF $(\mathsf{PRF.Gen}, f)$.

2.5   Verifiable Random Functions

Here we recall the definition of VRF, originally introduced in [MRV99], following the terminology of [Lys02, HJ16].

Definition 5. *A Verifiable Random Function is a triplet of* PPT *algorithms* $(\mathsf{VRF.Gen}, \mathsf{VRF.Eval}, \mathsf{VRF.Vfy})$ *satisfying:*

1. **Correctness.** *For any* $(\mathsf{vk}, \mathsf{sk})$ *in the image of* $\mathsf{VRF.Gen}(1^{\lambda})$ *and any* $x \in \mathcal{X}$

$$(y, \pi) \leftarrow \mathsf{VRF.Eval}(\mathsf{sk}, x) \quad \Rightarrow \quad \mathsf{VRF.Vfy}(\mathsf{vk}, x, y, \pi) \rightarrow 1.$$

2. **Unique Provability.** *For any* vk *(not necessarily in the range of* $\mathsf{VRF.Gen})$, *any input* $x \in \mathcal{X}$ *pair of outputs* $y_0, y_1 \in \mathcal{Y}$ *and pair of proofs* π_0, π_1 *it holds that*

$$\mathsf{VRF.Vfy}(\mathsf{vk}, x, y_0, \pi_0) \rightarrow 1, \quad \mathsf{VRF.Vfy}(\mathsf{vk}, x, y_1, \pi_1) \rightarrow 1 \quad \Rightarrow \quad y_0 = y_1.$$

3. **Pseudorandomness.** *For any* PPT *adversary* $\mathcal{A}$ *executed in experiment 3 there exists a negligible function* ε *such that*

$$\mathsf{Adv}(\mathcal{A}) = \left| \Pr\left[\mathsf{Exp}^{\mathsf{rnd}}(\mathcal{A}) \rightarrow 1 \right] - \frac{1}{2} \right| \leq \varepsilon(\lambda).$$

$\mathsf{Exp}^{\mathsf{rnd}}(\mathcal{A})$	$\mathcal{O}_{\mathsf{eval}}(x)$
1: Sample $b \leftarrow^{\$} \{0,1\}$	1: If $x \neq x^*$:
2: $\mathsf{vk}, \mathsf{sk} \leftarrow^{\$} \mathsf{VRF.Gen}(1^{\lambda})$ and set $x^* = \perp$	2: $(y, \pi) \leftarrow \mathsf{VRF.Eval}(\mathsf{sk}, x)$
3: $x^* \leftarrow \mathcal{A}^{\mathcal{O}_{\mathsf{eval}}}(\mathsf{vk})$	3: Return (y, π)
4: If x^* was previously queried:	4: Else: Return $\perp$
5: Return 0	
6: $y_0 \leftarrow^{\$} \mathcal{Y}$	
7: $(y_1, \pi) \leftarrow \mathsf{VRF.Eval}(\mathsf{sk}, x^*)$	
8: $\mathcal{A}^{\mathcal{O}_{\mathsf{eval}}}(\mathsf{vk}, y_b) \rightarrow b'$	
9: Return $b == b'$	

Fig. 3. The pseudorandomness security game with adversary $\mathcal{A}$.

Restricted Pseudorandomness. Relaxations of the pseudorandomness properties have been proposed over the years, for instance in [BGRV09] where *weak* pseudorandomness is defined by sampling the points for evaluation queries and for the challenge uniformly in the function's domain. In this work we will consider a notion we call *restricted pseudorandomness* where each message is interpreted as a tuple (x_0, x_1) and two messages $(x_0, x_1), (\bar{x}_0, \bar{x}_1)$ are considered to be the same by the challenger if $x_0 = \bar{x}_0$ (Fig. 4).

Definition 6. *A triplet* (VRF.Gen, VRF.Eval, VRF.Vfy) *with message space* $\mathcal{X} = \mathcal{X}_0 \times \mathcal{X}_1$ *satisfies restricted pseudorandomness with respect to* $\mathcal{X}_0$ *if for any* PPT *adversary* $\mathcal{A}$ *there exists a negligible function* ε *such that*

$$\mathsf{Adv}(\mathcal{A}) := \left| \Pr\left[\mathsf{Exp}^{\mathsf{res\text{-}rnd}}_{\mathcal{X}_0}(\mathcal{A}) = 1\right] - \frac{1}{2} \right| \leq \varepsilon(\lambda).$$

$\mathsf{Exp}^{\mathsf{res\text{-}rnd}}_{\mathcal{X}_0}(\mathcal{A})$	$\mathcal{O}_{\mathsf{eval}}(x_0, x_1)$
1: Sample $b \leftarrow^{\$} \{0,1\}$	1: If $x_0 \neq x_0^*$:
2: $\mathsf{vk}, \mathsf{sk} \leftarrow^{\$} \mathsf{VRF.Gen}(1^{\lambda})$ and set $x_0^* = \perp$	2: $(y, \pi) \leftarrow \mathsf{VRF.Eval}(\mathsf{sk}, x_0, x_1)$
3: $(x_0^*, x_1^*) \leftarrow \mathcal{A}^{\mathcal{O}_{\mathsf{eval}}}(\mathsf{vk})$	3: Return (y, π)
4: If $(x_0^*, \cdot)$ was previously queried:	4: Else: Return $\perp$
5: Return 0	
6: $y_0 \leftarrow^{\$} \mathcal{Y}$	
7: $(y_1, \pi) \leftarrow \mathsf{VRF.Eval}(\mathsf{sk}, x_0^*, x_1^*)$	
8: $\mathcal{A}^{\mathcal{O}_{\mathsf{eval}}}(\mathsf{vk}, y_b) \rightarrow b'$	
9: Return $b == b'$	

Fig. 4. The restricted pseudorandomness game with adversary $\mathcal{A}$.

Verifiable Unpredictable Functions. Another relaxation of the pseudorandomness property was defined in [MRV99] where Verifiable Unpredictable Functions (VUF) where introduced. A VUF is a tuple of algorithms (VUF.Gen, VUF.Eval, VUF.Vfy) satisfying correctness and unique provability as per Definition 5, but instead of pseudorandomness they are only required to satisfy unpredictability, i.e. for any PPT adversary $\mathcal{A}$, there exists a negligible $\varepsilon(\lambda)$ such that

$$\mathsf{Adv}(\mathcal{A}) := \Pr\left[\mathsf{Exp}^{\mathsf{unp}}(\mathcal{A}) = 1\right] \leq \varepsilon(\lambda).$$

With $\mathsf{Exp}^{\mathsf{unp}}(\mathcal{A})$ being as defined in Fig. 5.

$\mathsf{Exp}^{\mathsf{unp}}(\mathcal{A})$

1 : $\mathsf{vk}, \mathsf{sk} \xleftarrow{\$} \mathsf{VUF.Gen}(1^\lambda)$

2 : $(x^*, y^*, \pi^*) \leftarrow \mathcal{A}^{\mathsf{VUF.Eval(sk, \cdot)}}(\mathsf{vk})$

3 : **If** x^* was previously queried: **Return** 0

4 : $(y, \pi) \leftarrow \mathsf{VUF.Eval}(\mathsf{sk}, x^*)$

5 : **Return** $(y^*, \pi^*) == (y, \pi)$

Fig. 5. The unpredictability experiment with adversary $\mathcal{A}$.

3 Unbiasability

3.1 Definition

We define our notion of *unbiasability* through an experiment. Let us begin with an informal overview. Initially an adversary is asked to produce a list of distinct verification keys $\mathsf{vk}_1, \ldots, \mathsf{vk}_n$ along with a predicate p. Next, the challenger sample uniformly some inputs $x_1, \ldots, x_m$. The adversary then evaluates its VRFs on these points and return them along with their proofs. The challenger finally "filters" the values with an incorrect proof, replaces them with $\bot$, and returns this vector $\mathbf{y}$. The adversary's goal is to eventually make the probability of $p(\mathbf{y}) = 1$ significantly greater than that of $p(\mathbf{z}) = 1$ with $\mathbf{z} \sim U(\mathbb{F}_q)$ in the output space.

For technical reasons however we cannot allow p to be *any* predicate. One motivation is that adversaries can always "bias" the output by selectively revealing only certain outputs and not all of them. In order to factor out this class of trivial attacks from our definition, we introduce a class of predicates we call *monotone*.

Definition 7. *Over* $(\mathcal{Y} \cup \{\bot\})^n$ *we define a partial order*

$$(y_1, \ldots, y_n) \leq (z_1, \ldots, z_n) \quad \Leftrightarrow \quad \forall i \ (y_i = z_i \ \vee \ y_i = \bot).$$

A (probabilistic) predicate $p : (\mathcal{Y} \cup \{\bot\})^n \times \{0,1\}^r \to \{0,1\}$ *is monotone if, for a uniformly sampled random tape* $\rho \sim U(\{0,1\}^r)$

$$\mathbf{y} \leq \mathbf{z} \quad \Rightarrow \quad \Pr\left[p(\mathbf{y}; \rho) = 1\right] \leq \Pr\left[p(\mathbf{z}; \rho) = 1\right].$$

As usually done for probabilistic Turing machines, we will not explicitly write the random tape ρ, and assume that evaluating $p(\mathbf{x})$ really means sampling $\rho \leftarrow^\$ \{0,1\}^r$ and then computing $p(\mathbf{x}; \rho)$.

Definition 8. *A VRF is unbiasable if for any polynomially bounded integers n, m and PPT adversary $\mathcal{A}$, there exists a negligible function ε such that*

$$\mathsf{Adv}(\mathcal{A}) := \Pr\left[\mathsf{Exp}^{\mathsf{bias}}_{0,n,m}(\mathcal{A}) = 1\right] - \Pr\left[\mathsf{Exp}^{\mathsf{bias}}_{1,n,m}(\mathcal{A}) = 1\right] \leq \varepsilon(\lambda)$$

where the experiment $\mathsf{Exp}^{\mathsf{bias}}_{b,n,m}$ is defined in Fig. 6.

$\mathsf{Exp}^{\mathsf{bias}}_{b,n,m}(\mathcal{A})$

1: $(\mathsf{vk}_1, \ldots, \mathsf{vk}_n, p) \leftarrow \mathcal{A}$ such that:

2: $\quad \mathsf{vk}_1, \ldots, \mathsf{vk}_n$ are all distinct

3: $\quad p$ is a PPT computable monotone predicate

4: $(x_1, \ldots, x_m) \leftarrow^\$ \mathcal{X}$

5: $((y_{1,1}, \pi_{1,1}), \ldots, (y_{n,m}, \pi_{n,m})) \leftarrow \mathcal{A}(x_1, \ldots, x_m)$

6: **For all** $i \in [n]$, $j \in [m]$:

7: $\quad$ **If** $\mathsf{VRF.Vfy}(\mathsf{vk}_i, x_j, y_{i,j}, \pi_{i,j}) \to 0$: Set $y_{i,j} \leftarrow \perp$

8: Sample $(z_{1,1}, \ldots, z_{n,m}) \leftarrow^\$ \mathcal{Y}^{n,m}$

9: **If** $b = 0$: **Return** $p(y_{1,1}, \ldots, y_{n,m})$

10: **If** $b = 1$: **Return** $p(z_{1,1}, \ldots, z_{n,m})$

Fig. 6. The unbiasability experiment parametrized by $b \in \{0,1\}$.

Note that our notion of unbiasability requires the adversary to evaluate the VRFs linked to the chosen verification keys on the *same* set of points. A relaxation of this notion, which we call *unbiasability on independent points*, instead ask the adversary to evaluate each VRF on an independently sampled set of points. More formally

Definition 9. *A VRF is unbiasable on independent points if for all polynomially bounded integers $n, m \in \mathbb{N}$ and PPT adversary $\mathcal{A}$, there exists a negligible function ε such that*

$$\mathsf{Adv}(\mathcal{A}) := \Pr\left[\mathsf{Exp}^{\mathsf{ip-bias}}_{0,n,m}(\mathcal{A})) = 1\right] - \Pr\left[\mathsf{Exp}^{\mathsf{ip-bias}}_{1,n,m}(\mathcal{A})) = 1\right] \leq \varepsilon(\lambda)$$

where the experiment $\mathsf{Exp}^{\mathsf{ip-bias}}_{b,n,m}$ is defined in Fig. 7.

3.2   Properties

Having provided our unbiasability definition, we now show it to imply some desirable properties.

$$\mathsf{Exp}_{b,n,m}^{\mathsf{ip-bias}}(\mathcal{A})$$

1 : $(\mathsf{vk}_1, \ldots, \mathsf{vk}_n, p) \leftarrow \mathcal{A}$ such that:

2 : $\mathsf{vk}_1, \ldots, \mathsf{vk}_n$ are all distinct

3 : p is a PPT computable monotone predicate

4 : $(x_{1,1}, \ldots, x_{n,m}) \leftarrow^{\$} \mathcal{X}$

5 : $((y_{1,1}, \pi_{1,1}), \ldots, (y_{n,m}, \pi_{n,m})) \leftarrow \mathcal{A}(x_{1,1}, \ldots, x_{n,m})$

6 :   **For all** $i \in [n]$ and $j \in [m]$:

7 :   **If** $\mathsf{VRF.Vfy}(\mathsf{vk}_i, x_{i,j}, y_{i,j}, \pi_{i,j}) \to 0$: Set $y_{i,j} \leftarrow \perp$

8 :   Sample $(z_{1,1}, \ldots, z_{n,m}) \leftarrow^{\$} \mathcal{Y}^{n,m}$

9 :   **If** $b = 0$: **Return** $p(y_{1,1}, \ldots, y_{n,m})$

10 :   **If** $b = 1$: **Return** $p(z_{1,1}, \ldots, z_{n,m})$

Fig. 7. The unbiasability experiment with independently sampled points for each vk.

Pseudorandom Output. Informally if a VRF is unbiasable then its evaluations on random points also looks random (even with adversarially generated keys). This roughly follows as any PPT distinguisher $\mathcal{D}$ trying to distinguish the VRF output from uniformly random values, can be converted into a probabilistic monotone predicate $p^{\mathcal{D}}$ such that

$$p^{\mathcal{D}}(y_1, \ldots, y_m) = \begin{cases} 0 & \text{If } y_i = \perp \\ \mathcal{D}(y_1, \ldots, y_m) & \text{Otherwise} \end{cases}.$$

If $\mathcal{D}$ were to succeed with significant probability then the algorithm which computed $\mathsf{vk}_1, \ldots, \mathsf{vk}_n$ can be used to bias $p^{\mathcal{D}}$. More in detail, in order to make a meaningful statement about the "VRF output" even when the verification key is maliciously chosen, we will restrict the class of adversaries to those who always returns valid output and proofs on random inputs. For this class of adversaries we can state the following Proposition:

Proposition 1. *Let $\mathcal{A}$ be a PPT machine $\mathcal{A}$ initially computing $\mathsf{vk}_1, \ldots, \mathsf{vk}_n$ and then on input $x_1, \ldots, x_m \sim U(\mathcal{X}^m)$ always returning $y_{1,1}, \ldots, y_{n,m}$ along with valid proofs $\pi_{1,1}, \ldots, \pi_{n,m}$, i.e. such that $\mathsf{VRF.Vfy}(\mathsf{vk}_i, x_j, y_{i,j}, \pi_{i,j}) \to 1$.*

If the VRF satisfies unbiasability, sampling $\mathbf{z} \sim U(\mathcal{Y}^{n,m})$, then for any PPT distinguisher $\mathcal{D}$ there exists a negligible ε such that

$$\mathsf{Adv}(\mathcal{D}) := |\Pr[\mathcal{D}(\mathbf{y}) \to 1] - \Pr[\mathcal{D}(\mathbf{z}) \to 1]| \leq \varepsilon(\lambda).$$

Weak Unbiasability. In [EKS+21] another notion of unbiasability was proposed. Their definition informally says that any adversary generating one key vk cannot guess the VRF value on a random point significantly better than randomly guessing. More formally, given a PPT adversary $\mathcal{A}$ their experiment is defined as in Fig. 8. They then say that a VRF satisfies their security definition if there exists a negligible function ε such that

$$\mathsf{Adv}(\mathcal{A}) \;=\; \Pr\left[\mathsf{Exp}^{\mathsf{w-bias}}(\mathcal{A}) = 1\right] \;\le\; \frac{1}{|\mathcal{Y}|} + \varepsilon(\lambda).$$

$\mathsf{Exp}^{\mathsf{w-bias}}(\mathcal{A})$

1 : $(\mathsf{vk}, y^*) \leftarrow^{\$} \mathcal{A}(1^\lambda)$

2 : $x \leftarrow^{\$} \mathcal{X}$

3 : $(\pi, y) \leftarrow^{\$} \mathcal{A}(x)$

4 : $\beta \leftarrow \mathsf{VRF.Vfy}(\mathsf{vk}, x, y, \pi)$

5 : **Return** 1 iff $\beta = 1$ and $y = y^*$

Fig. 8. The weak-unbiasability experiment [EKS+21].

Our notion immediately implies this one up to observing that the adversary is attempting to bias the predicate $p_{y^*}(y)$ that is 0 if $y^* \ne y$ (which also includes the case $y = \perp$) and 1 otherwise. Note also that $|\mathcal{Y}|^{-1}$ is precisely the probability that $p_{y^*}(z) = 1$ for a randomly chosen z. We thus rename their notion as "weak-unbiasability" and formally state that

Proposition 2. *Every unbiasable VRF if also weakly unbiasable.*

In the full version's appendix we further justify the name "weak-unbiasability" by providing examples of weakly unbiasable VRF that are not unbiasable.

Fairness in VRF-Based Leader Election. The goal of secret leader election (SLE) protocols is to anonymously identify one user among many. VRF-based construction [CM16, KRDO17, DGKR17] generally follows the following blueprint: Initially each user P_i publishes a VRF key vk_i. Later a random input is sampled and the user with the lowest VRF output is the winner.

Among the properties such protocol should satisfy, *fairness* requires that no group of corrupted parties can win with probability higher than expected. More formally, a group C of t out of n corrupted parties should only contain a winner with probability $t/n + \varepsilon$. Assuming the VRF to be unbiasable, we can then prove VRF-based leader elections to be fair. Indeed, any adversary corrupting C parties and winning with high probability is also successfully biasing the predicate

$$p(y_1, \ldots, y_n) \;:\; \begin{cases} 0 & \text{If } y_i = \perp,\; i \notin C \\ \min_{i \in C}\{y_i\} \le \min_{i \notin C}\{y_i\} & \text{Otherwise} \end{cases}$$

where $\perp$ is treated as $+\infty$ in the min operations above. Note p is monotone as replacing any y_i with $\perp$ for $i \notin C$ makes the predicate false, and doing the same for $i \in C$ does not decrease the left hand side of the inequality.

4   Unbiasable VRF in the ROM

4.1   From Any VUF

In this section we analyze a folklore compiler that transforms any VUF into a VRF in the ROM, and show the resulting construction to be unbiasable as per Definition 8. The idea is simply to apply the RO on the VUF output, the verification key vk and the VUF input x. A full description is provided in Fig. 9

Notice that in order to obtain unbiasability hashing both vk and x along with the VUF output is necessary: If we were to remove x, it may be the case that for some maliciously generated verification key vk^*, the underlying function is constant. This would not contradict unpredictability as vk^* is only chosen with negligible probability. However, for several random inputs the RO applied to the VUF output and verification key would always yield the same value, implying that the resulting construction is not unbiasable.

If we were to remove vk we face similar issues: for some VUF there may exists two distinct verification keys vk_1^*, vk_2^* such that the underlying functions are identical. Again this does not contradict unpredictability, but the resulting construction would now give the same output when evaluated for vk_1^* and vk_2^* on the same inputs, which contradicts unbiasability.

$$\text{VRF.Gen}(1^\lambda)$$

$$1: \quad \textbf{Return } (\mathsf{vk}, \mathsf{sk}) \leftarrow^{\$} \text{VUF.Gen}(1^\lambda)$$

VRF.Eval(sk, x)	VRF.Vfy(vk, x, y, π)
$1: \quad (y^*, \pi^*) \leftarrow \text{VUF.Eval}(\mathsf{sk}, x)$	$1: \quad$ Parse $\pi = (\pi^*, y^*)$
$2: \quad y \leftarrow \mathsf{H}(\mathsf{vk}, x, y^*)$	$2: \quad \textbf{Return } 1$ if and only if:
$3: \quad \pi \leftarrow (\pi^*, y^*)$	$3: \quad \mathsf{H}(\mathsf{vk}, x, y^*) = y$
$4: \quad \textbf{Return } (y, \pi)$	$4: \quad \text{VUF.Vfy}(\mathsf{vk}, x, y^*, \pi^*) = 1$

Fig. 9. Unbiasable VRF based on a VUF using a Random Oracle H.

Theorem 1. *If $|\mathcal{X}| = \Omega(2^\lambda)$, with $\mathcal{X}$ being the VUF input space, the construction described in Fig. 9 is an Unbiasable VRF in the ROM.*

Proof of Theorem 1. Correctness, unique provability and pseudorandomness immediately follows from VUF properties and the usage of the ROM. We thus only focus on unbiasability.

Unbiasability. Let $\mathcal{A}$ be an adversary playing the game in Fig. 6. We will call Q the set of ROM queries it performs before returning $(\mathsf{vk}_1, \ldots, \mathsf{vk}_n, p)$ and define the two events

$$\text{Seen} := \exists i \in [n], \; j \in [m], \; y \in \{0,1\}^* \; : \; (\mathsf{vk}_i, x_j, y) \in Q$$
$$\text{Coll} := \exists j, j' \in [m] \; : \; x_j = x_{j'}$$

where Seen means a query with prefix (vk_i, x_j) was made and Coll means no collision occurs among the elements $x_1, \ldots, x_m$. These two events occur with negligible probability

$$\Pr[\text{Seen}] \leq \frac{m|Q|}{|\mathcal{X}|}, \qquad \Pr[\text{Coll}] \leq \frac{m^2}{|\mathcal{X}|}.$$

Let now $\mathbf{y}^*$ be the "filtered" output of $\mathcal{A}$ in the unbiasability experiment, so that values with invalid proofs are replaced with $\bot$. For all i and j we define $y_{i,j}$ to be $y_{i,j}^*$ if this value is not $\bot$ and otherwise sample $y_{i,j} \sim U(\mathcal{Y})$. According to Definition 7

$$\mathbf{y}^* \leq \mathbf{y} \quad \Rightarrow \quad \Pr[p(\mathbf{y}^*) = 1] \leq \Pr[p(\mathbf{y}) = 1]$$

with p being the monotone predicate chosen by $\mathcal{A}$. To conclude we observe than when conditioning on $\neg\text{Seen}, \neg\text{Coll}$, all the elements $y_{i,j}^* \neq \bot$ are evaluations of the random oracle on different[4] and not yet queried points, thus are uniformly random. Hence, setting $\mathbf{z} \sim U(\mathcal{Y}^{n,m})$

$$\Delta(\mathbf{y}, \mathbf{z}) \leq \Delta(\mathbf{y}_{|\neg\text{Seen}, \neg\text{Coll}}, \mathbf{z}_{|\neg\text{Seen}, \neg\text{Coll}}) + \Pr[\text{Seen} \vee \text{Coll}]$$
$$\leq \Pr[\text{Seen}] + \Pr[\text{Coll}]$$
$$\leq \frac{m|Q| + m^2}{|\mathcal{X}|}.$$

where the second inequality follows as $\mathbf{y}$ is uniform upon conditioning on $\neg\text{Seen}, \neg\text{Coll}$. We can then bound the advantage of $\mathcal{A}$ as

$$\mathsf{Adv}(\mathcal{A}) = \Pr[p(\mathbf{y}^*) = 1] - \Pr[p(\mathbf{z}) = 1] \leq$$
$$\leq \Pr[p(\mathbf{y}) = 1] - \Pr[p(\mathbf{z}) = 1] \leq \Delta(\mathbf{y}, \mathbf{z}) \leq \frac{m|Q| + m^2}{|\mathcal{X}|}.$$

4.2 From Weakly Unbiasable VUF

Although the compiler presented in Sect. 4.1 shows that any VUF can be converted into an unbiasable VRF in the random oracle model, not all schemes used in practice follow that blueprint. This most notably include the case of ECVRF [PWH+17] currently included in the standardization effort put forward in [GRPV23].

In order to capture ECVRF we propose a slightly different compiler, which does not include the verification key vk and input x in the RO query for evaluations. This, as discussed before, may lead to insecure constructions in general.

---

[4] Because $\mathsf{vk}_i \neq \mathsf{vk}_j$ by construction and $x_i \neq x_j$ by $\neg\text{Coll}$.

Therefore to prove security we will need the VUF to satisfy two extra properties, both achieved by the VUF used in ECVRF. First of all, we need that no adversary can guess the VUF output on a random input, even when it get to chose the VUF keys. In order words, we need the VUF to be weakly unbiasable (see Sect. 3.2). Moreover, we further need that for any given key vk, two distinct random inputs x_1, x_2 and their respective outputs y_1, y_2, then $\Pr[y_1 = y_2]$ is negligible. This second property is required to exclude VUFs with two keys defining (almost) the same function. Assuming these properties we can then prove our weaker compiler, presented in Fig. 10, to be a secure unbiasable VRF.

$$\text{VRF.Gen}(1^\lambda)$$

1 :   **Return** $(\text{vk}, \text{sk}) \leftarrow^{\$} \text{VUF.Gen}(1^\lambda)$

$\text{VRF.Eval}(\text{sk}, x)$

1 : $(y^*, \pi^*) \leftarrow \text{VUF.Eval}(\text{sk}, x)$
2 : $y \leftarrow H(y^*)$
3 : $\pi \leftarrow (\pi^*, y^*)$
4 :   **Return** (y, π)

$\text{VRF.Vfy}(\text{vk}, x, y, \pi)$

1 :   Parse $\pi = (\pi^*, y^*)$
2 :   **Return** 1 if and only if:
3 : $H(y^*) = y$
4 : $\text{VUF.Vfy}(\text{vk}, x, y^*, \pi^*) = 1$

Fig. 10. Unbiasable VRF based on a special VUF. Differences from the construction in Fig. 9 are highlighted.

Theorem 2. *Let* $(\text{VUF.Gen}, \text{VUF.Eval}, \text{VUF.Vfy})$ *be a weakly unbiasable (see Sect. 3.2) VUF so that there exists a negligible function* ε *such that for all* vk, $x_1, x_2 \sim U(\mathcal{X})$ *and* y_1, y_2 *for which there exists* π_1, π_2 *with*

$$\text{VUF.Vfy}(\text{vk}_1, x, y_1, \pi_1) = 1, \quad \text{VUF.Vfy}(\text{vk}_2, x, y_2, \pi_2) = 1$$

then $\Pr[y_1 = y_2] \leq \varepsilon(\lambda)$.

Then the construction presented in Fig. 10 is an Unbiasable VRF in the random oracle model.

A proof of this Theorem appears in the full version.

5   Constructions in the Standard Model

In this section we will first provide two unbiasable VRFs in the standard model achieving weaker notions of both pseudorandomness and unbiasability. More specifically both constructions achieve

1. Restricted pseudorandomness on the first component of their input space (see Definition 6).

2. Unbiasability on independent points (Definition 9) holding unconditionally, i.e. against computationally unbounded adversaries.

We target these properties as at the end of this Section we provide a compiler transforming any such VRF into a fully-fledged unbiasable VRF in the standard model.

5.1 1st Preliminary Construction: Padded VRF

Our first construction critically shows how targeting only restricted pseudorandomness and unbiasability with independent points simplifies the problem. The construction is based on two observations:

First, any (publicly computable) permutation is unbiasable with independent points (although not a VRF), as it preserves the input distribution. The easiest example is the identity function. The second idea is that, given a VRF $F_{\text{sk}}(\cdot) = \text{VRF.Eval}(\text{sk}, \cdot)$ and a publicly computable unbiasable function $f(\cdot)$, we can combine the two, returning on input $x = (u, v)$ the output $F_{\text{sk}}(u) \oplus f(v)$. This informally remains unbiasable because $f(v)$ preserves the entropy in v, and $F_{\text{sk}}(u)$ is independent from v. Moreover, this achieves restricted pseudorandomness on the first component because the adversary is not allowed to evaluate the VRF on two different points $x, \bar{x}$ with the same first component $u, \bar{u}$.

The resulting construction, given for $f = \text{id}$ and (VRF*.Gen, VRF*.Eval, VRF*.Vfy) a VRF, is described in Fig. 11, and we will refer to it as the *padded VRF* construction. There we assume that the VRF output space $\mathcal{Y}^*$ is a group $(\mathbb{G}, +)$. This generalizes the case $\mathcal{Y}^* = \{0, 1\}^\mu$ which is a group with the bit-wise xor. Our compiler in Sects. 5.5 however will only work for the special case in which the VRF's input space is a prime order group.

$\underline{\text{VRB.Gen}(1^\lambda)}$

   1 : **Return** $(\text{vk}, \text{sk}) \leftarrow^{\$} \text{VRF}^*.\text{Gen}(1^\lambda)$

$\underline{\text{VRB.Eval}(\text{sk}, x)}$	$\underline{\text{VRB.Vfy}(\text{vk}, x, y, \pi)}$
1 : Parse $x = (u, v)$	1 : Parse $x = (u, v)$
2 : $(w, \pi) \leftarrow \text{VRF}^*.\text{Eval}(\text{sk}, u)$	2 : $w \leftarrow y - v$
3 : $y \leftarrow w + v$	3 : **Return** 1 if and only if:
4 : **Return** y	4 : $\text{VRF.Vfy}(\text{vk}, w, u, \pi) \rightarrow 1$

Fig. 11. Padded VRF construction from a VRF (VRF*.Gen, VRF*.Eval, VRF*.Vfy) with output space a group $(\mathbb{G}, +)$.

Theorem 3. *If* (VRF*.Gen, VRF*.Eval, VRF*.Vfy) *is a secure VRF, then the construction in Fig. 11 is a VRF with restricted pseudorandomness. Moreover it satisfies unbiasability on independent points against computationally unbounded adversaries.*

A proof of this Theorem appears in the full version.

5.2 Verifiable Random Bijection

Our second approach to construct a VRF satisfying unbiasability on independent points is to guarantee that for each key, including maliciously generated ones, the resulting VRF is 1 to 1. In this section we formally defined this class of VRF, which we call *Verifiable Random Bijection* (VRB). For the sake of generality, we do not require each function to be always 1 to 1, which would exclude VRFs admitting "bad" keys that cannot be evaluated over the full domain. Instead, we more generally ask the function to have input and output space of the same cardinality and to always be injective. Formally

Definition 10. *A Verifiable Random Bijection is a VRF* (VRB.Gen, VRB.Eval, VRB.Vfy) *whose input space $\mathcal{X}$ and output space $\mathcal{Y}$ have the same cardinality $|\mathcal{X}| = |\mathcal{Y}|$ and furthermore satisfies*

4. **Injectivity.** *For any* vk *(not necessarily in the range of* VRF.Gen*), any output $y \in \mathcal{Y}$, pair of inputs $x_0, x_1 \in \mathcal{X}$ and proofs π_0, π_1 if holds that*

$$\textsf{VRF.Vfy}(\textsf{vk}, x_0, y, \pi_0) \to 1, \quad \textsf{VRF.Vfy}(\textsf{vk}, x_1, y, \pi_1) \to 1 \quad \Rightarrow \quad x_0 = x_1.$$

In the full version we provide a proof of the following theorem, stating that for any VRF (not even necessarily pseudorandom), injectivity suffices to achieve unconditionally unbiasability on independent points.

Theorem 4. *Any tuple* (VRF.Gen, VRF.Eval, VRF.Vfy) *with $|\mathcal{X}| = |\mathcal{Y}|$ satisfying correctness, unique provability and injectivity, then further satisfies unbiasability on independent points against computationally unbounded adversaries.*

5.3 2nd Preliminary Construction: 2-Feistel Rounds

In this section we observe that 2 Feistel rounds [LR88] suffice to transform any VRF into a VRB, at the cost of only achieving restricted pseudorandomness. Such weaker security notion is the reason why we do not need 3 or more rounds. Indeed, using notation from Fig. 1, known attacks to break 2 Feistel rounds require to perform queries with the same component z_1 but different w_1. This is disallowed when considering pseudorandomness restricted to the first component, where two queries with the same first entry are considered the same by the evaluation oracle.

Note that to instantiate this construction we do need the VRF's input space $\mathcal{X}$ to be a group $\mathbb{G}$ with some operation $+$ and that the output space is also $\mathbb{G}$.

The first condition is achieved assuming $\mathbb{G} \subseteq \mathcal{X}$ and then restricting the input space. The second one instead can be achieved by amplifying the VRF output length and then applying a universal hash to the group (in prime order groups, this hash can simply be the exponentiation by a generator). A full description of the scheme is presented in Fig. 12

VRB.Gen(1^λ)

1 : $vk_1, sk_1 \xleftarrow{\$} VRF.Gen(1^\lambda), \quad vk_2, sk_2 \xleftarrow{\$} VRF.Gen(1^\lambda)$
2 : $vk \leftarrow (vk_1, vk_2), \; sk \leftarrow (sk_1, sk_2)$
3 : **Return** (vk, sk)

VRB.Eval(sk, x)

1 : Parse $x = (z_1, w_1)$
2 : $(u_1, \pi_1) \leftarrow VRF.Eval(sk_1, z_1)$
3 : $(z_2, w_2) \leftarrow (z_1, w_1 + u_1)$
4 : $(u_2, \pi_2) \leftarrow VRF.Eval(sk_2, w_2)$
5 : $(z_3, w_3) \leftarrow (z_2 + u_2, w_2)$
6 : $y \leftarrow (z_3, w_3)$
7 : $\pi \leftarrow (u_1, u_2, \pi_1, \pi_2)$
8 : **Return** $y \leftarrow (z_3, w_3)$

VRF.Vfy(vk, x, y, π)

1 : Parse $x = (z_1, w_1)$
2 : Parse $\pi = (u_1, u_2, \pi_1, \pi_2)$
3 : $(z_2, w_2) \leftarrow (z_1, w_1 + u_1)$
4 : $(z_3, w_3) \leftarrow (z_2 + u_2, w_2)$
5 : **Return** 1 if and only if:
6 : $VRF.Vfy(vk_1, z_1, u_1, \pi_1) \rightarrow 1$
7 : $VRF.Vfy(vk_2, w_2, u_2, \pi_2) \rightarrow 1$
8 : $(z_3, w_3) = y$

Fig. 12. 2-Feistel round construction

Theorem 5. *If* $(VRF.Gen, VRF.Eval, VRF.Vfy)$ *is a secure VRF with input space* $\mathbb{G}$*, then the construction in Fig. 12 is a VRB with message space* $\mathbb{G} \times \mathbb{G}$ *and restricted pseudorandomness on the first component.*

The Theorem is again proven in the full version.

5.4 VRB Compiler

Before presenting in the next section a general compiler lifting our preliminary constructions to fully fledged unbiasable VRF, we discuss how to modify the 2-Feistel Round construction (or more generally, any VRB with constrained pseudorandomness) in order to obtain a VRB satisfying the regular pseudorandomness property. We see this as a useful stepping stone to introduce in a simpler setting some of the techniques used later on. Furthermore, security of this construction will eventually depend on simpler assumptions. Namely the underlying VRF security and the hardness of standard DLP.

The main issue of the construction in Sect. 5.3 is that pseudorandomness fails when an adversary evaluates the VRF in two different points sharing the same first component. A trivial fix could be to compose the 2-Feistel rounds with an hash functions, so that on input $x \in \mathbb{G}$, we evaluate that VRF on $(h(x), x)$. This however introduces collisions which, although hard to compute, would break injectivity.

Our solution is to rely on a Pedersen hash: given $\mathbf{x} \in \mathbb{F}_q^2$ and $[\mathbf{a}]$ a hash key, the hash of $\mathbf{x}$ is the inner product $[\mathbf{a}^\top \mathbf{x}]$. With this tool we can build a map from $\mathbb{F}_q^2 \to \mathbb{G}^2$ keyed on $[\mathbf{a}]$ such that

$$\mathbf{x} \mapsto \left([\mathbf{a}^\top \mathbf{x}], [\mathbf{e}_1^\top \mathbf{x}] \right).$$

were $\mathbf{e}_1 = (1, 0)$. This map is collision resistant on the first component when $\mathbf{a}$ is sampled by an honest user, which we needed for pseudorandomness. Moreover, even when $\mathbf{a}$ is sampled maliciously, it is possible to verify whether this map is a bijection or not by checking $[a_2] \neq 0$. Indeed in this case the matrix $A = (\mathbf{a}, \mathbf{e}_1)^\top$ has non-zero determinant and thus it is bijection. Our solution, consisting of the composition of this map and the construction of Sect. 5.3, is schematized in Fig. 13 and formally described in Fig. 14.

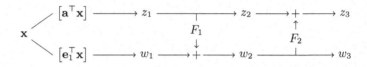

Fig. 13. 2-Feistel rounds with Petersen hash, where $F_i(\cdot) = \mathsf{VRF.Eval}(\mathsf{sk}_i, \cdot)$ and $\mathbf{a}, \mathbf{e}_1, \mathbf{x}$ are vectors in $\mathbb{F}_q^2$ with $\mathbf{e}_1 = (1, 0)$.

Theorem 6. *If* $(\mathsf{VRB}^*.\mathsf{Gen}, \mathsf{VRB}^*.\mathsf{Eval}, \mathsf{VRB}^*.\mathsf{Vfy})$ *is a VRB with domain* $\mathbb{G}^2$ *satisfying restricted pseudorandomness with respect to the first component, and DLP is hard, then the construction in Fig. 14 is a secure VRB.*

5.5   Unbiasable VRF Compiler

We finally provide our compiler lifting any VRF satisfying restricted pseudorandomness and unbiasability on independent points to fully fledged unbiasable VRF. Combining this with the constructions in Sect. 5.1 and 5.3 yields two compilers from VRF to unbiasable VRF. Note the resulting constructions are in the standard model, meaning without random oracles and setup assumptions, i.e. no CRS.

In order to enhance pseudorandomness we use the same technique of Sect. 5.4: Interpreting the input as a vector $\mathbf{x} \in \mathbb{F}_q^\mu$, we compute the first component as a Petersen Hash $[\mathbf{a}^\top \mathbf{x}]$ and the second one as a linear function $\mathbf{b}^\top \mathbf{x}$, with $[\mathbf{a}]$ and $\mathbf{b}$ being part of the public key.

VRB.Gen(1^λ)

---

1 :   Sample $\mathsf{vk}^*, \mathsf{sk}^* \leftarrow^{\$} \mathsf{VRB}^*.\mathsf{Gen}(1^\lambda)$

2 :   Sample $\mathbf{a} \leftarrow^{\$} \mathbb{F}_q^2$ with $a_2 \neq 0$

3 : $\mathsf{vk} \leftarrow (\mathsf{vk}^*, [\mathbf{a}]), \mathsf{sk} \leftarrow \mathsf{sk}^*$

4 :   **Return** $(\mathsf{vk}, \mathsf{sk})$

VRB.Eval($\mathsf{sk}, \mathbf{x}$)

---

1 :   // $\mathbf{x} \in \mathbb{F}_q^2$

2 : $z \leftarrow [\mathbf{a}^\top \mathbf{x}]$

3 : $w \leftarrow [\mathbf{e}_1^\top \mathbf{x}]$

4 : $(y, \pi) \leftarrow \mathsf{VRB}^*.\mathsf{Eval}(\mathsf{sk}^*, (z, w))$

5 :   **Return** (y, π)

VRB.Vfy(vk, x, y, π)

---

1 : $z \leftarrow [\mathbf{a}^\top \mathbf{x}]$

2 : $w \leftarrow [\mathbf{e}_1^\top \mathbf{x}]$

3 :   **Return** 1 if and only if:

4 : $\mathsf{VRB}^*.\mathsf{Vfy}(\mathsf{vk}^*, (z, w), y, \pi)$

5 : $[a_2] \neq 0$.

Fig. 14. Compiler returning a secure VRB from one with restricted pseudorandomness.

We now discuss how to obtain unbiasability. The challenge is that in Definition 8 we require the adversary to evaluate all of the VRFs on the *same* set of inputs, whereas the underlying VRF we start with is only unbiasable if each VRF is evaluated on *independently sampled* ones. Our idea is to derive those independently sampled sets, one for each key vk chosen by the adversary, from a common one using a PRF. In the introduction we discussed as non-working examples interpreting the input as a PRF key k and evaluating the VRF of $f_k(\mathsf{vk})$ or $(k, f_k(\mathsf{vk}))$. These however either break pseudorandomness if $k \mapsto f_k(\mathsf{vk})$ is not injective, or prevent us from using the PRF pseudorandomness in the proof. To fix notation, let Encode be the procedure performing such expansion (i.e. returning a vector $\mathbf{v}$ with entries in $\mathbb{F}_q$ which we pass as input to the Petersen Hash). Our solution improves on the trivial ones by relying on a perfectly binding commitment scheme Com:

- The input x is assumed to be of the form $(\mathbf{r}, k, \mathsf{pp}, \rho)$ with $\mathbf{r} \in \mathbb{F}_q$ and pp the public parameter of a perfectly binding commitment scheme.
- $\mathsf{Encode}(\mathbf{r}, k, \mathsf{pp}, \rho) = (\mathbf{r}, f_k(\mathsf{vk}), \mathsf{pp}, \mathsf{Com}_{\mathsf{pp}}(k; \rho))$ where $\mathbf{r} \in \mathbb{F}_q^2$ is used to turn the Pedersen hash into a chameleon hash, $f_k(\mathsf{vk}) \in \mathbb{F}_q^2$ randomizes the Petersen hash output *independently* for each vk.

Note that one key requirement of Encode is to be injective to preserve pseudorandomness. Hence the above solution only works if the map $(k, \mathsf{pp}, \rho) \mapsto \mathsf{Com}_{\mathsf{pp}}(k; \rho)$ is injective. Furthermore the commitment scheme must admit uniformly random public parameters. This unfortunately excludes a large class of constructions (e.g. lattice based). However all the above properties are true for ElGamal commitments, where, given a public group element $[\alpha]$ a commitment to k is defined as $[\beta], [\alpha\beta + k]$.

We eventually provide a full description of our solution for this specific choice of commitment scheme: first we let $\mathsf{repr} : \mathbb{G} \to \mathbb{F}_q^\eta$ be an efficiently computable and injective map. If $\mathbb{G} \subseteq \{0,1\}^\ell$ it exists with $\eta \leq \ell/\lfloor \log_2 q \rfloor$ by encoding $\lfloor \log_2 q \rfloor$ bits per field element. Given such representation map, we define $\mathsf{Encode} : \mathbb{F}_q^4 \times \mathcal{K} \to \mathbb{F}_q^{4+3\eta}$, with $\mathcal{K}$ being the set of possible verification keys vk, as

$$\mathsf{Encode}(r_1, r_2, \alpha, \beta, k, \mathsf{vk}) := (r_1, r_2, f_k(\mathsf{vk}), \mathsf{repr}([\alpha]), \mathsf{repr}([\beta]), \mathsf{repr}([\alpha\beta + k])).$$

Having defined the encoding procedure we can finally describe our compiler, taking as input a VRF (VRF*.Gen, , VRF*.Eval, VRF*.Vfy), described in Fig. 15. A proof of Theorem 7 is presented in the full version.

$\mathsf{VRF.Gen}(1^\lambda)$

1 : Sample $(\mathsf{vk}^*, \mathsf{sk}^*) \leftarrow^{\$} \mathsf{VRF^*.Gen}(1^\lambda)$

2 : Sample $\mathbf{a} \leftarrow^{\$} \mathbb{F}_q^{4+3\eta}$ with $a_2, a_4 \neq 0$

3 : Set $\mathsf{vk} \leftarrow (\mathsf{vk}^*, [\mathbf{a}])$ and $\mathsf{sk}^* \leftarrow \mathsf{sk}$

4 : **Return** $(\mathsf{vk}, \mathsf{sk})$

$\mathsf{VRF.Eval}(\mathsf{sk}, x)$

1 : $// \ x \in \mathbb{F}_q^5$

2 : $\mathbf{v} \leftarrow \mathsf{Encode}(x, \mathsf{vk})$

3 : $z \leftarrow [\mathbf{a}^\top \mathbf{v}]$

4 : $w \leftarrow [\mathbf{e}^\top \mathbf{v}]$ $// \ \mathsf{e} = \mathsf{e}_1 + \mathsf{e}_3$

5 : $(y, \pi) \leftarrow^{\$} \mathsf{VRF^*.Eval}(\mathsf{sk}^*, (z, w))$

6 : **Return** (y, π)

$\mathsf{VRF.Vfy}(\mathsf{vk}, x, y, \pi)$

1 : $\mathbf{v} \leftarrow \mathsf{Encode}(x, \mathsf{vk})$

2 : $z \leftarrow [\mathbf{a}^\top \mathbf{v}]$

3 : $w \leftarrow [\mathbf{e}^\top \mathbf{v}]$ $// \ \mathsf{e} = \mathsf{e}_1 + \mathsf{e}_3$

4 : **Return** 1 if and only if:

5 : $[a_2] \neq 0, \ [a_4] \neq 0$

6 : $\mathsf{VRF^*.Vfy}(\mathsf{vk}^*, (z, w), y, \pi) \to 1$

Fig. 15. Compiler returning an unbiasable VRF.

Theorem 7. *Let* (VRF*.Gen, VRF*.Eval, VRF*.Vfy) *be a VRF with domain* $\mathbb{G} \times \mathbb{G}$, *restricted pseudorandomness on the first component, and unconditional unibasability on independent points (i.e. holding against unbounded adversaries). If* DLPrep-DDH *is hard in* $\mathbb{G}$ *and* f *is a PRF secure against* PPT *adversaries with preprocessing in* $\mathsf{PPT}^{\mathsf{DL}}$ *(see Sect. 2.3), then the construction described in Fig. 15 is an Unbiasable VRF.*

6   Conclusions

In conclusion we initiated the study of unbiasable verifiable random functions and proved them to be useful for applications and realizable in the plain model. Regarding future research directions, we list some problems we leave open whose solution would improve our understanding of these objects.

First of all, it is unclear to us under what hypothesis it is possible into compile any VRF to an unbiasable one. For instance, having a simpler construction based only on symmetric key primitives would narrow down the efficiency gap between plain model and ROM constructions. A simpler problem would be to understand whether unbiasability can be based only on plausibly post-quantum hypothesis. We further leave open understanding whether preprocessing is necessary to achieve unbiasability in the plain model. This was the case in our proof as the reduction uses the adversary as a black-box oracle to evaluate the VRF, and eventually needs to evaluate such VRF on a partially unknown point. This means it must violate the pseudorandomness property, and super polynomial preprocessing is the extra edge to do so. We hence believe that overcoming such limitations would also likely lead to novel proof techniques.

Acknowledgments. The authors would like to thanks Handan Kılınç Alper for the helpful discussions regarding the UC-Security of VRF. This work has been partially supported by PRODIGY Project (TED2021-132464B-I00) funded by MCIN/AEI/10.13039/501100011033/ and the European Union NextGenerationEU/PRTR.

References

[ACF09] Abdalla, M., Catalano, D., Fiore, D.: Verifiable random functions from identity-based key encapsulation. In: Joux, A. (ed.) EUROCRYPT 2009. LNCS, vol. 5479, pp. 554–571. Springer, Heidelberg (2009). https://doi.org/10.1007/978-3-642-01001-9_32

[BASV23a] Burdges, J., Alper, H.K., Stewart, A., Vasilyev, S.: Ethical identity, ring VRFs, and zero-knowledge continuations. Cryptology ePrint Archive, Report 2023/002 (2023). https://eprint.iacr.org/2023/002

[BASV23b] Burdges, J., Alper, H.K., Stewart, A., Vasilyev, S.: Sassafras and semi-anonymous single leader election. Cryptology ePrint Archive, Report 2023/031 (2023). https://eprint.iacr.org/2023/031

[BGK+18] Badertscher, C., Gazi, P., Kiayias, A., Russell, A., Zikas, V.: Ouroboros genesis: Composable proof-of-stake blockchains with dynamic availability. In: Lie, D., Mannan, M., Backes, M., Wang, X. (eds.) ACM CCS 2018, pp. 913–930. ACM Press, October 2018

[BGQR22] Badertscher, C., Gazi, P., Querejeta-Azurmendi, I., Russell, A.: A composable security treatment of ECVRF and batch verifications. In: Atluri, V., Di Pietro, R., Jensen, C.D., Meng, W. (eds.) ESORICS 2022. LNCS, vol. 13556, pp. 22–41. Springer, Cham (2022). https://doi.org/10.1007/978-3-031-17143-7_2

[BGRV09] Brakerski, Z., Goldwasser, S., Rothblum, G.N., Vaikuntanathan, V.: Weak verifiable random functions. In: Reingold, O. (ed.) TCC 2009. LNCS, vol. 5444, pp. 558–576. Springer, Heidelberg (2009). https://doi.org/10.1007/978-3-642-00457-5_33

[BMR10] Boneh, D., Montgomery, H.W., Raghunathan, A.: Algebraic pseudorandom functions with improved efficiency from the augmented cascade. In: Al-Shaer, E., Keromytis, A.D., Shmatikov, V., (eds.) ACM CCS 2010, pp. 131–140. ACM Press, October 2010

[BY96]   Bellare, M., Yung, M.: Certifying permutations: noninteractive zero-knowledge based on any trapdoor permutation. J. Cryptol. **9**(3), 149–166 (1996)

[Can01]   Canetti, R.: Universally composable security: a new paradigm for cryptographic protocols. In: 42nd FOCS, pp. 136–145. IEEE Computer Society Press, October 2001

[CD17]   Cascudo, I., David, B.: SCRAPE: Scalable randomness attested by public entities. In: Gollmann, D., Miyaji, A., Kikuchi, H. (eds.) ACNS 17. LNCS, vol. 10355, pp. 537–556. Springer, Heidelberg (2017)

[CD20]   Cascudo, I., David, B.: ALBATROSS: publicly attestabLe BATched randomness based on secret sharing. In: Moriai, S., Wang, H. (eds.) ASIACRYPT 2020. LNCS, vol. 12493, pp. 311–341. Springer, Cham (2020). https://doi.org/10.1007/978-3-030-64840-4_11

[CDG+18] Camenisch, J., Drijvers, M., Gagliardoni, T., Lehmann, A., Neven, G.: The wonderful world of global random Oracles. In: Nielsen, J.B., Rijmen, V. (eds.) EUROCRYPT 2018. LNCS, vol. 10820, pp. 280–312. Springer, Cham (2018). https://doi.org/10.1007/978-3-319-78381-9_11

[CK18]   Corrigan-Gibbs, H., Kogan, D.: The discrete-logarithm problem with preprocessing. In: Nielsen, J.B., Rijmen, V. (eds.) EUROCRYPT 2018. LNCS, vol. 10821, pp. 415–447. Springer, Cham (2018). https://doi.org/10.1007/978-3-319-78375-8_14

[CL07]   Chase, M., Lysyanskaya, A.: Simulatable VRFs with applications to multi-theorem NIZK. In: Menezes, A. (ed.) CRYPTO 2007. LNCS, vol. 4622, pp. 303–322. Springer, Heidelberg (2007). https://doi.org/10.1007/978-3-540-74143-5_17

[CM16]   Chen, J., Micali, S.: Algorand. arXiv preprint arXiv:1607.01341 (2016)

[DGKR17] David, B., Gaži, P., Kiayias, A., Russell, A.: Ouroboros praos: an adaptively-secure, semi-synchronous proof-of-stake protocol. Cryptology ePrint Archive, Report 2017/573 (2017). https://eprint.iacr.org/2017/573

[EKS+21] Esgin, M.F., Kuchta, V., Sakzad, A., Steinfeld, R., Zhang, Z., Sun, S., Chu, S.: Practical post-quantum few-time verifiable random function with applications to Algorand. In: Borisov, N., Diaz, C. (eds.) FC 2021. LNCS, vol. 12675, pp. 560–578. Springer, Heidelberg (2021). https://doi.org/10.1007/978-3-662-64331-0_29

[ESLR22] Esgin, M.F., Steinfeld, R., Liu, D., Ruj, S.: Efficient hybrid exact/relaxed lattice proofs and applications to rounding and VRFs. Cryptology ePrint Archive, Report 2022/141 (2022). https://eprint.iacr.org/2022/141

[FKL18]   Fuchsbauer, G., Kiltz, E., Loss, J.: The algebraic group model and its applications. In: Shacham, H., Boldyreva, A. (eds.) CRYPTO 2018. LNCS, vol. 10992, pp. 33–62. Springer, Cham (2018). https://doi.org/10.1007/978-3-319-96881-0_2

[FLS90]   Feige, U., Lapidot, D., Shamir, A.: Multiple non-interactive zero knowledge proofs based on a single random string (extended abstract). In: 31st FOCS, pp. 308–317. IEEE Computer Society Press, October 1990

[Fuc14]   Fuchsbauer, G.: Constrained verifiable random functions. In: Abdalla, M., De Prisco, R. (eds.) SCN 14. LNCS, vol. 8642, pp. 95–114. Springer, Heidelberg (2014)

[GGM86]   Goldreich, O., Goldwasser, S., Micali, S.: How to construct random functions. J. ACM (JACM) **33**(4), 792–807 (1986)

[GLOW21] Galindo, D., Liu, J., Ordean, M., Wong, J.-M.: Fully distributed verifiable random functions and their application to decentralised random beacons, pp. 88–102 (2021)

[GNP+14] Goldberg, S., Naor, M., Papadopoulos, D., Reyzin, L., Vasant, S., Ziv, A.: NSEC5: provably preventing DNSSEC zone enumeration. Cryptology ePrint Archive, Report 2014/582 (2014). https://eprint.iacr.org/2014/582

[GRPV23] Goldberg, S., Reyzin, L., Papadopoulos, D., Včelák, J.: Verifiable Random Functions (VRFs). RFC 9381, August 2023

[HJ16] Hofheinz, D., Jager, T.: Verifiable random functions from standard assumptions. In: Kushilevitz, E., Malkin, T. (eds.) TCC 2016. LNCS, vol. 9562, pp. 336–362. Springer, Heidelberg (2016). https://doi.org/10.1007/978-3-662-49096-9_14

[HW10] Hohenberger, S., Waters, B.: Constructing verifiable random functions with large input spaces. In: Gilbert, H. (ed.) EUROCRYPT 2010. LNCS, vol. 6110, pp. 656–672. Springer, Heidelberg (2010). https://doi.org/10.1007/978-3-642-13190-5_33

[Koh19] Kohl, L.: Hunting and gathering – verifiable random functions from standard assumptions with short proofs. In: Lin, D., Sako, K. (eds.) PKC 2019. LNCS, vol. 11443, pp. 408–437. Springer, Cham (2019). https://doi.org/10.1007/978-3-030-17259-6_14

[KR98] Krawczyk, H., Rabin, T.: Chameleon hashing and signatures. Cryptology ePrint Archive, Report 1998/010 (1998). https://eprint.iacr.org/1998/010

[KRDO17] Kiayias, A., Russell, A., David, B., Oliynykov, R.: Ouroboros: a provably secure proof-of-stake blockchain protocol. In: Katz, J., Shacham, H. (eds.) CRYPTO 2017. LNCS, vol. 10401, pp. 357–388. Springer, Cham (2017). https://doi.org/10.1007/978-3-319-63688-7_12

[Lai23] Lai, Y.-F.: CAPYBARA and TSUBAKI: verifiable random functions from group actions and isogenies. Cryptology ePrint Archive, Report 2023/182 (2023). https://eprint.iacr.org/2023/182

[LBM20] Liang, B., Banegas, G., Mitrokotsa, A.: Statically aggregate verifiable random functions and application to e-lottery. Cryptography 4(4), 37 (2020)

[LR88] Luby, M., Rackoff, C.: How to construct pseudorandom permutations from pseudorandom functions. SIAM J. Comput. 17(2), 373–386 (1988)

[Lys02] Lysyanskaya, A.: Unique signatures and verifiable random functions from the DH-DDH separation. In: Yung, M. (ed.) CRYPTO 2002. LNCS, vol. 2442, pp. 597–612. Springer, Heidelberg (2002)

[MR02] Micali, S., Rivest, R.L.: Micropayments revisited. In: Preneel, B. (ed.) CT-RSA 2002. LNCS, vol. 2271, pp. 149–163. Springer, Heidelberg (2002). https://doi.org/10.1007/3-540-45760-7_11

[MRV99] Micali, S., Rabin, M.O., Vadhan, S.P.: Verifiable random functions. In: 40th FOCS, pp. 120–130. IEEE Computer Society Press, October 1999

[PWH+17] Papadopoulos, D., et al.: Making NSEC5 practical for DNSSEC. Cryptology ePrint Archive, Report 2017/099 (2017). https://eprint.iacr.org/2017/099

[Sho94] Shor, P.W.: Algorithms for quantum computation: discrete logarithms and factoring. In: 35th FOCS, pp. 124–134. IEEE Computer Society Press, November 1994

Monotone-Policy Aggregate Signatures

Maya Farber Brodsky[1], Arka Rai Choudhuri[2], Abhishek Jain[2,3],
and Omer Paneth[1($\boxtimes$)]

[1] Tel Aviv University, Tel Aviv, Israel
omerpa@tauex.tau.ac.il
[2] NTT Research, Sunnyvale, USA
{arkarai.choudhuri,abhishek.jain}@ntt-research.com
[3] Johns Hopkins University, Baltimore, USA
abhishek@cs.jhu.edu

Abstract. The notion of aggregate signatures allows for combining signatures from different parties into a short certificate that attests that *all* parties signed a message. In this work, we lift this notion to capture different, more expressive signing policies. For example, we can certify that a message was signed by a (weighted) threshold of signers.

We present the first constructions of aggregate signatures for monotone policies based on standard polynomial-time cryptographic assumptions. The aggregate signatures in our schemes are succinct, i.e., their size is *independent* of the number of signers. Moreover, verification is also succinct if all parties sign the same message (or if the messages have a succinct representation). All prior work requires either interaction between the parties or non-standard assumptions (that imply SNARKs for NP).

Our signature schemes are based on non-interactive batch arguments (BARGs) for monotone policies [Brakerski-Brodsky-Kalai-Lombardi-Paneth, Crypto'23]. In contrast to previous constructions, our BARGs satisfy a new notion of *adaptive* security which is instrumental to our application. Our new BARGs for monotone policies can be constructed from standard BARGs and other standard assumptions.

1 Introduction

Suppose that a group of parties wish to jointly sign a message m such that anyone can verify that a majority of the parties signed m. Such a scenario is commonplace in applications such as byzantine agreement [49], crypto wallets [2] and many other settings involving decentralization of trust [1,15,26,27,44].

Consider the following notion of digital signatures that captures several properties desirable for such applications: each of the k parties locally computes and publishes a verification key for its preferred signature scheme and uses the corresponding secret key to sign messages. Later, an untrusted party called the "aggregator" can combine the signatures of multiple parties into a joint signature σ to certify that at least t out of k parties signed a message. The combined signature σ can be verified given a digest of all k verification keys and the vector of messages signed (but without knowing the identity of the t signers). The key requirement is succinctness:

M. Joye and G. Leander (Eds.): EUROCRYPT 2024, LNCS 14654, pp. 168–195, 2024.
https://doi.org/10.1007/978-3-031-58737-5_7

- The size of the aggregate signature should be *sublinear* in k and even t, and ideally only depend on the security parameter.
- If all parties sign the *same* message (or, more generally, if the vector of messages has some succinct representation), the verification time should also be *sublinear* in t.
- Ideally, the aggregation time should grow with the number of signatures t as opposed to the number of parties k.

The security requirement is that no polynomial-time adversary that corrupts less than t parties in an *adaptive* manner should be able to create valid signatures.

This notion combines the best features of two central notions of multiparty signatures: threshold signatures [23,24] and aggregate signatures [9,34].[1] Threshold signatures, widely used in the blockchain ecosystem, support threshold signing with succinct verification but require *interactive* protocols for key setup and (in most cases) signing. Aggregate signatures dispense with the necessity of interaction but can only attest that *all* k parties signed (i.e., they do not support threshold signing). Therefore, the above notion can be viewed as a threshold variant of aggregate signatures or as an ad-hoc variant of threshold signatures. To see the appeal of this notion, consider decentralized autonomous organizations (DAO) where members vote on proposals to make joint decisions on governance of assets. Threshold signatures are a natural cryptographic tool for implementing such voting; however, running an interactive key setup between all members is unrealistic. Our notion eliminates this barrier.

Monotone-Policy Aggregate Signatures. We can generalize the above notion to capture more expressive signing policies. For example, consider weighted thresholds, where each party has a different weight and the signing policy is defined with respect to the sum of the party weights. Such a policy is useful in proof-of-stake blockchains [42]. Another example is threshold of thresholds capturing users with some hierarchical structure. In general, the signing policy might be described by a monotone function that takes as input a list of signers and decides whether they are authorized. We refer to this primitive as monotone-policy aggregate signatures.

It is not difficult to see that this primitive can be realized by combining standard signature schemes with (adaptively sound) succinct non-interactive arguments of knowledge (SNARKs) for NP [6,41]. The aggregate signature on a message m simply consists of a SNARK that proves the existence of valid signatures on m from an authorized set of signers. The succinctness property of the SNARK translates to the succinctness of aggregate signature. Sublinear verification time can be achieved by additionally relying on collision-resistant hash functions to compute verification key digests.

---

[1] In the literature, there are two distinct notions of signature schemes that support signature aggregation: multisignatures [34], where all parties sign the same message, and aggregate signatures [9], where parties may sign distinct messages. For simplicity of exposition, we use the terminology of aggregate signatures to refer to both settings.

SNARKs for NP are currently only known based on heuristics or non-standard assumptions [7,41]. Moreover, SNARK constructions with an explicit knowledge extractor are not known and are subject to strong barriers [8].

We ask:

Can we realize monotone policy aggregate signatures from standard assumptions?

Signatures from Batch Arguments. Non-interactive batch arguments (BARGs) [12,18,38] allow an efficient prover to compute a publicly verifiable proof of the validity of multiple NP statements, with size sublinear in the total witness length. If at least one statement is false, no polynomial-time adversary should be able to compute an accepting proof.

A recent sequence of works [17–19,35,50] provided constructions of BARGs for NP in the common reference string (CRS) model from various standard assumptions including learning with errors (LWE), decisional linear assumption (DLIN) over pairing groups, and sub-exponential decisional Diffie Hellman (DDH). Notably, these works achieve a *somewhere extraction* property that guarantees (given a CRS "trapdoor") efficient extraction of the witness of one statement in the batch from any accepting proof. This guarantee holds in the adaptive setting where the adversary can choose the NP statements as a function of the CRS. Using this property, recent works obtained the first constructions of aggregate signatures from standard assumptions [18,25,50].

It is easy to see that there is a direct correspondence between the k-out-of-k (i.e., conjunction) policies supported by BARGs and aggregate signatures. In light of this connection, and towards answering the above question, we ask whether there exist batch arguments that support more expressive policies of the following form: given a batch of statements $(x_1, \ldots, x_k)$ and a monotone policy $f : \{0,1\}^k \to \{0,1\}$, a valid proof should attest whether $f(b_1, \ldots, b_k) = 1$, where b_i indicates the veracity of x_i.

A very recent work [11] investigates this problem for the setting where the policy f is described by a polynomial-size monotone circuit.

They achieve an extraction property that extends the prior notion of somewhere extraction to general monotone policies. However, as we discuss in Sect. 2, this guarantee turns out to be inadequate for achieving monotone-policy aggregate signatures.

1.1   Our Results

We present the first constructions of aggregate signatures from standard assumptions that support expressive monotone policies and achieve poly-logarithmic signature size and verification time. Our constructions are in the common reference string (CRS) model where the size of the CRS grows only poly-logarithmically in the number of signers.

Before we state our results, we elaborate on our notion of aggregate signatures for monotone policies.

Monotone-Policy Aggregate Signatures. In an aggregate signature scheme for a monotone policy f, each party P_i publishes its own verification key vk_i, and there is a deterministic public algorithm that aggregates the verification keys of all k parties into a single aggregated verification key $\widehat{vk}$. Given a collection of signatures $\{\sigma_i\}_{i \in I}$ on a message m, an aggregator can produce an aggregated signature $\widehat{\sigma}$ on m. The signature $\widehat{\sigma}$ verifies with respect to $\widehat{vk}$ if $f(b_1, \ldots, b_k) = 1$, where $b_j = 1$ for every j such that signature σ_j verifies with respect to vk_j.

In terms of security, we require that no efficient adversary can win the following game with non-negligible probability. The adversary may ask the challenger for the verification key of any party, and it can ask for a signature on any message under any of these verification keys. These queries can be completely *adaptive*. Finally, the adversary produces a sequence of verification keys $vk_1, \ldots, vk_k$ that may include keys that were not generated by the challenger. Intuitively, we think of the keys generated by the challenger as belonging to honest parties while the other keys come from parties corrupted by the adversary. Together with the verification keys, the adversary also produces a target message m and a signature $\widehat{\sigma}$. The adversary wins if $\widehat{\sigma}$ verifies with respect to m and the key $\widehat{vk}$ aggregated from $vk_1, \ldots, vk_k$, and if the forgery is non-trivial. Intuitively, the forgery is non-trivial if the set of honest parties that signed m together with all corrupted parties does not satisfy the policy. That is, $f(b_1, \ldots, b_k) = 0$ where $b_j = 1$ for every j such that either the adversary asked for signature on m with respect to vk_j, or vk_j was not generated by the challenger.

Aggregate Signatures for Bounded-Space Monotone Policies. Our first construction supports read-once, bounded-space monotone policies. Such policies are given by a monotone function $f : \{0,1\}^k \to \{0,1\}$ that is computable by an algorithm that reads each bit of the input once, and maintains a state of size S that is updated after reading each bit. This class of monotone policies includes, for example: the t-out-of-k threshold function with state of size $S = \log k$, or the weighted threshold function for weights in $[B]$ with state of size $S = \log kB$.

Theorem 1 (Informal). *Assuming the existence of somewhere extractable BARGs with 2^S-security, there exists an aggregate signature scheme for all read-once $O(S)$ space polynomial-time monotone policies. The size of the CRS, the size of the aggregated signature, and the verification time are $\mathsf{poly}(\log k, S, \lambda)$ where λ denotes the security parameter.*

In particular, for $k = \mathsf{poly}(\lambda)$ and $S = \log(k)$ the theorem only requires BARGs with polynomial security.

Under the same assumptions as in Theorem 1, we can also construct aggregate signatures for monotone policies f that are computable by monotone circuits of fan-in two and $\log(\lambda)$-depth (or more generally, d-depth under 2^d-secure BARGs). This result is incomparable to Theorem 1. We refer the reader to the supplementary material for further details.

Fast Aggregator. For threshold policies, our result in Theorem 1 can be extended to achieve a more efficient aggregator whose running time only depends on the number of signatures t as opposed to the total number of parties k.

Theorem 2 (Informal). *Assuming the existence of somewhere extractable BARGs, there exist aggregate signature schemes for threshold policies such that the size of the CRS, the size of an aggregated signature and the verification time are* $\mathsf{poly}(\log k, \lambda)$, *and the aggregation time is* $\mathsf{poly}(t, \lambda)$ *for threshold* t.

Weakly Unforgeable Aggregate Signatures for Polynomial-Size Monotone Policies. Our last construction of aggregate signatures supports any policy computable by polynomial-size monotone circuits. It achieves the same (polylogarithmic) CRS size, signature size and verification time as in Theorem 1 but satisfies a weaker notion of security. Intuitively, this notion only guarantees that the adversary cannot forge signatures on messages that were not signed by any honest party. This definition relaxes the fully adaptive definition discussed above as follows: in the security game, signing queries on the challenge message m under any verification key generated by the challenger are not allowed. (The adversary is still free to output its own verification keys.) A similar relaxation was studied in the context of threshold signatures [3,48] where the stronger notion of full-security has proven to be more useful, but also more challenging to achieve.[2]

Theorem 3 (Informal). *Assuming fully homomorphic encryption and somewhere extractable BARGs, there exist* weakly unforgeable *aggregate signature schemes for all polynomial-size monotone circuits. The size of the CRS, the size of an aggregated signature and the verification time is* $\mathsf{poly}(\log k, \lambda)$.

Universal Aggregation and Updatability. We now highlight some additional properties of our constructions of aggregate signatures. First, our scheme supports *universal aggregation* [32]: we allow each user to use a different signature without modifying the way that individual verification keys or signatures are generated.[3] As a result, a signature issued by a party i can be *reused* for computing aggregate signatures with respect to different aggregate verification keys for different set of parties (that include i). Second, our schemes allow new users to *dynamically* join the system without the need to rerun system setup. The aggregate verification key defined for any subset of users can be efficiently updated to add new users. (The aggregated verification key in our scheme is simply a root of a hash tree computed over the individual verification keys.)

On Multi-hop Aggregation. Recently, [25] used rate-1 BARGs to construct multi-hop n-out-of-n aggregate signatures, where signatures can be aggregate incrementally. While, our schemes are only presented for the single-hop setting, we follow the same BARG based approach as [25]. Therefore, it is plausible that similar ideas could be applied to our schemes to support multi-hop aggregation; we leave further exploration of this topic to future work.

---

[2] See single- vs. dual-parameter threshold scheme in [48] and TS-UF-0 vs. TS-UF-1 in [3].

[3] For Theorem 3 the verification keys of the base signature are required to satisfy some natural property. See the full version for further details.

Monotone-Policy Aggregate Signatures from Batch Arguments. Our aggregate signatures constructions are based on new notions of monotone-policy BARGs. To realize Theorem 1 we rely on monotone-policy BARGs with a new notion of security that we called *adaptive subset extraction*. Our definition models an adaptive adversary that given the CRS outputs a batch of k statements, a proof π and a necessary subset J for the monotone policy f. Here, we say that a subset $J \subset [k]$ is *necessary* for f if for every input $b_1, \ldots, b_k$ such that $f(b_1, \ldots, b_k) = 1$, there exists a $j \in J$ such that $b_j = 1$. Our definition requires an efficient extractor algorithm that extracts from π a witness w such that conditioned on π being an accepting proof and J being a necessary subset, the extractor outputs a valid witness w_j for an index $j \in J$ with probability at least $\frac{1}{k}$. Since the extractor outputs a witness without knowing the set J, hitting J with probability $\frac{1}{k}$ is optimal.[4]

This notion is incomparable to the notion of subset extraction for monotone-policy BARGs from [11]. In their definition, the necessary subset J is chosen non-adaptively and programmed into the CRS, but the extraction algorithm is required to succeed with probability negligibly close to 1. Our construction of monotone-policy aggregate signatures crucially relies on the adaptive nature of our new security definition.

We construct BARGs with adaptive subset extraction for read-once bounded-space monotone policies.

Theorem 4 (Informal). *Assuming the existence of somewhere extractable BARGs with 2^S-security, there exist BARGs with adaptive subset extraction for all read-once $O(S)$ space polynomial-time monotone policies. The proofs are of size $|w| \cdot \text{poly}(\log k, S, \lambda)$ and the CRS is of size $\text{poly}(\log k, \lambda)$, where λ denotes the security parameter and $|w|$ is the length of a single witness.*

We also give a variant of the BARGs in Theorem 4 where the running time of the prover grows with the number of witnesses it is given instead of the total number of statements k. This gives Theorem 2.

Finally, we realize Theorem 3 based on BARGs for monotone policies with a new notion of security called *functional subset extraction* which generalizes the notion of subset extraction from [11]. In BARGs with subset extraction, we program a necessary subset J into the CRS. In contrast, in functional subset extraction, we program a function g into the CRS. We also add a tag y that is given as an additional input to the BARG prover and verifier. The requirement is that given any proof π that is accepted with respect to a tag y, if $J = g(y)$ is a necessary subset then we can extract from π a valid witness w_j for an index $j \in J$ with probability negligibly close to 1.

Based on the construction of [11], we obtain BARGs with functional subset extraction for all policies computable by polynomial-size monotone circuits. The

---

[4] For example in the case of k-out-of-k threshold, each singleton set $\{j\}$ for $j \in [k]$ is necessary.

proof is of size $|w| \cdot \text{poly}(\log k, \lambda)$ where $|w|$ is the size of a witness, and the CRS is of size $B \cdot \text{poly}(\log k, \lambda)$, where B is a bound on the description size of a function that can be programmed into the CRS.

1.2 Related Work

Threshold Signatures. There is an extensive body of work dedicated to the study of threshold signatures [23,24]. The de facto design of such schemes involves a distributed setup phase to compute a verification key and a threshold secret sharing [47] of the signing key. Subsequently, the parties can jointly sign messages using their key shares, typically using an interactive signing protocol.

While any signature scheme can be "thresholdized" using secure multiparty computation [5,13,31], prior work has primarily focused on designing efficient thresholdizers for popular signature schemes used in practice such as Schnorr [46], ECDSA [14] and BLS [10]. All such solutions, however, require *interactive* protocols for key setup and (except for BLS) signature computation. Furthermore, by their very design, such solutions do not support universal aggregation of signatures from different signature schemes. Very recently, [22,30] overcame the former limitation by presenting an efficient instantiation of the generic SNARK-based approach discussed earlier. The security of their schemes is proven in idealized models.

Aggregate Signatures. Aggregate signatures [9] support aggregation of signatures from different parties on possibly different messages. The key requirement is succinctness of the aggregated signature. Most known schemes also support succinct verification given a digest of the verification key of all the signers. A variation of aggregate signatures where all signers sign the same message is referred to as multisignatures [34]. For simplicity of exposition, we use the common terminology of aggregate signatures for both of these settings throughout this work.

Until recently, aggregate signatures were only known in (i) the Random Oracle model from pairing-based assumptions [9]; or (ii) the standard model utilizing heavy tools such as multilinear maps [29,45] or indistinguishability obfuscation [32], or only achieved weaker properties (e.g., multisignatures or sequential aggregation) [39,40]. Recently, using non-interactive BARGs, new constructions in the common reference string (CRS) model were obtained based on a variety of standard assumptions including LWE [19,25,43], DLIN assumption over pairing groups [50], and sub-exponential DDH [16].

Batch Arguments. [37] gave the first construction of BARGs for NP from a non-standard but falsifiable assumption over bilinear maps. Recently, a sequence of works [17–19,33,50] constructed BARGs for NP from a variety of standard assumptions with proof sizes ranging from slightly sublinear to poly-logarithmic in the number of statements. Two lines of work devised efficiency boosting compilers for BARGs: [36] show how to achieve poly-logarithmic proof sizes generically from sublinear-size proofs, and [25,43] construct rate-1 BARGs from BARGs with low rate. Very recently, [11] constructed BARGs for monotone circuits from polynomial hardness of LWE.

Sigma Protocols. Sigma protocols are three-round public-coin zero-knowledge proof systems with special soundness [20]. They have many applications including efficient constructions of digital signatures via the Fiat-Shamir heuristic [28]. Sigma protocols are known to be closed under different types of composition such as monotone span programs [21] and more. In the composition of sigma protocols, the communication complexity typically grows with the number of instances and the primary emphasis is on preserving the zero knowledge property. In contrast, our focus is on succinctness and our signatures do not have any hiding property.

2   Technical Overview

In this section, we provide an overview of our definitions and constructions. Our starting point is a simple template construction of aggregate signatures from BARGs. By instantiating this template with existing BARG constructions, we get aggregate signatures for the k-out-of-k (i.e., conjunction) policy. In what follows, we instantiate the template construction with more general notions of BARGs resulting in aggregate signature for more expressive policies. We start by describing the template construction focusing on the simple case of conjunctions.

Template Aggregate Signature from BARGs. The CRS of the aggregate signature scheme consists of a CRS for the BARG and a description of a collision-resistant hash function H. Fix a base signature scheme S that is used by each party to generate keys and sign/verify messages. To aggregate a sequence of verification keys $\mathsf{vk}_1, \ldots, \mathsf{vk}_k$ we compute a hash tree over them using H and set the aggregate verification key $\widehat{\mathsf{vk}}$ to its root. An aggregate signature $\widehat{\sigma}$ on a message m under $\widehat{\mathsf{vk}}$ is a BARG proof that m has a signature under each of the verification keys. In more detail, let $\mathcal{L}$ be the NP language that contains tuples $(\widehat{\mathsf{vk}}, m, i)$ if and only if there exists a verification key vk_i, a path authenticating vk_i as the i-th leaf of the hash tree rooted at $\widehat{\mathsf{vk}}$, and a valid signature σ_i on m under vk_i using the base scheme S. Given verification keys $\mathsf{vk}_1, \ldots, \mathsf{vk}_k$, a message m and signatures $\sigma_1, \ldots, \sigma_k$, we set the aggregate signature $\widehat{\sigma}$ to be a BARG proof for the k statements $(\widehat{\mathsf{vk}}, m, i) \in \mathcal{L}$ for $i \in [k]$. To verify the aggregate signature we simply verify that the BARG proof is accepting.

The succinctness of this construction follows from that of the hash tree and the BARG. The size of the aggregate verification key (i.e. the root of the hash tree) is $\mathsf{poly}(\lambda)$ where λ is the security parameter. By the succinctness of the BARG, the size of the aggregate signature (i.e. the BARG proof) is polynomial in λ and the size of the witness for a single statement $(\widehat{\mathsf{vk}}, m, i) \in \mathcal{L}$. The witness consists of a key and signature of the base scheme S and an authentication path in the hash tree and it is, therefore, of size $\mathsf{poly}(\lambda, \log k)$. To get efficient verification we rely on BARGs with efficient verification known as BARGs for the index language [19]. In such BARGs, verifying the k statements that differ from each other only in the index $i \in [k]$ takes time that is polynomial in the size of just one statement and the proof. Therefore, verifying the k statements $(\widehat{\mathsf{vk}}, m, i) \in \mathcal{L}$ for $i \in [k]$, takes time $\mathsf{poly}(\lambda, \log k)$.

To show the security of the construction, consider an adversary A that outputs verification keys $vk_1, \ldots, vk_k$, a message m, and an aggregate signature $\hat{\sigma}$ such that $\hat{\sigma}$ is a valid signature on m under the aggregate key $\widehat{vk}$ and there exists at least one index $j^* \in [k]$ such that the challenger generated the key vk_{j^*} and did not sign m under vk_{j^*}. Our goal is to give a reduction that can extract from the aggregate signature $\hat{\sigma}$ (i.e. the BARG proof) a forged signature on m under vk_j (or, alternatively, a collision in H). This seems to call for BARGs that are not only sound, but also extractable (i.e. BARGs of knowledge). Moreover, the BARGs should be adaptively secure since the statements depend on $\widehat{vk}, m$ which A may choose as a function of the CRS.

Existing BARG constructions, however, are not known to satisfy full-fledged knowledge soundness in the adaptive setting. Indeed, such BARGs would imply SNARKs for all of NP [12]. Instead, existing BARGs provide a weaker guarantee known as *somewhere extractablilty* [19]. In a somewhere extractable BARG we can generate, for every index $j \in [k]$, a CRS that is "programmed" at j and is computationally indistinguishable from an honestly generated CRS. Under the programmed CRS, we can extract a witness for the j-th statement from any accepting BARG proof using a trapdoor. Using somewhere extractable BARGs, the security reduction for the aggregate signature is as follows. The reduction generates a CRS for the BARG that is programmed at a random index $j \in [k]$. If A produces a valid aggregate signature $\hat{\sigma}$ (i.e. an accepting BARG proof) the reduction extracts a witness for the j-th statement $(\widehat{vk}, m, j) \in \mathcal{L}$. Such a witness contains a verification key $\widetilde{vk}_j$, a path authenticating $\widetilde{vk}_j$ under $\widehat{vk}$, and a valid signature σ_j on m under $\widetilde{vk}_j$. If $\widetilde{vk}_j \neq vk_j$ the reduction finds a collision in H. Otherwise, if $j = j^*$, the reduction finds a forged signature on m under vk_{j^*}. It remains to show that indeed $j = j^*$ with noticeable probability. This follows from the fact that the programmed CRS hides the index j. (Note that the reduction finds j^* efficiently and without the CRS trapdoor).

Towards More Expressive Policies. Going beyond conjunctions, we turn our attention to aggregate signatures for more expressive monotone policies. Before describing our schemes, we start with a simple construction of an aggregate signature scheme for general monotone policies, albeit, with weak succinctness. The high-level idea is to use the aggregate signature scheme for conjunctions described above and restrict it to the subset of the parties that signed the message. In more detail, given verification keys $vk_1, \ldots, vk_k$ we again set the aggregate verification key $\widehat{vk}$ to be the root of the hash tree over the k keys. Let $\{\sigma_i\}_{i \in I}$ be a collection of signatures on a message m by a subset of the parties $I \subseteq [k]$ that satisfies the policy f. We aggregate $\{\sigma_i\}_{i \in I}$ into a signature $\hat{\sigma}$ under $\widehat{vk}$ as follows. First, we use the conjunction scheme to aggregate $\{vk_i\}_{i \in I}$ into an key $\widehat{vk}_I$ and aggregate $\{\sigma_i\}_{i \in I}$ into a signature $\hat{\sigma}_I$ under $\widehat{vk}_I$. The aggregate signature $\hat{\sigma}$ contains contains a description of the set I, the keys $\{vk_i\}_{i \in I}$ together with their authentication paths under $\widehat{vk}$, and the signature $\hat{\sigma}_I$. To verify $\hat{\sigma}$ under $\widehat{vk}$ we first check that the set I satisfies the policy and that all the authentication paths are valid. Then we use the conjunction scheme to recompute the aggregate key $\widehat{\mathsf{vk}}_I$ and verify the signature $\widehat{\sigma}_I$. The main drawback of this approach is that size of the aggregate signature $\widehat{\sigma}$ can grow with the size of the authorized subset I. For example, for the t-out-of-k threshold policy, the signature will grow with the threshold t. In contrast, our results give succinct aggregate signatures of size $\mathsf{poly}(\log k, \lambda)$ even for policies where the authorized subsets may be much larger.

Aggregate Signatures from Monotone-Policy BARGs. Our aggregate signature constructions follow a different approach: starting from the template construction of aggregate signature, we replace the BARGs with the stronger notion of BARGs for monotone policies. Intuitively, a BARG for a monotone policy f, can prove that a batch of statements $x_1, \ldots, x_k$ satisfies f. That is, $f(b_1, \ldots, b_k) = 1$, where b_i indicates the veracity of x_i. Recall that in our template aggregate signature construction, a valid statement x_i corresponds to a signature under the i-th party's verification key. BARGs for all policies given by polynomial-size monotone circuits were constructed by a recent work of Brakerski, Brodsky, Kalai, Lombardi and Paneth [11], however, the security notion guaranteed by their BARGs seems insufficient to prove the security of the aggregate signatures. Instead, our results are based on new monotone-policy BARG constructions that satisfy different security notions. Before expanding on these contributions, we start by reviewing the security notion of [11] and explain why it is insufficient.

The work of [11] puts forward a generalization of the somewhere extractability property of [19] to the settings of monotone-policy BARGs: Instead of programming the CRS on a single index $j \in [k]$, we can program the CRS on any *necessary subset* of indices $J \subseteq [k]$ and the programmed CRS hides J. A subset $J \subseteq [k]$ is necessary if any other subset J' that satisfies the policy intersects J. Or, equivalently, J is necessary if its complement $[k] \setminus J$ does not satisfy the policy.[5] Using the programmed CRS, we can extract from any accepting BARG proof, a witness for the j-th statement for some $j \in J$. This holds even if the adversary can choose the BARG statements $x_1, \ldots, x_k \in \mathcal{L}$ adaptively, as a function of the CRS. For example, for the conjunction policy, every singleton set $\{j\}$ for $j \in [k]$ is necessary, and thus, we recover the original notion of somewhere extractability for BARGs.

We can instantiate the template aggregate signature construction with somewhere extractable monotone-policy BARGs, but we do not know how to argue the security of the resulting scheme.[6] Going back to the aggregate signatures security game, consider an adversary A that is given a CRS, and, after interacting with the challenger, outputs verification keys $\mathsf{vk}_1, \ldots, \mathsf{vk}_k$, a target message m and an aggregate signature $\widehat{\sigma}$ on m that verifies under the aggregate key $\widehat{\mathsf{vk}}$. Let $J \subseteq [k]$ be the subset of indices of honest parties that did not sign m. That is, J contains every index j such that the challenger generated vk_j but did not sign m under it. Recall that A's forgery is considered non-trivial if the set of honest parties that signed m together with all corrupted parties does not sat-

---

[5] We assume that the policy is not a constant function.

[6] Another issue is that in the construction of [11] the CRS size grows linearly with k, while we are aiming for CRS of size $\mathsf{poly}(\lambda, \log k)$.

isfy the policy. In other words, if A wins the game then J must be a necessary subset. Therefore, if we had programmed the CRS on the set J, we could have extracted from $\hat{\sigma}$ (i.e. the BARG proof) a witness for the j-th BARG statement $(\widehat{vk}, m, j) \in \mathcal{L}$ for some $j \in J$. Such a witness must contain a forged signature σ_j on m under vk_j (or, a collision in the hash H) and, since $j \in J$, this is a non-trivial forgery of the base signature scheme S. The problem with this argument is that the necessary subset J is defined by A's queries and output and, therefore, it is not known at the time the CRS is generated. In fact, A can even choose J adaptively as a function of the CRS.[7]

To get around this hurdle we introduce new notions of security of monotone-policy BARGs where the extraction guarantee holds for necessary subsets that can be chosen *adaptively*, after the CRS is fixed. The BARGs behind Theorems 1 and 3 are described in Sects. 2.1 and 2.2 respectively.

2.1   Aggregate Signatures for Bounded-Space Monotone Policies

In this section we first describe our new notion of monotone-policy BARGs with *adaptive subset extraction* which is the main tool behind Theorem 1.

Then we overview our construction of monotone-policy BARGs with adaptive subset extraction for the class of read-once, bounded-space monotone policies based on somewhere-extractable BARGs. A monotone policy $f : \{0,1\}^k \to \{0,1\}$ is read-once, space S if there exists a polynomial time Turing machine Γ and a pair of states $s_0, s_k \in \{0,1\}^S$ such that $f(b_1, \ldots, b_k) = 1$ if and only if there exist states $s_1, \ldots, s_{k-1} \in \{0,1\}^S$ such that $s_i = \Gamma(s_{i-1}, b_i)$ for every $i \in [k]$.

Monotone-Policy BARGs with Adaptive Subset Extraction. In BARGs with adaptive subset extraction the CRS is generated together with an extraction trapdoor. However, in contrast to the notion of somewhere extractability, the CRS is not programmed on any particular subset. Instead, the adversary outputs a description of a subset $J^* \subseteq [k]$ together with the statements $x_1, \ldots, x_k \in \mathcal{L}$ and the proof, after receiving the CRS. Ideally, we would like to require that whenever J^* is necessary and the proof is accepting, we can extract a witness for the j-th statement for some $j \in J^*$ using a trapdoor. However, this requirement seems too strong since it implies full-fledged knowledge soundness. (I.e. we can extract witnesses for i-th statement for any $i \in I$ for some subset I that satisfies the policy.[8]) Instead, we only require that if the adversary outputs a necessary subset J^* and an accepting proof with some probability α, then we can extract a witness for the j-th statement for some $j \in J^*$ with probability that is at most negligibly smaller than α/k. We note that as long as we only extract a single witness from each proof, losing a factor of k in the extraction probability

---

[7] Note that if the policy has necessary subsets that are sufficiently large, then guessing the set J may result in security loss that is exponential in k. Tolerating such loss would mean losing succinctness.

[8] To extract, start from the necessary subset $J^* = [k]$, run the extractor, and obtain a witness for the j-th statement for some $j \in J^*$. Remove j from J^* and repeat until J^* is no longer necessary.

is inherent. Taking, for example, the conjunction policy, if the adversary outputs a necessary subset $\{j\}$ for a random $j \in [k]$, then the extracted witness fits the j-th statement with probability at most $1/k$.[9]

By instantiating the template aggregate signature construction with monotone-policy BARGs that satisfy adaptive subset extraction (instead of somewhere extraction), we can fix the flawed analysis above: Consider an adversary A that wins the aggregate signatures security game with some noticeable probability α. As before, we let J^* be the subset that contains every index j such that the challenger generated vk_j but did not sign m under it. If A wins the game then the aggregate signature $\hat{\sigma}$ is valid (i.e. the BARG proof is accepting) and the set J^* is necessary. Therefore, we are guaranteed to extract a witness for the j-th BARG statement $(\widehat{\mathsf{vk}}, m, j) \in \mathcal{L}$ for some $j \in J^*$ with noticeable probability $\alpha/k - \mathsf{negl}$. Such a witness must contain a non-trivial forged signature σ_j under vk_j (or, a collision in the hash H).

BARGs with Adaptive Subset Extraction For Low-Depth Policies. Our first construction of BARGs with adaptive subset extraction is based on any somewhere extractable BARG, and it supports policies that are computable by monotone circuits of fan-in two and $\log(\lambda)$-depth (or, more generally, d-depth under 2^d-secure BARGs). The work of [11] gives a simple construction of BARGs for such policies. We observe that their analysis naturally extends to achieve adaptive subset extraction. For completeness, we describe this construction and its analysis in the full version of the paper. We note, however, that the main construction from [11] that supports more expressive policies does *not* guarantee adaptive subset extraction out of the box.

On Adaptive Subset Extraction from Somewhere Extraction. A natural approach for constructing monotone-policy BARGs with adaptive subset extraction would be to start from any somewhere-extractable monotone-policy BARG and transform it into a BARG with adaptive subset extraction for the same policy. Indeed, for the conjunction policy such a transformation exists: simply program the CRS on a necessary subset $\{j\}$ for a random $j \in [k]$. To argue that the resulting BARG satisfies adaptive subset extraction, consider an adversary that outputs a necessary subset J^* and an accepting proof for some batch of statements with probability α. The somewhere extraction property guarantees that we can extract a witness for the j-th statement from any accepting proof. Moreover, since the CRS hides the index j, the probability of extracting a witness for the j-th statement for $j \in J^*$ is at least $\alpha/k - \mathsf{negl}$.

This transformation, however, does not seem to extend to other policies. Consider, for example, the $(k-1)$-out-of-k threshold policy where every set with more than one index is necessary. We focus on transformations where the CRS is programmed with a subset J sampled from some distribution over necessary subsets. Let A be an adversary that outputs a random subset J^* of size exactly

---

[9] We can relax adaptive subset extraction by considering a different bound $\beta \leq 1/k$ on the loss in the extraction probability. The notion remains meaningful for any inverse polynomial β and is still sufficient for constructing aggregate signatures.

2 together with an accepting proof. The somewhere extraction property guarantees that we can extract a witness for the j-th statement for some $j \in J$ with probability $1 - \mathsf{negl}$. Now, suppose that whenever $J \setminus J^*$ is not empty, the extracted index j is in $J \setminus J^*$. Indeed, we cannot rule out such an adversary since the extracted index j may depend both on the programmed set J and on A's proof (which may be correlated with J^*).[10] Since J is of size at least 2 and J^* is a set of size exactly 2 chosen at random after J is already fixed, the probability that $J \setminus J^*$ is empty is at most $\frac{2}{k(k-1)}$. Therefore, $j \in J^*$ with probability that is noticeably smaller than $1/k$.[11]

Extracting at an Index Instead of a Subset. In the above attempt to transform somewhere extraction into adaptive subset extraction, the high level idea was to guess some necessary subset J and program it into the CRS. The problem is that we had no control over the statement in J for which we extract a witness. As a result, we had to guess a subset J that is entirely contained in the subset J^* chosen by the adversary. For some policies, however, this loss in the probability of extraction is too high.

We therefore follow a different approach: instead of guessing a necessary subset J, we guess the particular index $j \in [K]$ of the statement x_j we wish to extract a witness for, and program j into the CRS. Indeed, since j is hidden from the adversary, the probability that $j \in J^*$ is at least $1/k - \mathsf{negl}$. However, now we can no longer expect to extract a witness for the j-statement from any accepting proof. Unless the subset $\{j\}$ happens to be necessary, the adversary might output statements $x_1, \ldots, x_k \in \mathcal{L}$ where the subset $I \subseteq [k]$ of true statements satisfies the policy, but $x_j \notin \mathcal{L}$ and so extraction must fail. Moreover, we cannot rule out an adversary that outputs such statements with probability 1, even when j is sampled randomly. The issue is that the adversary may choose the statements adaptively, as a function of the CRS, without knowing which of the statements are true.

A possible solution to this problem is to have the adversary prove that it knows the subset I of true statements. Indeed, if the adversary outputs a subset J^* that is necessary, then J^* and I intersect. Therefore, if the adversary knows I (i.e. we can efficiently extract I from the adversary) then we can use the fact that j is hidden to argue that, conditioned on J^* being necessary, $j \in J^* \cap I$ with probability at least $1/k - \mathsf{negl}$. The problem with this solution is without resorting to SNARKs for NP, we do not know how to prove knowledge of I without losing succinctness. Nonetheless, this approach turns out to be useful: instead of requiring the prover to know the subset I of true statements, in our solution we make a weaker requirement. Very roughly, we require that it is

---

[10] We can even construct a contrived BARG for which this attack is feasible based on the scheme of [11].

[11] More generally, if a policy f has exactly T "minimal" necessary subsets (that do not contain smaller necessary subsets) then we can transform any somewhere-extractable BARG for f into a BARG for f with adaptive subset extraction where the loss in extraction probability is bounded by $\beta = 1/T$. However for $\beta > 1/T$ we do not know of such a transformation.

possible to simulate a subset $\tilde{I}$ that satisfies the policy and is, in some useful sense, indistinguishable from the actual subset I of true statements chose by the adversary. We show how to enforce this weaker requirement using weaker machinery that can be based on BARGs.

Verifiable PIR. The main tool we use to construct monotone-policy BARGs with adaptive subset extraction is verifiable private information retrieval (vPIR) recently introduced by Ben-David, Kalai, and Paneth [4]. In a plain PIR protocol a server holds a database $D = (r_1, \ldots, r_k)$ and a client can query a row r_i while keeping the index i hidden from the server. Each party sends one message, and the size of the server's answer should be sublinear in k. In vPIR, we additionally require the server to use a database that satisfies some predicate P. Otherwise, its answer should be rejected by the (public) verification algorithm. This security requirement is formalized via the real-ideal paradigm: for every efficient malicious server A, we require that there exists an efficient simulator Sim such that for every index i the output of the following two experiments are indistinguishable:[12]

Real: Query A on index i. If the answer verifies output the decrypted row r. Otherwise output $\bot$.

Ideal: Sim samples a database $D = (r_1, \ldots, r_k)$. If $P(D) = 1$ output r_i. Otherwise output $\bot$.

One may consider a stronger secure computation style notion where Sim is required to simulate also the view of A in the real experiment (i.e. the query). However, we do not know how to satisfy this stronger notion. The work of [4] constructs vPIR for read-once, log-space predicates based on somewhere-extractable BARGs. (More generally, they can handle read-once space S predicates based on 2^S-secure BARGs.) We say that a predicate P is read-once space S if there exists a polynomial time Turing machine Γ and a pair of states $s_0, s_k \in \{0,1\}^S$ such that $P(r_1, \ldots, r_k) = 1$ if and only if there exist states $s_1, \ldots, s_{k-1} \in \{0,1\}^S$ such that $s_i = \Gamma(s_{i-1}, r_i)$ for every $i \in [k]$.

Verifiable PIR for Policies. When constructing monotone-policy BARGs for a policy f, we use vPIR for particular predicates P_f that evaluates the policy f where the i-th input bit to the policy is computed by some local polynomial-time predicate L on the i-th database row. Moreover, it would be useful to allow the local predicate to depend on some row-specific instance. That is, given instances $x_1, \ldots, x_k$ and a database $D = (r_1, \ldots, r_k)$, we have $P(D) = f(b_1, \ldots, b_k)$ where $b_i = L(x_i, r_i)$ for every $i \in [k]$. Observe that if f is a read-once space S policy, then P_f is also a read-once space S predicate.

Looking ahead, the instances will correspond to the BARG statements $x_1, \ldots, x_k \in \mathcal{L}$ and, therefore, when defining security, we need to allow the adversary to choose these instances adaptively as a function of CRS. While the analysis of [4] only supports predicates that are chosen non-adaptively, we extend their construction and show that for predicates of form P_f, it satisfies a useful

---

[12] The actual notion we work with is slightly weaker: for every polynomial q there exists a simulator Sim such that the outputs are $1/q$-indistinguishable.

notion of security in the adaptive setting.[13] For every efficient malicious server A
we require that there exists an efficient simulator Sim such that for every index
i the output of the following two experiments are indistinguishable:

Real: Query A on index i and obtain instances $(x_1, \ldots, x_k)$ and an answer a. If
the answer verifies output (x_i, r) where r is the decryption of a. Otherwise
output $\perp$.

Ideal: Sim samples instances $(\tilde{x}_1, \ldots, \tilde{x}_k)$ and a database $D = (r_1, \ldots, r_k)$. If
$P(D) = 1$ output $(\tilde{x}_i, r_i)$. Otherwise output $\perp$.

One may consider a stronger notion where Sim is required to simulate all the
instances $x_1 \ldots, x_k$ chosen by A in the real experiment instead of just x_i. However, we do not know how to satisfy this stronger notion. See the full version for
further details on the notion and construction of vPIR for policies.

BARGs with Adaptive Subset Extraction from vPIR: First Attempt.
We start with a simple construction of monotone-policy BARGs from vPIR.
(We will eventually need to modify this construction to show adaptive subset
extraction.)

To construct BARGs for a policy f we will use vPIR for a related predicate
P_f over the database of witnesses: for statements $x_1, \ldots, x_k$, and database $D = (w_1, \ldots, w_k)$, we have that $P(D) = f(b_1, \ldots, b_k)$, where $b_i = 1$ if and only if
w_i is a valid witness for the i-th statement. The CRS of the BARG is a vPIR
query for a random index $j \in [k]$. The prover computes the vPIR answer using
the database of witnesses $D = (w_1, \ldots, w_k)$ (if the prover is not given a witness
for x_i it sets $w_i = \perp$) and outputs it as the proof. The verifier accepts the proof
if the vPIR answer verifies. To extract a witness from the proof we decrypt the
vPIR answer.

To explain the difficulty in proving adaptive subset extraction, consider the
following (flawed) argument. Let A be an adversary that given a CRS (i.e. a
vPIR query), outputs a statement $x_1, \ldots, x_k$, an accepting proof (i.e. a vPIR
answer) and a necessary subset J^* with probability α. By vPIR security, there is a
simulator Sim that samples instances $\tilde{x}_1, \ldots, \tilde{x}_k$ and a database $\tilde{D} = (\tilde{w}_1, \ldots, \tilde{w}_k)$
such that $P_f(\tilde{D}) = 1$ with probability $\alpha - \mathsf{negl}$. Moreover, if j is the random
index queried in the CRS, then the output $(\tilde{x}_j, \tilde{w}_j)$ of the ideal experiment is
indistinguishable from the output (x_j, w) of the real experiment where w denotes
the decrypted vPIR answer (this is conditioned on the outputs being different
than $\perp$). If $P_f(\tilde{D}) = 1$ then any necessary subset J^* must contain some index $i \in J^*$ such that $\tilde{w}_i$ is a valid witness for $\tilde{x}_i \in \mathcal{L}$. Since $\tilde{D}$ is sampled independently
of j we have that $i = j$ with probability $1/k$. That is, with probability at least
$\alpha/k - \mathsf{negl}$, $\tilde{w}_j$ is a valid witness for $\tilde{x}_j \in \mathcal{L}$ and $j \in J^*$. By vPIR security, it
follows that also in the real experiment, the extracted value, w is a valid witness
for $x_j \in \mathcal{L}$ and $j \in J^*$ with probability at least $\alpha/k - \mathsf{negl}$. The problem is

---

[13] To get BARGs for the index language, our vPIR construction additionally supports
fast verification for instances $x_1, \ldots, x_k$ that differ from each other only on the index
$i \in [k]$.

that while this argument holds for any fixed necessary subset J^*, it may fail if A chooses J^* adaptively, as a function of the CRS (i.e. the vPIR query). Indeed, vPIR security does not guarantee simulation of both w and the view of A together.

A Simple Analysis for Threshold Policies. We start by describing an alternative analysis tailored to the case of threshold policies. The solution for general policies is more complex and we discuss it next. For the t-out-of-k threshold policy, if the simulated database $\tilde{D} = (\tilde{w}_1, \ldots, \tilde{w}_k)$ satisfies the predicate, then, since the index j is random and independent of $\tilde{D}$, we have that $\tilde{w}_j$ is a valid witness for $\tilde{x}_j \in \mathcal{L}$ with probability at least $\alpha \cdot t/k$. By vPIR security, it follows that also in the real experiment, w is a valid witness for $x_j \in \mathcal{L}$ with probability at least $\alpha \cdot t/k - $ negl. (Note that we can use vPIR security here since this event does not depend on the set J^* or the view of A.) For the t-out-of-k threshold policy, every necessary subset is of size at least $k - t + 1$. Therefore, in the real experiment, since A outputs a necessary subset J^* and since the index j is random and hidden from A, we have that $j \in J^*$ with probability at least $\alpha \cdot (k - t + 1)/k - $ negl. Therefore, by the Union bound, w is a valid witness for $x_j \in \mathcal{L}$ and $j \in J^*$ with probability at least $\alpha/k - $ negl.

Going Beyond Threshold Policies via Composable vPIR. The analysis above crucially relies on the symmetric structure of threshold policies and it does not seem to extend beyond that. As suggested by failed attempt above, to support general read-once bounded space polices, it is sufficient to simulate the witness w extracted from the proof together with the subset J^* chosen by A. While we do not know if such simulation is possible, our new simulation strategy will take into account the subset J^*. Very roughly, the main idea behind our simulation is to encode the set J^* as another database, and simulate both databases together using the machinery of vPIR. To this end, we introduce a stronger notion of vPIR that remains secure under composition. Intuitively, in a t-composable vPIR protocol for predicates $P^1, \ldots, P^t$, the same query can be answered using t different databases, where the i-th database is required to satisfy the predicate P^i. To capture this, we modify the real and ideal experiments as follows:

Real: Query A on index i and obtain instances $(x_1, \ldots, x_k)$ and t answers $a^1, \ldots, a^t$. If all the answers verify output $(x_i, r^1, \ldots, r^t)$ where r^j is the decryption of a^j. Otherwise output $\bot$.
Ideal: Sim samples instances $(\tilde{x}_1, \ldots, \tilde{x}_k)$ and t databases $D^1, \ldots, D^t$ where $D^i = (r_1^j, \ldots, r_k^j)$. If $P^j(D^j) = 1$ for every $j \in [t]$ output $(\tilde{x}_i, r_i^1, \ldots, r_i^t)$. Otherwise output $\bot$.

We show that the vPIR construction of [4] is t-composable for any $t = O(1)$. Very roughly, what enables such composition is that evaluating read-once S space predicates over $O(1)$ different databases can be done by a singe read-once $O(S)$ space predicate operating over all the databases simultaneously. See the full version for further details on our composition theorem.

BARGs with Adaptive Subset Extraction from Composable vPIR. Our final construction of BARGs from vPIR remains unchanged, except that in the analysis we rely on the fact that the vPIR is 2-composable. To argue adaptive subset extraction, consider an adversary A against the BARG that given a CRS (i.e. a vPIR query) outputs statement $x_1, \ldots, x_k$, a proof (i.e. a vPIR answer a) and a subset J^*. We turn A into a 2-composable vPIR adversary A' that outputs the instances $x_1, \ldots, x_k$, A's vPIR answer a and an additional answer a' that encodes J^* as follows: Let $D' = (b_1', \ldots, b_k')$ be the database such that $b_i' = 1$ if and only if $i \notin J^*$. Let P_f' be the predicate such that $P_f'(D') = 1$ if and only if $f(D') = 0$ (i.e. if and only if J^* is necessary). Using vPIR for the predicate P_f', compute the answer a' to the query in the CRS from the database D'.

Say A outputs an accepting proof and a necessary subset J^* with probability α. When this occurs, A' outputs two accepting vPIR answers. Therefore, by 2-composable vPIR security, there is a simulator Sim that samples instances $\tilde{x}_1, \ldots, \tilde{x}_k$ and a pair of databases $\tilde{D} = (\tilde{w}_1, \ldots, \tilde{w}_k)$ and $\tilde{D}' = (\tilde{b}_1', \ldots, \tilde{b}_k')$ such that $P_f(\tilde{D}) = 1$ and $P_f'(\tilde{D}') = 1$ with probability $\alpha -$ negl. Moreover, if j is the random index queried in the CRS, then the output $(\tilde{x}_j, \tilde{w}_j, \tilde{b}_j')$ of the ideal experiment is indistinguishable from the output (x_j, w, b') of the real experiment where w and b' denote the decryption of the answers a and a' respectively (this is conditioned on the outputs being different than $\bot$). If $P_f(\tilde{D}) = 1$ and $P_f'(\tilde{D}') = 1$ then there must exist some index $i \in [k]$ such that $\tilde{w}_i$ is a valid witness for $\tilde{x}_i \in \mathcal{L}$ and $\tilde{b}_i' = 0$. Since $\tilde{D}, \tilde{D}'$ are sampled independently of j we have that $i = j$ with probability $1/k$. That is, with probability at least $\alpha/k -$ negl, $\tilde{w}_j$ is a valid witness for $\tilde{x}_j \in \mathcal{L}$ and $\tilde{b}_j' = 0$. By vPIR security, it follows that also in the real experiment, the extracted value, w is a valid witness for $x_j \in \mathcal{L}$ and $b' = 0$ with probability at least $\alpha/k -$ negl. Finally, by the definition of a' (which was computed honestly) we have that $b' = b_j'$ and, therefore, w is a valid witness for $x_j \in \mathcal{L}$ and $j \in J^*$ with probability at least $\alpha/k -$ negl.

Fast Prover/Aggregator. For general read-once bounded-space policies, the number of true statements required to satisfy the policy may be large. Therefore, the running time of the honest prover must, in general, grow with k. When constructing aggregate signatures from BARGs this affects the time required to aggregate signatures. However, for specific policies we can hope to do better. For example, for the t-out-of-k threshold policy, we construct a BARG with adaptive subset extraction where the prover time grows with t instead of k. Plugging this BARG into the template aggregate signature construction gives Theorem 2. Going beyond thresholds, the ideas behind our construction can be extended to give schemes with fast prover/aggregator for other policies as well. We discuss such extensions in the full version.

We modify our construction of BARG from vPIR to use a more efficient encoding of the database of witnesses. In the scheme above, the prover constructs a database with k rows where the witness for the i-th statement is stored in the i-th row, and the remaining rows contain $\bot$. In the modified scheme, the prover constructs a database D with t rows such that each row contains a witness w and an index $j \in [k]$ such that w is a valid witness for the j-th statement and, the sequence of t indices stored in the database is strictly increasing. Indeed, such a database exists if and only if at least t out of the k statements are true. Checking that the database satisfies these two properties can be done by a read-once predicate P using $\log k + 1$ bits of space.[14]

The analysis of the new construction is similar to that above, with some key modifications. We again turn any adversary A against the BARG into a 2-composable vPIR adversary A'. When A outputs a vPIR answer a and a necessary subset J^*, A' outputs an additional answer a' as above, however, a' is computed in a different way: The answer a' is computed from a database D' using vPIR for a predicate P' where D', P' are as follows: Let $\bar{J}$ be a set of size $t - 1$ such that $J^* \cup \bar{J} = [k]$ (such a set exists since J^* is necessary). Let $j_1, \ldots, j_{t-1}$ be the indices in $\bar{J}$ in increasing order. For $i \in [t]$, the i-th row of D' contains the pair of indices (j_{i-1}, j_i) where at the edges we set $j_0 = 0$ and $j_t = k + 1$. We can think of the row (j_{i-1}, j_i) as describing an open interval. The predicate P' checks that the intervals in D' are indeed ordered and cover all indices in $[k]$ except for the $t - 1$ end points in $\bar{J}$. (Note that P' is indeed a read-once $\log k + 1$ space predicate.) The key property that enables the analysis to go through is that in the ideal experiment, if the simulator samples a pair of databases $\tilde{D}, \tilde{D}'$ such that $P(\tilde{D}) = 1$ and $P'(\tilde{D}') = 1$ then there must exist some index $i \in [t]$ such that if the i-th rows of $\tilde{D}$ and $\tilde{D}'$ are $(\tilde{w}, \tilde{j})$ and $(\tilde{j}_{i-1}, \tilde{j}_i)$ respectively, then $\tilde{w}$ is a valid witness for the $\tilde{j}$-th statement and $\tilde{j}_{i-1} < \tilde{j} < \tilde{j}_i$. Intuitively, the latter guarantees that in the real world, the extracted index j is outside the set $\bar{J}$ (and therefore, inside J^*) with sufficiently high probability. See the full version for further details.

2.2 Weakly Unforgeable Aggregate Signatures for Polynomial-Size Monotone Policies

In this section we overview the proof of Theorem 3 for constructing aggregate signatures for all monotone policies given by polynomial-size circuits with weakly unforgeable security. Recall that in the aggregate signatures security game, the adversary outputs verification keys $\mathsf{vk}_1, \ldots, \mathsf{vk}_k$, a target message m and a signature $\hat{\sigma}$. The adversary wins if $\hat{\sigma}$ is a valid signature on m under the aggregate key and if the forgery is non-trivial. In the case of weakly unforgeable security, the forgery is considered non-trivial if the set of corrupted parties, whose keys where not generated by the challenger, does not satisfy the policy, and if no honest party signed m. (This is in contrast to the fully adaptive notion where honest parties are allowed to sign m, but the set of honest parties that signed m together with all corrupted parties should not satisfy the policy.)

Our construction is, once again, based on the template aggregate signature construction instantiated with a new notion of monotone-policy BARGs. To motivate this new notion we briefly recall our previous attempts: in a nutshell, our proof strategy was to define a necessary subset of indices J^* based on the

---

[14] The predicate can store the index of the last row read using $\log k$ bits and use another bit to remember if any of the previously read rows violated the constraints.

adversary's queries and then try to extract a witness for the j-th BARG statement for some $j \in J^*$. Since J^* was only fixed at the time the adversary outputs its forgery, we could not program J^* into the CRS. Instead, we relied on the stronger notion of adaptive subset extraction where the subset J^* can be chosen by the adversary, as a function of the CRS. Our construction of BARGs with adaptive subset extraction, however, is limited to read-once bounded space policies.

The main idea behind our construction in Theorem 3 is to fix the subset J^* as a function of the BARG statements. This will allow us to target J^* not only during extraction, but already in the construction and verification of the BARG proof. In more detail, in the weakly unforgeable aggregate signatures security game, the subset J^* contains the indices of all honest parties whose verification keys were generated by the challenger. (This is in contrast to the fully adaptive notion where J^* does not contain indices of honest parties that signed m.) Therefore, to recover the subset J^* from the BARG statements (i.e. the verification keys $\mathsf{vk}_1, \ldots, \mathsf{vk}_k$) it is sufficient to distinguish keys generated by the challenger from keys generated by the adversary. To this end, we rely on an underlying signature scheme that supports *trapdoor keys*. In such a signature scheme, it is possible to generate "marked" verification keys that can be recognized using a trapdoor. Without the trapdoor, however, the adversary cannot distinguish the marked keys from honestly generated keys, or generate new marked keys.[15]

To implement this idea, we instantiate the template aggregate signature construction with a new notion of monotone-policy BARGs with *functional subset extraction* that generalise the somewhere extraction property. A construction satisfying this notion is implicit in [11]. Recall that in BARGs with somewhere extraction, if we program the CRS on a necessary subset J, then, using a trapdoor, we can extract a witness for the j-th statement for some $j \in J$ from any accepting proof. In functional subset extraction, the subset J depends both on the programmed CRS and on an additional input that is fixed together with the BARG statements. In more detail, the CRS is programmed with a function g and it is indistinguishable from an honestly generated CRS.[16] The BARG prover and verifier take an additional input y. The guarantee is that if $J = g(y)$ is a necessary subset, then we can extract a witness for the j-th statement for some $j \in J$ from any accepting proof using a trapdoor. We additionally require that the verification time does not grow with the running time of g. Moreover, in case the input y is itself long, the verifier only requires a short digest of y and its running time does not grow with $|y|$.

We plug in BARGs with functional subset extraction into the template aggregate signature construction. To aggregate a signature under a sequence of verification keys $\mathsf{vk}_1, \ldots, \mathsf{vk}_k$, we use this sequence as the input y to the BARG prover. We also include a short digest (a hash root) of y in the aggregate verification key,

---

[15] Starting from any signature scheme, we can construct a scheme with trapdoor keys by adding a random string to each verification key. To mark a key, we replace the random string with a PRF-based MAC.

[16] The length of the CRS grows with an upper bound on the description of g.

and the BARG verifier uses this digest to verify an aggregate signature. In the analysis, we consider an alternative challenger that gives the adversary marked verification keys, and programs the CRS with a function g that is hard-coded with the trapdoor for the base signature. Given an input $y = (\mathsf{vk}_1, \ldots, \mathsf{vk}_k)$, g uses the trapdoor to recognize the marked keys and outputs the subset J containing their indices. We note that this analysis does not extend to the fully adaptive setting. In the fully adaptive security game, the adversary can ask the challenger to sign the target message m under some of the marked verification keys. In this case, the indices of these keys should not be included in the subset J, or we may extract a trivial forgery. In our weakly unforgeable construction, however, the subset J is fixed only as a function of the verification keys chosen by the adversary, regardless of its signing queries.

Our construction of monotone-policy BARGs with functional subset extraction is based on the somewhere extractable BARGs for monotone policies given by polynomial-size circuits from [11]. In their construction, the CRS contains the programmed subset J encrypted with a fully homomorphic encryption scheme. Therefore, given an input y and a CRS that contains an encryption of a function g, the prover homomorphically evaluates a CRS that is programmed on $g(y)$ and computes its BRAG proof with respect to the evaluated CRS. The verifier given the input y can recompute the evaluated CRS itself and verify the proof. To allow verification given only the hash of y and to reduce the verification time to be independent of the running time of g, we use a RAM SNARK for deterministic computation [19] to delegate the computation of the evaluated CRS to the prover.

2.3 Full Version

In the remainder of this paper we include only the formal definition of aggregate signature schemes, batch arguments with adaptive subset extraction, and a transformation from batch arguments with adaptive subset extraction to aggregate signatures. We refer the reader to the full version of this submission for the remaining constructions and full proofs.

3 Aggregate Signatures for Monotone Policies

In this section we define aggregate signature schemes for monotone policies. We additionally define a weaker notion, and define a special case of aggregate signatures where the prover time depends only on the number of instances for which it has witnesses.

Syntax. Let $F = \{F_\lambda\}_{\lambda \in \mathbb{N}}$ be a family of monotone policies, such that each $f \in F_\lambda$ is a monotone function $f \colon \{0, 1\}^k \to \{0, 1\}$. Let $\mathsf{S} = (\mathsf{KeyGen}, \mathsf{Sign}, \mathsf{Verify})$ be a digital signature scheme. An F-aggregation scheme for S consists of the following polynomial-time algorithms:

$\mathsf{Setup}(1^\lambda) \to \mathsf{crs}$. This is a probabilistic setup algorithm that takes as input the security parameter 1^λ. It outputs a common reference string crs.

KeyAgg(crs, $\{vk_i\}_{i \in [k]}$) → $\widehat{vk}$. This is a deterministic key aggregation algorithm that takes as input the common reference string crs, and a collection of verification keys $\{vk_i\}_{i \in [k]}$. It outputs an aggregate verification key $\widehat{vk}$.

SigAgg(crs, f, $\{vk_i, \sigma_i\}_{i \in [k]}$, m) → $\widehat{\sigma}$. This is a deterministic signature aggregation algorithm that takes as input the common reference string crs, a policy f, a collection of verification keys and signatures $\{vk_i, \sigma_i\}_{i \in [k]}$, and a message m. It outputs an aggregate signature $\widehat{\sigma}$.

AggVerify(crs, f, $\widehat{vk}$, m, $\widehat{\sigma}$) → 0/1. This is a deterministic aggregate verification algorithm that takes as input the common reference string crs, a policy f, an aggregate verification key $\widehat{vk}$, a message m, and an aggregate signature $\widehat{\sigma}$. It outputs a bit (1 to accept, 0 to reject).

Remark 1 For simplicity, in this work we focus on a notion that only allows for aggregating many signatures on the same message. One might consider a more general notion where each party can sign a different message. In this case the verification algorithm AggVerify should take as input a vector $\{m_i\}_{i \in [k]}$ of messages signed instead of a single message m. Note that AggVerify is not given the subset set of parties that produced one of the signatures aggregated. Therefore, we give AggVerify one message for each party, even if the party did not sign any message.

In general, if we sign different messages, the running time of AggVerify must grow with k. However, in case the messages signed have some succinct representation, we may require that the running time of AggVerify grows with the representation size instead of k. Indeed, our constructions in subsequent section can be extended to support such succinct verification.

Definition 1 (Aggregation Scheme). An F-aggregation scheme (Setup, KeyAgg, SigAgg, AggVerify) for S = (KeyGen, Sign, Verify) is required to satisfy the following properties:

Correctness. For any $\lambda \in \mathbb{N}$, any policy $f \in F_\lambda$, any message m $\in \{0,1\}^\lambda$, and any collection of verification keys and signatures $\{vk_i, \sigma_i\}_{i \in [k]}$ such that for $b_i = $ Verify(vk_i, m, σ_i) it holds that $f(b_1, \ldots, b_k) = 1$,

$$\Pr\left[\text{AggVerify}(crs, f, \widehat{vk}, m, \widehat{\sigma}) = 1 \; : \; \begin{array}{l} crs \leftarrow \text{Setup}(1^\lambda) \\ \widehat{vk} \leftarrow \text{KeyAgg}(crs, \{vk_i\}_{i \in [k]}) \\ \widehat{\sigma} \leftarrow \text{SigAgg}(crs, f, \{vk_i, \sigma_i\}_{i \in [k]}, m) \end{array} \right] = 1 .$$

Efficiency. There exists a fixed polynomial poly such that in the correctness experiment above, $|\widehat{vk}| + |\widehat{\sigma}| = \text{poly}(\lambda)$.

Unforgeability. For any $\lambda \in \mathbb{N}$ and $f \in F_\lambda$, define the unforgeability game between an adversary $\mathcal{A}$ and a challenger as follows:

- The challenger samples crs ← Setup(1^λ), and gives crs to $\mathcal{A}$.
- The adversary can now make queries to the challenger. Each query is of one of three types:

- Verification key queries: $\mathcal{A}$ can request a verification key from the challenger. The challenger generates $(\mathsf{sk}, \mathsf{vk}) \leftarrow \mathsf{KeyGen}(1^\lambda)$, gives vk to $\mathcal{A}$ and saves the pair $(\mathsf{sk}, \mathsf{vk})$.
- Signing queries: Given a verification key vk and a message $\mathsf{m} \in \{0, 1\}^\lambda$, if the challenger previously saved the pair $(\mathsf{sk}, \mathsf{vk})$ it gives $\mathsf{Sign}(\mathsf{sk}, \mathsf{m})$ to $\mathcal{A}$. Otherwise, it gives $\bot$.
- Signing key queries: Given a verification key vk, if the challenger previously saved the pair $(\mathsf{sk}, \mathsf{vk})$ it gives sk to $\mathcal{A}$. Otherwise, it gives $\bot$.

– At the end of the game the adversary outputs a collection of verification keys $\{\mathsf{vk}_i\}_{i \in [k]}$, a message $\mathsf{m} \in \{0, 1\}^\lambda$, and an aggregate signature $\widehat{\sigma}$.

– Let $\widehat{\mathsf{vk}} = \mathsf{KeyAgg}(\mathsf{crs}, \{\mathsf{vk}_i\}_{i \in [k]})$. For $i \in [k]$, let $b_i = 1$ if one of the following conditions holds. Otherwise, let $b_i = 0$:
  - $\mathcal{A}$ did not make a verification key query that was answered with vk_i (that is, if vk_i is a maliciously generated key).
  - $\mathcal{A}$ made a signing query for $\mathsf{vk}_i, \mathsf{m}$.
  - $\mathcal{A}$ made a signing key query for vk_i

– The adversary $\mathcal{A}$ wins the game if $f(b_1, \ldots, b_k) = 0$ and $\mathsf{AggVerify}(\mathsf{crs}, f, \widehat{\mathsf{vk}}, \mathsf{m}, \widehat{\sigma}) = 1$.

For any poly-size adversary $\mathcal{A}$, there exists a negligible function $\mathsf{negl}(\cdot)$ such that for all $\lambda \in \mathbb{N}$ and $f \in F_\lambda$, $\mathcal{A}$ wins the unforgeability game with probability at most $\mathsf{negl}(\lambda)$.

4   Batch Arguments for Monotone Policies

In this section we provide new a definitions for batch arguments, specifically BARGs with adaptive subset extraction for monotone policies. The definitions extend the definition of BARGs for monotone policies considered in [11]. We then show how to construct aggregate signatures from BARGs with adaptive subset extraction. We defer the definition of our other notions of BARGs, and construction of these BARGs to the supplementary material. Our BARGs are going to be defined for the following batch language considered in [11].

Definition 1. *The language* $\mathsf{MonotonePolicyTMSAT}$ *consists of instances of the form* $x = (f, M, z, T)$, *where:* $f \colon \{0, 1\}^k \to \{0, 1\}$ *is the description of a monotone function,* M *is the description of a Turing machine,* z *is an input string (to* M), *and* T *is a running time.*

An instance $x = (f, M, z, T)$ *is in* $\mathsf{MonotonePolicyTMSAT}$ *if it satisfies the following witness relation* $\mathcal{R}_{\mathsf{full}}$. *A* $\mathcal{R}_{\mathsf{full}}$-*witness for* x *is* $w = (w_1, \ldots, w_k)$ *such that* $f(b_1, \ldots, b_k) = 1$, *where* $b_i \in \{0, 1\}$ *are defined by* $b_i = 1$ *if and only if* $M(z, i, w_i)$ *accepts within* T *steps.*

Further, let $F = \{F_\lambda\}_{\lambda \in \mathbb{N}}$ be a family of policies, where each $f \in F_\lambda$ is a monotone function $f \colon \{0, 1\}^k \to \{0, 1\}$. We say that a subset $J \subseteq [k]$ is necessary for a monotone function f if $f(\mathbb{1}_{[k] \setminus J}) = 0$.

4.1   Batch Arguments with Adaptive Subset Extraction

The syntax of batch arguments with adaptive subset extraction is similar to the syntax of somewhere-extractable BARGs for monotone policy in [11], except that the trapdoor generated by the setup algorithm does not depend on a particular subset of indices (or on a single index as in standard somewhere extractable batch arguments [19]). Instead the adaptive subset extraction guarantee will be defined with respect to necessary subsets chosen by the prover as a function of the crs.

Syntax. Let $\mathcal{R}(=\mathcal{R}_{\mathsf{full}})$ be the witness relation for MonotonePolicyTMSAT. Let $\alpha = \alpha(\lambda)$ be a polynomial. A F-batch argument with α-adaptive subset extraction for relation $\mathcal{R}$ consists of the following polynomial-time algorithms:

Setup$(1^\lambda) \to (\mathsf{crs}, \mathsf{td})$. This is a probabilistic setup algorithm that takes as input the security parameter 1^λ. It outputs a common reference string crs and a trapdoor td.

$\mathcal{P}(\mathsf{crs}, f, M, z, 1^T, w) \to \pi$. This is a deterministic prover algorithm that takes as input the common reference string crs, policy f, Turing machine M, input z, runtime 1^T, and witness w (for the relation $\mathcal{R}$). It outputs a proof π.

$\mathcal{V}(\mathsf{crs}, x, \pi) \to 0/1$. This is a deterministic verification algorithm that takes as input the common reference string crs, instance $x = (f, M, z, T)$, and a proof π. It outputs a bit (1 to accept, 0 to reject).

Extract$(\mathsf{td}, \pi) \to (i, w_i)$. This is a deterministic extraction algorithm that takes as input the trapdoor td, and a proof π. It outputs an index $i \in [k]$, and a witness w_i.

Definition 2 (Batch Argument for Policies with Adaptive Subset Extraction). A F-batch argument with α-adaptive subset extraction (Setup, $\mathcal{P}, \mathcal{V}$, Extract) for relation $\mathcal{R}$ is required to satisfy the following properties:

Completeness. For any $\lambda \in \mathbb{N}$, any $n, m, T \leq 2^\lambda$, any instance $x = (f, M, z, T) \in$ MonotonePolicyTMSAT with $|M|+|z|= n$ and corresponding witness w such that $(x, w) \in \mathcal{R}$ and $|w_i|= m$,

$$\Pr\left[\mathcal{V}(\mathsf{crs}, x, \pi) = 1 \ : \ \begin{array}{l} (\mathsf{crs}, \mathsf{td}) \leftarrow \mathsf{Setup}(1^\lambda) \\ \pi \leftarrow \mathcal{P}(\mathsf{crs}, f, M, z, 1^T, w) \end{array} \right] = 1 \ .$$

Succinctness. In the completeness experiment above, $|\pi| \leq m \cdot \mathsf{poly}(\lambda)$. The running time of the verifier is at most $\mathsf{poly}(|\mathsf{crs}|+|\pi|) + \mathsf{poly}(\lambda) \cdot |x|$.

α-Adaptive Subset Extraction. For any polynomial $T(\lambda)$, any poly-size cheating prover $\mathcal{P}^*$, and any sequence $\{f_\lambda \in F_\lambda\}_{\lambda \in \mathbb{N}}$, there exists a negligible function $\mathsf{negl}(\cdot)$ such that for every $\lambda \in \mathbb{N}$,

$$\Pr_{\mathsf{EXP}}\left[i \in J \ \wedge \ M(z, i, w_i) = 1 \right] \geq \frac{1}{\alpha(\lambda)} \cdot \Pr_{\mathsf{EXP}}\left[\begin{array}{l} \mathcal{V}(\mathsf{crs}, x, \pi) = 1 \ \wedge \\ f(\mathbb{1}_{[k] \setminus J}) = 0 \end{array} \right] - \mathsf{negl}(\lambda) \ ,$$

where EXP is the experiment defined as follows:
 - Generate $(\mathsf{crs}, \mathsf{td}) \leftarrow \mathsf{Setup}(1^\lambda)$.
 - Run the cheating prover and obtain $(M, z, \pi, J) \leftarrow \mathcal{P}^*(\mathsf{crs})$, and let $x = (f_\lambda, M, z, T)$.
 - Extract $(i, w_i) \leftarrow \mathsf{Extract}(\mathsf{td}, \pi)$.

Setup(1^λ):
  1. Generate hk $\leftarrow$ Gen$_{\text{HT}}(1^\lambda)$.
  2. Generate (crs$_{\text{BARG}}$, td$_{\text{BARG}}$) $\leftarrow$ Setup$_{\text{BARG}}(1^\lambda)$.
  3. Output crs = (hk, crs$_{\text{BARG}}$).
KeyAgg(crs, $\{vk_i\}_{i \in [k]}$):
  1. Parse crs = (hk, crs$_{\text{BARG}}$).
  2. Output $\widehat{vk}$ = Hash$_{\text{HT}}$(hk, $(vk_1, \ldots, vk_k)$).
SigAgg(crs, f, $\{vk_i, \sigma_i\}_{i \in [k]}$, m):
  1. Parse crs = (hk, crs$_{\text{BARG}}$).
  2. Compute $\widehat{vk}$ = Hash$_{\text{HT}}$(hk, $(vk_1, \ldots, vk_k)$).
  3. Let $z = $ (hk, $\widehat{vk}$, m), and define the Turing machine $M(z, j, w_j)$ which operates as follows:
     – Parse $z = $ (hk, $\widehat{vk}$, m).
     – Parse $w_j = (\rho_j, vk_j, \sigma_j)$.
     – Check that Verify$_{\text{HT}}$(hk, $\widehat{vk}$, j, vk_j, ρ_j) = 1.
     – Check that Verify(vk_j, m, σ_j) = 1.
     Let $T = \text{poly}(\lambda)$ so that the above pseudocode terminates.
  4. For every $j \in [k]$, construct a witness w_j such that $M(z, j, w_j) = 1$, using the Open$_{\text{HT}}$ algorithm to produce the appropriate openings. Let $w = (w_1, \ldots, w_k)$.
  5. Output $\widehat{\sigma} = \mathcal{P}_{\text{BARG}}(\text{crs}_{\text{BARG}}, f, M, z, 1^T, w)$.
AggVerify(crs, f, $\widehat{vk}$, m, $\widehat{\sigma}$):
  1. Parse crs = (hk, crs$_{\text{BARG}}$).
  2. Define M, T as above and $z = $ (hk, $\widehat{vk}$, m), and let $x = (f, M, z, T)$.
  3. Output $\mathcal{V}_{\text{BARG}}(\text{crs}_{\text{BARG}}, x, \widehat{\sigma})$.

Fig. 1. Aggregate Signatures from BARGs

4.2 From Adaptive Subset Extraction to Aggregate Signatures

We present our first transformation, where we construct aggregate signatures from BARGs with adaptive subset extraction, and any signature scheme. Specifically, let $F = \{F_\lambda\}$ be a family of monotone policies. We construct an F-aggregation scheme for S (Definition 1) from the following building blocks:

– A digital signature scheme S = (KeyGen, Sign, Verify).
– A F-batch argument with α-adaptive subset extraction (Definition 2) (Setup$_{\text{BARG}}$, $\mathcal{P}_{\text{BARG}}$, $\mathcal{V}_{\text{BARG}}$, Extract$_{\text{BARG}}$) for $\mathcal{R}_{\text{full}}$ with polynomial α.
– A hash family with local opening (Gen$_{\text{HT}}$, Hash$_{\text{HT}}$, Open$_{\text{HT}}$, Verify$_{\text{HT}}$).

We describe the aggregate signature algorithms in Fig. 1, and prove the following theorem in the full version of the paper.

Theorem 5. *Assuming the existence of a digital signature scheme, hash family and F-batch argument with α-adaptive subset extraction, the construction given in Fig. 1 is an F-aggregation scheme for S.*

Acknowledgements. Disclosure of Interests.Maya Farber Brodsky was supported by an ISF grant 1789/19. Omer Paneth is a member of the Checkpoint Institute of Information Security and is supported by an Azrieli Faculty Fellowship, Len Blavatnik and the Blavatnik Foundation and ISF grant 1789/19. Supported in part by AFOSR Award FA9550-23-1-0312. Any opinions, findings and conclusions or recommendations expressed in this material are those of the author(s) and do not necessarily reflect the views of the United States Government or AFOSR.

References

1. drand: Randomness Beacon Service (2017). https://drand.love/docs/cryptography/
2. Threshold Signature Wallets (2021). https://sepior.com/mpc-blog/threshold-signature-wallets
3. Bellare, M., Tessaro, S., Zhu, C.: Stronger security for non-interactive threshold signatures: BLS and FROST. IACR Cryptol. ePrint Archive, p. 833 (2022). https://eprint.iacr.org/2022/833
4. Ben-David, S., Kalai, Y.T., Paneth, O.: Verifiable private information retrieval. In: Kiltz, E., Vaikuntanathan, V. (eds.) TCC 2022, Part III. LNCS, vol. 13749, pp. 3–32. Springer, Heidelberg (2022). https://doi.org/10.1007/978-3-031-22368-6_1
5. Ben-Or, M., Goldwasser, S., Wigderson, A.: Completeness theorems for non-cryptographic fault-tolerant distributed computation (extended abstract). In: 20th ACM STOC, pp. 1–10. ACM Press, May 1988. https://doi.org/10.1145/62212.62213
6. Bitansky, N., et al.: The hunting of the SNARK. J. Cryptol. **30**(4), 989–1066 (2017)
7. Bitansky, N., Canetti, R., Chiesa, A., Tromer, E.: Recursive composition and bootstrapping for SNARKS and proof-carrying data. In: Boneh, D., Roughgarden, T., Feigenbaum, J. (eds.) 45th ACM STOC, pp. 111–120. ACM Press, June 2013. https://doi.org/10.1145/2488608.2488623
8. Bitansky, N., Canetti, R., Paneth, O., Rosen, A.: On the existence of extractable one-way functions. SIAM J. Comput. **45**(5), 1910–1952 (2016)
9. Boneh, D., Gentry, C., Lynn, B., Shacham, H.: Aggregate and verifiably encrypted signatures from bilinear maps. In: Biham, E. (ed.) EUROCRYPT 2003. LNCS, vol. 2656, pp. 416–432. Springer, Heidelberg (2003). https://doi.org/10.1007/3-540-39200-9_26
10. Boneh, D., Lynn, B., Shacham, H.: Short signatures from the Weil pairing. In: Boyd, C. (ed.) ASIACRYPT 2001. LNCS, vol. 2248, pp. 514–532. Springer, Heidelberg (Dec 2001). https://doi.org/10.1007/3-540-45682-1_30
11. Brakerski, Z., Brodsky, M.F., Kalai, Y.T., Lombardi, A., Paneth, O.: SNARGs for monotone policy batch NP. In: Handschuh, H., Lysyanskaya, A. (eds.) CRYPTO 2023, Part II. LNCS, vol. 14082, pp. 252–283. Springer, Heidelberg (2023). https://doi.org/10.1007/978-3-031-38545-2_9
12. Brakerski, Z., Holmgren, J., Kalai, Y.T.: Non-interactive delegation and batch NP verification from standard computational assumptions. In: Hatami, H., McKenzie, P., King, V. (eds.) 49th ACM STOC. pp. 474–482. ACM Press, June 2017. https://doi.org/10.1145/3055399.3055497
13. Chaum, D., Crépeau, C., Damgård, I.: Multiparty unconditionally secure protocols (abstract). In: Pomerance, C. (ed.) CRYPTO 1987. LNCS, vol. 293, pp. 462–462. Springer, Heidelberg (1988). https://doi.org/10.1007/3-540-48184-2_43

14. Chen, L., Moody, D., Regenscheid, A., Robinson, A.: Digital signature standard (DSS) (2023). https://www.nist.gov/publications/digital-signature-standard-dss-3

15. Chia Network: BLS signatures in C++ using the RELIC toolkit. https://github.com/Chia-Network/bls-signatures. Accessed 06 May 2019

16. Choudhuri, A.R., Garg, S., Jain, A., Jin, Z., Zhang, J.: Correlation intractability and SNARGs from sub-exponential DDH. Cryptology ePrint Archive, report 2022/1486 (2022). https://eprint.iacr.org/2022/1486

17. Choudhuri, A.R., Garg, S., Jain, A., Jin, Z., Zhang, J.: Correlation intractability and SNARGs from sub-exponential DDH. In: Handschuh, H., Lysyanskaya, A. (eds.) CRYPTO 2023, Part IV. LNCS, vol. 14084, pp. 635–668. Springer, Heidelberg (2023). https://doi.org/10.1007/978-3-031-38551-3_20

18. Choudhuri, A.R., Jain, A., Jin, Z.: Non-interactive batch arguments for NP from standard assumptions. In: Malkin, T., Peikert, C. (eds.) CRYPTO 2021. LNCS, vol. 12828, pp. 394–423. Springer, Cham (2021). https://doi.org/10.1007/978-3-030-84259-8_14

19. Choudhuri, A.R., Jain, A., Jin, Z.: SNARGs for $\mathcal{P}$ from LWE. In: 62nd FOCS, pp. 68–79. IEEE Computer Society Press, February 2022. https://doi.org/10.1109/FOCS52979.2021.00016

20. Cramer, R.: Modular Design of Secure yet Practical Cryptographic Protocols. Ph.D. thesis, University of Amsterdam, January 1997

21. Cramer, R., Damgård, I., MacKenzie, P.D.: Efficient zero-knowledge proofs of knowledge without intractability assumptions. IACR Cryptol. ePrint Archive, p. 45 (2000). http://eprint.iacr.org/2000/045

22. Das, S., Camacho, P., Xiang, Z., Nieto, J., Bünz, B., Ren, L.: Threshold signatures from inner product argument: Succinct, weighted, and multi-threshold. IACR Cryptology ePrint Archive, p. 598 (2023)

23. Desmedt, Y.: Society and group oriented cryptography: a new concept. In: Pomerance, C. (ed.) CRYPTO 1987. LNCS, vol. 293, pp. 120–127. Springer, Heidelberg (1988). https://doi.org/10.1007/3-540-48184-2_8

24. Desmedt, Y., Frankel, Y.: Threshold cryptosystems. In: Brassard, G. (ed.) CRYPTO 1989. LNCS, vol. 435, pp. 307–315. Springer, New York (1990). https://doi.org/10.1007/0-387-34805-0_28

25. Devadas, L., Goyal, R., Kalai, Y., Vaikuntanathan, V.: Rate-1 non-interactive arguments for batch-NP and applications. In: 63rd FOCS, pp. 1057–1068. IEEE Computer Society Press, October/November 2022. https://doi.org/10.1109/FOCS54457.2022.00103

26. DFINITY: go-dfinity-crypto. https://github.com/dfinity/go-dfinity-crypto. Accessed 06 May 2019

27. Ellis, S., Juels, A., Nazarov, S.: ChainLink: a decentralized oracle network (2017). Accessed 11 Mar 2018

28. Fiat, A., Shamir, A.: How to prove yourself: practical solutions to identification and signature problems. In: Odlyzko, A.M. (ed.) CRYPTO 1986. LNCS, vol. 263, pp. 186–194. Springer, Heidelberg (1987). https://doi.org/10.1007/3-540-47721-7_12

29. Freire, E.S.V., Hofheinz, D., Paterson, K.G., Striecks, C.: Programmable hash functions in the multilinear setting. In: Canetti, R., Garay, J.A. (eds.) CRYPTO 2013, Part I. LNCS, vol. 8042, pp. 513–530. Springer, Heidelberg (2013). https://doi.org/10.1007/978-3-642-40041-4_28

30. Garg, S., Jain, A., Mukherjee, P., Sinha, R., Wang, M., Zhang, Y.: Cryptography with weights: MPC, encryption and signatures. Cryptology ePrint Archive, Report 2022/1632 (2022). https://eprint.iacr.org/2022/1632

31. Goldreich, O., Micali, S., Wigderson, A.: How to play any mental game or A completeness theorem for protocols with honest majority. In: Aho, A. (ed.) 19th ACM STOC. pp. 218–229. ACM Press, May 1987. https://doi.org/10.1145/28395. 28420

32. Hohenberger, S., Koppula, V., Waters, B.: Universal signature aggregators. In: Oswald, E., Fischlin, M. (eds.) EUROCRYPT 2015. LNCS, vol. 9057, pp. 3–34. Springer, Heidelberg (2015). https://doi.org/10.1007/978-3-662-46803-6_1

33. Hulett, J., Jawale, R., Khurana, D., Srinivasan, A.: SNARGs for P from sub-exponential DDH and QR. In: Dunkelman, O., Dziembowski, S. (eds.) EUROCRYPT 2022, Part II. LNCS, vol. 13276, pp. 520–549. Springer, Heidelberg (2022). https://doi.org/10.1007/978-3-031-07085-3_18

34. Itakura, K., Nakamura, K.: A public key cryptosystem suitable for digital multisignatures. In: NEC Research and Development (1983)

35. Kalai, Y., Lombardi, A., Vaikuntanathan, V., Wichs, D.: Boosting batch arguments and RAM delegation. In: STOC, pp. 1545–1552. ACM (2023)

36. Kalai, Y., Lombardi, A., Vaikuntanathan, V., Wichs, D.: Boosting batch arguments and RAM delegation. In: Saha, B., Servedio, R.A. (eds.) Proceedings of the 55th Annual ACM Symposium on Theory of Computing, STOC 2023, Orlando, FL, USA, 20–23 June 2023. pp. 1545–1552. ACM (2023). https://doi.org/10.1145/3564246.3585200, https://doi.org/10.1145/3564246.3585200

37. Kalai, Y.T., Paneth, O., Yang, L.: How to delegate computations publicly. In: Charikar, M., Cohen, E. (eds.) 51st ACM STOC. pp. 1115–1124. ACM Press (Jun 2019). https://doi.org/10.1145/3313276.3316411

38. Kalai, Y.T., Paneth, O., Yang, L.: Delegation with updatable unambiguous proofs and PPAD-hardness. In: Micciancio, D., Ristenpart, T. (eds.) CRYPTO 2020. LNCS, vol. 12172, pp. 652–673. Springer, Cham (2020). https://doi.org/10.1007/978-3-030-56877-1_23

39. Lu, S., Ostrovsky, R., Sahai, A., Shacham, H., Waters, B.: Sequential aggregate signatures and multisignatures without random oracles. In: Vaudenay, S. (ed.) EUROCRYPT 2006. LNCS, vol. 4004, pp. 465–485. Springer, Heidelberg (2006). https://doi.org/10.1007/11761679_28

40. Lysyanskaya, A., Micali, S., Reyzin, L., Shacham, H.: Sequential aggregate signatures from trapdoor permutations. In: Cachin, C., Camenisch, J.L. (eds.) EUROCRYPT 2004. LNCS, vol. 3027, pp. 74–90. Springer, Heidelberg (2004). https://doi.org/10.1007/978-3-540-24676-3_5

41. Micali, S.: CS proofs (extended abstracts). In: 35th FOCS, pp. 436–453. IEEE Computer Society Press, November 1994. https://doi.org/10.1109/SFCS.1994.365746

42. Nguyen, C.T., Hoang, D.T., Nguyen, D.N., Niyato, D., Nguyen, H.T., Dutkiewicz, E.: Proof-of-stake consensus mechanisms for future blockchain networks: fundamentals, applications and opportunities. IEEE Access 7, 85727–85745 (2019). https://doi.org/10.1109/ACCESS.2019.2925010

43. Paneth, O., Pass, R.: Incrementally verifiable computation via rate-1 batch arguments. In: 63rd FOCS, pp. 1045–1056. IEEE Computer Society Press, October/November 2022. https://doi.org/10.1109/FOCS54457.2022.00102

44. Poly Network: Poly Network (2020). https://poly.network/

45. Rückert, M., Schröder, D.: Aggregate and verifiably encrypted signatures from multilinear maps without random oracles. In: Park, J.H., Chen, H.-H., Atiquzzaman, M., Lee, C., Kim, T., Yeo, S.-S. (eds.) ISA 2009. LNCS, vol. 5576, pp. 750–759. Springer, Heidelberg (2009). https://doi.org/10.1007/978-3-642-02617-1_76

46. Schnorr, C.P.: Efficient identification and signatures for smart cards. In: Brassard, G. (ed.) CRYPTO 1989. LNCS, vol. 435, pp. 239–252. Springer, New York (1990). https://doi.org/10.1007/0-387-34805-0_22

47. Shamir, A.: How to share a secret. Commun. ACM **22**(11), 612–613 (1979). https://doi.org/10.1145/359168.359176

48. Shoup, V.: Practical threshold signatures. In: Preneel, B. (ed.) EUROCRYPT 2000. LNCS, vol. 1807, pp. 207–220. Springer, Heidelberg (2000). https://doi.org/10.1007/3-540-45539-6_15

49. Toueg, S.: Randomized byzantine agreements. In: Proceedings of the Third Annual ACM Symposium on Principles of Distributed Computing, pp. 163–178. PODC 1984, Association for Computing Machinery (1984)

50. Waters, B., Wu, D.J.: Batch arguments for sfNP and more from standard bilinear group assumptions. In: Dodis, Y., Shrimpton, T. (eds.) CRYPTO 2022, Part II. LNCS, vol. 13508, pp. 433–463. Springer, Heidelberg (2022). https://doi.org/10.1007/978-3-031-15979-4_15

Leakage-Tolerant Circuits

Yuval Ishai[1]([⊠]) and Yifan Song[2,3]

[1] Technion, Haifa, Israel
yuvali@cs.technion.ac.il
[2] Institute for Theoretical Computer Science, Institute for Interdisciplinary Information Sciences, Tsinghua University, Beijing, People's Republic of China
yfsong@mail.tsinghua.edu.cn
[3] Shanghai Qi Zhi Institute, Shanghai, People's Republic of China

Abstract. A *leakage-resilient circuit* for $f : \{0,1\}^n \to \{0,1\}^m$ is a randomized Boolean circuit C mapping a randomized encoding of an input x to an encoding of $y = f(x)$, such that applying any leakage function $L \in \mathcal{L}$ to the wires of C reveals essentially nothing about x. A *leakage-tolerant circuit* achieves the stronger guarantee that even when x and y are not protected by any encoding, the output of L can be simulated by applying some $L' \in \mathcal{L}$ to x and y alone. Thus, C is as secure as an ideal hardware implementation of f with respect to leakage from $\mathcal{L}$.

Leakage-resilient circuits were constructed for low-complexity classes $\mathcal{L}$, including (length-t output) $\mathcal{AC}0$ functions, parities, and functions with bounded communication complexity. In contrast, leakage-*tolerant* circuits were only known for the simple case of *probing* leakage, where L outputs the values of t wires in C.

We initiate a systematic study of leakage-tolerant circuits for natural classes $\mathcal{L}$ of *global* leakage functions, obtaining the following main results.

- **Leakage-tolerant circuits for depth-1 leakage.** Every circuit C_f for f can be efficiently compiled into an $\mathcal{L}$-tolerant circuit C for f, where $\mathcal{L}$ includes all leakage functions L that output either t *parities* or t *disjunctions* (alternatively, conjunctions) of any number of wires or their negations. In the case of parities, our simulator runs in $2^{O(t)}$ time. We provide partial evidence that this may be inherent.
- **Application to stateful leakage-resilient circuits.** Using a general transformation from leakage-tolerant circuits, we obtain the first construction of *stateful* t-leakage-resilient circuits that tolerate a *continuous* parity leakage, and the first such construction for disjunction/conjunction leakage in which the circuit size grows subquadratically with t. Interestingly, here we can obtain poly(t)-time simulation even in the case of parities.

1 Introduction

A dream goal in cryptography is to design hardware that can perform general computations on secret inputs while resisting arbitrary side-channel attacks that reveal partial information about the computation. An extreme version of this goal requires ideal (and unrealizable) flavors of obfuscation. However, when

© International Association for Cryptologic Research 2024
M. Joye and G. Leander (Eds.): EUROCRYPT 2024, LNCS 14654, pp. 196–225, 2024.
https://doi.org/10.1007/978-3-031-58737-5_8

settling for security against limited classes of side channels, this goal becomes realizable and has been the topic of a large body of theoretical and applied work.

A simple formal model for studying this problem is a *leakage-resilient circuit* (LRC) [24]. Let $\mathcal{L}$ be a class of leakage functions with t-bit output. A (stateless) LRC for a function $f : \{0,1\}^n \rightarrow \{0,1\}^m$ is a randomized Boolean circuit $C :$ $\{0,1\}^{\hat{n}} \rightarrow \{0,1\}^{\hat{m}}$ mapping a randomized encoding (or secret-sharing) $\hat{x}$ of an input x to an encoding $\hat{y}$ of $y = f(x)$, such that applying any leakage function $L \in \mathcal{L}$ to the wires of C reveals essentially nothing about x in an information-theoretic sense. Assuming the availability of an ideal (leak-free) input encoder and output decoder[1], this gives an end-to-end solution to the problem of protecting the computation of f against leakage class $\mathcal{L}$.

There is a long line of works studying different flavors of the LRC question. The vast majority of these works focus on the simple class $\mathcal{L}$ of *probing* leakage, where L can only output the values of t (physical) wires in C. This baseline model has been extended in two orthogonal ways:

From Local to Global Leakage. While the "local" leakage resilience captured by the probing model is practically relevant and implies resilience against certain kinds of noisy leakage [13], it does not capture global leakage that applies *jointly* to an unbounded number of wires. This type of leakage may arise in realistic side-channels attacks such as timing or power analysis that measure global information about the computation. The study of such global leakage functions was initiated in [16,25]. Most relevant to the current work are constructions of LRCs against $\mathcal{AC}0$ leakage, consisting of constant-depth polynomial-size circuits over AND, OR, NOT gates with unbounded fan-in [5,6,16,30], and LRCs against *parity* leakage and (more broadly) bounded-communication leakage [18,21]. See Sect. 1.2 for more work in this direction.

From Stateless to Stateful Circuits. The simplicity of the LRC model makes it an attractive object of study. However, this model is limited in two significant ways. First, it assumes *leak-free* input encoder and output decoder. Second, it is limited to a *one-shot* scenario where a single computation is performed and is subject to a small amount of leakage. In contrast, real-world computers or embedded devices need to maintain a persistent secret state, and are subject to *continuous* leakage which may be unbounded over time. The *stateful* variant of LRCs [15,16,24] addresses both limitations by considering circuits with memory that can be initialized with an encoded secret state, and can then "refresh" the encoded state in each invocation. The main challenge in converting stateless LRCs into stateful ones is to ensure sufficient independence between the encoded input and the encoded output conditioned on the leakage. While there is a variety of techniques for achieving this in the case of probing leakage [2,9,10,20,29], it is not clear how to extend them even to very simple types of global leakage.

---

[1] To avoid trivial solutions in which the computation is carried out by the input encoder or the output decoder, it is required that the encoding of the inputs and outputs be *universal* in the sense that it depends only on their length and not on C.

Indeed, most stateless LRCs are not known to have stateful analogues without relying on leak-free components [5,14,16,21,26].

Leakage-Tolerant Circuits. In this work we focus on a different extension of the baseline LRC model, which is strongly motivated by the combination of the two extensions discussed above. Recall that the basic LRC model does not address the question of protecting the input encoding and output decoding steps, which are assumed to be leak-free. A more desirable goal is to obtain a *leakage-tolerant* circuit (LTC), where C maps an unprotected input x to an unprotected output $y = f(x)$ while providing the following best-possible security guarantee: the output of any leakage function $L \in \mathcal{L}$ can be *simulated* (up to a negligible statistical distance) by applying a similar leakage $L' \in \mathcal{L}$ to (x, y). Thus, C is "as secure" as an ideal (leak-free) hardware implementation of f.

Note that an LTC against $\mathcal{L}$ can be readily converted into an LRC against $\mathcal{L}$ by using an arbitrary $\mathcal{L}$-resilient encoding to protect the input x and the output y. More interestingly, the strong security guarantee of LTCs allows them to serve as a *general-purpose* replacement for ideal hardware with respect to leakage class $\mathcal{L}$. Jumping ahead, this may help bridge the gap between stateless and stateful LRCs for natural classes $\mathcal{L}$ of *global* leakage.

The starting point for the current work is the observation that we currently know virtually nothing about LTCs for general leakage classes. While LTCs are quite easy to realize in the baseline case of probing leakage [1,23], this goal seems much more challenging even for simple classes of global leakage. Indeed, no such results are currently known. We thus ask:

Is leakage tolerance possible for any nontrivial class of global leakage?

1.1 Our Results

We initiate a systematic study of leakage-tolerant circuits for natural classes $\mathcal{L}$ of global leakage functions. Concretely, we focus on the case of *depth-1* leakage, which consists of two distinct classes $\mathcal{L}$ that strictly generalize t-probing:

- Depth-1 $\mathcal{AC}0$ leakage. This includes all leakage functions L that output t *disjunctions* (alternatively, conjunctions) of any number of wires or their negations. This simple kind of leakage is motivated by *selective failure* attacks (such as buffer overflows), where a system fails if at least one of several components fail. Existing LRCs for this class that do not rely on trusted hardware either incur a high asymptotic overhead, increasing the circuit size by a factor of $\Omega(t^2)$ [6,30] (in fact, this is known even for higher-depth $\mathcal{AC}0$ leakage), or alternatively are restricted to the stateless case [5].
- Parity leakage. Here L may output t *parities* of any number of wires. In theoretical computer science, parities often serve as the natural next step beyond probing: for instance, whereas a t-wise independent PRG fools t-probing distinguishers, a small-bias PRG [27] fools a parity distinguisher. From a more applied perspective, parity leakage can be viewed as going "half way" towards more realistic classes of global leakage, such as leaking the Hamming weight

of subsets of wires. Finally, from a technical perspective this case seems challenging, because the standard LRC construction of [24] completely breaks down in the presence of parity leakage. Nevertheless, efficient LRCs for this class (in fact, for the broader class of *bounded-communication leakage*) were obtained in [18, 21]. The question of obtaining *stateful* LRCs against parities was left open.

We note that the question of obtaining LTCs for these classes is nontrivial even for simple functions f, such as the mod-2 inner-product of two input vectors.

Feasibility of LTCs. Our main technical contribution is a general construction of LTCs for depth-1 leakage, establishing the first feasibility result for leakage-tolerance with respect to nontrivial global leakage classes. Concretely, we show that every circuit C_f computing a function f can be efficiently compiled into an LTC C for f in which any t disjunctions/conjunctions/parities of the wires of C or their negations can be simulated, with negligible statistical error, by making t queries of the same kind to the inputs and outputs of C.

A limitation of our parity-tolerant circuit compiler is that the associated *simulator* runs in time $2^{O(t)}$. We give a (weak) partial evidence for the necessity of inefficient simulation, showing that a related leakage-tolerant encoding scheme requires inefficient simulation assuming the hardness of the learning parity with noise (LPN) problem.

Application to Stateful LRCs. Finally, we observe that LTCs can be used to bridge the gap between stateless and stateful LRCs. Extending a technique of Faust et al. [16], we show how to obtain a stateful LRC for $\mathcal{L}$ by combining two ingredients: (1) an LTC for $\mathcal{L}$, and (2) a leakage-resilient encoding for $\mathcal{L}$ that resists two *adaptive* leakage queries. Using this general transformation, we apply our LTC constructions to obtain the first construction of *stateful* t-leakage-resilient circuits that resist a *continuous* parity leakage, and the first such construction for disjunction/conjunction leakage in which the circuit size grows sub-quadratically with t. Somewhat surprisingly, we show how to ensure that the stateful LRC has an efficient simulator even if the underlying LTC does not. In particular, our stateful LRC for parities has a poly(t)-time simulator.

Future Directions. Several natural questions are left open for future work.

- Can we narrow the gap between LRCs and LTCs by obtaining LTC constructions for other classes? While our construction for parity leakage is closely related to the LRC against bounded-communication leakage from [21] (see Sect. 2 for an overview), we are unable to extend our results to this class, or even to the subclass of leakage functions that output the Hamming weight of a subset of wires. In particular, our LTC for the parity case crucially relies on a technique for reducing any parity query to a small number of probing queries, which we are not able to extend to the case of Hamming weight leakage. The LTC question is also still open for depth-2 $\mathcal{AC}0$ (capturing polynomial-size CNF/DNF formulas) and other classes for which LRCs are known to exist (see Sect. 1.2).

– Is there a t-parity-tolerant circuit with a poly(t)-time simulator? Our simulator needs to find a short vector in a linear code defined by the parity queries, and we are only able to show that this is inherent for a related encoding problem. Note, however, that we can get around this limitation in the context of the application to stateful LRCs.

1.2 Related Work

We survey here some related works on leakage-resilient circuits. While in this work we focus on information-theoretic security, we are not aware of computationally secure constructions that achieve our goals. See [11] and references therein for constructions with computational security.

Global Leakage. Simple classes $\mathcal{L}$ of global leakage considered in the literature include AC^0 leakage [5,6,16,30], "only computation leaks" leakage [14,19,25] and its extension to bounded-communication leakage [18,21], and even NC^1 leakage [26]. Some of these constructions require trusted hardware components in the stateful case or input encoder which is as big as the circuit for f in the stateless case [14,16,26] and some rely on unproven conjectures [5,26,30]. Another class of global leakage that was previously studied is captured by the *noisy leakage* model [28], where a small amount of information about every wire is independently leaked. However, the independence assumption makes this type of global leakage reducible to local leakage [13].

Composable Probing Resilience. The notion of LTC provides general-purpose composition guarantees. However, more refined notions of composable security can suffice in specific application scenarios. Such notions for the relatively simple case of *probing* leakage have been considered in several previous works (see [3,4,8,20] and references therein), with the *primary* goal of improving the practical efficiency of t-probing resilient circuits for small values of t.

2 Technical Overview

This work initiates a systematic study of *leakage-tolerant circuits* (LTCs). We start by describing the application of LTCs to building *stateful* leakage-resilient circuits (LRCs) that achieve security against *continuous leakage*. This application serves as a primary motivation behind this work.

2.1 Application: Stateful Leakage-Resilient Circuits

The notion of a *stateful* LRC aims to protect a general-purpose computing device, which can be invoked any number of times and possibly update the contents of its memory in each invocation. What makes this problem challenging is that the total amount of information leaked across multiple invocations is unbounded, and in particular is higher than the entropy of the secret state used to initialize this. This explains the fact that stateful LRCs are often much more challenging to construct than stateless ones.

We consider here the model of stateful LRCs that was introduced by Ishai et al. [24] for the special case of "probing" leakage and later extended by Faust et al. [16] to general leakage classes. In this model, the ideal computation is defined by a stateful circuit $C[s]$ that starts with a secret initial state $s = s_0$. In the i-th invocation, given its current secret state s_{i-1} and an external public input x_i, the circuit C updates its secret state to s_i and produces an external public output y_i, where (s_i, y_i) are a function of (s_{i-1}, x_i). For example, consider a stateful AES circuit in which the internal state is the AES secret key, and in each invocation the circuit takes a plaintext x_i as input and outputs the corresponding ciphertext y_i. In this example, the state in different invocations remains the same.

For an ideal stateful circuit $C[s]$ as above, a leakage-resilient implementation consists of a randomized stateful circuit $C'[s']$ along with a randomized mapping from an initial secret state s_0 of C to the initial state s'_0 of C', satisfying the following correctness and security requirements: (1) $C'[s'_0]$ has the same (reactive) functionality as $C[s_0]$, and (2) any adversary who interacts with the stateful circuit $C'[s'_0]$, adaptively choosing inputs x_i and leakage queries $L_i \in \mathcal{L}$ to the circuit wires for each invocation, should learn essentially nothing about the secret state (in any invocation) of the stateful circuit $C[s_0]$. In other words, the view of such an adversary should be simulatable given the public inputs x_i and public outputs y_i alone. Note that we do not protect external inputs and outputs and in fact the adversary may arbitrarily choose the external inputs in each invocation of $C'[s'_0]$.

The simpler notion of a *stateless* LRC considers a one-shot computation of a function f on a secret input x. To avoid a direct leakage on the input x or output $y = f(x)$, the inputs and outputs are protected by an input encoder and an output decoder, respectively. Concretely, a stateless leakage-resilient circuit is defined by a triple (I, C, O), where I is a randomized input encoder, C is a randomized circuit mapping the encoded input to an encoded output, and O is an output decoder. Here we assume that the (single) leakage function $L \in \mathcal{L}$ applies only to the wires in C but not to the wires in I or O, and require that the output of L reveals essentially nothing about the private input.

Note that LTCs are in a sense strictly stronger than (stateless) LRCs. Indeed, we can use LTCs to construct LRCs by having the input encoder I encode the input x using a leakage-resilient encoding (which is typically easy to construct), then use an LTC C to map the encoded input to a leakage-resilient encoding of the output, and finally let the output decoder O apply the decoding function of the leakage-resilient encoding. It turns out, however, that the stronger leakage-tolerance property plays a crucial role in the context of composition. One primary example is the construction of *stateful* LRCs. We start by discussing the challenges in converting stateless LRCs into stateful ones, and then explain how LTCs give rise to a conceptually simple transformation.

Transforming Stateless LRCs into Stateful LRCs? In [24], the authors consider *t-probing attacks*, where the leakage class $\mathcal{L}$ includes all *t*-projection functions that output *t* fixed input bits. To construct a stateful LRC, they first augment a stateless LRC (I, C, O) to support additional public input and output, and then simply concatenate such LRCs together. In more detail: (1) The initial state is first encoded under the input encoder I. (2) Then in each invocation, an LRC C takes the encoded input and a public input, and computes the encoded secret output and the public output. (3) The encoded output corresponds to an encoding of the current state, which is used as the encoded input in the next invocation.[2]

It is important to highlight the fact that the security of the above transformation relies on specific properties of the underlying stateless LRC and does not work in general. To illustrate this, consider a stateful LRC that has no public input or output and simply keeps its state unchanged. That is, the ideal stateful circuit C simply computes the identity function on the state. A trivial stateless LRC for the identity function can simply output the encoded input. However, applying the ad-hoc transformation from [24] does *not* yield a secure stateful LRC since in each invocation the attacker may probe *t* wires of the same encoding and eventually learn the whole encoding, which reveals the secret state.

This problem is inherent when using stateless LRCs because there is no separation between the randomness used in the input encoding and the randomness used in the output encoding. When using a general stateless LRC to construct a stateful LRC, the same randomness may be under attack in different invocations and eventually revealed to the attacker. In this case, the encoding no longer gives any protection to the secret state. While there are several formulations of sufficient "separation" requirements for the simple case of probing leakage [2,10,20], it is not clear how to meaningfully extend them to more powerful leakage classes. Indeed, most previous works on stateful LRCs for global leakage classes could only address this problem by assuming an ideal trusted hardware that helps perform "refreshing" operations to guarantee the required separation [5,14,16,26], or alternatively settling for computational security and relying on indistinguishability obfuscation [11].

From LTCs to Stateful LRCs. We now describe a general approach for obtaining stateful LRCs via a black-box combination of LTCs and a suitable type of leakage-resilient encoding, extending a previous approach from [16] for constructing stateful LRCs using small trusted hardware components.

Suppose we are given a randomized encoding function Enc which is secure against *two adaptive leakage queries* in the following sense: for all pairs of messages m_0, m_1, any (computationally unbounded) adversary who can adaptively choose $L_0, L_1 \in \mathcal{L}$ and learn $L_0(\text{Enc}(m_b)), L_1(\text{Enc}(m_b))$, where b is a random bit, cannot guess b with non-negligible advantage. Given such an encoding, the construction starts by letting $s_0' = \text{Enc}(s_0)$. Then, in the i-th invocation, we use

---

[2] One can use an encoded output as an encoded input since I and O are compatible, in the sense that inputs and outputs are encoded in the same way.

an LTC $\tilde{C}'$ to decode the internal state s_{i-1} from s'_{i-1}, invoke the ideal stateful circuit $C[s_{i-1}]$, and encode the new state s_i using a fresh invocation of Enc. Relying on the leakage tolerance of $\tilde{C}'$, the leakage queries made by the adversary to the wires in $\tilde{C}'$ can be reduced to leakage queries to the encoded states. Since the states are protected by *fresh* leakage-resilient encodings, the leakage queries to the encoded states can be simulated without knowing the states. This concludes the stateful LRC construction.

Note that we need Enc to provide security against two adaptive leakage queries since an encoded state s'_i is under attack in both the $(i-1)$-th invocation and the i-th invocation, and moreover the leakage query made in the i-th invocation can depend on the result of the leakage query made in the $(i-1)$-th invocation. We summarize this transformation by the following informal theorem. We refer the readers to the full version of this paper for the formal statement.

Theorem 1 (Stateful LRC via LTC, Informal). *Let $\mathcal{L}$ be a leakage class. Suppose there is a 2-adaptive $\mathcal{L}$-leakage-resilient encoding, and an efficient compiler transforming any (stateless) circuit C to an equivalent $\mathcal{L}$-LTC C'. Then, there is an efficient compiler transforming any stateful circuit $C[s_0]$ to an equivalent stateful $\mathcal{L}$-LRC $C'[s'_0]$.*

Combining the above theorem with the LTC constructions we describe next, together with simple leakage-resilient encoding schemes, we obtain the first feasibility results for stateful LRCs against parity leakage, as well as the first *efficient* constructions of stateful LRCs against depth-1 $\mathcal{AC}0$ leakage.

On Efficient Simulation. We note that the simulation efficiency of the stateful LRC construction described above is inherited from the underlying LTC $\tilde{C}'$. If $\tilde{C}'$ requires inefficient simulation (in the output length of the leakage query), then the LRC $C'[s'_0]$ also requires inefficient simulation. This will be the case when using our construction for t-parity-tolerant circuits to build a stateful t-parity-resilient circuit. In the full version of this paper, we provide evidence that the inefficient simulation of our t-parity-tolerant circuits may be inherent; see Sect. 2.4 for an overview.

Fortunately, in the context of the stateful LRC application, we can still obtain efficient simulation regardless of the efficiency of the LTC simulator. At a high level, our idea is to include a control bit b in the initial state. We modify the functionality computed in each invocation by taking an auxiliary input: If $b = 0$, then we ignore the auxiliary input and compute the output by using the internal state and the public input as the original stateful circuit. Otherwise, we keep the state unchanged and output the decoding of the auxiliary input. To achieve the same functionality as the original stateful circuit, the control bit is set to be 0 by default and we just use random bits as the auxiliary input. Now the construction of the $\mathcal{L}$-leakage-resilient stateful circuit is applying the above compiler to the modified stateful circuit.

To obtain efficient simulation, the simulator will set the initial state to some default value and the control bit to 1. In each invocation, after learning the public input and output, the simulator will replace the auxiliary input by an encoding of the public output. In this way, the simulator can simply evaluate the $\mathcal{L}$-leakage-resilient stateful circuit with a fake initial state and compute the leakage queried by the adversary. This can be viewed as an information-theoretic analogue of the technique from [17] for converting witness-indistinguishability to zero knowledge. We refer the readers to the full version of this paper for a formal treatment.

2.2   Overview of Feasibility Results

Motivated in part by the application discussed above, our main technical contribution is establishing the feasibility of LTCs for simple classes of *global* leakage. We focus on the following two "depth-1" leakage classes:

- The first contains all depth-1 $\mathcal{AC}0$ functions. That is, every leakage function L has t output bits, each obtained by choosing a subset S of its inputs and computing the OR (alternatively AND) of bits in S or their negations.
- The second leakage class contains all parity functions. That is, each of the t output bits of L is obtained by choosing a subset S of input bits and computing their XOR.

We will give feasibility results of these two leakage classes separately in the following two subsections.

But to illustrate the non-triviality of the question, we start by showing a counter-intuitive result for the OR leakage class, where L outputs the OR of a subset of input bits without negating them.

Negative Result for the ISW Construction. The standard ISW construction [24] implements an LRC against t-probing leakage (i.e., the adversary can learn any t chosen wires) using the following natural approach. Given a circuit C that computes the function $f : \{0,1\}^n \to \{0,1\}^m$, each wire w in C is transformed to a bundle of wires w_i whose parity is equal to value of w. One may interpret this as generating an *additive secret sharing* for each wire value. This ensures that learning t wires gives no information about the wire values in C.

It turns out that the same construction achieves leakage resilience against $\mathcal{AC}0$ leakage when setting t to be a security parameter κ [6]. This intuitively follows from the well-known fact that $\mathcal{AC}0$ cannot compute parities (though the actual proof is much more subtle). Given this result, it is natural to conjecture that the κ-probing-tolerant variant of the ISW construction also achieves leakage *tolerance* against the OR leakage class, which is much weaker than the $\mathcal{AC}0$ leakage class. Surprisingly, we show that this is not the case even for a linear function f.

Counterexample. Consider the function $f(x_1, x_2, x_3) = x_1 \oplus x_2 \oplus x_3$. The probing-tolerant variant of the ISW construction for f works as follows.

1. Input Encoding Phase: For all $i \in \{1, 2, 3\}$, do the following.
   - Prepare κ random bits $x_{i,0}, \ldots, x_{i,\kappa-1}$.

- Compute $x_{i,\kappa} = x_i \oplus x_{i,0} \oplus \ldots \oplus x_{i,\kappa-1}$ in order.
- Set $[x_i] = (x_{i,0}, \ldots, x_{i,\kappa})$. Note that the parity of bits in $[x_i]$ is x_i.
2. Circuit Emulation Phase: Compute $[y] = [x_1] \oplus [x_2] \oplus [x_3]$ coordinate by coordinate in order.
3. Output Decoding Phase: Set $(y_0, \ldots, y_\kappa) = [y]$. Compute $y = y_\kappa \oplus y_{\kappa-1} \oplus \ldots \oplus y_0$ in order.

One can show that the above construction achieves κ-probing tolerance for f.

Consider the following attack: $(x_1 \oplus x_{1,0}) \vee (x_2 \oplus x_{2,0}) \vee (x_{1,0} \oplus x_{2,0})$, where $x_1 \oplus x_{1,0}, x_2 \oplus x_{2,0}$ are the inner wires in the input encoding phase when computing $x_{1,\kappa}$ and $x_{2,\kappa}$, and $x_{1,0} \oplus x_{2,0}$ is the inner wire in the circuit emulation phase when computing $[y]$. Using Boolean algebra identities, we have

$$(x_1 \oplus x_{1,0}) \vee (x_2 \oplus x_{2,0}) \vee (x_{1,0} \oplus x_{2,0}) = (x_1 \oplus x_{1,0}) \vee (x_2 \oplus x_{2,0}) \vee (x_1 \oplus x_2).$$

Let $r_1 = x_1 \oplus x_{1,0}$ and $r_2 = x_2 \oplus x_{2,0}$. Then the above attack reveals $r_1 \vee r_2 \vee (x_1 \oplus x_2)$, which is equal to 1 with probability $3/4$ and leaks $x_1 \oplus x_2$ with probability $1/4$. If the construction were OR-tolerant, then such an attack could be simulated by computing the OR of a subset of $x_1, x_2, x_3, y = x_1 \oplus x_2 \oplus x_3$. However, intuitively, the OR operation is not able to compute $x_1 \oplus x_2$ from the above, which leads to a contradiction. We refer the readers to the full version of this paper for the details.

2.3   Leakage Tolerance Against Depth-1 $\mathcal{AC}0$ Leakage

It turns out that if we extend the OR leakage class to depth-1 $\mathcal{AC}0$, by allowing both the real and the ideal leakage to apply negations, then the ISW construction becomes leakage-tolerant.

The reason for this unexpected phenomenon is that when we switch to a richer leakage class, we strengthen not only the "real" leakage L that applies to all wires, but also the "ideal" leakage L' that applies only to the input and output bits. Thus, for two leakage classes $\mathcal{L} \subset \hat{\mathcal{L}}$, an $\hat{\mathcal{L}}$-LTC is not necessarily an $\mathcal{L}$-LTC.

Single Bit of Depth-1 $\mathcal{AC}0$ Leakage. Consider a linear function $f(x_1, \ldots, x_n) = (y_1, \ldots, y_m)$ where each y_j is a linear combination of $\{x_i\}_{i=1}^n$. Let κ be the security parameter. Recall the κ-probing-tolerant variant of the ISW construction for the linear function f:

1. Input Encoding Phase: For all $i \in \{1, \ldots, n\}$, do the following.
   - Prepare κ random bits $x_{i,0}, \ldots, x_{i,\kappa-1}$.
   - Compute $x_{i,\kappa} = x_i \oplus x_{i,0} \oplus \ldots \oplus x_{i,\kappa-1}$ in order.
   - Set $[x_i] = (x_{i,0}, \ldots, x_{i,\kappa})$.
2. Circuit Emulation Phase: The circuit computes $[y_j]$ via a proper linear combination of $[x_1], \ldots, [x_n]$.
3. Output Decoding Phase: For all $j \in \{1, \ldots, m\}$, set $(y_{j,0}, \ldots, y_{j,\kappa}) = [y]$ and compute $y_j = y_{j,\kappa} \oplus y_{j,\kappa-1} \oplus \ldots \oplus y_{j,0}$ in order.

For all $j \in \{0, \dots, \kappa\}$, let $\mathcal{I}_j$ be the set of wires that are non-zero linear combinations of $\{x_{i,j}\}_{i=1}^n$ in the circuit emulation phase. We note that if we arbitrarily pick a variable $w_j \in \mathcal{I}_j$ for all $j \in \{0, \dots, \kappa\}$, then any κ variables in $\{w_j \in \mathcal{I}_j\}_{j=0}^{\kappa}$ are uniformly random. This is because for all $S \subset \{0, \dots, \kappa\}$ with $|S| = \kappa$, $\{x_{i,j}\}_{j \in S, i \in \{1,\dots,n\}}$ are uniformly random bits. Then for all $j \in S$, each w_j is uniformly random given $\{x_{i,j'}\}_{j' \in S, j' \neq j, i \in \{1,\dots,n\}}$.

Now consider a single bit of depth-1 $\mathcal{AC}0$ leakage, obtained as follows.

1. An adversary first chooses an arbitrary set W of wires in C.
2. Then the adversary may arbitrarily flip some wires in W. Denote the resulting set of literals (wire variables or their negations) by $\widetilde{W}$.
3. Finally, the leakage is defined to be $\mathtt{OR}(\widetilde{W})$, where $\mathtt{OR}(S)$ denotes the result of $\mathtt{OR}$ of all bits in S.

Our main observation is that, if for all $j \in \{0, \dots, \kappa\}$, $W \cap \mathcal{I}_j \neq \emptyset$, then there are at least κ variables in $\widetilde{W}$ that are uniformly random. In this case $\mathtt{OR}(\widetilde{W}) = 1$ with probability at least $1 - 2^{-\kappa}$. Thus, we may simply output 0 as the simulation of $\mathtt{OR}(\widetilde{W})$.

It is therefore sufficient to focus on the case where there is $j^\star \in \{0, \dots, \kappa\}$ such that $W \cap \mathcal{I}_{j^\star} = \emptyset$. We observe that in this case, every wire in W only depends on a single input or output bit. In this way, $\mathtt{OR}(\widetilde{W})$ naturally corresponds to a depth-1 $\mathcal{AC}0$ leakage on the input and output bits. At a high level, this can be achieved by the following two steps.

1. Simulate all wire values in $\bigcup_{j \neq j^\star} \mathcal{I}_j$. We note that this can be done without knowing the input and output bits.
2. Given wire values in $\bigcup_{j \neq j^\star} \mathcal{I}_j$, every intermediate wire in the input encoding phase and the output decoding phase only depends on a single input or output bit.

In the full version of this paper, we show how to extend the above idea to handle multiple bits of depth-1 $\mathcal{AC}0$ leakage.

Towards General Functions. Based on the positive result of the ISW construction for linear functions against depth-1 $\mathcal{AC}0$ leakage, we show how to construct leakage-tolerant circuits for general functions.

Let $f : \{0,1\}^n \to \{0,1\}^m$ be an arbitrary binary function with circuit implementation C. At a high level, for each wire w in C, we will compute an additive secret sharing of w. Then we will use the ISW construction to compute every $\mathtt{XOR}$ gate and every $\mathtt{AND}$ gate.

1. For each input bit x_i, we sample κ random bits $(x_{i,0}, \dots, x_{i,\kappa-1})$. To obtain $[x_i]$, we want to compute $x_{i,\kappa} = x_i \oplus (\bigoplus_{\ell=0}^{\kappa-1} x_{i,\ell})$. We view the computation of $x_{i,\kappa}$ as a linear function and apply the ISW construction to it.
2. For each $\mathtt{XOR}$ gate with two input additive sharings $[a]$, $[b]$, we sample random bits $c_0, \dots, c_{\kappa-1}$. To obtain $[c] = [a+b]$, we want to compute $c_\kappa = (\bigoplus_{\ell=0}^{\kappa} a_\ell) \oplus (\bigoplus_{\ell=0}^{\kappa} b_\ell) \oplus (\bigoplus_{\ell=0}^{\kappa-1} c_\ell)$. We view the computation of c_κ as a linear function and apply the ISW construction to it.

3. For each AND gate with two input additive sharings $[a]$, $[b]$, we sample random bits $c_0, \ldots, c_{\kappa-1}$. Then we compute $a_{\ell_1} \cdot b_{\ell_2}$ for all $\ell_1, \ell_2 \in \{0, \ldots, \kappa\}$. Our goal is to compute $c_\kappa = (\bigoplus_{\ell_1,\ell_2=0}^{\kappa} a_{\ell_1} \cdot b_{\ell_2}) \oplus (\bigoplus_{\ell=0}^{\kappa-1} c_\ell)$. We view the computation of c_κ as a linear function and apply the ISW construction to it.

4. After obtaining an additive secret sharing $[y_j]$ for each output y_j, we want to reconstruct $y_j = \bigoplus_{\ell=0}^{\kappa} y_{j,\ell}$. We view the computation of y_j as a linear function and apply the ISW construction to it.

Intuitively, by using the ISW construction for every linear function, it is sufficient to focus on an adversary which only has access to the input and output wires of the linear functions. These wires can be summarized as follows:

- The input and output bits of f: $(x_1, \ldots, x_n)$ and $(y_1, \ldots, y_m)$
- A random additive secret sharing for every wire w: $[w] = (w_0, w_1, \ldots, w_\kappa)$.
- For each AND gate with two input additive sharings $[a]$, $[b]$, the cross multiplications between shares: $\{a_{\ell_1} \cdot b_{\ell_2}\}_{\ell_1=0,\ell_2=0}^{\kappa}$.

Note that 1 bit of depth-1 $\mathcal{AC}0$ leakage on these wires can be viewed as the OR of two separated bits of depth-1 $\mathcal{AC}0$ leakage: the first part is depth-1 $\mathcal{AC}0$ leakage on the input and output bits, and the second part is depth-1 $\mathcal{AC}0$ leakage on the random additive secret sharings and the cross multiplications between shares. We note that the second part can be further viewed as a depth-2 $\mathcal{AC}0$ leakage on the random additive secret sharings. Since we know that an $\mathcal{AC}0$ leakage cannot distinguish a random additive secret sharing of 0 from a random additive secret sharing of 1, we may just replace random additive secret sharings for wire values in C by random additive secret sharings of 0 and compute the cross multiplications between shares accordingly. In this way, the second part can be computed directly while the first part is just a depth-1 $\mathcal{AC}0$ leakage on the input and output bits of the function. Thus, we have the following theorem.

Theorem 2 (LTC Against Depth-1 $\mathcal{AC}0$, Informal). *Let $\mathcal{L}$ denote the leakage class that contains all depth-1 $\mathcal{AC}0$ leakage functions. For all binary function $f : \{0,1\}^n \rightarrow \{0,1\}^m$ with circuit implementation C, there exists an $\mathcal{L}$-leakage-tolerant circuit for C.*

Using General Linear Secret Sharing Schemes. In Sect. 4, we show that our construction can be modified slightly to support any linear secret sharing scheme. In particular, we can use packed Shamir sharings to achieve a better circuit complexity for computing SIMD circuits. Relying on [12], which transforms a general circuit to a SIMD circuit, we obtain the following corollary.

Corollary 1 (Informal). *Let $\mathcal{L}$ denote the leakage class that contains all depth-1 $\mathcal{AC}0$ leakage functions. For all binary function $f : \{0,1\}^n \rightarrow \{0,1\}^m$ with circuit implementation C of size s and depth h, there exists an $\mathcal{L}$-leakage-tolerant circuit for C with circuit size $\tilde{O}(\kappa s + \kappa^2 h + \kappa^3)$, where $\tilde{O}$ omits logarithmic factors and κ is the security parameter.*

2.4   Leakage Tolerance Against Parity Leakage

Unlike the depth-1 $\mathcal{AC}0$ leakage, one cannot hope the ISW construction to be parity-tolerant (i.e., leakage-tolerant against parity leakage) since we can easily recover an intermediate wire value by XOR. At a high level, our result is obtained in two steps.

Step 1. We first define a new notion which we refer to as *parity-to-probing* circuits. Very informally, given a circuit $\tilde{C}$ representing the function we want to compute, a (t, k)-parity-to-probing implementation of $\tilde{C}$ is a triple (I, C, O), where I is a randomized input encoder, C is a randomized circuit, and O is an output decoder, such that the following properties hold.

- For any input x, we have $O(C(I(x))) = \tilde{C}(x)$ (with probability 1).
- Any t parity queries to the wires of C can be simulated by k probing queries to the wires of $\tilde{C}$. We refer to this property as parity-to-probing security.
- I and O admit circuit implementations in which any inner wire is a linear combination of the input and output wires. We refer to this property as trivial parity tolerance. Note that this property can be satisfied even by nonlinear functions, such as $x_1 \cdot x_2$.

We observe that when $\tilde{C}$ is a k-probing-tolerant circuit, any t parity queries to the wires of C can be simulated by k probing queries to the inputs and outputs of $\tilde{C}$. We utilize this property and show that a t-parity-tolerant circuit can be constructed from a (t, k)-parity-to-probing circuit.

We remark that without the last property, a parity-to-probing circuit is strictly weaker than a parity-resilient circuit since the latter requires that any parity query to the wires in C should give essentially no information about the inputs and outputs of $\tilde{C}$. However, our construction relies on the property of trivial parity tolerance for the input encoder and the output decoder. On the other hand, we show that the input encoder and the output decoder of a parity-resilient circuit cannot be trivially parity-tolerant (see Claim 5.1).

Step 2. Then, we show how to construct a parity-to-probing circuit for any underlying circuit $\tilde{C}$. Our construction is inspired by the construction of [21]. We observe that the construction in [21] implies a (t, k)-parity-to-probing circuit with the aid of a secure NAND gadget. In this step, we construct a circuit that realizes the secure NAND gadget and show that after replacing the NAND gadget by our construction in [21], the (t, k)-parity-to-probing security remains. Combining with the first step, we obtain a feasibility result for t-parity-tolerant circuits.

In the following we give a more detailed exposition of the above 2 steps.

Step 1: Parity-to-Probing Implies Parity Tolerance

Parity Tolerance vs. Parity Resilience. A natural attempt of constructing a parity-tolerant circuit is to use a parity-resilient circuit (I, C, O) and implement I and O by parity-tolerant circuits. However there are two issues with this attempt:

- *Constructing parity-tolerant circuits for I and O is not trivial.*

The only previous construction of parity-resilient circuits is from [21]. While the input encoder and the output decoder in this construction are not complicated, it is still not clear how to implement them in a parity-tolerant way. In fact, even constructing a parity-tolerant circuit for the mod-2 inner-product function $f(x_1, x_2, y_1, y_2) = x_1 \cdot y_1 + x_2 \cdot y_2$ is not an easy task. The naive implementation, which first computes $x_1 \cdot y_1, x_2 \cdot y_2$ and then computes their sum, is *not* parity-tolerant. This is because the inner wire $x_1 \cdot y_1$ cannot be simulated by one parity query to the input wires (x_1, x_2, y_1, y_2) and the output wire $x_1 \cdot y_1 + x_2 \cdot y_2$.

- *There is a quantitative loss when composing two parity-tolerant circuits.*

Even if we have constructed t-parity-tolerant circuits for I and O (meaning that any t parities of the wires can be simulated by t parities of the circuit inputs and outputs), the implementation of (I, C, O) may not achieve t-parity tolerance. Consider the following natural simulation strategy: For each parity query, we view it as the summation of three parity queries, the first one for the wires in I, the second one for the wires in C, and the last one for the wires in O. The t parity queries to the wires in C are not a problem, since (by parity resilience) they can be simulated independently of the function inputs and outputs. However, to simulate the t parity queries to the wires in I, we need to make t parity queries to the inputs and outputs of I, which translate to t parity queries to the function inputs and outputs. Similarly, to simulate the t parity queries to the wires in O, we need to make another t parity queries to the function inputs and outputs. These add up to $2t$ parity queries to the function inputs and outputs. In summary, to simulate t parity queries to the implementation of (I, C, O), we may have to make $2t$ parity queries to the function inputs and outputs.

Constructing Parity-Tolerant Circuits from Parity-to-Probing Circuits. Let f be a function. Our goal is to construct a parity-tolerant circuit implementation of f. We focus on a single parity query for simplicity.

Our first attempt is to start with a k-probing-tolerant implementation $\tilde{C}$ of f and then consider the $(1, k)$-parity-to-probing circuit (I, C, O) of $\tilde{C}$. Now consider the parity of a set W of wires of the circuit implementation of (I, C, O). Recall that for a parity-to-probing circuit, its input encoder and output decoder satisfies the trivial parity tolerance. Therefore, parity(W) can be computed by some parity of (1) the function inputs and outputs, and (2) the wires in C. (Here and in the following, parity(W) denotes the parity of all wires in W.) Now by the parity-to-probing security, the parity of wires in C can be simulated by k wires in $\tilde{C}$, which can be simulated by k inputs and outputs of $\tilde{C}$ due to the property of probing tolerance.

In summary, parity(W) can be simulated by (1) a parity of the function inputs and outputs and (2) k wires of the function inputs and outputs. This requires us to not only make one parity query but also k probing queries.

To address this issue, for each bit x of the function inputs and outputs, we split it to $k + 1$ random additive shares with parity x. Then we apply the above idea to compute $\hat{f}$ which maps additive sharings of the inputs of f to additive sharings of the outputs of f. We note that

- The k probings of additive sharings of the function inputs and outputs can be simulated by choosing k random values.
- Given the k probings, any parity query to the additive sharings of the function inputs and outputs can be reduced to a parity query to the function inputs and outputs. Furthermore, the encoding and decoding processes of an additive sharing achieve parity tolerance for free, since every inner wire can be computed by a linear combination of the additive shares.

Thus, our construction of a parity-tolerant circuit $C^\star$ is as follows (See Fig. 2 for the complete description):

1. The circuit $C^\star$ first encodes each bit of the input $\boldsymbol{x}$ of f by a random additive sharing. Let $\hat{\boldsymbol{x}}$ denotes the encoding of $\boldsymbol{x}$.
2. Then let $\hat{f}$ be the (randomized) function that maps an encoded input $\hat{\boldsymbol{x}}$ to a freshly encoded output $\hat{\boldsymbol{y}}$. Let $\tilde{C}$ be a k-probing-tolerant implementation of $\hat{f}$, and let (I, C, O) be a $(1, k)$-parity-to-probing circuit implementation of $\tilde{C}$. Then $C^\star$ runs (I, C, O) on $\hat{\boldsymbol{x}}$ and outputs $\hat{\boldsymbol{y}}$.
3. Finally, the circuit $C^\star$ decodes $\hat{\boldsymbol{y}}$ by computing the parity of each additive sharing and obtains $\boldsymbol{y}$.

The above idea is naturally extended to constructing t-parity-tolerant circuits from (t, k)-parity-to-probing circuits and k-probing-tolerant circuits. We refer the readers to Sect. 5.1 for more details.

Step 2: Constructing Parity-to-Probing Circuits. Now we turn our focus to parity-to-probing circuits. Our starting point is the construction in [21], which implicitly gives a (t, k)-parity-to-probing circuit with the aid of a secure NAND gadget. We first give an overview of the construction in [21].

Overview of [21]. Let $\tilde{C}$ denote the input circuit. The goal is to construct a (t, k)-parity-to-probing circuit implementation of $\tilde{C}$. Without loss of generality, we assume that $\tilde{C}$ only contains NAND gates. The idea in [21] is to encode each wire in $\tilde{C}$ by a small-bias encoding scheme. Very informally, an ϵ-bias encoding scheme ensures that the parity of any non-empty subset bits of the encoding has bias (i.e., difference from a uniform bit) at most ϵ. An example of a $1/2$-bias encoding is presented in Fig. 1. In the following, we will stick to the small-bias encoding scheme in Fig. 1. The construction of $(\hat{I}, \hat{C}, \hat{O})$ is as follows:

- $\hat{I}$ takes $\boldsymbol{x} \in \{0,1\}^{n_i}$ as input and computes a small-bias encoding for each input bit: $\{\texttt{Enc}(x_i)\}_{i=1}^{n_i}$.
- $\hat{C}$ takes $\{\texttt{Enc}(x_i)\}_{i=1}^{n_i}$ as input. Then $\hat{C}$ computes a small-bias encoding for each wire value in C'. Concretely, for each NAND gate in C' with input x_0, x_1, $\hat{C}$ uses a secure NAND gadget to compute $\texttt{Enc}(x_0 \text{ NAND } x_1)$ from $\texttt{Enc}(x_0), \texttt{Enc}(x_1)$.
- $\hat{O}$ takes $\{\texttt{Enc}(y_i)\}_{i=1}^{n_o}$ as input and outputs $\{y_i = \texttt{Dec}(\texttt{Enc}(y_i))\}_{i=1}^{n_o}$.

1/2-Bias Encoding Scheme (Enc, Dec)

$$\text{Enc}(x; r_0, r_1) = (r_0, r_1, r_0 \cdot r_1 \oplus x)$$
$$\text{Dec}(\hat{x}_0, \hat{x}_1, \hat{x}_2) = \hat{x}_0 \cdot \hat{x}_1 \oplus \hat{x}_2.$$

Fig. 1. An Example of Small-bias Encoding Scheme

We first verify that this construction achieves parity-to-probing security. Consider a parity query which chooses a set W of wires in $\hat{C}$. Intuitively, if W touches more than k different small-bias encodings in $\hat{C}$, then $\text{parity}(W)$ would have bias at most 2^{-k}, indicating that $\text{parity}(W)$ is statistically close to a uniform bit. On the other hand, if W touches at most k different small-bias encodings in $\hat{C}$, then $\text{parity}(W)$ can be perfectly simulated by probing the underlying k wires in C'. In Sect. 5.2, we show that the above analysis can be extended to t parity queries.

As for the trivial parity tolerance, one can easily verify that this property is satisfied in the following two circuit constructions for $\hat{I}$ and $\hat{O}$ respectively.

- For $\hat{I}$, which computes a 1/2-bias encoding of each bit x, the encoding is computed by first computing $r_0 \cdot r_1$, and then computing $(r_0 \cdot r_1) \oplus x$.
- For $\hat{O}$, which decodes a 1/2-bias encoding for each output bit, the decoding is computed by first computing $\hat{x}_0 \cdot \hat{x}_1$, and then computing $(\hat{x}_0 \cdot \hat{x}_1) \oplus \hat{x}_2$.

Instantiating NAND *Gadgets.* Our initial attempt is to utilize the instantiation in [21]. We note that the construction in [21] only focuses on parity-resilient circuits. Unfortunately, we do not know whether the (t, k)-parity-to-probing property remains after applying their instantiation for NAND gadgets. In the full version of this paper, we discuss their solution in details and show that:

- By using the parity-simulation lemma, the construction in [21] is a $(1, k)$-parity-to-probing circuit. Together with our main theorem in Step 1, we can compile their construction into a 1-parity-tolerant circuit. The parity-simulation lemma and its proof may be of independent interest.
- On the other hand, we show that the parity-simulation lemma cannot handle more than 1 bit of parity leakage. We also give a counter example which shows that in general, a 1-parity-tolerant circuit may not achieve 2-parity tolerance.

In the following, we discuss our solution that gives a (t, k)-parity-to-probing circuit. Our solution is specific to the use of the small-bias encoding presented in Fig. 1. Let $(\hat{I}, \hat{C}, \hat{O})$ be the (t, k)-parity-to-probing circuit with the aid of a secure NAND gadget from [21]. Recall that $\hat{C}$ computes a small-bias encoding for every wire of the underlying circuit $\tilde{C}$. Suppose $\boldsymbol{w} = (w_1, \ldots, w_{|\tilde{C}|})$ are the wires in $\tilde{C}$ and $\boldsymbol{u}, \boldsymbol{v} \in \{0,1\}^{|\tilde{C}|}$ are two vectors of random bits. Then, the wires in $\hat{C}$ are

$$(u_1, v_1, u_1 \cdot v_1 \oplus w_1), \ldots, (u_{|\tilde{C}|}, v_{|\tilde{C}|}, u_{|\tilde{C}|} \cdot v_{|\tilde{C}|} \oplus w_{|\tilde{C}|}),$$

or equivalently, $(\boldsymbol{u}, \boldsymbol{v}, \boldsymbol{u} * \boldsymbol{v} \oplus \boldsymbol{w})$.

Our main observation is that, the (t, k)-parity-to-probing property is preserved even if the adversary knows $\boldsymbol{v}$ and can do any computation on $\boldsymbol{v}$. To be more precise: For all subset W of wires in $\hat{C}$, the joint view of $(\texttt{parity}(W), \boldsymbol{v})$ can be simulated with statistical error negligible in k by probing k wires in $\tilde{C}$.

Intuitively, it follows the fact that $\texttt{parity}(W)$ is masked by $\oplus_{i \in \mathcal{I}} u_i \cdot v_i$ for some set $\mathcal{I}$. When $|\mathcal{I}| \geq k$, as long as one of v_i is not 0, which happens with probability $1 - 2^{-k}$ the mask value is uniformly distributed. As long as $\boldsymbol{v}$ is sampled uniformly random and the adversary only learns $\boldsymbol{v}$ after choosing W, learning $\boldsymbol{v}$ does not help the adversary to learn any information about $\boldsymbol{w}$. This observation allows us to do any computation on $\boldsymbol{v}$ when instantiating $\texttt{NAND}$ gadgets while preserving the parity-to-probing property.

Example: Using Our Observation to Instantiate $\texttt{XOR}$ *Gadgets.* To explain our high level idea, we show how our observation allows us to instantiate $\texttt{XOR}$ gadgets. Our instantiation for $\texttt{NAND}$ gadgets follows a similar idea which is discussed later. Given two encodings $(u_1, v_1, z_1 = u_1 \cdot v_1 \oplus w_1), (u_2, v_2, z_2 = u_2 \cdot v_2 \oplus w_2)$, we want to compute an encoding $(u_0, v_0, z_0 = u_0 \cdot v_0 \oplus w_1 \oplus w_2)$. Since u_0, v_0 are random bits, we just need to compute $z_0 = u_0 \cdot v_0 \oplus u_1 \cdot v_1 \oplus u_2 \cdot v_2 \oplus z_1 \oplus z_2$. The main observation is that, given v_0, v_1, v_2, this equation becomes a linear combination of $(u_0, u_1, u_2, z_1, z_2)$, which can be implemented directly since the intermediate results can also be obtained under parity attack on $(u_0, u_1, u_2, z_1, z_2)$. Therefore, we first compute z_0 under all possible assignments of $(v_0, v_1, v_2) = (a_0, a_1, a_2)$. In the meantime, we also compute a bit indicating whether $(v_0, v_1, v_2) = (a_0, a_1, a_2)$. Note that the computation of indicating bits only depends on $\boldsymbol{v}$. As we argued above, these intermediate wires do not break the parity-to-probing security. Finally, we use the indicating bits to choose the proper z_0. In the actual construction, we will first prepare a random bit ρ and compute $z_0 + \rho$ using the above approach to protect the secrecy of $w_1 \oplus w_2$. The overall construction is as follows:

1. We first sample a random bit ρ. Let $f(v_0, v_1, v_2) = u_0 \cdot v_0 \oplus u_1 \cdot v_1 \oplus u_2 \cdot v_2 \oplus z_1 \oplus z_2 \oplus \rho$, which is just $z_0 \oplus \rho$.
2. For all $(a_0, a_1, a_2) \in \{0,1\}^3$, compute $f(a_0, a_1, a_2)$ by a linear combination of $(u_0, u_1, u_2, z_1, z_2, \rho)$.
3. For all $(a_0, a_1, a_2) \in \{0,1\}^3$, compute $\prod_{i=0}^{2}(v_i \oplus a_i \oplus 1)$, which indicates whether $(v_0, v_1, v_2) = (a_0, a_1, a_2)$.
4. Compute $z_0 \oplus \rho = \sum_{a \in \{0,1\}^3} f(a_0, a_1, a_2) \cdot \prod_{i=0}^{2}(v_i \oplus a_i \oplus 1)$.
5. Compute $z_0 = (z_0 \oplus \rho) \oplus \rho$.

Note that the intermediate wires introduced in Step 2 are linear combination of the input and output bits. The intermediate wires introduced in Step 3 only depends on $\boldsymbol{v}$. As for the intermediate wires introduced in Step 4, let $\rho' =$

$z_0 \oplus \rho$. We may sample a random bit as ρ' and compute $\rho = z_0 \oplus \rho'$. Then the intermediate wires introduced in Step 4 only depends on random bits v and ρ', which does not break the parity-to-probing security.

Moving to NAND *Gadgets.* For NAND gadgets, what we need to compute becomes $z_0 = u_0 \cdot v_0 \oplus (u_1 \cdot v_1 \oplus z_1) \cdot (u_2 \cdot v_2 \oplus z_2)$. Even if given v_0, v_1, v_2, this equation is not a linear combination of $(u_0, u_1, u_2, z_1, z_2)$, which means that computing z_0 given (v_0, v_1, v_2) is no longer for free under parity attacks. To address this issue, our idea is to also fix (u_1, z_1) (or (u_2, z_2)) so that z_0 is a linear combination of (u_0, u_2, z_2) (or (u_0, u_1, z_1)). To be more concrete, we first refresh the encoding of w_1 (and w_2), i.e., computing $(u'_1, v'_1, z'_1 = u'_1 \cdot v'_1 \oplus w_1)$ from (u_1, v_1, w_1). This can be viewed as a Refresh gadget and can be instantiated in a similar way to XOR gadgets. In this way, when analyzing the intermediate wires related to (u_2, z_2), we fix the refreshed encoding (u'_1, v'_1, z'_1) and now the computation of z_0 is linear as that in XOR gadgets. We refer readers to Sect. 5.2 for more details.

In the full version of this paper, we show that our construction maintains the (t, k)-parity-to-probing security of $(\hat{I}, \hat{C}, \hat{O})$. Therefore, combining our result in the first step, we obtain a t-parity-tolerant circuit for any function f.

On the Need for Inefficient Simulation. A limitation of our construction of (t, k)-parity-to-probing circuits is that the running time of the simulation is exponential in t. This implies that our construction of t-parity tolerant circuits also has exponential-time simulation. We demonstrate this problem by taking the parity-to-probing circuit $(\hat{I}, \hat{C}, \hat{O})$ constructed in [21] as an example. To simplify the description, for two sets W_1, W_2, we define $W_1 \oplus W_2 = W_1 \cup W_2 \setminus (W_1 \cap W_2)$. Then $\mathtt{parity}(W_1) \oplus \mathtt{parity}(W_2) = \mathtt{parity}(W_1 \oplus W_2)$.

Recall that for a set W of wires in $\hat{C}$, if W touches more than k small-bias encodings, then $\mathtt{parity}(W)$ can be simulated by a random bit. Otherwise, we need to probes the set of wires of the underlying circuit $\tilde{C}$ whose encodings are touched by W to simulate $\mathtt{parity}(W)$. We denote this set by $\mathcal{V}(W)$. Given W, we can find $\mathcal{V}(W)$ efficiently.

When we have t sets $W_1, \ldots, W_t$, only finding the sets $\mathcal{V}(W_1), \ldots, \mathcal{V}(W_t)$ is not sufficient since we have to consider the joint distribution of all parities. For example, if W_1 and W_2 both touches more than k encodings, then $\mathcal{V}(W_1) = \mathcal{V}(W_2) = \emptyset$. On the other hand $W_1 \oplus W_2$ may only touch less than k encodings. In this case, we have to find the set $\mathcal{V}(W_1 \oplus W_2)$ to simulate $\mathtt{parity}(W_1) \oplus \mathtt{parity}(W_2)$. In general, to simulate t parities, we have to compute the set $V = \cup_{S \subset \{1,\ldots,t\}} \mathcal{V}(\oplus_{i \in S} W_i)$ which takes time exponential in t. (A remark about the size of V: Although it is a union set of 2^t subsets, we show that the size of V is bounded by kt. See more details in Sect. 5.2 and the proof of Theorem 4 in the full version of this paper.)

In the full version of this paper, we consider a relaxed notion of t-parity tolerance which we refer to as (t, t')-parity-tolerant functions. Concretely, a (t, t')-parity-tolerant function requires that any t parities of the output of the function can be simulated by t' parities of the input of the function. Intuitively, one may view a parity-tolerant circuit as a special kind of parity-tolerant function where the function's input is the circuit input and output, and the function's output is the wires of the circuit.

We give an example of a (t, t')-parity-tolerant function that requires superpolynomial simulation time in t under the standard LPN assumption. This may serve as partial evidence that inefficient simulation may be inherent for parity tolerance as well.

3   Preliminaries

In this section, we define the notion of leakage-resilient circuits and leakage-tolerant circuits for general leakage classes. We assume that the leakage classes considered in this work are closed under restrictions, i.e., for all $L : \{0,1\}^n \to \{0,1\}^m$ in $\mathcal{L}$, for all $S \subset \{1, \ldots, n\}$, and for all $\boldsymbol{x}_S \in \{0,1\}^{|S|}$, we require that $L(\boldsymbol{x})$ given $\boldsymbol{x}_S$ is also in $\mathcal{L}$. We note that all natural leakage classes (or their simple variants[3]) considered in the literature satisfy this property. We borrow the definition of leakage-resilient circuits from [21] as follows.

Definition 1 ([21]). *For a (possibly randomized) function* $f : \{0,1\}^{n_i} \to \{0,1\}^{n_o}$, *a leakage-resilient circuit for* f *is defined by* (I, C, O), *where*

- $I : \{0,1\}^{n_i} \to \{0,1\}^{\hat{n}_i}$ *is a randomized input encoder, which maps an input* $\boldsymbol{x}$ *to an encoded input* $\hat{\boldsymbol{x}}$,
- C *is a randomized circuit, mapping an encoded input* $\hat{\boldsymbol{x}} \in \{0,1\}^{\hat{n}_i}$ *to an encoded output* $\hat{\boldsymbol{y}} \in \{0,1\}^{\hat{n}_o}$,
- $O : \{0,1\}^{\hat{n}_o} \to \{0,1\}^{n_o}$ *is a deterministic output decoder, mapping* $\hat{\boldsymbol{y}}$ *to an output* $\boldsymbol{y}$.

Let $\mathcal{L}$ *be a class of leakage functions. We say* C *is an* $(\mathcal{L}, \epsilon)$-*leakage-resilient implementation of* f *if*

- *Correctness: For any input* $\boldsymbol{x} \in \{0,1\}^{n_i}$, *the following two distributions are identical:*

$$f(\boldsymbol{x}) \equiv O(C(I(\boldsymbol{x}))).$$

- *Leakage Resilience: For all* $L \in \mathcal{L}$ *with input size* $|C|$ *and for all* $\boldsymbol{x}, \boldsymbol{x}' \in \{0,1\}^{n_i}$, *the statistical distance between the distributions* $L(\tau(C, I(\boldsymbol{x})))$ *and* $L(\tau(C, I(\boldsymbol{x}')))$ *is at most* ϵ, *where* $\tau(C, \hat{\boldsymbol{x}})$ *denotes the wire values of* C *when taking* $\hat{\boldsymbol{x}}$ *as input.*

For leakage-tolerant circuits for general leakage classes, we generalize the notion of t-probing-tolerant circuits from [1,22,24].

---

[3] For example, for parity leakage, we may include functions that compute the flip of the parity of a subset of input bits. For probing leakage, we may include the constant functions that always output 0 or 1. These expansions of the leakage classes do not bring more power to the adversary.

Definition 2 (Leakage-Tolerant Circuit). *For a (possibly randomized) function $f : \{0,1\}^{n_i} \rightarrow \{0,1\}^{n_o}$, a leakage-tolerant circuit for f is defined by a randomized circuit C mapping an input $\boldsymbol{x} \in \{0,1\}^{n_i}$ to an output $\boldsymbol{y} \in \{0,1\}^{n_o}$. Let $\mathcal{L}$ be a class of leakage functions. We say C is an $(\mathcal{L}, \epsilon)$-leakage-tolerant implementation of f if*

- *Correctness: For any input $\boldsymbol{x} \in \{0,1\}^{n_i}$, the following two distributions are identical:*

$$f(\boldsymbol{x}) \equiv C(\boldsymbol{x}).$$

- *Leakage Tolerance: There exists a simulator $\mathtt{Sim} = (\mathtt{Sim}_1, \mathtt{Sim}_2)$ with the following syntax:*
  - *$\mathtt{Sim}_1$ takes as input a leakage function $L \in \mathcal{L}$ with input size $|C|$ and outputs a state $\mathtt{st}$ as well as a leakage function $L' \in \mathcal{L}$ with input size $n_i + n_o$,*
  - *$\mathtt{Sim}_2$ takes as input a state $\mathtt{st}$ and the output of the ideal leakage $L'(\cdot)$ on the input and output of f, and outputs a string $\boldsymbol{b}$,*
  such that for all input $\boldsymbol{x} \in \{0,1\}^{n_i}$ and for all $L \in \mathcal{L}$, the following two distributions are ϵ-close (in statistical distance):

$$(L(\tau(C, \boldsymbol{x})), C(\boldsymbol{x})) \approx_\epsilon (\mathtt{Sim}_2(\mathtt{st}, L'(\boldsymbol{x}, \boldsymbol{y})), \boldsymbol{y}) : \boldsymbol{y} \leftarrow f(\boldsymbol{x}), (\mathtt{st}, L') \leftarrow \mathtt{Sim}_1(L)$$

where $\tau(C, \boldsymbol{x})$ denotes the random variables of the wire values of C when the input is $\boldsymbol{x}$.

In this work, we are interested in three different leakage classes.

- Probing Leakage Class: This leakage class contains all leakage functions $L : \{0,1\}^n \rightarrow \{0,1\}$ defined by $i \in \{1, \ldots, n\}$ such that $L(\boldsymbol{x}) = x_i$.
- Depth-1 $\mathcal{AC}0$ Leakage Class (D1 Leakage Class for short): This leakage class contains all leakage functions $L : \{0,1\}^n \rightarrow \{0,1\}$ defined by $S_0, S_1 \subset \{1, \ldots, n\}$ such that $L(\boldsymbol{x}) = (\bigvee_{i \in S_0} x_i) \vee (\bigvee_{i \in S_1} (x_i \oplus 1))$.
- Parity Leakage Class: This leakage class contains all leakage functions $L : \{0,1\}^n \rightarrow \{0,1\}$ defined by $S \subset \{1, \ldots, n\}$ such that $L(\boldsymbol{x}) = \bigoplus_{i \in S} x_i$.

We say $\mathcal{L}$ is the t-leakage class of $\mathcal{L}'$ (denoted by $(\mathcal{L}')^{\otimes t}$) if $\mathcal{L}$ contains all leakage functions L such that there exists $L'_1, \ldots, L'_t \in \mathcal{L}'$ with the same input length as L and $L(\boldsymbol{x}) = (L'_1(\boldsymbol{x}), \ldots, L'_t(\boldsymbol{x}))$. Thus, the above three leakage classes can be naturally extended to their t-leakage versions: t-probing leakage class, t-D1 leakage class, and t-parity leakage class.

In the following, we use (t, ϵ)-D1 tolerance to denote leakage tolerance against t-D1 leakage with error ϵ. Similarly, we use (t, ϵ)-parity tolerance to denote leakage tolerance against t-parity leakage with error ϵ. Since there are known results [1,24] that can achieve leakage tolerance against t-probing leakage without error, we simply write t-probing tolerance for probing leakage.

4   Sketch of Depth-1 $\mathcal{AC}0$ Leakage Tolerance

In this section, we give a sketch of our construction for leakage tolerant circuits against depth-1 $\mathcal{AC}0$ leakage (D1 leakage for short). We follow the overview in Sect. 2.3 and show that the ISW construction [24] for linear functions achieves D1 tolerance. Then D1-tolerant circuits for general functions can be easily obtained following the compiler in Sect. 2.3. We give the formal description in the full version of this paper.

Recall that in Sect. 2.3, we show that the ISW construction for linear functions achieve 1-D1 tolerance. The high-level idea is to separate the wires in the computation phase to $\kappa+1$ disjoint sets $\mathcal{I}_0, \ldots, \mathcal{I}_\kappa$ such that if we arbitrarily pick a variable $w_j \in \mathcal{I}_j$ for all $j \in \{0, \ldots, \kappa\}$, then any κ variables in $\{w_j \in \mathcal{I}_j\}_{j=0}^{\kappa}$ are uniformly random. Based on this fact, if the leakage query touches wires in all $\kappa+1$ sets, then the output is 1 with overwhelming probability. Otherwise, say $\mathcal{I}_{j^*}$ is not touched. Then every wire in C except those in $\mathcal{I}_{j^*}$ only depends on a single input or output bit. So the D1-leakage query to the wires in the circuit is also a D1-leakage query to the input and output bits.

When considering t-D1 leakage, we use a $(t\kappa + 1)$-probing tolerant construction. We may similarly separate the wires in the computation phase to $\{\mathcal{I}_j\}_{j=0}^{t\kappa}$. The observation is that for each D1-leakage query, if it touches wires in more than κ sets, then the output of this leakage bit is 1 with overwhelming probability. By a standard hybrid argument, it is sufficient to only focus on leakage queries that touch at most κ sets. Then at most $t\kappa$ sets are touched by all D1-leakage queries, and there is one set, say $\mathcal{I}_{j^*}$, which is not touched by and D1-leakage query. Since every wire in C except those in $\mathcal{I}_{j^*}$ only depends on a single input or output bit, the t D1-leakage queries to the wires in the circuit become t D1-leakage queries to the input and output bits.

Supporting General Linear Secret Sharings. We note that our construction for general functions can be modified slightly to support any linear secret sharing scheme that is $t\kappa$-wise independent. On one hand, it is known from [7] that a $t\kappa$-wise independent secret sharing scheme is t-D1-resilient. On the other hand, reconstructing secrets and computing a fresh random secret sharing can be done by linear circuits for a linear secret sharing scheme. Note that for a general linear secret sharing scheme, the multiplication of two secret sharings can still be done by multiplying every two shares, one from each secret sharing. Reconstructing the secrets of the multiplication result can be done by a linear circuit.

When using (packed) Shamir sharings, the multiplication of two secret sharings can be done by multiplying two vector of shares coordinate-by-coordinate, which reduces the overhead from $O(k^2)$ to $O(k)$, where k is the number of shares. What's more, the packed Shamir secret sharing scheme allows to multiply a vector of $O(k)$ secrets in parallel. Thus, our construction with packed Shamir secret sharing scheme allows efficient evaluation of SIMD circuits that compute $O(k)$ copies of the same sub-circuits. In [12], a general boolean circuit C with size s and depth h can be transformed to a SIMD circuit with size $\tilde{O}(s + kh + k^2)$, where the $\tilde{O}$ notation omits logarithmic factors. Since the ISW construction for linear circuits blows up the circuit size by $O(t\kappa)$, we have the following corollary.

Corollary 2. *Let κ denote the security parameter. For all positive integer t and for all $f : \{0,1\}^n \to \{0,1\}^m$ that admits a circuit of size s and depth h, there exists a $(t, t(s+1)2^{-\kappa})$-D1-tolerant implementation with size $\tilde{O}(t\kappa s + t^2\kappa^2 h + t^3\kappa^3)$.*

5   Parity Leakage Tolerance

5.1   Parity-to-Probing Implies Parity Tolerance

In this subsection, we focus on the first step discussed in Sect. 2.4. We first define the notions of trivial parity tolerance and parity-to-probing circuits. Then we give a general transformation from parity-to-probing circuits to parity-tolerant circuits.

In the full version of this paper, we review the construction in [21] and show that their construction is a parity-to-probing circuit against 1 parity query. We also give an example showing that in general 1-parity tolerance does not imply 2-parity tolerance in the full version of this paper.

Definition 3 (Trivial Parity Tolerance). *We say a randomized circuit C is trivially parity-tolerant if every wire of C can be expressed as a linear combination of its inputs and outputs. We say a function $f : \{0,1\}^{n_i} \to \{0,1\}^{n_o}$ is trivially parity-tolerant if it admits a trivially parity-tolerant implementation.*

Definition 4 (Parity-to-Probing Circuits). *For a (possibly randomized) circuit $\tilde{C} : \{0,1\}^{n_i} \to \{0,1\}^{n_o}$, a parity-to-probing circuit implementation of $\tilde{C}$ is a tuple (I, C, O) with the same syntax as leakage-resilient circuits defined in Definition 1 such that*

- *Correctness: For all input $x \in \{0,1\}^{n_i}$, the following distributions are identically distributed:*
$$\tilde{C}(x) \equiv O(C(I(x))).$$
- *Trivial Parity Tolerance: The input encoder I and the output decoder O are trivially parity-tolerant.*
- *Parity-to-Probing Security: There exists a simulator $\mathtt{Sim} = (\mathtt{Sim}_1, \mathtt{Sim}_2)$ with the following syntax:*
  - *$\mathtt{Sim}_1$ takes as input t sets $W_1, \ldots, W_t$ of wires in C and outputs a state $\mathtt{st}$ as well as a set V of at most k wires in $\tilde{C}$,*
  - *$\mathtt{Sim}_2$ takes as input a state $\mathtt{st}$ and the wire values in V and outputs t bits $(b_1, \ldots, b_t)$,*

  such that for all input $x \in \{0,1\}^{n_i}$ and for all sets $W_1, \ldots, W_t$ of wires in C, the following two distributions are statistically close with error ϵ:

$$(\mathtt{parity}(W_1), \ldots, \mathtt{parity}(W_t), O(C(I(x))))$$
$$\approx_\epsilon (\mathtt{Sim}_2(\mathtt{st}, \mathsf{val}(V)), \tilde{C}(x)) : (\mathtt{st}, V) \leftarrow \mathtt{Sim}_1(W_1, \ldots, W_t).$$

Here $\mathsf{val}(V)$ denotes the values of the wires of $\tilde{C}$ in V.

As we mentioned in Sect. 2.4, without requiring I, O to be trivially parity-tolerant, the notion of parity-to-probing circuits is strictly weaker than parity-resilient circuits as the latter requires to hide all the wires of the input circuit $\tilde{C}$. On the other hand, a parity-resilient circuit usually requires more complicated input encoder and output decoder. In fact, we have the following claim stating that any encoding scheme $(\mathsf{Enc}, \mathsf{Dec})$ cannot be both trivially parity-tolerant and parity-resilient. To be more concrete, for a randomized function $\mathsf{Enc} : \{0, 1\} \to \{0, 1\}^n$,

- We say Enc is an encoding function if $\{\mathsf{Enc}(0; r)\}_r$ and $\{\mathsf{Enc}(1; r)\}_r$ have disjoint support sets.
- We say Enc is ϵ-parity-resilient if for all subset W of the output of Enc, $\mathsf{parity}(W(\mathsf{Enc}(0)))$ and $\mathsf{parity}(W(\mathsf{Enc}(1)))$ are statistically close with distance ϵ.

Let $\mathsf{Enc} : \{0, 1\} \to \{0, 1\}^n$ be an encoding function. If Enc admits a trivially parity-tolerant implementation C, then Enc is not ϵ-parity-resilient, where $\epsilon = \frac{1}{4|C|}$.

We refer the readers to the full version of this paper for the proof of Claim 5.1.

Theorem 3. *Let t, k be integers. Assume that*

- *For all function f, there is a k-probing-tolerant implementation of f;*
- *For all circuit $\tilde{C}$, there is a (t, k, ϵ)-parity-to-probing circuit implementation of $\tilde{C}$.*

Then for all function $f : \{0, 1\}^{n_i} \to \{0, 1\}^{n_o}$, there is a (t, ϵ)-parity-tolerant implementation of f.

Proof. Let $f : \{0, 1\}^{n_i} \to \{0, 1\}^{n_o}$ be the input function. Let $n = \max\{n_i, n_o\}$. Our construction works for all encoding scheme $(\mathsf{Enc}, \mathsf{Dec})$ with the following properties:

- $\mathsf{Enc} : \{0, 1\}^n \to \{0, 1\}^{\hat{n}}$ is a randomized function such that (1) Enc outputs its random tape, (2) each output bit is a linear combination of its input and random tape, and (3) when the random tape of Enc are sampled uniformly, any k bits of the output of Enc are independent and uniformly distributed.
- $\mathsf{Dec} : \{0, 1\}^{\hat{n}} \to \{0, 1\}^n$ is a deterministic function such that (1) for all $x \in \{0, 1\}^n$, $\Pr[\mathsf{Dec}(\mathsf{Enc}(x)) = x] = 1$, where the probability is over the randomness of Enc, and (2) each output bit of Dec is a linear combination of its input.

A direct instantiation of $(\mathsf{Enc}, \mathsf{Dec})$ is that

- $\mathsf{Enc} : \{0, 1\}^n \to \{0, 1\}^{(k+1)n}$ computes a random additive secret sharing with $k + 1$ shares for each input bit.
- $\mathsf{Dec} : \{0, 1\}^{(k+1)n} \to \{0, 1\}^n$ parses the input as n additive secret sharings, each with $k + 1$ shares, and computes each output bit by the parity of the $k + 1$ shares.

Parity-Tolerant Circuit for f

1. Encoding the Input: The circuit $C^\star$ samples random bits r for Enc, pads the input x to be $x\|0 \in \{0,1\}^n$, and computes $\hat{x} := \text{Enc}(x\|0; r)$ by only using XOR gates.
2. Computing Encoded Output from Encoded Input:
   (a) Let ℓ be the number of random bits used in Enc. Let $f' : \{0,1\}^{\hat{n}} \times \{0,1\}^{\ell} \to \{0,1\}^{\hat{n}}$ be the function defined by

   $$f'(\hat{x}, r') \quad : \quad x\|* \leftarrow \text{Dec}(\hat{x}), \text{ where } x \in \{0,1\}^{n_i}$$
   $$y \leftarrow f(x)$$
   $$\hat{y} \leftarrow \text{Enc}(y\|0; r'), \text{ where } y\|0 \in \{0,1\}^n.$$

   (b) Let $\tilde{C}$ be a k-probing-tolerant implementation of f'. Note that $\tilde{C}$ is a randomized circuit. Let (I, C, O) be a (t, k, ϵ)-parity-to-probing circuit implementation of $\tilde{C}$.
   (c) The circuit $C^\star$ samples random bits r' and computes $\hat{y} = O(C(I(\hat{x}, r')))$.
3. Decoding the Output: The circuit $C^\star$ computes $\text{Dec}(\hat{y})$ and outputs the first n_o bits.

Fig. 2. Construction of Parity-Tolerant Circuits from Parity-to-Probing Circuits

We describe the parity-tolerant circuit for f (Fig. 2).

Lemma 1. *The circuit $C^\star$ constructed in Fig. 2 is a (t, ϵ)-parity-tolerant implementation of f.*

We refer the readers to the full version of this paper for the proof of Lemma 1.

5.2 Feasibility of Parity-Tolerant Circuits

According to Theorem 3, to obtain a (t, ϵ)-parity-tolerant circuit, it is sufficient to construct a (t, k, ϵ)-parity-to-probing circuit defined in Definition 4.

Our starting point is the construction in [21]. Let $\tilde{C}$ be a circuit that only consists of NAND gates. Recall that the idea is to encode each wire value in $\tilde{C}$ by a small-bias encoding scheme. In the following, we will focus on the $1/2$-bias encoding scheme in Fig. 1. Suppose

- $w = (w_1, \ldots, w_{|\tilde{C}|})$ are the wire values in $\tilde{C}$.
- $u, v \in \{0,1\}^{|\tilde{C}|}$ are two vectors of random bits.

Then, the compiler in [21] takes $\tilde{C}$ as input and outputs $(\hat{I}, \hat{C}, \hat{O})$ where the wire values in $\hat{C}$ are

$$(u_1, v_1, u_1 \cdot v_1 \oplus w_1), \ldots, (u_{|\tilde{C}|}, v_{|\tilde{C}|}, u_{|\tilde{C}|} \cdot v_{|\tilde{C}|} \oplus w_{|\tilde{C}|}),$$

or equivalently, $(\boldsymbol{u}, \boldsymbol{v}, \boldsymbol{u} * \boldsymbol{v} \oplus \boldsymbol{w})$.

We observe that $(\hat{I}, \hat{C}, \hat{O})$ is already a (t, k, ϵ)-parity-to-probing circuit assuming NAND gadget for some proper k and ϵ. The intuition is as follows.

Intuitions. First, for each subset W of wires in $\hat{C}$, there is a *deterministic* set $\mathcal{V}(W)$ of wires in $\tilde{C}$ of size at most k' such that $\mathtt{parity}(W)$ can be simulated with statistical error $2^{-k'-1}$ if we learn $\mathsf{val}(\mathcal{V}(W))$. More concretely, for a set W of wires in $\hat{C}$, we may define a set $\mathcal{V}(W)$ of wires in $\tilde{C}$ as follows:

- If W touches more than k' different encodings, then we set $\mathcal{V}(W) = \emptyset$.
- Otherwise, we set $\mathcal{V}(W) = \{w_i \mid \text{some bit of } \mathtt{Enc}(w_i) = (u_i, v_i, u_i \cdot v_i \oplus w_i) \text{ is in } W\}$.

Then, if $|\mathcal{V}(W)| \neq \emptyset$, $\mathtt{parity}(W)$ can be perfectly simulated if we learn $\mathsf{val}(\mathcal{V}(W))$. If $|\mathcal{V}(W)| = \emptyset$, then either W is an empty set, indicating that $\mathtt{parity}(W) = 0$, or W touches more than k' different encodings, indicating that $\mathtt{parity}(W)$ is statistically close to a uniform bit with error $2^{-k'-1}$ (See more details in the full version of this paper). In any case, $\mathtt{parity}(W)$ can be simulated with statistical error $2^{-k'-1}$ when learning wire values in $\mathcal{V}(W)$.

Now, for two sets W and W', we define $W \oplus W' = (W \cup W') \backslash (W \cap W')$. Then we have $\mathtt{parity}(W) \oplus \mathtt{parity}(W') = \mathtt{parity}(W \oplus W')$. Now for t subsets $W_1, \ldots, W_t$, we want to simulate the joint distribution of $\mathtt{parity}(W_1), \ldots, \mathtt{parity}(W_t)$. Let $V = \cup_{S \subset \{1, \ldots, t\}} (\mathcal{V}(\oplus_{i \in S} W_i))$. Then if we learn all wire values in V, we can simulate $\mathtt{parity}(\oplus_{i \in S} W_i)$ with statistical error $2^{-k'-1}$ for all subset $S \subset \{1, \ldots, t\}$. By the XOR lemma (See more details in the full version of this paper), we can simulate the joint distribution of $\mathtt{parity}(W_1), \ldots, \mathtt{parity}(W_t)$ with statistical error $2^{t/2-k'-1}$ from the wire values in V.

Regarding the size of V, we note that $\mathcal{V}(\cdot)$ satisfies that for all subsets W, W', if $\mathcal{V}(W), \mathcal{V}(W')$ are not the empty set, then $\mathcal{V}(W \oplus W') \subset \mathcal{V}(W) \cup \mathcal{V}(W')$. Indeed,

- If $\mathcal{V}(W \oplus W') = \emptyset$, then $\mathcal{V}(W \oplus W') \subset \mathcal{V}(W) \cup \mathcal{V}(W')$.
- If $\mathcal{V}(W \oplus W') \neq \emptyset$, then for all $w_i \in \mathcal{V}(W \oplus W')$, some bit of $\mathtt{Enc}(w_i)$ is in $W \oplus W'$. This implies that at least one of W and W' contains some bit of $\mathtt{Enc}(w_i)$, indicating that $w_i \in \mathcal{V}(W) \cup \mathcal{V}(W')$. Thus, $\mathcal{V}(W \oplus W') \subset \mathcal{V}(W) \cup \mathcal{V}(W')$.

With this property, we can prove that $|V| \leq t \cdot k'$. Thus $(\hat{I}, \hat{C}, \hat{O})$ is a $(t, t \cdot k', 2^{t/2-k'-1})$-parity-to-probing circuit.

Realizing NAND Gadgets. Thus, to obtain a (t, k, ϵ)-parity-to-probing circuit compiler in the plain model, our goal is to remove the NAND gadget in the construction in [21].

We summarize our construction for NAND in Fig. 3 and refer the readers to Sect. 2.4 for intuitions about our construction.

Our Construction. We summarize our construction in Fig. 4.

Circuit for NAND

– Input: $(u_1, v_1, z_1), (u_2, v_2, z_2), u_0, v_0$
– Auxiliary Input: $(u'_1, v'_1), (u'_2, v'_2), \rho_1, \rho_2, \rho_3$
– Output: $z_0 := u_0 \cdot v_0 \oplus (z_1 \oplus u_1 \cdot v_1) \cdot (z_2 \oplus u_2 \cdot v_2) \oplus 1$.

1. Refresh Input Encoding: The goal of the first step is to compute

$$z'_1 = u'_1 \cdot v'_1 \oplus (z_1 \oplus u_1 \cdot v_1), \quad z'_2 = u'_2 \cdot v'_2 \oplus (z_2 \oplus u_2 \cdot v_2).$$

The circuit is constructed as follows.
   (a) For all $\boldsymbol{a} \in \{0,1\}^2$, the circuit computes $\alpha_{1,\boldsymbol{a}} := u'_1 \cdot a_1 \oplus (z_1 \oplus u_1 \cdot a_2) \oplus \rho_1$
   and $\alpha_{2,\boldsymbol{a}} := u'_2 \cdot a_1 \oplus (z_2 \oplus u_2 \cdot a_2) \oplus \rho_2$.
   (b) For all $\boldsymbol{a} \in \{0,1\}^2$, the circuit computes $\beta_{1,\boldsymbol{a}} := (v'_1 \oplus a_1 \oplus 1) \cdot (v_1 \oplus a_2 \oplus 1)$
   and $\beta_{2,\boldsymbol{a}} := (v'_2 \oplus a_1 \oplus 1) \cdot (v_2 \oplus a_2 \oplus 1)$.
   (c) For all $\boldsymbol{a} \in \{0,1\}^2$, the circuit computes $\gamma_{1,\boldsymbol{a}} := \alpha_{1,\boldsymbol{a}} \cdot \beta_{1,\boldsymbol{a}}$ and $\gamma_{2,\boldsymbol{a}} :=$
   $\alpha_{2,\boldsymbol{a}} \cdot \beta_{2,\boldsymbol{a}}$.
   (d) The circuit computes

$$z'_1 = \left(\oplus_{\boldsymbol{a} \in \{0,1\}^2} \gamma_{1,\boldsymbol{a}}\right) \oplus \rho_1, \quad z'_2 = \left(\oplus_{\boldsymbol{a} \in \{0,1\}^2} \gamma_{2,\boldsymbol{a}}\right) \oplus \rho_2.$$

2. Computing NAND on Refreshed Input Encodings: The goal of the second step is to compute z_0 from $(u'_1, v'_1, z'_1), (u'_2, v'_2, z'_2), u_0, v_0$:

$$z_0 = u_0 \cdot v_0 \oplus (z'_1 \oplus u'_1 \cdot v'_1) \cdot (z'_2 \oplus u'_2 \cdot v'_2) \oplus 1.$$

The circuit is constructed as follows.
   (a) The circuit computes $z'_1 \cdot z'_2, z'_1 \cdot u'_2, u'_1 \cdot z'_2, u'_1 \cdot u'_2$.
   (b) For all $\boldsymbol{a} \in \{0,1\}^3$, the circuit computes

$$\alpha_{3,\boldsymbol{a}} := u_0 \cdot a_0 \oplus (z'_1 \oplus u'_1 \cdot a_1) \cdot (z'_2 \oplus u'_2 \cdot a_2) \oplus 1 \oplus \rho_3$$
$$= u_0 \cdot a_0 \oplus (z'_1 \cdot z'_2) \oplus a_2 \cdot (z'_1 \cdot u'_2) \oplus a_1 \cdot (u'_1 \cdot z'_2)$$
$$\oplus a_1 a_2 \cdot (u'_1 \cdot u'_2) \oplus 1 \oplus \rho_3.$$

   by a proper linear combination of $u_0, z'_1 \cdot z'_2, z'_1 \cdot u'_2, u'_1 \cdot z'_2, u'_1 \cdot u'_2, \rho_3$.
   (c) For all $\boldsymbol{a} \in \{0,1\}^3$, the circuit computes $\beta_{3,\boldsymbol{a}} := (v_0 \oplus a_0 \oplus 1) \cdot (v'_1 \oplus a_1 \oplus 1) \cdot (v'_2 \oplus a_2 \oplus 1)$.
   (d) For all $\boldsymbol{a} \in \{0,1\}^3$, the circuit computes $\gamma_{3,\boldsymbol{a}} := \alpha_{3,\boldsymbol{a}} \cdot \beta_{3,\boldsymbol{a}}$.
   (e) The circuit computes

$$z_0 = \left(\oplus_{\boldsymbol{a} \in \{0,1\}^3} \gamma_{3,\boldsymbol{a}}\right) \oplus \rho_3.$$

Fig. 3. Circuit Implementation of NAND Gadget

(t, k, ϵ)-Parity-to-Probing Circuit (I, C, O)

- Input: A randomized circuit $\tilde{C}$ with input size $\{0,1\}^{n_i}$ and output size $\{0,1\}^{n_o}$
- Output: A tuple (I, C, O)

Input Encoder I: For input $\boldsymbol{x} \in \{0,1\}^{n_i}$, $I(\boldsymbol{x}) = \{(u_i, v_i, u_i \cdot v_i \oplus x_i)\}_{i=1}^{n_i}$, where u_i, v_i are random bits for all $i \in \{1, \ldots, n_i\}$.

Circuit C:

1. Suppose the wires in $\tilde{C}$ are denoted by $w_1, \ldots, w_{|\tilde{C}|}$. For simplicity, assume that the first n_i wires are the input wires, and the last n_o wires are the output wires. The circuit C takes $I(\boldsymbol{x})$ as input and samples the following random bits:
   - $\boldsymbol{u}, \boldsymbol{u}^{(1)}, \boldsymbol{u}^{(2)} \in \{0,1\}^{|\tilde{C}|}$ where the first n_i bits of $\boldsymbol{u}$ are set to be the same as those in $I(\boldsymbol{x})$.
   - $\boldsymbol{v}, \boldsymbol{v}^{(1)}, \boldsymbol{v}^{(2)} \in \{0,1\}^{|\tilde{C}|}$ where the first n_i bits of $\boldsymbol{v}$ are set to be the same as those in $I(\boldsymbol{x})$.
   - $\boldsymbol{\rho}, \boldsymbol{\rho}^{(1)}, \boldsymbol{\rho}^{(2)} \in \{0,1\}^{|\tilde{C}|}$.
2. For each random wire w_i in $\tilde{C}$, the circuit C samples a random bit as z_i and sets the encoding of w_i as (u_i, v_i, z_i).
3. We label the NAND gates in $\tilde{C}$ by the indices of their output wires. I.e., the output of the ℓ-th NAND gate is the ℓ-th wire w_ℓ. Let $\pi_1(\cdot)$ be the function that maps ℓ to the index of the first input of the ℓ-th NAND gate, and $\pi_2(\cdot)$ be the function that maps ℓ to the index of the second input of the ℓ-th NAND gate. Then the ℓ-th NAND gate takes as input $w_{\pi_1(\ell)}, w_{\pi_2(\ell)}$ and outputs $w_\ell = w_{\pi_1(\ell)}$ NAND $w_{\pi_2(\ell)}$.
4. For each NAND gate in $\tilde{C}$, suppose this is the ℓ-th NAND gate and the input encodings are $(u_{\pi_1(\ell)}, v_{\pi_1(\ell)}, z_{\pi_1(\ell)})$ and $(u_{\pi_2(\ell)}, v_{\pi_2(\ell)}, z_{\pi_2(\ell)})$. The circuit C computes the subcircuit for the NAND gadget described in Figure 3 with
   - Input: $(u_{\pi_1(\ell)}, v_{\pi_1(\ell)}, z_{\pi_1(\ell)}), (u_{\pi_2(\ell)}, v_{\pi_2(\ell)}, z_{\pi_2(\ell)}), u_\ell, v_\ell$
   - Auxiliary Input: $(u_\ell^{(1)}, v_\ell^{(1)}), (u_\ell^{(2)}, v_\ell^{(2)}), \rho_\ell^{(1)}, \rho_\ell^{(2)}, \rho_\ell$
   We set z_ℓ to be the output of the subcircuit.
5. The output of C is $\{(u_i, v_i, z_i)\}_{i=|\tilde{C}|-n_o+1}^{|\tilde{C}|}$

Output Decoder O: O takes the output of C, denoted by $\{(u_i, v_i, z_i)\}_{i=|\tilde{C}|-n_o+1}^{|\tilde{C}|}$, as input, and outputs $\boldsymbol{y} = (u_{|\tilde{C}|-n_o+1} \cdot v_{|\tilde{C}|-n_o+1} \oplus z_{|\tilde{C}|-n_o+1}, \ldots, u_{|\tilde{C}|} \cdot v_{|\tilde{C}|} \oplus z_{|\tilde{C}|})$.

Fig. 4. (t, k, ϵ)-Parity-to-Probing Circuit

Theorem 4. *For all circuit $\tilde{C}$, the construction in Fig. 4 is a (t, k, ϵ)-parity-to-probing circuit, where*

$$\epsilon = 2^{\frac{t}{2}+1} \cdot \left(\frac{7}{8}\right)^{\frac{k}{2t}}.$$

We prove Theorem 4 in the full version of this paper.

Towards t-Parity-Tolerant Circuits. By Theorem 3 and Theorem 4, we have the following corollary.

Corollary 3. *There exists a polynomial-time circuit compiler that takes as input $(C_f, 1^t, 1^\kappa)$, where C_f is a circuit of size s that computes f, and outputs a $(t, 2^{-\kappa})$-parity-tolerant implementation of f with circuit size $poly(t, \kappa, s)$.*

Acknowledgements. Y. Ishai was supported by ERC grant NTSC (742754), BSF grant 2022370, ISF grant 2774/20, and ISF-NSFC grant 3127/23. Y. Song was supported in part by the National Basic Research Program of China Grant 2011CBA00300, 2011CBA00301, the National Natural Science Foundation of China Grant 61033001, 61361136003.

References

1. Ananth, P., Ishai, Y., Sahai, A.: Private circuits: a modular approach. In: Shacham, H., Boldyreva, A. (eds.) CRYPTO 2018, Part III. LNCS, vol. 10993, pp. 427–455. Springer, Cham (2018). https://doi.org/10.1007/978-3-319-96878-0_15

2. Barthe, G., et al.: Strong non-interference and type-directed higher-order masking. In: Weippl, E.R., Katzenbeisser, S., Kruegel, C., Myers, A.C., Halevi, S. (eds.) Proceedings of the 2016 ACM SIGSAC Conference on Computer and Communications Security, Vienna, Austria, October 24–28, 2016, pp. 116–129. ACM (2016)

3. Belaïd, S., Cassiers, G., Rivain, M., Taleb, A.R.: Unifying freedom and separation for tight probing-secure composition. In: Handschuh, H., Lysyanskaya, A. (eds.) CRYPTO 2023. LNCS, pp. 440–472. Springer, Cham (2023). https://doi.org/10.1007/978-3-031-38548-3_15

4. Belaïd, S., Goudarzi, D., Rivain, M.: Tight private circuits: achieving probing security with the least refreshing. In: Peyrin, T., Galbraith, S. (eds.) ASIACRYPT 2018. LNCS, vol. 11273, pp. 343–372. Springer, Cham (2018). https://doi.org/10.1007/978-3-030-03329-3_12

5. Bogdanov, A., Dinesh, K., Filmus, Y., Ishai, Y., Kaplan, A., Srinivasan, A.: Bounded indistinguishability for simple sources. In: Braverman, M. (ed.) 13th Innovations in Theoretical Computer Science Conference, ITCS 2022, LIPIcs, January 31 - February 3, 2022, Berkeley, CA, USA, vol. 215, pp. 26:1–26:18. Schloss Dagstuhl - Leibniz-Zentrum für Informatik (2022)

6. Bogdanov, A., Ishai, Y., Srinivasan, A.: Unconditionally secure computation against low-complexity leakage. J. Cryptol. **34**(4), 38 (2021)

7. Braverman, M.: Poly-logarithmic independence fools bounded-depth Boolean circuits. Commun. ACM **54**(4), 108–115 (2011)

8. Cassiers, G., Grégoire, B., Levi, I., Standaert, F.-X.: Hardware private circuits: from trivial composition to full verification. IEEE Trans. Comput. **70**(10), 1677–1690 (2021)

9. Coron, J.-S., Greuet, A., Prouff, E., Zeitoun, R.: Faster evaluation of SBoxes via common shares. In: Gierlichs, B., Poschmann, A.Y. (eds.) CHES 2016. LNCS, vol. 9813, pp. 498–514. Springer, Heidelberg (2016). https://doi.org/10.1007/978-3-662-53140-2_24

10. Coron, J.-S., Prouff, E., Rivain, M., Roche, T.: Higher-order side channel security and mask refreshing. In: Moriai, S. (ed.) FSE 2013. LNCS, vol. 8424, pp. 410–424. Springer, Heidelberg (2014). https://doi.org/10.1007/978-3-662-43933-3_21
11. Dachman-Soled, D., Liu, F.-H., Zhou, H.-S.: Leakage-Resilient Circuits Revisited – Optimal Number of Computing Components Without Leak-Free Hardware. In: Oswald, E., Fischlin, M. (eds.) EUROCRYPT 2015, Part II. LNCS, vol. 9057, pp. 131–158. Springer, Heidelberg (2015). https://doi.org/10.1007/978-3-662-46803-6_5
12. Damgård, I., Ishai, Y., Krøigaard, M.: Perfectly secure multiparty computation and the computational overhead of cryptography. In: Gilbert, H. (ed.) EUROCRYPT 2010. LNCS, vol. 6110, pp. 445–465. Springer, Heidelberg (2010). https://doi.org/10.1007/978-3-642-13190-5_23
13. Duc, A., Dziembowski, S., Faust, S.: Unifying leakage models: from probing attacks to noisy leakage. J. Cryptol. 32(1), 151–177 (2019)
14. Dziembowski, S., Faust, S.: Leakage-resilient circuits without computational assumptions. In: Cramer, R. (ed.) TCC 2012. LNCS, vol. 7194, pp. 230–247. Springer, Heidelberg (2012). https://doi.org/10.1007/978-3-642-28914-9_13
15. Dziembowski, S., Pietrzak, K.: Leakage-resilient cryptography. In: 49th Annual IEEE Symposium on Foundations of Computer Science, FOCS 2008, October 25-28, 2008, Philadelphia, PA, USA, pp. 293–302. IEEE Computer Society (2008)
16. Faust, S., Rabin, T., Reyzin, L., Tromer, E., Vaikuntanathan, V.: Protecting circuits from computationally bounded and noisy leakage. SIAM J. Comput. 43(5), 1564–1614 (2014)
17. Feige, U., Lapidot, D., Shamir, A.: Multiple noninteractive zero knowledge proofs under general assumptions. SIAM J. Comput. 29(1), 1–28 (1999)
18. Genkin, D., Ishai, Y., Weiss, M.: How to construct a leakage-resilient (stateless) trusted party. In: Kalai, Y., Reyzin, L. (eds.) TCC 2017. LNCS, vol. 10678, pp. 209–244. Springer, Cham (2017). https://doi.org/10.1007/978-3-319-70503-3_7
19. Goldwasser, S., Rothblum, G.N.: How to compute in the presence of leakage. SIAM J. Comput. 44(5), 1480–1549 (2015)
20. Goudarzi, D., Prest, T., Rivain, M., Vergnaud, D.: Probing security through input-output separation and revisited quasilinear masking. IACR Trans. Cryptogr. Hardw. Embed. Syst. 2021(3), 599–640 (2021)
21. Goyal, V., Ishai, Y., Maji, H.K., Sahai, A., Sherstov, A.A.: Bounded-communication leakage resilience via parity-resilient circuits. In: 2016 IEEE 57th Annual Symposium on Foundations of Computer Science (FOCS), pp. 1–10 (2016)
22. Goyal, V., Ishai, Y., Song, Y.: Private circuits with quasilinear randomness. In: Dunkelman, O., Dziembowski, S. (eds.) EUROCRYPT 2022. LNCS, vol. 13277, pp. 192–221. Springer, Cham (2022). https://doi.org/10.1007/978-3-031-07082-2_8
23. Ishai, Y., et al.: Robust pseudorandom generators. In: Fomin, F.V., Freivalds, R., Kwiatkowska, M., Peleg, D. (eds.) ICALP 2013. LNCS, vol. 7965, pp. 576–588. Springer, Heidelberg (2013). https://doi.org/10.1007/978-3-642-39206-1_49
24. Ishai, Y., Sahai, A., Wagner, D.: Private circuits: securing hardware against probing attacks. In: Boneh, D. (ed.) CRYPTO 2003. LNCS, vol. 2729, pp. 463–481. Springer, Heidelberg (2003). https://doi.org/10.1007/978-3-540-45146-4_27
25. Micali, S., Reyzin, L.: Physically observable cryptography. In: Naor, M. (ed.) TCC 2004. LNCS, vol. 2951, pp. 278–296. Springer, Heidelberg (2004). https://doi.org/10.1007/978-3-540-24638-1_16
26. Miles, E., Viola, E.: Shielding circuits with groups. In: Boneh, D., Roughgarden, T., Feigenbaum, J. (eds.) Symposium on Theory of Computing Conference, STOC'13, Palo Alto, CA, USA, June 1–4, 2013, pp. 251–260. ACM (2013)

27. Naor, J., Naor, M.: Small-bias probability spaces: efficient constructions and applications. In: Proceedings of the Twenty-Second Annual ACM Symposium on Theory of Computing, STOC 1990, page 213–223, New York, NY, USA, 1990. Association for Computing Machinery (1990)

28. Prouff, E., Rivain, M.: Masking against side-channel attacks: a formal security proof. In: Johansson, T., Nguyen, P.Q. (eds.) EUROCRYPT 2013. LNCS, vol. 7881, pp. 142–159. Springer, Heidelberg (2013). https://doi.org/10.1007/978-3-642-38348-9_9

29. Rivain, M., Prouff, E.: Provably secure higher-order masking of AES. In: Mangard, S., Standaert, F.-X. (eds.) CHES 2010. LNCS, vol. 6225, pp. 413–427. Springer, Heidelberg (2010). https://doi.org/10.1007/978-3-642-15031-9_28

30. Rothblum, G.N.: How to compute under $\mathcal{AC}^0$ leakage without secure hardware. In: Safavi-Naini, R., Canetti, R. (eds.) CRYPTO 2012. LNCS, vol. 7417, pp. 552–569. Springer, Heidelberg (2012). https://doi.org/10.1007/978-3-642-32009-5_32

Pseudorandom Isometries

Prabhanjan Ananth[(✉)], Aditya Gulati, Fatih Kaleoglu, and Yao-Ting Lin

UCSB, Santa Barbara, USA
prabhanjan@cs.ucsb.edu, {adityagulati,kaleoglu,yao-ting_lin}@ucsb.edu

Abstract. We introduce a new notion called $\mathcal{Q}$-secure pseudorandom isometries (PRI). A pseudorandom isometry is an efficient quantum circuit that maps an n-qubit state to an $(n+m)$-qubit state in an isometric manner. In terms of security, we require that the output of a q-fold PRI on ρ, for $\rho \in \mathcal{Q}$, for any polynomial q, should be computationally indistinguishable from the output of a q-fold Haar isometry on ρ.

By fine-tuning $\mathcal{Q}$, we recover many existing notions of pseudorandomness. We present a construction of PRIs and assuming post-quantum one-way functions, we prove the security of $\mathcal{Q}$-secure pseudorandom isometries (PRI) for different interesting settings of $\mathcal{Q}$.

We also demonstrate many cryptographic applications of PRIs, including, length extension theorems for quantum pseudorandomness notions, message authentication schemes for quantum states, multi-copy secure public and private encryption schemes, and succinct quantum commitments.

1 Introduction

Pseudorandomness has played an important role in theoretical computer science. In classical cryptography, the notions of pseudorandom generators and functions have been foundational, with applications to traditional and advanced encryption schemes, signatures, secure computation, secret sharing schemes, and proof systems. On the other hand, we have only just begun to scratch the surface of understanding the implications pseudorandomness holds for quantum cryptography, and there is still a vast uncharted territory waiting to be explored.

When defining pseudorandomness in the quantum world, there are two broad directions one can consider.

Quantum States. Firstly, we can study pseudorandomness in the context of quantum states. Ji, Liu, and Song (JLS) [JLS18] proposed the notion of a pseudorandom quantum state generator, which is an efficient quantum circuit that on input a secret key k produces a quantum state (referred to as a pseudorandom quantum state) that is computationally indistinguishable from a Haar state as long as k is picked uniformly at random and moreover, the distinguisher is given many copies of the state. JLS and the followup works by Brakerski and Shmueli [BS19,BS20b] presented constructions of pseudorandom quantum state generators from one-way functions. Ananth, Qian, and Yuen [AQY22] defined the notion of a pseudorandom function-like quantum state generator, which is similar to pseudorandom quantum state generators, except that the same key can be used to

© International Association for Cryptologic Research 2024
M. Joye and G. Leander (Eds.): EUROCRYPT 2024, LNCS 14654, pp. 226–254, 2024.
https://doi.org/10.1007/978-3-031-58737-5_9

generate multiple pseudorandom quantum states. These two notions have many applications, including in quantum gravity theory [BFV20, ABF+23], quantum machine learning [HBC+22], quantum complexity [Kre21], and quantum cryptography [AQY22, MY22]. Other notions of pseudorandomness for quantum states have also been recently explored [ABF+23, ABK+23, GLG+23].

Quantum Operations. Secondly, we can consider pseudorandomness in the context of quantum operations. This direction is relatively less explored. One prominent example, proposed in the same work of [JLS18], is the notion of pseudorandom unitaries, which are efficient quantum circuits such that any efficient distinguisher should not be able to distinguish whether they are given oracle access to a pseudorandom unitary or a Haar unitary. Establishing the feasibility of pseudorandom unitaries could have ramifications for quantum gravity theory (as noted under open problems in [GLG+23]), quantum complexity theory [Kre21], and cryptography [GJMZ23]. Unfortunately, to date, we do not have any provably secure construction of pseudorandom unitaries, although some candidates have been proposed in [JLS18]. A recent independent work by Lu, Qin, Song, Yao, and Zhao [LQS+23] takes an important step towards formulating and investigating the feasibility of pseudorandomness of quantum operations. They define a notion called pseudorandom state scramblers that isometrically maps a quantum state $|\psi\rangle$ into another state $|\psi'\rangle$ such that t copies of $|\psi'\rangle$, where t is a polynomial, is computationally indistinguishable from t copies of a Haar state. They establish its feasibility based on post-quantum one-way functions. In the same work, they also explored cryptographic applications of pseudorandom state scramblers.

Although pseudorandom state scramblers can be instantiated from one-way functions, the definition inherently allows for scrambling only a single state. On the other extreme, pseudorandom unitaries allow for scrambling polynomially many states but unfortunately, establishing their feasibility remains an important open problem. Thus, we pose the following question:

Is there a pseudorandomness notion that can scramble polynomially many states and can be provably instantiated based on well studied cryptographic assumptions?

Our Work in a Nutshell. We address the above question in this work. Our contribution is three-fold:

1. NEW DEFINITIONS: We introduce a new notion called $\mathcal{Q}$-secure pseudorandom isometries that can be leveraged to scramble many quantum states coming from the set $\mathcal{Q}$.
2. CONSTRUCTION: We present a construction of pseudorandom isometries and investigate its security for different settings of $\mathcal{Q}$.
3. APPLICATIONS: Finally, we explore many cryptographic applications of pseudorandom isometries.

1.1 Our Results

Roughly speaking, a pseudorandom isometry is an efficient quantum circuit, denoted by PRI_k, parameterized by a key[1] $k \in \{0,1\}^\lambda$ that takes as input an n-qubit state and outputs an $(n + m)$-qubit state with the guarantee that PRI_k is functionally equivalent to an isometry. In terms of security, we require that any efficient distinguisher should not be able to distinguish whether they are given oracle access to PRI_k or a Haar isometry[2] $\mathcal{I}$. We consider a more fine-grained version of this definition in this work, where we could fine-tune the set of allowable queries.

More precisely, we introduce a concept called $(n, n + m)$-$\mathcal{Q}$-secure- pseu-dorandom isometries (PRIs). Let us first consider a simplified version of this definition. Suppose $n(\lambda), q(\lambda)$ are polynomials and $\mathcal{Q}_{n,q,\lambda}$ is a subset of nq-qubit (mixed) states. Let $\mathcal{Q} = \{\mathcal{Q}_{n,q,\lambda}\}_{\lambda \in \mathbb{N}}$. The definition states that it should be computationally infeasible to distinguish the following two distributions: for any polynomials q,

- $\left(\rho,\ \mathsf{PRI}_k^{\otimes q}(\rho)\right)$,
- $\left(\rho,\ \mathcal{I}^{\otimes q}(\rho)(\mathcal{I}^\dagger)^{\otimes q}\right)$,

where $\rho \in \mathcal{Q}_{n,q,\lambda}$ and $\mathcal{I}$ is a Haar isometry.

Let us consider some examples.

1. If $\mathcal{Q}_{n,q,\lambda} = \{|0^n\rangle^{\otimes q}\}$ then this notion implies a pseudorandom state generator (PRSG) [JLS18].
2. If $\mathcal{Q}_{n,q,\lambda}$ consists of all possible q computational basis states then this notion implies a pseudorandom function-like state generator (PRFSG) [AQY22, AGQY22].
3. If $\mathcal{Q}_{n,q,\lambda}$ consists of q-fold tensor of all possible n-qubit states then this notion implies a pseudorandom state scrambler (PSS) [LQS+23].

We can generalize this definition even further. Specifically, we allow the adversary to hold an auxiliary register that is entangled with the register on which the q-fold isometry (PRI_k or Haar) is applied and we could require the stronger security property that the above indistinguishability should hold even in this setting.

In more detail, ρ is now an $(nq + \ell)$-qubit state and the distinguisher is given either of the following:

- $\left(\rho, \left(I_\ell \otimes \mathsf{PRI}_k^{\otimes q}\right)(\rho)\right)$,
- $\left(\rho, \left(I_\ell \otimes \mathcal{I}_k^{\otimes q}\right)\rho\left(I_\ell \otimes \mathcal{I}_k^{\dagger \otimes q}\right)\right)$

---

[1] We denote λ to be the security parameter.

[2] The Haar distribution of isometries is defined as follows: first, sample a unitary from the Haar measure, and then set the isometry, that on input a quantum state $|\psi\rangle$, first initializes an ancilla register containing zeroes and then applies the Haar unitary on $|\psi\rangle$ and the ancilla register.

where I_ℓ is an ℓ-qubit identity operator. We can correspondingly define $\mathcal{Q}$ to be instead parameterized by n, q, ℓ, λ, and we require $\rho \in \mathcal{Q}_{n,q,\ell,\lambda}$.

The above generalization captures the notion of pseudorandom isometries (discussed in the beginning of Sect. 1.1) against selective queries. Specifically, if PRI_k is a $\mathcal{Q}$-secure pseudorandom isometry (according to the above-generalized definition), where $\mathcal{Q}$ is the set of all possible $nq + \ell$-qubit states then indeed it is infeasible for an efficient distinguisher making selective queries[3] to distinguish whether it has oracle access to PRI_k or a Haar isometry oracle.

Thus, by fine-tuning $\mathcal{Q}$, we recover many notions of pseudorandomness in the context of both quantum states and operations.

Construction. We first study the feasibility of PRIs.

We present a construction of PRIs and investigate its security for different settings of $\mathcal{Q}$. On input an n-qubit state $|\psi\rangle = \sum_{x \in \{0,1\}^n} \alpha_x |x\rangle$, define $\mathsf{PRI}_k |\psi\rangle$ as follows:

$$\mathsf{PRI}_k |\psi\rangle = \frac{1}{\sqrt{2^m}} \sum_{x \in \{0,1\}^n, y \in \{0,1\}^m} \alpha_x \cdot \omega_p^{f_{k_1}(x||y)} |g_{k_2}(x||y)\rangle$$

In the above construction, we parse k as a concatenation of two λ_1-bit strings k_1 and k_2, where $\lambda = 2\lambda_1$. The first key k_1 would serve as a key for a pseudorandom function $f : \{0,1\}^{\lambda_1} \times \{0,1\}^{n+m} \to \mathbb{Z}_p$, where $p \sim 2^{\lambda_1}$ is an integer. The second key k_2 would serve as a key for a pseudorandom permutation $g : \{0,1\}^{\lambda_1} \times \{0,1\}^{n+m} \to \{0,1\}^{n+m}$. Both f and g should satisfy quantum query security. Moreover, both of them can be instantiated from post-quantum one-way functions [Zha12, Zha16]. We require n to be a polynomial in λ, larger than λ, and similarly, we set m to be a polynomial in λ, larger than λ.

The above construction was first studied by [BBSS23, ABF+23], perhaps surprisingly, in completely different contexts. Brakerski, Behera, Sattath, and Shmueli [BBSS23] introduced a new notion of PRSG and PRFSG and instantiated these two notions using the above construction. Aaronson, Bouland, Fefferman, Ghosh, Vazirani, Zhang, and Zhou [ABF+23] introduced the notion of pseudo-entanglement and instantiated this notion using the above construction. An important property of this construction is that it is *invertible*, that is, given the key k, it is efficient to implement Inv_k such that $\mathsf{Inv}_k \mathsf{PRI}_k$ is the identity map.

It is natural to wonder if it is possible to modify the above construction to have binary phase as against p^{th} roots of unity, for a large p. There is some recent evidence to believe since [HBK23] showed that pseudorandom unitaries cannot just have real entries.

---

[3] Roughly speaking, the selective query setting is one where all the queries are made at the same time. In contrast, in the adaptive query setting, each query could depend on the previous queries and answers.

Security. We look at different possible settings of $\mathcal{Q}$ and study their security[4].

I. HAAR STATES. Our main contribution is showing that the output of PRI_k on many copies of many n-qubit Haar states, namely, $(|\psi_1\rangle^{\otimes t}, \ldots, |\psi_s\rangle^{\otimes t})$ with t being a polynomial and $|\psi_1\rangle, \ldots, |\psi_s\rangle$ are Haar states, is computationally indistinguishable from a Haar isometry on $(|\psi_1\rangle^{\otimes t}, \ldots, |\psi_s\rangle^{\otimes t})$. Moreover, the computational indistinguishability should hold even if $(|\psi_1\rangle^{\otimes t}, \ldots, |\psi_s\rangle^{\otimes t})$ is given to the QPT adversary. In other words, PRI_k can be used to map maximally mixed states on smaller dimensional symmetric subspaces onto pseudorandom states on larger dimensional symmetric subspaces. We consider the following setting:

- Let $t(\lambda)$ and $s(\lambda)$ be two polynomials. Let $q = s \cdot t$ and $\ell = n \cdot q$.
- We define $\mathcal{Q}_{\mathsf{Haar}} = \{\mathcal{Q}_{n,q,\ell,\lambda}\}_{\lambda \in \mathbb{N}}$, where $\mathcal{Q}_{n,q,\ell,\lambda}$ is defined as follows[5]:

$$\mathcal{Q}_{n,q,\ell,\lambda} = \left\{ \mathbb{E}_{|\psi_1\rangle,\ldots,|\psi_s\rangle \leftarrow \mathscr{H}_n} \left[\bigotimes_{i=1}^{s} |\psi_i\rangle\langle\psi_i|^{\otimes t} \otimes \bigotimes_{i=1}^{s} |\psi_i\rangle\langle\psi_i|^{\otimes t} \right] \right\}$$

Recall that the first ℓ qubits (in the above case, it is the first t red-colored copies of n-qubit Haar states $|\psi_1\rangle, \ldots, |\psi_s\rangle$) are not touched. On the next q n-qubit states (colored in blue), either $\mathsf{PRI}_k^{\otimes q}$ or $\mathcal{I}^{\otimes q}$ is applied.

We prove the following.

Theorem 1 (Informal). *Assuming post-quantum one-way functions exist, PRI_k is a $\mathcal{Q}_{\mathsf{Haar}}$-secure pseudorandom isometry.*

This setting is reminiscent of the *weak* pseudorandom functions [DN02, ABG+14] studied in the classical cryptography literature, where we require the pseudorandomness to hold only on inputs chosen from the uniform distribution on binary strings.

APPLICATION: LENGTH EXTENSION THEOREM. As an application, we demonstrate a length extension theorem for PRSGs and PRFSGs. Specifically, we show how to extend the output length of both these pseudorandomness notions assuming PRIs secure against Haar queries[6]. Specifically, we show the following.

Theorem 2 (Length Extension Theorem; Informal). *Assuming $\mathcal{Q}_{\mathsf{Haar}}$-secure pseudorandom isometry, mapping n qubits to $n+m$ qubits, and an n-qubit PRSG, there exists an $n + m$-qubit PRSG.*

Similarly, assuming a $\mathcal{Q}_{\mathsf{Haar}}$-secure pseudorandom isometry, mapping n qubits to $n + m$ qubits, and n-qubit PRFSG, there exists an $(n + m)$-qubit PRFSG.

---

[4] We only consider a simplified version of these settings here and in the technical sections, we consider the most general version.

[5] $\mathscr{H}_n$ denotes the Haar distribution on n-qubit Haar states.

[6] An $(n, n + m)$-pseudorandom isometry secure against any $\mathcal{Q}$ trivially gives a PRSG or PRFSG on $n + m$ qubits. However, our length extension theorem requires the underlying PRI to only be secure against Haar queries.

Prior to our work, the only known length extension theorem was by Gunn, Ju, Ma, and Zhandry [GJMZ23] who demonstrated a method to increase the output length of pseudorandom states and pseudorandom unitaries but at the cost of reducing the number of copies given to the adversary. That is, the resulting PRSG in their transformation is only secure if the adversary is given one copy. On the other hand, in the above theorem, the number of copies of the PRSG is preserved in the above transformation.

II. MANY COPIES OF AN n-QUBIT STATE. We also consider the setting where we have multiple copies of a single state. Specifically, we consider the following setting:

- Let $q = q(\lambda)$ be a polynomial. Let $\ell = n \cdot q$.
- We define $\mathcal{Q}_{\mathsf{Single}} = \{\mathcal{Q}_{n,q,\ell,\lambda}\}_{\lambda \in \mathbb{N}}$, where $\mathcal{Q}_{n,q,\ell,\lambda}$ is defined as follows:

$$\mathcal{Q}_{n,q,\ell,\lambda} = \left\{ |\psi\rangle^{\otimes q} \otimes |\psi\rangle^{\otimes q} \; : \; |\psi\rangle \in \mathcal{S}(\mathbb{C}^{2^n}) \right\}$$

We prove the following.

Theorem 3 (Informal). *Assuming post-quantum one-way functions exist,* PRI_k *is a* $\mathcal{Q}_{\mathsf{Single}}$-*secure pseudorandom isometry.*

Informally, the above theorem ensures that even if an efficient distinguisher is given polynomially many copies of $|\psi\rangle$, for an arbitrary n-qubit state $|\psi\rangle$, it should not be able to efficiently distinguish q copies of $\mathsf{PRI}_k|\psi\rangle$ versus q copies of $\mathcal{I}|\psi\rangle$, for any polynomial $q(\lambda)$.

APPLICATION: PSEUDORANDOM STATE SCAMBLERS.
A recent work [LQS+23] shows how to isometrically scramble a state such that many copies of the scrambled state should be computationally indistinguishable from many copies of a Haar state. Our notion of $\mathcal{Q}_{\mathsf{Single}}$-secure pseudorandom isometry is equivalent to pseudorandom state scramblers. Thus, we have the following.

Theorem 4 (Informal). $\mathcal{Q}_{\mathsf{Single}}$-*secure pseudorandom isometry exists if and only if pseudorandom state scramblers exist.*

The work of [LQS+23] presents an instantiation of pseudorandom scramblers from post-quantum one-way functions. While our result does not give anything new for pseudorandom scramblers in terms of assumptions, we argue that our construction and analysis are (in our eyes) much simpler than [LQS+23]. In addition to pseudorandom permutations and functions, they also use rotation unitaries in the construction. Their analysis also relies on novel and sophistical tools such as Kac random walks whereas our analysis is more elementary.

APPLICATION: MULTI-COPY SECURE PUBLIC-KEY ENCRYPTION. There is a simple technique to encrypt a quantum state, say $|\psi\rangle$: apply a quantum one-time pad on $|\psi\rangle$ and then encrypt the one-time pad keys using a post-quantum encryption scheme. However, the disadvantage of this construction is that the security is not guaranteed to hold if the adversary receives many copies of the ciphertext state. A natural idea is to apply a unitary t-design on $|\psi\rangle$ rather than a quantum one-time pad but this again only guarantees security if the adversary receives at most t queries. On the other hand, we formalize a security notion called multi-copy secure public-key and private-key encryption schemes, where the security should hold even if the adversary receives arbitrary polynomially many copies of the ciphertext.

Theorem 5 (Informal). *Assuming $\mathcal{Q}_{\mathsf{Single}}$-secure pseudorandom isometry[7], there exists multi-copy secure private-key and public-key encryption schemes.*

The investigation of multi-copy security was independently conducted by [LQS+23]. However, they only studied multi-copy security in the context of one-time encryption schemes whereas we introduce the definition of multi-copy security for private-key and public-key encryption schemes and establish their feasibility for the first time.

CONJECTURE. Unfortunately, we currently do not know how to prove that PRI_k is a $\mathcal{Q}$-secure pseudorandom isometry for every $\mathcal{Q}$. We leave the investigation of this question as an interesting open problem.

Conjecture 1. For every $\mathcal{Q} = \{\mathcal{Q}_{n,q,\ell,\lambda}\}_{\lambda \in \mathbb{N}}$, where $\mathcal{Q}_{n,q,\ell,\lambda}$ consists of nq-qubit states, PRI_k is a $\mathcal{Q}$-secure pseudorandom isometry.

Other Applications. We explore other applications of PRIs that were not covered before.

APPLICATION: QUANTUM MACs. We explore novel notions of message authentication codes (MAC) for quantum states. Roughly speaking, in a MAC for quantum states, there is a signing algorithm using a signing key sk that on input a state, say $|\psi\rangle$, outputs a tag that can be verified using the same signing key sk. Intuitively, we require that any adversary who receives tags on message states of their choice should not be able to produce a tag on a challenge message state. For the notion to be meaningful, we require that the challenge message state should be orthogonal (or small fidelity) to all the message states seen so far.

There are different settings we consider:

- In the first setting, the verification algorithm gets as input multiple copies of the message state $|\psi\rangle$ and the tag state. In this case, we require the probability that the adversary should succeed is negligible.

---

[7] We additionally require that the pseudorandom isometry satisfy an invertibility condition. We define this more formally in the technical sections.

– In the second setting, the verification algorithm gets as input many copies of the message state but only a single copy of the tag. In this case, we weaken the security by only requiring that the adversary should only be able to succeed with inverse polynomial probability.

– Finally, we consider the setting where we restrict the type of message states that can be signed. Specifically, we impose the condition that for every message state $|\psi\rangle$, there is a circuit C that on input an all-zero state outputs $|\psi\rangle$. Moreover this circuit C is known to the verification algorithm. In this case, we require that the adversary only be able to succeed with negligible probability.

We show how to achieve all of the above three settings using PRIs.

APPLICATION: LENGTH EXTENSION THEOREM. Previously, we explored a length extension theorem where we showed how to generically increase the output length of pseudorandom (function-like) state generators assuming only PRIs secure against Haar queries. We explore a qualitatively different method to extend the output length of pseudorandom states. Specifically, we show the following.

Theorem 6 (Informal). *Assuming the existence of $(n, n + m)$-secure pseudorandom isometry and an $(2n)$-output PRSG secure against $o(m)$ queries, there exists a $(2n+m)$-output PRSG secure against the same number of queries. Moreover, the key of the resulting PRSG is a concatenation of the $(2n)$-output PRSG and the $(n, n + m)$-secure PRI.*

One might be tempted to conclude that a unitary $o(m)$-design can be used to get the above result. The main issue with using a $o(m)$-design is that it increases the key size significantly [BCH+21]. However, in the above theorem, if we start with a PRI with short keys (i.e., $\lambda \ll m$) then the above transformation gets a PRSG with a much larger stretch without increasing the key size by much.[8]

1.2   Technical Overview

Haar Unitaries: Observations. Before we talk about proving security of our construction, we point out some useful properties of Haar unitaries. Note that Haar isometries are closely related to Haar unitaries since the former can be implemented by appending suitably many zeroes[9] followed by a Haar random unitary.

Behavior on Orthogonal Inputs. In the classical world, a random function f with polynomial output length is indistinguishable from the corresponding random permutation g against a query-bounded black-box adversary $\mathcal{A}$. One can prove this fact in three simple steps:

---

[8] The proofs can be found in the full version https://eprint.iacr.org/2023/1741.

[9] The state being appended and the position of the new qubits is not important.

1. Without loss of generality one can assume $\mathcal{A}$ only makes distinct queries $\{x_1, \ldots, x_q\}$.
2. f is perfectly indistinguishable from g conditioned on the fact that $f(x_i) \neq f(x_j)$ for $i \neq j$.
3. If the number q is polynomial, then the probability that f has a collision on $\{x_1, \ldots, x_q\}$ is negligible.

Now consider the quantum analogue of the same problem. Namely, consider two oracles O_1, O_2 that can only be queried on classical inputs, where: (1) O_1 on input x outputs $\mathcal{U}|x\rangle$, where $\mathcal{U}$ is a Haar unitary; and (2) O_2 for each distinct input x, outputs an i.i.d. Haar-random state $|\psi_x\rangle$. Our goal is to show that O_1, O_2 are indistinguishable against a query-bounded quantum adversary $\mathcal{A}$. If we try to replicate the classical proof above, we run into problems: we can no longer assume distinct queries due to the principle of no-cloning, and we need to generalize step 3 in a non-trivial to an almost-orthogonality argument. Instead, we consider an alternative proof for the classical case.

Fix the set of queries $\{x_1, \ldots, x_q\}$ and for $0 \leq i \leq q$ define a hybrid oracle O_i as follows:

- For $1 \leq j \leq q$, if $x_j \in \{x_1, \ldots, x_{q-1}\}$, then output consistently as the previous instance of the same query.
- Otherwise, for $1 \leq j \leq i$: On input x_j, sample $y_j \notin \{y_1, \ldots, y_{j-1}\}$ uniformly at random and output y_j. For $i + 1 \leq j \leq q$, sample an i.i.d. random answer y_j and output y_j.

Now, one can argue that O_i is perfectly indistinguishable from O_{i+1} conditioned on the answer y_{i+1} sampled by O_i satisfying $y_{i+1} \notin \{y_1, \ldots, y_i\}$. It turns out this argument is more easily generalizable to the quantum case, where we can define oracle $\widetilde{O}_i$ as answering $x_1, \ldots, x_i$ using a random isometry and answering $x_{i+1}, \ldots, x_q$ using i.i.d. Haar-random states (while maintaining consistency). Indistinguishability of $\widetilde{O}_i$ and $\widetilde{O}_{i+1}$ follows from an analysis comparing the dimensions of the subspaces the hybrid oracles sample outputs from.

Almost-Invariance Property. The security definition for a pseudorandom unitary, and similarly isometry, can be cumbersome to work with. Let us focus on the information-theoretic setting first, i.e. when there is no computational assumption on the adversary besides a query bound. We investigate what it means for a candidate pseudorandom unitary F_k to be information theoretically indistinguishable from a Haar unitary $\mathcal{U}$ for different query sets $\mathcal{Q}$; in other words, we consider *statistical $\mathcal{Q}$-security* of F_k. Rather than attempting to directly calculate the trace distance between the output of F_k on a given query ρ and the output of a Haar unitary $\mathcal{U}$ on the same input, which may look significantly different for different values of ρ, we are naturally drawn to look for a simpler condition that suffices for security.

Accordingly, we show that F_k is statistically $\mathcal{Q}$-secure if and only if for every $\rho \in \mathcal{Q}$ which describes q queries to F_k, we have that $F_k^{\otimes q} \rho (F_k^\dagger)^{\otimes q}$ changes only negligibly (in trace distance) under the action of q-fold Haar unitary

$\mathcal{U}^{\otimes q}(\cdot)(\mathcal{U}^\dagger)^{\otimes q}$. We prove this fact for any quantum channel Φ (in particular for $\Phi(\cdot) = F_k(\cdot)F_k^\dagger$) as long as Φ is a mixture of unitary maps, and the proof follows by the unitary invariance of the Haar measure.

We note that the argument above can be easily generalized to a pseudo-random isometry (PRI), since an isometry can be decomposed into appending zeroes followed by applying a unitary.

Next, we will describe our construction, then discuss its security and applications in more detail.

Construction. We describe how to naturally arrive at our construction of pseudorandom isometry, which was recently studied by [BBSS23, ABF+23] in different contexts. Given an input state $|\psi\rangle = \sum \alpha_x |x\rangle$, we will first apply an isometry $\tilde{I}$ to get a state $|\varphi\rangle = \sum \theta_z |z\rangle$, followed by unitary operations. A commonly used technique to scramble a given input state $|\varphi\rangle$ is to apply a random binary function f with a phase kickback [JLS18], i.e. apply the unitary $O_f|\psi\rangle = \sum(-1)^{f(z)}\theta_z|z\rangle$. The action of O_f on a mixed state q-query input $\rho = \sum_{\vec{z},\vec{z}'} \beta_{\vec{z},\vec{z}'} |\vec{z}\rangle\langle\vec{z}'|$ can be calculated as

$$\mathop{\mathbb{E}}_f\left[O_f^{\otimes q}\rho(O_f^\dagger)^{\otimes q}\right] = \mathop{\mathbb{E}}_f\left[\sum_{\vec{z},\vec{z}'}(-1)^{\sum_i f(z_i)+f(z_i')}\beta_{\vec{z},\vec{z}'}|\vec{z}\rangle\langle\vec{z}'|\right]$$

$$= \sum_{\vec{z},\vec{z}'}\beta_{\vec{z},\vec{z}'}|\vec{z}\rangle\langle\vec{z}'|\mathop{\mathbb{E}}_f\left[(-1)^{\sum_i f(z_i)+f(z_i')}\right].$$

Observe that if $\vec{z}$ and $\vec{z}'$ are related by a permutation[10], then $(-1)^{\sum_i f(z_i)+f(z_i')} = 1$. Otherwise, if there exists z, which occurs odd number of times in $\vec{z}$ and even number of times in $\vec{z}'$ (or vice versa), we get $(-1)^{\sum_i f(z_i)+f(z_i')} = 0$. Ideally we would like all terms $|\vec{z}\rangle\langle\vec{z}'|$ to vanish when $\vec{z}$ and $\vec{z}'$ are not related by a permutation. We can easily fix this by switching to p-th root of unity phase kickback, i.e. apply $\tilde{O}_f$ for a random function f with codomain $\mathbb{Z}_p$, where $\tilde{O}_f|\psi\rangle = \sum_x \omega_p^{f(x)}|x\rangle$ and $\omega_p = e^{2\pi i/p}$. As long as $q \ll p$ (e.g. q is polynomial and p is super-polynomial), we get that

$$\mathop{\mathbb{E}}_f\left[\tilde{O}_f^{\otimes q}\rho(\tilde{O}_f^\dagger)^{\otimes q}\right] = \sum_{\substack{\vec{z},\vec{z}' \\ \exists\sigma: \vec{z}'=\sigma(\vec{z})}} \beta_{\vec{z},\vec{z}'}|\vec{z}\rangle\langle\vec{z}'|.$$

Now we would like to scramble the remaining terms $|\vec{z}\rangle\langle\vec{z}'|$ in the equation above. A natural try is to apply a random permutation π in the computational basis, denoted by O_π as a unitary operation. Such an operation would scramble the term above as $O_\pi^{\otimes q}|\vec{z}\rangle\langle\vec{z}'|(O_\pi^\dagger)^{\otimes q}$, which only depends on σ as long as $\vec{z}$ has distinct entries. Hence, to achieve maximal scrambling we would like $|\varphi\rangle$ to have negligible weight on states $|\vec{z}\rangle$ with collisions of the form $z_i = z_j$.

---

[10] This condition will later be referred to as $\vec{z}$ and $\vec{z}'$ having the same *type*.

In order to make sure that the weight on $|\vec{z}\rangle$ with distinct entries is close to 1, we pick $\widetilde{I}$ to append a uniform superposition of strings[11], which brings us to the information-theoretic inefficient construction

$$G_{(f,\pi)}|\psi\rangle = \frac{1}{\sqrt{2^m}} \sum_{x\in\{0,1\}^n, y\in\{0,1\}^m} \alpha_x \cdot \omega_p^{f(x||y)} |\pi(x||y)\rangle, \qquad (1)$$

To make the construction efficient, we instantiate f and g with a post-quantum pseudorandom function and a post-quantum pseudorandom permutation, respectively, hence reaching our construction

$$F_{(k_1,k_2)}|\psi\rangle = \frac{1}{\sqrt{2^m}} \sum_{x\in\{0,1\}^n, y\in\{0,1\}^m} \alpha_x \cdot \omega_p^{f_{k_1}(x||y)} |g_{k_2}(x||y)\rangle.$$

Security Proof. As a first step, we argue that a QPT adversary cannot distinguish the PRF (f_{k_1}) and the PRP (g_{k_2}) from a random function and a random permutation, respectively. To show this we use a $2q$-wise independent hash function as an intermediate hybrid for f_{k_1} to get an efficient reduction, following [Zha12] who showed that such a hash function is indistinguishable from a random function under q queries. Combining this with [Zha16] who showed how to instantiate the PRP (g_{k_2}) from post-quantum one-way functions, we successfully invoke computational assumptions.

Now that we have invoked the computational assumptions as per the existence of quantum-secure PRF and PRP, we are left with the information theoretic construction given by $G_{(f,\pi)}$ (Eq. (1)), which is parametrized by a random function f and a random permutation π. Below, we write $\rho \in \mathcal{Q}$ as a short-hand to mean $\rho \in \mathcal{Q}_{n,q,\ell,\lambda}$ for some $\lambda \in \mathbb{N}$. To show that $G_{(f,\pi)}$ is *statistically $\mathcal{Q}$-secure* for different query sets $\mathcal{Q}$, we will show that the output of $G_{(f,\pi)}$ under any query $\rho \in \mathcal{Q}$ is *almost-invariant* under q-fold Haar unitary as per our second observation above. We achieve this in two steps:

Step 1: Find a particular mixed state ρ_{uni}, to be defined later, which is almost-invariant under q-fold Haar unitary. Conclude that if the output of $G_{(f,\pi)}$ under any query $\rho \in \mathcal{Q}$ is negligibly close (in trace distance) to ρ_{uni}, then it is q-fold Haar almost invariant, hence $G_{(f,\pi)}$ satisfies statistical $\mathcal{Q}$-security.

Step 2: For 3 different instantiations of $\mathcal{Q}$, prove that the condition in Step 1 is satisfied, hence $G_{(f,\pi)}$ is statistically $\mathcal{Q}$-secure.

Note that our proof-strategy outlined above is a top-down approach, and the first two steps can be viewed as reducing the problem of PRI-security to a simpler condition that is easier to check for different query sets, and is independent of the action of Haar isometry on $\mathcal{Q}$. In Step 3, we show instantiations of $\mathcal{Q}$ that satisfy the simpler condition. Next, we delve into the details of each step.

---

[11] Note that this step crucially relies on the fact that we are constructing a pseudorandom isometry, not a pseudorandom unitary.

Step 1: An Almost-Invariant State: ρ_{uni}. Having established q-fold Haar almost-invariance as a sufficient condition for statistical security of $G_{(f,\pi)}$, it is natural to ask the question:

Can we find a state ρ^* which is both:
(a) close to the output of $G_{(f,\pi)}$ on certain inputs, and
(b) q-fold Haar almost-invariant?

This would allow us to use negligible closeness to ρ^* as a sufficient condition for q-fold Haar almost-invariance, hence for statistical security of $G_{(f,\pi)}$. We start by analyzing condition (a).

We restrict our attention to queries with a particular, yet quite general, structure. Namely, suppose $\mathcal{Q} = \{\mathcal{Q}_{n,q,\ell,\lambda}\}$ is such that every $\rho \in \mathcal{Q}$ is a mixture of pure states of the form $\bigotimes_{i=1}^{s}|\psi_i\rangle^{\otimes t}$, where $q = st$. In other words, the adversary makes queries in the form of s states with t-copies each, or formally queries from the s-fold tensor product of symmetric subspaces, denoted by $\mathcal{H} = \left(\vee^t \mathbb{C}^N\right)^s$. For such inputs, the output of the isometry will belong to the corresponding tensor product of symmetric subspaces $\mathcal{H}' := \left(\vee^t \mathbb{C}^{NM}\right)^s$, where $N = 2^n$ and $M = 2^m$. It is known [Har13] that $\mathcal{H}$ is spanned by s-fold tensor product of *type states* $|\psi_{T_1,\ldots,T_s}\rangle = \bigotimes_{i=1}^{s}|\text{type}_{T_i}\rangle$, where $|\text{type}_{T_i}\rangle$ is a uniform superposition over computational basis states $|\vec{x}\rangle \in \mathbb{C}^{Nt}$ of the same *type* (T_i), where $\vec{x}$ and $\vec{y}$ are said to have the same type if $\vec{y} = \sigma \vec{x}$ for some permutation $\sigma \in S_t$ over t elements.

To understand the action of $G_{(f,\pi)}$ on $\mathcal{Q}$, we consider its action on a basis state $|\psi_{T_1,\ldots,T_s}\rangle$ of $\mathcal{H}$. We first look at the action of a random isometry $\mathcal{I}$ on $|\psi_{T_1,\ldots,T_s}\rangle$ and see that

$$\underset{\mathcal{I}}{\mathbb{E}}\left[\mathcal{I}^{\otimes q}|\psi_{T_1,\ldots,T_s}\rangle\langle\psi_{T_1,\ldots,T_s}|\mathcal{I}^{\otimes q}\right] = \underset{T_1',\ldots,T_s'}{\mathbb{E}}\left[|\psi_{T_1',\ldots,T_s'}\rangle\langle\psi_{T_1',\ldots,T_s'}|\right]$$

is maximally mixed over $\mathcal{H}'$, where $T_1',\ldots,T_s'$ are types over $\mathbb{C}^{NMt}$. The same fact is not quite true for $G_{(f,\pi)}$ due to cross terms. Nonetheless, such terms cancel out whenever $(T_1,\ldots,T_s)$ form a set of *unique* types, denoted by $(T_1,\ldots,T_s) \in \mathcal{T}_{\text{uni}_{s,t}^n}$, meaning collectively they span st distinct computational basis states $|x\rangle \in \mathbb{C}^N$, thanks to the nice algebraic structure of the image of f, i.e. $\mathbb{Z}_p$. As a result, we get

$$\underset{f,\pi}{\mathbb{E}}\left[G_{(f,\pi)}^{\otimes q}|\psi_{T_1,\ldots,T_s}\rangle\langle\psi_{T_1,\ldots,T_s}|G_{(f,\pi)}^{\otimes q}\right]$$

$$= \underset{(T_1',\ldots,T_s') \leftarrow \mathcal{T}_{\text{uni}_{s,t}^{n+m}}}{\mathbb{E}}\left[|\psi_{T_1',\ldots,T_s'}\rangle\langle\psi_{T_1',\ldots,T_s'}|\right] =: \rho_{\text{uni}} \qquad (2)$$

for any $(T_1,\ldots,T_s) \in \mathcal{T}_{\text{uni}_{s,t}^n}$. Fortunately, ρ_{uni} satisfies[12] property (b) as well. The reason is that the q-fold unique type states $|\psi_{T_1,\ldots,T_s}\rangle$ constitute the

---

[12] We note that $\rho_{\text{uni}} = \rho_{\text{uni}_{s,t}}$ is parametrized by s,t in the tecnhical sections, which we omit here for simplicity of notation.

vast majority[13] of the basis for $\mathcal{H}'$, so that ρ_{uni} is negligibly close to the maximally mixed state over $\mathcal{H}'$, which is invariant under q-fold unitary operations. Therefore, if $G^{\otimes q}_{(f,\pi)}\rho(G^{\dagger}_{(f,\pi)})^{\otimes q}$ is negligible close to ρ_{uni}, then it is q-fold Haar almost-invariant, hence we have a simpler sufficient condition to check for PRI security as desired. Note that so far we have ignored the ℓ-qubit (purification) register held by the adversary, but the arguments generalize without trouble.

Step 2: Closeness to ρ_{uni}. In the final step of our security proof, we show that $G_{(f,\pi)}$ is statistically $\mathcal{Q}$-secure for three instantiations of $\mathcal{Q}$ by showing that the output of $G_{(f,\pi)}$ is close to ρ_{uni} in each case.

<u>DISTINCT TYPES:</u> By Eq. (2), it follows that $G_{(f,\pi)}$ is $\mathcal{Q}$-secure for[14] $\mathcal{Q} = \mathcal{T}_{\text{uni}^n_{s,t}}$. We can generalize this to *distinct* type states $|\psi_{T_1,\ldots,T_s}\rangle$, which are defined by the condition that the computational basis states spanned by the types T_i are mutually disjoint, denoted by $(T_1,\ldots,T_s) \in \mathcal{T}_{\text{dis}^n_{s,t}}$. Note that $\mathcal{T}_{\text{uni}^n_{s,t}} \subset \mathcal{T}_{\text{dis}^n_{s,t}}$ since for types $(T_1,\ldots,T_s) \in \mathcal{T}_{\text{dis}^n_{s,t}}$ each T_j may contain repetitions. Fortunately, a careful analysis shows that the output of $G_{(f,\pi)}$ on a distinct type state acquires a nice form and is close to ρ_{uni} as well. Intuitively, the reason for this is that the first step in our construction appends a random string $\vec{a}$ to the input query, and after this step the internal collisions in $\mathcal{T}_{\text{dis}^n_{s,t}}$ get eliminated except with negligible weight. Accordingly, we get security for the query set

$$\mathcal{Q}_{\text{distinct}_{t,s}} = \left\{ \bigotimes_{i=1}^{s} |\text{type}_{T_i}\rangle\langle\text{type}_{T_i}| : (T_1,\cdots,T_s) \in \mathcal{T}_{\text{dis}^n_{s,t}} \right\}.$$

As a corollary, we conclude that our construction is secure against computational basis queries.

MANY COPIES OF AN n-QUBIT STATE: Next, we show security for many copies of the same pure state, defined by the query set

$$\mathcal{Q}_{\text{Single}} = \left\{ |\psi\rangle^{\otimes t} \otimes |\psi\rangle^{\otimes t} \; : \; |\psi\rangle \in \mathcal{S}(\mathbb{C}^{2^n}) \right\},$$

which allows for the adversary to keep t copies of the state that are not fed into the PRI, with $\ell = q = t$. We can write the input state in the type-basis of the symmetric subspace as

$$|\psi\rangle\langle\psi|^{\otimes t} = \sum_{T,T'} \alpha_{T,T'} |\text{type}_T\rangle\langle\text{type}_{T'}|.$$

Thanks to the algebraic structure of $\mathbb{Z}_p$, the terms with $T \neq T'$ vanish under the application of $G^{\otimes q}_{(f,\pi)}(\cdot)(G^{\dagger}_{(f,\pi)})^{\otimes q}$. The rest of the terms are approximately

---

[13] This follows from the fact that a random type will contain no repetitions with overwhelming probability as long as $t = \text{poly}(\lambda)$.

[14] The reader may observe that we can also consider the convex closure of $\mathcal{T}_{\text{uni}^n_{s,t}}$.

mapped to ρ_{uni} as we showed in $\mathcal{Q}_{\mathsf{distinct}_{t,s}}$-security above (by taking $s = 1$). Hence, the result follows.

HAAR STATES: Finally, we consider the case when the query contains a collection of s i.i.d. Haar states, with t copies of each kept by the adversary and t copies given as input to the PRI, i.e. the query set is

$$\mathcal{Q}_{\mathsf{Haar}} = \left\{ \mathbb{E}_{|\psi_1\rangle,\dots,|\psi_s\rangle \leftarrow \mathcal{H}_n} \left[\bigotimes_{i=1}^{s} |\psi_i\rangle\langle\psi_i|^{\otimes t} \otimes \bigotimes_{i=1}^{s} |\psi_i\rangle\langle\psi_i|^{\otimes t} \right] \right\}.$$

Note that without the red part, the security would simply follow by taking an expectation over unique types in Eq. (2). Since the adversary will keep t copies of each Haar state to herself, she holds an entangled register (purification) to the query register, hence we need to work more. We first recall that the query $\rho_{\mathsf{Haar}} \in \mathcal{Q}_{\mathsf{Haar}}$ is negligibly close to the uniform mixture of unique s-fold type states (for $2t$ copies). We combine this with the useful expression

$$|\mathsf{type}_T\rangle\langle\mathsf{type}_T| = \frac{1}{(2t)!} \sum_{\sigma \in S_{2t}} \sum_{\substack{\vec{v} \in [N]^{2t} \\ \mathsf{type}(\vec{v})=T}} |\vec{v}\rangle\langle\sigma(\vec{v})|. \tag{3}$$

to express the output as

$$\rho \propto \underset{\substack{(f,\pi) \\ T_1,\dots,T_s \\ (\vec{x_1},\cdots,\vec{x_s}) \in (T_1,\cdots,T_s) \\ \sigma_1,\cdots,\sigma_s \in S_{2t}}}{\mathbb{E}} \left[\bigotimes_{i=1}^{s} \left(\left(I_{nt} \otimes \left(G_{(f,\pi)} \right)^{\otimes t} \right) |\vec{x_i}\rangle\langle\sigma_i(\vec{x_i})| \right. \right.$$

$$\left. \left. \cdot \left(I_{nt} \otimes \left(G^\dagger_{(f,\pi)} \right)^{\otimes t} \right) \right) \right].$$

Above, due to the nice structure of $G_{(f,\pi)}$, the only terms that do not vanish are those with permutations σ_i that act separately on the first and the last n qubits, i.e. $\sigma_i(\vec{x_i}) = \sigma_i^1(\vec{x_i^1})||\sigma_i^2(\vec{x_i^2})$ with $\sigma_i^b \in S_n, x_i^b \in \{0,1\}^n$. With this observation, and using Eq. (3) in reverse, we see that the q-fold application of $G_{(f,\pi)}$ effectively *unentangles* the state, which was the only barrier against security.

Applications. We discuss applications of PRIs, giving an overview of Sect. 4.

Multi-Copy Secure Encryption. As a first application, we achieve multi-copy secure public-key and private-key encryption for quantum messages. Multi-copy security is defined via a chosen-plaintext attack (CPA) with the modification that the CPA adversary gets polynomially many copies of the ciphertext in the security experiment. This modification only affects security in the quantum setting due to the no-cloning principle, with the ciphertexts being quantum states. We note that using t-designs one can achieve multi-copy security if the number of copies is fixed a-priori before the construction, whereas using PRI we can achieve it for *arbitrary* polynomially many copies. Multi-copy security was independently studied by [LQS+23] albeit in the one-time setting.

We will focus on the public-key setting, for the private-key setting is similar. Formally, we would like an encryption scheme (Setup, Enc, Dec) with the property that no QPT adversary, given $\rho^{\otimes t}$, where $\rho \leftarrow \mathsf{Enc}(|\psi_b\rangle)$, can distinguish the cases $b = 0$ and $b = 1$ with non-negligible advantage, for any quantum messages $|\psi_0\rangle, |\psi_1\rangle$. In the construction, we will use a post-quantum public-key encryption scheme (setup, enc, dec) and a secure pseudorandom isometry PRI. The public-secret keys are those generated by $\mathsf{setup}(1^\lambda)$. To encrypt a quantum message $|\psi\rangle$, we sample a PRI key k and output (ct, φ), where ct is encryption of k using enc, and $\varphi \leftarrow \mathsf{PRI}_k(|\psi\rangle)$. Note that for correctness we need the ability to efficiently invert the PRI, which is a property satisfied by our PRI construction.

To show security, we deploy a standard hybrid argument where we invoke the security of (setup, enc, dec) as well as the $\mathcal{Q}_{\mathsf{Single}}$-security of PRI. This suffices since we only run PRI on copies of the same pure-state input (the quantum message).

Succinct Commitments. [GJMZ23] showed how to achieve succinct quantum commitments using pseudorandom unitaries (PRU) by first achieving one-time secure quantum encryption, and then showing that one-time secure quantum encryption implies succinct commitments. We adapt their approach to achieve succinct quantum commitments from PRIs. [LQS+23] uses the work of [GJMZ23] in a similar fashion to achieve succinct commitments from quantum pseudorandom state scramblers.

To one-time encrypt a quantum message, we apply in order: (1) inverse Schur transform, (2) PRI, and (3) Schur transform. Note that in contrast with [GJMZ23], the Schur transforms in (1) and (3) have different dimensions. The security proof follows that of [GJMZ23] closely and relies on Schur's Lemma.

Quantum MACs. We show how to achieve a restricted version of quantum message authentication codes (QMACs) using an invertible pseudorandom isometry PRI. We face definitional challenges in this task.

Similar to an injective function, an isometry does not have a unique inverse[15]. We discuss this and give a natural definition of the inverse in Sect. 2.1.

There is extensive literature [BCG+02, DNS12, GYZ17, AM17] on *one-time*, private-key quantum state authentications, i.e., the honest parties can detect whether the signed quantum state has been tempered. However, defining *many-time* security, such as existentially unforgeable security under a chosen-message attack, is quite challenging. In particular, defining QMACs is non-trivial for several reasons, explicitly pointed out by [AGM18]. Firstly, one needs to carefully define what constitutes a *forgery*, and secondly, verification may require multiple copies of the message and/or the tag. We give a new syntax which differs from

---

[15] We remind the reader that the map $\mathcal{I}^\dagger$ is not a physical map (quantum channel) for a general isometry $\mathcal{I}$.

the classical setting in that the verification algorithm outputs a message instead of Accept/Reject.

In our construction, the signing algorithm simply applies PRI to the quantum message, whereas the verification applies the inverse of PRI. Given this syntax, we show that our construction satisfies three different security notions:

- In the first setting, the verification algorithm is run polynomially many times in parallel on fresh (message, tag) pairs, and the outputs of the verifier is compared with the message using a SWAP test. We argue that during a forgery, each swap test succeeds with constant probability, hence the forgery succeeds with exponentially small probability due to independent repetition of SWAP tests.
- In the second setting, the verification is run once on the tag, and the output is compared to polynomially many copies of the message using a generalized SWAP test called *the permutation test* [BBD+97, KNY08, GHMW15, BS20a]. The upside of this security notion is that it requires only one copy of the tag, yet the downside is that the it yields inverse polynomial security rather than negligible security.
- In the third setting, the adversary is asked to output the description of an invertible quantum circuit that generates the forgery message on input $|0^n\rangle$, together with the tag. In this setting, the verification is run on the tag, and the inverse of the circuit is computed on the output to see if the outcome is $|0^n\rangle$. We show that negligible security in this setting follows as a direct consequence of PRI security.

Now we will describe the security proof for the first and the second settings. Firstly, we can replace the PRI with a Haar isometry $\mathcal{I}$ using PRI security. Next, suppose the adversary $\mathcal{A}$ makes q queries $|\psi_1\rangle, \ldots, |\psi_q\rangle$ to the signing oracle, receiving tags $|v_1\rangle, \ldots, |v_q\rangle$ in return. Let the forgery output by $\mathcal{A}$ be $(|\psi^*\rangle, |\phi^*\rangle)$. It is forced by definition that $|\psi^*\rangle$ is orthogonal to $V := \mathsf{span}(|\psi_1\rangle, \ldots, |\psi_q\rangle)$. From $\mathcal{A}$'s point of view, $\mathcal{I}|\psi^*\rangle$ is a Haar-random state sampled from $V^\perp$. Therefore, any $|\phi^*\rangle \in V$ will be mapped to a state orthogonal to $|\psi^*\rangle$ by the verification, whereas a forgery satisfying $|\phi^*\rangle \in V^\perp$ is as good as any other such forgery. Putting these together, a straightforward calculation using the fact that $\dim V \leq q \ll 2^\lambda$ suffices for the proof in both settings.

PRS Length Extension. We show how to generically extend the length of a Haar-random state using a small amount of randomness assuming the existence of PRIs. Formally, we show that if PRI is a secure $(n, n + m)$-pseudorandom isometry, then given t copies of a $2n$-qubit Haar-random state $|\theta\rangle$, the state $(I_n \otimes \mathsf{PRI}_k)^{\otimes t}|\theta\rangle^{\otimes t}$, obtained by applying PRI_k to the last n qubits, is computationally indistinguishable from t copies of a $(2n + m)$-qubit Haar-random state $|\gamma\rangle^{\otimes t}$.

In the proof, we can replace PRI with a random isometry $\mathcal{I}$ up to negligible loss invoking security. After writing $|\theta\rangle\langle\theta|^{\otimes t}$ as a uniform mixture of type states, we obtain the expression

$$\rho' = \mathop{\mathbb{E}}_{T, \mathcal{I}} \left[(I_n \otimes \mathcal{I})^{\otimes t} |\mathsf{type}_T\rangle\langle\mathsf{type}_T| (I_n \otimes \mathcal{I}^\dagger)^{\otimes t} \right],$$

where by a collision-bound we can assume (up to a negligible loss) that T is sampled as a *good* type, meaning if it contains strings $\{x_1\|y_1 \ldots x_t\|y_t\}$, then $x_i \neq x_j$ and $y_i \neq y_j$ for $i \neq j$. For such good types T, we can show that the state ρ' is close to the uniform mixture of type states $|\text{type}_{T'}\rangle\langle\text{type}_{T'}|$ spanning states of the form $|\vec{x}\rangle|\vec{z}\rangle$, where $\vec{z} \in \{0,1\}^{(n+m)t}$ is a random vector with pairwise distinct coordinates. This is because the mapping $(I_n \otimes \mathcal{I})^{\otimes t}$ scrambles $\vec{y}$ and leaves $\vec{x}$ untouched. In the proof we use our (first) observation about how t-fold Haar unitary acts on orthogonal inputs.

For technical reasons, our loss in this step is proportional to $t!$, which necessitates the assumption that t must be sublinear in the security parameter (e.g. $t = \text{poly}\log(\lambda)$). In more detail, we expand ρ' by expressing the type state $|\text{type}_T\rangle$ as superposition of computational basis states pairwise related by a permutation to get

$$\rho' = \frac{1}{t!} \sum_{\sigma, \pi \in S_t} |\sigma(\vec{x})\rangle\langle\pi(\vec{x})| \otimes \underset{\mathcal{I}}{\mathbb{E}}[\mathcal{I}^{\otimes t}|\sigma(\vec{y})\rangle\langle\pi(\vec{y})|(\mathcal{I}^\dagger)^{\otimes t}]$$

$$= \frac{1}{t!} \sum_{\sigma, \pi \in S_t} |\sigma(\vec{x})\rangle\langle\pi(\vec{x})| \otimes P_\sigma \underset{\mathcal{I}}{\mathbb{E}}[\mathcal{I}^{\otimes t}|\vec{y}\rangle\langle\vec{y}|(\mathcal{I}^\dagger)^{\otimes t}]P_\pi^\dagger,$$

where we used the fact that the permutation operators P_σ, P_π commute[16] with the t-fold isometry $\mathcal{I}^{\otimes t}$. We can show that the term between the permutation operators $P_\sigma, P_\pi^\dagger$ is maximally scrambled for any given σ, π, which can be combined with a union bound over σ, π that yields a factor of $t!$ in the loss. Unfortunately we do not know how to relate the terms across different σ, π to avoid this loss. Finally, the uniform mixture we obtained is negligibly close to the distribution of $|\gamma\rangle^{\otimes t}$ by another collision-bound.

2   Pseudorandom Isometry: Definition

For a given class of inputs $\mathcal{Q}$, we propose the following definition of $\mathcal{Q}$-secure psuedorandom isometries. Throughout the rest of the paper, for a polynomial $p(\cdot)$, we denote p to be $p(\lambda)$, where λ is the security parameter.

Definition 1 ($\mathcal{Q}$-Secure Pseudorandom Isometry (PRI)). *Let n, m, q, ℓ be polynomials in λ. Suppose $\mathcal{Q} = \{\mathcal{Q}_{n,q,\ell,\lambda}\}_{\lambda \in \mathbb{N}}$, where $\mathcal{Q}_{n,q,\ell,\lambda} \subseteq \mathcal{D}(\mathbb{C}^{2^{nq+\ell}})$. We say that $\mathsf{PRI} = \{F_\lambda\}_{\lambda \in \mathbb{N}}$ is an $(n, n+m)$-$\mathcal{Q}$-secure pseudorandom isometry if the following holds:*

- *For every $k \in \{0,1\}^\lambda$, $F_\lambda(k, \cdot)$ is a QPT algorithm implementing a quantum channel such that it is functionally equivalent to $\mathcal{I}_k$, where $\mathcal{I}_k$ is an isometry that maps n qubits to $n + m$ qubits.*

---

[16] Technically the permutation operator acts on a larger Hilbert space after applying the isometry, but it applies the same permutation to the order of t copies.

– *For sufficiently large $\lambda \in \mathbb{N}$, any QPT distinguisher $\mathcal{A}$, the following holds: for every $\rho \in \mathcal{Q}_{n,q,\ell,\lambda}$,*

$$\left|\Pr\left[\mathcal{A}\left((I_\ell \otimes F_k^{\otimes q})(\rho)\right) = 1\right] - \Pr\left[\mathcal{A}\left((I_\ell \otimes \mathcal{I}^{\otimes q})(\rho)\right) = 1\right]\right| \leq \mathsf{negl}(\lambda),$$

where:
- *$\mathcal{I}(\cdot)$ is the channel implementing a Haar-random isometry that takes an n-qubit input $|\psi\rangle$ and outputs an $(n+m)$-qubit output $\mathcal{I}(|\psi\rangle)$,*
- *I_ℓ is an identity operator on ℓ qubits.*

We sometimes write $\mathcal{Q}$-secure with m, n being implicit. We consider the following set of queries. We color the part of the query given to I_ℓ with red and color the part of the query given to F_k or $\mathcal{I}$ with blue.

Computational basis queries. We define $\mathcal{Q}_{n,q,\ell,\lambda}^{(\mathsf{Comp})}$ as follows.

$$\mathcal{Q}_{n,q,\ell,\lambda}^{(\mathsf{Comp})} = \mathcal{D}(\mathbb{C}^{2^\ell}) \otimes \left\{(|x_1\rangle\langle x_1| \otimes \ldots \otimes |x_q\rangle\langle x_q|) \; : \; x_1, \ldots, x_q \in \{0,1\}^n\right\}.$$

Let $n(\cdot), q(\cdot), \ell(\cdot)$ be polynomials. We also define $\mathcal{Q}_{\mathsf{Comp}}$ (implicitly parameterized by $n(\cdot), q(\cdot), \ell(\cdot)$) to be $\mathcal{Q}_{\mathsf{Comp}} = \left\{\mathcal{Q}_{n,q,\ell,\lambda}^{(\mathsf{Comp})}\right\}_{\lambda \in \mathbb{N}}$.

Multiple copies of a single pure state. We define $\mathcal{Q}_{n,q,\ell,\lambda}^{(\mathsf{Single})}$ as follows:

$$\mathcal{Q}_{n,q,\ell,\lambda}^{(\mathsf{Single})} = \mathcal{D}(\mathbb{C}^{2^\ell}) \otimes \left\{(|\psi\rangle\langle\psi|^{\otimes q}) \; : \; |\psi\rangle \text{ is an } n\text{-qubit pure state}\right\}.$$

Let $n(\cdot), q(\cdot), \ell(\cdot)$ be polynomials. We also define $\mathcal{Q}_{\mathsf{Single}}$ (implicitly parameterized by $n(\cdot), q(\cdot), \ell(\cdot)$) to be $\mathcal{Q}_{\mathsf{Single}} = \left\{\mathcal{Q}_{n,q,\ell,\lambda}^{(\mathsf{Single})}\right\}_{\lambda \in \mathbb{N}}$.

Haar queries. We first define $\mathcal{Q}_{n,s,t,\ell',\lambda}^{(\mathsf{Haar})}$ as follows, for some polynomials $s(\cdot), t(\cdot), \ell'(\cdot)$,

$$\mathcal{Q}_{n,s,t,\ell',\lambda}^{(\mathsf{Haar})} = \mathcal{D}(\mathbb{C}^{2^{\ell'(\lambda)}}) \otimes \left\{ \underset{|\psi_1\rangle,\ldots,|\psi_{s(\lambda)}\rangle \leftarrow \mathscr{H}_n}{\mathbb{E}} \left[\bigotimes_{i=1}^{s(\lambda)} |\psi_i\rangle\langle\psi_i|^{\otimes t(\lambda)} \otimes \bigotimes_{i=1}^{s(\lambda)} |\psi_i\rangle\langle\psi_i|^{\otimes t(\lambda)}\right]\right\}.$$

Next, we define $\mathcal{Q}_{n,q,\ell,\lambda}^{(\mathsf{Haar})}$ as follows

$$\mathcal{Q}_{n,q,\ell,\lambda}^{(\mathsf{Haar})} = \bigcup_{\substack{s,t,\ell' \\ \text{such that } q=st \\ \text{and } \ell=\ell'+st}} \mathcal{Q}_{n,s,t,\ell',\lambda}^{(\mathsf{Haar})}.$$

Let $n(\cdot), q(\cdot), \ell(\cdot)$ be polynomials. We also define $\mathcal{Q}_{\mathsf{Haar}}$ (implicitly parameterized by $n(\cdot), q(\cdot), \ell(\cdot)$) to be $\mathcal{Q}_{\mathsf{Haar}} = \left\{ \mathcal{Q}_{n,q,\ell,\lambda}^{(\mathsf{Haar})} \right\}_{\lambda \in \mathbb{N}}$.

Distinct Querries We define a class of states

$$\mathcal{Q}_{n,t,s,\ell,\lambda}^{(\text{distinct})} := \mathcal{D}(\mathbb{C}^{2^{\ell'(\lambda)}}) \otimes \left\{ \bigotimes_{i=1}^{s} |\mathsf{type}_{T_i}\rangle\langle\mathsf{type}_{T_i}| : (T_1, \cdots, T_s) \in \mathcal{T}_{\mathsf{dis}_{s,t}^n} \right\}.$$

Next, we define the following class:

$$\mathcal{Q}_{n,q,\ell,\lambda}^{(\text{distinct})} := \bigcup_{\substack{s,t \\ \text{such that } q=st}} \mathcal{Q}_{n,t,s,\ell,\lambda}^{(\text{distinct})}.$$

We define $\mathcal{Q}_{(\text{distinct})} := \{ \mathcal{Q}_{n,q,\ell,\lambda}^{(\text{distinct})} \}_{\lambda \in \mathbb{N}}$.

Selective PRI. Above, we considered the security of PRI in the setting where the queries came from a specific query set. However, we can consider an alternate definition where the indistinguishability holds against computationally bounded adversaries making a single parallel query to an oracle that is either PRI or Haar. We term such a PRI to be a selectively secure PRI.

Definition 2 (Selective Pseudorandom Isometry). $\mathsf{PRI} = \{F_\lambda\}_{\lambda \in \mathbb{N}}$ *is an* $(n, n + m)$-*selective pseudorandom isometry if the following holds:*

- *For every* $k \in \{0,1\}^\lambda$, $F_\lambda(k, \cdot)$ *is a QPT algorithm such that it is functionally equivalent to* $\mathcal{I}_k$, *where* $\mathcal{I}_k$ *is an isometry that maps n qubits to $n + m$ qubits.*
- *For sufficiently large* $\lambda \in \mathbb{N}$, *for any* $q = \mathsf{poly}(\lambda)$, *any QPT distinguisher* $\mathcal{A}$ *making 1 query to the oracle, the following holds:*

$$\left| \Pr\left[\mathcal{A}^{(F_\lambda(k,\cdot))^{\otimes q}} = 1 \right] - \Pr\left[\mathcal{A}^{(\mathcal{I}(\cdot))^{\otimes q}} = 1 \right] \right| \le \mathsf{negl}(\lambda),$$

where:
- $F_\lambda(k, \cdot)$ *takes as input* $|\psi\rangle$ *and outputs* $F_\lambda(k, |\psi\rangle)$
- $\mathcal{I}(\cdot)$ *is a Haar-random isometry that takes as n-qubit input* $|\psi\rangle$ *and outputs an $(n + m)$-qubit output* $\mathcal{I}(|\psi\rangle)$.

The following claim is immediate.

Claim. Let $n(\cdot), m(\cdot)$ be two polynomials. Suppose PRI is an $(n, n + m)$-$\mathcal{Q}_{n,q,\ell}$-secure pseudorandom isometry for every polynomial $q(\cdot), \ell(\cdot)$, and, $\mathcal{Q}_{n,q,\ell} = \{\mathcal{Q}_{n,q,\ell,\lambda}\}_{\lambda \in \mathbb{N}}$, where $\mathcal{Q}_{n,q,\ell,\lambda} = \mathcal{D}(\mathbb{C}^{2^{nq+\ell}})$. Then, PRI is a selective pseudorandom isometry.

Similarly, the other direction is true as well.

Claim. Let $n(\cdot), m(\cdot)$ be two polynomials. Suppose PRI is an $(n, n + m)$-secure pseudorandom isometry. Then PRI is a $(n, n + m)$-$\mathcal{Q}_{n,q,\ell}$-secure pseudorandom isometry for every polynomial $q(\cdot), \ell(\cdot)$, and, $\mathcal{Q}_{n,q,\ell} = \{\mathcal{Q}_{n,q,\ell,\lambda}\}_{\lambda \in \mathbb{N}}$, where $\mathcal{Q}_{n,q,\ell,\lambda} = \mathcal{D}(\mathbb{C}^{2^{nq+\ell}})$.

Adapive PRI. We also define an adaptive version of the pseudorandom isometries below. In this definition, the adversary can make an arbitrary number of queries to the oracle.

Definition 3 (Adaptive Pseudorandom Isometry). PRI $= \{F_\lambda\}_{\lambda \in \mathbb{N}}$ *is an* $(n, n + m)$-*adaptive pseudorandom isometry if the following holds:*

- *For every* $k \in \{0, 1\}^\lambda$, $F_\lambda(k, \cdot)$ *is a QPT algorithm such that it is functionally equivalent to* $\mathcal{I}_k$, *where* $\mathcal{I}_k$ *is an isometry that maps* n *qubits to* $n + m$ *qubits.*
- *For sufficiently large* $\lambda \in \mathbb{N}$, *for any* $t = \mathsf{poly}(\lambda)$, *any QPT distinguisher* $\mathcal{A}$ *making* t *queries to the oracle, the following holds:*

$$\left| \Pr\left[\mathcal{A}^{F_\lambda(k, \cdot)} = 1 \right] - \Pr\left[\mathcal{A}^{\mathcal{I}(\cdot)} = 1 \right] \right| \leq \mathsf{negl}(\lambda),$$

where:
- $F_\lambda(k, \cdot)$ *takes as input* $|\psi\rangle$ *and outputs* $F_\lambda(k, |\psi\rangle)$
- $\mathcal{I}(\cdot)$ *is a Haar-random isometry that takes as* n-*qubit input* $|\psi\rangle$ *and outputs an* $(n + m)$-*qubit output* $\mathcal{I}(|\psi\rangle)$.

Observations. It should be immediate that pseudorandom unitaries, introduced in [JLS18], imply adaptive PRI, which in turn implies selectively secure PRI. Whether pseudorandom isometries are separated from pseudorandom unitaries or there is a transformation from the former to the latter is an interesting direction to explore.

If we weaken our definition of pseudorandom isometries further, where we a priori fix the number of queries made by the adversary and allow the description of the pseudorandom isometry to depend on this then this notion is implied by unitary t-designs [AE07, BHH16].

In terms of implications of pseudorandom isometries to other notions of pseudorandomness in the quantum world, we note that pseudorandom isometries imply both PRSGs and PRFSGs.

2.1   Invertibility

Invertible Pseudorandom Isometries. In applications, we need a stronger notion of *invertible* pseudorandom isometries.

Definition 4 (Invertible $\mathcal{Q}$-Secure Pseudorandom Isometry). *We say that* $\mathsf{PRI} = \{F_\lambda\}_{\lambda \in \mathbb{N}}$ *is an invertible* $(n, n+m)$-$\mathcal{Q}$*-secure pseudorandom isometry if first and foremost, it is a* $\mathcal{Q}$*-secure pseudorandom isometry (Definition 1) and secondly, there is a QPT algorithm* Inv *with the following guarantee: for every* $|\psi\rangle \in \mathcal{S}\left(\mathbb{C}^{2^n}\right)$ *and* $k \in \{0, 1\}^\lambda$,

$$\mathrm{TD}(|\psi\rangle\langle\psi|, \mathsf{Inv}\left(k, F_\lambda(k, |\psi\rangle)\right)) = \mathsf{negl}(\lambda).$$

Remark 1. Similarly, we can define invertible versions of $\mathcal{Q}$-secure PRIs and selectively secure PRIs. Also, note that for $|\phi\rangle$ which is orthogonal to the range of $F_\lambda(k, \cdot)$, being invertible has no guarantee on $\mathsf{Inv}(k, |\phi\rangle)$.

Inverse of Isometries. For a (fixed) isometry $\mathcal{I}$ maps n-qubit states to $(n + m)$-qubit states, the "inverse" of $\mathcal{I}$ is not unique. However, under the view of *Stinespring dilation*, it is possible to naturally define a quantum channel $\mathcal{I}^{-1}$ such that $\mathcal{I}^{-1} \circ (\mathcal{I}|\psi\rangle\langle\psi|\mathcal{I}^\dagger) = |\psi\rangle\langle\psi|$ for every $|\psi\rangle \in \mathcal{S}\left(\mathbb{C}^{2^n}\right)$.[17] Consider an arbitrary unitary $U_\mathcal{I}$ on $n + m$ qubits such that $U_\mathcal{I}$ is *consistent* with $\mathcal{I}$, that is, $U_\mathcal{I}|\psi\rangle|0^m\rangle_{\mathsf{Aux}} = \mathcal{I}|\psi\rangle$ for every $|\psi\rangle \in \mathcal{S}\left(\mathbb{C}^{2^n}\right)$. One can easily verify that $\mathrm{Tr}_{\mathsf{Aux}}\left(U_\mathcal{I}^\dagger \mathcal{I}|\psi\rangle\langle\psi|\mathcal{I}^\dagger U_\mathcal{I}\right) = |\psi\rangle\langle\psi|$ for every $|\psi\rangle \in \mathcal{S}\left(\mathbb{C}^{2^n}\right)$. Furthermore, one can even provide a distribution over such unitaries. This yields the following candidate definition: let $\mu_\mathcal{I}$ be some distribution over unitaries that are consistent with $\mathcal{I}$, the inverse of $\mathcal{I}$ can be defined as

$$\mathcal{I}^{-1}(X) = \underset{U_\mathcal{I} \leftarrow \mu_\mathcal{I}}{\mathbb{E}} \mathrm{Tr}_{\mathsf{Aux}}\left(U_\mathcal{I}^\dagger X U_\mathcal{I}\right).$$

Since we focus on Haar isometries in this work, we'll choose the distribution $\mu_\mathcal{I}$ to be Haar random conditioned on being consistent with $\mathcal{I}$. Formally, we have the following definition.

Definition 5 (Inverse of Isometries). *Let* $\mathcal{I}$ *be an isometry from* n *qubits to* $n + m$ *qubits. The inverse of* $\mathcal{I}$ *is a quantum channel from* $n + m$ *qubits to* n *qubits defined to be*

$$\mathcal{I}^{-1}(X) := \underset{U \leftarrow \mathscr{H}_{n+m}|_\mathcal{I}}{\mathbb{E}} \mathrm{Tr}_{\mathsf{Aux}}\left(U^\dagger X U\right),$$

for any $X \in \mathcal{L}(\mathbb{C}^{2^{n+m}})$, *where register* Aux *refers to the last* m *qubits and* $\mathscr{H}_{n+m}|_\mathcal{I}$ *denotes the Haar measure over* $(n + m)$*-qubit unitaries* U *conditioned on* $U|\psi\rangle|0^m\rangle_{\mathsf{Aux}} = \mathcal{I}|\psi\rangle$ *for any* $|\psi\rangle \in \mathcal{S}\left(\mathbb{C}^{2^n}\right)$.

---

[17] The readers should not confuse $\mathcal{I}^\dagger$, the conjugate transpose of $\mathcal{I}$, with the channel $\mathcal{I}^{-1}$.

The inverse of a Haar isometry satisfies the following:

Fact 7. *Let $\mathcal{I}$ be a Haar isometry from n qubits to $n + m$ qubits. Then the joint distribution of $(\mathcal{I}, \mathcal{I}^{-1})$ is identically distributed to the following procedures: (1) Sample $U \leftarrow \mathscr{H}_{n+m}$. (2) Define $\mathcal{I}$ to be the first 2^n columns of U. That is, $\mathcal{I}$ satisfies $\mathcal{I}|\psi\rangle = U|\psi\rangle|0^m\rangle_{\mathsf{Aux}}$ for any $|\psi\rangle \in \mathcal{S}\left(\mathbb{C}^{2^n}\right)$. (3) Define $\mathcal{I}^{-1}(X) := \mathrm{Tr}_{\mathsf{Aux}}(U^\dagger X U)$.*

Strong Invertible Adaptive PRI. In order to achieve more applications, we define the following stronger security definition in which the adversary is given the inversion oracle.

Definition 6 (Strong Invertible Adaptive Pseudorandom Isometry). $\mathsf{PRI} = \{F_\lambda\}_{\lambda \in \mathbb{N}}$ *is a strong invertible $(n, n + m)$-pseudorandom isometry if it satisfies the following conditions for every $\lambda \in \mathbb{N}$:*

- *For every $k \in \{0,1\}^\lambda$, $F(k, \cdot)$ is a QPT algorithm such that it is functionally equivalent to $\mathcal{I}_k$, where $\mathcal{I}_k$ is an isometry that maps n qubits to $n + m$ qubits.*
- *For every $k \in \{0,1\}^\lambda$, $\mathsf{Inv}(k, \cdot)$ is a QPT algorithm such that it is functionally equivalent to $\mathcal{I}_k^{-1}$, where $\mathcal{I}_k^{-1}$ is the inverse of $\mathcal{I}_k$ (Definition 5) that maps $n + m$ qubits to n qubits.*
- *For any polynomial $t = \mathsf{poly}(\lambda)$, any QPT distinguisher $\mathcal{A}$ making a total of t queries to the oracles, the following holds:*

$$\left| \Pr_{k \leftarrow \{0,1\}^\lambda} \left[\mathcal{A}^{F(k,\cdot), \mathsf{Inv}(k,\cdot)} = 1 \right] - \Pr_{\mathcal{I} \leftarrow \mathscr{H}_{n,n+m}} \left[\mathcal{A}^{\mathcal{I}(\cdot), \mathcal{I}^{-1}(\cdot)} = 1 \right] \right| \leq \mathsf{negl}(\lambda).$$

3   Construction

Let $m(\cdot), n(\cdot)$ be polynomials. Let $p = p(\lambda)$ be a λ-bit integer. Let $\lambda = 2\lambda_1$. We use the following tools in the construction of PRI.

- $f : \{0,1\}^{\lambda_1} \times \{0,1\}^{n(\lambda_1)+m(\lambda_1)} \to \mathbb{Z}_p$ is a quantum-query secure pseudorandom function (QPRF).
- $g : \{0,1\}^{\lambda_1} \times \{0,1\}^{n(\lambda_1)+m(\lambda_1)} \to \{0,1\}^{n(\lambda_1)+m(\lambda_1)}$ is a quantum-query secure pseudorandom permutation (QPRP).

We present the construction of psuedorandom isometry $\{F_\lambda\}_{\lambda \in \mathbb{N}}$ in Fig. 1. Note that the construction presented is functionally equivalent to an isometry even though it performs a partial trace.

3.1   Main Results

Our construction is secure against inputs of the form: (1) distinct type state, (2) multiple copies of the same pure state, (3) i.i.d. Haar states. We state the formal theorem below:

On input a key $k \in \{0,1\}^\lambda$ and an n-qubit register $\mathbf{X}$. We define the operation of $F_\lambda(k, \cdot)$ as follows.
- Parse the key k as $k_1 \| k_2$, where $k_1 \in \{0,1\}^{\lambda_1}$ is a QPRF key and $k_2 \in \{0,1\}^{\lambda_1}$ is a QPRP key.
- Append an m-qubit register $\mathbf{Z}$ initalized with $|0^m\rangle_{\mathbf{Z}}$ to register $\mathbf{X}$.
- Apply $H^{\otimes m}$ to register $\mathbf{Z}$.
- Apply $O_{f_{k_1}}$ to registers $\mathbf{X}$ and $\mathbf{Z}$.
- Apply $O_{g_{k_2}}$ to registers $\mathbf{X}$ and $\mathbf{Z}$.

Explicitly, $F_\lambda(k, \cdot)$ maps the basis vector $|x\rangle_{\mathbf{X}}$ to

$$\frac{1}{\sqrt{2^m}} \sum_{z \in \{0,1\}^m} \omega_p^{f(k_1, x\|z)} |g(k_2, x\|z)\rangle_{\mathbf{XZ}} .$$

Fig. 1. Description of F_λ.

Theorem 8 (Main Theorem). *Let* $n, m, s, t, \ell, q = \mathsf{poly}(\lambda)$. *Let* $\mathcal{Q}_{n,t,s,\ell,\lambda}^{(\mathsf{distinct})}$, $\mathcal{Q}_{n,q,\ell,\lambda}^{(\mathsf{Haar})}$ *and* $\mathcal{Q}_{n,q,\ell,\lambda}^{(\mathsf{Single})}$ *be as defined in Sect. 2. then, assuming the existence of post-quantum one-way functions, the construction of* PRI *given in Fig. 1 is* $\mathcal{Q}$-*secure for* $\mathcal{Q} \in \left\{ \mathcal{Q}_{n,t,s,\ell,\lambda}^{(\mathsf{distinct})}, \mathcal{Q}_{n,q,\ell,\lambda}^{(\mathsf{Haar})}, \mathcal{Q}_{n,q,\ell,\lambda}^{(\mathsf{Single})} \right\}$.

Although we are not able to prove stronger security of our construction, we observe that our construction naturally mimics the steps of sampling a Haar isometry by truncating columns of a Haar unitary. We have the following conjecture.

Conjecture 2. Assuming the existence of post-quantum one-way functions, the construction of PRI given in Fig. 1 is a strong invertible adaptive PRI (Definition 6)

4   Applications

We explore the cryptographic applications of pseudorandom isometries. Notably, some applications in this section only require invertible $\mathcal{Q}$-secure (Definition 4), for classes of $\mathcal{Q}$ which can be initiated by post-quantum one-way functions, as we showed in Sect. 3. In Sect. 4.2, we present quantum message authentication codes. In Sect. 4.3, we present length extension theorems.

4.1   PRI Implies PRSG and PRFSG

Theorem 9 (PRI implies PRSG and PRFSG). *Assuming* $(n, n + m)$-$\mathcal{Q}_{\mathsf{Comp}}$-*pseudorandom isometries exist, there exist an* $(n + m)$-PRSG *and a selectively-secure* $(n, n + m)$-PRFSG.

4.2   Quantum Message Authentication Codes

The scheme of authenticating *quantum messages* was first studied by Barnum et al. [BCG+02] in which they considered *one-time private-key* authentication schemes. The definition in [BCG+02] is generalized in the following works [DNS12, GYZ17]. In particular, Garg, Yuen, and Zhandry [GYZ17] defined the notion of *total authentication*, which is tailored for one-time (information-theoretic) security. They showed that total authentication implies unforgeability (in certain settings[18]) and *key reusability* — conditioned on successful verification of an authentication scheme that satisfies total authentication, the key can be reused by the honest parties. Moreover, they constructed a total-authenticating scheme from unitary 8-designs. Later, the works of [Por17, AM17] independently improved the construction by using only unitary 2-designs to achieve total authentication.

In the fully classical setting, many-time security of an authentication scheme is defined via *unforgeability* — no efficient adversary can forge an un-queried message-tag pair. A message authentication code (MAC) is a common primitive that satisfies the desired properties. However, consider MACs for classical messages: when the adversary is allowed to query the signing oracle in superposition [BZ13, AMRS20], defining the *freshness* of the forgery is already nontrivial. For quantum message authentication schemes, it is well-known that authentication implies encryption [BCG+02]. Furthermore, due to the quantum nature of no-cloning and entanglement, it is challenging to define a general many-time security notion [AGM18, AGM21]. Nevertheless, we consider a strict version of MACs for quantum messages in this subsection. We'll focus on several weak yet nontrivial notions of unforgeability and show how to achieve them using PRIs.

Syntax. A message authentication codes (MAC) scheme for quantum messages of length $n(\lambda)$ is a triple of algorithms (Setup, Sign, Ver).

- Setup(1^λ): on input the security parameter λ, output a key $k \leftarrow \{0,1\}^\lambda$.
- Sign($k, |\psi\rangle$): on input $k \in \{0,1\}^\lambda$ and a quantum message $|\psi\rangle \in \mathcal{S}\left(\mathbb{C}^{2^n}\right)$, output a quantum tag[19] $|\phi\rangle \in \mathcal{S}\left(\mathbb{C}^{2^s}\right)$ where $s(\lambda) = \mathsf{poly}(\lambda)$ is the tag length.
- Ver($k, |\phi\rangle$): on input $k \in \{0,1\}^\lambda$ and a quantum tag $|\phi\rangle \in \mathcal{S}\left(\mathbb{C}^{2^s}\right)$, output a mixed quantum state $\rho \in \mathcal{D}(\mathbb{C}^{2^n})$.

Definition 7 (Correctness). *There exists a negligible function $\varepsilon(\cdot)$ such that for every $\lambda \in \mathbb{N}$, $k \in \{0,1\}^\lambda$, and quantum message $|\psi\rangle \in \mathcal{S}\left(\mathbb{C}^{2^n}\right)$,*

$$\mathsf{TD}(\mathsf{Ver}(k, \mathsf{Sign}(k, |\psi\rangle)), |\psi\rangle\langle\psi|) \leq \varepsilon(\lambda).$$

---

[18] In more detail, they show total authentication implies unforgeability for MACs for classical messages with security against a single superposition message query.

[19] We emphasize that here we explicitly require the tag to be a pure state. We can relax this condition to allow for the signature algorithm to output a state that is close to a pure state without changing the notion much.

Security Definitions. Defining security for MACs for quantum states is quite challenging, as discussed in prior works, notably in [AGM18]. Nonetheless, our goal is to present some reasonable, although restrictive, definitions of MACs for quantum states whose feasibility can be established based on the existence of pseudorandom isometries. We believe that our results shed light on the interesting connection between pseudorandom isometries and MACs for quantum states and we leave the exploration of presenting the most general definition of MACs for quantum states (which in our eyes is an interesting research direction by itself!) for future works.

When the adversary is only asked to output a single copy of the (quantum) forgery, it is unclear how to achieve negligible security error. For example, if the verification is done by simply applying a SWAP test[20], then the success probability of the forger is at least $1/2$. In the following, we introduce several notions capturing unforgeability. First, in order to boost security, a straightforward way is to simply ask the adversary to send $t = \mathsf{poly}(\lambda)$ copies of the forgery message and tag.

Definition 8 (Many-Copies-Unforgeability). *Let* $t = \mathsf{poly}(\lambda)$. *For every polynomial* $q(\cdot)$ *and every non-uniform QPT adversary, there exists a function* $\varepsilon(\cdot)$ *such that for sufficiently large* $\lambda \in \mathbb{N}$, *the adversary wins with probability at most* $\varepsilon(\lambda)$ *in the following security game:*

1. *Challenger samples* $k \leftarrow \{0,1\}^\lambda$.
2. *The adversary sends* $|\psi_1\rangle, \ldots, |\psi_q\rangle \in \mathcal{S}\left(\mathbb{C}^{2^n}\right)$ *and receives* $\mathsf{Sign}(k, |\psi_i\rangle)$ *for* $i = 1, \ldots, q$.
3. *The adversary outputs* $(|\psi^*\rangle \otimes |\phi^*\rangle)^{\otimes t}$ *where* $|\psi^*\rangle \in \mathcal{S}\left(\mathbb{C}^{2^n}\right)$ *is orthogonal to* $|\psi_i\rangle$ *for* $i = 1, \ldots, q$.
4. *Challenger runs* $\mathsf{SwapTest}(|\psi^*\rangle\langle\psi^*|, \mathsf{Ver}(k, |\phi^*\rangle))$ t *times in parallel. The adversary wins if and only if every SWAP test outputs 1.*

Remark 2. We note that, in general, the forgery message and the tag could be entangled. Here, we focus on a restricted case in which the message and tag are required to be a product state. We leave the exploration of stronger security notions for future works.

In some cases, it is unsatisfactory to ask the adversary to output multiple copies of the forgery tag due to the no-cloning theorem and in this case, we can consider the following definition in which the adversary needs to output multiple copies of the forgery message but only a single copy of the forgery tag. The winning condition of the adversary is defined by passing the generalized SWAP test — called the *permutation test* [BBD+97, KNY08, GHMW15, BS20a].

Lemma 1 (Permutation Test). *The permutation test is an efficient quantum circuit* $\mathsf{PermTest}$ *that takes as input* $\rho \in \mathcal{D}((\mathbb{C}^d)^{\otimes t})$, *outputs 1 with probability* $p := \mathrm{Tr}(\Pi_{\mathsf{sym}}^{d,t}\rho)$, *and outputs 0 with probability* $1 - p$.

---

[20] The SWAP test is an efficient quantum circuit that takes as input two density matrices ρ, σ of the same dimension and output 1 with probability $\frac{1+\mathrm{Tr}(\rho\sigma)}{2}$.

Definition 9 ((PermTest, t, ε)-unforgeability). *For every polynomial $q(\cdot)$ and every non-uniform QPT adversary, there exists a function $\varepsilon(\cdot)$ such that for sufficiently large $\lambda \in \mathbb{N}$, the adversary wins with probability at most $\varepsilon(\lambda)$ in the following security game:*

1. *Challenger samples $k \leftarrow \{0,1\}^{\lambda}$.*
2. *The adversary sends $|\psi_1\rangle, \ldots, |\psi_q\rangle \in \mathcal{S}\left(\mathbb{C}^{2^n}\right)$ and receives $\mathsf{Sign}(k, |\psi_i\rangle)$ for $i = 1, \ldots, q$.*
3. *The adversary outputs $|\psi^*\rangle^{\otimes t} \otimes |\phi^*\rangle$ where $|\psi^*\rangle \in \mathcal{S}\left(\mathbb{C}^{2^n}\right)$ and is orthogonal to $|\psi_i\rangle$ for $i = 1, \ldots, q$.*
4. *The adversary wins if $\mathsf{PermTest}(|\psi^*\rangle\langle\psi^*|^{\otimes t} \otimes \mathsf{Ver}(k, |\phi^*\rangle)) = 1$.*

Finally, suppose $\mathsf{Sign}(k, \cdot)$ is an isometry for every $k \in \{0,1\}^{\lambda}$. We consider another definition in which we ask the adversary to send the classical description of the quantum circuit that generates the forgery message and only one copy of the corresponding tag.

Definition 10 (Uncompute-Unforgeability). *For every polynomial $q(\cdot)$ and every non-uniform QPT adversary, there exists a negligible function $\varepsilon(\cdot)$ such that for every $\lambda \in \mathbb{N}$, the adversary wins with probability at most $\varepsilon(\lambda)$ in the following security game:*

1. *Challenger samples $k \leftarrow \{0,1\}^{\lambda}$.*
2. *The adversary sends $|\psi_1\rangle, \ldots, |\psi_q\rangle \in \mathcal{S}\left(\mathbb{C}^{2^n}\right)$ and receives $\mathsf{Sign}(k, |\psi_i\rangle)$ for $i = 1, \ldots, q$.*
3. *The adversary outputs a pair $(C, |\phi^*\rangle)$ where C is the classical description of a quantum circuit containing no measurements such that $C|0^n\rangle$ is orthogonal to $|\psi_i\rangle$ for $i = 1, \ldots, q$.*
4. *Challenger applies $C^{\dagger}\mathsf{Ver}(k, \cdot)$ on $|\phi^*\rangle$ and performs a measurement on all qubits in the computational basis. The adversary wins if and only if the measurement outcome is 0^n.*

Let $\mathsf{PRI} = \{F_{\lambda}\}_{\lambda \in \mathbb{N}}$ be a strong invertible adaptive $(n, n+m)$-PRI (Definition 6) where $n(\cdot), m(\cdot)$ are polynomials. We construct a MAC for quantum messages from PRI.

Construction 10 (MAC for quantum messages).

1. $\mathsf{Sign}(k, |\psi\rangle)$: *on input $k \in \{0,1\}^{\lambda}$ and a message $|\psi\rangle \in \mathcal{S}\left(\mathbb{C}^{2^n}\right)$, output $F_{\lambda}(k, |\psi\rangle) \in \mathcal{S}\left(\mathbb{C}^{2^{m+n}}\right)$.*

2. $\mathsf{Ver}(k, |\phi\rangle)$: *on input $k \in \{0,1\}^{\lambda}$ and a tag $|\phi\rangle \in \mathcal{S}\left(\mathbb{C}^{2^{m+n}}\right)$, output $\mathsf{Inv}(k, |\phi\rangle)$.*

The correctness of Construction 10 follows from the invertibility of PRI.

Theorem 11. *For every $t \in \mathbb{N}$, Construction 10 satisfies (PermTest, t, $O(1/t)$)-unforgeability.*

Theorem 12. *Construction 10 satisfies uncompute-unforgeability.*

4.3 Length Extension of Pseudorandom States

We introduce methods to increase the *length* of pseudorandom quantum states while preserving the *number of copies*. In the classical setting, the length extension of pseudorandom strings can be accomplished by repeatedly applying PRGs. On the other hand, since pseudorandom random states are necessarily (highly) pure and entangled [JLS18, AQY22], no such method was known that would not decrease the number of copies.

Theorem 13 (Length Extension Theorem). *Assuming* $\mathcal{Q}_{\text{Haar}}$*-secure pseudorandom isometry, mapping n qubits to $n + m$ qubits, and an n-qubit PRSG, there exists an $(n + m)$-PRSG. Similarly, assuming* $\mathcal{Q}_{\text{Haar}}$*-secure pseudorandom isometry, mapping n qubits to $n + m$ qubits, and classical-accessible selectively-secure (ℓ, n)-PRFSG, there exists a classical-accessible selectively-secure $(\ell, n + m)$-PRFSG.*

Theorem 14 (Another Length Extension Theorem). *Let $\{F_\lambda\}_{\lambda \in \mathbb{N}}$ be an $(n, n + m)$-PRI, $t = t(\lambda)$,*

$$\rho := \underset{|\theta\rangle \leftarrow \mathscr{H}_{2n}, k \in \{0,1\}^\lambda}{\mathbb{E}} \left[(I_n \otimes F_k)^{\otimes t} |\theta\rangle\langle\theta|^{\otimes t} (I_n \otimes F_k^\dagger)^{\otimes t} \right],$$

where F_k means $F_\lambda(k, \cdot)$ and I_n is the identity operator on n qubits, and

$$\sigma := \underset{|\gamma\rangle \leftarrow \mathscr{H}_{2n+m}}{\mathbb{E}} \left[|\gamma\rangle\langle\gamma|^{\otimes t} \right].$$

Then any non-uniform QPT adversary has at most $O(t! t^2 / 2^{n+m} + t^2 / 2^n)$ advantage in distinguishing ρ from σ.

Acknowledgements. We thank Fermi Ma for useful discussions.

References

[ABF+23] Aaronson, S., et al.: Quantum Pseudoentanglement (2023). arXiv:2211. 00747

[ABG+14] Akavia, A., Bogdanov, A., Guo, S., Kamath, A., Rosen, A.: Candidate weak pseudorandom functions in $AC^0 \circ Mod_2$. In: Proceedings of the 5th Conference on Innovations in Theoretical Computer Science, pp. 251–260 (2014)

[ABK+23] Arvind, R., Bharti, K., Khoo, J.Y., Koh, D.E., Kong, J.F.: A quantum tug of war between randomness and symmetries on homogeneous spaces. arXiv preprint arXiv:2309.05253 (2023)

[AE07] Ambainis, A., Emerson, J.: Quantum t-designs: t-wise independence in the quantum world. In: Twenty-Second Annual IEEE Conference on Computational Complexity (CCC'07), pp. 129–140. IEEE (2007)

[AGM18] Alagic, G., Gagliardoni, T., Majenz, C.: Unforgeable quantum encryption. In: Nielsen, J.B., Rijmen, V. (eds.) EUROCRYPT 2018. LNCS, vol. 10822, pp. 489–519. Springer, Cham (2018). https://doi.org/10.1007/978-3-319-78372-7_16

[AGM21] Alagic, G., Gagliardoni, T., Majenz, C.: Can you sign a quantum state? In: Quantum **5**, 603 (2021). https://doi.org/10.22331/q-2021-12-16-603

[AGQY22] Ananth, P., Gulati, A., Qian, L., Yuen, H.: Pseudorandom (Function-Like) quantum state generators: new definitions and applications. In: Theory of Cryptography Conference, pp. 237–265. Springer (2022). https://doi.org/10.1007/978-3-031-22318-1_9

[AM17] Alagic, G., Majenz, C.: Quantum non-malleability and authentication. In: Katz, J., Shacham, H. (eds.) CRYPTO 2017. LNCS, vol. 10402, pp. 310–341. Springer, Cham (2017). https://doi.org/10.1007/978-3-319-63715-0_11

[AMRS20] Alagic, G., Majenz, C., Russell, A., Song, F.: Quantum-access-secure message authentication via blind-unforgeability. In: Canteaut, A., Ishai, Y. (eds.) EUROCRYPT 2020. LNCS, vol. 12107, pp. 788–817. Springer, Cham (2020). https://doi.org/10.1007/978-3-030-45727-3_27

[AQY22] Ananth, P., Qian, L., Yuen, H.: Cryptography from pseudorandom quantum states. In: CRYPTO (2022)

[BBD+97] Barenco, A., Berthiaume, A., Deutsch, D., Ekert, A., Jozsa, R., Macchiavello, C.: Stabilization of quantum computations by symmetrization. SIAM J. Comput. **26**(5), 1541–1557 (1997)

[BBSS23] Behera, A., Brakerski, Z., Sattath, O., Shmueli, O.: Pseudorandomness with proof of destruction and applications. In: Cryptology ePrint Archive (2023)

[BCG+02] Barnum, H., Crépeau, C.M., Gottesman, D., Smith, A., Tapp, A.: Authentication of quantum messages. In: The 43rd Annual IEEE Symposium on Foundations of Computer Science, 2002. Proceedings, pp. 449–458. IEEE (2002)

[BCH+21] Brandão, F.G.S.L., Chemissany, W., Hunter-Jones, N., Kueng, R., Preskill, J.: Models of quantum complexity growth. PRX Quantum **2**(3), 030316 (2021)

[BFV20] Bouland, A., Fefferman, B., Vazirani, U.V.: Computational Pseudorandomness, the Wormhole Growth Paradox, and Constraints on the AdS/CFT Duality (Abstract). In: 11th Innovations in Theoretical Computer Science Conference, ITCS 2020, January 12-14, 2020, Seattle, Washington, USA, vol. 151, 63:1–63:2 (2020). https://doi.org/10.4230/LIPIcs.ITCS.2020.63

[BHH16] Brandao, F.G.S.L., Harrow, A.W., Horodecki, M.: Local random quantum circuits are approximate polynomial-designs. Commun. Math. Phys. **346**, 397–434 (2016)

[BS19] Brakerski, Z., Shmueli, O.: (Pseudo) Random quantum states with binary phase. In: Theory of Cryptography - 17th International Conference, TCC 2019, Nuremberg, Germany, December 1-5, 2019, Proceedings, Part I, vol. 11891, pp. 229–250 (2019). https://doi.org/10.1007/978-3-030-36030-6_10

[BS20a] Behera, A., Sattath, O.: Almost public quantum coins. arXiv preprint arXiv:2002.12438 (2020)

[BS20b] Brakerski, Z., Shmueli, O.: Scalable pseudorandom quantum states. In: Advances in Cryptology - CRYPTO 2020 - 40th Annual International Cryptology Conference, CRYPTO 2020, Santa Barbara, CA, USA, August 17-21, 2020, Proceedings, Part II, vol. 12171, pp. 417–440 (2020). https://doi.org/10.1007/978-3-030-56880-1_15

[BZ13] Boneh, D., Zhandry, M.: Quantum-secure message authentication codes. In: Johansson, T., Nguyen, P.Q. (eds.) EUROCRYPT 2013. LNCS, vol. 7881, pp. 592–608. Springer, Heidelberg (2013). https://doi.org/10.1007/978-3-642-38348-9_35

[DN02] Damgård, I., Nielsen, J.B.: Expanding pseudorandom functions; or: from known-plaintext security to chosen-plaintext security. In: Yung, M. (ed.) CRYPTO 2002. LNCS, vol. 2442, pp. 449–464. Springer, Heidelberg (2002). https://doi.org/10.1007/3-540-45708-9_29

[DNS12] Dupuis, F., Nielsen, J.B., Salvail, L.: Actively secure two-party evaluation of any quantum operation. In: Safavi-Naini, R., Canetti, R. (eds.) CRYPTO 2012. LNCS, vol. 7417, pp. 794–811. Springer, Heidelberg (2012). https://doi.org/10.1007/978-3-642-32009-5_46

[GHMW15] Gutoski, G., Hayden, P., Milner, K., Wilde, M.M.: Quantum interactive proofs and the complexity of separability testing. Theory Comput. 11(3), 59–103 (2015). https://doi.org/10.4086/toc.2015.v011a00310.4086/toc.2015.v011a003

[GJMZ23] Gunn, S., Ju, N., Ma, F., Zhandry, M.: Commitments to quantum states. In: Proceedings of the 55th Annual ACM Symposium on Theory of Computing, pp. 1579–1588 (2023)

[GLG+23] Gu, A., Leone, L., Ghosh, S., Eisert, J., Yelin, S., Quek, Y.: A little magic means a lot. In: arXiv preprint arXiv:2308.16228 (2023)

[GYZ17] Garg, S., Yuen, H., Zhandry, M.: New security notions and feasibility results for authentication of quantum data. In: Katz, J., Shacham, H. (eds.) CRYPTO 2017. LNCS, vol. 10402, pp. 342–371. Springer, Cham (2017). https://doi.org/10.1007/978-3-319-63715-0_12

[Har13] Harrow, A.W.: The church of the symmetric subspace. arXiv preprint arXiv:1308.6595 (2013)

[HBC+22] Huang, H.-Y., et al.: Quantum advantage in learning from experiments. Science 376(6598), 1182–1186 (2022)

[HBK23] Haug, T., Bharti, K., Koh, D.E.: Pseudorandom unitaries are neither real nor sparse nor noise-robust. arXiv preprint arXiv:2306.11677 (2023)

[JLS18] Ji, Z., Liu, Y.-K., Song, F.: Pseudorandom quantum states. In: Advances in Cryptology - CRYPTO 2018 - 38th Annual International Cryptology Conference, Santa Barbara, CA, USA, August 19-23, 2018, Proceedings, Part III. Ed. by Hovav Shacham and Alexandra Boldyreva, vol. 10993, pp. 126–152 (2018). https://doi.org/10.1007/978-3-319-96878-0_5

[KNY08] Kada, M., Nishimura, H., Yamakami, T.: The efficiency of quantum identity testing of multiple states. J. Phys. A: Math. Theor. 41(39), 395309 (2008)

[Kre21] Kretschmer, W.: Quantum pseudorandomness and classical complexity. In: 16th Conference on the Theory of Quantum Computation, Communication and Cryptography, TQC 2021, July 5-8, 2021, Virtual Conference, vol. 197, pp. 2:1–2:20 (2021). https://doi.org/10.4230/LIPIcs.TQC.2021.2

[LQS+23] Lu, C., Qin, M., Song, F., Yao, P., Zhao, M.: Quantum pseudorandom scramblers. arXiv preprint arXiv:2309.08941 (2023)

[MY22] Morimae, T., Yamakawa, T.: Quantum commitments and signatures without one-way functions. CRYPTO (2022)

[Por17] Portmann, C.: Quantum authentication with key recycling. In: Coron, J.-S., Nielsen, J.B. (eds.) EUROCRYPT 2017. LNCS, vol. 10212, pp. 339–368. Springer, Cham (2017). https://doi.org/10.1007/978-3-319-56617-7_12

[Zha12] Zhandry, M.: Secure identity-based encryption in the quantum random oracle model. cryptology ePrint archive, Paper 2012/076. https://eprint.iacr.org/2012/076 (2012)

[Zha16] Zhandry, M.: A note on quantum-secure PRPs. arXiv preprint arXiv:1611.05564 (2016)

New Limits of Provable Security and Applications to ElGamal Encryption

Sven Schäge[(✉)] [iD]

Eindhoven University of Technology, Eindhoven, Netherlands
s.schage@tue.nl

Abstract. We provide new results showing that ElGamal encryption cannot be proven CCA1-secure – a long-standing open problem in cryptography. Our result follows from a very broad, meta-reduction-based impossibility result on random self-reducible relations with efficiently rerandomizable witnesses. The techniques that we develop allow, for the first time, to provide impossibility results for very weak security notions where the challenger outputs fresh challenge statements at the end of the security game. This can be used to finally tackle encryption-type definitions that have remained elusive in the past. We show that our results have broad applicability by casting several known cryptographic setups as instances of random self-reducible and re-randomizable relations. These setups include general semi-homomorphic PKE and the large class of certified homomorphic one-way bijections. As a result, we also obtain new impossibility results for the IND-CCA1 security of the PKEs of Paillier and Damgård–Jurik, and many one-more inversion assumptions like the one-more DLOG or the one-more RSA assumption.

1 Introduction

The ElGamal public-key encryption (PKE) scheme from 1984 is, besides RSA, the most well-known asymmetric encryption system today and its importance for the development of cryptography can hardly be overestimated [19]. It is conceptually simple and, since it supports the use of elliptic curves, can provide very high efficiency. In the past, ElGamal encryption has served as a fruitful template for the development of new schemes that are based on novel mathematical structures like bilinear pairings or lattices and, via further modifications, paved the way for new powerful primitives like IBE and functional encryption. Most PKE systems that are used in practice are enhancements of the basic ElGamal scheme that additionally armor it from strong active attacks. The scheme has become so much part of the cryptographic canon, that introductory academic courses on cryptography that do not cover ElGamal are hardly imaginable.

Security Guarantees of ElGamal PKE. ElGamal is well-known to be IND-CPA secure (under the DDH assumption) which states that an attacker A who is

---

S. Schäge—The author has partially been supported by the CONFIDENTIAL6G project that is co-funded by the European Union (grant agreement ID: 101096435).

M. Joye and G. Leander (Eds.): EUROCRYPT 2024, LNCS 14654, pp. 255–285, 2024.
https://doi.org/10.1007/978-3-031-58737-5_10

given a challenge ciphertext c^* cannot distinguish if it encrypts message m_0^* or m_1^*, even if both messages have been chosen by A. Unfortunately, it turns out that without further modifications ElGamal PKE cannot fulfill the stronger, standard notion of IND-CCA2 security, where the attacker is also allowed to query a decryption oracle at any point in the security game (with the restriction that the challenge ciphertext may not be queried). Essentially this is due to the malleability of the ciphertexts in ElGamal encryption, making it possible to query a slight modification c'^* of c^* to the decryption oracle and use the answer to c'^* to find the message within c^*. This impossibility result is unconditional and there is no hope to circumvent it. However, there is another widespread but slightly weaker notion of security called lunchtime attacks or IND-CCA1 security. According to this notion, the attacker is allowed to also query the decryption oracle but only *before* she receives the challenge ciphertext. Now the above attack cannot be applied anymore since decryption queries cannot depend on c^*. For decades, the exact state of ElGamal's security against lunchtime attacks has remained unclear and, despite the theoretical and practical importance of this scheme, hardly any progress towards that goal has been made. In this paper, we provide new, major contributions to the following long-standing open question.[1]

Can ElGamal PKE be shown IND-CCA1 secure?

We answer this question negatively in a very strong sense as detailed below.

Main Result. Our result on ElGamal encryption immediately follows from two fundamental results on random self-reducible and re-randomizable relations (RRRs) that are assumed to be hard to invert. In a nutshell, an RRR consists of a special relation R that is accompanied by a set of efficient algorithms for sampling, self-reducibility of statements, and re-randomizability of witnesses. A variant of RRRs that we call strong RRR additionally provides an efficient but indirect membership test. Although (strong) RRRs have a comparatively rich structure, we show that many cryptographic setups can be captured via the notion of RRRs. Remarkably, this includes general semi-homomorphic PKE (including ElGamal, Paillier, and Damgård–Jurik PKE) where statement/witness pairs correspond to ciphertext/plaintext pairs, and certified homomorphic one-way bijections (e.g., RSA, DLOG), where statement/witness pairs correspond to output/input pairs.

In our central result, we consider a security game (Fig. 1) in which an attacker has to invert an RRR (i.e. find witnesses w^*) on a set of random challenge statements s^* (such that $(s^*, w^*) \in R$) that are specified at the *very end* of the security game. Deriving impossibility results for this challenging scenario has proven elusive in the past and our work is the first to provide an approach to this problem by exploiting the properties of RRRs. In a nutshell, our result shows that if the attacker is allowed to make $t + 1$ inversion queries, we cannot

---

[1] To provide some examples of explicit accounts on the importance of the question by well-known researchers, Yehuda Lindell calls the problem a "big open question" [27], whereas Helga Lipmaa terms it a "well-known open problem" [29].

Lunchtime Inversion (LI) Game

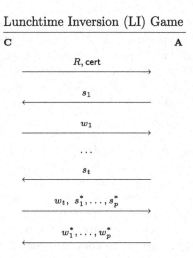

Fig. 1. Security game considered in this work. We consider a relation R with statements s and witnesses w that is used in a security game played between a challenger **C** and an attacker **A**. The certificate cert proves that R is a re-randomizable and self-reducible relation. **A** has access to t adaptive inversion queries s_i and for each query receives back w_i such that $(s_i, w_i) \in R$. For every challenge statement s_i^*, **A** must output w_i^* such that $(s_i^*, w_i^*) \in R$.

have a security reduction that is based on a security assumption that allows up to t oracle calls (we call this a t-interactive complexity assumption or tICA for short). This is in some sense *optimal* as any security game with t oracle calls could easily be proven (tautologically) secure using security assumptions that allow t oracle calls — simply by assuming the security of the security game. We prove the following results.

Theorem 1 (First Main Result, Informal). *Let* RRR *be a RRR. Let* ICA *be a secure tICA. Then, there is no* simple[2] *Turing reduction that can reduce the lunchtime security of* RRR *with $t + 1$ adaptive inversion queries to the security of* ICA.

Theorem 2 (Second Main Result, Informal). *Let* RRR *be a strong RRR. Let* ICA *be a secure tICA. Then, there is no (general) Turing reduction that, while creating up to u attacker instances, can reduce the lunchtime security of* RRR *with $t + u$ adaptive inversion queries to the security of* ICA.

One mere corollary of this result is that the number of calls to an inversion oracle granted to the attacker induces a complexity hierarchy of problems.[3] Transferred to semi-homomorphic PKE this says that its t-OW-CCA1 security (OW-CCA1 security when granted up to t decryption queries) cannot be based on its $(t-1)$-OW-CCA1 security. For $t = 1$ this already separates

---

[2] Simple reductions call the attacker only once and do not rewind.
[3] For a more general discussion of both results let us for simplicity consider $u = 1$ in the following.

IND-CPA security from 1-OW-CCA1 security, i.e. OW-CCA1 security with only one-time access to a decryption oracle. However, we stress that our result on semi-homomorphic PKE is much more general than that. Since OW-CCA1 security is weaker than IND-CCA1 security, our result shows that semi-homomorphic PKE, and in particular ElGamal PKE, cannot be shown $(t+1)$-IND-CCA1 under *any* tICA under simple reductions. To obtain our results we have to overcome several challenges.

Challenge 1: Passing the Barrier towards Weaker Security Notions. We emphasize that, in general, the security game that we examine in our main impossibility result as depicted in Fig. 1 considers an extremely weak security notion. However, for our purpose, this is of course advantageous as our impossibility result transfers to any security notion that is strictly stronger. Previous impossibility results that use related techniques already considered remarkably weak security notions. The weakest of them have in common that they formulate a so-called one-more inversion problem, where the attacker is given $t + 1$ challenge statements at the beginning of the security game together with subsequent t-time access to an inversion oracle [34]. However, our security notion is even weaker than that, and in fact, passing this barrier towards a weaker security notion has been the main obstacle to achieving further progress. In the notion that we consider, the attacker still has t-time access to an inversion oracle. However, the attacker's challenge statements are only decided on at the end of the security game by the challenger. In particular, all queries to the inversion oracle are thus independent of the final statement. For this challenging case, we show how to derive impossibility results based on the meta-reduction approach when dealing with efficiently random self-reducible and re-randomizable relations.

Proof Framework. Our result is obtained using the meta-reduction technique that was introduced by Boneh and Venkatesan [6]. The proof is by contradiction, where we start to simply assume that an appropriate PPT reduction B exists. According to the meta-reduction methodology, we first specify an ideal attacker that breaks the security game (with unbounded resources). Since the attacker A is successful, the reduction B must be able to use it to break some complexity assumption C with only a polynomial overhead in running time and an at most polynomial loss of success probability. In the second step, we show how to efficiently simulate the attacker toward the reduction. To this end, we define an efficient meta-reduction M that runs and controls the reduction algorithm. Crucially, we have to show that from B's perspective, M behaves indistinguishably from A. This shows that the combination of B and M breaks the underlying security assumption C efficiently, thus contradicting the starting assumption. From a more abstract angle, this approach shows that the reduction, if it exists, has already the power to break the security assumption itself.

Proof Idea. Our result holds for RRRs, relations that are random self-reducible and re-randomizable. On a high level, we intuitively exploit that any output of the reduction, and in particular any challenge statement, can be blinded and then relayed back to the reduction B as a query – without B noticing. More concretely, our notion of random self-reducibility guarantees that we can generate from any challenge statement s_i^* a derived statement $s_i'^*$ such that, crucially, the reduction has no way of recognizing that $s_i'^*$ was constructed from s_i^*. (Recall that to transfer the following discussion to the ElGamal setting, we simply can identify statements s with ciphertexts c and witnesses w with plaintexts m.) Next, the meta-reduction *rewinds* the reduction to some earlier point in the execution and sends $s_i'^*$ as an inversion query to B which in turn responds with the corresponding witness $w_i'^*$. Since the relation is random self-reducible, the meta-reduction can compute from $w_i'^*$ a challenge witness $w_i''^*$ for s_i^*. However, as $w_i'^*$ has been computed by B, the challenge witness $w_i''^*$ still might depend (in a way recognizable by the reduction) on $w_i'^*$. This is where we re-randomize $w_i''^*$ to obtain the final response w_i^* to s_i^*. We perform this last step since, similarly to before, the meta-reduction needs to make sure that the reduction is not able to recognize that the final output w_i^* has been computed from one of its responses. Here we exploit the properties of the re-randomization process, which state that for any witness pair, the output distributions of the re-randomization process are statistically close.

Certified Relations. So far, we have described how to ensure that the reduction cannot recognize any dependencies between the challenge statement/witness pair and the queried pairs of the relation. However, there is another important but rather subtle issue that we need to take care of. To closely model practice, we have included in our security model that the challenger sends the description of the relation to the attacker in the first step. Intuitively this may, for example, correspond to a public key in a cryptographic system along with the public system parameters. To make our technique work, the attacker needs to be able to efficiently verify that the so-specified relation is indeed an RRR. In practice, there might be several ways to ensure this. Most of the relations that we give as examples will allow to immediately verify the properties of the RRR. However, we may also consider relations where this is not possible and where instead relation descriptions are accompanied by appropriate (statistically or perfectly sound, non-interactive) proofs. Furthermore, we may consider trusted third parties that provide both parties with the relation such that the RRR properties are always fulfilled. This issue is indeed very subtle and in early works on related meta-reductions has not been addressed explicitly [26].

First Result: Exploiting RRRs. We present two main results. These results depend on whether the attacker may efficiently implement an (indirect) algorithm for deciding for given (s, w) if we have $(s, w) \in R$ or not. The first case assumes that no such algorithm exists. Our result for this case considers a more general relation type but achieves a weaker impossibility result. In particular, the impossibility result restricts the class of considered reductions considerably and only works for what is commonly called simple reductions where the reduction runs the attacker a single time without rewinding. Still, we believe that this rules out a very widespread type of reduction in cryptography. However, as we show, it becomes clear that if we allow the reduction to rewind the attacker even only once then this strategy becomes useless immediately. In a nutshell, the reason is that the reduction can use a simple strategy to distinguish the ideal attacker from the meta-reduction in case it can rewind the attacker, see Sect. 10.

Second Result: Exploiting Strong RRRs. In the second case, the RRR additionally admits an efficient algorithm called RSRTest that, given witness w, checks whether $(s, w) \in R$ where, importantly, s has in turn been derived from some given statement s^* using random coins r. We call such a relation a strong RRR. Intuitively, this algorithm can work as a weak form of membership test for values s that have been crafted in some specific way while having access to all the information that was used in the process of constructing s. (We stress that this does not constitute a direct, offline membership tester for R.)

Challenge 2: Dealing with Arbitrary Reductions. In contrast to before, our second main result rules out general (non-uniform) reductions. In this setting, we additionally have to deal with rewinding reductions that concurrently execute several instances of the attacker. In general, this is known to considerably complicate the analysis of impossibility results based on meta-reductions. And indeed, in our proof, we have to address several technical challenges.

One of these challenges is to ensure that a rewinding reduction cannot obtain more information from the meta-reduction than from the ideal attacker, for example by rewinding the attacker and answering a query once again, but this time with a distinct response. To this end, we extend recent techniques by [34] and [30] to guarantee that the meta-reduction essentially behaves deterministically overall but independent of the concrete witnesses received as long as they are correct.

Another challenge is to avoid exponential blow-ups in the simulation time when dealing with rewinding reductions that execute several, u, attackers concurrently. To this end, we utilize some of the technical tools that were developed in [34] and which were in turn inspired by a line of research on resettable zero-knowledge [9,10,15,35,38]. However, our strategy fundamentally deviates from [34] and rather follows [30]. In particular, we do not describe a recursive rewinding strategy to deal with reductions that execute several attackers concurrently. Arguably, this makes our exposition more accessible since we do not have to formalize concepts like slots. At the same time, we obtain a result that is *concrete*. More precisely, let t' be the number of queries granted in the lunchtime inversion game and t be the number of queries in the security game of the interactive complexity assumption. Previous works like [34,41] require that the attacker makes $t' = \omega(\kappa + t + 1)$ queries for security parameter κ while requiring an upper bound on the number of overall queries M exchanged between the reduction and the attacker. Of course, bounding M implicitly also bounds u, the number of attacker instances created by the reduction. In contrast, our result solely requires an upper bound on the number of instances u created by the reduction while concretely assuming $t' = u + t$. For reductions that call a single attacker ($u = 1$), this gives an optimal bound $t' = t + 1$, since for $t' \leq t$ we cannot hope to obtain a separation result from general interactive complexity assumptions with t queries.

Challenge 3: Casting Semi-Homomorphic PKE as a Strong RRR. To rule out general reductions via our second and main result, we also show how to cast ElGamal PKE as a strong RRR. Essentially this translates to an attacker that can check if the responses to inversion (decryption) queries are correct, although statement/witness pairs are in general not efficiently recognizable! This task is considerably more complicated than for mere RRRs and requires novel additional techniques. Solving this problem for general (semi-)homomorphic PKE is one of our main contributions.

Additional Encryption of MACed Plaintext. On a high level, we approach this problem by defining a strong RRR where statements consist of pairs of cipher-texts and witnesses of pairs of plaintexts. It is now possible to prepare pairs of ciphertexts such that the first one contains some message m while the second ciphertext contains a tag on m that is computed with a homomorphic MAC (under some freshly drawn MAC key) featuring statistical security (implemented as a pairwise-independent hash function). Since the MAC is homomorphic, this can be done even if the plaintext in the first ciphertext is unknown. Using this approach the attacker can check whether the reduction provides correct responses to the queries even for unknown ciphertexts. This is critical when relaying challenge statements back to the reduction in the presence of reductions that can rewind the attacker. Our final argument will show that when instantiating the lunchtime security game for RRRs with this strong RRR we end up in a very weak security game for (semi-homomorphic) PKE termed Paired OW-CCA1 that is (strictly) weaker than the OW-CCA1 security game. In particular, the main difference is that the Paired OW-CCA1 security game is less adaptive since *pairs* of ciphertexts are queried to the decryption oracle (which in turn responds with the corresponding plaintext pairs). On the one hand, this makes our second impossibility result more general as we rely on a weaker security game. However, relying on strong RRRs also influences our bounds for PKE quantitatively, increasing the number of allowed decryption queries overall from $t + u$ to $2t + 2u$:

Corollary 1. *Let* PKE *be a semi-homomorphic PKE. Let* ICA *be a tICA. Then, there is no (general) Turing reduction that, while creating at most u instances of the attacker, can reduce the Paired OW-CCA1 security of* PKE *with $2t + 2u$ decryption queries to the security of* ICA.

Broad Applicability: Certified Homomorphic One-Way Bijections and Semi-Homomorphic PKE. Our impossibility results are very general. The first application of our main theorems is to general semi-homomorphic PKE. This not only includes ElGamal PKE, but also the well-known public-key encryption system by Paillier and its generalization by Damgård–Jurik. To underline the broad applicability of our results further, we single out another practically important application that relies on certified homomorphic one-way bijections (CHOWB) like discrete exponentiation or the RSA permutation. It is not hard to show that these functions immediately give rise to suitable strong RRRs and our result applies. Since CHOWBs are so common in (asymmetric) cryptography, our result has a plethora of interesting applications (for example in the realm of one-more inversion assumptions, here improving on some existing impossibility results).

Scope and Interpretation. Our work provides fundamental impossibility results in the standard model under a very liberal notion of reduction where the only restrictions are i) that the reduction treats inefficient attackers in a black-box way (Turing reduction) and ii) that the number of queries allowed in the security assumption is strictly less than the number of queries in the security game. The latter condition seems necessary to rule out tautological results. The former condition states that our result does not exclude reductions that depend on the attacker. However we stress that, although there has been considerable progress in recent years, it seems that current techniques for general non-black box reductions are still not able to tackle this problem without major breakthroughs. At the same time, we note that there are several arguments for considering reductions that use attackers in a black-box sense as more natural — and in the context of security reductions even semantically more meaningful. One such argument that was for example invoked by Pass [34] is that such reductions will also work against attackers where parts of it are hard to be transformed into an explicit formal description, for example, if they consist of combinations of algorithms and humans. We emphasize that our result captures constructions that can rely on the underlying building block in a non-black-box manner (in contrast to, for example, most oracle separation techniques and idealized models like generic groups). Moreover, the reduction may also use the security assumptions in a non-black-box way. The only requirement that we have is that the reduction treats the attacker as black-box. In terms of the fine-grained hierarchy developed in [3], a refined version of [37], this corresponds to a so-called NBN reduction. We also emphasize that, as [3] have pointed out, if we only consider efficient attackers then knowledge of the code of the adversary does not lend additional power to the reduction (i.e. NBNa-type reductions exist iff NNNa-type do). So our result in fact only requires that *inefficient* attackers are treated in a black-box way by the reduction. This gives a somewhat complete picture since it is well-known that ElGamal can be proven CCA1 secure under some non-interactive assumption in idealized models like the algebraic group model (AGM) where the reduction also has access to the attacker's internal representation of group elements as shown in [22]. (In the AGM, essentially *all* algorithms are assumed to (i) create new group elements X only via the application of the group operation to some fixed base B of group elements and (ii) always also output the internal representation of X with respect to B.) We note that in [22], the power to access the internal representation of *the attacker* specifically seems to be the main leverage towards obtaining a security proof. Requiring access to the internal representation of the *reduction only* in contrast yields an impossibility result under non-interactive security assumptions (for ElGamal KEM) [24].

Take-Home Message on ElGamal PKE. Conceptually, our arguments heavily exploit the random self-reducibility of ciphertexts in ElGamal PKE. In a sense, random self-reducibility can be viewed as a form of perfect malleability. In fact, it is so strong that no party, including the reduction, is able to recognize the original ciphertext given the derived one. Thus, one way to view our results on ElGamal is that:

While the malleability of the ciphertexts shows that ElGamal PKE is not IND-CCA2 secure, its "perfect" malleability shows its lack of provable IND-CCA1 security.

2   Related Work and Overview

ElGamal PKE [19] has been invented in 1984 and can be regarded as a non-interactive twist of the famous 1976 Diffie–Hellman protocol [16], where one of the exchanged public keys is made static. In particular, it is the first PKE scheme based on discrete-logarithm-type assumptions. Since then, many results have used or extended this scheme. Some important milestone results are the Cramer–Shoup encryption scheme that can be proven IND-CCA secure in the standard model [13], and the Boneh–Franklin scheme, the first identity-based encryption system in bilinear groups [5]. Meta-reductions have been introduced by Boneh and Venkatesan [6] in 1998 and since then have proven a flexible and powerful technique for deriving strong impossibility results besides oracle separation. In the standard model, previous works have used meta-reductions mostly to derive impossibility or efficiency results for concrete primitives like signatures schemes [4,17,18,20,21,23,32,39], and encryption systems [33]. Starting with the seminal work of Coron [12], many recent works like [2,25,26,30] use meta-reductions to prove bounds on the (non-exponential) security loss of cryptographic constructions for one-more-forgery type problems. Other results like [7,8] use meta-reductions to derive relationships among cryptographic one-more type problems. Probably closest to ours is the seminal work of Pass that showed a very general impossibility result on one-more inversion problems [34] with unique witnesses. As mentioned before, one of our main novelties is that by focusing on RRRs and a new simulation approach, we can provide results for a much weaker security notion that could not be covered by the previous techniques. In this way, our result is somewhat incomparable to [34] as it at the same time increases and decreases in generality albeit in distinct directions (since our security games are weaker but we have more restrictions on the relations by requiring them to be random self-reducible as well). Besides the already mentioned differences, our result provides several technical improvements that have not been considered in [34], like the broad treatment of re-randomizable relations via new and general notions. Finally, we point out that [34] does only hold for recognizable relations. Intuitively, this means that it requires the existence of Strong RRRs with explicit membership tests, to begin with. This makes it in general impossible to apply it to classical encryption-type definitions for probabilistic encryption where challenges correspond to ciphertexts and witnesses to plaintexts since the ability to recognize valid ciphertext/plaintext pairs could easily be used to simply break (even) IND-CPA security. Two papers have specifically worked on the impossibility of proving ElGamal PKE IND-CCA1 secure [29, 40]. However, they both relate tICAs to ElGamal with t decryption queries. As stated, this may allow for tautological results:

- The result in [29] relates ElGamal PKE to DDH/CDH type assumptions. It shows a reduction from the security of ElGamal PKE with t decryption queries to a tICA. And indeed, the author himself regards this as a "tautology", "which is mainly useful to simplify further results".
- Similarly to this, [40] relates the OW-CCA1 security of ElGamal PKE with t decryption queries to a tICA called DTCDHA (or a combination of a weaker tICA called DTDLA and a knowledge type assumption).

Finally, we stress that the meta-reduction framework has recently been extended in several directions. These extensions are typically quite generic such that they can often be applied to many works that use a similar meta-reduction technique. Some important stepping stones are the extension of the meta-reduction framework to rule out so-called memory-tight reduction as initiated in [1], or the application of the meta-reduction technique to non-uniform reductions [11].

3   Preliminaries

Relations. We use κ to denote the security parameter. Let S and W be sets and assume that there are efficient membership tests to check whether $s \in S$ and $w \in W$. We call S the set of statements and W the set of witnesses. Assume we have a relation $R \subseteq S \times W$. For any $s \in S$ let $W_s := \{w | (s, w) \in R\} \subseteq W$ be the *witness set* of s. Furthermore, we say that $s \in S$ has $t \in \mathbb{N}$ witnesses if $|W_s| = t$. If for a relation R we have that any statement $s \in S$ has at least one witness, we call it total. For simplicity, we will in the following only be interested in total relations. Moreover, we say that a relation is unique if for all statements s we have $|W_s| \leq 1$. We will use $[1; \ell]$ for $\ell \in \mathbb{N}$ to denote the set of natural numbers $1, \ldots, \ell$ and $[\ell]$ as a shorthand for $[1; \ell]$. In the following, we will always be interested in relations with superpolynomial statement set $|S|$.

Algorithms for Relations. We use $y = A(x; r)$ to denote a deterministic algorithm A that takes as input x and randomness r (for $r \in D = \{0, 1\}^d$ with some polynomial $d = d(\kappa)$) to compute output y. Equally, we may make the random coins implicit, view A as a probabilistic algorithm, and simply write $y \leftarrow A(x)$ assuming that A is provided with uniformly random $r \in D$. In the following, we will for simplicity assume that every randomized algorithm uses random coins in $D = \{0, 1\}^d$ for some appropriate polynomial d unless specified explicitly otherwise. If A is an algorithm and $(a_1, \ldots, a_\ell) \leftarrow A(x)$ for $\ell \in \mathbb{N}$ we use $[A(x)]_i$ for $i \in [\ell]$ to denote the ith output a_i. Similarly, we use $[A(x)]_{[i;j]}$ to denote the projection of the output of $A(x)$ on the coordinates i up to j. In the same way, we use $[B]_i$ for any tuple $B = (b_1, \ldots, b_\ell)$ to denote the projection on the ith component b_i and $[B]_{[i;j]}$ for the projection $(b_i, \ldots, b_j)$ on components i to j. In case $s \in S^k$ and $w \in W^k$ are tuples, we more generally write $(s, w) \in R$ to denote that for all $i \in [k]$ it holds that $([s]_i, [w]_i) \in R$. If D is a set we use $r \leftarrow D$ to denote that r is drawn uniformly at random from D. Let X be some random variable that is drawn according to some discrete distribution D' over some set. We use $H_\infty(X) = k$ if $\max_x \Pr[X = x] = 2^{-k}$. In this case we also say that distribution D has min-entropy $H_\infty(X) = k$.

Reductions. Let us now explain what type of reductions we consider. We mainly follow [34] here. For an alternative, more general, and very formal treatment we refer to [3] where the reductions that we focus on are called NBN reductions. Commonly, these types of reductions are simply called Turing reductions. In a nutshell, a black-box reduction for basing the security of a primitive X on the hardness of a primitive Y, is a probabilistic polynomial-time oracle machine B such that B^A "breaks" Y, whenever the oracle A (the attacker) "breaks" X. Typically a successful break is defined in a security game played between a challenger and an attacker with precise conditions under which the attacker wins. When the oracles are interactive, we only consider deterministic attacker oracles that may be given random coins as first input. If B gives the oracle A fresh random coins at the beginning of the security game, we also say that the reduction has *created an instance* (of A). Having explicit random coins given to a deterministic oracle allows general reductions to restart and "rewind" its oracle. Simple reductions, however, can only send these initial random coins to the oracle once. To model probabilistic reductions we assume that each reduction is given access to random coins $r_B \in D_B$. In this work, we concentrate on uniform algorithms and in particular uniform reductions. In the full version, we sketch how our result could be transferred to non-uniform algorithms.

Success Probability after Rewinding. In our proofs we will make use of the well-known Splitting Lemma, see for example [36].

Lemma 1 (Splitting Lemma). *Let U and V be finite sets. Call $G \subseteq U \times V$ the set of good elements. For any element $(u, v) \in U \times V$ we define $k_u = |\{(u, v') \mid (u, v') \in G\}|$, i.e. k_u is the number of $v' \in V$ such that (u, v') is good. Suppose there is a lower bound on the number of good elements such that $|G| \geq \epsilon |U \times V|$. Define the set of super-good elements G' as a subset of G with $G' = \{(u, v) \in G \mid k_u \geq \epsilon/2 |V|\}$. Then it holds that*

$$|G'| \geq \epsilon/2 \, |U \times V|.$$

4   Notions for PKE and CHOWBs

In this section, we formally introduce semi-homomorphic public-key encryption. We will later use the well-known notion of OW-CCA1 in a corollary of our first main result. A further, even weaker notion is called Paired OW-CCA1 security. According to this notion pairs of ciphertexts are sent to the challenger for decryption. Each time, the challenger responds with the corresponding pair of plaintexts. (Likewise, in the final phase, the challenger sends a pair of challenge ciphertexts to the attacker which in turn responds with the corresponding plaintext pair.) Paired OW-CCA1 can later be used when applying our second main result (Sect. 10) to semi-homomorphic PKE. (A formal definition of Paired OW-CCA1 can be found in the full version.)

4.1 Public-Key Encryption

A public-key encryption (PKE) system $\mathsf{PKE} = (\mathsf{PKEKGen}, \mathsf{PKEEnc}, \mathsf{PKEDec})$ consists of three algorithms.

1. $\mathsf{PKEKGen}(1^\kappa)$: the probabilistic key generator $\mathsf{PKEKGen}$ takes as input the security parameter in unary and outputs an asymmetric key pair with public key $pk \in \mathcal{PK}$ and secret key $sk \in \mathcal{SK}$.
2. $\mathsf{PKEEnc}(pk, m)$: the probabilistic encryption algorithm takes as input the public key $pk \in \mathcal{PK}$ and a message m from some message space $\mathcal{M}$ and outputs some ciphertext c in the ciphertext space $\mathcal{C}$.
3. $\mathsf{PKEDec}(sk, c)$: the deterministic decryption algorithm takes as input the secret key $sk \in \mathcal{SK}$ and a ciphertext c. It either outputs a message $m \in \mathcal{M}$ if $c \in \mathcal{C}$ or a dedicated error symbol $\perp$ if $c \notin \mathcal{C}$.

We say that PKE is perfectly correct if for all $(pk, sk) \leftarrow \mathsf{PKEKGen}(1^\kappa)$ we have for all $m \in \mathcal{M}$ that $\Pr[\mathsf{PKEDec}(sk, \mathsf{PKEEnc}(pk, m)) = m] = 1$. In the following, we will only be interested in perfectly correct PKE systems. We call a PKE system certified if i) there is an efficient algorithm that can check whether indeed $pk \in \mathcal{PK}$ and ii) it holds that $[\mathsf{PKEKGen}(1^\kappa)]_1 = \mathcal{PK}$, meaning that the set of public keys output by the key generator is efficiently recognizable.

4.2 Semi-Homomorphic PKE

We will particularly be interested in (semi-)homomorphic PKE. We say that $\mathsf{PKE} = (\mathsf{PKEKGen}, \mathsf{PKEEnc}, \mathsf{PKEDec})$ is homomorphic if the following several properties are fulfilled:

1. For all κ and all $(pk, sk) \leftarrow \mathsf{PKEKGen}(1^\kappa)$ it is possible to define (finite, cyclic) groups $(G, +)$ and $(H, \cdot)$ such that the set G is equal to the plaintext space $\mathcal{M}$ and H is equal to the ciphertext space $\mathcal{C}$. We require that membership in G and H can be efficiently tested.
2. $|G|$ grows exponentially in the security parameter.
3. There is an efficient algorithm that can draw $t \in \mathbb{N}$ uniformly from $t \leftarrow [|G|]$ with only statistically small error probability.

4. For any $m, m' \in G$ and any scalar $t \in [|G|]$ it holds that

$$PKEDec(sk, \prod_{i=1}^{t} PKEEnc(pk, m) \cdot PKEEnc(pk, m')) = \sum_{i=1}^{t} m + m'$$
$$= tm + m'.$$

5. We have that $\mathcal{C} = PKEEnc(pk, \mathcal{M}; D)$, that is, for every pk and each ciphertext c in the ciphertext space there exists message m and randomness r such that $c = PKEEnc(pk, m; r)$.
6. For uniformly random message $m \in \mathcal{M}$ and uniformly random $r \in D$, we have that $PKEEnc(pk, m; r)$ is distributed like a uniformly sampled ciphertext.

Property 3 allows us to not only model groups G of known order where we can directly draw $t \leftarrow [|G|]$ but also groups of unknown order like RSA (or Paillier) setups where randomly drawing from $[(N-1)/4]$ is statistically close to drawing from $[\phi(N)]$.

It is well-known that ElGamal PKE is a semi-homomorphic PKE. However, in the cryptographic literature, we can find several other well-known PKE systems that fulfill our definition of homomorphic PKE. Among them, there is the well-known PKE by Paillier [31] and its generalization by Damgård–Jurik [14]. For brevity, we refer to the original papers for the description of the other schemes. These works also show that all required properties are fulfilled if the public keys are set up as defined in the scheme's description. For these cryptosystems, it is also relatively easy to actually provide cryptographic proofs cert showing that the key material has been set up as given in the description. Such a proof can thus ultimately guarantee that all the above properties are fulfilled. For example, for Paillier encryption such a corresponding proof simply boils down to proving that $gcd(N, \phi(N)) = 1$ as shown in [28]. If such a proof can be computed and verified efficiently, we call the PKE scheme *certified*. It is important to stress that, since we require that plaintexts and ciphertexts are efficiently recognizable, our definition excludes PKE systems like the Cramer–Shoup scheme [13] or its IND-CCA1-secure lite version where real ciphertexts $(g_1^r, g_2^r, \ldots)$ are indistinguishable from "malformed" ciphertexts $(g_1^r, g_2^{r'}, \ldots)$ for $r' \neq r$ that the reduction can produce. Another interpretation of this condition is that we require that the validity of ciphertexts can be *publicly* verified.

4.3 Certified Homomorphic One-Way Bijections

For each κ let F be a family of efficiently sampleable homomorphic one-way bijections such that $|F|$ grows exponentially in security parameter κ. We assume that the input and output space of each $f \in F$ is efficiently sampleable. Moreover, we assume that all the functions in F are *certified* so that there exists an efficient algorithm which given some f outputs 1 if $f \in F$ and 0 otherwise. We assume that each $f \in F$ maps elements from finite group $(A, \oplus)$ to group $(B = range(f), \odot)$ of the same order. We thus have $f(x \oplus y) = f(x) \odot f(y)$ for all $x, y \in A$. We assume that all group operations are efficient. Finally, let us also assume that the evaluation of f is efficient for all $f \in F$. We will now consider a security notion in which the attacker makes a polynomial number, $t = t(\kappa)$, of inversion queries before it has to compute the pre-images of p challenge outputs.

1. The challenger draws $f \in F$ and sends f to the attacker A.
2. The attacker A may query up to t inversion queries to C. Each query y_i consists of a value in the image of f.
3. The challenger C responds to each such query with input x_i such that $y_i = f(x_i)$. If $i = t$, the challenger additionally sends random outputs $\hat{y}_1^*, \ldots, \hat{y}_p^*$ to A.
4. A responds with the corresponding inputs $x_1^*, \ldots, x_p^*$.

The attacker wins and breaks the security of F if the probability that for all $i \in [p]$ we have $y_i^* = f(x_i^*)$ is non-negligible. There are many well-known examples of CHOWBs in cryptography like the discrete exponentiation function or the (certified) RSA permutation. The above security notion formalizes a form of adaptive security for CHOWBs that is a very weak variant of a so-called one-more assumption where the challenge is given to the attacker only at the end of the security game.

5   Random Self-Reducible and Re-Randomizable Relations (RRRs)

In the following, we will define the class of relations that we are interested in. To this end, we formally specify several algorithms that work with some total relation R. After that, we will provide some detailed intuition for these algorithms and how we make use of them later. Additional intuition will be provided via the concrete examples of RRRs in Sect. 6.

5.1   Algorithms

To formally capture the intuition behind RRRs, we introduce the notion of RRR systems that comprise several efficient algorithms RRR = (RGen, RSample, RSubSample, ReRand, ReCheck, RSRStatement, RSRWitness, RVerify). We parameterize our notion by some integer k which we call the *fan-out* of RRR. We will in the following assume that $k = 1$ unless explicitly specified otherwise. We also introduce the notion of strong RRR systems that have an additional efficient algorithm RSRTest: RRR$'$ = (RGen, RSample, RSubSample, ReRand, ReCheck, RSRStatement, RSRWitness, RSRTest, RVerify).

- RGen(1^κ): The probabilistic *relation generator* RGen takes as input the security parameter κ and outputs the description of a relation $R \subseteq S \times W$ along with a proof cert $\in U$. For simplicity, we assume that R implicitly also specifies the spaces S, W, U, and $S' \subseteq S$ with superpolynomial $|S'|$.
- RSample(R): The probabilistic *sampler* RSample outputs $(s, w) \in S \times W$ for uniformly random $s \in S$.

- RSubSample(R): The probabilistic *sub-sampler* RSubSample outputs $(s', w) \in R$, where $s' \in S'$ is drawn according to some distribution X with min-entropy $H_\infty(X) \geq \kappa$.
- ReRand(R, s, w): The probabilistic *re-randomizer* ReRand is given relation R and $(s, w) \in R$. It outputs a new witness $w' \in W$.
- ReCheck(R, s, w, w'): The deterministic *checker* ReCheck is given relation R, $(s, w) \in R$, and $w' \in W$ as input. It outputs a bit c indicating whether $(s, w') \in R$.
- RSRStatement($R, s^*; r$): The *statement transformer* RSRStatement is given as input relation R, a statement $s^* \in S$, and random coins r. The output is a vector of statements, $s \in S'^k$ for $k \in \mathbb{N}$, and the state $st = (s^*, r) \in S \times \{0, 1\}^*$. We also say that s is the *transformed statement* of s^* (and r).
- RSRWitness(R, w, st): The deterministic *derivation algorithm* RSRWitness is given R, witness vector $w \in W^k$, and state $st = (s^*, r) \in S \times \{0, 1\}^*$. It outputs a new witness $w^* \in W$. We also call w^* the *derivation* of w.
- RSRTest(R, w, k', st): The deterministic *tester* RSRTest is given R, a single witness $w \in W$, an index $k' \in [k]$, and a state $st = (s^*, r) \in S \times \{0, 1\}^*$. The output is a bit t indicating whether the k'th component of the transformed statement of s^* and r has witness w.
- RVerify(R, cert): The deterministic *verifier* RVerify is given as input the description R and proof $\text{cert} \in U$. The output is a bit v indicating whether the proof is correct.

If R is clear from the context, we might omit R as an input in our notation. If we do not specify an explicit value for cert, we implicitly assume that $\text{cert} = \bot$ is set. Also, if $k = 1$ for some concrete RRR we may use RSRTest(R, w, st) short for RSRTest($R, w, 1, st$).

Properties of R. Let us now, for some given relation R, define several properties that we might require from the algorithms of a (strong) RRR system.

P-1: Correctness of RSample:

$$\forall r \in D : \mathsf{RSample}(R; r) \in R.$$

P-2: Correctness of RSubSample:

$$\forall r \in D : \mathsf{RSubSample}(R; r) \in R.$$

P-3: Correctness of ReRand:

$$\forall (s, w) \in S \times W, r \in D : (s, w) \in R \Rightarrow (s, \mathsf{ReRand}(R, s, w; r)) \in R.$$

P-4: Witness indistinguishability of ReRand:

$$\forall s \in S, w, w', w'' \in W_s :$$
$$\Pr[w'' = \mathsf{ReRand}(R, s, w)] = \Pr[w'' = \mathsf{ReRand}(R, s, w')].$$

P-5: Correctness and soundness of ReCheck:

$$\forall (s, w) \in R, w' \in W : \ \mathsf{ReCheck}(R, s, w, w') = 1 \Leftrightarrow (s, w') \in R.$$

P-6: Correctness of (RSRStatement, RSRWitness):

$$\forall s^* \in S, r \in D, w \in W^k :$$
$$([\mathsf{RSRStatement}(R, s^*; r)]_{[k]}, w) \in R$$
$$\Rightarrow \mathsf{RSRWitness}(R, w, [\mathsf{RSRStatement}(R, s^*; r)]_{k+1}) \in W_{s^*}.$$

P-7: Statement indistinguishability of RSRStatement:

$$\forall s^*, s' \in S :$$
$$[\mathsf{RSRStatement}(R, s^*)]_{[k]} \approx_s [\mathsf{RSRStatement}(R, s')]_{[k]}.$$

P-8: Indistinguishable sampleability of RSubSample:

$$\forall s^* \in S, i \in [k] : \ [\mathsf{RSubSample}(R)]_1 \approx_s [\mathsf{RSRStatement}(R, s^*)]_i.$$

P-9: Statistical correctness and soundness of (RSRStatement, RSRTest):

$$\forall s^* \in S, w \in W, k' \in [k]$$
$$\Pr[(\mathsf{RSRStatement}(R, s^*; r)]_{k'}, w) \in R]$$
$$\approx_s \Pr[\mathsf{RSRTest}(R, w, k', [\mathsf{RSRStatement}(R, s^*; r)]_{k+1}) = 1],$$
$$\textit{where the probability is over } r \leftarrow D.$$

Let us finally define what a *certified* (strong) RRR system is.

Definition 1. *Let* RRR *be an RRR system. We say that* RRR *is a certified RRR system if properties P-10 to P-11 are fulfilled where:*

P-10: Correctness of RGen*:*

$$\forall r \in D : \mathsf{RGen}(1^\kappa; r) = (R, \mathsf{cert}) \Rightarrow \textit{P-1 to P-8 are fulfilled on input } R.$$

P-11: Soundness of RVerify*:*

$$\forall R \subseteq S \times W, \mathsf{cert} \in U : \mathsf{RVerify}(R, \mathsf{cert}) = 1 \Leftrightarrow \textit{P-1 to P-8 hold on input } R.$$

Certified RRR systems will be utilized in our first result. In our second result, we need certified strong RRRs.

Definition 2. *Let* RRR$'$ *be an RRR system. We say that* RRR$'$ *is a certified strong RRR system if properties P-12 to P-13 are fulfilled where:*

P-12: Correctness of RGen*:*

$$\forall r \in D : \mathsf{RGen}(1^\kappa; r) = (R, \mathsf{cert}) \Rightarrow \textit{P-1 to P-9 are fulfilled on input } R.$$

P-13: Soundness of RVerify*:*

$$\forall R \subseteq S \times W, \mathsf{cert} \in U : \mathsf{RVerify}(R, \mathsf{cert}) = 1 \Leftrightarrow \textit{P-1 to P-9 hold on input } R.$$

Intuition. Let us provide some intuition for these algorithms and the properties that we require. The pair of algorithms RGen and RVerify, along with properties P-10 and P-11 (respectively P-12 and P-13) are used to capture that we can test if a given relation R is indeed a (strong) RRR. To this end, we have that RGen may output a corresponding proof cert alongside R that can be verified by RVerify. We remark that this notion also captures situations where a dedicated proof is not necessary, such that the verifier can be convinced by performing some efficient computations on R. An example that will also underlie our analysis of ElGamal is when R specifies a generator g of a cyclic group that has prime order p. We assume that in these cases cert is set to cert $= \perp$.

Our notion of re-randomizability of witnesses is captured via ReRand, ReCheck, and P-4 to P-5. ReRand outputs when given $(s, w) \in R$ a new witness $\tilde{w} \in W_s$. At the same time, we guarantee a strong form of witness indistinguishability by requiring that the output distributions of ReRand(R, s, w) and ReRand(R, s, w'), for any s and $w, w' \in W_s$, are equal. Finally, we have that the algorithm ReCheck can recognize, given arbitrary $(s, w) \in R$, if a new witness w' is also in W_s. As mentioned before, if R has unique witnesses the algorithm is trivial: it simply outputs 1 iff $w' = w$. In this case, we also say that the re-randomization of R is trivial. To capture random self-reducibility we make use of RSRStatement, RSRWitness along with P-6 and P-7. To model strong RRRs we also exploit RSRTest and require that P-9 is fulfilled. The algorithm RSRStatement simply constructs from statement s^* a derived vector of statements s. Similar to before, we have that the output of this algorithm does not reveal the input value s^*, capturing a strong form of statement indistinguishability. Moreover, we require that whenever we indeed obtain a witness w for s, we can use that to compute a witness w^* for the original statement s^*.

Finally, for strong RRRs, we require that we have a weak membership test via RSRTest for derived s and arbitrary w. However, it requires as input the state st, which has been used to construct s from s^*. In contrast to RSRWitness that only works on a full vector $w' \in W^k$, we can run RSRTest with a single component $w \in W$ indexed by k'. Observe that nevertheless both algorithms are fed with the same state. In this way, we can use RSRTest to stepwisely test whether the components of $w' \in W^k$ are correct in the sense that a full vector w' can later indeed be used by RSRWitness to output witness w^*. We stress that property P-9 must hold for *all* possible witnesses w, including those that could be computed from the transformed statement RSRStatement$(R, s^*; r)$. For most relations that we detail below, we have $k = 1$. However, for our final analysis of semi-homomorphic PKE, and in particular ElGamal PKE, we have that $k = 2$ (intuitively indicating that statements consist of pairs of ciphertexts).

Finally, we introduce two sampling algorithms RSample and RSubSample. The first is used to generate relation pairs $(s, w) \in R$. The second is used to generate a new pair $(s', w') \in S' \times W$ such that $(s', w') \in R$. Importantly, the output distribution of this algorithm should be statistically close to that of the first k components of RSRStatement as encoded in P-8. So, using RSubSample we can output k distinct values that are distributed statistically close to the statements that are output by RSRStatement. At the same time, the output s of RSubSample should have high min-entropy. This guarantees that we can generate hard instances of statements s such that it is difficult to compute w with $(s, w) \in R$ at all. In the algorithms that we consider we usually have that RSubSample(R) simply does the same as RSample(R) and we have that $S' = S$. In our security proof, the attacker will use RSubSample to generate pairs of the relation while the reduction may use either RSubSample or RSample to create statements.

6 Important RRRs

In the following, we will provide an important example of an RRR that is based on semi-homomorphic PKE. In the full version, we also show how we can easily obtain a strong RRR RRR_F from certified homomorphic one-way bijections when statement/witness pairs correspond to output/input pairs. We emphasize that all these RRRs are not built from concrete algebraic setups, like RSA groups, but from entire classes of building blocks ultimately leading to very broad impossibility results.

6.1 RRRs from Semi-Homomorphic PKE

Let us now present an RRR, denoted $\mathrm{RRR}_{\mathrm{HomPKE}}$, that is derived from a semi-homomorphic PKE system PKE with associated groups $G = \mathcal{M}$ and $H = \mathcal{C}$. Intuitively, the statements correspond to ciphertexts while the witnesses are plaintexts. For simplicity, we assume that for each pk, PKE is certified via some cert, to begin with. To prove that all properties of RRRs are fulfilled, we exploit perfect correctness of the PKE such that for every ciphertext we have a unique plaintext.

- RGen(1^κ) calls PKEKGen(1^κ) to obtain secret key sk and public key pk. This specifies the relation of ciphertext/plaintext pairs.

$$R_{\mathrm{HomPKE}} = \{(\ s, w = \mathsf{PKEDec}(sk, s)\ )\}$$
$$= \{(\ \mathsf{PKEEnc}(pk, w; r), w\ )\}_{r \in D} \subseteq \mathcal{C} \times \mathcal{M}.$$

We have $S = S' = \mathcal{C}$ and $W = \mathcal{M}$. The output is R_{HomPKE}, i.e. pk, and cert.
- RSample(R_{HomPKE}) draws randomness $r \in D$ and random $w \in \mathcal{M}$ and outputs
$$(s, w) = (\ \mathsf{PKEEnc}(pk, w; r), w\ ).$$
- RSubSample(R_{HomPKE}) simply outputs $(s, w) \leftarrow$ RSample(R_{HomPKE}).
- ReRand(s, w) outputs w.
- ReCheck(s, w, w') outputs 1 iff $w' = w$.
- RSRStatement($s^*; r$) draws uniformly random $m \in \mathcal{M}$ and randomness $r' \in D$ to output
$$(s, st) = (\ (s^* \cdot \mathsf{PKEEnc}(pk, m; r')), (s^*, r', m)\ ).$$

- RSRWitness(w, st) parses $st = (s^*, r', m)$ and outputs $w^* = w + (-m)$ where $-m$ is the inverse of m.
- RVerify(pk, cert) outputs 1 iff cert is a valid certificate for PKE.

Lemma 2. RRR_{HomPKE} *is a certified RRR.*

Proof. Observe that all algorithms are efficient, and due to perfect correctness for every statement there is a unique witness if R_{HomPKE} is certified. This makes re-randomization trivial. At the same time, RVerify perfectly tests whether a purported output of RGen is correct since PKE is certified. Finally, RSRStatement statistically hides s^* while RSRWitness perfectly recovers w^*. Since the output s of RSRStatement is uniformly random it is perfectly distributed like the output of RSubSample. $\square$

6.2 Strong RRRs from Semi-Homomorphic PKE

Let us now present an RRR, denoted $\text{RRR}_{2\text{HomPKE}}$, that is derived from a semi-homomorphic PKE system PKE. This transformation is one of our main contributions as it allows a proof under arbitrary reductions in the first place later on. We believe that the technique can be useful in many other contexts of cryptography as well. Intuitively, the statements now correspond to pairs of ciphertexts while the witnesses are pairs of plaintexts. Again, we assume that the PKE is certified. Moreover, we now rely on the fact that the group of plaintexts $|G| = |\mathcal{M}|$ has exponential size in the security parameter.

Before we begin, let us briefly provide some intuition for the novel techniques that we use to implement an online membership test. To provide some context, the technical challenge is to provide a technique such that the attacker can be sure that the reduction's responses are correct. At the most critical part of the proof, we need this to hold even if the attacker does not know the plaintext of one of the ciphertexts. The main idea is as follows: we make the attacker encrypt a message in the first ciphertext and the MAC tag of that message in the second one. The MAC is homomorphic and implemented via a two-wise independent hash function. Moreover, the MAC is a one-time MAC and its key material $u \in [|G|]$, $w' \in G$ is freshly drawn with each query. This gives statistical security. Crucially, exploiting the homomorphic properties, the attacker can use this technique to create from a given ciphertext s'^* encrypting w'^* a new ciphertext that encrypts the tag $uw'^* + w'$ *without knowledge of* w'^*. Of course, these two ciphertexts can also be blinded and, after rewinding, be sent to the reduction as a single query (recall that we are considering pairs of ciphertexts as statements). The other ciphertext in the challenge is treated in the same way. For each challenge ciphertext, the attacker so generates two ciphertexts, one for the blinded ciphertext and one for the MAC of this value, to extract a single challenge plaintext. We thus have fan-out $k = 2$.

- RGen(1^κ) calls PKEKGen(1^κ) to obtain secret key sk and public key pk. This specifies the relation of ciphertext/plaintext pairs:

$$R_{2\mathrm{HomPKE},sk} = \{(\,(s',s''),\ (\mathsf{PKEDec}(sk,s'),\mathsf{PKEDec}(sk,s''))\,)\}$$
$$= \{(\,s,\ w\,)\} \subseteq \mathcal{C}^2 \times \mathcal{M}^2$$

with $s = (s',s'')$ and $w = (\mathsf{PKEDec}(sk,s'),\mathsf{PKEDec}(sk,s''))$. We have $S = S' = \mathcal{C}^2$ and $W = \mathcal{M}^2$.
- RSample($R_{2\mathrm{HomPKE},sk}$) draws randomness $r',r'' \in D$ and random $w',w'' \in \mathcal{M}$ and outputs

$$((s',s''),(w',w''))$$

where

$$s' \leftarrow \mathsf{PKEEnc}(pk,w';r') \text{ and } s'' \leftarrow \mathsf{PKEEnc}(pk,w'';r'').$$

We set $r = (r',r'')$ to denote the overall randomness and $w = (w',w'')$ for the witness.
- RSubSample($R_{2\mathrm{HomPKE},x}$) simply outputs $(s,w) \leftarrow$ RSample($R_{2\mathrm{HomPKE},x}$).
- ReRand(s,w) outputs w.
- ReCheck(s,w,w') outputs 1 iff $w' = w$.
- RSRStatement($s^*;r$) takes as input a pair of ciphertexts $s^* = (s'^*, s''^*)$. From that it generates four ciphertexts that are organized as pairs $\hat{s} = (\hat{s}', \hat{s}'')$ and $\tilde{s} = (\tilde{s}', \tilde{s}'')$ along with some state information. First, the algorithm draws randomness $\hat{r}'$ and random witness $\hat{w}'$ and blinds[4] the ciphertext s'^* to

$$\hat{s}' = s'^* \cdot \mathsf{PKEEnc}(pk, \hat{w}'; \hat{r}').$$

Next, we draw randomness $\hat{r}''$ and random witness $\hat{w}''$ as well as random scalar $\hat{u} \leftarrow [\lVert G \rVert]$ (or statistically close to that as required by our definition of semi-homomorphic PKE). The pair $\hat{u}$ and $\hat{w}''$ correspond to a key of a statistically secure, homomorphic MAC that is implemented with a pairwise independent hash function. Then, we compute the encrypted MAC by setting

$$\hat{s}'' = \prod_{i=1}^{\hat{u}} (\hat{s}'^*) \cdot \mathsf{PKEEnc}(pk, \hat{w}''; \hat{r}'') = (\hat{s}'^*)^{\hat{u}} \cdot \mathsf{PKEEnc}(pk, \hat{w}''; \hat{r}'')$$

using standard multiplicative notation. We proceed similarly for the second pair of ciphertexts and obtain

$$\tilde{s}' = s''^* \cdot \mathsf{PKEEnc}(pk, \tilde{w}'; \tilde{r}')$$

and

$$\tilde{s}'' = \prod_{i=1}^{\tilde{u}} (\tilde{s}'^*) \cdot \mathsf{PKEEnc}(pk, \tilde{w}''; \tilde{r}'') = (\tilde{s}'^*)^{\tilde{u}} \cdot \mathsf{PKEEnc}(pk, \tilde{w}''; \tilde{r}'').$$

The output is $s = (\hat{s}, \tilde{s})$, where $\hat{s} = (\hat{s}', \hat{s}'')$ and $\tilde{s} = (\tilde{s}', \tilde{s}'')$, and the state consists of s^* and all the random values drawn throughout the game, i.e., $st = (s^*, (\hat{w}', \hat{r}', \hat{w}'', \hat{r}'', \hat{u}), (\tilde{w}', \tilde{r}', \tilde{w}'', \tilde{r}'', \tilde{u}))$.

---

[4] This perfectly hides s'^*.

- RSRTest(w, k', st) parses w as $w = (\hat{w}, \tilde{w})$ with $\hat{w} = (\hat{w}_1, \hat{w}_2)$ and $\tilde{w} = (\tilde{w}_1, \tilde{w}_2)$ and the state st as $st = (s^*, (\hat{w}', \hat{r}', \hat{w}'', \hat{r}'', \hat{u}), (\tilde{w}', \tilde{r}', \tilde{w}'', \tilde{r}'', \tilde{u}))$. The algorithm first recomputes $s = (\hat{s}, \tilde{s})$ using RSRStatement where $\hat{s} = (\hat{s}', \hat{s}'')$ and $\tilde{s} = (\tilde{s}', \tilde{s}'')$. Next, the algorithm essentially verifies the MACs on the plaintexts received, depending on $k' \in \{1, 2\}$. If $k' = 1$ the algorithm checks if

$$\sum_{i=1}^{\hat{u}} \hat{w}_1 + \hat{w}'' = \hat{u}\hat{w}_1 + \hat{w}'' = \hat{w}_2$$

using standard additive notation. If $k' = 2$ the algorithm checks if

$$\sum_{i=1}^{\tilde{u}} \tilde{w}_1 + \tilde{w}'' = \tilde{u}\tilde{w}_1 + \tilde{w}'' = \tilde{w}_2.$$

On failure, it outputs 0. On success, it outputs 1.
- RSRWitness(w, st) parses $st = (s^*, (\hat{w}', \hat{r}', \hat{w}'', \hat{r}'', \hat{u}), (\tilde{w}', \tilde{r}', \tilde{w}'', \tilde{r}'', \tilde{u}))$ and $w = (\hat{w}, \tilde{w})$ with $\hat{w} = (\hat{w}_1, \hat{w}_2)$ and $\tilde{w} = (\tilde{w}_1, \tilde{w}_2)$. It computes $w'^* = \hat{w}_1 + (-\hat{w}')$ where $-\hat{w}'$ is the inverse of $\hat{w}'$ and $w''^* = \tilde{w}_1 + (-\tilde{w}')$. This undoes the blinding in the plaintext space. The output is $w^* = (w'^*, w''^*)$.
- RVerify(u) outputs 1 iff the key is certified.

Lemma 3. $RRR_{2HomPKE}$ *is a strong certified RRR.*

Due to space limitations, the proof of Lemma 3 is given in the full version.

7   A New Weak Security Notion for Relations

Let us now formalize the main security notion that we will consider in this work (as depicted in Fig. 1). In the rest of the paper, we always assume that t, p are polynomials in the security parameter unless specified otherwise. We state the security game using some of the syntax of certified RRRs. However, we stress that the security game is very general and stating it does not require the existence of most of the algorithms that are associated to RRR systems. However, our main results will only apply if we indeed have access to all the algorithms of RRR systems.

Security Game: Lunchtime Inversion with t Adaptive Queries. The central security notion that we consider for $t \in \mathbb{N}$, $t \geq 1$ is very simple. It is formalized as a game played between two algorithms, a challenger C and attacker A.

1. The challenger C calls $(R, \text{cert}) \leftarrow \text{RGen}(1^\kappa)$. The output is sent to A.
2. The parties repeat the following steps for all $i \in [1; t]$.
   2.i.1 The attacker A outputs statement $s_i \in S$.
   2.i.2 The challenger C responds with uniformly random witness $w_i \in W_{s_i}$ such that $(s_i, w_i) \in R$. If $i = t$ the challenger also sends challenge statement $s_1^*, \dots, s_p^* \in S$.
3. The attacker outputs the challenge witness $w_1^*, \dots, w_p^* \in W$.

We say that the attacker wins if for all $i \in [p]$ we have $(s_i^*, w_i^*) \in R$. If in any execution of the security game algorithm C finishes Step 2.i.2, we say that C *accepts* the $s_1, \ldots, s_i$.

To generalize our security notion, we also define the case for $t = 0$ where the attacker is not allowed to query any statement for its corresponding witness.

Security Game: Lunchtime Inversion with $t = 0$ (No) Adaptive Queries.

1. The challenger C calls $(R, \text{cert}) \leftarrow \text{RGen}(1^\kappa)$. The output is sent to the attacker A along with p challenge statements $s_1^*, \ldots, s_p^* \in S$.
2. The attacker outputs the challenge witnesses $w_1^*, \ldots, w_p^* \in W$.

Again, we say that the attacker wins if for all $i \in [p]$ we have $(s_i^*, w_i^*) \in R$.

Definition 3. *We say that certified (strong) RRR system* RRR *is secure against (lunchtime) inversion (attacks) with t adaptive queries if no PPT attacker A can have non-negligible success probability to win in the above security game.*

8   Interactive Complexity Assumption

t-Interactive Complexity Assumptions. To model interactive complexity assumptions with t queries we will rely on a generalization of the formulation introduced in [2] that originally focuses on non-interactive assumptions only. It is slightly more general than the notion in [34] which uses fixed thresholds. Intuitively, the notion we use allows arbitrary algorithms to implement a trivial guessing strategy. A t-interactive complexity assumption (tICA) consists of $t + 3$ Turing machines $\text{ICA} = (\text{ICAGen}, \text{ICAVer}, \text{ICATriv}, \text{ICAQuery}_1, \ldots, \text{ICAQuery}_t)$.

- The efficient probabilistic instance generator $\text{ICAGen}(1^\kappa) \rightarrow (c, st_0)$ computes on input the security parameter in unary a problem instance c and initial state st_0.
- On input the i-th query q_i and state st_{i-1} for $i \in [1; t]$, the efficient algorithm ICAQuery_i outputs the i-th response p_i and state st_i. For convenience, we will also consider the set of all the ICAQuery_i as a stateful algorithm ICAQuery in the natural way.
- The efficient algorithm ICATriv is given a problem instance c and t-time oracle access to a stateful algorithm ICAQuery. It outputs a candidate solution s. This algorithm implements a trivial attack.
- The verification algorithm ICAVer takes as input a problem instance c, the final state st_t, and a purported solution s and outputs a bit b. If $\text{ICAVer}(c, st_t, s) = 1$ we say that s is a valid solution.

If ICAVer is efficient, we call ICA falsifiable.

Security Game for t-Interactive Complexity Assumptions (tICAs). Let us consider the following security experiment ICA_N^A involving attacker A.

1. The experiment runs $\mathsf{ICAGen}(1^\kappa) \rightarrow (c, st_0)$.
2. A is given c and oracle access to $\mathsf{ICAQuery}$ (run with random coins r_P) for up to t queries.
3. Finally, the attacker outputs a candidate solution s.
4. The experiment returns whatever $\mathsf{ICAVer}(c, st_t, s)$ returns.

Definition 4. *We say that A efficiently breaks $tICA$ ICA if A runs in polynomial time and*

$$|\Pr[\mathsf{ICA}^A_{\mathsf{ICA}}(1^\kappa) \Rightarrow 1] - \Pr[\mathsf{ICA}^{\mathsf{ICATriv}}_{\mathsf{ICA}}(1^\kappa) \Rightarrow 1]| = \epsilon$$

is non-negligible where the probability is over the random coins consumed by $\mathsf{ICAGen}, \mathsf{ICATriv}, \mathsf{ICAQuery}$ and A. We say that $tICA$ ICA is secure if no probabilistic polynomial algorithm can break ICA.

9   First Result: Impossibility of Simple Reductions for General RRR Systems

In this section, we will establish our first result. Before we begin, let us describe the restrictions that we make on the considered reductions.

9.1   Simple Reductions

Our first result will consider a restricted form of reduction algorithms that we call simple reductions. We stress that most of the reductions in cryptography seem to be of this type, including all reductions that are used for security proofs of ElGamal PKE and derived schemes. In particular, we will consider reductions B with the following properties.

- B treats the attacker in a black-box way, as in our general result.
- B only calls a single attacker.
- B does not rewind the attacker.

9.2   First Main Result

Now let us formally state our first result.

Theorem 1. *Let RRR be a certified RRR system with constant fan-out k. Let p be a constant that indicates the number of statements that the attacker must invert in the lunchtime-inversion game. Then there is no simple PPT reduction B that can reduce the security of the lunchtime-inversion game with $t+1$ adaptive queries to the security of any t-interactive complexity assumption ICA.*

9.3   Proof of Theorem 1

Let us provide an overview of the proof. At first, we specify an ideal (unbounded) attacker A for which the reduction has to work. Next, we present an efficient meta-reduction M that simulates the ideal attacker. Finally, we analyze the difference between the behavior of a reduction B in the two cases. We show that the reduction will not be able to tell the two settings apart. Thus, the reduction also has to work for the efficient M. The combination of B and M will therefore break the underlying tICA. The meta-reduction gains its power from rewinding the reduction.

In a nutshell, the proof relies on the fact that we can always find *a useful rewinding spot* after rewinding. The useful rewinding spot is an attacker query such that i) the reduction provides a (correct) response to that query and ii) the reduction does not query its tICA challenger before delivering the response. Intuitively, the meta-reduction will repeatedly try to hit a useful rewinding spot and send new queries that are derived from the challenge statements to the reduction. The proof exploits that in each of these runs, with non-negligible probability, the reduction will behave as in the first run if presented with a new query since new queries are distributed statistically close to queries of the first run. Let us now be more formal.

9.4   The Ideal Attacker A

1. The attacker A receives random coins r, and R, cert. It aborts in case RVerify$(R, \text{cert}) \neq 1$. Otherwise, it continues.
2. The parties repeat the following steps for all $i \in [1; t+1]$.
   2.i.1 The attacker A draws $(s_i, w_i) \leftarrow \text{RSubSample}(R)$ and sends s_i to the challenger.
   2.i.2 The challenger responds with witness w_i'. If $i = t$, the challenger also sends challenge statements $s_1^*, \ldots, s_p^* \in S$. The attacker aborts in the case that $\text{ReCheck}(s_i, w_i, w_i') \neq 1$. Otherwise, it continues.
3. The attacker checks if $s_1^*, \ldots, s_p^* \in S$ and aborts otherwise. Next, the attacker uses its unbounded power to compute a challenge witness $w_\ell^* \in W$ for each $\ell \in [p]$. To this end it could for example compute $\text{RSample}(R; r)$ for all possible random coins and generate the set $W_{s_\ell^*}$ for each $\ell \in [p]$. From this, it can draw an arbitrary witness $w_\ell' \in W_{s_\ell^*}$. Next, it re-randomizes witness w_ℓ' by computing $w_\ell^* \leftarrow \text{ReRand}(s_\ell^*, w_\ell')$. The final output consists of $w_1^*, \ldots, w_p^*$.

9.5   The Meta-Reduction M Can Rewind Reduction B

We will now consider a meta-reduction M that acts as an attacker against the purported reduction B. In particular, we assume that M can store the full execution state state_i of B after B has sent some message and awaits a corresponding response. With these states, M can rewind B to a previous point in time by loading the corresponding execution states. Let us now specify how the meta-reduction simulates the ideal attacker.

9.6   The Simulated Attacker

0. The meta-reduction M receives the tICA instance c and relays it to B along with random coins $r_B \in D_B$.
1. The attacker M receives r, R, cert from B and aborts if $\mathsf{RVerify}(R, \mathsf{cert}) \neq 1$. Otherwise, it continues.
2. The parties repeat the following steps for all $i \in [1; t+1]$.

   2.i.1 First the attacker M stores B's execution state state_i. Next, the attacker M calls $(s_i, w_i) \leftarrow \mathsf{RSubSample}(R)$ and sends s_i to the reduction.

   2.i.2 The reduction responds with a witness $w_i' \in W$. If the reduction B outputs a query to its tICA challenger, this query is simply relayed by M to its tICA challenger. Likewise, all responses are relayed back to B. The attacker M aborts if $\mathsf{ReCheck}(s_i, w_i, w_i') \neq 1$. Otherwise, it continues. If $i = t$ the reduction also sends challenge statements $s_1^*, \ldots, s_p^* \in S$ to M.

2' The attacker checks if $s_1^*, \ldots, s_p^* \in S$. On failure it aborts. Otherwise, it halts B and stores the current execution state state^* of B. Then, for each $\ell \in [p]$ the attacker M repeats the following loop:

   2'.ℓ The attacker M computes $(s_\ell', st_\ell^*) \leftarrow \mathsf{RSRStatement}(R, s_\ell^*)$ with $s_\ell' = (s_{\ell,1}', \ldots, s_{\ell,k}')$. Next, M iterates through all k components of s_ℓ'. To this end, it repeats the following loop for all $j \in [k]$:

   2'.ℓ.j The attacker M iterates through all possible states state_v. To this end, it repeats the following loop for all state indices $v \in [t+1]$:

   2'.ℓ.j.v The attacker M rewinds the reduction B back to the point before [2.v.1] by loading state_v. Next it sends $s_{\ell,j}'$ to B. If M receives a response $w_{\ell,j}' \in W$ and no external query to its tICA challenger has been made by the reduction in the time between sending $s_{\ell,j}'$ and receiving $w_{\ell,j}'$, M leaves this loop immediately (break[5]). Otherwise, it checks whether $v = t+1$. In case $v = t + 1$,[6] attacker M jumps back to 2'.ℓ and repeats the entire computation calling $\mathsf{RSRStatement}(R, s_\ell^*)$ with fresh randomness.

3. The meta-reduction computes the value $w_\ell'^* \leftarrow \mathsf{RSRWitness}(R, st_\ell^*, w_\ell')$ for each $\ell \in [p]$ and from this $w_\ell^* \leftarrow \mathsf{ReRand}(R, s_\ell^*, w_\ell'^*)$ for all $\ell \in [p]$. Next it loads B's state state^*, and outputs the challenge witnesses $w_1^*, \ldots, w_p^* \in W$.
4. B responds with a solution to the tICA challenge.
5. Finally, meta-reduction M relays that solution to the tICA challenger.

9.7   Analysis

Due to space limitations, the proof of the following lemma can be found in the full version.

---

[5] The attacker M continues at Step 2'.ℓ.j' for $j' = j + 1$.

[6] This means, that M has not received $w_{\ell,j}' \in W$ as a response to $s_{\ell,j}'$ in any of the states state_v or if the reduction has always made external queries.

Lemma 5. *The following four conditions are fulfilled:*

1. *M runs in expected polynomial time.*
2. *M always outputs $w_1^*, \ldots, w_p^*$ if it finishes its computations.*
3. *All values $w'_{\ell,j}$ received by M as responses to $s'_{\ell,j}$ in the rewinding process of M are correct with non-negligible probability, i.e. $(s'_{\ell,j}, w'_{\ell,j}) \in R$.*
4. *With probability statistically close to one, the reduction B can never distinguish M from A.*
5. *M makes at most t queries to the ICA challenger.*

With Lemma 5 we are guaranteed that B, after expected polynomial time, outputs a solution to the tICA challenge when given $w_1^*, \ldots, w_p^*$ with non-negligible probability. This concludes the proof of Theorem 1. We note that previous results on meta-reductions like [34] also require the reduction to run in expected polynomial time. By an application of the Markov inequality, we can then truncate the execution of the machine while still guaranteeing an inverse polynomial success probability for infinitely many security parameters in strict polynomial time.

10   Second Main Result

On the Neccessity of Non-Rewinding Reductions. For our first result it is important that the reduction cannot rewind the attacker. Otherwise it could (in Step 2.i.2) first try to send some incorrect w' to M such that $(s, w') \notin R$ when answering an inversion query for s. Only if the attacker aborts, the reduction would rewind M and retry to respond to the query s with a correct w. However, since M can *in a rewound run* not notice if w' is correct while the ideal attacker can always notice this, the reduction can easily tell A and M apart. This is a fundamental problem when dealing with RRRs.

Tackling Rewinding Reductions. In our second main result, we will thus extend and refine the above idea to deal with general reductions. In particular, we need to take care of rewinding reductions. At the same time we take care of reductions that execute several, u, attackers concurrently. To this end, we make use of novel and known techniques. However, what is crucial is that because of the generic problem that we described we now have to rely on strong RRR systems when dealing with rewinding reductions. This has important consequences. First, we will end up showing an impossibility result for the weaker notion of Paired OW-CCA1 security (where statements correspond to ciphertext pairs and witnesses to plaintext pairs) when applying our result to strong RRRs based on semi-homomorphic PKE. This makes our result seemingly stronger than the last one since Paired OW-CCA1 is weaker than OW-CCA1 security and thus IND-CCA1 security. However, crucially, the result now holds only if the reduction makes at most half the number of queries $\lfloor t/2 \rfloor$ to its $\lfloor t/2 \rfloor$ICA challenger where t is the number of queries by the attacker. This also makes our result somewhat weaker. Finally, we will consider reductions that make at most arbitrary u instances overall.

Theorem 2. *Let* RRR *be a certified strong RRR system with constant fan-out* k. *Let* p *be a polynomial. There is no PPT reduction* B *that can reduce the security of the lunchtime inversion game with* $t' \geq (u+t)$ *adaptive queries to the security of any tICA while creating at most* u *instances of the attacker overall.*

Lazy Simulation. For space reasons, the proof can be found in the full version. Here we provide a brief sketch of the proof. Let us provide some intuition for the simulation strategy of our final meta-reduction. Assume the reduction B creates u instances of the attacker A. Intuitively, we employ a careful generalization of the previous proof strategy that is applied to each simulated attacker, one after the other. The meta-reduction M simulates all of these runs. Since it has to deal with rewinding reductions, the proof makes sure that the ideal attacker and the meta-reduction behave deterministically from the point of view of the reduction. Thus rewindings do not help the reduction to obtain additional information. Corresponding to the lunchtime inversion game (Figure 1, Sect. 7), in the first phase of each of the simulated attackers, the meta-reduction only queries the reduction on $t + 1$ random statements. At the end of each of these phases, the meta-reduction has received back the corresponding witnesses to its random queries and also the set of challenge statements $s_1^*, \ldots, s_p^*$. Let A' be the instance of the simulated attacker that receives the challenge statements *first*. This starts the second phase of the simulation of A' which is similar to the proof of the first main theorem. First, the meta-reduction stores the state of the reduction at this point to later come back to it. Next, M repeatedly rewinds R back to hit a useful rewinding spot with a derived statement. However, in this proof, a useful rewinding spot fulfills three conditions. It is an index i, such that in the time span between query s_i from A' and corresponding response w_i sent to A', the reduction has i) *not* made any external query to the complexity assumption, ii) has responded with a correct response (this can now be tested), and iii) not required any of the $u - 1$ other instances of the (simulated) attacker to output a forgery. As in the first proof, i) ensures that the outside communication between B and its challenger is not disturbed. The third condition is crucial to avoid that simulation runtimes can grow exponentially when the communication with the attacker is nested by the reduction *after* rewinding [34]. Since there are only t queries from the reduction to the complexity assumption overall and since we only have at most u instances (and at most $u - 1$ that are different from A') there will always be at least one such index if $t' \geq u + t$ by the pigeon-hole principle. Now, the reduction, as in the first proof, proceeds according to a lazy strategy that tries to extract *all* p challenge witnesses by exploiting that M can repeatedly send new query s_i to B and that, with high probability, B behaves as in the first run. As a first step, it randomizes the first challenge statement s_1^* (exploiting random self-reducibility) and sends the result as a new query s_i' at index i to B. Since the distribution of the two queries s_i, s_i' are statistically close, the reduction will with high probability behave as after the first query and output a witness without calling the challenger of the complexity challenge. On failure, M simply generates another randomization of s_1^* and tries again. Observe that since we now rely on strong RRRs, the meta-reduction can, like the ideal attacker, *always* check if the responses from the reduction are correct. On success, M can exploit the response to s_i' and the properties of the RRR (random self-reducibility and re-randomizability) to obtain a solution w_1^* to the first challenge statement. After that, M repeats the process with all of its other challenge statements, one after the other. Since M can now *immediately* check if a witness w_i^* is indeed correct (exploiting the indirect membership test of strong RRRs at the end of Step $2'.\ell.j$ in the meta-reduction), the meta-reduction can proceed in a step-by-step manner and only continue if the previous witness was successfully found. In this way, the meta-reduction can slowly but surely accumulate all witnesses. Next, the meta-reduction returns to the original execution state and, after re-randomization, outputs the solutions to the challenge queries. By the properties of the RRR, the reduction will accept these values with high probability. The simulation continues until the next simulated attacker receives its challenge statements and the process of extracting solutions to the challenge statements is repeated. This increases the runtime of the meta-reduction at most by an additional factor of u. Finally, if M has computed responses to all challenge statements, B will output the solution to the tICA.

References

1. Auerbach, B., Cash, D., Fersch, M., Kiltz, E.: Memory-tight reductions. In: Katz, J., Shacham, H. (eds.) CRYPTO 2017, Part I, LNCS, vol. 10401, pp. 101–132. Springer, Heidelberg, August 2017. https://doi.org/10.1007/978-3-319-63688-7_4

2. Bader, C., Jager, T., Li, Y., Schäge, S.: On the impossibility of tight cryptographic reductions. In: Fischlin, M., Coron, J.S. (eds.) EUROCRYPT 2016, Part II. LNCS, vol. 9666, pp. 273–304. Springer, Heidelberg, May 2016.https://doi.org/10.1007/978-3-662-49896-5_10

3. Baecher, P., Brzuska, C., Fischlin, M.: Notions of black-box reductions, revisited. In: Sako, K., Sarkar, P. (eds.) ASIACRYPT 2013, Part I. LNCS, vol. 8269, pp. 296–315. Springer, Heidelberg, December 2013. https://doi.org/10.1007/978-3-642-42033-7_16

4. Baldimtsi, F., Lysyanskaya, A.: On the security of one-witness blind signature schemes. In: Sako, K., Sarkar, P. (eds.) ASIACRYPT 2013, Part II. LNCS, vol. 8270, pp. 82–99. Springer, Heidelberg, December 2013. https://doi.org/10.1007/978-3-642-42045-0_5

5. Boneh, D., Franklin, M.K.: Identity-based encryption from the Weil pairing. In: Kilian, J. (ed.) CRYPTO 2001. LNCS, vol. 2139, pp. 213–229. Springer, Heidelberg, August 2001. https://doi.org/10.1007/3-540-44647-8_13

6. Boneh, D., Venkatesan, R.: Breaking RSA may not be equivalent to factoring. In: Nyberg, K. (ed.) EUROCRYPT'98. LNCS, vol. 1403, pp. 59–71. Springer, Heidelberg, May/June 1998. https://doi.org/10.1007/BFb0054117

7. Bresson, E., Monnerat, J., Vergnaud, D.: Separation results on the "one-more" computational problems. In: Malkin, T. (ed.) CT-RSA 2008. LNCS, vol. 4964, pp. 71–87. Springer, Heidelberg, April 2008. https://doi.org/10.1007/978-3-540-79263-5_5

8. Brown, D.R.L.: Irreducibility to the one-more evaluation problems: more may be less. Cryptology ePrint Archive, Report 2007/435 (2007). http://eprint.iacr.org/

9. Canetti, R., Goldreich, O., Goldwasser, S., Micali, S.: Resettable zero-knowledge (extended abstract). In: 32nd ACM STOC, pp. 235–244. ACM Press, May 2000. https://doi.org/10.1145/335305.335334
10. Canetti, R., Lin, H., Pass, R.: Adaptive hardness and composable security in the plain model from standard assumptions. In: 51st FOCS, pp. 541–550. IEEE Computer Society Press, October 2010. https://doi.org/10.1109/FOCS.2010.86
11. Chung, K., Lin, H., Mahmoody, M., Pass, R.: On the power of nonuniformity in proofs of security. In: Kleinberg, R.D. (ed.) ITCS '13, Berkeley, CA, USA, 9-12 January 2013, pp. 389–400. ACM (2013). https://doi.org/10.1145/2422436.2422480
12. Coron, J.S.: Optimal security proofs for PSS and other signature schemes. In: Knudsen, L.R. (ed.) EUROCRYPT 2002, LNCS, vol. 2332, pp. 272–287. Springer, Heidelberg, Apr/May 2002. https://doi.org/10.1007/3-540-46035-7_18
13. Cramer, R., Shoup, V.: A practical public key cryptosystem provably secure against adaptive chosen ciphertext attack. In: Krawczyk, H. (ed.) CRYPTO'98, LNCS, vol. 1462, pp. 13–25. Springer, Heidelberg, August 1998. https://doi.org/10.1007/BFb0055717
14. Damgård, I., Jurik, M.: A generalisation, a simplification and some applications of Paillier's probabilistic public-key system. In: Kim, K. (ed.) PKC 2001. LNCS, vol. 1992, pp. 119–136. Springer, Heidelberg, February 2001. https://doi.org/10.1007/3-540-44586-2_9
15. Deng, Y., Goyal, V., Sahai, A.: Resolving the simultaneous resettability conjecture and a new non-black-box simulation strategy. In: 50th FOCS, pp. 251–260. IEEE Computer Society Press, October 2009. https://doi.org/10.1109/FOCS.2009.59
16. Diffie, W., Hellman, M.E.: New directions in cryptography. IEEE Trans. Inf. Theory $22(6)$, 644–654 (1976). https://doi.org/10.1109/TIT.1976.1055638
17. Dodis, Y., Oliveira, R., Pietrzak, K.: On the generic insecurity of the full domain hash. In: Shoup, V. (ed.) CRYPTO 2005. LNCS, vol. 3621, pp. 449–466. Springer, Heidelberg, August 2005. https://doi.org/10.1007/11535218_27
18. Dodis, Y., Reyzin, L.: On the power of claw-free permutations. In: Cimato, S., Galdi, C., Persiano, G. (eds.) SCN 02. LNCS, vol. 2576, pp. 55–73. Springer, Heidelberg, September 2003. https://doi.org/10.1007/3-540-36413-7_5
19. ElGamal, T.: A public key cryptosystem and a signature scheme based on discrete logarithms. In: Blakley, G.R., Chaum, D. (eds.) CRYPTO'84. LNCS, vol. 196, pp. 10–18. Springer, Heidelberg, August 1984
20. Fischlin, M., Fleischhacker, N.: Limitations of the meta-reduction technique: the case of Schnorr signatures. In: Johansson, T., Nguyen, P.Q. (eds.) EUROCRYPT 2013. LNCS, vol. 7881, pp. 444–460. Springer, Heidelberg, May 2013. https://doi.org/10.1007/978-3-642-38348-9_27
21. Fleischhacker, N., Jager, T., Schröder, D.: On tight security proofs for Schnorr signatures. In: Sarkar, P., Iwata, T. (eds.) ASIACRYPT 2014, Part I. LNCS, vol. 8873, pp. 512–531. Springer, Heidelberg, December 2014. https://doi.org/10.1007/978-3-662-45611-8_27
22. Fuchsbauer, G., Kiltz, E., Loss, J.: The algebraic group model and its applications. In: Shacham, H., Boldyreva, A. (eds.) CRYPTO 2018, Part II. LNCS, vol. 10992, pp. 33–62. Springer, Heidelberg, August 2018. https://doi.org/10.1007/978-3-319-96881-0_2
23. Garg, S., Bhaskar, R., Lokam, S.V.: Improved bounds on security reductions for discrete log based signatures. In: Wagner, D. (ed.) CRYPTO 2008. LNCS, vol. 5157, pp. 93–107. Springer, Heidelberg, August 2008. https://doi.org/10.1007/978-3-540-85174-5_6

24. Hanaoka, G., Matsuda, T., Schuldt, J.C.N.: On the impossibility of constructing efficient key encapsulation and programmable hash functions in prime order groups. In: Safavi-Naini, R., Canetti, R. (eds.) CRYPTO 2012. LNCS, vol. 7417, pp. 812–831. Springer, Heidelberg, August 2012. https://doi.org/10.1007/978-3-642-32009-5_47

25. Hofheinz, D., Jager, T., Knapp, E.: Waters signatures with optimal security reduction. In: Fischlin, M., Buchmann, J., Manulis, M. (eds.) PKC 2012. LNCS, vol. 7293, pp. 66–83. Springer, Heidelberg, May 2012. https://doi.org/10.1007/978-3-642-30057-8_5

26. Kakvi, S.A., Kiltz, E.: Optimal security proofs for full domain hash, revisited. In: Pointcheval, D., Johansson, T. (eds.) EUROCRYPT 2012. LNCS, vol. 7237, pp. 537–553. Springer, Heidelberg, April 2012. https://doi.org/10.1007/978-3-642-29011-4_32

27. Lindell, Y.: Is ElGamal IND-CCA1 Secure? – answer. https://crypto.stackexchange.com/questions/26867/is-elgamal-ind-cca1 (2015). Accessed 03 April 2022

28. Lindell, Y.: Fast secure two-party ECDSA signing. In: Katz, J., Shacham, H. (eds.) CRYPTO 2017, Part II. LNCS, vol. 10402, pp. 613–644. Springer, Heidelberg, August 2017. https://doi.org/10.1007/978-3-319-63715-0_21

29. Lipmaa, H.: On the CCA1-security of Elgamal and Damgård's Elgamal. Cryptology ePrint Archive, Report 2008/234 (2008). https://ia.cr/2008/234

30. Morgan, A., Pass, R.: On the security loss of unique signatures. In: Beimel, A., Dziembowski, S. (eds.) TCC 2018, Part I. LNCS, vol. 11239, pp. 507–536. Springer, Heidelberg, November 2018. https://doi.org/10.1007/978-3-030-03807-6_19

31. Paillier, P.: Public-key cryptosystems based on composite degree residuosity classes. In: Stern, J. (ed.) EUROCRYPT'99. LNCS, vol. 1592, pp. 223–238. Springer, Heidelberg, May 1999. https://doi.org/10.1007/3-540-48910-X_16

32. Paillier, P., Vergnaud, D.: Discrete-log-based signatures may not be equivalent to discrete log. In: Roy, B.K. (ed.) ASIACRYPT 2005. LNCS, vol. 3788, pp. 1–20. Springer, Heidelberg, December 2005. https://doi.org/10.1007/11593447_1

33. Paillier, P., Villar, J.L.: Trading one-wayness against chosen-ciphertext security in factoring-based encryption. In: Lai, X., Chen, K. (eds.) ASIACRYPT 2006. LNCS, vol. 4284, pp. 252–266. Springer, Heidelberg, December 2006. https://doi.org/10.1007/11935230_17

34. Pass, R.: Limits of provable security from standard assumptions. In: Fortnow, L., Vadhan, S.P. (eds.) 43rd ACM STOC. pp. 109–118. ACM Press, June 2011. https://doi.org/10.1145/1993636.1993652

35. Pass, R., Venkitasubramaniam, M.: On constant-round concurrent zero-knowledge. In: Canetti, R. (ed.) TCC 2008. LNCS, vol. 4948, pp. 553–570. Springer, Heidelberg, March 2008. https://doi.org/10.1007/978-3-540-78524-8_30

36. Pointcheval, D., Stern, J.: Security proofs for signature schemes. In: Maurer, U.M. (ed.) EUROCRYPT'96. LNCS, vol. 1070, pp. 387–398. Springer, Heidelberg, May 1996. https://doi.org/10.1007/3-540-68339-9_33

37. Reingold, O., Trevisan, L., Vadhan, S.P.: Notions of reducibility between cryptographic primitives. In: Naor, M. (ed.) TCC 2004. LNCS, vol. 2951, pp. 1–20. Springer, Heidelberg, February 2004. https://doi.org/10.1007/978-3-540-24638-1_1

38. Richardson, R., Kilian, J.: On the concurrent composition of zero-knowledge proofs. In: Stern, J. (ed.) EUROCRYPT'99. LNCS, vol. 1592, pp. 415–431. Springer, Heidelberg, May 1999. https://doi.org/10.1007/3-540-48910-X_29

39. Seurin, Y.: On the exact security of Schnorr-type signatures in the random oracle model. In: Pointcheval, D., Johansson, T. (eds.) EUROCRYPT 2012. LNCS, vol. 7237, pp. 554–571. Springer, Heidelberg, April 2012. https://doi.org/10.1007/978-3-642-29011-4_33

40. Wu, J., Stinson, D.R.: On the security of the ElGamal encryption scheme and Damgård's variant. IACR Cryptol. ePrint Arch. p. 200 (2008). http://eprint.iacr.org/2008/200

41. Zhang, J., Zhang, Z., Chen, Y., Guo, Y., Zhang, Z.: Black-box separations for one-more (static) CDH and its generalization. In: Sarkar, P., Iwata, T. (eds.) ASIACRYPT 2014, Part II. LNCS, vol. 8874, pp. 366–385. Springer, Heidelberg, December 2014. https://doi.org/10.1007/978-3-662-45608-8_20

Constructing Leakage-Resilient Shamir's Secret Sharing: Over Composite Order Fields

Hemanta K. Maji[1], Hai H. Nguyen[2([⊠])], Anat Paskin-Cherniavsky[3], and Xiuyu Ye[1]

[1] Department of Computer Science, Purdue University, West Lafayette, USA
{hmaji,ye151}@purdue.edu
[2] Department of Computer Science, ETH Zurich, Zurich, Switzerland
haihoang.nguyen@inf.ethz.ch
[3] Department of Computer Science, Ariel University, Ariel, Israel
anatpc@ariel.ac.il

Abstract. Probing physical bits in hardware has compromised cryptographic systems. This work investigates how to instantiate Shamir's secret sharing so that the physical probes into its shares reveal statistically insignificant information about the secret.

Over prime fields, Maji, Nguyen, Paskin-Cherniavsky, Suad, and Wang (EUROCRYPT 2021) proved that choosing random evaluation places achieves this objective with high probability. Our work extends their randomized construction to composite order fields – particularly for fields with characteristic 2. Next, this work presents an algorithm to classify evaluation places as secure or vulnerable against physical-bit probes for some specific cases.

Our security analysis of the randomized construction is Fourier-analytic, and the classification techniques are combinatorial. Our analysis relies on (1) contemporary Bézout-theorem-type algebraic complexity results that bound the number of simultaneous zeroes of a system of polynomial equations over composite order fields and (2) characterization of the zeroes of an appropriate generalized Vandermonde determinant.

1 Introduction

Threshold secret-sharing schemes, like *Shamir's secret-sharing* [37], distribute a secret among parties so that a quorum can reconstruct the secret. Their security

Hemanta K. Maji, and Xiuyu Ye are supported in part by an NSF CRII Award CNS–1566499, NSF SMALL Awards CNS–1618822 and CNS–2055605, the IARPA HEC-TOR project, MITRE Innovation Program Academic Cybersecurity Research Awards (2019–2020, 2020–2021), a Ross-Lynn Research Scholars Grant (2021–2022), a Purdue Research Foundation (PRF) Award (2017–2018), and The Center for Science of Information, an NSF Science and Technology Center, Cooperative Agreement CCF–0939370. Hai H. Nguyen is supported by the Zurich Information Security & Privacy Center (ZISC). Anat Paskin-Cherniavsky is supported by the Ariel Cyber Innovation Center in conjunction with the Israel National Cyber directorate in the Prime Minister's Office.

M. Joye and G. Leander (Eds.): EUROCRYPT 2024, LNCS 14654, pp. 286–315, 2024.
https://doi.org/10.1007/978-3-031-58737-5_11

is against an adversary who obtains the shares of a group of parties (who do not form the quorum) and has no information on the remaining shares. Side-channel attacks have repeatedly circumvented such "all-or-nothing" corruption models and revealed partial information about the secret by accumulating small leakage from all shares. A broad mathematical model for such side-channel attacks considers independent leakage from each share, i.e., local leakage.

Locally leakage-resilient secret sharing, introduced by Benhamouda et al. [5, 6] and (also implicit in) Goyal & Kumar [20], is a security metric that ensures the statistical independence of the secret and the local leakage from the shares. Inspired by real-world side-channel attacks, Ishai et al. [24] introduced the prominent physical bit probing model that locally leaks physical bits from memory storing the shares. Given the ubiquity of Shamir's secret sharing in privacy and cryptography technologies, it is natural to wonder:

> How do we instantiate Shamir's secret sharing
> to protect its secret against physical bit probes on the shares?

Maji, Nguyen, Paskin-Cherniavsky, Suad, and Wang [27] proved that for large prime moduli and reconstruction threshold ≥ 2, choosing the evaluation places for Shamir's secret sharing at random results in a locally leakage-resilient scheme secure against physical bit leakage with high probability. This work investigates the secret sharing over composite order fields, specifically large characteristic-2 fields used widely in practice.

Additional Motivation. Our research contributes to NIST's recent standardization efforts for threshold cryptographic schemes [9]. The security of Shamir's secret sharing is critical to this effort due to its applications in distributed key generation (for private and public-key primitives) and as a gadget in other higher-level primitives like secure computation. Section 1.3 presents another motivation for the question investigated in this work from the perspective of side-channel attacks.

1.1 Basic Preliminaries

This section presents basic definitions to facilitate the presentation of our results. Consider Shamir's secret sharing among n parties with reconstruction threshold k. Let F be a finite field of order $q = p^d$, where $p \geq 2$ is a prime and $d \in \{1, 2, \dots\}$. Elements of F are stored as length-d vectors of F_p elements, each stored in their binary representation. The security parameter λ is the number of bits required to represent each share, i.e., $\lambda = d \cdot \lceil \log_2 p \rceil$. Shamir's secret sharing chooses a random F-polynomial $P(Z)$ of degree $< k$ such that $P(0) = s$, the secret. The shares are $s_i = P(X_i)$, for $i \in \{1, 2, \dots, n\}$, where $X_1, X_2, \dots, X_n \in F^*$ are distinct evaluation places.

For a secret $s \in F$, represent the leakage joint distribution by $\ell(s)$, where $\ell(\cdot)$ represents the leakage function. Following [5,6], the insecurity of a secret sharing against a leakage class $\mathcal{L}$ is

$$\max_{\ell \in \mathcal{L}} \max_{s, s' \in F} \mathsf{SD}\left(\ell(s), \ell(s')\right). \tag{1}$$

Here, $\mathsf{SD}\,(\ell(s)\,,\,\ell(s'))$ represents the statistical distance between the leakage distributions when the secrets are s and s'.

This work considers physical bit leakages introduced by [24]. They leak arbitrary m_i physical bits from the i-th share, for $i \in \{1,2,\ldots,n\}$ and $m_i \in \{0,1,\ldots\}$. The total leakage $M = m_1 + m_2 + \cdots + m_n$ parameterizes our leakage class; this family of local leakages is represented by $\mathsf{PHYS}(M)$. This leakage class, in particular, allows the adversary to obtain the entire shares of a few parties and partial information from the remaining shares.[1]

1.2   Our Results

Result 1 (Randomized Construction for Composite Order Finite Fields)

Consider Shamir's secret sharing with evaluation places $X_1, X_2, \ldots, X_n \in F^*$ chosen uniformly at random. Suppose the total leakage $m_1 + m_2 + \cdots + m_n \leqslant \rho \cdot (k-1) \cdot \lambda$, where

$$\rho := \begin{cases} (1 - 1/p), & \text{for } 2 \leqslant p < (k-1), \\ 1, & \text{otherwise.} \end{cases}$$

With probability $1 - \mathsf{poly}(k)/\sqrt{q}$ over the choice of evaluation places, the resulting secret sharing has $\mathsf{poly}(k)/\sqrt{q}$ insecurity against physical bit leakages.

A randomness beacon [34] or coin-tossing protocol (depending on the application scenario) can generate public randomness to instantiate our randomized construction. In cryptographic applications, the number of parties n and the reconstruction threshold k are (at most) $\mathsf{poly}(\lambda)$ and, in several scenarios, constants as well. On the other hand, the order of the field F_q is exponential in the security parameter λ. Therefore, our result guarantees that the insecurity is exponentially small with probability exponentially close to 1. Section 1.4 presents the technical overview of our randomized construction.

Remark 1 (Clarification). The result above ignores a $\mathsf{poly}\log(\lambda)$ term for clarity of presentation. Corollary 2, Theorem 3, and Theorem 4 present the exact technical statement.

Comparison with the Result over Prime Fields. For prime fields (i.e., $q = p$), Maji, Nguyen, Paskin-Cherniavsky, Suad, Wang [27] proved that randomly choosing evaluation places results in a secure scheme as long as the total physical bit leakage $m_1 + m_2 + \ldots + m_n$ is less than the total entropy in the secret shares of the secret 0, which is (roughly) $(k-1) \cdot \lambda$. In our result, the permissible leakage tolerance may be slightly smaller for composite order fields, depending on the field characteristic. When $p \geqslant (k-1)$, our tolerance coincides with theirs.

---

[1] Leakage-resilient secure computation considers adversaries that corrupt parties to obtain their shares and leak additional information from honest parties' shares.

For small characteristic fields $2 \leqslant p < (k-1)$, our tolerance is $(1 - 1/p)$ times smaller.

Ideally, it is desirable to derandomize such randomized constructions because adversarially set randomness can make the scheme insecure, unbeknownst to the honest parties. Even for a fixed leakage ℓ, non-trivial techniques to estimate the insecurity expression in Eq. 1 are unknown. Toward this objective, we present a classification algorithm that identifies secure evaluation places for $k = 2$ against single *block-leakage* per share. Recall that the $x \in F_q$ is represented as a length-d vector of F_p elements. The adversary can leak one F_p element from this vector representation of x. Single block leakage can simulate multiple physical bit leakages from the same block of the share.

Result 2 *Against single block leakage from each share, Shamir's secret sharing is either perfectly secure or completely insecure. Given evaluation places* $X_1, X_2, \ldots, X_n$ *as input, our algorithm (Fig. 1) correctly classifies them as secure or not.*

The leakage distribution is independent of the secret in a perfectly secure secret sharing. A completely insecure secret sharing has two secrets the leakage can always distinguish. We also identify a block leakage attack if the evaluation places are insecure. Evaluation places satisfy a dichotomy; they are either perfectly secure or completely insecure – there is no "partial" insecurity. We prove that at least $1 - d^n p^{n-1}/q$ fraction of the evaluation places are secure, which is close to 1 for n close to d. The run-time of our algorithm is $d^n \text{poly}(lambda)$, which may be inefficient for large n. However, avoiding this factor seems challenging because there are d^n different block leakage attacks, and our algorithm outputs the leakage attack when evaluation places are vulnerable. Section 1.5 presents the technical overview of our classification result.

1.3 Prior Related Works

Physical Bit Probing Attacks. Motivated by attacks on cryptosystems, Ishai et al. [24] introduced a powerful leakage model that *probes physical bits* in the memory storing the shares. On the *additive secret-sharing* scheme over prime fields F_p among n parties, Maji et al. [27] introduced a local attack that leaks the parity of each share by probing their least significant bit (namely, the parity-of-the-parities attacker). This attack can distinguish two secrets with $(2/\pi)^n \approx (0.63)^n$ advantage [1,27,28] for any prime p. Thus, additive secret sharing is vulnerable when the number of shares is small. Furthermore, the distinguishing advantage of the attack increases as the order p of the prime field decreases. In particular, over F_2, this leakage can always distinguish secrets 0 and 1, irrespective of the number of parties.

Shamir's secret sharing inherits these vulnerabilities if its evaluation places are carelessly chosen [13,27]. Over composite order fields, the threat of these attacks is determined by the field's characteristic – the smaller the characteristic, the more devastating the attack. For example, over characteristic-2 fields, the parity-of-the-parities attacker can distinguish the secret $0, 1 \in F_{2^d}$ with certainty, where $d \in \{1, 2, \dots\}$.

The set of these specific vulnerable evaluation places is known to have an exponentially small density in the set of all possible evaluation places.

Given this background, it is natural to wonder: *Are there additional vulnerable evaluation places? What is the density of the set of all vulnerable evaluation places against physical bit probing attacks? Can we identify the vulnerable evaluation places?* Our work proves that the density of these vulnerable evaluation places is exponentially small, even when allowing multiple probes per share. We also characterize all vulnerable evaluation places for a few parameter choices.

Other Related Works. A large body of works constructs non-linear leakage-resilient secret-sharing schemes [2,3,7,8,10,11,16,17,23,26,32,38]. Benhamouda et al. [5] initiated the investigation of the security of additive and Shamir's secret sharing against local leakage attacks. A sequence of works considers arbitrary single-bit local leakage from each share of Shamir's secret sharing. Against such schemes, when the ratio of the reconstruction threshold to the number of parties is $\geqslant 0.69$, the secret sharing is secure for all evaluation places [5,6,25,29,31]. However, such schemes *cannot facilitate secure multiplication*, which requires the ratio to be < 0.5. The scope of our work includes small reconstruction thresholds, for example, $k \geqslant 2$, and many parties. So, our results lead to leakage-resilient secure multiplication of secrets against physical bit probes.

Codeword Repairing – An Antithetical Objective. Guruswami and Wootters [21, 22] introduced repairing Reed-Solomon codewords. There is a vast literature on this topic [12,14,15,18,19,35,36,39,40,42,43]; refer to [12, Section 6] for the applicability of these results to the security of Shamir's secret sharing. These repairing algorithms reconstruct the entire secret using small leakage per share, a strongly antithetical objective to leakage resilience. Leakage resilience insists that leakage from the shares reveals no statistically significant information about the secret, not just ruling out the possibility of reconstructing the entire secret. Nielsen and Simkin [33] demonstrated such attacks that reconstruct the secret with some probability. Unsurprisingly, leakage resilience has been significantly challenging to achieve.

1.4   Technical Overview: Randomized Construction

We will prove that Shamir's secret sharing is leakage-resilient against physical probes for most evaluation places $\boldsymbol{X} = (X_1, X_2, \dots, X_n)$. We illustrate the technical ideas using $m = 1$, i.e., a single physical bit probe per share. The extension of the analysis for the general case is included at the end of this section. Our analysis will follow the blueprint of [27].

Reduction 1. **Fix two secrets** $s.s' \in F$. We prove the following two bounds. By now, standard Fourier-analytic techniques in the literature [5,27] upper bound the statistical distance of the leakage as follows (see Proposition 3),

$$\mathsf{SD}\left(\ell(s)\,,\,\ell(s')\right) \leqslant \sum_{t\in\{0,1\}^n} \sum_{\alpha\in C_X^\perp\backslash\{0\}} \left(\prod_{i=1}^n \left|\widehat{\mathbb{1}_{t_i}}(\alpha_i)\right|\right),$$

where $\mathbb{1}_{t_i}$ is the indicator of the set $\{x \in F: \ell_i(x) = t_i\}$, C_X is the generalized Reed-Solomon code and is the set of all possible secret shares of secret 0 in Shamir's scheme with evaluation places X, and $C_X^\perp$ is the dual code of C_X.

Next, we prove that this upper bound is small in expectation over randomly chosen evaluation places $X \in (F^*)^n$ (Lemma 8). That is,

$$\mathbb{E}_X\left[\sum_{t\in\{0,1\}^n} \sum_{\alpha\in C_X^\perp\backslash\{0\}} \left(\prod_{i=1}^n \left|\widehat{\mathbb{1}_{t_i}}(\alpha_i)\right|\right)\right] \leqslant \exp(-\Theta(\lambda)).$$

This upper bound is sufficient for our objective. We use a union bound over all possible leakage functions in the family to conclude that most evaluation places result in a locally leakage-resilient Shamir's secret sharing. Next, a Markov inequality leads to the conclusion that nearly all evaluation places are leakage-resilient, except an exponentially small fraction.

Reduction 2. We use Fourier analysis over composite order fields to establish the above second bound. The left-hand side of the inequality is rewritten as

$$\sum_{t\in\{0,1\}^n} \sum_{\alpha\in F^n\backslash\{0\}} \left(\prod_{i=1}^n \left|\widehat{\mathbb{1}_{t_i}}(\alpha_i)\right|\right) \cdot \Pr_X\left[\alpha \in C_X^\perp\right]$$

Section 5 reduces this estimation to the following two subproblems.

Subproblem 1: Our aim is to upper-bound the probability that a vector α belongs to the dual code $C_X^\perp$. Estimating this probability is equivalent to counting the simultaneous zeroes of the equation below.

$$\begin{pmatrix} X_1 & X_2 & \cdots & X_n \\ X_1^2 & X_2^2 & \cdots & X_n^2 \\ \vdots & \vdots & \ddots & \vdots \\ X_1^{k-1} & X_2^{k-1} & \cdots & X_n^{k-1} \end{pmatrix} \cdot \begin{pmatrix} \alpha_1 \\ \alpha_2 \\ \vdots \\ \vdots \\ \alpha_n \end{pmatrix} = \begin{pmatrix} 0 \\ 0 \\ \vdots \\ 0 \end{pmatrix}.$$

Our objective is to count the number of $X \in (F^*)^n$ satisfying the equation above such that $X_1, X_2, \ldots, X_n$ are distinct.

We rely on a contemporary Bézout-like theorem, particularly a form with an easy-to-verify analytic test (refer to Imported Theorem 1), to claim that the number of solutions is bounded. [27] used [41]'s result for prime fields; we use

[4]'s very recent result for composite order fields. There are further nuances when working over composite order fields highlighted below. Consider the following cases:

1. If $p \geqslant k$, then we fix $(n - k + 1)$ variables to reduce the above equation to a square system of polynomials with $(k-1)$ variables and $(k-1)$ polynomials. By Imported Theorem 1, there will be at most $(k-1)!$ solutions. Consequently, overall, the number of solutions $X \in (F^*)^n$ is at most $(k-1)! \cdot p^{n-k+1}$ (Lemma 1).

2. If $p = 2$, we have to do a more subtle analysis, reducing the equation to a square system with $k/2$ variables and $k/2$ polynomials. The subtlety arises because we cannot use even powers in our system of equations, a concern similar to Example 1 in Sect. 1.6. Instead, we will use equations with odd powers, cutting the size of the system of equations to (roughly) $k/2$, down from $(k - 1)$. Like the previous case, the number of solutions is at most $(k - 1)! \cdot p^{n-k/2}$ (Lemma 2).

3. If $3 \leqslant p < k$, we prove the result for $p = (k-1)$ or $p = k-2$ explicitly (Lemma 4). We can also write the solution in general with roughly $2k^2/(q-1)$ density of roots (Lemma 3).

Section 1.6 elaborates on this aspect of our technical analysis.

Subproblem 2: After problem 1 is solved, we bound the ℓ_1-Fourier norm of the physical bit leakage function (Sect. 4). That is, for every $t_i \in \{0,1\}$, the objective is to upper bound

$$\left\| \widehat{\mathbb{1}_{t_i}} \right\|_1 := \sum_{\alpha_i \in F} \left| \widehat{\mathbb{1}_{t_i}(\alpha_i)} \right|$$

Our proof heavily relies on the composite order field F having subgroups (subspaces). We show that ℓ_1-Fourier norm of a one-bit physical leakage function over F is (less than or) equal to that over the base (prime) field F_p. Then, we apply the bound for ℓ_1-Fourier norm of physical leakage over the prime field in [27] when $p > 2$. Using a different analysis, we provide a stronger bound when $p = 2$. See Sect. 4 for details.

Resolving the two problems above completes the proof of Theorem 1.

Extension to multiple-bit leakage. Suppose that the adversary leaks m_i bits from the i-th share. We employ the approach in [27] to prove the result. Consider secret sharing, where the i-th share is repeated m_i times. The leakage distribution induced by the m_i-bit physical leakage on Shamir's scheme is identical to that induced by the one-bit physical leakage on the new scheme with repeated shares. Then, the technical analysis proceeds analogously to the presentation above. Theorem 2 summarizes this result.

1.5 Technical Overview: Classification Algorithm

Consider $n = 2$ parties and reconstruction threshold $k = 2$. Consider Shamir's secret sharing over F_q, where $q = p^d$ and $d \in \{2, 3, \dots\}$. To begin, suppose the evaluation places are $(X_1, X_2) \in (F_q)^n$.

Interpret $F_q \cong F_p[\zeta]/\Pi(\zeta)$, where $\Pi(\zeta)$ is an irreducible F_p-polynomial with degree d. Represent elements of F_q as a length-d vector of F_p elements. An element $x \in F_q$ that is the polynomial $x_0 + x_1\zeta + \cdots + x_{d-1}\zeta^{d-1}$ is represented as the vector $(x_0, x_1, \ldots, x_{d-1}) \in F_p^d$. This section considers *single block leakage* – leaking the i-th block of $x \in F_q$ reveals $x_i \in F_p$, where $i \in \{0, 1, \ldots, d-1\}$. *Our objective is to determine whether Shamir's secret sharing (with the specific evaluation places) is secure against single block leakage from each share.*

Consider a secret $s \in F_q$. The polynomial to generate its shares is $P(Z) = s + P_1 \cdot Z$, where $P_1 \in F_p$ is chosen uniformly at random. The two shares are

$$(s + P_1 X_1 , s + P_1 X_2).$$

Consider arbitrary $i, j \in \{0, 1, \ldots, d-1\}$ and the leakage function that leaks the first share's i-th block and the second share's j-th block. So, the leakage joint distribution is:

$$\left((s + P_1 X_1)_i , (s + P_1 X_2)_j \right).$$

By a change of random variable, this distribution is identical to

$$\left((Q)_i , (Q \cdot (X_2 X_1^{-1}) + s')_j \right),$$

where $s' = s \cdot \left(1 - X_2 X_1^{-1}\right)$, an F_q linear automorphism and $Q \in F_q$ is chosen uniformly at random.

We prove a technical result (Proposition 4) similar to the proof strategy of [30]: There is $\eta^{(i)} \in F_q$ such that $(x)_i = \left(x \cdot \eta^{(i)}\right)_0$, for all $x \in F_q$ and $i \in \{0, 1, \ldots, d-1\}$. Therefore, the leakage is identical to

$$\left(\left(Q \cdot \eta^{(i)}\right)_0 , \left(Q \cdot (X_2 X_1^{-1}) \cdot \eta^{(j)} + s''\right)_0 \right),$$

where $s \mapsto s''$ is a linear automorphism over F_q. Next, by renaming the random variables, the leakage distribution is:

$$\left((R)_0 , \left(R \cdot (X_2 X_1^{-1}) \cdot \left(\eta^{(j)} \eta^{(i)^{-1}}\right) + s''\right)_0 \right).$$

To conclude, the leakage joint distribution is

$$(R_0 , (R \cdot \beta(i, j) + s'')_0),$$

where $\beta(i, j) := X_2 X_1^{-1} \cdot \eta^{(j)} (\eta^{(i)})^{-1}$.

Fix the leakage $r_0 := R_0 \in F_p$. Define $V = \{x \in F_q : x_0 = 0\}$. We know that R is a uniformly random sample from the set $V + r_0 \subseteq F_q$. We will present a technical result (Lemma 9) proving the following: For any $\beta \in F_q \setminus F_p$, for x sampled uniformly at random from $V + q_0$, the distribution $(x \cdot \beta)_0$ is uniformly at random over F_p.[2]

---

[2] Looking ahead, we will prove a significantly stronger generalization of Lemma 9 for arbitrary number of parties.

Using this result, we conclude that the distribution $(R \cdot \beta(i,j) + s''')_0$ is uniformly at random over F_p, conditioned on the leakage from the first share being q_0. Therefore, the leakage is uniformly distributed over $(F_p)^2$, irrespective of the secret s, as long as

$$\beta(i,j) := X_2 X_1^{-1} \cdot \eta^{(i)} (\eta^{(j)})^{-1} \in F_q \setminus F_p.$$

So, Shamir's secret sharing with evaluation places (X_1, X_2) is perfectly secure against block leakage if the above condition holds for all $i, j \in \{0, 1, \ldots, d-1\}$.

Furthermore, this characterization is tight. When $\beta(i,j) \in F_p$, then two appropriate secrets can always be distinguished. Without loss of generality, consider $i = j = 0$ and $X_2 = c \cdot X_1$, for some $c \in F_p$. For secret $s = 0$, the identity $c \cdot (s_1)_0 + (s_2)_0 = 0$ will be satisfied, where s_1, s_2 are the two shares. For secret $s = 1$, this identity will never be satisfied.

Based on this analysis, the following algorithm tests the security of evaluation places (X_1, X_2):

1. Initialize the bad set $B = \emptyset$.
2. For each $i, j \in \{0, 1, \ldots, d-1\}$: Update $B \longleftarrow B \bigcup F_p \cdot (\eta^{(i)})^{-1} \eta^{(j)}$.
3. If $\alpha_2 \alpha_1^{-1} \notin B$: return "Secure;" else, return "Insecure."

This proves that at least $1 - d^2 p/q$ fraction of evaluation places are secure.

Extension to Larger Number n of Parties. Consider Shamir's secret sharing for n parties and reconstruction threshold $k = 2$. The evaluation places are $X_1, X_2, \ldots, X_n \in F^*$ and the shares are $s_1, s_2, \ldots, s_n$. Consider leaking blocks $i_1, i_2, \ldots, i_n$ from shares $s_1, s_2, \ldots, s_n$, respectively, where $i_1, i_2, \ldots, i_n \in \{0, 1, \ldots, d-1\}$. The joint leakage distribution is:

$$\Big((s_1)_{i_1} , (s_2)_{i_2} , \ldots, (s_n)_{i_n} \Big),$$

where $s_i = s + P_1 \cdot X_i$, for $i \in \{1, 2, \ldots, n\}$ and uniformly at random $P_1 \in F_q$.

Similar to the analysis for $(n, k) = (2, 2)$ above, the previous distribution is identical to the leakage distribution:

$$\Big(\big(Q X_1 \eta^{(i_1)}\big)_0 , \big(Q X_2 \eta^{(i_2)}\big)_0 + t_2 , \ldots, \big(Q X_n \eta^{(i_n)}\big)_0 + t_n \Big),$$

where $s \mapsto t_j$ are appropriate linear automorphisms over F_q, for all $j \in \{2, 3, \ldots, n\}$ and uniformly at random $Q \in F_q$. Similar to the approach before, our objective is to show that the evaluation places $X_1, X_2, \ldots, X_n$ are secure if (and only if) the following elements

$$X_1 \eta^{(i_1)}, X_2 \eta^{(i_2)}, \ldots, X_n \eta^{(i_n)} \in F_q$$

are all F_p-linearly independent.

If some of these elements are linearly dependent over F_p, then the leakages also satisfy the same linear dependence when the secret $s = 0$. For $s = 1$, this particular linear dependence will not hold. We prove a technical result (Lemma 10) showing that if these elements above are linearly independent, then the distribution

$$\left(\left(QX_1\eta^{(i_1)} \right)_0 , \left(QX_2\eta^{(i_2)} \right)_0 , \ldots, \left(QX_n\eta^{(i_n)} \right)_0 \right)$$

is identical to the uniform distribution over $(F_p)^n$ for uniformly random $Q \in F_q$. From this fact, it is clear that the leakage distribution is also uniformly random over $(F_p)^n$. So, the secret sharing is perfectly secure against this particular leakage.

Building on this, we have the following algorithm to test the security of evaluation places $X_1, X_2, \ldots, X_n$:

1. For each $i_1, i_2, \ldots, i_n \in \{0, 1, \ldots, d - 1\}$: If the set $\{X_1\eta^{(i_1)}, X_2\eta^{(i_2)}, \ldots, X_n\eta^{(i_n)}\} \subseteq F_q$ is *not* F_p-linearly independent, return "Insecure."
2. Return "Secure."

This algorithm demonstrates that (roughly) at least $1 - d^n p^{n-1}/q$ fraction of the evaluation places are secure. This fraction is $1 - o(1)$ for $d = \lambda - o(\lambda)$. The running time of our algorithm is $d^n \mathsf{poly}(lambda)$, which may be inefficient for large n.

1.6   Discussion: Jacobian Test & the Number of Isolated Zeroes

Overview. Generally speaking, there are two types of "bad" cases for our randomized construction: (1) zeroes of a Jacobian and (2) (isolated) zeroes of a system of polynomial equations. The zeroes of the Jacobian are due to "redundancies" in the system of equations; for example, two evaluation places being identical. For prime fields, this was the only form of badness it captured. For composite order fields, there are additional such bad cases; worked-out examples below will illustrate them. However, the density of the set of these zeroes is $\mathsf{poly}(k)/q$, an exponentially small number. Outside the Jacobian's zeroes, the (isolated) zeroes of the system of polynomial equations (specifically corresponding to a generalized Vandermonde matrix being rank deficient) are the "Bézout-like" zeroes. Their number is upper-bounded by $k!$ (the product of degree), and their density is $k!/q^k \ll k/q$, exponentially small as well.

The Details. This section closely follows the notation and presentation in [4], which we felt was more approachable. Let $f_j \in F[X_1, X_2, \ldots, X_k]$ be a polynomial of degree $d_j \in \{1, 2, \ldots\}$, where $j \in \{1, 2, \ldots, k\}$ and F is an arbitrary finite field. The objective is to count the simultaneous zeroes of $f_j = 0$ for all $j \in \{1, 2, \ldots, k\}$. We represent the system as $\mathbf{f} = 0$ for brevity. We define the corresponding Jacobian as the determinant below:

$$J(\mathbf{f}) := \det \left(\frac{\partial f_j}{\partial X_i} \right)_{i,j \in \{1,2,\ldots,k\}} \in F[X_1, X_2, \ldots, X_k].$$

For $\mathbf{a} \in F^k$, $\mathbf{f}(\mathbf{a})$ represents the evaluation of the system of polynomials at $\mathbf{a}$, and $J(\mathbf{f}; \mathbf{a})$ represents the evaluation of the Jacobian $J(\mathbf{f})$ at $\mathbf{a}$.

Definition 1 (Isolated Zero). *An* $\mathbf{a} \in F^k$ *is an* isolated zero *of the system* $\mathbf{f} = 0$, *if* $\mathbf{f}(\mathbf{a}) = 0$ *but* $J(\mathbf{f}; \mathbf{a}) \neq 0$.

Counting all the zeroes of $\mathbf{f} = 0$ is challenging. However, [4] presents a bound for the number of *isolated zeroes* of a system of polynomial equations.

Imported Result 1 (Corollary 1.3 in [4]) *Let* $\mathcal{N}(\mathbf{f})$ *represent the number of isolated zeroes of the system of equations* $\mathbf{f} = 0$, *then* $\mathcal{N}(\mathbf{f}) \leqslant d_1 \cdot d_2 \cdots d_k$.

Wooley [41] proved this result for prime fields F, and Maji et al. [27] used Wooley's result to prove the leakage resilience of Shamir's secret sharing over prime fields. Zhao [44] extended Wooley's result to arbitrary finite fields, and Bafna et al. [4] present an elementary proof for this result (and fill some missing gaps in the proof of [44]).

Our high-level strategy for using this imported result is the following. We will pick random $\mathbf{a} \in F^k$ and hope that only a few of them will satisfy $J(\mathbf{f}; \mathbf{a}) = 0$ or $\mathbf{f}(\mathbf{a}) = 0$. For the remaining $\mathbf{a}$ (whose density will be close to 1), our analysis will show that they correspond to "secure Shamir's scheme."

Worked-Out Examples. Example 1. Let F be a finite field of characteristic 2. Consider the system of equations $f_1 = X_1 + X_2 = 0$ and $f_2 = X_1^2 + X_2^2 = 0$, where $k = 2$. Note that the Jacobian of this system of equations is

$$J(\mathbf{f}) = \det \begin{pmatrix} 1 & 2 \cdot X_1 \\ 1 & 2 \cdot X_2 \end{pmatrix} = 0,$$

for all $(X_1, X_2) \in F^k$, because F has characteristic 2 and $2 \cdot X = 0$ for any $X \in F$. Since the Jacobian is (identical to) the 0 polynomial, there are no isolated zeroes.

Example 2. Let F be a finite field of characteristic 2. Consider the system of equations $f_1 = X_1 + X_2 = 0$ and $f_2 = X_1^3 + X_2^3 = 0$, where $k = 2$. Note that the Jacobian of this system of equations is

$$J(\mathbf{f}) = \det \begin{pmatrix} 1 & 3 \cdot X_1^2 \\ 1 & 3 \cdot X_2^2 \end{pmatrix} = 3 \cdot (X_1^2 - X_2^2).$$

Note that (for a characteristic 2 field F) the Jacobian $J(\mathbf{f}; \mathbf{a}) \neq 0$ if (and only if) a_1, a_2 are distinct. So, among all $\mathbf{a} \in F^k$, the number of isolated solution (i.e., where $J(\mathbf{f}; \mathbf{a}) \neq 0$) is at most $d_1 \cdot d_2 = 1 \cdot 3 = 3$.

Example 3. Let F be a finite field of characteristic 3. Consider the system of equations $f_1 = X_1 + X_2 + X_3 = 0$, $f_2 = X_1^2 + X_2^2 + X_3^2 = 0$, and $f_3 = X_1^4 + X_2^4 + X_3^4 = 0$, where $k = 3$. The Jacobian is

$$J(\mathbf{f}) = \det \begin{pmatrix} 1 & 2 \cdot X_1 & 4 \cdot X_1^3 \\ 1 & 2 \cdot X_2 & 4 \cdot X_2^3 \\ 1 & 2 \cdot X_3 & 4 \cdot X_3^3 \end{pmatrix} = 8 \cdot (X_1 - X_2)(X_2 - X_3)(X_3 - X_1) \cdot (X_1 + X_2 + X_3).$$

Note that $J(\mathbf{f}; \mathbf{a}) = 0$ if (and only if)

1. a_1, a_2, a_3 are not distinct, or
2. $a_1 + a_2 + a_3 = 0$.

This example highlights that the Jacobian can also be 0 in many new and unexpected ways over composite order fields. Such determinants are referred to as *generalized Vandermonde* determinants, and identifying their zeroes is an open research problem in mathematics. When the Jacobian is not zero, there are at most $d_1 \cdot d_2 \cdot d_3 = 8$ values of $\mathbf{a} \in F^k$ such that $\mathbf{f}(\mathbf{a}) = 0$.

Example 4. A more typical example will be the following. Suppose F is a finite field of characteristic $p > k$. For $j \in \{1, 2, \ldots, k\}$, consider the equation $f_j = \sum_{i=1}^{k} X_i^j = 0$. In this case, the Jacobian is the standard Vandermonde matrix

$$J(\mathbf{f}) = \det \left(j X_i^{j-1} \right)_{i,j \in \{1,2,\ldots,k\}} = k! \cdot \prod_{1 \leqslant i < j \leqslant k} (X_i - X_j).$$

The Jacobian is 0 if (and only if) $X_1, X_2, \ldots, X_k$ are not all distinct. When, $X_1, X_2, \ldots, X_k$ are all distinct, then $\mathbf{f}(\mathbf{a}) = 0$ has at most $d_1 \cdot d_2 \cdots d_k = k!$ isolated zeroes.

2   Preliminaries

We always use F to denote a finite field of order p^d for some prime p and positive integer d. The set $F[X_1, X_2, \ldots, X_n]$ denotes the set of all multivariate polynomials on $X_1, X_2, \ldots, X_n$ whose coefficients are in F. We use bold letters $\mathbf{X}, \boldsymbol{\ell}, \boldsymbol{\alpha}, \ldots$ to denote vectors whose length will be apparent in the context. For example, $\mathbf{X}$ usually denotes the vector $(X_1, X_2, \ldots, X_n)$ of length n.

For any set S, we use U_S to denote the uniform distribution over the set S. The $\mathbb{1}_S$ represents its indicator function.

Statistical Distance. For any two distributions P and Q over a countable sample space, the statistical distance between the two distributions, represented by $\mathsf{SD}(P, Q)$, is defined as $\frac{1}{2} \sum_x |\Pr[P = x] - \Pr[Q = x]|$.

We shall use $f(\lambda) \sim g(\lambda)$ if $f(\lambda) = (1 + o(1)) g(\lambda)$. Additionally, we write $f(\lambda) \lesssim g(\lambda)$ if $f(\lambda) \leqslant (1 + o(1)) g(\lambda)$.

2.1   Secret Sharing Schemes

Definition 2 ($(n, k, \mathbf{X})_F$-Shamir Secret Sharing). *Let F be a finite field and n, k be positive integers such that $k \leqslant n$. Let $\mathbf{X} = (X_1, X_2, \ldots, X_n) \in (F^*)^n$ be n distinct evaluation places. The corresponding $(n, k, \mathbf{X})_F$-Shamir secret sharing, denoted as $\mathsf{ShamirSS}(n, k, \mathbf{X})_F$, is defined as follows.*

1. *Sharing phase: For any secret $s \in F$, $\mathsf{Share}^{\mathbf{X}}(s)$ randomly picks a F-polynomial $P(z)$ of degree strictly less than k such that $P(0) = s$. The shares are $s_i = P(X_i)$ for $i \in \{1, 2, \ldots, n\}$.*
2. *Reconstruction phase: Given any $s_{i_1}, s_{i_2}, \ldots, s_{i_t}$ shares for some $t \geqslant k$, the reconstruction algorithm $\mathsf{Rec}^{\mathbf{X}}$ interpolates to obtain the unique polynomial $f \in F[X]/X^k$ satisfying $f(X_{i_j}) = s_{i_j}$ for every $1 \leqslant j \leqslant t$, and outputs $f(0)$ to be the reconstructed secret.*

2.2   Physical-Bit Leakages and Leakage-Resilient Secret Sharing

Every element $x = x_0 + x_1\zeta + \cdots + x_{d-1}\zeta^{d-1} \in F$ is equivalently represented as $\boldsymbol{x} = (x_0, x_1, \ldots, x_{d-1})$. Effectively, each element of F is stored as a length-d vector of F_p elements, each stored as $\lceil \log_2 p \rceil$-bit in their binary representation. The security parameter $\lambda = d \lceil \log_2 p \rceil$ is the number of bits for each element in F. For example, in the finite field F_{5^2} with 25 elements, $\lambda = 6$, the element 3 is stored as $(011, 000)$, and the element $1 + 4\zeta$ is stored as $(001, 100)$.

Definition 3. *An m-bit physical leakage function $\boldsymbol{\ell} = (\ell_1, \ell_2, \ldots, \ell_n)$ on $(n, k, \boldsymbol{X})_F$-Shamir secret sharing leaks m physical bits from every share locally, where each $\ell_i \colon F \to \{0, 1\}^m$ for $1 \leqslant i \leqslant n$. For a secret $s \in F$, the joint leakage distribution, denoted as $\boldsymbol{\ell}(s)$, is defined as the following experiment.*

1. *Sample $(s_1, s_2, \ldots, s_n) \leftarrow \mathsf{Share}^{\boldsymbol{X}}(s)$,*
2. *Output $(\ell_1(s_1), \ell_2(s_2), \ldots, \ell_n(s_n))$.*

Definition 4 ($(\boldsymbol{m}, \varepsilon)_F$-LLRSS). *Let $\boldsymbol{m} = (m_1, m_2, \ldots, m_n)$. An $(n, k, \boldsymbol{X})_F$-Shamir secret sharing scheme is an $(\boldsymbol{m}, \varepsilon)$-local-leakage-resilient secret sharing scheme against $\boldsymbol{m}$ physical-bit leakage (represented as $(\boldsymbol{m}, \varepsilon)_F$-LLRSS), if it provides the following guarantee. For any two secrets $s, s' \in F$ and any $\boldsymbol{m}$-bit physical leakage function $\boldsymbol{\ell} = (\ell_1, \ell_2, \ldots, \ell_n)$, where $\ell_i \colon F \to \{0, 1\}^{m_i}$ for $1 \leqslant i \leqslant n$, it holds that*

$$\mathsf{SD}\left(\boldsymbol{\ell}(s), \, \boldsymbol{\ell}(s')\right) \leqslant \varepsilon.$$

2.3   Generalized Reed-Solomon Codes and Vandermonde Matrices

Definition 5 ($(n, k, \boldsymbol{X}, \boldsymbol{\alpha})_F$-GRS). *A generalized Reed-Solomon code over a finite field F with message length k and block length n consists of an encoding function $\mathsf{Enc} \colon F^k \to F^n$ and decoding function $\mathsf{Dec} \colon F^n \to F^k$. It is specified by the evaluation places $\boldsymbol{X} = (X_1, \ldots, X_n) \in (F^*)^n$ such that X_i's are all distinct, and a scaling vector $\boldsymbol{\alpha} = (\alpha_1, \ldots, \alpha_n) \in (F^*)^n$. Given $\boldsymbol{X}$ and $\boldsymbol{\alpha}$, the encoding function is defined as*

$$\mathsf{Enc}(m_1, \ldots, m_k) := (\alpha_1 \cdot f(X_1), \ldots, \alpha_n \cdot f(X_n)),$$

where $f(X) := m_1 + m_2 X + \cdots + m_k X^{k-1}$.

In particular, the generator matrix of the linear $(n, k, \boldsymbol{X}, \boldsymbol{\alpha})_F$-GRS code is

$$\begin{pmatrix} \alpha_1 \cdot 1 & \alpha_2 \cdot 1 & \cdots & \alpha_n \cdot 1 \\ \alpha_1 \cdot X_1 & \alpha_2 \cdot X_2 & \cdots & \alpha_n \cdot X_n \\ \vdots & \vdots & \ddots & \vdots \\ \alpha_1 \cdot X_1^{k-1} & \alpha_2 \cdot X_2^{k-1} & \cdots & \alpha_n \cdot X_n^{k-1} \end{pmatrix}.$$

We denote $C_{\boldsymbol{X}}$ as the set of all possible secret shares of secret 0 for $(n, k, \boldsymbol{X})_F$-Shamir secret sharing. The following fact will be useful.

Fact 1 *The set $C_{\boldsymbol{X}}$ is a $(n, k-1, \boldsymbol{X}, \boldsymbol{X})_F$-GRS code.*

Definition 6 (Generalized Vandermonde Matrix). *A generalized Vander-monde matrix over a finite field F is an $n \times n$ matrix of the form*

$$V_n(\boldsymbol{\mu}) = \begin{pmatrix} x_1^{\mu_1} & x_1^{\mu_2} & \cdots & x_1^{\mu_n} \\ x_2^{\mu_1} & x_2^{\mu_2} & \cdots & x_2^{\mu_n} \\ \vdots & \vdots & \ddots & \vdots \\ x_n^{\mu_1} & x_n^{\mu_2} & \cdots & x_n^{\mu_n} \end{pmatrix} = \left(x_i^{\mu_j} \right)_{i,j \in \{1,2,\dots,n\}}.$$

where $x_i \in F$ and $\mu_i \in \{0, 1, 2, \dots\}$. In particular, $V_n(0, 1, \dots, n-1)$ is the classical Vandermonde matrix.

Observe that if μ_i's are not all distinct, then $\det V_n(\boldsymbol{\mu}) = 0$. The following result is a well-known fact about the determinant of the Vandermonde matrix.

Fact 2 *It hold that $\det V_n(0, 1, \dots, n-1) = \prod_{1 \leqslant i < j \leqslant n}(x_i - x_j)$.*

Note that $\det V_n(\boldsymbol{\mu})$ is divisible by $\det V_n(0, 1, \dots, n-1)$ for any $\boldsymbol{\mu}$.

Fact 3 *It holds that $\det V_n(\boldsymbol{\mu}) = \det(V_n(0, 1, \dots, n-1)) \cdot \Phi(x_1, x_2, \dots, x_n)$, where $\Phi(x_1, x_2, \dots, x_n)$ is a symmetric multivariate polynomial in $x_1, x_2, \dots, x_n$.*

Note that $\det V_n(\boldsymbol{\mu})$ can be computed efficiently in $\mathsf{poly}(n)$-time.[3]

2.4 Field Trace

Definition 7. *The trace of an extension field $F = F_{p^d}$ over a base field F_p is a mapping, denoted as Tr_{F/F_p}, from F to F_p such that $\mathsf{Tr}_{F/F_p}(y) := \sum_{i=0}^{d-1} y^{p^i}$.*

Proposition 1. *The trace $\mathsf{Tr}_{F/F_p} \colon F \to F_p$ is a linear map. That is, for every $a, b \in F_p$ and $x, y \in F$,*

$$\mathsf{Tr}_{F/F_p}(ax + by) = a\mathsf{Tr}_{F/F_p}(x) + b\mathsf{Tr}_{F/F_p}(y).$$

2.5 Fourier Analysis

We shall use Fourier analysis over the additive group of a finite field $F = F_{p^d}$ for some $d \in \{1, 2, \dots\}$. Let $q = p^d$. Define $\omega := \exp(2\pi\imath/p)$. Define the Fourier function $\widehat{f} \colon F \to \mathbb{C}$ as follows. For any $\alpha \in F$,

$$\widehat{f}(\alpha) = \frac{1}{q} \sum_{x \in F} f(x) \cdot \omega^{\mathsf{Tr}_{F/F_p}(\alpha \cdot x)}.$$

The value $\widehat{f}(\alpha)$ is called the *Fourier coefficient* of f at α. The ℓ_1-*Fourier norm* of f is defined as $\left\| \widehat{f} \right\|_1 := \sum_{\alpha \in F} \left| \widehat{f}(\alpha) \right|$.

Fact 4 (Fourier Inversion Formula) $f(x) = \sum_{\alpha \in F} \widehat{f}(\alpha) \cdot \omega^{-\mathsf{Tr}_{F/F_p}(\alpha \cdot x)}$.

Fact 5 (Parseval's Identity) $\frac{1}{q} \sum_{x \in F} |f(x)|^2 = \sum_{\alpha \in F} \left| \widehat{f}(\alpha) \right|^2$.

---

[3] First perform Gaussian elimination, and then the determinant is the product of the diagonal elements.

2.6   Counting Isolated Roots

Definition 8 (Derivative, Determinant, and Jacobian).

1. *Let $f = a_t X_i^t + a_{t-1} X_i^{t-1} + \cdots + a_1 X_i + a_0$. Then, the derivative of f with respect to X_i is the polynomial in $F[X_1, X_2, \ldots, X_n]$ defined below.*

$$\frac{\partial f}{\partial X_i} := (t \cdot a_t) X_i^{t-1} + ((t-1) \cdot a_{t-1}) X_i^{t-2} + \cdots + (2 \cdot a_2) X_i + a_1.$$

2. *For a $k \times k$ matrix M with elements in $F[X_1, X_2, \ldots, X_n]$, the determinant of M, denoted as $\det(M)$, is defined as follows.*

$$\det(M) := \sum_{\substack{\sigma: \{1,2,\ldots,k\} \to \{1,2,\ldots,k\} \\ \sigma \text{ is a permutation}}} \text{sign}(\sigma) \cdot \prod_{i=1}^{k} M_{i,\sigma(i)},$$

where $\text{sign}(\sigma)$ represents the $\{+1, -1\}$ sign of the permutation σ. Note that $\det(M) \in F[X_1, X_2, \ldots, X_n]$.

3. *For a system of polynomials $\boldsymbol{f} = (f_1, \ldots, f_k) \in (F[X_1, X_2, \ldots, X_n])^k$, the Jacobian of $\boldsymbol{f}$ is defined as*

$$\boldsymbol{J}(\boldsymbol{f}) := \det \begin{pmatrix} \frac{\partial f_1}{\partial X_1} & \frac{\partial f_2}{\partial X_1} & \cdots & \frac{\partial f_k}{\partial X_1} \\ \frac{\partial f_1}{\partial X_2} & \frac{\partial f_2}{\partial X_2} & \cdots & \frac{\partial f_k}{\partial X_2} \\ \vdots & \vdots & \ddots & \vdots \\ \frac{\partial f_1}{\partial X_n} & \frac{\partial f_2}{\partial X_n} & \cdots & \frac{\partial f_k}{\partial X_n} \end{pmatrix}.$$

For $\boldsymbol{a} \in F^k$, we use $J(\boldsymbol{f}; \boldsymbol{a})$ to denote the evaluation of $J(\boldsymbol{f})$ at $\boldsymbol{a}$.

Definition 9 (Isolated Roots). *For a system of polynomials $\boldsymbol{f} = (f_1, f_2, \ldots, f_k) \in (F[X_1, X_2, \ldots, X_k])^k$, we say that $\boldsymbol{a} \in F^k$ is an isolated root of $\boldsymbol{f}$ if $f_i(a) = 0$ for every $i \in \{1, 2, \ldots, k\}$ and $\det(J(\boldsymbol{f}; \boldsymbol{a})) \neq 0$. Let $\mathcal{N}(\boldsymbol{f})$ denote the number of isolated roots of $\boldsymbol{f}$.*

Imported Theorem 1 (Bézout-like Theorem [4]) *Let $\boldsymbol{f} = (f_1, f_2, \ldots, f_k)$ be a system of polynomials in $F[X_1, X_2, \ldots, X_k]$ with $\deg(f_i) \leqslant d_i$ for every $i \in \{1, 2, \ldots, k\}$. Then $\mathcal{N}(f) \leqslant d_1 \cdot d_2 \cdots d_k$.*

3   Bounding the Number of Solutions of an Equation

This section presents one of our main technical results. An important step in proving the leakage-resilient Shamir's secret sharing is to upper bound the number of solutions of the equation $G_{\boldsymbol{X}} \cdot \boldsymbol{\alpha}^T = 0$ (refer to Problem 1 in Sect. 1.4), where $\boldsymbol{X} = (X_1, X_2, \ldots, X_n) \in (F^*)^n$ is randomly chosen such that they are all distinct, $\boldsymbol{\alpha} \in F^n$, and $G_{\boldsymbol{X}}$ is a $(k-1) \times n$ matrix such that $G_{\boldsymbol{X}} = (X_j^i)_{i \in \{1, \ldots, k-1\}, j \in \{1, \ldots, n\}}$. Let $\mathcal{S}(G_{\boldsymbol{X}}, \boldsymbol{\alpha})_F$ denote the number of solutions of the above equation over the finite field F. The following subsections provide the bounds for different parameter settings.

3.1   Over Finite Fields with Large Characteristics

Lemma 1. *Let F be a finite field with characteristic $p \geqslant k$. It holds that*

$$\mathcal{S}(G_X, \alpha)_F \leqslant (q-1)(q-2)\cdots(q-(n-k+1)) \cdot (k-1)!.$$

The proof of Lemma 1 follows closely to the proof of the prime field case in [27]. The key difference is that our proof employs the contemporary Bézout-like theorem [4,44], while [27] used the result by Wooley [41].

Proof. Observe that $G_X \cdot \alpha^T = 0$ implies that $\alpha \in C_X^\perp$, where C_X is the code containing all possible secret share of secret 0 of $(n, k, X)_F$-Shamir secret sharing. Note that $C_X^\perp$ is an $(n, n-k+1, k)$-GRS. Thus, the codeword α has at least k non-zero entries. Without loss of generality, assume $\alpha_i \neq 0$ for every $1 \leqslant i \leqslant k$. We rewrite the equation $G_X \cdot \alpha^T = 0$ as a system of polynomial equations with n variables and $(k-1)$ equations as follows.

$$f_i(X_1, X_2, \ldots, X_n) := \alpha_1 X_1^i + \alpha_2 X_2^i + \ldots + \alpha_n X_n^i = 0 \text{ for } i \in \{1, 2, \ldots, n\}$$

Observe that the above system is not a square system of polynomials. To make it a square system and apply Imported Theorem 1, we fix X_i to be distinct non-zero values in F for $i = k, k+1, \ldots, n$. Notice that there are $(q-1)(q-2)\cdots(q-(n-k+1))$ ways of doing the fixing. Define $c_i := \sum_{j=k}^n \alpha_j X_j^i$ for $i = 1, 2, \ldots, k-1$. The above system is now rewritten as, for $i \in \{1, 2, \ldots, k-1\}$,

$$g_i(X_1, X_2, \ldots, X_{k-1}) := \alpha_1 X_1^i + \alpha_2 X_2^i + \ldots + \alpha_{k-1} X_{k-1}^i + c_i = 0$$

Since $\alpha_i \neq 0$, it is a square polynomials system with $\deg(f_i) = i$ for every $1 \leqslant i \leqslant k-1$. Next, we shall show that

$$\mathbf{J}(g_1, g_2, \ldots, g_{k-1})(X_1, X_2, \ldots, X_{k-1}) \neq 0 \text{ if } X_i \neq X_j \text{ for every } i \neq j.$$

One can compute the Jacobian of the above system as follows.

$$\mathbf{J}(g_1, g_2, \ldots, g_{k-1})(X_1, X_2, \ldots, X_{k-1})$$

$$= \det \begin{pmatrix} \alpha_1 & 2\alpha_1 X_1 & \cdots & (k-1)\alpha_1 X_1^{k-2} \\ \alpha_2 & 2\alpha_2 X_2 & \cdots & (k-1)\alpha_2 X_2^{k-2} \\ \vdots & \vdots & \ddots & \vdots \\ \alpha_{k-1} & 2\alpha_{k-1} X_{k-1} & \cdots & (k-1)\alpha_{k-1} X_{k-1}^{k-2} \end{pmatrix}$$

$$= \left(\prod_{i=1}^{k-1} \alpha_i \right) \cdot (k-1)! \cdot \prod_{1 \leqslant i < j \leqslant k-1} (X_i - X_j) \qquad \text{(Fact 2)}$$

We show that all three terms in the last equation are non-zero. The first term $\prod_{i=1}^{k-1} \alpha_i$ is non-zero since $\alpha_i \neq 0$ for every $1 \leqslant i \leqslant k-1$. Since $p \geqslant k$, it is clear that the second term $(k-1)! \neq 0 \mod p$. The third term is non-zero since X_i's are distinct. Thus, the determinant is non-zero. By Imported Theorem 1, $\mathcal{N}(f_1, f_2, \ldots, f_{k-1}) \leqslant (k-1)!$. Hence, the total number of solutions $\mathcal{S}(G_X, \alpha)_F$ is at most $(q-1)(q-2)\cdots(q-(n-k+1)) \cdot (k-1)!$. □

3.2 Over Finite Fields with Characteristic Two

Lemma 2. *Let F be a finite field with characteristic two. It holds that*

$$S(G_X, \alpha)_F \leqslant (q-1)(q-2)\cdots(q-(n-\lfloor k/2 \rfloor))\cdot(k-1)!.$$

Proof. If $k = 2$, then a similar proof as of Lemma 1 works since $(k-1)! = 1$ is not divisible by 2. Therefore, the total number of solutions for $G_X \cdot \alpha^T = 0$ is at most $(q-1)(q-2)\ldots(q-(n-1))$.

From now on, we consider $k \geqslant 3$. We first note that a similar proof for Lemma 1 does not work since $(k-1)!$ is divisible by 2, so the determinant is zero. Our idea is to remove all the equations with even powers. Without loss of generality, assume k is odd (the proof for even k is similar). Let $t = (k-1)/2$. Observe that $S(G_X, \alpha)_F$ is upper bounded by the number of solutions for the system removing the equations $f_{2i}(X_1, X_2, \ldots, X_n) = 0$ for $1 \leqslant i \leqslant t$. So, there will be only t equations left. We construct a square polynomial system as follows. Fix $X_{t+1}, \ldots, X_n$ as arbitrary distinct non-zero elements in F. Define $c_i = \sum_{j=t+1}^{n} \alpha_j X_j^{2i-1}$ for $1 \leqslant i \leqslant t$. Consider the following square polynomial system with t variables and also t equations. For $i \in \{1, 2, \ldots, t\}$,

$$h_i(X_1, X_2, \ldots, X_t) := \alpha_1 X_1^{2i-1} + \alpha_2 X_2^{2i-1} + \ldots + \alpha_t X_t^{2i-1} + c_i = 0$$

Using a similar idea as in the case $p \geqslant k$, we have

$$\mathbf{J}(h_1, h_2, \ldots, h_t)(X_1, X_2, \ldots, X_t)$$

$$= \left(\prod_{i=1}^{t} \alpha_i\right) \cdot \left(\prod_{i=1}^{t}(2i-1)\right) \cdot \prod_{1 \leqslant i < j \leqslant t}(X_i^2 - X_j^2) \tag{Fact 2}$$

$$= \left(\prod_{i=1}^{t} \alpha_i\right) \cdot \left(\prod_{i=1}^{t}(2i-1)\right) \cdot \prod_{1 \leqslant i < j \leqslant t}(X_i - X_j)^2 \qquad (X = -X \text{ for } X \in F_{2^d})$$

Note that the first two terms are non-zero. The last term $\prod_{1 \leqslant i < j \leqslant k-1}(X_i - X_j)^2$ is also non-zero since X_i's are all distinct. These imply that the Jacobian is not zero. Applying Imported Theorem 1 yields that the number of solutions for the square polynomial system is at most $1 \cdot 3 \cdots (2t-1)$. Therefore, the number of solutions for $G_X \cdot \alpha^T = 0$ is at most

$$(q-1)(q-2)\cdots(q-(n-t))\cdot 1 \cdot 3 \cdots (2t-1) \leqslant (q-1)(q-2)\cdots(q-(n-t))\cdot(k-1)!,$$

which is $(q-1)(q-2)\cdots(q-(n-(k-1)/2))\cdot(k-1)!$. □

3.3 Over Finite Fields with Small Characteristic

Finally, we consider the finite field F with characteristic $3 \leqslant p < k$. Inspired by the proof of Lemma 2, it is natural to remove all the equations whose powers (degrees) are divisible by p to avoid the determinant being equal to zero. That is, consider the following square system of equations.

$$h_i(X_1, X_2, \ldots, X_t) = \alpha_1 X_1^i + \alpha_2 X_2^i + \cdots + \alpha_t X_t^i + c_i = 0 \text{ for } i \in I,$$

where $I = \{i : 1 \leqslant i \leqslant k - 1,\ i \text{ is not divisible by } p\}$, $c_i \in F$, and $t = (k - 1) - \lfloor (k - 1)/p \rfloor$. Note that both the number of variables and the number of equations are t. Let $\boldsymbol{h}_I = (h_i : i \in I)$. The Jacobian is

$$\mathbf{J}(\boldsymbol{h}_I) = \left(\prod_{i=1}^{t} \alpha_i \right) \cdot \left(\prod_{j \in I} j \right) \cdot \det(V_t(\boldsymbol{\mu}))$$

Here $\boldsymbol{\mu} = (i - 1 : i \in I)$, and $V_t(\boldsymbol{\mu}) = \left(X_i^{\mu_j} \right)_{i,j \in \{1,2,\ldots,t\}}$ is the generalized Vandermonde matrix (refer to Sect. 2.3). Now, we are done if $\mathbf{J}(\boldsymbol{h}_I) \neq 0$, which is equivalent to $\det(V_t(\boldsymbol{\mu})) \neq 0$. However, it is not always non-zero. The following result claims that the determinant is non-zero with high probability.

Lemma 3. *It holds that* $\det(V_t(\boldsymbol{\mu})) \neq 0$ *with probability at least* $1 - \frac{2k^2}{q-1}$, *where the probability is taken over randomly chosen $\boldsymbol{X}$.*

Proof (of Lemma 3). It follows from Fact 3 that

$$\det(V_t(\boldsymbol{\mu})) = \Phi(X_1, X_2, \ldots, X_t) \cdot \prod_{1 \leqslant i < j \leqslant t} (X_i - X_j),$$

where $\Phi(X_1, X_2, \ldots, X_t)$ is a (symmetric) multivariate polynomial. Observe that $\deg(P) \leqslant k^2$ since $\det(V_t(\boldsymbol{\mu}))$ is a multivariate polynomial with degree at most $\sum_{i \in I} i \leqslant k^2$. Consider $\boldsymbol{X} = (X_1, X_2, \ldots, X_t)$ in which each X_i is independently and randomly chosen from F^*. The Schwartz-Zipple lemma for multivariate polynomials implies that

$$\Pr_{\boldsymbol{X}}[\Phi(X_1, X_2, \ldots, X_n) = 0] \leqslant k^2/(q-1).$$

Applying union bound twice yields

$$\Pr_{\boldsymbol{X}}[\det(V_t(\boldsymbol{\mu})) = 0] \leqslant \Pr_{\boldsymbol{X}}[\Phi(\boldsymbol{X}) = 0] + \Pr_{\boldsymbol{X}}[\exists 1 \leqslant i < j \leqslant t : X_i = X_j]$$

$$\leqslant k^2/(q-1) + \sum_{1 \leqslant i < j \leqslant t} \Pr_{\boldsymbol{X}}[X_i = X_j]$$

$$\leqslant k^2/(q-1) + k^2 \cdot 1/(q-1)$$

$$= 2k^2/(q-1).$$

Next, we show that for some particular values of p, we can derive a good upper bound on the number of solutions $\mathcal{S}(G_{\boldsymbol{X}}, \boldsymbol{\alpha})_F$.

Lemma 4. *Let F be a finite field with characteristic $p = k - 1$ or $p = k - 2$. It holds that*

$$\mathcal{S}(G_{\boldsymbol{X}}, \boldsymbol{\alpha})_F \leqslant (q - 1)(q - 2) \cdots (q - (n - p + 1)) \cdot (p - 1)!.$$

Proof. For $p = k - 1$, the index set $I = \{1, 2, \ldots, k - 2\}$. This implies that $\boldsymbol{\mu} = \{0, 1, \ldots, k - 3\}$. Thus, $V_t(\boldsymbol{\mu})$ is a Vandermonde matrix whose determinant is always non-zero as long as all X_i are distinct. So we have $\mathcal{S}(G_X, \boldsymbol{\alpha})_F \leqslant (q - 1)(q - 2) \cdots (q - (n - p + 1)) \cdot (p - 1)!$.

For $p = k - 2$, we choose $I = \{1, 2, \ldots, k - 3\}$. With a similar argument, we have $\mathcal{S}(G_X, \boldsymbol{\alpha})_F \leqslant (q - 1)(q - 2) \cdots (q - (n - p + 1)) \cdot (p - 1)!$. □

4   Bounding ℓ_1-Fourier Norms of Physical-Bit Leakages

This section shows that the ℓ_1-Fourier norm of physical-bit leakage is small.

Lemma 5. *Let $f \colon F \to \{0, 1\}$ be a one-bit physical leakage function. Then, for any leakage value $t \in \{0, 1\}$, the ℓ_1-Fourier norm of f is bounded as follows.*

1. $\left\| \widehat{1_{f^{-1}(t)}} \right\|_1 = 1$ *if the finite field F has characteristic two.*

2. $\left\| \widehat{1_{f^{-1}(t)}} \right\|_1 \lesssim (\log_2 p)^3 / \pi^2$ *otherwise.*

We first study the ℓ_1-Fourier norm of physical leakage function over finite fields with characteristic two. We need the following technical result.

Proposition 2. *Let G be a subgroup of $F = F_{p^d}$ and $\alpha \in F$. We abuse notation and define the distribution $\mathsf{Tr}_{F/F_p}(\alpha \cdot G)$ as the following experiment.*

1. *Sample x uniformly at random over G,*
2. *Output $\mathsf{Tr}_{F/F_p}(\alpha x)$*

Then, it holds that

$$\mathsf{Tr}_{F/F_p}(\alpha G) = \begin{cases} U_{\{0\}} & \text{if } \alpha = 0 \text{ or } \alpha G \subseteq \ker(\mathsf{Tr}_{F/F_p}) \\ U_{F_p} & \text{otherwise.} \end{cases}$$

Proof. The first case is straightforward from the definition. So, we will focus on showing the second case. Let $\phi_\alpha \colon G \to F_p$ be a function defined as $\phi_\alpha(x) = \mathsf{Tr}_{F/F_p}(\alpha x)$. For any $a, b \in F_p$ and $x, y \in F$, by the linear property of the trace function (Proposition 1),

$$\phi_\alpha(ax + by) = \mathsf{Tr}_{F/F_p}(\alpha(ax + by)) = a\mathsf{Tr}_{F/F_p}(\alpha x) + b\mathsf{Tr}_{F/F_p}(\alpha y).$$

Thus, the mapping ϕ_α is linear over F_p.

Next, we will show that, if $\alpha \neq 0$ and αG is not a subset of $\ker(\mathsf{Tr}_{F/F_p})$, then ϕ_α is surjective. First, by the assumption, there must exist a $x^* \in G$ such that $\phi_\alpha(x^*) = \mathsf{Tr}_{F/F_p}(\alpha x^*) \neq 0$. Let $b = \phi_\alpha(x^*)$. Since G is a subgroup of F, $ax^* \in G$ for every $a \in F_p$. Therefore, for every $c \in F_p$, we have

$$\phi_\alpha(cb^{-1}x^*) = cb^{-1}\phi_\alpha(x^*) = cb^{-1}b = c.$$

It implies that ϕ_α is surjective. Together with the linear property, for every $c, c' \in F_p$,

$$\left| \phi_\alpha^{-1}(c) \right| = \left| \phi_\alpha^{-1}(c') \right|.$$

Hence, the distribution $\mathsf{Tr}_{F/F_p}(\alpha G)$ is uniform over F_p when $\alpha \neq 0$ and αG is not a subset of $\ker(\mathsf{Tr}_{F/F_p})$, which completes the proof. □

Lemma 6. *Let F be a finite field with characteristic two. Let $f: F \to \{0,1\}$ be an one-bit physical leakage function that outputs the bit x_i on input $x = x_0 + x_1\zeta + \ldots + x_{d-1}\zeta^{d-1} \in F$ for some $i \in \{0,1,\ldots,d-1\}$. Let $C = \{x \in F: x_i = 0\}$. Then, for any $t \in \{0,1\}$ and $\alpha \in F$,*

$$\left|\widehat{\mathbb{1}_{f^{-1}(t)}}(\alpha)\right| = \begin{cases} 1/2 & \text{if } \alpha C = \ker(\text{Tr}_{F/F_p}) \\ 0 & \text{otherwise,} \end{cases}$$

where $\ker(\text{Tr}_{F/F_p}) := \{x \in F: \text{Tr}_{F/F_p}(x) = 0\}$. Consequently, $\left\|\widehat{\mathbb{1}_{f^{-1}(t)}}\right\|_1 = 1$.

Proof. Observe that $f^{-1}(t) = v + C$ for some $v \in \{0, \zeta^i\}$. For any $\alpha \in F$,

$$\left|\widehat{\mathbb{1}_{f^{-1}(t)}}(\alpha)\right| = \left|\frac{1}{q}\sum_{x \in v+C} \omega^{\text{Tr}_{F/F_p}(\alpha \cdot x)}\right| \qquad \text{(Since } f^{-1}(t) = v + C\text{)}$$

$$= \left|\frac{1}{q}\omega^{\text{Tr}_{F/F_p}(\alpha \cdot v)} \cdot \sum_{y \in C} \omega^{\text{Tr}_{F/F_p}(\alpha \cdot y)}\right|$$

By Proposition 2, the sum $\sum_{y \in C} \omega^{\text{Tr}_{F/F_p}(\alpha \cdot y)}$ is equal to $|C| = 2^{d-1}$ if $\alpha C = \ker(\text{Tr}_{F/F_p})$, and is equal to 0 otherwise. This yields

$$\left|\widehat{\mathbb{1}_{f^{-1}(t)}}(\alpha)\right| = \begin{cases} 1/2 & \text{if } \alpha C = \ker(\text{Tr}_{F/F_p}) \\ 0 & \text{otherwise.} \end{cases}$$

Note that there are exactly two $\alpha \in F$ such that $\alpha C = \ker(\text{Tr}_{F/F_p})$. Consequently, we have $\left\|\widehat{\mathbb{1}_{f^{-1}(t)}}\right\|_1 = 1$, which completes the proof. □

Next, we state the bound for a finite field with a characteristic greater than 2.

Lemma 7. *Let F be a finite field. Let $f: F \to \{0,1\}^n$ be a 1-bit physical leakage function. Then, for every $t \in \{0,1\}$, it holds that*

$$\left\|\widehat{\mathbb{1}_{f^{-1}(t)}}\right\|_1 \lesssim \frac{(\log_2 p)^3}{\pi^2}.$$

Proof (of Lemma 7). Suppose f leaks one bit on the i-th block. Let $C = \{x \in F: x_i = 0\}$. Unlike in the characteristic 2 case, now we have $f^{-1}(t) = V + C$, where $V \subseteq D = \{0, \zeta^i, \ldots, (p-1)\zeta^i\}$. We have

$$\left|\widehat{\mathbb{1}_{f^{-1}(t)}}(\alpha)\right| = \left|\frac{1}{q}\sum_{v \in V} \omega^{\text{Tr}_{F/F_p}(\alpha \cdot v)} \cdot \sum_{y \in C} \omega^{\text{Tr}_{F/F_p}(\alpha \cdot y)}\right|$$

By Proposition 2, if $\alpha C \neq \ker(\text{Tr}_{F/F_p})$, then $\left|\widehat{\mathbb{1}_{f^{-1}(t)}}(\alpha)\right| = 0$. Otherwise,

$$\left|\widehat{\mathbb{1}_{f^{-1}(t)}}(\alpha)\right| = \frac{1}{p}\left|\sum_{v \in V} \omega^{\text{Tr}_{F/F_p}(\alpha \cdot v)}\right| = \frac{1}{p}\left|\sum_{c \in V_i} \omega^{\text{Tr}_{F/F_p}(\alpha c \zeta^i)}\right| = \frac{1}{p}\left|\sum_{c \in V_i} \omega^{c \cdot \text{Tr}_{F/F_p}(\alpha \zeta^i)}\right|,$$

where $V_i = \{x_i \colon x \in V\}$. This implies that $\left| \widehat{\mathbb{1}_{f^{-1}(t)}}(\alpha) \right| = \widehat{\mathbb{1}_{V_i}}(\mathsf{Tr}_{F/F_p}(\alpha\zeta^i))$.

Observe that $\{\mathsf{Tr}_{F/F_p}(\alpha\zeta^i) \colon \alpha D \neq \ker(\mathsf{Tr}_{F/F_p})\} = F_p$. This implies that $\left\| \widehat{\mathbb{1}_{f^{-1}(t)}} \right\|_1 = \left\| \widehat{\mathbb{1}_{V_i}} \right\|_1$. To prove our result, we shall use a result from [27] saying that V can be partitioned into at most $\log_2 p$ generalized arithmetic progressions (GAPs) of rank two, and the ℓ_1-Fourier norm of these GAPs bounded. It follows from the result in [27](see corollary 1) that $\left\| \widehat{\mathbb{1}_{f^{-1}(t)}} \right\|_1 \leqslant (\log_2 p)^3/\pi^2$.   □

It is easy to see that Lemma 5 follows from Lemma 6 and 7.

5   Leakage Resilience: Characteristic Two Finite Fields

This section considers Shamir's secret sharing schemes over finite fields with characteristic 2. We will prove the following theorem.

Theorem 1. *Let F be a finite field with characteristic two. For any $\varepsilon > 0$, the following bound holds.*

$$\Pr_{X}[\mathsf{ShamirSS}(n, k, \boldsymbol{X})_F \text{ is not an } (1, \varepsilon)\text{-LLRS}] \lesssim \frac{1}{\varepsilon} \cdot \frac{2^n \cdot \lambda^n \cdot (k-1)!}{(q-n)^{\lfloor k/2 \rfloor}}$$

We recall that $\boldsymbol{X} = (X_1, X_2, \ldots, X_n) \in (F^*)^n$ is the uniform distribution over the set of distinct evaluation places. We interpret the Theorem 1 as follows.

Corollary 1. *Let F be a finite field with order 2^d. For any number of parties $n \in \{2, 3, \ldots, \}$, reconstruction threshold $k \leqslant n$, and insecurity parameter $\varepsilon = 2^{-t}$, if the security parameter $\lambda = d \cdot \lceil \log_2 p \rceil$ satisfies $\lambda \geqslant 2t/k + 2n(1 + \log_2 \lambda)/k$, then $\mathsf{ShamirSS}(n, k, \boldsymbol{X})_F$ is an $(1, \varepsilon)$-LLRSS with probability at least $1 - \exp(-\Theta(\lambda))$.*

Our result extends to multiple-bit leakage, which is summarized as follows.

Theorem 2. *Let F be a finite field with characteristic two. For any $m \in \{1, 2, \ldots\}$ and $\varepsilon > 0$, the following bound holds.*

$$\Pr_{X}[\mathsf{ShamirSS}(n, k, \boldsymbol{X})_F \text{ is not an } (m, \varepsilon)\text{-LLRS}] \lesssim \frac{1}{\varepsilon} \cdot \left(\frac{\lambda}{m}\right)^n \cdot \frac{2^{mn} \cdot (k-1)!}{(q-n)^{\lfloor k/2 \rfloor}}$$

Remark 2. The above result extends to the setting where m_i bits are leaked from the i-th share for $1 \leqslant i \leqslant n$. The probability that $\mathsf{ShamirSS}(n, k, \boldsymbol{X})_F$ is not $(\boldsymbol{m}, \varepsilon)$-LLRSS is upper-bounded by

$$\frac{1}{\varepsilon} \cdot \binom{\lambda}{m_1}\binom{\lambda}{m_2}\cdots\binom{\lambda}{m_n} \cdot \frac{2^{mn} \cdot (k-1)!}{(q-n)^{\lfloor k/2 \rfloor}} \leqslant \frac{1}{\varepsilon} \cdot \left(\frac{\lambda}{M/n}\right)^n \cdot \frac{2^M (k-1)!}{(q-n)^{\lfloor k/2 \rfloor}}.$$

This bound is maximized when all $m_i = M/n$, where M is the total number of physical bits probed.

Corollary 2. *Let F be a finite field with order 2^d. For any number of parties $n \in \{2, 3, \ldots, \}$, reconstruction threshold $k \leqslant n$, the number of leaked bits m, and insecurity parameter $\varepsilon = 2^{-t}$, if the security parameter $\lambda = d$ satisfies $\lambda \geqslant 2tM/(nk) + 2M(1 + \log_2 \lambda)/k$, then $\mathsf{ShamirSS}(n, k, \boldsymbol{X})_F$ is an (m, ε)-LLRSS with probability at least $1 - \exp(-\Theta(\lambda))$.*

In the following subsections, we provide a proof of Theorem 1. The proof of Theorem 2 is analogous. The main idea is to reduce the m-bit physical leakage on n secret shares to the 1-bit physical leakage on mn secret shares. We make m copies of each secret share. Then, leaking m bits on the secret share is identical to leaking one bit from the i-th copy for $i \in \{1, 2, \ldots, m\}$.

5.1   Claims Needed for Theorem 1

Proposition 3. *Let $\boldsymbol{\ell} = (\ell_1, \ell_2, \ldots, \ell_n)$ be an arbitrary m-bit physical leakage function, where $\ell_i \colon F \to \{0, 1\}^m$ for $1 \leqslant i \leqslant n$. The following bound holds for every pair of secret $s, s' \in F$.*

$$\mathsf{SD}\left(\boldsymbol{\ell}(s), \boldsymbol{\ell}(s')\right) \leqslant \sum_{t \in (\{0,1\}^m)^n} \sum_{\alpha \in C_{\boldsymbol{X}}^{\perp} \setminus \{\boldsymbol{0}\}} \left(\prod_{i=1}^{n} \left| \widehat{\mathbb{1}_{t_i}}(\alpha_i) \right| \right)$$

The following result states that the average of the upper bound over randomly chosen evaluation places $\boldsymbol{X}$ is sufficiently small.

Lemma 8. *Let F be a finite field with characteristic 2. It holds that*

$$\mathop{\mathbb{E}}_{\boldsymbol{X}}\left[\sum_{t \in \{0,1\}^n} \sum_{\alpha \in C_{\boldsymbol{X}}^{\perp} \setminus \{\boldsymbol{0}\}} \left(\prod_{i=1}^{n} \left| \widehat{\mathbb{1}_{t_i}}(\alpha_i) \right| \right) \right] \lesssim \frac{2^n \cdot (k-1)!}{(q-n)^{\lfloor k/2 \rfloor}}$$

5.2   Proof of Theorem 1

Our proof closely follows the idea in [27]. We have

$$\mathop{\mathrm{Pr}}_{\boldsymbol{X}}\left[\mathsf{ShamirSS}(n, k, \boldsymbol{X}, F) \text{ is not a } (m, \varepsilon) - LLRS\right]$$

$$= \mathop{\mathrm{Pr}}_{\boldsymbol{X}}\left[\exists s, s', \boldsymbol{\ell} \text{ s.t. } \mathsf{SD}\left(\boldsymbol{\ell}(s), \boldsymbol{\ell}(s')\right) \geqslant \varepsilon\right]$$

$$\leqslant \mathop{\mathrm{Pr}}_{\boldsymbol{X}}\left[\exists s, s', \boldsymbol{\ell} \text{ s.t. } \sum_{t \in (\{0,1\}^m)^n} \sum_{\alpha \in C_{\boldsymbol{X}}^{\perp} \setminus \{\boldsymbol{0}\}} \left(\prod_{i=1}^{n} \left| \widehat{\mathbb{1}_{t_i}}(\alpha_i) \right| \right) \geqslant \varepsilon\right]$$
$$\hspace{10cm} \text{(Proposition 3)}$$

$$= \mathop{\mathrm{Pr}}_{\boldsymbol{X}}\left[\exists \boldsymbol{\ell} \text{ s.t. } \sum_{t \in (\{0,1\}^m)^n} \sum_{\alpha \in C_{\boldsymbol{X}}^{\perp} \setminus \{\boldsymbol{0}\}} \left(\prod_{i=1}^{n} \left| \widehat{\mathbb{1}_{t_i}}(\alpha_i) \right| \right) \geqslant \varepsilon\right] \hspace{1cm} \text{(Ind. of } s, s')$$

$$= \sum_{\ell} \Pr_{X} \left[\sum_{t \in (\{0,1\}^m)^n} \sum_{\alpha \in C_X^{\perp} \setminus \{0\}} \left(\prod_{i=1}^{n} \left| \widehat{\mathbb{1}_{t_i}}(\alpha_i) \right| \right) \geqslant \varepsilon \right] \qquad \text{(Union bound)}$$

$$\leqslant \sum_{\ell} \frac{1}{\varepsilon} \cdot \mathbb{E}_X \left[\sum_{t \in (\{0,1\}^m)^n} \sum_{\alpha \in C_X^{\perp} \setminus \{0\}} \left(\prod_{i=1}^{n} \left| \widehat{\mathbb{1}_{t_i}}(\alpha_i) \right| \right) \right] \qquad \text{(Markov's inequality)}$$

$$\lesssim \sum_{\ell} \frac{1}{\varepsilon} \cdot \frac{2^n \cdot (k-1)!}{(q-n)^{\lfloor k/2 \rfloor}} \qquad \text{(Lemma 8)}$$

$$= \frac{1}{\varepsilon} \cdot \frac{2^n \cdot \lambda^n \cdot (k-1)!}{(q-n)^{\lfloor k/2 \rfloor}}$$

Therefore, we have completed the proof of Theorem 1.

6   Leakage Resilience: Large Characteristic Fields

This section presents the results over finite fields with characteristics greater than two. The following theorems summarize our results.

Theorem 3. *Let the reconstruction threshold $k \in \{2, 3, \dots\}$. Let F be a finite field with characteristic $p \geqslant k$ and M be the total leaked bits. For $\varepsilon > 0$, the following bound holds.*

$$\Pr_{X}[\text{ShamirSS}(n, k, X)_F \text{ is not an } (M/n, \varepsilon)\text{-LLRS}]$$

$$\lesssim \frac{1}{\varepsilon} \cdot \left(\frac{\lambda}{M/n} \right)^n \cdot \frac{2^M \cdot (\log_2 p)^M \cdot (k-1)!}{\pi^M \cdot (q-n)^{k-1}}.$$

Theorem 4. *Let the reconstruction threshold $k \in \{2, 3, \dots\}$. Let F be a finite field with characteristic $p = k - 1$ or $p = k - 2$ and M be the total leaked bits. For any $\varepsilon > 0$, the following bound holds.*

$$\Pr_{X}[\text{ShamirSS}(n, k, X)_F \text{ is not an } (M/n, \varepsilon)\text{-LLRS}]$$

$$\lesssim \frac{1}{\varepsilon} \cdot \left(\frac{\lambda}{M/n} \right)^n \cdot \frac{2^M \cdot (\log_2 p)^M \cdot (p-1)!}{\pi^M \cdot (q-n)^{p-1}}.$$

The proofs of Theorem 3 and Theorem 4 are analogous to the proof presented in Sect. 5. The main differences are that these proofs (1) use Lemma 7 to bound ℓ_1-Fourier norm, and (2) use Lemma 1 and Lemma 4 to upper bound the number of solutions of the equation, respectively.

7   Our Classification Algorithm

This section presents an explicit algorithm to identify secure evaluation places for Shamir secret sharing against the single block leakage from every share.

Consider the finite field $F = F_{p^d}$ where $d \in \{2, 3, \dots\}$. We will interpret F as $F_p[\zeta]/\Pi(\zeta)$, where $\Pi(\zeta)$ is an irreducible degree-d F_p-polynomial. Every element $x \in F$ can be written as a length-d vector of F_p elements. We represent $x \in F$ as $x = (x_0, x_1, \dots, x_{d-1}) \in (F_p)^d$ when $x = x_0 + x_1\zeta + \cdots + x_{d-1}\zeta^{d-1}$. We define the *single block leakage* function $\ell_i^{\mathrm{block}} \colon F \to F_p$ as the $\lceil \log_2(p) \rceil$-bit physical leakage function that leaks the i-th coefficient $x_i \in F_p$ for $x \in F$, i.e. $\ell_i^{\mathrm{block}}(x) = x_i$.

Theorem 5. *Let F be a finite field with characteristic $p \geqslant 2$. Consider the $(n, 2, (X_1, \dots, X_n))$-Shamir secret-sharing scheme over F. Consider the block physical bit leakage function $\ell^{\mathrm{block}} = (\ell_{i_1}^{\mathrm{block}}, \ell_{i_2}^{\mathrm{block}}, \dots, \ell_{i_n}^{\mathrm{block}})$ where $i_1, i_2, \dots, i_n \in \{0, 1, 2, \dots, d-1\}$ and $\ell_{i_j}^{\mathrm{block}} \colon F \to F_p$ for all $j \in \{0, 1, \dots, n\}$. Define the shifting factor $\eta^{(i_j)} \in F_q$ such that $(x)_{i_j} = \left(x \cdot \eta^{(i_j)}\right)_0$, for all $x \in F_q$. For any secret $s \in F$, if $X_1\eta^{(i_1)}, X_2\eta^{(i_2)}, \dots, X_n\eta^{(i_n)} \in F_q$ are all F_p-linearly independent, then*

$$\mathrm{SD}\left(\ell^{\mathrm{block}}(0), \, \ell^{\mathrm{block}}(s)\right) = 0.$$

Theorem 5 implies that all evaluation places $(X_1, \dots, X_n) \in F_q^n$ satisfying

$$X_1\eta^{(i_1)}, X_2\eta^{(i_2)}, \dots, X_n\eta^{(i_n)} \in F_q$$

being all F_p-linearly independent, are perfectly secure against single block leakage attack. Figure 1 shows a test to identify secure evaluation places $(X_1, \dots, X_n) \in F_q^n$ for $(n, 2, (X_1, \dots, X_n))$-Shamir secret sharing over finite field F_q with characteristic $p \geqslant 2$ against the single block leakage from every share. Note that the algorithm outputs secure for at least $1 - d^n p^{n-1}/q$ fraction of evaluation places.

Input. Distinct evaluation places $X_1, X_2, \dots, X_n \in F$, and p is a prime

Output. Decide whether the evaluation places $(X_1, \dots, X_n)$ are secure to all single-block leakage attacks.

Algorithm.
1. For $i \in \{0, 1, \dots, d-1\}$:
   (a) Compute the shift factor $\eta^{(i,0)}$ as defined in Proposition 4
2. For $i_1, i_2, \dots, i_n \in \{0, 1, \dots, d-1\}$:
   (a) If $\left\{ X_1\eta^{(i_1)}, X_2\eta^{(i_2)}, \dots, X_n\eta^{(i_n)} \right\} \subseteq F_q$ is *not* F_p-linearly independent, return "Insecure."
3. Return "Secure."

Fig. 1. Identify secure evaluation places for Shamir's secret-sharing scheme against all single-block leakage attacks.

7.1 Proof of Theorem 5

Consider leakage distribution $\left((s + P \cdot X_1)_{i_1}, (s + P \cdot X_2)_{i_1}, \ldots, (s + P \cdot X_n)_{i_n}\right)$ where $i_1, i_2, \ldots, i_n \in \{0, 1, \ldots, d-1\}$ and $P \in F_q$ is chosen uniformly at random. Then, the above distribution is identical to

$$\left((Q \cdot X_1)_{i_1}, (Q \cdot X_2 + t_2)_{i_1}, \ldots, (Q \cdot X_n + t_n)_{i_n}\right)$$

where $(s \cdot X_1^{-1} + P) \mapsto Q$ is an automorphism over F_q and $t_i = s \cdot (1 - X_i \cdot X_1^{-1})$ By Proposition 4, the shifting factor $\eta^{(i_1)}, \eta^{(i_2)}, \ldots, \eta^{(i_n)} \in F_q$ allow us to equivalent study the leakage distribution on the 0-th block

$$\left(\left(QX_1\eta^{(i_1)}\right)_0, \left(QX_2\eta^{(i_2)} + t_2'\right)_0, \ldots, \left(QX_n\eta^{(i_n)} + t_n'\right)_0\right)$$

where Q is uniformly at random from F_q and $t_j' = t_j \cdot \eta^{(i_j)}$ for $j \in \{1, 2, \ldots, n\}$. Finally, the previous distribution is identical to

$$\left(\left(QX_1\eta^{(i_1)}\right)_0, \left(QX_2\eta^{(i_2)}\right)_0 + t_2'', \ldots, \left(QX_n\eta^{(i_n)}\right)_0 + t_n''\right),$$

where Q is uniformly at random from F_q and $s \mapsto t_j''$ are appropriate linear automorphisms over F_q, for all $j \in \{2, 3, \ldots, n\}$. By Lemma 10, the distribution

$$\left(\left(QX_1\eta^{(i_1)}\right)_0, \left(QX_2\eta^{(i_2)}\right)_0, \ldots, \left(QX_n\eta^{(i_n)}\right)_0\right)$$

is equivalent as a uniform distribution over $(F_p)^n$ for uniformly random $Q \in F_q$. Thus, if $X_1\eta^{(i_1)}, X_2\eta^{(i_2)}, \ldots, X_n\eta^{(i_n)} \in F_q$ are all F_p-linearly independent,

$$\mathsf{SD}\left(\ell^{\mathsf{block}}(0), \ell^{\mathsf{block}}(s)\right) = 0.$$

7.2 Technical Results

The below result says that a block leakage is emulated by another block leakage.

Proposition 4. For $i \in \{0, 1, \ldots, d-1\}$, define $C_i := \{x \in F \colon x_i = 0\}$. For $i, j \in \{0, 1, \ldots, d-1\}$, there exists $\eta^{(i,j)} \in F^*$ such that $C_i \cdot \eta^{(i,j)} = C_j$.

Proof. Let D be the set of all subgroups of order p^{d-1} of the additive group $(F, +)$. Observe that $x \cdot C_i \in D$ for every $x \in F^*$. Consider the following map $\phi_{C_i} \colon F^* \to D$ such that $\phi_{C_i}(x) := x \cdot C_i$. One can easily verify that ϕ_{C_i} is one-to-$(p-1)$ mapping. That is, $\phi_{C_i}(x) = \phi_{C_i}(ax)$ for every $a \in F_p^*$, and $\phi_{C_i}(x) \neq \phi_{C_i}(y)$ if $x \neq ay$ for some $a \in F_p^*$. Observe now that $|D| = (p^d - 1)/(p-1)$ and $|F^*| = p^d - 1$. Therefore, $\left|\phi_{C_i}^{-1}(C)\right| = p - 1$ for every $C \in D$. This implies that there exists some $\eta^{(i,j)} \in F^*$ such that $C_j = \eta^{(i,j)} \cdot C_i$ since $C_j \in D$. $\square$

Lemma 9. *For $i \in \{0, 1, \ldots, d-1\}$, define $C_i := \{x \in F : x_i = 0\}$. Then, the following statements hold.*

1. *If $\alpha = 0$, $C_i \cdot \alpha = \{0\}$.*
2. *If $\alpha \in F_p^* \subseteq F$, then $C_i \cdot \alpha = C_i$ and $(C_i \cdot \alpha)_i = \{0\}$.*
3. *If $\alpha \in F \setminus F_p$, then $(U_{C_i} \cdot \alpha)_i = U_{F_p}$.*

Proof. The first two cases are straightforward from the definition. Suppose $\alpha \in F \setminus F_p$. Let D be the set of all subgroups of order p^{d-1} of F. Consider the mapping $\psi_\alpha : C_i \to F_p$ defined as $\psi_\alpha(x) = (\alpha \cdot x)_i$. One can verify that this mapping is linear over F_p. Therefore, to complete the proof, it suffices to show that there is an $x \in F$ such that $\psi_\alpha(x) \neq 0$. By the property of the mapping ϕ_{C_i} in the proof of Proposition 2, it is clear that $\alpha \cdot C_i \neq C_i$. This implies that, there exists $x' \in F$ such that $\psi_\alpha(x') = (\alpha \cdot x')_i \neq 0$ since C_i is the only subgroup of order p^{d-1} satisfying $x_i = 0$ for element x in that subgroup. Thus, for every $a, b \in F_p$, $|\psi_\alpha^{-1}(a)| = |\psi_\alpha^{-1}(b)|$, which completes the proof. $\qquad\square$

Corollary 3. *For $i \in \{0, 1, \ldots, d-1\}$, define $C_i := \{x \in F : x_i = 0\}$. If $\alpha \in F \setminus F_p$, then for all $c \in F$, $(U_{C_i} \cdot \alpha + c)_i = U_{F_p}$.*

Lemma 10. *Fix arbitrary elements $Y^{(1)}, Y^{(2)}, \ldots, Y^{(n)} \in F_q$ such that the set of vectors $\{Y^{(1)}, Y^{(2)}, \ldots, Y^{(n)}\} \subseteq (F_p)^d$ is F_p-linearly independent, where $n \in \{1, 2, \ldots\}$. Then, the joint distribution $\left((QY^{(1)})_0, (QY^{(2)})_0, \ldots, (QY^{(n)})_0 \right)$ is uniformly random over $(F_p)^n$, for uniformly random $Q \in F_q$.*

Note that, for the set to be independent, it must be the case that $d \leqslant n$ because the ambient space F_q is an F_p-vector space of dimension d. The proof of this result will crucially rely on the fact that the elements belong to a field.

Proof. At the outset, our objective is to formalize the linear map $Q \longmapsto (QY)_0$ behaves for $Q, Y \in F_q$, where $q = p^d$. Note that it is identical to the map

$$(Q_0, \ldots, Q_{d-1}) \longmapsto \left((Q_0, \ldots, Q_{d-1}) \cdot \begin{pmatrix} (Y \cdot 1)_0 & \cdots & (Y \cdot 1)_{d-1} \\ (Y \cdot \zeta)_0 & \cdots & (Y \cdot \zeta)_{d-1} \\ \vdots & \ddots & \vdots \\ (Y \cdot \zeta^{d-1})_0 & \cdots & (Y \cdot \zeta^{d-1})_{d-1} \end{pmatrix} \right)_0$$

In the matrix above, we clarify that $(Y \cdot \zeta^i)_j$ represents the coefficient of ζ^j in the polynomial representation of the product of $Y \in F_q$ and $\zeta^i \in F_q$. So, the $Q \longmapsto (Q \cdot Y)_0$ map is equivalent to the $F_q \longmapsto F_p$ linear map:

$$Q \equiv (Q_0, Q_1, \ldots, Q_{d-1}) \longmapsto Q_0 \cdot (Y \cdot 1)_0 + Q_1 \cdot (Y \cdot \zeta)_0 + \cdots + Q_{d-1} \cdot (Y \cdot \zeta^{d-1})_0$$

Now, we begin proving the lemma. We are given $Y^{(1)}, Y^{(2)}, \ldots, Y^{(n)} \in F_q$. Each $Y^{(i)} \in F_q$ is equivalently interpreted as $(Y_0^{(i)}, Y_1^{(i)}, \ldots, Y_{d-1}^{(i)}) \in (F_p)^d$, where $i \in \{1, 2, \ldots, n\}$. We are given that the following set of $(F_p)^d$ vectors are linearly independent: $\left\{ \left(Y_0^{(i)}, Y_1^{(i)}, \ldots, Y_{d-1}^{(i)} \right) : i \in \{1, 2, \ldots, n\} \right\}$.

We aim to prove that, for uniformly random $Q \in F_q$, the joint distribution $\left((QY^{(1)})_0 , (QY^{(2)})_0 , \ldots, (QY^{(n)})_0 \right)$ is uniform over $(F_p)^n$. Note that this joint distribution is identical to the following distribution, where $Q_0, Q_1, \ldots, Q_{d-1} \in (F_p)^d$ are chosen uniformly and independently at random (due to Eq. 7.2).

$$(Q_0, Q_1, \ldots, Q_{d-1}) \cdot \begin{pmatrix} (Y^{(1)} \cdot 1)_0 & (Y^{(2)} \cdot 1)_0 & \cdots & (Y^{(n)} \cdot 1)_0 \\ (Y^{(1)} \cdot \zeta)_0 & (Y^{(2)} \cdot \zeta)_0 & \cdots & (Y^{(n)} \cdot \zeta)_0 \\ \vdots & \vdots & \ddots & \vdots \\ (Y^{(1)} \cdot \zeta^{d-1})_0 & (Y^{(2)} \cdot \zeta^{d-1})_0 & \cdots & (Y^{(n)} \cdot \zeta^{d-1})_0 \end{pmatrix}$$

So, it is equivalent to showing the below set of vectors is linearly independent:

$$\left\{ \left(\left(Y^{(i)} \cdot 1 \right)_0 , \left(Y^{(i)} \cdot \zeta \right)_0 , \ldots, \left(Y^{(i)} \cdot \zeta^{d-1} \right)_0 \right) \; : \; i \in \{1, 2, \ldots, n\} \right\}.$$

It suffices to prove that the following $(F_p)^d \longmapsto (F_p)^d$ is a full-rank map:

$$(Y_0, Y_1, \ldots, Y_{d-1}) \longmapsto \left((Y \cdot 1)_0, (Y \cdot \zeta)_0, \ldots, (Y \cdot \zeta^{d-1})_0 \right). \tag{2}$$

Let $\Pi(\zeta) = \zeta^d - \Pi_{d-1}\zeta^{d-1} - \cdots - \Pi_0$ be the irreducible polynomial, where $\Pi_0, \Pi_1, \ldots, \Pi_{d-1} \in F_p$. Here is an essential observation. For $i \in \{1, 2, \ldots, d-1\}$ the following identity holds: $(\zeta^i \cdot \zeta^{d-i})_0 = \Pi_0 \neq 0$. Using this essential observation, Eq. 2 establishes the following maps of the basis vectors.

$$(1, 0, 0, \ldots, 0) \longmapsto (1, 0, 0, \ldots, 0, 0)$$
$$(0, 1, 0, \ldots, 0) \longmapsto (0, 0, 0, \ldots, 0, \Pi_0)$$
$$(0, 0, 1, \ldots, 0) \longmapsto (0, 0, 0, \ldots, \Pi_0, *)$$
$$\vdots$$
$$(0, 0, 0, \ldots, 1) \longmapsto (0, \Pi_0, *, \ldots, *, *)$$

In the maps above, $*$ elements represent arbitrary elements of F_p. Let $A \in (F_p)^{d \times d}$ be the matrix such that for all $Y_0, Y_1, \ldots, Y_{d-1} \in F_p$ and $Y = Y_0 + Y_1\zeta + \cdots Y_{d-1}\zeta^{d-1} \in F_q$, the following identity is satisfied.

$$(Y_0, Y_1, \ldots, Y_{d-1}) \cdot A = \left((Y \cdot 1)_0, (Y \cdot \zeta)_0, \ldots, (Y \cdot \zeta^{d-1})_0 \right).$$

From the basis maps above, we conclude that the matrix $A \in (F_p)^{d \times d}$ has the following structure.

$$A = \begin{pmatrix} 1 & 0 & 0 & \cdots & 0 & 0 \\ 0 & 0 & 0 & \cdots & 0 & \Pi_0 \\ 0 & 0 & 0 & \cdots & \Pi_0 & * \\ \vdots & \vdots & \vdots & \ddots & \vdots & \vdots \\ 0 & \Pi_0 & * & \cdots & * & * \end{pmatrix}$$

This structure shows that the matrix A has full rank, whence the lemma. $\square$

References

1. Adams, D.Q., et al.: Lower bounds for leakage-resilient secret sharing schemes against probing attacks. In: ISIT 2021 (2021)
2. Aggarwal, D., et al.: Stronger leakage-resilient and non-malleable secret sharing schemes for general access structures. In: Boldyreva, A., Micciancio, D. (eds.) CRYPTO 2019. LNCS, vol. 11693, pp. 510–539. Springer, Cham (2019). https://doi.org/10.1007/978-3-030-26951-7_18
3. Badrinarayanan, S., Srinivasan, A.: Revisiting non-malleable secret sharing. In: Ishai, Y., Rijmen, V. (eds.) EUROCRYPT 2019. LNCS, vol. 11476, pp. 593–622. Springer, Cham (2019). https://doi.org/10.1007/978-3-030-17653-2_20
4. Bafna, M., Sudan, M., Velusamy, S., Xiang,D.: Elementary analysis of isolated zeroes of a polynomial system (2021). arXiv preprint arXiv:2102.00602
5. Benhamouda, F., Degwekar, A., Ishai, Y., Rabin, T.: On the local leakage resilience of linear secret sharing schemes. In: Shacham, H., Boldyreva, A. (eds.) CRYPTO 2018. LNCS, vol. 10991, pp. 531–561. Springer, Cham (2018). https://doi.org/10.1007/978-3-319-96884-1_18
6. Benhamouda, F., Degwekar, A., Ishai, Y., Rabin, T.: On the local leakage resilience of linear secret sharing schemes. J. Cryptol. **34**(2), 10 (2021). https://doi.org/10.1007/s00145-021-09375-2
7. Bishop, A., Pastro, V., Rajaraman, R., Wichs, D.: Essentially optimal robust secret sharing with maximal corruptions. In: Fischlin, M., Coron, J.-S. (eds.) EUROCRYPT 2016. LNCS, vol. 9665, pp. 58–86. Springer, Heidelberg (2016). https://doi.org/10.1007/978-3-662-49890-3_3
8. Bogdanov, A., Ishai, Y., Srinivasan, A.: Unconditionally secure computation against low-complexity leakage. In: Boldyreva, A., Micciancio, D. (eds.) CRYPTO 2019. LNCS, vol. 11693, pp. 387–416. Springer, Cham (2019). https://doi.org/10.1007/978-3-030-26951-7_14
9. Brandão, L.T.A.N., Peralta, R.: NIST first call for multi-party threshold schemes, 25 January 2023. https://csrc.nist.gov/publications/detail/nistir/8214c/draft
10. Chandran, N., Kanukurthi, B., Lakshmi, S., Obbattu, B., Sekar, S.: Short leakage resilient and non-malleable secret sharing schemes. In: Dodis, Y., Shrimpton, T. (eds.) CRYPTO 2022, Part I, vol. 13507, LNCS, pp. 178–207. Springer, Heidelberg (2022). https://doi.org/10.1007/978-3-031-15802-5_7
11. Chattopadhyay, E., et al.: Extractors and secret sharing against bounded collusion protocols. In: 61st FOCS, pp. 1226–1242. IEEE Computer Society Press, November 2020. https://doi.org/10.1109/FOCS46700.2020.00117
12. Con, R., Tamo, I.: Nonlinear repair of reed-Solomon codes. IEEE Trans. Inf. Theory **68**(8), 5165–5177 (2022). https://doi.org/10.1109/TIT.2022.3167615
13. Costes, N., Stam, M.: Redundant code-based masking revisited. IACR TCHES. 2021(1), 426–450 (2021). https://tches.iacr.org/index.php/TCHES/article/view/8740, https://doi.org/10.46586/tches.v2021.i1.426-450
14. Dimakis, A.G., Godfrey, P.B., Wu, Y., Wainwright, M.J., Ramchandran, K.: Network coding for distributed storage systems. IEEE Trans. Inf. Theory **56**(9), 4539–4551 (2010)
15. El Rouayheb, S., Ramchandran,K.: Fractional repetition codes for repair in distributed storage systems. In: 2010 48th Annual Allerton Conference on Communication, Control, and Computing (Allerton), pp. 1510–1517. IEEE (2010)

16. Fehr, S., Yuan, C.: Towards optimal robust secret sharing with security against a rushing adversary. In: Ishai, Y., Rijmen, V. (eds.) EUROCRYPT 2019. LNCS, vol. 11478, pp. 472–499. Springer, Cham (2019). https://doi.org/10.1007/978-3-030-17659-4_16

17. Fehr, S., Yuan, C.: Robust secret sharing with almost optimal share size and security against rushing adversaries. In: Pass, R., Pietrzak, K. (eds.) TCC 2020. LNCS, vol. 12552, pp. 470–498. Springer, Cham (2020). https://doi.org/10.1007/978-3-030-64381-2_17

18. Goparaju, S., El Rouayheb, S., Calderbank, R., Vincent Poor, H.: Data secrecy in distributed storage systems under exact repair. In: 2013 International Symposium on Network Coding (NetCod), pp. 1–6. IEEE (2013)

19. Goparaju, S., Fazeli, A., Vardy, A.: Minimum storage regenerating codes for all parameters. IEEE Trans. Inf. Theory 63(10), 6318–6328 (2017)

20. Goyal, V., Kumar, A.: Non-malleable secret sharing. In: Diakonikolas, I., Kempe, D., Henzinger, M. eds. 50th ACM STOC, pp. 685–698. ACM Press, June 2018. https://doi.org/10.1145/3188745.3188872

21. Guruswami, V., Wootters, M.: Repairing reed-Solomon codes. In: Wichs, D., Mansour, Y., (eds.) 48th ACM STOC, pp. 216–226. ACM Press, June 2016. https://doi.org/10.1145/2897518.2897525

22. Guruswami, V., Wootters, M.: Repairing reed-Solomon codes. IEEE Trans. Inf. Theory 63(9), 5684–5698 (2017). https://doi.org/10.1109/TIT.2017.2702660

23. Hazay, C., Venkitasubramaniam, M., Weiss, M.: The price of active security in cryptographic protocols. In: Canteaut, A., Ishai, Y. (eds.) EUROCRYPT 2020. LNCS, vol. 12106, pp. 184–215. Springer, Cham (2020). https://doi.org/10.1007/978-3-030-45724-2_7

24. Ishai, Y., Sahai, A., Wagner, D.: Private circuits: securing hardware against probing attacks. In: Boneh, D. (ed.) CRYPTO 2003. LNCS, vol. 2729, pp. 463–481. Springer, Heidelberg (2003). https://doi.org/10.1007/978-3-540-45146-4_27

25. Klein, O., Komargodski, I.: New bounds on the local leakage resilience of Shamir's secret sharing scheme. In: Handschuh, H., Lysyanskaya, A. (eds.) Advances in Cryptology–CRYPTO 2023. CRYPTO 2023. LNCS, vol. 14081, pp. 139–170. Springer, Cham (2023). https://doi.org/10.1007/978-3-031-38557-5_5

26. Kumar, A., Meka, R., Sahai, A.: Leakage-resilient secret sharing against colluding parties. In: Zuckerman, D., (ed.) 60th FOCS, pp. 636–660. IEEE Computer Society Press, November 2019. https://doi.org/10.1109/FOCS.2019.00045

27. Maji, H.K., Nguyen, H.H., Paskin-Cherniavsky, A., Suad, T., Wang, M.: Leakage-resilience of the Shamir secret-sharing scheme against physical-bit leakages. In: Canteaut, A., Standaert, F.-X. (eds.) EUROCRYPT 2021. LNCS, vol. 12697, pp. 344–374. Springer, Cham (2021). https://doi.org/10.1007/978-3-030-77886-6_12

28. Maji, H.K., et al.:. Tight estimate of the local leakage resilience of the additive secret-sharing scheme & its consequences. In: Dachman-Soled, D. (ed.) 3rd Conference on Information-Theoretic Cryptography, ITC 2022, July 5-7, 2022, Cambridge, MA, USA, vol. 230, LIPIcs, pp. 16:1–16:19. Schloss Dagstuhl - Leibniz-Zentrum für Informatik (2022). https://doi.org/10.4230/LIPIcs.ITC.2022.16

29. Maji, H.K., Nguyen, H.H., Paskin-Cherniavsky, A., Wang, M.: Improved bound on the local leakage-resilience of Shamir's secret sharing. In: IEEE International Symposium on Information Theory, ISIT 2022, Espoo, Finland, June 26–July 1, 2022, pp. 2678–2683. IEEE (2022). https://doi.org/10.1109/ISIT50566.2022.9834695

30. Maji, H.K., Nguyen, H.H., Paskin-Cherniavsky, A., Ye, X.: Security of Shamir's secret-sharing against physical bit leakage: Secure evaluation places (2023). https://www.cs.purdue.edu/homes/hmaji/papers/MNPY23.pdf

31. Maji, H.K., Paskin-Cherniavsky, A., Suad, T., Wang, M.: Constructing locally leakage-resilient linear secret-sharing schemes. In: Malkin, T., Peikert, C. (eds.) CRYPTO 2021. LNCS, vol. 12827, pp. 779–808. Springer, Cham (2021). https://doi.org/10.1007/978-3-030-84252-9_26

32. Manurangsi, P., Srinivasan, A., Vasudevan, P.N.: Nearly optimal robust secret sharing against rushing adversaries. In: Micciancio, D., Ristenpart, T. (eds.) CRYPTO 2020. LNCS, vol. 12172, pp. 156–185. Springer, Cham (2020). https://doi.org/10.1007/978-3-030-56877-1_6

33. Nielsen, J.B., Simkin, M.: Lower bounds for leakage-resilient secret sharing. In: Canteaut, A., Ishai, Y. (eds.) EUROCRYPT 2020. LNCS, vol. 12105, pp. 556–577. Springer, Cham (2020). https://doi.org/10.1007/978-3-030-45721-1_20

34. NIST. Randomness beacon project. http://www.nist.gov/itl/csd/ct/nist_beacon.cfm

35. Papailiopoulos, D.S., Dimakis, A.G., Cadambe, V.R.: Repair optimal erasure codes through Hadamard designs. IEEE Trans. Inf. Theory **59**(5), 3021–3037 (2013)

36. Vinayak Rashmi, K., Shah, N.B., Vijay Kumar, P.: Optimal exact-regenerating codes for distributed storage at the MSR and MBR points via a product-matrix construction. IEEE Trans. Inf. Theory **57**(8), 5227–5239 (2011)

37. Shamir, A.: How to share a secret. Commun. Assoc. Comput. Mach. **22**(11), 612–613 (1979)

38. Srinivasan, A., Vasudevan, P.N.: Leakage resilient secret sharing and applications. In: Boldyreva, A., Micciancio, D. (eds.) CRYPTO 2019. LNCS, vol. 11693, pp. 480–509. Springer, Cham (2019). https://doi.org/10.1007/978-3-030-26951-7_17

39. Tamo, I., Wang, Z., Bruck, J.: Zigzag codes: MDS array codes with optimal rebuilding. IEEE Trans. Inf. Theory **59**(3), 1597–1616 (2012)

40. Wang, Z., Tamo, I., Bruck, J.: Explicit minimum storage regenerating codes. IEEE Trans. Inf. Theory **62**(8), 4466–4480 (2016)

41. Wooley, T.D.: A note on simultaneous congruences. J. Number Theory. **58**(2), 288–297 (1996)

42. Ye, M., Barg, A.: Explicit constructions of high-rate MDS array codes with optimal repair bandwidth. IEEE Trans. Inf. Theory **63**(4), 2001–2014 (2017)

43. Ye, M., Barg, A.: Explicit constructions of optimal-access MDS codes with nearly optimal sub-packetization. IEEE Trans. Inf. Theory **63**(10), 6307–6317 (2017)

44. Zhao, X.: A note on multiple exponential sums in function fields. Finite Fields Appl. **18**(1), 35–55 (2012)

Connecting Leakage-Resilient Secret Sharing to Practice: Scaling Trends and Physical Dependencies of Prime Field Masking

Sebastian Faust[1], Loïc Masure[2], Elena Micheli[1]([✉]), Maximilian Orlt[1], and François-Xavier Standaert[3]

[1] Department of Computer Science, Technical University of Darmstadt, Darmstadt, Germany
{sebastian.faust,elena.micheli}@tu-darmstadt.de
[2] LIRMM, Univ. Montpellier, CNRS, Montpellier, France
[3] Crypto Group, ICTEAM Institute, UCLouvain, Louvain-la-Neuve, Belgium

Abstract. Symmetric ciphers operating in (small or mid-size) prime fields have been shown to be promising candidates to maintain security against low-noise (or even noise-free) side-channel leakage. In order to design prime ciphers that best trade physical security and implementation efficiency, it is essential to understand how side-channel security evolves with the field size (i.e., scaling trends). Unfortunately, it has also been shown that such scaling trends depend on the leakage functions and cannot be explained by the standard metrics used to analyze Boolean masking with noise. In this work, we therefore initiate a formal study of prime field masking for two canonical leakage functions: bit leakages and Hamming weight leakages. By leveraging theoretical results from the leakage-resilient secret sharing literature, we explain formally why (1) bit leakages correspond to a worst-case and do not encourage operating in larger fields, and (2) an opposite conclusion holds for Hamming weight leakages, where increasing the prime field modulus p can contribute to a security amplification that is exponential in the number of shares, with $\log(p)$ seen as security parameter like the noise variance in Boolean masking. We combine these theoretical results with simulated experiments and show that the interest masking in larger prime fields can degrade gracefully when leakage functions slightly deviate from the Hamming weight abstraction, motivating further research towards characterizing (ideally wide) classes of leakage functions offering such guarantees.

1 Introduction

Security against differential side-channel analysis [26], where an adversary continuously accumulates leakage about a long-term secret, is needed for any symmetric authentication or encryption scheme with embedded security guaran-

© International Association for Cryptologic Research 2024
M. Joye and G. Leander (Eds.): EUROCRYPT 2024, LNCS 14654, pp. 316–344, 2024.
https://doi.org/10.1007/978-3-031-58737-5_12

tees [5]. Masking is the main countermeasure to mitigate such attacks [16,23].[1] It can be viewed as multi-party computation on silicon, where the (e.g., symmetric) cryptographic algorithm is executed on d shares. Informally, masking forces the adversary to combine the leakage of different shares in order to gain information on the long-term secret. A broad sequence of works has investigated the theoretical security guarantees that such schemes provide and connected them to practical (e.g., noisy leakage) models [18,19,25,34,39,40]: they show that under some noise and independence assumptions, masking can lead to exponential security amplification. The independence assumption has been the focus of significant research efforts over the last decade and established design and proof techniques enable to ensure it to a sufficient extent [14,21,36,38]. The noise condition has been more investigated from the adversarial viewpoint and several works showed that the requirement is strict for binary ciphers [2,11,24,35], hence calling for masked operations that manipulate each share minimally [1,13].

Concretely, the weakness of masking in low-noise settings is due to the strong algebraic compatibility between leakage functions observed in practice, such as the Hamming Weight (HW) leakage function, and operations performed in binary fields. For example, say an adversary is able to observe the noise-free HW of Boolean shares (processed in serial or in parallel). Then, just observing the parity of the leakages provides easily exploitable information about the secret, regardless of the number of shares [43]. By adding noise to the leakages, designers essentially ensure that this algebraic compatibility is sufficiently hidden so that the only remaining attack path is statistical (i.e., requires to estimate a high-order moment of the leakage distribution [37,41]). A bit more formally, the reason of this weakness is that the finite group over which masking operates has non-trivial subgroups in the binary case. If the support of the Probability Mass Function (PMF) of each share given the leakage is contained in a coset of a non-trivial subgroup, then the PMF of the corresponding secret is also contained in a coset of the same subgroup [44]. As a consequence, the support of the secret PMF cannot be full, which results in an amount of informative leakage about the secret that cannot be arbitrarily low, regardless of the number of shares.

In order to circumvent this issue, Dziembowski et al. showed that the finite group in which the masking operates should not have any non-trivial subgroup, which characterizes prime fields [20]. This seed result has recently triggered an interest for prime-field masking in symmetric cryptography. Early works in this direction show that ciphers that natively operate in prime fields have a good potential to leverage the excellent properties of prime-field masking. They could in turn enable better implementation security vs. efficiency tradeoffs than binary ciphers, especially in low-noise settings, and with only mild overheads when side-channel attacks are not a concern [12,33]. Yet, these results also show that taking full advantage of this potential requires understanding the scaling trends of prime-field masking. In particular, one central open question of which the

---

[1] The only known alternative is to rely on fresh re-keying with a leakage-resilient PRF [4], which is only exploitable in tailored designs such as ISAP [17].

answer could guide the design of new prime ciphers is whether increasing the prime modulus is beneficial to side-channel security (and by how much)?

Both the empirical evaluations in [33] and the theoretical results in [20] suggest that answering this question is non-trivial. On the empirical side, Masure et al. showed that the interest of increasing the prime modulus depends on the leakage function. For example, a larger modulus improves the security amplification of masking for (noise-free) HW leakages while it does not for (noise-free) LSB leakages. Such a dependency on the (deterministic part of) the leakage function implies that the standard tools and metrics used to characterize Boolean masking are unlikely to explain the scaling trends of prime-field masking. This is because Boolean masking is only effective if leakages are sufficiently noisy, so that the deterministic part of the leakage function is essentially lifted in this case. As a result, the security amplification of Boolean masking only depends on the informativeness of the shares' leakages, classically measured with the Mutual Information (MI) or Statistical Distance (SD). But the HW of a value is more informative than a single-bit leakage according to these metrics, which does not back up the observations of [33]. As for the theoretical side, the noise amplification bounds provided in [20] are not tight for our purpose and do not suggest that increasing the size of the field in which masking operates is beneficial.

Based on this state of the art, the main goal of this paper is to provide theoretical explanations for previous empirical observations on prime-field masking, in order to establish foundations on which prime ciphers could be designed. Interestingly, it turns out that the case of bit (e.g., LSB) leakages has been the topic of (for now mostly theoretical) investigations in the context of leakage-resilient secret sharing, and extended towards any deterministic leakage model with a bounded range [7,8,27–31]. Among others, these works show that bit leakages are in some sense the most powerful leakage functions with bounded range, which therefore raises the question whether more positive results could be obtained for other, ideally more realistic, leakage functions.

In order to provide a complete analysis, we study the leakage resilience with respect to average-case and worst-case metrics. The average-case metric considers leakage from a masked *random* secret and is prominently used by the physical security community (since choosing plaintexts otherwise than uniformly at random has been shown to bring limited gains in this context [45]). On the other hand, worst-case security considers the resistance of masking for a worst-case choice of the secret. The latter is a standard notion in the cryptographic theory community, and, e.g., is used by the aforementioned results on leakage-resilient secret sharing. Interestingly, we show that for the LSB leakage function the analysis can be tightened when considering the weaker, yet realistic, average-case metric. To sum up, we achieve the following theoretical results:

– *For bit leakages*, we show that for both the average-case and worst-case metric, increasing the prime modulus in prime-field masking cannot lead to increased security. This confirms formally the experimental observations from [33]. On the positive side, our analysis for the average-case improves existing bounds from the worst-case setting by a constant factor.

– *For Hamming weight leakages* (which, to the best of our knowledge, were not formally studied so far), we show that for both the average-case and worst-case metric, increasing the prime modulus p can contribute to a security amplification that is exponential in the number of shares, with $\log(p)$ serving as a security parameter like the noise variance in Boolean masking. In contrast to prior work on leakage-resilient secret sharing, our analysis takes into account that the range of the HW leakage function scales with the underlying field size. Concretely, we show that the distinguishing advantage approaches 0, while naively applying bounds from the literature on leakage-resilient secret sharing only gives a trivial upper bound of 1.

In Table 1, we provide a summary of our contribution within the existing literature, with references to the corresponding theorems in this paper. We remark that, for Hamming weight leakage, this work only considers upper bounds. The rationale behind this decision is our primary focus in arguing about how the security improves when increasing the field size. Nonetheless, we recognize the interest in quantifying the minimal information derived from a Hamming-weight leakage attack, which we leave as an open research question.

Table 1. Overview of the results for the security of additive secret sharing against bit and HW leakage, for both the worst-case and the average-case metric.

	Bit Leakage	Hamming Weight
Worst-case	*upper bound:* Theorem 1 [7]	*upper bound:* Theorem 6
	lower bound: Theorem 4 [29]	*lower bound:* open problem
Average-case	*upper bound:* Theorem 1 [7]	*upper bound:* Theorem 8
	lower bound: Theorem 5	*lower bound:* open problem

Hence, our results indicate that for the Hamming weight leakage function, there is theoretical support to design ciphers that operate in larger prime fields (which should then be weighted with the performance overheads this increase leads to). Quite naturally, they also raise the question whether concrete leakage functions that are close to but not exactly equal to the Hamming weight function maintain this interest. In order to stimulate research in this direction, we combine our theoretical analyzes with a simulated experiment, where we evaluate linear leakage functions that gradually deviate from the Hamming weight function. While extreme deviations lead to bit-like leakages where increasing p does not help (e.g., if a single bit leaks with such a high contribution to the overall leakage that it can be isolated), we show that this loss is gradual and that a broad class of leakage functions maintains the interest of Hamming weight leakages.

Finally, and despite we primarily use techniques in the context of leakage-resilient secret sharing to improve the understanding of masking in prime fields, our results come with observations that could be relevant for (more theoretical) research on leakage-resilient secret sharing as well. For example, the average-case security notion allows us to obtain tighter bounds for LSB leakages, and it would be interesting to study whether similar gains can be obtained for other practically-relevant leakage functions. In this respect, we note that for many applications of leakage-resilient secret sharing (e.g., in threshold cryptography for sharing a random secret key), the average-case notion suffices. In addition, our work highlights the importance of achieving good bounds when the range of a leakage function increases with the underlying field. We believe this is a quite natural generalization that could also be relevant in the domain of leakage-resilient secret sharing and opens up avenues for future research.

2   Background

Notations. In this paper, calligraphic letters like $\mathcal{S}$ denote sets, small letters like x denote elements of a given set, and capital letters like X denote random variables over a given set. The notation $X \leftarrow \mathcal{S}$ means that X is uniformly drawn from $\mathcal{S}$. If $f : \mathcal{A} \to \mathcal{B}$ denotes a function mapping a set $\mathcal{A}$ to an image set $\mathcal{B}$, and $y \in \mathcal{B}$, $f^{-1}(y)$ denotes the pre-image set of all values $x \in \mathcal{A}$ such that $f(x) = y$. For a set $\mathcal{S} \subseteq \mathcal{A}$, we denote by $1_{\mathcal{S}} : \mathcal{A} \to \{0,1\}$ the function mapping any $x \in \mathcal{A}$ to 1 if and only if (i.f.f.) $x \in \mathcal{S}$ and to 0 otherwise. In particular, when considering characteristic functions over pre-image sets, we may use the shortcut notation 1_y to denote $1_{f^{-1}(y)}$ as long as there is no ambiguity on f.

Masking. For a finite field $\mathcal{Y} = \mathbb{F}_p$ of prime size p, let $Y \in \mathcal{Y}$ be a *sensitive* value—*i.e.*, depending on a chunk of secret. To protect Y against a too much informative leakage, let $Y_1, \ldots, Y_d$ be d random variables uniformly drawn from $\mathcal{Y}$, such that $Y = Y_1 + \ldots + Y_d$. This encoding is commonly referred to as masking, and the corresponding random variables are called shares. The adversary is then given access to a random vector $\mathbf{L} = (L_1, \ldots, L_d)$ such that each random variable L_i, also known as *leakage*, solely depends on the realization of Y_i. In the remaining of this paper, we make the additional assumption that we are in a *low-noise* setting, *i.e.* that each leakage L_i is a deterministic (non-injective) function randomized by its input Y_i.[2]

2.1   Quantifying the Distance to Uniform

To quantify the distance to the uniform distribution over $\mathcal{Y}$, we will use different metrics. Let p, m be two Probability Mass Functions (PMFs) over the finite set $\mathcal{Y}$. We denote by $TV(p; m)$ the Total Variation (TV) between p and m:

$$TV(p; m) = \frac{1}{2} \sum_{y \in \mathcal{Y}} |p(y) - m(y)| \ . \tag{1}$$

---

[2] The literature of noise amplification bounds does not directly assume a noise-free setting, as it can be encompassed in the noisy leakage framework. On the opposite, to the best of our knowledge it is more common in the literature about the leakage-resilience of linear secret sharing schemes to rely on this assumption [8,29].

We will sometimes denote with $\mathrm{TV}\left(X^{(0)}; X^{(1)}\right)$ the total variation for the PMFs corresponding to the random variables $X^{(0)}, X^{(1)}$. Adapting the terminology from Prouff & Rivain [40], we define the *statistical bias* as Duc et al. [18]:

$$\beta(Y|L) = \underset{L}{\mathbb{E}}\left[\mathrm{TV}\left(p_{Y \mid L}; p_Y\right)\right] = \mathrm{TV}\left(p_{Y,L}; p_Y \otimes p_L\right), \tag{2}$$

where $\otimes$ denotes the Cartesian product between two marginal probability distributions.[3] Notice that β is symmetric in its arguments, *i.e.*, $\beta(Y|L) = \beta(L|Y) = \underset{Y}{\mathbb{E}}\left[\mathrm{TV}\left(p_{L \mid Y}; p_L\right)\right]$. In the particular case of masking—which will be the main focus in this paper—the latter one can be rephrased as

$$\underset{y \leftarrow y}{\mathbb{E}}\left[\mathrm{TV}(L\left(\mathsf{AddEnc}\left(y\right)\right); L\left(\mathsf{AddEnc}\left(Y\right)\right))\right],$$

where $\mathsf{AddEnc}\left(\cdot\right)$ is a random function that maps a secret value with one of its additive encodings. The bias is actually the *average* Total Variation (TV) between two PMFs. This definition is usual in papers dealing with masking against side-channel analysis. Note that this metric depends not only on the chosen leakage model, but also on the underlying distribution of the secret. That is why some related works [7] also considered a variant of this metric that we call *worst-case bias*:

$$M_\infty\left(L\right) = \max_{y^{(0)}, y^{(1)} \in \mathcal{Y}} \mathrm{TV}\left(L\left(\mathsf{AddEnc}\left(y^{(0)}\right)\right); L\left(\mathsf{AddEnc}\left(y^{(1)}\right)\right)\right).$$

Here, the expectation is replaced by a maximum over the product set of secrets $\mathcal{Y}$. As a result, it follows that for all random variable Y:

$$\beta(Y|L) \leq M_\infty\left(L\right) \leq p \cdot \beta(Y|L). \tag{3}$$

2.2   The Limits of Generic Noise Amplification Bounds

So far, the literature of masking security proofs provides bounds on the statistical bias of the following shape:

$$\beta(Y|L) \leq f(\delta_1, \ldots, \delta_d), \quad \text{if } \delta_i < t \text{ for all } i,$$

where δ_i stands for the statistical bias between one share Y_i and its corresponding leakage L_i, t is a threshold for which the bound is valid, and f is a decreasing function with its arguments and converging exponentially fast with d towards 0 [3,20]. These so-called *noise amplification* bounds in the literature have the main strength of being *tight*, *i.e.*, there exists a leakage model such that the

---

[3] The first equality is used in noise amplification papers [20,34,40] and aims at quantifying how the distribution of the secret deviates from the prior knowledge whenever some side information L is available. The second equality is used in simulation-based proofs [18], and rather aims at quantifying how the side information L changes whenever the secret is known.

inequality becomes an equality. They also have the advantage of being *universal*, which means that they do not depend on the nature of the underlying leakage model, provided that the latter one verifies $\beta(Y_i|L_i) \leq \delta_i$ for all $i \in [\![0, d]\!]$. This would strongly suggest the intuitive idea that when comparing two leakage models applied on each share, the higher the δ_i for all i, the higher the bias $\beta(Y|L)$. In other words, the leakier each share, the leakier the resulting secret.

To discuss this intuition, let us take as an example two well-known leakage models. The first one is the Hamming Weight (HW), the leakage function returning the sum of bits of the underlying leaky variable, *i.e.*, $\mathsf{HW}(y) = \sum_{i=0}^{n} y_i$.

Lemma 1 (Bias of Hamming weight). *For $n \in \mathbb{N}^\star$ and $p = 2^n - 1$, let $Y \leftarrow \mathbb{Z}_p$ and let $L = \mathsf{HW}(Y)$. Then the statistical bias between Y and L verifies*

$$\beta(Y|L) = 1 - \frac{\binom{2n}{n} - 1}{(2^n - 1)^2} \approx 1 - \frac{1}{\sqrt{\pi n}}. \tag{4}$$

We also consider a second leakage model where a proportion α of the n bits leaks. In other words, the leakage function ℓ^S returns the bits $y_{s_1}, \ldots, y_{s_{\alpha n}}$ where $S = \{s_1, \ldots, s_{\alpha n}\}$ is a set of αn indices.

Lemma 2 (Proportion of leaky bits). *For $n \in \mathbb{N}^\star$ and $p = 2^n - 1$, let $Y \leftarrow \mathbb{Z}_p$ and let $L = (Y_{s_1}, \ldots, Y_{s_{\alpha n}})$. Then the statistical bias between Y and L verifies*

$$\beta(Y|L) = 1 - \frac{2^{n(1-\alpha)}}{2^n - 1} + \frac{2^{n(1-\alpha)} - 1}{(2^n - 1)^2}. \tag{5}$$

In particular, for the LSB leakage model, $\alpha = \frac{1}{n}$, we have $\beta(Y|L) \approx \frac{1}{2} - 2^{-(n+1)}$.

Lemma 1 and Lemma 2, proven in Appendix B, tell us that a share leaking in Hamming Weight (HW) is leakier than the same share leaking in Least Significant Bit (LSB).[4] Even more, for the HW leakage model, the amount of leakage increases with the field size, whereas it remains nearly constant in the LSB leakage model. We would therefore expect a target device protected with masking and leaking the LSB of each share to be more secure than the same device leaking in HW. Furthermore, we would expect that in the latter case, increasing the field size could be harmful. But the observations of Masure *et al.* [33, Fig. 3]—measured in terms of MI—contradict both intuitions: not only the HW behaves not worse than the LSB leakage with masking in $\mathbb{F}_p$, but increasing the field size seems helpful to get a better leakage-resilience.

2.3   Refined Bounds Through Fourier Analysis

A recent line of works have studied the so-called *local leakage resilience* of secret-sharing schemes designed over prime fields [7]. As a perhaps unexpected application of their framework (initially devoted to the security of MPC protocols),

---

[4] This is true regardless of the choice of the metric, *i.e.*, similar trends hold when considering the Mutual Information (MI).

Benhamouda *et al.*'s framework can be used to refine the noise amplification bounds prone to the limitations emphasized at the previous subsection.

Their framework relies on the Fourier analysis of leakage functions of each share. That is why we first recall a few facts about Fourier analysis.

Definition 1 (Discrete Fourier Transform). *Let $f : \mathbb{Z}_p \to \mathbb{C}$ be a function over the cyclic group $\mathbb{Z}_p$. Then the Discrete Fourier Transform (DFT) of f of harmonic α—or the α-th Fourier coefficient of f for short—is defined as*

$$\widehat{f}(\alpha) = \frac{1}{p} \sum_{y \in \mathbb{Z}_p} f(y) e^{-\frac{2\pi \alpha y}{p} i}. \tag{6}$$

Next, we list some interesting properties of the discrete Fourier transform.

Proposition 1 (Parseval). *Let $f, g : \mathbb{Z}_p \to \mathbb{C}$. Then*

$$\frac{1}{p} \sum_{y \in \mathbb{Z}_p} f(y) \cdot g(y) = \sum_{\alpha \in \mathbb{Z}_p} \widehat{f}(\alpha) \cdot \overline{\widehat{g}(\alpha)}.$$

In particular, this implies

$$\frac{1}{p} \sum_{y \in \mathbb{Z}_p} |f(y)|^2 = \sum_{\alpha \in \mathbb{Z}_p} \left| \widehat{f}(\alpha) \right|^2. \tag{7}$$

Proposition 1 tells us that the DFT is an isometry for the Euclidean norm, up to a normalizing field-size factor. We next need another well-known formula from Fourier analysis, namely the Poisson summation formula.[5]

Proposition 2 (Poisson Summation Formula). *Let $\mathbb{F}$ be a finite field, and let $C \subseteq \mathbb{F}^d$ be a linear code with dual code $C^\perp$. Let $f_1, \ldots, f_d : \mathbb{F} \to C$ be functions. Then the following inequality holds:*

$$\mathop{\mathbb{E}}_{x \leftarrow C} \left[\prod_{j=1}^{d} f_j(x_j) \right] = \sum_{\alpha \in C^\perp} \prod_{j=1}^{d} \widehat{f}_j(\alpha_j).$$

As observed in [7], the Poisson Summation Formula can be leveraged to link total variation and Fourier coefficients.

Proposition 3. *Let $\mathbb{F}_p$ be a prime field of size p. Then, for all $y^{(0)}, y^{(1)} \in \mathbb{F}_p$:*

$$\mathsf{TV}\left(\mathbf{L} \left(\mathsf{AddEnc} \left(y^{(0)} \right) \right) ; \mathbf{L} \left(\mathsf{AddEnc} \left(y^{(1)} \right) \right) \right)$$
$$= \frac{1}{2} \sum_{\ell \in \mathcal{L}^d} \left| \sum_{\alpha \in \mathbb{F}^\star} \left(\prod_{j=1}^{d} \widehat{1_{L_j^{-1}(\ell_j)}}(\alpha) \right) \left(e^{-\frac{2i\pi \alpha y^{(0)}}{p}} - e^{-\frac{2i\pi \alpha y^{(1)}}{p}} \right) \right|. \tag{8}$$

---

[5] For a more general statement of Proposition 2 concerning any linear code, see [7].

Furthermore, if Y follows the uniform distribution over $\mathbb{F}_p$, then for every $y \in \mathbb{F}_p$, $\text{TV}(\mathbf{L}(\text{AddEnc}(y)); \mathbf{L}(\text{AddEnc}(Y)))$ equals

$$\frac{1}{2} \sum_{\ell \in \mathcal{L}^d} \left| \sum_{\alpha \in \mathbb{F}^*} \left(\prod_{j=1}^{d} \widehat{1_{L_j^{-1}(\ell_j)}}(\alpha) \right) e^{-\frac{2i\pi\alpha y}{p}} \right|. \tag{9}$$

Stated as is, the right-hand sides of the equalities in Proposition 3 are not numerically tractable, as they sum over $\mathcal{L}^d$, which becomes quickly hard when the range of $\mathcal{L}$ or d increase. Monte-Carlo estimations can be used to partially circumvent the problem [33]. But the core idea of such simulations is to leverage the phenomenon of *concentration* of probability distributions in high-dimensional spaces [9]. In this respect, they are efficient whenever the dimensionality of the leakage space—d here—increases, but not necessarily whenever the range of $\mathcal{L}$ increases, which is the core question of this paper. That is why we leverage another corollary from Benhamouda *et al.*[6]

Corollary 1 (Cauchy-Schwarz [8, p. 30, restated]). *Let $\mathbf{L} = (L_1, \ldots, L_d)$ be any family of leakage. Then, $\text{M}_\infty(\mathbf{L})$ is upper bounded by*

$$\frac{1}{p} \left(\sum_{\ell_1} \left\| 1_{L_1^{-1}(\ell_1)} \right\|_2 \right) \cdot \left(\sum_{\ell_2} \left\| 1_{L_2^{-1}(\ell_2)} \right\|_2 \right) \cdot \prod_{j=3}^{d} \left(\sum_{\ell_j} \max_{\alpha \in \mathbb{F}^*} \left| \widehat{1_{L_j^{-1}(\ell_j)}}(\alpha) \right| \right). \tag{10}$$

Corollary 1 provides an upper bound for the worst-case metric as a product of d sums over $\mathcal{L}$, whose complexity grows linearly with both the range of $\mathcal{L}$ and d. Hence, the right-hand side of Eq. 10 is much more tractable and can be exactly computed—up to negligible numerical errors. Benhamouda *et al.* also leverage Corollary 1 to establish an upper bound of the worst-case metric for any noise-free m-bounded leakage function, *i.e.*, any function that can take up to 2^m different values, for some integer m.

Theorem 1 ([7, Thm. 4.7], restated). *For a secret $Y \leftarrow \mathbb{F}_p$ protected with additive secret sharing, let $\mathbf{L} = (L_1, \ldots, L_d)$ be any family of leakage functions where $L_i : \mathbb{F}_p \to \{0,1\}^m$. Let $c_m = \frac{2^m \sin(\pi/2^m)}{p \sin(\pi/p)} < 1$ (when $2^m < p$). Then,*

$$\text{M}_\infty(\mathbf{L}) \leq 2^m \cdot c_m^{d-2}. \tag{11}$$

For the average-case metric with uniform Y, the upper bound stays the same, but with the additional multiplicative factor $\frac{1}{2}$.

Equation 11 provides a non-trivial upper bound on the worst-case bias whenever the field size p increases. This upper bound is asymptotically tight, as Maji *et al.* have exhibited a leakage function, namely the LSB, for which there is a lower bound asymptotically matching the right-hand side of Eq. 11, up to a small

---

[6] The Cauchy-Schwarz trick has already been used in the noise amplification bound of Prouff & Rivain [40, Thm. 1], although applied to another metric.

constant factor. Theorem 1 thereby provides an upper bound on the statistical bias, as it can be trivially upper bounded by the worst-case bias. Therefore, the only missing inequality to get a comprehensive view of the leakage-resilience of m-bounded leakage functions is a lower bound on the statistical bias. This will be the focus of Sect. 3. Furthermore, we note that in Theorem 1 the right-hand side of Eq. 11 is non-trivial when p increases if and only if the range m of the leakage function is constant. This assumption does not always hold, and there are concrete counter-examples of leakage functions for which the range m depends on the field size, such as the HW—where $m \approx \log \log p$. As a result, one should go back to Corollary 1 to tighten the upper bound through a refined analysis of the Fourier coefficients of the specific leakage function under study. We will instantiate this approach for the HW leakage in Sect. 4.

3   Bit Leakages

In this section, we investigate how the information derived from bit leakage is affected by the field size. Our findings indicate that this leakage model exhibits limited sensitivity to changes in the field size, up to the point that we can lower-bound the amount of information by a constant in p. As an initial step, we provide an outlook on a prior result of Maji et al. [29]. In their work, they already showed that the information deriving from LSB leakage can be lower-bounded by a constant in p in the worst-case scenario. Following, we demonstrate that the weak noise amplification observed in the worst-case setting actually occurs for a large fraction of secrets. In other words, we provide a lower bound that is independent of p for the LSB in the average-case metricl. Eventually, we move out of the LSB leakage model and achieve the same lower bounds for the more general case of bit probing. We conclude that there is a barrier beyond which security against bit probing cannot be enhanced by increasing the field size.

In the first part of this section, we consistently work in the LSB leakage model. Henceforth, unless specified differently, we use the more general notation $\mathbf{L} : \mathbb{F}_p^{d+1} \to \{0,1\}^{d+1}$ for the function returning the LSB of every component.

3.1   Worst-Case Characterization

With the following theorem, we recall the LSB analysis in the worst-case metric of [29]. Their main observation is that the information obtained from LSB leakage can be lower-bounded by a constant in p in the worst-case scenario.

Theorem 2 ([29, Thm. 10], restated). *Let p be a prime ≥ 3. Then, for every number of shares $d \in \mathbb{N}$*

$$\mathsf{M}_\infty\left(\mathbf{L}\right) \geq \frac{1}{2} \cdot \left(\frac{2}{\pi}\right)^d \cdot \left[\frac{3}{2} - 4\left(\left(\frac{2}{3}\right)^d + \frac{1}{d+1}\left(\frac{1}{3}\right)^{d+1}\right)\right]. \tag{12}$$

We note that the above result is non-trivial only when the right-hand side is non negative, which happens for every $d \geq 3$. We remark that Theorem 2 slightly differs from [29, Thm. 10]. This is because the latter is only stated asymptotically, while the actual parameters only appear inside the corresponding proof. In Theorem 2, we condense the information from [29] to provide a more comprehensive version of the same statement.

3.2   Average-Case Characterization

Given that $M_\infty(\mathbf{L}) \leq p \cdot \beta(Y|\mathbf{L})$ (from Eq. (1)), Theorem 2 already yields a lower bound to the average-case metric, that is

$$\beta(Y|\mathbf{L}) \geq \frac{1}{2p} \cdot \left(\frac{2}{\pi}\right)^d \cdot \left[\frac{3}{2} - 4\left(\left(\frac{2}{3}\right)^d + \frac{1}{d+1}\left(\frac{1}{3}\right)^{d+1}\right)\right]. \tag{13}$$

In contrast with the worst-case result, this lower bound could suggest that increasing the field size may result in a more effective strategy against LSB attacks for random secrets. In other words, the possible tightness of Eq. (13) would reveal that only a handful of secrets yield the weak noise amplification observed in the worst-case scenario. In fact, we show that the lower bound of Eq. (13) can be improved to remove the dependence on p. This means that the weak noise amplification involves the majority of secrets, and thus must be considered in the randomized setting as well. We make this finding formal with Theorem 3. From a technical standpoint, our key observation is that Eq. (12) can be slightly modified to lower-bound the information derived from at least half of the possible secrets. Later in the section, we provide a discussion of our results, and explore their applicability within the broader bit-probing model.

Theorem 3. *Let p be a prime ≥ 3 and $d \in \mathbb{N}$ be any number of shares. Let Y be the uniform distribution over $\mathbb{F}_p$. Then $\beta(Y|\mathbf{L})$ is lower-bounded by*

$$\frac{1}{2} \cdot \left(\frac{2}{\pi}\right)^d \cdot \left[\frac{p+1}{2p} \cdot \sqrt{2} \cdot \sqrt{1 - \sin\left(\frac{\pi}{2p}\right)} - 2 \cdot \left(\left(\frac{2}{3}\right)^d + \frac{1}{d+1}\left(\frac{1}{3}\right)^{d+1}\right)\right].$$

As for the worst-case analysis of [29], this lower bound is non-trivial whenever $d \geq 3$.

We now outline the proof of Theorem 3. As in [29], the first step is to rewrite the Statistical Distance (SD) in the Fourier domain. Using Eq. (9) from Theorem 3, we get

$$\beta(Y|\mathbf{L}) = \frac{1}{2p} \sum_{y \in \mathbb{F}_p} \sum_{\ell \in \{0,1\}^d} \left| \sum_{\alpha \in \mathbb{F}^*} \left(\prod_{j=1}^{d} \widehat{1_{L_j^{-1}(\ell_j)}}(\alpha) \right) e^{-\frac{2i\pi\alpha y}{p}} \right|. \tag{14}$$

As observed in [29, Claim 15], the LSB Fourier coefficients for $\alpha \in \mathbb{F}^*$ satisfy

$$\widehat{1_{L_j^{-1}(0)}}(\alpha) = -\widehat{1_{L_j^{-1}(1)}}(\alpha) = \frac{1}{2p} \cdot \frac{1}{\cos(\pi\alpha/p)} \cdot e^{\frac{i\pi\alpha}{p}}.$$

Therefore, Eq. (14) becomes

$$\beta(\mathbf{Y}|\mathbf{L}) = \frac{2^{d-1}}{p} \sum_{y \in \mathbb{F}_p} \left| \sum_{\alpha \in \mathbb{F}^*} \left(\frac{1}{2p} \cdot \frac{1}{\cos(\pi \alpha/p)} \cdot e^{\frac{i\pi\alpha}{p}} \right)^d e^{-\frac{2i\pi\alpha y}{p}} \right|.$$

Similar to [29], we observe that the dominant terms are those corresponding to $\alpha = \{\frac{p-1}{2}, \frac{p+1}{2}\}$. However, since we consider an *average-case* metric, the above observation needs to hold for a large enough set of field elements $y \in \mathcal{Y}$. Therefore, the proof relies on the following lemmas.

Lemma 3. *Let $p \geq 3$. There exist a subset $\tilde{\mathcal{Y}} \subseteq \mathbb{F}_p$ such that every $y \in \tilde{\mathcal{Y}}$ satisfies*

$$\left| \sum_{\alpha \in \{\frac{p-1}{2}, \frac{p+1}{2}\}} \left(\frac{1}{2p} \cdot \frac{1}{\cos(\pi\alpha/p)} \cdot e^{\frac{i\pi\alpha}{p}} \right)^d \cdot e^{-\frac{2i\pi\alpha y}{p}} \right| \tag{15}$$
$$\geq \pi^{-d} \cdot \sqrt{2} \cdot \sqrt{1 - \sin\left(\frac{\pi}{2p} \right)}.$$

Lemma 4. *Let $p \geq 3$. For every secret $y \in \mathbb{F}_p$, it holds*

$$\left| \sum_{\alpha \in \mathbb{F}^* \setminus \{\frac{p-1}{2}, \frac{p+1}{2}\}} \left(\frac{1}{2p} \cdot \frac{1}{\cos(\pi\alpha/p)} \cdot e^{\frac{i\pi\alpha}{p}} \right)^d \cdot e^{-\frac{2i\pi\alpha y}{p}} \right|$$
$$\leq 2\pi^{-d} \cdot \left(\left(\frac{2}{3} \right)^d + \frac{1}{d+1} \left(\frac{1}{3} \right)^{d+1} \right).$$

Given that Lemma 3 holds for $\frac{p+1}{2}$ elements, and Lemma 4 is true for every field element, Theorem 3 follows by triangular inequality

Proof of Theorem 3.

$$\beta(\mathbf{Y}|\mathbf{L}) \geq \frac{2^{d-1}}{p} \sum_{y \in \mathbb{F}_p} \left| \sum_{\alpha \in \{\frac{p-1}{2}, \frac{p+1}{2}\}} \left(\frac{1}{2p} \cdot \frac{1}{\cos(\pi\alpha/p)} \cdot e^{\frac{i\pi\alpha}{p}} \right)^d e^{-\frac{2i\pi\alpha y}{p}} \right|$$

$$- \frac{2^{d-1}}{p} \sum_{y \in \mathbb{F}_p} \left| \sum_{\alpha \in \mathbb{F}_p^* \setminus \{\frac{p-1}{2}, \frac{p+1}{2}\}} \left(\frac{1}{2p} \cdot \frac{1}{\cos(\pi\alpha/p)} \cdot e^{\frac{i\pi\alpha}{p}} \right)^d e^{-\frac{2i\pi\alpha y}{p}} \right|.$$

$$\geq \frac{1}{2} \left(\frac{2}{\pi} \right)^d \left[\frac{p+1}{2p} \sqrt{2} \sqrt{1 - \sin\left(\frac{\pi}{2p} \right)} - 2 \left(\left(\frac{2}{3} \right)^d + \frac{1}{d+1} \left(\frac{1}{3} \right)^{d+1} \right) \right]$$

$\square$

To complete the analysis, we present the proofs of Lemma 3 and Lemma 4.

Proof of Lemma 3. We first restate the left-hand side of Eq. (15) as

$$\left| \frac{1}{2p} \cdot \frac{1}{\sin\left(\frac{\pi}{2p}\right)} \right|^d \cdot \left| 1 + (-1)^d e^{\frac{i\pi d}{p}} e^{-\frac{2i\pi y}{p}} \right|$$

and observe that it can be lower-bounded by $\pi^{-d} \cdot \left| 1 + e^{i\pi\left(d + \frac{d}{p} - \frac{2y}{p}\right)} \right|$ because $\frac{1}{x\sin(1/x)}$ is a decreasing function in x, and $\lim_{x\to\infty} \frac{1}{x\sin(1/x)} = 1$. So it remains to find $\tilde{\mathcal{Y}}$ so that, for every $y \in \tilde{\mathcal{Y}}$, we can lower-bound $\left| 1 + e^{i\pi\left(d + \frac{d}{p} - \frac{2y}{p}\right)} \right|$.

We use the fact that, whenever x lies in $\left[-\frac{p+1}{2p}, \frac{p+1}{2p} \right]$, then

$$\left| 1 + e^{i\pi x} \right| = \sqrt{2} \cdot \sqrt{1 + \cos(\pi x)} \geq \sqrt{2} \cdot \sqrt{1 - \sin\left(\frac{\pi}{2p}\right)},$$

as cos is symmetric in $\left[-\frac{p+1}{2p}\pi, \frac{p+1}{2p}\pi \right]$ and decreasing in $\left[0, \frac{p+1}{2p}\pi \right]$.

This means that, whenever y belongs to the interval

$$\mathcal{I} = \left[\frac{p}{2}\left(-\frac{p+1}{2p} + d + \frac{d}{p} \right), \frac{p}{2}\left(\frac{p+1}{2p} + d + \frac{d}{p} \right) \right] \quad \text{mod } p,$$

then

$$\left| 1 + e^{i\pi\left(d + \frac{d}{p} - \frac{2y}{p}\right)} \right| \geq \sqrt{2} \cdot \sqrt{1 - \sin\left(\frac{\pi}{2p}\right)}.$$

Let $\tilde{\mathcal{Y}} = \mathbb{F}_p \cap \mathcal{I}$. Since $\mathcal{I}$ has length $\frac{p+1}{2}$, then $\tilde{\mathcal{Y}}$ has at least $\frac{p+1}{2}$ elements. This concludes the proof. □

Proof of Lemma 4. Using the triangular inequality on the left-hand side of Lemma 4, we get

$$\left| \sum_{\alpha \in \mathbb{F}^* \backslash \left\{ \frac{p-1}{2}, \frac{p+1}{2} \right\}} \left(\frac{1}{2p} \cdot \frac{1}{\cos(\pi\alpha/p)} \cdot e^{\frac{i\pi\alpha}{p}} \right)^d \cdot e^{-\frac{2i\pi\alpha y}{p}} \right|$$

$$\leq \sum_{\alpha \in \mathbb{F}^* \backslash \left\{ \frac{p-1}{2}, \frac{p+1}{2} \right\}} \left| \frac{1}{2p} \cdot \frac{1}{\cos(\pi\alpha/p)} \cdot e^{\frac{i\pi\alpha}{p}} \right|^d.$$

Then, the lemma follows from the following observation of [29] (proof of Claim 17)

$$\sum_{\alpha \in \mathbb{F}^* \setminus \{\frac{p-1}{2}, \frac{p+1}{2}\}} \left| \frac{1}{2p} \cdot \frac{1}{\cos(\pi\alpha/p)} \cdot e^{\frac{i\pi\alpha}{p}} \right|^d$$

$$\leq 2\pi^{-d} \cdot \left(\left(\frac{2}{3}\right)^d + \frac{1}{d+1} \left(\frac{1}{3}\right)^{d+1} \right).$$

$\square$

3.3 Discussion

On the Field Size (In)Dependence. Asymptotically in p, both the worst-case and the average-case metrics are lower-bounded by a value independent of p. The latter defines a barrier beyond which security cannot be enhanced by increasing the field size. This property is inherent to the LSB leakage model, as its maximal Fourier coefficients over $\mathbb{F}_p^*$ do not converge towards zero as p approaches infinity. This observation is already made formal in Theorem 2 and Theorem 3, but we can provide a more pictorial intuition of why it's true.

First note that, for every $\alpha \in \mathbb{F}_p$ and for every $S \subseteq \mathbb{F}_p$, we can restate

$$\widehat{1_S}(\alpha) = \frac{|S|}{p} \cdot \frac{1}{|S|} \sum_{z \in \alpha S} e^{-\frac{2\pi z i}{p}}.$$

That is, $\widehat{1_S}(\alpha)$ equals the barycenter of the roots of unity corresponding to αS up to the multiplicative factor $\frac{|S|}{p}$. When $S = \mathsf{lsb}^{-1}(0)$, then both $\frac{p-1}{2}S$ and $\frac{p+1}{2}S$ yield sets of $\frac{p+1}{2}$ consecutive field elements. That is, the corresponding Fourier coefficients converge to the barycenter of half of the unit circle up to a constant, which is not zero. Figure 1 shows the Fourier spectrum of $1_{L_j^{-1}(0)}$ in the LSB model for different primes p.

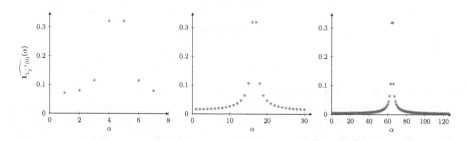

Fig. 1. α vs $\widehat{1_{L_j^{-1}(0)}}(\alpha)$ for $\alpha \in \mathbb{F}^*$ in the LSB leakage model, for $p = 7, 31, 127$.

On Tightness. As observed in [29], the lower bounds for the LSB leakage model can be used to argue about the tightness of the upper bounds of [7]. In particular, Theorem 1 states that the information provided by any leakage function with range 1 satisfies

$$\mathsf{M}_\infty\left(\mathbf{L}\right) \leq 2 \cdot \left(\frac{2}{p \cdot \sin\left(\frac{\pi}{p}\right)}\right)^{d-2},$$

which converges to $\frac{\pi^2}{2} \cdot \left(\frac{2}{\pi}\right)^d$ asymptotically in p. When excluding the factor 2, the same upper bound extends to the average-case metric. As seen in this section, both the worst-case and the average-case metric in the LSB model are lower-bounded by $\left(\frac{2}{\pi}\right)^d$ modulo a factor that only depends on d. Therefore, these result witness that Theorem 1 is asymptotically tight for leakage functions with range 1, modulo a factor that only depends on d.

In Fig. 2, we compare the LSB lower and upper bounds with the corresponding numerical computation in both the average and worst-case metrics.

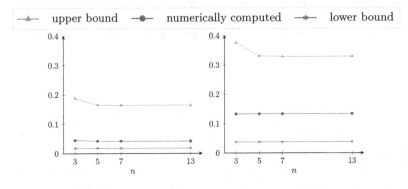

Fig. 2. Both images illustrate the comparison between the upper bound from [7] and the lower bounds discussed in this section with the corresponding numerical computation. The values displayed correspond to different field size values, computed as $p = 2^n - 1$, and fixed number of shares $d = 6$. The left image pertains to the average-case metric, while the right one refers to the worst-case metric.

On Arbitrary Bit Leakage. As observed in [22], the above remark readily extends to the case where the adversary can probe an arbitrary bit location. This follows from the fact that shifting backwards $n - k$ times a string whose k-th significant bit is zero yields one whose LSB is zero. More formally, denote with ksb the function returning the k-th significant bit. Then

$$2^k \mathsf{ksb}^{-1}(0) = \mathsf{lsb}^{-1}(0).$$

This property defines a bijection between the Fourier coefficients of all single-bit probing models, *i.e.* for every $\alpha \in \mathbb{F}_p$ and $k \in [\![1, n]\!]$,

$$\widehat{1_{\mathsf{lsb}^{-1}(0)}}(\alpha) = \widehat{1_{\mathsf{ksb}^{-1}(0)}}(2^k \alpha).$$

As a consequence, the maximizing Fourier coefficients in the ksb leakage model are those for $\alpha \in \{2^{k-1}, p - 2^{k-1}\}$, and there is no convergence towards zero when the field size goes to infinity. In line with this observation, we can extend Theorem 2 and Theorem 3 to the ksb leakage model.

Theorem 4 (Generalizing Theorem 2 to the ksb model). *Let p be a prime ≥ 3 and let $\mathbf{L} : \mathbb{F}_p^d \rightarrow \{0,1\}^d$ be the function returning the ksb of every component. Then, for every $d \in \mathbb{N}$*

$$\mathsf{M}_\infty(\mathbf{L}) \geq \frac{1}{2} \cdot \left(\frac{2}{\pi}\right)^d \cdot \left[\frac{3}{2} - 4\left(\left(\frac{2}{3}\right)^d + \frac{1}{d+1}\left(\frac{1}{3}\right)^{d+1}\right)\right].$$

Theorem 5 (Generalizing Theorem 3 to the ksb model). *Let p be a prime ≥ 3, $\mathbf{L} : \mathbb{F}_p^d \rightarrow \{0,1\}^d$ be the function returning the ksb of every component, and $d \in \mathbb{N}$ be the number of shares. Let Y be the uniform distribution over $\mathbb{F}_p$. Then, $\beta(Y|\mathbf{L})$ is lower-bounded by*

$$\frac{1}{2} \cdot \left(\frac{2}{\pi}\right)^d \cdot \left[\frac{p+1}{2p} \cdot \sqrt{2} \cdot \sqrt{1 - \sin\left(\frac{\pi}{2p}\right)} - 2 \cdot \left(\left(\frac{2}{3}\right)^d + \frac{1}{d+1}\left(\frac{1}{3}\right)^{d+1}\right)\right].$$

Proof Sketch. The proofs of Theorem 4 and Theorem 5 follow the same structure as those for the LSB leakage model, but instead of isolating $\alpha \in \{\frac{p-1}{2}, \frac{p+1}{2}\}$, we isolate the terms corresponding to the maximal Fourier coefficients in the ksb model, *i.e.* $\alpha \in \{2^{k-1}, p - 2^{k-1}\}$. We upper-bound the sum of the terms different from $\{2^{k-1}, p - 2^{k-1}\}$ using the same strategy as in the proof of Lemma 4. Namely, we upper-bound it with the sum of all the corresponding Fourier coefficients. Given the bijection with the non-dominant Fourier coefficients for LSB, the same upper bound holds. It remains to lower-bound the summands corresponding to $\{2^{k-1}, p - 2^{k-1}\}$. Note that by changing the variable y to 2^ky, the problem reduces to the estimation of the dominant terms corresponding to $\{\frac{p-1}{2}, \frac{p+1}{2}\}$ in the LSB model. Therefore, the same statement holds.   □

From Leaking a Single-Bit to a Proportion of Bits. We close this section by discussing to which extent the results established for a single-bit leakage apply as well when several of the bits are revealed to the adversary. In this respect, we first emphasize that the upper bound from Theorem 1 already covers this case. As for the lower bound, we observe that a "single-bit" adversary can be trivially simulated by an adversary having access to several bits of each share. As a consequence, the lower bounds of Theorems 4 and 5 remain true.[7] Hence, leaking a proportion of bits keeps the conclusion of this section unchanged.

---

[7] This can be formalized by applying the data processing inequality to the TV.

4   Hamming Weight Leakages

The previous section has focused on the LSB leakage function, as it is "a realistic and analytically-tractable leakage function" [29, p. 2]. From the physical viewpoint, observing such bit leakages is quite challenging though, and a more realistic leakage function, on which we focus in this section, is the HW, which maps a value to the sum of its bits [32]. As argued at the end of Sect. 2, Theorem 1 does not cover such leakage functions, as their range increases with the field size leading ultimately to trivial bounds. To circumvent this issue, we need to go one step backwards by starting our analysis from Corollary 1, and trying to refine the Fourier analysis of our specific leakage function under scrutiny.

Hereupon, notice how the right-hand side of Eq. 10 depends on the quantity $\sum_h \max_{\alpha \neq 0} \left| \widehat{1_{\mathsf{HW}^{-1}(h)}}(\alpha) \right|$. This quantity illustrates how sensitive is the highest Fourier coefficient of the leakage function for the resulting security bound. In order to get some insights into the quantity behavior, Fig. 3 plots the exemplary Fourier spectra for the bit leakage function studied in the previous section, and for the Hamming weight model that we study now.

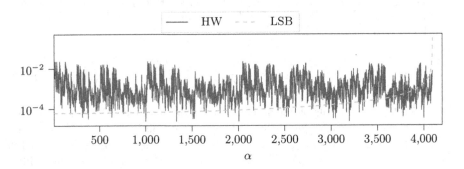

Fig. 3. First half of Fourier spectra of $1_{\mathsf{HW}^{-1}(n/2)}$ (Hamming weight leakage) and $1_{LSB^{-1}(0)}$ (bit leakage) for $n = 13, p = 2^n - 1$ (the second half is symmetric).

On the one hand, the orange curve denotes the spectrum of a pre-image set of the LSB. This spectrum is described by a very smooth curve with a peak close to the value $p/2$, as more formally discussed in the proof outline of Sect. 3. On the other hand, the blue curve denotes the spectrum of a pre-image set of the HW leakage function. This curve is much less smooth than the orange curve, but even worse, there is no concentration of the spectrum around one peak as for the LSB leakage. The missing peak means that we cannot isolate dominant terms as in Lemma 3 and Lemma 4 with $\alpha \in \{ \frac{p-1}{2}, \frac{p+1}{2} \}$. Hence, the proof technique used in Sect. 3 does not provide sufficiently tight security bounds for the HW leakage function, and this section requires an alternative approach.

Nevertheless, the security bound is strongly related to the quantity

$$\sum_h \max_{\alpha \neq 0} \left| \widehat{1_{\mathsf{HW}^{-1}(h)}}(\alpha) \right|.$$

That is why Fig. 4 numerically plots this quantity of interest for an increasing Mersenne number. This will help us derive some insights before diving into a more formal result, as it shows that the quantity decreases with increasing field sizes. In particular, the blue curve denoting the quantity of interest is decreasing at a polynomial rate between $\mathcal{O}\left(\frac{1}{\sqrt{n}}\right)$ and $\mathcal{O}\left(\frac{1}{n}\right)$, represented as the green and orange curve, respectively. In other words, the plot provides a numerical evidence of a bias in $\mathcal{O}\left(\log(p)^{-r \cdot d}\right)$, where $r \in \left[\frac{1}{2}, 1\right]$. In the remaining part of this section, we move towards the formalization of this observation, which in turn allows us to provide a proof for a more conservative upper bound.

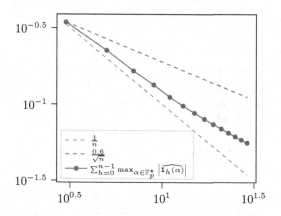

Fig. 4. $\sum_{h=0}^{n-1} \max_{\alpha \neq 0} \left| \widehat{1_h}(\alpha) \right|$ vs. $n \in [\![3, 29]\!]$ odd, and $p = 2^n - 1$.

4.1   Worst-Case Characterization

We start with an upper bound valid for the worst-case bias.

Theorem 6. *For n odd, let $p = 2^n - 1$ be a Mersenne number. Let $\mathbf{L} : \mathbb{F}_p^d \to [\![0, n-1]\!]^d$ be the function returning* $\mathsf{HW}(\cdot)$ *for each component. Then the following inequality is valid:*

$$\mathsf{M}_\infty\left(\mathbf{L}\right) \leq \frac{1}{2} \cdot \left(\sum_{h=0}^{n-1} \sqrt{\binom{n}{h}}\right)^d \cdot p^{-\frac{d}{2}} \cdot (2n)^{\frac{d}{2}} = \mathcal{O}\left(n^{1-\frac{d}{4}}\right). \tag{16}$$

Compared to the numerical computations depicted in Fig. 4 suggesting a convergence in $\mathcal{O}\left(\log(p)^{-r \cdot d}\right)$ for $r \in \left[\frac{1}{2}, 1\right]$, Theorem 6 only guarantees that $r \geq \frac{1}{4}$, and would require at least $d \geq 5$ to be non-trivial. So our provable bound is not completely tight. Still, it proves that the HW leakage model is more leakage-resilient with the help of masking in Mersenne prime fields.

The remaining of this subsection gives an outline of the proof of Theorem 6. It is derived from Corollary 1 thanks to the following theorem bounding the highest Fourier coefficient of each pre-image set of the HW leakage model.

Theorem 7. *For n odd, $p = 2^n - 1$ a Mersenne number and $0 \le h \le n - 1$,*

$$\max_{\alpha \ne 0} \left| \widehat{1_h}(\alpha) \right|^2 \le \frac{\binom{n}{h}}{p} \cdot \frac{1 - \frac{\binom{n}{h}}{p}}{2 \cdot n} \, . \tag{17}$$

The full proof of Theorem 7 is deferred to Appendix B. In essence, it starts from Eq. 7 in Parseval's theorem applied to the characteristic function 1_h, and leverages the following lemma, stating that each term in the right-hand side of Eq. 7 applied to $1_{\mathsf{HW}^{-1}(h)}$ has $2 \cdot n$ similar values in other terms.

Lemma 5. *Let $p = 2^n - 1$. Then, for all $\alpha \in \mathbb{F}_p^\star$ and for all $k \in \mathbb{N}$,*

$$\left| \widehat{1_h}\left(2^k \alpha\right) \right| = \left| \widehat{1_h}(\alpha) \right| \, . \tag{18}$$

Proof of Lemma 5. We leverage the property spotted in [33]: multiplying x by a power of two modulo a Mersenne number, *i.e.* of the shape, $p = 2^n - 1$, is just a rotation of the bits of x. Hence it is invariant for the Hamming weight. Let us then express the left hand-side of Eq. 18. For any $k \in \mathbb{N}$,

$$\widehat{1_h}\left(2^k \alpha\right) = \frac{1}{p} \sum_{x : \mathsf{HW}(x) = h} e^{-\frac{2 i \pi 2^k \alpha x}{p}} \, . \tag{19}$$

We make the following change of variable: let $x' = 2^k x$. Then the sum goes over the same values for x' as for x since multiplying by a power of two modulo a Mersenne prime keeps the Hamming weight unchanged. Meanwhile, the exponent in each term becomes $-\frac{2 i \pi \alpha x'}{p}$. We thus identify the Fourier coefficient of harmonic α. $\qquad\square$

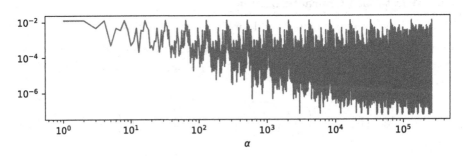

Fig. 5. First half of the Fourier spectrum of $1_{\lfloor \frac{n}{2} \rfloor}$, $n = 19, p = 2^n - 1$. Notice some regular patterns in the peaks, when displaying the x-axis in log-scale.

As a result of Lemma 5 (illustrated in Fig. 5), the sum of squared Fourier coefficients can be factorized by $2 \cdot n$, hence the denominator in Eq. 17, making the upper-bound non-trivial for all the observed leakage values h.

4.2   Average-Case Characterization

As discussed in Subsect. 4.1, we have established an upper bound for the worst-case bias, which approaches zero as the field size p tends to infinity. Since the average-case bias can be trivially upper bounded by the worst-case bias with $\beta(Y|\mathbf{L}) \leq \mathsf{M}_\infty(\mathbf{L})$ (Eq. 3), the upper bound derived in the right-hand side of Theorem 6 (Eq. 16) is also a valid upper bound of the average-case bias.

Theorem 8. *For n odd, let $p = 2^n - 1$ be a Mersenne number. Let $\mathbf{L} : \mathbb{F}_p^d \to [\![0, n-1]\!]^d$ be the function returning $\mathsf{HW}(\cdot)$ for each component. Then the following inequality is valid:*

$$\beta(Y|\mathbf{L}) \leq \frac{1}{2} \cdot \left(\sum_{h=0}^{n-1} \sqrt{\binom{n}{h}} \right)^d \cdot p^{-\frac{d}{2}} \cdot (2n)^{\frac{d}{2}} = \mathcal{O}\left(n^{1-\frac{d}{4}} \right). \tag{20}$$

4.3   Discussion

On the Field Size Dependence. Asymptotically with the field size p, the worst-case bias is upper bounded by a value following a poly-log trend, whereas asymptotically with the number of shares, the bias goes to zero exponentially fast. In a sense, the $n = \log(p)$ value in Eq. 16 and Eq. 20 may be seen as a surrogate of the Gaussian noise parameter in the early security analysis of Chari *et al.* [16], hence the interest of turning masking into prime fields in the particular setting of noise-free Hamming weight leakages.

On the Tightness. So far in this section, we have explained why the techniques used for the LSB analysis could not be applied for the HW, before providing upper bounds for the latter leakage using another approach through Parseval's identity, and we have said that the derived upper bounds are not completely tight with what is observed on numerical computation. We may therefore wonder where this gap comes from. Essentially, the core idea of our proof was to upper bound the maximum Fourier coefficient—in squared absolute value—by a sum provably containing this maximum coefficient. This approach provides a tight bound only if the Fourier spectrum is concentrated in its maximum coefficient—like for the bit leakage. Looking at Fig. 5, it is clear that many more Fourier coefficients are dominant, *i.e.*, of the same order of magnitude as the maximum one, without being exactly equal to the maximum. Therefore, one possible way to improve the inequalities could be to first prove which value of α maximizes the Fourier transform.[8] Then, one could find other values of α for which the Fourier transform is close in absolute value to the maximum coefficient, and to bound them by a quantity depending the latter one. Hence the hope would be to increase the $2 \cdot n$ denominator of the right-hand side of Eq. 17.

---

[8] We conjecture based on the numerical calculations of the spectrum that for $n \geq 13$, $\left| \widehat{\mathbf{1}_h}(1) \right|$ maximizes the Fourier transform.

5   Empirical Evaluation

The results in Sects. 3 and 4 provide formal confirmation that increasing the size of the modulus used in prime-field masking leads to significant security gains for the HW leakage function and does not lead to any gains for the LSB one. While the HW function is a more realistic abstraction for the power consumption of actual implementations [32], it remains a quite abstract one and in practice, implementations may show up leakage models that are highly correlated with the HW function without exactly matching it [10]. This raises the question whether such small deviations from the HW leakage function directly bring us back to the LSB case, or whether a more graceful degradation takes place. Formally answering this question will require to characterize classes of leakage functions for which similar results as in Sects. 3 and 4 can be obtained. As a first step in this direction, we next extend the simulated experiments of Masure et al. from [33] towards linear leakage functions that generalize the HW one. Precisely, and inspired by [42], we consider a leakage function that outputs a weighted sum of bits, like the HW one, but with less constraints on the weights:

$$L(Y) = \sum_{i=1}^{\lceil \log(p) \rceil} \omega_i \cdot Y(i),$$

with $Y(i)$ the ith bit of Y. In the HW case, $\omega_i = 1$ for all i's. We propose two generalizations: the *Skewed Hamming Weight (SHW)* function where only the LSB gets a higher weight s, and the *Random Linear (Rlin)* functions where all coefficients are picked up uniformly at random between 1 and s.

We then ran Monte-Carlo simulations: we uniformly drew $N = 1,000$ additive encodings $\mathsf{AddEnc}(Y)_i \leftarrow \mathbb{F}_p^d$ for which we applied the leakage model L under study to each share. It leads to a dataset of leakages $\{L_1, \dots, L_N\}$ and their corresponding PMF. The statistical bias is therefore estimated as follows:

$$\beta(Y|L) = \mathop{\mathbb{E}}_{L}\left[\mathsf{TV}\Big(\mathsf{p}_{Y\,|\,L}; \mathsf{p}_Y\Big)\right] \approx \frac{1}{N}\sum_{i=1}^{N}\mathsf{TV}\Big(\mathsf{p}_{Y\,|\,L=\ell_i}; \mathsf{p}_Y\Big).$$

The simulations are repeated for different field sizes, and for different number of shares d. The masked PMF takes the shape of a discrete convolution product that can be seen as an instance of a so-called SASCA attack, which is efficiently implemented in the SCALib library for estimating this statistical bias up to $d = 6$ shares [15]. All simulations depicted in Fig. 6 assume noise-free leakages.

Starting with the upper plots, which correspond to the SHW case, we can see that increasing s gradually decreases the interest of increasing the prime modulus p. This can be explained by the "isolating effect" of increasing s (i.e., with sufficiently large s, a single-bit is leaked on top of the HW information). There is a single curve per size of p in this case since we only vary the single coefficient ω_1. A similar gradual degradation effect can be observed for the lower plots, which correspond to the RLin case. Here we have multiple curves per size of p since coefficients ω_i are picked up uniformly at random.

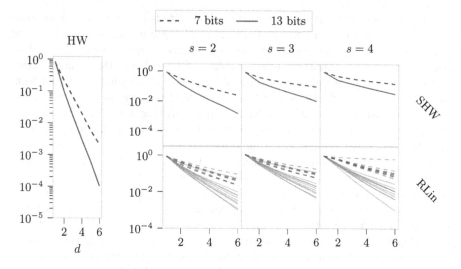

Fig. 6. Estimation of the average-case bias vs. number of shares d.

Both sets of plots motivate the further characterization of these generalized leakages. For the SHW case, it is for example questionable whether the "isolating effect" that is caused by an increase of s can be mitigated by an increase of the field size. But experimenting with large fields is computationally-intensive and putting forward a theoretical trend would be handy. For the Rlin case, we observe a significant variation for different functions with coefficients having the same range. So it suggests a need to characterize the leakage functions with another parameter than s in order to capture our empirical observations.

6   Conclusions and Open Problems

By combining theoretical advances from the leakage-resilient secret sharing literature with a formal analysis of two representative leakage functions, our results make an important step towards understanding the potential of prime-field masking and motivating the design of dedicated ciphers for this purpose. In particular, they show that for practically-relevant leakage functions like the Hamming weight one (and small variations thereof), increasing the size of the prime modulus p can lead to important security gains, so that $\log(p)$ can serve as a security parameter like the noise variance in Boolean masking. Such increases should in turn be compared with the (possibly limited [12]) performance overheads that computations in prime field imply. We conjecture that using small primes (e.g., 8- to 16-bit) can lead to excellent results for hardware implementations and that software implementations (with efficient multipliers) will benefit from prime sizes up to 32-bit. The careful investigations of symmetric designs enabling to back up this claim is an important scope for further investigations.

Besides, our formal results are for now limited to two canonical leakage functions, and we rely on our empirical evaluations to gain confidence that the good properties of the Hamming weight leakage function can be generalized. This leads to the other important open problem of formalizing this generalization and providing theoretical evidence that large classes of practically-relevant leakage functions can actually benefit from prime-field masking in larger fields. We believe the investigation of linear leakage functions that we initiate in work are natural candidates for this purpose, as they provide a good characterization of the physical measurements met in practice [42]. In this respect, another important problem will be to investigate how much the increase of the prime modulus p can be combined with an increase of the noise level. On the one hand, both have been shown to combine gracefully in the experiments of [33]. On the other hand, linear leakage functions with increasing granularity (i.e., larger s parameter in the experiments of Sect. 5) will inevitably end up being bijective (and therefore trivially insecure) in the noise-free setting. Yet, it is unlikely that it poses an insurmountable security issue, since for many relevant leakage functions, we expected that a mild noise addition will be enough to lift this granularity.

We hope these questions and observations stimulate further research towards analyzing prime-field masking under increasingly realistic assumptions.

Acknowledgments. François-Xavier Standaert is a senior research associate of the Belgian Fund for Scientific Research (FNRS-F.R.S.). This work has been funded in parts by the German Research Foundation (DFG) CRC 1119 CROSSING (project S7), by the German Federal Ministry of Education and Research and the Hessen State Ministry for Higher Education, Research and the Arts within their joint support of the National Research Center for Applied Cybersecurity ATHENE, by the ERC Consolidator Grant 101044770 (CRYPTOLAYER) and by the ERC Advanced Grant 101096871 (BRIDGE). Views and opinions expressed are those of the authors only and do not necessarily reflect those of the European Union or the European Research Council. Neither the European Union nor the granting authority can be held responsible for them.

A   Proofs of Section 2

Proof of Lemma 1. By definition we have

$$\Pr(Y = y \mid L = h) = \frac{1_{\mathsf{HW}\, y = h}}{\binom{n}{h}}, h \in [\![0, n-1]\!],$$

$$\Pr(Y = y) = \frac{1}{2^n - 1},$$

$$\Pr(L = h) = \frac{\binom{n}{h}}{2^n - 1}, h \in [\![0, n-1]\!].$$

It follows that the statistical distance for Hamming weight is

$$\beta(Y|L) = \frac{1}{2} \sum_{h=0}^{n-1} \sum_{y \in \mathcal{Y}} \left| \frac{1_{HW\,y=h}}{2^n - 1} - \frac{\binom{n}{h}}{(2^n - 1)^2} \right|$$

$$= \frac{1}{2^n - 1} \sum_{h=0}^{n-1} \binom{n}{h} \left(1 - \frac{\binom{n}{h}}{2^n - 1} \right).$$

We may then leverage Vandermonde's convolution equality to replace the sum of squared binomial coefficients by $\binom{2n}{n} - 1$. Finally, using Stirling's formula, we get the desired result.

As per the MI, notice that it is equal to the entropy of a binomial distribution, truncated from its maximum value n, and re-normalized by a factor $\frac{2^n}{2^n-1} \approx 1 + 2^{-n}$. We argue hereafter that this slight change to the binomial distribution does not change the entropy approximation. First, the re-normalization factor does not change much the non-truncated terms of the entropy. As per the truncated term, it initially contributed to the entropy at a value $\frac{n}{2^n} \ll \log(n)$.   □

Proof of Lemma 2. The MI of this leakage model is trivially $\alpha \cdot n$. As per the bias, first, assume $\alpha < 1$. Then, for every $h \in \{0,1\}^{\alpha n}$

$$\Pr(Y = y) = \frac{1}{2^n - 1},$$

$$\Pr(Y = y \mid L = h) = \begin{cases} 0 & \text{if } h \neq \ell^S(y) \\ \frac{1}{2^{n(1-\alpha)}} & \text{else if } h \neq 1^{\alpha n} \\ \frac{1}{2^{n(1-\alpha)}-1} & \text{else if } h = 1^{\alpha n} \end{cases},$$

$$\Pr(L = h) = \begin{cases} \frac{2^{n(1-\alpha)}}{2^n - 1} & \text{if } h \neq 1^{\alpha n} \\ \frac{2^{n(1-\alpha)}-1}{2^n - 1} & \text{if } h = 1^{\alpha n}. \end{cases}$$

Therefore

$$\beta(Y|L) = \frac{1}{2} \sum_{\substack{h \in \{0,1\}^{\alpha n} \\ h \neq 1^{\alpha n}}} \sum_{y \in \mathcal{Y}} \left| \frac{1_{\ell^S(y)=h}}{2^n - 1} - \frac{2^{n(1-\alpha)}}{(2^n - 1)^2} \right| + \frac{1}{2} \sum_{y \in \mathcal{Y}} \left| \frac{1_{\ell^S(y)=1^{\alpha n}}}{2^n - 1} - \frac{2^{n(1-\alpha)} - 1}{(2^n - 1)^2} \right|.$$

The result follows from further algebraic computation.

If $\alpha = 1$, then the event $\{L = 1^n\}$ has probability 0, and thus we cannot directly use the above analysis. On the other hand, $\alpha = 1$ describes the case where the secret is completely leaked, that is

$$\beta(Y|L) = 1 - \frac{1}{|\mathbb{F}_p|}.$$

Since the above equation corresponds to Eq. (5) for $\alpha = 1$, the lemma follows. □

B   Proofs of Section 4

The following lemma tells us that the symmetry property of the HW leakage function, coming from the symmetry of the binomial distribution, also translates in the Fourier transform.

Lemma 6 (Symmetry). *Let $n \in \mathbb{N}$ and $p = 2^n - 1$. Then, for all $h \in [\![0, n]\!]$, and for all $\alpha \in \mathbb{Z}_p$,*

$$\left| \widehat{1_h}(\alpha) \right| = \left| \widehat{1_{n-h}}(\alpha) \right|. \tag{21}$$

Proof. We start by recalling the identity $\mathsf{HW}(x \oplus y) = \mathsf{HW}(x) + \mathsf{HW}(y) - 2\,\mathsf{HW}(x \wedge y)$. In particular, for $y = 2^n - 1 = 1...1$, and by observing that $1...1 \oplus x = 2^n - 1 - x$, we get that

$$\mathsf{HW}(x) = n - \mathsf{HW}(2^n - 1 - x).$$

Therefore, applying the change of variable $x \mapsto 2^n - 1 - x$ in Eq. 6 gives us that

$$\widehat{1_{n-h}}(\alpha) = \overline{\widehat{1_h}(\alpha)}.$$

Finally, taking the absolute value in both side gives us the desired result.   □

Proof of Theorem 7. Using the Parseval formula, and the fact that $\widehat{1_h}(0) = \frac{\binom{n}{h}}{p}$ by definition of a PMF, we get that

$$\left(\frac{\binom{n}{h}}{p} \right)^2 + \sum_{\alpha=1}^{p-1} \left| \widehat{1_h}(\alpha) \right|^2 = \frac{1}{p} \cdot \sum_{i=0}^{p-1} |1_h(i)|^2 = \frac{\binom{n}{h}}{p}. \tag{22}$$

We will use the fact that the maximum squared absolute value of the Fourier coefficients (for non-zero harmonic) is upper bounded by the sum in the left hand-side of Eq. 22. However, stated as such, Eq. 22 would imply trivial upper bounds. Nevertheless, we will show that the sum of the left hand-side contains many identical terms. Thus by factoring the sum, we will tighten the bound.

Let $1 \leq \alpha \leq p - 1$. Lemma 5 tells us that we can find at least n other Fourier coefficients sharing the same absolute value as $\left| \widehat{1_h}(\alpha) \right|$—they can be derived by cyclically shifting the bits of α. Therefore, we can partition the set $[\![1, p-1]\!]$ of harmonics into classes of harmonics α sharing the same absolute value of Fourier coefficients, each classes containing at least n elements. We shall prove that each class actually contains at least $2 \cdot n$ elements.

Claim. Each class contains at least $2 \cdot n$ elements.

Proof. Since 1_h is real-valued, we have for all $\alpha \neq 0$, $\left| \widehat{1_h}(\alpha) \right| = \left| \widehat{1_h}(p - \alpha) \right|$. In other words, for each of the n harmonics that are in the same class, we can derive another harmonic having the same Fourier coefficient in absolute value, hence in the class as well. We shall prove that this *conjugate* harmonic does not coincide with any of the first n harmonics emphasized. To see why, observe that

$$\mathsf{HW}(p - \alpha) = n - \mathsf{HW}(\alpha)$$

(*cf.* proof of Lemma 6). Moreover, by assumption n is odd, so the parity of both hand-sides differ. It implies that the Hamming weight of α is always different from the Hamming weight of $p - \alpha$. As a consequence, none of the harmonics derived by shifting the bits of $p - \alpha$ can never coincide with any of the harmonics derived by shifting the bits of α. Hence, there is at least $2 \cdot n$ elements in each class. □

We can now conclude the proof. Let $\mathcal{F}_\alpha = \left\{ \alpha' \in \mathbb{F}_p : \left| \widehat{1_h}(\alpha') \right| = \left| \widehat{1_h}(\alpha) \right| \right\}$. Then for all class $\mathcal{F}_i$, let $\alpha_{\mathcal{F}_\alpha} = \frac{|\mathcal{F}_i|}{2n}$. Observe that $\alpha_{\mathcal{F}_\alpha} \geq 1$ by virtue of the claim.[9] Then we can rephrase Eq. 22 as follows:

$$\left(\frac{\binom{n}{h}}{p} \right)^2 + 2n \cdot \sum_{\mathcal{F}_\alpha} \alpha_i \left| \widehat{1_h}(\alpha) \right|^2 = \frac{\binom{n}{h}}{p}, \tag{23}$$

therefore for any α, we get that

$$\left| \widehat{1_h}(\alpha) \right|^2 \leq \sum_{\mathcal{F}_\alpha} \alpha_{\mathcal{F}_\alpha} \left| \widehat{1_h}(\alpha) \right|^2 \leq \left(\frac{\binom{n}{h}}{p} - \left(\frac{\binom{n}{h}}{p} \right)^2 \right) \cdot \frac{1}{2n}.$$

□

Remark 1. We may even prove that for Mersenne primes, the $\alpha_{\mathcal{F}_\alpha}$ coefficients in Eq. 23 are integer values. To see why, observe that if p is a Mersenne prime, then n is necessarily an odd prime. It follows from Fermat's little theorem that $2n$ divides $p - 1$, *i.e.* the number of terms in Eq. 22.

Proof of Theorem 6. We start from Eq. 17 from which we derive the following inequality.

$$\sum_\ell \max_{\alpha \in \mathbb{F}^*} \left| \widehat{1_{\mathsf{HW}^{-1}(\ell)}} \right| \leq \frac{1}{\sqrt{2np}} \sum_{h=0}^{n-1} \sqrt{\binom{n}{h}}.$$

The latter inequality is injected into Eq. 10, where we also use the following equality, by definition of the Hamming weight leakage model:

$$\sum_\ell \left\| 1_{\mathsf{HW}^{-1}(\ell)} \right\|_2 = \frac{1}{\sqrt{p}} \sum_{h=0}^{n-1} \sqrt{\binom{n}{h}}.$$

It then comes that

$$\mathsf{M}_\infty^{\mathsf{Y}}(\mathbf{L}, \mathbf{Y}) \leq \frac{1}{2} \cdot \left(\sum_{h=0}^{n-1} \sqrt{\binom{n}{h}} \right)^{d+1} \cdot \frac{1}{2^{\frac{d+1}{2}-1}} \cdot \frac{1}{p^{\frac{d+1}{2}}} \cdot \frac{1}{n^{\frac{d+1}{2}-1}},$$

---

[9] We empirically observe that all the α_i are equal to one, however this stronger claim would not seem to improve the upper bound.

hence the inequality in Eq. 16. The asymptotic estimation of the right hand-side is then derived from the following claim [6, Sec. 3.1]:

$$\sum_{h=0}^{n} \sqrt{\binom{n}{h}} \sim 2^{\frac{n}{2}+\frac{1}{4}} \cdot (\pi n)^{1/4}.$$

□

References

1. Andrychowicz, M., Dziembowski, S., Faust, S.: Circuit compilers with $O(1/\log(n))$ leakage rate. In: Fischlin, M., Coron, J.-S. (eds.) EUROCRYPT 2016. LNCS, vol. 9666, pp. 586–615. Springer, Heidelberg (2016). https://doi.org/10.1007/978-3-662-49896-5_21

2. Battistello, A., Coron, J.-S., Prouff, E., Zeitoun, R.: Horizontal side-channel attacks and countermeasures on the ISW masking scheme. In: Gierlichs, B., Poschmann, A.Y. (eds.) CHES 2016. LNCS, vol. 9813, pp. 23–39. Springer, Heidelberg (2016). https://doi.org/10.1007/978-3-662-53140-2_2

3. Béguinot, J., et al.: Removing the field size loss from Duc et al.'s conjectured bound for masked encodings. In: Kavun, E.B., Pehl, M. (eds.) COSADE 2023. LNCS, vol. 13979, pp. 86–104. Springer, Cham (2023). https://doi.org/10.1007/978-3-031-29497-6_5

4. Belaïd, S., et al.: Towards fresh re-keying with leakage-resilient PRFs: cipher design principles and analysis. J. Cryptogr. Eng. 4(3), 157–171 (2014)

5. Bellizia, D., et al.: Mode-level vs. implementation-level physical security in symmetric cryptography. In: Micciancio, D., Ristenpart, T. (eds.) CRYPTO 2020. LNCS, vol. 12170, pp. 369–400. Springer, Cham (2020). https://doi.org/10.1007/978-3-030-56784-2_13

6. Bender, E.A.: Asymptotic methods in enumeration. SIAM Rev. 16(4), 485–515 (1974)

7. Benhamouda, F., Degwekar, A., Ishai, Y., Rabin, T.: On the local leakage resilience of linear secret sharing schemes. In: Shacham, H., Boldyreva, A. (eds.) CRYPTO 2018. LNCS, vol. 10991, pp. 531–561. Springer, Cham (2018). https://doi.org/10.1007/978-3-319-96884-1_18

8. Benhamouda, F., Degwekar, A., Ishai, Y., Rabin, T.: On the local leakage resilience of linear secret sharing schemes. J. Cryptol. 34(2), 10 (2021)

9. Boucheron, S., Lugosi, G., Massart, P.: Concentration Inequalities: A Nonasymptotic Theory of Independence. OUP Oxford (2013)

10. Brier, E., Clavier, C., Olivier, F.: Optimal statistical power analysis. IACR Cryptology ePrint Archive, p. 152 (2003)

11. Bronchain, O., Standaert, F.-X.: Breaking masked implementations with many shares on 32-bit software platforms or when the security order does not matter. IACR Trans. Cryptogr. Hardw. Embed. Syst. 2021(3), 202–234 (2021)

12. Cassiers, G., Masure, L., Momin, C., Moos, T., Standaert, F.-X.: Prime-field masking in hardware and its soundness against low-noise SCA attacks. IACR Trans. Cryptogr. Hardw. Embed. Syst. 2023(2), 482–518 (2023)

13. Cassiers, G., Standaert, F.-X.: Towards globally optimized masking: From low randomness to low noise rate or probe isolating multiplications with reduced randomness and security against horizontal attacks. IACR Trans. Cryptogr. Hardw. Embed. Syst. 2019(2), 162–198 (2019)

14. Cassiers, G., Standaert, F.-X.: Provably secure hardware masking in the transition- and glitch-robust probing model: better safe than sorry. IACR Trans. Cryptogr. Hardw. Embed. Syst. **2021**(2), 136–158 (2021)
15. Cassiers, G., Bronchain, O.: Scalib: a side-channel analysis library. J. Open Source Softw. **8**(86), 5196 (2023)
16. Chari, S., Jutla, C.S., Rao, J.R., Rohatgi, P.: Towards sound approaches to counteract power-analysis attacks. In: Wiener, M. (ed.) CRYPTO 1999. LNCS, vol. 1666, pp. 398–412. Springer, Heidelberg (1999). https://doi.org/10.1007/3-540-48405-1_26
17. Dobraunig, C., et al.: ISAP v2.0. IACR Trans. Symmetric Cryptol. **2020**(S1), 390–416 (2020)
18. Duc, A., Dziembowski, S., Faust, S.: Unifying leakage models: from probing attacks to noisy leakage. In: Nguyen, P.Q., Oswald, E. (eds.) EUROCRYPT 2014. LNCS, vol. 8441, pp. 423–440. Springer, Heidelberg (2014). https://doi.org/10.1007/978-3-642-55220-5_24
19. Duc, A., Faust, S., Standaert, F.-X.: Making masking security proofs concrete - or how to evaluate the security of any leaking device. In: Oswald, E., Fischlin, M. (eds.) EUROCRYPT 2015. LNCS, vol. 9056, pp. 401–429. Springer, Heidelberg (2015). https://doi.org/10.1007/978-3-662-46800-5_16
20. Dziembowski, S., Faust, S., Skórski, M.: Optimal amplification of noisy leakages. In: Kushilevitz, E., Malkin, T. (eds.) TCC 2016. LNCS, vol. 9563, pp. 291–318. Springer, Heidelberg (2016). https://doi.org/10.1007/978-3-662-49099-0_11
21. Faust, S., Grosso, V., Pozo, S.M.D., Paglialonga, C., Standaert, F.-X.: Composable masking schemes in the presence of physical defaults & the robust probing model. IACR Trans. Cryptogr. Hardw. Embed. Syst. **2018**(3), 89–120 (2018)
22. Galbraith, S.D., Laity, J., Shani, B.: Finding significant Fourier coefficients: clarifications, simplifications, applications and limitations (2018)
23. Goubin, L., Patarin, J.: DES and differential power analysis the "duplication" method. In: Koç, Ç.K., Paar, C. (eds.) CHES 1999. LNCS, vol. 1717, pp. 158–172. Springer, Heidelberg (1999). https://doi.org/10.1007/3-540-48059-5_15
24. Grosso, V., Standaert, F.-X.: Masking proofs are tight and how to exploit it in security evaluations. In: Nielsen, J.B., Rijmen, V. (eds.) EUROCRYPT 2018. LNCS, vol. 10821, pp. 385–412. Springer, Cham (2018). https://doi.org/10.1007/978-3-319-78375-8_13
25. Ishai, Y., Sahai, A., Wagner, D.: Private circuits: securing hardware against probing attacks. In: Boneh, D. (ed.) CRYPTO 2003. LNCS, vol. 2729, pp. 463–481. Springer, Heidelberg (2003). https://doi.org/10.1007/978-3-540-45146-4_27
26. Kocher, P., Jaffe, J., Jun, B.: Differential power analysis. In: Wiener, M. (ed.) CRYPTO 1999. LNCS, vol. 1666, pp. 388–397. Springer, Heidelberg (1999). https://doi.org/10.1007/3-540-48405-1_25
27. Maji, H.K., Nguyen, H.H., Paskin-Cherniavsky, A., Suad, T., Wang, M.: Leakage-resilience of the shamir secret-sharing scheme against physical-bit leakages. In: Canteaut, A., Standaert, F.-X. (eds.) EUROCRYPT 2021. LNCS, vol. 12697, pp. 344–374. Springer, Cham (2021). https://doi.org/10.1007/978-3-030-77886-6_12
28. Maji, H.K., et al.: Leakage-resilient linear secret-sharing against arbitrary bounded-size leakage family. In: Kiltz, E., Vaikuntanathan, V. (eds.) TCC 2022. LNCS, vol. 13747, pp. 355–383. Springer, Cham (2022). https://doi.org/10.1007/978-3-031-22318-1_13
29. Maji, H.K., et al.: Tight estimate of the local leakage resilience of the additive secret-sharing scheme & its consequences. In: ITC. LIPIcs, vol. 230, pp. 16:1–16:19. Schloss Dagstuhl - Leibniz-Zentrum für Informatik (2022)

30. Maji, H.K., Nguyen, H.H., Paskin-Cherniavsky, A., Wang, M.: Improved bound on the local leakage-resilience of Shamir's secret sharing. In: ISIT, pp. 2678–2683. IEEE (2022)
31. Maji, H.K., Paskin-Cherniavsky, A., Suad, T., Wang, M.: Constructing locally leakage-resilient linear secret-sharing schemes. In: Malkin, T., Peikert, C. (eds.) CRYPTO 2021. LNCS, vol. 12827, pp. 779–808. Springer, Cham (2021). https://doi.org/10.1007/978-3-030-84252-9_26
32. Mangard, S., Oswald, E., Popp, T.: Power Analysis Attacks - Revealing the Secrets of Smart Cards. Springer, New York (2007). https://doi.org/10.1007/978-0-387-38162-6
33. Masure, L., Méaux, P., Moos, T., Standaert, F.-X.: Effective and efficient masking with low noise using small-mersenne-prime ciphers. In: Hazay, C., Stam, M. (eds.) EUROCRYPT 2023. LNCS, vol. 14007, pp. 596–627. Springer, Cham (2023). https://doi.org/10.1007/978-3-031-30634-1_20
34. Masure, L., Standaert, F.X.: Prouff and Rivain's formal security proof of masking, revisited - tight bounds in the noisy leakage model. In: Handschuh, H., Lysyanskaya, A. (eds.) CRYPTO 2023. LNCS, vol. 14083, pp. 343–376. Springer, Cham (2023). https://doi.org/10.1007/978-3-031-38548-3_12
35. Moos, T.: Static power SCA of sub-100 nm CMOS ASICS and the insecurity of masking schemes in low-noise environments. IACR Trans. Cryptogr. Hardw. Embed. Syst. **2019**(3), 202–232 (2019)
36. Moos, T., Moradi, A., Schneider, T., Standaert, F.-X.: Glitch-resistant masking revisited or why proofs in the robust probing model are needed. IACR Trans. Cryptogr. Hardw. Embed. Syst. **2019**(2), 256–292 (2019)
37. Moradi, A., Standaert, F.-X.: Moments-correlating DPA. In: TIS@CCS, pp. 5–15. ACM (2016)
38. Nikova, S., Rijmen, V., Schläffer, M.: Secure hardware implementation of nonlinear functions in the presence of glitches. J. Cryptol. **24**(2), 292–321 (2011)
39. Prest, T., Goudarzi, D., Martinelli, A., Passelègue, A.: Unifying leakage models on a Rényi day. In: Boldyreva, A., Micciancio, D. (eds.) CRYPTO 2019. LNCS, vol. 11692, pp. 683–712. Springer, Cham (2019). https://doi.org/10.1007/978-3-030-26948-7_24
40. Prouff, E., Rivain, M.: Masking against side-channel attacks: a formal security proof. In: Johansson, T., Nguyen, P.Q. (eds.) EUROCRYPT 2013. LNCS, vol. 7881, pp. 142–159. Springer, Heidelberg (2013). https://doi.org/10.1007/978-3-642-38348-9_9
41. Prouff, E., Rivain, M., Bevan, R.: Statistical analysis of second order differential power analysis. IEEE Trans. Comput. **58**(6), 799–811 (2009)
42. Schindler, W., Lemke, K., Paar, C.: A stochastic model for differential side channel cryptanalysis. In: Rao, J.R., Sunar, B. (eds.) CHES 2005. LNCS, vol. 3659, pp. 30–46. Springer, Heidelberg (2005). https://doi.org/10.1007/11545262_3
43. Standaert, F.-X.: How (not) to use Welch's T-test in side-channel security evaluations. In: Bilgin, B., Fischer, J.-B. (eds.) CARDIS 2018. LNCS, vol. 11389, pp. 65–79. Springer, Cham (2019). https://doi.org/10.1007/978-3-030-15462-2_5
44. Stromberg, K.: Probabilities on a compact group. Trans. Am. Math. Soc. **94**(2), 295–309 (1960)
45. Veyrat-Charvillon, N., Standaert, F.-X.: Adaptive chosen-message side-channel attacks. In: Zhou, J., Yung, M. (eds.) ACNS 2010. LNCS, vol. 6123, pp. 186–199. Springer, Heidelberg (2010). https://doi.org/10.1007/978-3-642-13708-2_12

From Random Probing to Noisy Leakages Without Field-Size Dependence

Gianluca Brian[1]([✉])[ID], Stefan Dziembowski[2][ID], and Sebastian Faust[3][ID]

[1] ETH Zurich, Zurich, Switzerland
gianluca.brian@inf.ethz.ch
[2] University of Warsaw and IDEAS NCBR, Warsaw, Poland
stefan.dziembowski@crypto.edu.pl
[3] Technical University of Darmstadt, Darmstadt, Germany
sebastian.faust@tu-darmstadt.de

Abstract. Side channel attacks are devastating attacks targeting cryptographic implementations. To protect against these attacks, various countermeasures have been proposed – in particular, the so-called masking scheme. Masking schemes work by hiding sensitive information via secret sharing all intermediate values that occur during the evaluation of a cryptographic implementation. Over the last decade, there has been broad interest in designing and formally analyzing such schemes. The random probing model considers leakage where the value on each wire leaks with some probability ϵ. This model is important as it implies security in the noisy leakage model via a reduction by Duc et al. (Eurocrypt 2014). Noisy leakages are considered the "gold-standard" for analyzing masking schemes as they accurately model many real-world physical leakages. Unfortunately, the reduction of Duc et al. is non-tight, and in particular requires that the amount of noise increases by a factor of $|\mathbb{F}|$ for circuits that operate over $\mathbb{F}$ (where $\mathbb{F}$ is a finite field). In this work, we give a generic transformation from ε-random probing to δ-average probing, with $\delta \approx \varepsilon^2$, which avoids this loss of $|\mathbb{F}|$. Since the average probing is identical to the noisy leakage model (Eurocrypt 2014), this yields for the first time a security analysis of masked circuits where the noise parameter in the noisy leakage model is independent of $|\mathbb{F}|$. The latter is particularly important for cryptographic schemes operating over large fields, e.g., the AES or the recently standardized post-quantum schemes.

1 Introduction

Side-channel attacks target cryptographic implementations by exploiting physical phenomena such as the power consumption or running time of a device [20, 21]. They extract sensitive information about the internals of the computation, often leading to devastating attacks against cryptographic implementations. One of the most prominent countermeasures to defeat side-channel attacks is the

---

G. Brian—Work partially done while at Sapienza University of Rome and University of Warsaw.

M. Joye and G. Leander (Eds.): EUROCRYPT 2024, LNCS 14654, pp. 345–374, 2024.
https://doi.org/10.1007/978-3-031-58737-5_13

masking scheme [12,19]. The basic idea of masking is to hide sensitive information by randomizing all internal values that occur during the computation. This typically works by encoding all internal values $v \in \mathbb{F}$ via a randomized encoding scheme $(v_1, \ldots, v_n) \leftarrow \mathsf{Enc}(v)$ and designing algorithms that securely compute on these encodings. Since designing secure masking schemes is challenging, most state-of-the-art masking schemes are proven secure within a *security model*. The security model captures the power of the adversary, which in particular requires us to accurately model the side-channel *leakage* emitting from a device. Over the last decade, there has been lots of interest in designing and analyzing masking schemes (see, e.g., [2,8,11,13–16,19,24] and many more), where one of the most fundamental challenges is to come up with an accurate model for real-world side-channel attacks. Below we briefly recap the history of leakage models that have been considered for masking schemes.

The t-Probing Model. The t-probing model was introduced in the seminal work of Ishai, Sahai, and Wagner [19]. The authors model (cryptographic) computation as a Boolean circuit $\mathcal{C}$, where the wires of the circuit carry the sensitive values. In the t-probing model, the adversary obtains the values of up to t wires in $\mathcal{C}$, which should not reveal more information about the cryptographic computation than what can be learned by just black-box access to the device. As this is a highly relevant attack in practice, security analysis in the t-probing model is the de-facto standard when designing and analyzing masking schemes.

Noisy Leakages. While the t-probing model is an excellent first step for verifying the security of a masking scheme, it has two shortcomings for modeling real-world leakages accurately. On the one hand, it is too restrictive as it requires that the leakage is quantitatively bounded. This is in contrast to real-world leakages, which rarely can be described by a small number of bits; e.g., a physical power measurement typically results in megabytes of data that the adversary has to store. On the other hand, the t-probing leakage model is too generous. It allows the adversary to learn the *exact* value on some of the wires of the computation. Non-invasive real-world leakages, however, are typically rather noisy, and that noise is precisely what makes a side-channel attack difficult to carry out in practice. To address this shortcoming, Prouff and Rivain introduce the important model of *noisy leakages* [24]. Here, the adversary obtains a noisy version of each value carried on a wire during the computation of the circuit (e.g., the value perturbed by a Gaussian distribution).

More formally, consider a uniform random variable $\mathbf{X}$ over some finite field $\mathbb{F}$. A leakage function ν is said to be δ noisy if the statistical distance between the uniform distribution $\mathbf{X}$ and the conditional distribution $\mathbf{X}|\nu(\mathbf{X})$ is upper bounded by δ. Hence, by choosing δ appropriately, we can cover a broad range of different noise distributions. Moreover, the noisy leakage model eliminates the quantitative bound on the amount of leakage that an adversary obtains, thus incorporating many realistic leakages such as the horizontal side-channel attacks [4]. Hence, it is considered the practically most relevant leakage model for a security evaluation of masked circuits. Unfortunately, however, the noisy leakage model has a significant drawback. An analysis in this model is highly complex, which was one of the reasons why in their original work, Prouff and Rivain were only able to give a security proof assuming that some parts of the masked computation is leak free.

Random Probing Model. In a follow-up work, Duc, Dziembowski, and Faust [15] observed that, somewhat surprisingly, the noisy leakage model is equivalent to the random probing model [19]. In the random probing model, we consider a particular noise distribution, where each wire leaks with some probability ε. More concretely, for a ε-random probing leakage function ρ, we have for all $x \in \mathbb{F}$ that $\Pr[\rho(x) \neq \bot] = \epsilon$. The main result of Duc et al. is then to show that any δ-noisy leakage function can be simulated via some ε random probing function (for some ε related to δ). As analyzing security in the random probing model is much simpler than a security proof in the noisy leakage model, Duc et al. can show that the original ISW construction is δ noisy leakage resilient for some parameter δ without requiring any leak-free computation.

Because of the connection between noisy leakages and the random probing model, there has been significant interest in proposing new constructions and analyzing their security in the random probing model [1–3,6–8,10]. Important goals are finding new constructions that achieve security for a (nearly) optimal noise parameter δ, optimizing overheads of the masked algorithms, and presenting new composition results and automated tools for easing the analysis of masking schemes in the random probing model.

Shortcoming of an Analysis in the Random Probing Model. While δ-noisy leakage and ε-random probing leakage functions are related via the reduction of Duc et al., there is a significant loss between these two models. Concretely, for some $\delta > 0$ to simulate the output of the δ-noisy leakage function $\nu(\cdot)$ via an ε-random probing $\rho(\cdot)$, we need that $\varepsilon = \delta \cdot |\mathbb{F}|$. Put differently: suppose that for some $\varepsilon > 0$ we prove the security of the masking scheme in the ε-random probing model. When we transfer this result via the reduction of Duc et al. [15] to the more realistic δ-noisy leakage model, we lose a factor of $|\mathbb{F}|$. While such a loss is generally undesirable, it is particularly problematic when $|\mathbb{F}|$ is large. Examples of such cases include the masking of the AES, which works in $GF(2^8)$, or even worse when masking some of the recent post-quantum schemes that typically operate in much larger fields.

Average Probing Model. To address the loss in the reduction of [15], Dziembowski, Faust and Skorski [17] introduce the average probing model. The average probing model makes a subtle but important change to the random probing model. In particular, a function α is said to be δ-average probing if for a uniformly random $\mathbf{X} \leftarrow \mathbb{F}$, we have that $\Pr[\alpha(\mathbf{X}) \neq \bot] = \delta$. Here, the probability is taken over the randomness of α and the choice of $\mathbf{X}$. As a main result, Dziembowski et al. present a tight reduction between average probing and noisy leakages. Concretely, for any field $\mathbb{F}$, any δ-noisy leakage function ν can efficiently be simulated by some δ-average probing leakage function.

While at first sight average probing looks very similar to random probing leakage, it turns out that a security analysis in the average probing model is significantly more challenging. Concretely, in [17] the authors present a masking compiler that while eliminating the loss of $|\mathbb{F}|$ again requires that certain parts of the computation are leak-free.

Related Work. By changing the metric for the computation of the noisy leakage, Prest, Goudarzi, Martinelli and Passelègue [23] prove a tighter bound. Namely, the authors consider two *worst-case* metrics, Relative Error and Average Relative Error, to measure the noisy leakage. The advantage of using such metrics is that they allow for proofs that do not have a security loss in the size of the field; in particular, they are able to reduce ε-random probing to ε-ARE-noisy leakage. However, the ARE metric incurs in bigger overheads, compared to Statistical Distance, when measuring leakage of functions; as an example, they consider the hamming weight with gaussian noise, which has a overhead of $\sqrt{\log(|\mathbb{F}|)}$ in the ARE setting compared to the SD setting.

Other ways to get rid of the loss in the field size is to consider arithmetic *programs* [18] instead of circuits or consider fields of characteristic 2 [5]. In the first case, in particular, even if arithmetic programs and circuits are equivalent, a program allows to split the computation in smaller logical instructions (i.e., the word size of the computer) and consider the noisy leakage from those instructions. This, in turns, allows for a security loss of just $\log(|\mathbb{F}|)$.

1.1 Our Contribution

The main result of our work is to present a generic compiler that transforms any circuits $\mathcal{C}$ with security against random probing into a circuit $\hat{\mathcal{C}}$ with security in the average probing model. Our transformation does not require leak free computation. Thus, using the tight relation between average probing and noisy leakages, we can show that any circuit $\mathcal{C}$ working over an arbitrary field $\mathbb{F}$ which is ε-random probing secure, can be transformed into a circuit $\hat{\mathcal{C}}$ that is δ-noisy leakage resilient, where (a) $\hat{\mathcal{C}}$ does not require leak-free computation, and (b) δ is independent of $|\mathbb{F}|$. In particular, if ε is a constant, then $\delta \approx \varepsilon^2$ is a constant (independent of $|\mathbb{F}|$ and the security parameter λ).

High-Level Idea. The main idea of our compiler is to ensure that any value $x \in \mathbb{F}$ occurring in the original circuit $\mathcal{C}$ is "encoded" into a sharing $(x_1, x_2) \in \mathbb{F}^2$ where individually each share x_i is (almost) uniformly distributed over $\mathbb{F}$. Let us briefly discuss the main idea by taking a look at the most simple case of a circuit that consists only of a single wire x. In our transformed circuit $\hat{\mathcal{C}}$ the value x is represented by a secret sharing (x_1, x_2), where x_1, x_2 are uniformly random in $\mathbb{F}$ subject to the constrained that $x_1 + x_2 = x$. Our approach now works by using random probing leakage from x to simulate the average probing leakage from (x_1, x_2). More concretely, we show that for any δ-average probing leakage function α the leakage $(\alpha(x_1), \alpha(x_2))$ can be simulated from $\varepsilon = 2\delta$-random probing leakage of x.

The basic idea to show the above statement is as follows. Since (x_1, x_2) is a secret sharing of x, each one of x_1, x_2 is uniformly random when considered independently, and therefore the marginal probability that any of them leaks is exactly δ. Then, by the union bound, the probability that any of x_1, x_2 leaks is bounded by 2δ. The strategy is then to construct a simulator Sim that outputs $(\bot, \bot)$ (i.e., no leakage occurred) when the random probing leakage is $\bot$, and is able to fully simulate the values on the wires (and, therefore, the corresponding leakage) when the random probing leakage is $x \in \mathbb{F}$. Clearly, upon input $x \in \mathbb{F}$, the simulator Sim(x) cannot naively output the real distribution, since otherwise $(\bot, \bot)$ would be output too often and the simulated average probing leakage would not be identically distributed to the real one; instead, Sim(x) adjusts the probabilities so that $(\bot, \bot)$ is output less often, in order to match the real distribution. This can be done efficiently, e.g., by rejection sampling.

In the previous paragraph, we only described the most simple case where we simulate average probing leakage from a single encoding $(x_1, x_2) \leftarrow$ Enc(x). Our analysis gets much more involved, when we move to the setting where the adversary obtains leakage from the entire computation. For a high-level overview how we can simulate average random probing leakage of an encoded complex circuit from random probing leakage of an (unencoded) circuit, we refer the reader to the technical overview in Sect. 1.2.

Impact. We believe that our work shows a missing piece for the analysis of masking schemes. As discussed above, currently there is lots of interest in designing new masking countermeasures in the random probing model. However, to transform these results to the noisy leakage model, all these works will require a noise parameter δ that decreases by $1/|\mathbb{F}|$.[1] Our result shows that any of the existing constructions for random probing leakage can be transformed into a construction that is secure against noisy leakage *without* suffering this loss. One direct application of our result is to show that for any field $\mathbb{F}$ the ISW construction is noisy leakage resilient for $\delta \approx 1/n^2$ (where n is the number of shares used in the ISW-masked circuit). Earlier results required either leak-free gates [17] or required a noise parameter of $\delta \approx 1/(n|\mathbb{F}|)$ [15]. We leave it as an important open question to apply our result to some of the existing constructions for random probing security and further optimize their parameters.

1.2   Technical Overview

In the previous section, we showed how to simulate average probing leakage of a single encoding $(x_1, x_2) \leftarrow$ Enc(x) given random probing leakage from x. To extend our analysis to complex circuits, we follow a standard gate-by-gate approach. More precisely, we show that for each gate g in $\mathcal{C}$ there is an efficient gadget $\hat{g}$ in $\hat{\mathcal{C}}$ (in fact, the overhead is a small constant), where average probing leakage from $\hat{g}$ can be simulated by random probing leakage from the inputs of g.

---

[1] Notice that means that we need an amount of noise that is at least proportional to $|\mathbb{F}|$.

The simulation and analysis of this transformation is significantly more involved, and in particular requires us to take care of internal wires that are not uniformly distributed.[2] For instance, this is the case for the multiplication gadget, where internally we compute values $x \cdot y$, where x and y are uniform over $\mathbb{F}$.

Then, we also need to show that the gadgets we construct are composable in a "safe" way, meaning that one cannot break the simulatability of a gadget by looking at other parts of the circuit. This turns out to be quite involved, as in particular the simulation must be careful with sampling the outputs of the gadgets that are consistent with whatever an adversary has observed in the past. To explain the main technical challenge, let us consider a concrete toy example that highlights the technical difficulty of our analysis. Suppose that we are working in the finite field $\mathbb{F} = \mathbb{F}_5$ with 5 elements and that the leakage function α leaks 0 with probability 1 and everything else with probability 0. Clearly, α is a $\frac{1}{5}$-average probing function. We show two different ways to construct a uniform encoding of $4 \in \mathbb{F}_5$ which lead to two different leakage distributions when we consider leakage from the the whole circuit.

First, suppose the simplest way to generate an encoding $(x_1, x_2) \xleftarrow{\$} \mathsf{Enc}(4)$ by sampling from the distribution $\mathsf{Enc}(4)$. Assuming that the leakage from the encoding is $(\perp, \perp)$, then the possible encodings given the leakage are $(1, 3), (2, 2), (3, 1)$. Notice that they also all appear with the same probability of $\frac{1}{3}$.

A second circuit that produces an encoding of 4 is through a sum of encodings of 3 and 1. Suppose again that nothing in the circuit leaks, then the possible encodings for 3 are $(4, 4), (2, 1), (1, 2)$ and the possible encodings for 1 are $(4, 2), (3, 3), (2, 4)$. By writing a table with all the possible sums, we can eliminate some of the outcomes as they are impossible (since they contain 0, which leaks with probability 1, and we assumed that nothing leaks); the remaining outcomes are, again, $(1, 3), (2, 2), (3, 1)$. However, this time $(2, 2)$ appears slightly less often as shown in the table below.

+	$(4, 4)$	$(2, 1)$	$(1, 2)$
$(4, 2)$	$(3, 1)$	$(1, 3)$	$(0, 4)$
$(3, 3)$	$(2, 2)$	$(0, 4)$	$(4, 0)$
$(2, 4)$	$(1, 3)$	$(4, 0)$	$(3, 1)$

This, in turn, means that the probability of the outcome being $(2, 2)$ is $\frac{1}{5}$, compared to $(1, 3)$ and $(3, 1)$ which appear with probability $\frac{2}{5}$. As can be seen from the above example, the simulation of the leakage from a gadget depends on the leakage that occured in other parts of the circuit. Notably, this is even true, when nothing leaked, i.e., when the leakage was only $\perp$. This is unlike in the random probing model, where leaking $\perp$ gives freedom to the gadget simulator and thus allows for much simpler composition results.

---

[2] Recall that in the case of the encoding each of the x_i is individual uniform over $\mathbb{F}$.

Approximation. In the above example, a naive simulation that does not take into account leakage from other parts of the circuit fails because even if the output distribution is uniform, it is not uniform anymore if we condition on some event such as "something leaks from the circuit computation" or "nothing leaks from the computation". However, the above example also shows a way to deal with such dependencies. Indeed, we can see that, even if the output distribution of the gadget (i.e., the encoding of 4) is not uniform conditioned on the leakage, it is still somewhat close to the simplest case in which we only consider leakage from the encoding and nothing else. We exploit this observation to construct a simulator that is able to approximate the output distribution of gadgets even when the simulator knows nothing about the input or the rest of the circuit. Then, we can follow a similar strategy as the one for simulating average probing leakage from the simple encoding. Concretely, as previously, when the simulator receives some additional information that allows to simulate the exact distributions, we can compensate for the above approximation error such that the final distribution output by the simulator is identical to the real distribution, even conditioned on the exact input encoding and leakage from the gadget.

In order to apply the above strategy, we need two additional properties from our gadgets. The first one is that all the wires on the gadget need to be uniform when considered independently, so that we can apply the same idea as in the simple encoding $(x_1, x_2) \leftarrow \mathsf{Enc}(x)$. Unfortunately, this is not possible due to the presence of multiplication gates (recall that, when $\mathbf{x}, \mathbf{y}$ are uniform over $\mathbb{F}$, the product $\mathbf{xy}$ takes the value 0 slightly more often); however, we are able to show that the strategy still holds if we relax this requirement and only ask for *close-to-uniform* wires. The second property, which we call *output-independence*, states that the values on the wires of the gadget are (close-to-)uniform even when the output of the gadget is known in full, and, additionally, the output of the gadget is identically distributed to the one of a fresh encoding. Looking ahead, this is needed so that the simulator is always able to approximate the output distribution.

Fortunately, it turns out that the above two properties are not hard to achieve. Indeed, the internal wires are close-to-uniform when all the input encodings are re-randomized and, additionally, re-randomizing the output of the gadget allows to achieve the output-independence property. Furthermore, some of the gadgets (i.e., addition, subtraction) already satisfy the output-independence property due to the properties of Enc (i.e., $\mathsf{Enc}(x) + \mathsf{Enc}(y)$ is identically distributed to $\mathsf{Enc}(x + y)$).

Gadget Simulators. Now that we established the main strategy to construct the gadgets and the basic idea to simulate their leakage, we will provide the high-level idea of the composition. We start by describing the security guarantee that the gadget simulator has to satisfy and which will suffice for composition. For simplicity assume that the gate g only has 1 input and 1 output. A first attempt to define the gadget simulator $\mathsf{Sim}_{\widehat{g}}$ is to require for any input encoding $\widehat{x}$ to the gadget $\widehat{g}$ that the following holds:

$$\Lambda \overset{?}{\equiv} \mathsf{Sim}_{\widehat{g}}\left(\rho(x)\right),$$

where Λ is the random variable of the average-probing leakage from the gadget $\widehat{g}$ on input $\widehat{x}$ and $x \in \mathbb{F}$ is the input value on the unmasked circuit. Unfortunately, as discussed above, this is not sufficient, because the simulator needs to receive some additional information from the environment to produce the output encoding of the gadget as well:[3]

$$\mathsf{Real}_{\widehat{g}}(\widehat{x}) \equiv \mathsf{Sim}_{\widehat{g}}\left(\rho(x), \mathsf{info}\right),$$

where $\mathsf{Real}_{\widehat{g}}(\widehat{x}) = (\Lambda, \widehat{\mathbf{y}})$ is the joint distribution of the real leakage and the real output upon input $\widehat{x}$. Moreover, info denotes some auxiliary information that we will explain in a moment.

Unfortunately, the input $\rho(x)$ does not suffice for the gadget simulator to produce $\mathsf{Real}_{\widehat{g}}(\widehat{x})$ and hence we slightly strengthen the power of the simulator by giving it as input $\mathsf{Blind}_{\rho(x)}(\widehat{x})$ which outputs $\widehat{x}$ if $\rho(x) = x$ and outputs $\bot$ otherwise. This allows us to let the simulator play "safe" and make it output everywhere $\bot$ when $\rho(x) = \bot$ and compensate for this "overestimation" when getting $\widehat{x}$ as input. Hence, we get:

$$\mathsf{Real}_{\widehat{g}}(\widehat{x}) \equiv \mathsf{Sim}_{\widehat{g}}\left(\mathsf{Blind}_{\rho(x)}(\widehat{x}), \mathsf{info}\right),$$

where we explain the meaning of info next. Observe that the simulator needs to correctly sample $\widehat{\mathbf{y}}$ as discussed in the previous paragraph. However, this cannot be done if $\rho(x) = \bot$. Looking ahead, the final observation here is that $\widehat{\mathbf{y}}$ is only needed by the simulator of the next gadget if the random probing of the output value $y = g(x)$ reveals y. When this is the case, we can give y to the simulator, which can then *approximate* the correct distribution $\widehat{\mathbf{y}}$ as we described above; the simulator will then compensate for this approximation error in the case in which it receives $\widehat{x}$ in full. Hence, the final notion of a composable gadget simulator is given by:

$$(\Lambda, \mathsf{Blind}_{y_?}(\widehat{\mathbf{y}})) \equiv \mathsf{Sim}_{\widehat{g}}\left(\mathsf{Blind}_{\rho(x)}(\widehat{x}), y_?\right),$$

where $(\Lambda, \widehat{\mathbf{y}}) = \mathsf{Real}_{\widehat{g}}(\widehat{x})$, $y_? = \rho(y)$ denotes the outcome of random probing $y = g(x)$, and the above holds for all $\widehat{x}$ and all $\widehat{y} = \widehat{g}(\widehat{x})$. This notion states that the above simulator outputs a leakage distribution Λ and a "blinded" output distribution $\widehat{\mathbf{y}}$ that is identical to the real distribution even when considered jointly.

Sadly, this approach only works when all the inputs of the gate are given to the simulator, which, for gates with fan-in 2, causes the leakage parameter to be squared, i.e., $\delta \approx \varepsilon^2$ when starting from ε-random probing. We leave the problem of filling this gap open for future work.

---

[3] Looking ahead, this information is needed for composition in order to produce a consistent simulation.

Composition of Gadget Simulators. Now that we established the correct notion for the simulatable gadgets, we want to apply it to prove simulatability of the whole circuit. We plan to do so by hybrid argument. Namely, we define as many hybrid experiments as there are gates in the circuit, and we replace the real gadgets with the simulated gadgets one by one; then, we show that two consecutive hybrids are identically distributed, by a reduction to the simulatability of the gadgets. More in detail, the reduction would first run the real circuit until the challenge gadget, then receives some either real or simulated leakage/output pair and finally continues with the simulated gadgets. This is enabled by the above notion of simulatability, which states that the distribution of the output does not change when moving from the real to the simulated gadget. In turns, this means that we can completely replace the real gadget with the corresponding simulator and use the output of the simulator to feed the subsequent simulators in the circuit.

Structure of the Paper. We state formally all the necessary notions for the gadgets in Sect. 3, in which we also show how to achieve such notions. Then, in Sect. 4 we state the simulatability notions for circuits, and we show how to use the simulatable gadgets to achieve the simulatable circuit. Finally, we conclude in Sect. 5 and pose some open problems for future research.

2 Preliminaries

Notation. For a number $n \in \mathbb{N}$, we denote by $[n]$ the set $\{1, \ldots, n\}$. We denote sets by uppercase calligraphic letters $\mathcal{A}, \mathcal{B}, \mathcal{X}, \mathcal{Y}, \ldots$ and random variables by bold letters $\mathbf{A}, \mathbf{B}, \mathbf{x}, \mathbf{y}, \ldots$; similarly, we use bold letters for randomized functions, like $\mathbf{f}, \mathbf{g}, \boldsymbol{\alpha}, \boldsymbol{\rho}$. For a set $\mathcal{X}$, we denote by $x \xleftarrow{\$} \mathcal{X}$ the fact that x is uniformly sampled from $\mathcal{X}$. For two random variables $\mathbf{X}, \mathbf{Y}$ over the same set $\mathcal{X}$, the *statistical distance between $\mathbf{X}$ and $\mathbf{Y}$* is denoted as $\Delta(\mathbf{X}, \mathbf{Y})$ and defined as

$$\Delta(\mathbf{X}, \mathbf{Y}) := \frac{1}{2} \sum_{x \in \mathcal{X}} |\Pr[\mathbf{X} = x] - \Pr[\mathbf{Y} = x]|.$$

Whenever $\Delta(\mathbf{X}, \mathbf{Y}) = 0$, we say that $\mathbf{X}$ and $\mathbf{Y}$ are *identically distributed*, and we denote this fact by writing $\mathbf{X} \equiv \mathbf{Y}$. We denote by $d(\mathbf{X}) := \Delta(\mathbf{X}, \mathbf{U})$ the distance between $\mathbf{X}$ and the uniform random variable $\mathbf{U}$ over $\mathcal{X}$. In general, we will refer to $\mathbf{X}$ as *uniform* if $d(\mathbf{X}) = 0$, and, for $\gamma \in [0, 1]$, as *γ-close-to-uniform* if $d(\mathbf{X}) \leq \gamma$.

For a function $f : \mathcal{X} \to \mathcal{Y}$ and a vector $x = (x_1, \ldots, x_n) \in \mathcal{X}^n$, we overload the notation and write $f(x)$ for the function $(x_1, \ldots, x_n) \mapsto (f(x_1), \ldots, f(x_n))$; this applies to randomized functions $\mathbf{f}$ as well. Furthermore, for $x \in (\mathcal{X} \cup \{\perp\})^n$, we overload the notation of $\perp$ as well and write $x = \perp$ if $x = (\perp, \ldots, \perp)$.

Circuits. We model computation as an arithmetic circuit $\mathcal{C}$ carrying values from an (arbitrary) finite field $\mathbb{F}$ on their wires and using the following gates to carry out computation in $\mathbb{F}$:

- ADD, SUB, MUL, which compute, respectively, the sum, the difference and the product in $\mathbb{F}$ of their inputs,
- IN, which has no input and models either some constant or the external input to the circuit,
- OUT, which has one input and no output, and models the output produced by the circuit,
- RND, which has no input and produces a uniformly random and independent element of $\mathbb{F}$,
- and CPY, which takes as input a single value and outputs two copies.

We say that the gates ADD, SUB, MUL, CPY are *functional gadgets*, in that they compute a function (respectively, $(x, y) \mapsto x + y, (x, y) \mapsto x - y, (x, y) \mapsto xy, x \mapsto (x, x)$). Furthermore, we view the circuit as a directed acyclic graph $\mathcal{C} = (\mathcal{G}, \mathcal{W})$ in which

- $\mathcal{G}$ is the set of the gates of the circuit, seen as a set of nodes of the graph,
- $\mathcal{W}$ is the set of the wires of the circuit, seen as a set of edges of the graph.

We also assume that $\mathcal{C}$ is connected (otherwise, it suffices to look at each connected component separately, since they act independently) and that $\mathcal{G}$ is topologically sorted. Namely, for every two gates $g_i, g_j \in \mathcal{G}$ with $i < j$, then g_i comes *before* g_j. Intuitively, this means that g_j is not needed to compute g_i.

A circuit $\mathcal{C}$ models computation on some (possibly randomized) input $x \in \mathbb{F}^{m^*}$ and produces some output $y \in \mathbb{F}^{n^*}$; we denote this by writing $y \leftarrow \mathcal{C}(x)$. The numbers m^* and n^* are respectively the *fan-in* and the *fan-out* of the circuit, and they correspond respectively to the number of input gates and the number of output gates of $\mathcal{C}$. Sometimes, we need more detail about the computation of the circuit. In this case, we denote by $\mathbf{W}(x)$ the list of all the values that the wires of the circuit take upon input x.

Circuit Compiler. A circuit compiler Γ takes as input the original circuit $\mathcal{C}$ and produces a new circuit $\widehat{\mathcal{C}} = \Gamma(\mathcal{C})$. Unless stated otherwise, we denote by regular letters everything that belongs to the original circuit, like $\mathcal{C}, x, g \in \mathcal{G}, w \in \mathcal{W}$, and by letters with hats everything that belongs to the transformed circuit, like $\widehat{\mathcal{C}}, \widehat{x}, \widehat{g} \in \widehat{\mathcal{G}}, \widehat{w} \in \widehat{\mathcal{W}}$.

The compiler Γ is associated with an encoding scheme $\mathsf{Enc} : \mathbb{F} \to \mathbb{F}^\ell, \mathsf{Dec} : \mathbb{F}^\ell \to \mathbb{F}$ such that, for all $x \in \mathbb{F}$, $\mathsf{Dec}(\mathsf{Enc}(x)) = x$ (or, more formally, this happens with probability 1 over the randomness of the encoding). Then, the wires of the original circuit $\mathcal{C}$ are represented in the transformed circuit $\widehat{\mathcal{C}}$ as *wire bundles* that carry the value of the wire in encoded form. The input $x \in \mathbb{F}^{m^*}$ to $\mathcal{C}$ is then transformed into the encoded input $\mathsf{Enc}(x)$ to $\widehat{\mathcal{C}}$. The main challenge to compile $\mathcal{C}$ to $\widehat{\mathcal{C}}$ is to describe how to transform the gates. For each gate $g \in \mathcal{G}$, the compiler constructs a sub-circuit $\widehat{g}$, the so-called *gadget*, that represents the computation of $\widehat{g}$ in $\widehat{\mathcal{C}}$ and carries out the output of g in encoded form. We emphasize that the computation in the gadgets use the standard gates defined in the previous section. Notice also that, for simplicity, we focus in this work on *stateless* circuits, i.e., the circuits do not have memory gates. Hence, we require that compiled circuits $\widehat{C}$ receive their inputs in encoded form.

In what follows, we partition the wires of every gadget $\widehat{g}$ into three disjoint subsets:

- the *input* wires are the wires that carry the input encoding $\widehat{x}$;
- the *output* wires are the wires that carry the output encoding $\widehat{y} = \widehat{g}(\widehat{x})$;
- all the other wires belong to the set of the *internal* wires, which carry the computation inside $\widehat{g}$.

Notice that, whenever a gadget $\widehat{g_1}$ is connected to $\widehat{g_2}$, the wires from $\widehat{g_1}$ to $\widehat{g_2}$ are both input wires for $\widehat{g_2}$ and output wires for $\widehat{g_1}$. Since every value that is output by a gadget is then input into another gadget, we can ignore the input wires and consider every gadget to be just its internal and output wires.

Finally, we now establish some notation that is useful when reasoning about gadgets. For a gadget $\widehat{g}$, we denote by $\mathcal{In}_{\widehat{g}}$ the set of the possible inputs and by $\mathcal{Out}_{\widehat{g}}(\widehat{x})$ the set of the possible outputs upon input $\widehat{x}$.

Leakage. A *leakage* function is a (possibly randomized) function $\mathbf{f} : \mathbb{F} \to \Omega$ for some set Ω. As discussed in detail in the introduction, in this work we focus on *probing* functions, and we use two probing models. Let $\mathbb{F}$ be a finite field. A randomized function $\varphi : \mathbb{F} \to \mathbb{F} \cup \{\bot\}$ is called a *(wire) probing function (over the field $\mathbb{F}$)* if for every $x \in \mathbb{F}$ we have that $\varphi(x)$ is equal either to x or to $\bot$, where $\bot$ is a special symbol that denotes that the probing function failed to probe the wire. For $\varepsilon \in (0,1)$, such a function is called:

- ε-*random* if for every $x \in \mathbb{F}$, $\Pr[\varphi(x) = x] = \varepsilon$, and
- ε-*average* if for the uniform random variable $\mathbf{x}$ over $\mathbb{F}$, $\Pr[\varphi(\mathbf{x}) = \mathbf{x}] = \varepsilon$.

In what follows, we use the letter ρ to denote random probing and the letter α to denote average probing.

Sometimes we need to keep or discard values depending on the outcome of a probing function. Towards this, for any $x \in \mathbb{F} \cup \{\bot\}$ and any $\widehat{x} \in \mathbb{F}^{\ell}$, we define the function

$$\mathsf{Blind}_x(\widehat{x}) := \begin{cases} \widehat{x} & \text{if } x \in \mathbb{F}, \\ \bot & \text{if } x = \bot. \end{cases}$$

We extend Blind_x to a function $\mathbb{F}^n \to \mathbb{F}^{\ell n}$ in the usual way, i.e., by applying it to every component of $x = (x_1, \ldots, x_n)$ and $\widehat{x} = (\widehat{x_1}, \ldots, \widehat{x_n})$:

$$\mathsf{Blind}_x(\widehat{x}) := (\mathsf{Blind}_{x_1}(\widehat{x_1}), \ldots, \mathsf{Blind}_{x_n}(\widehat{x_n})).$$

Furthermore, we consider an *all-or-nothing* function Blind_x^* defined for every $x \in (\mathbb{F} \cup \{\bot\})^n$ such that

$$\mathsf{Blind}_x^*(\widehat{x}) := \begin{cases} \widehat{x} & \text{if } x \in \mathbb{F}^n, \\ \bot & \text{otherwise.} \end{cases}$$

2.1 Simple Facts

In this section we list some results that we are going to use later in this work.

First of all, we state two general fact about products of uniform distributions.

Lemma 1. *Let $\mathbb{F}$ be a field and let $\mathbf{x}, \mathbf{y}$ be two independent and uniform random variables over $\mathbb{F}$. Then, the product $\mathbf{xy}$ is $\frac{1}{|\mathbb{F}|}$-close to uniform.*

Lemma 2 ([22]). *Let $\mathbb{G}$ be a group $\mathbf{x}, \mathbf{y}$ be two independent random variables over $\mathbb{G}$. Then,*

$$d(\mathbf{x} + \mathbf{y}) \leq 2d(\mathbf{x})d(\mathbf{y}).$$

A consequence of the above is the following.

Lemma 3. *Let $\gamma \in \left[0, \frac{1}{2}\right]$ be a parameter, let $\mathbb{F}$ be a field and let $\mathbf{x}, \mathbf{y}$ be two independent and γ-close-to-uniform distributions over $\mathbb{F}$. Then, $\mathbf{x} + \mathbf{y}$ is γ-close-to-uniform.*

The following lemma states that, informally, if a distribution over a set of values is "uniform enough", then it is always possible that nothing leaks even in the stronger model of average probing.

Lemma 4. *Let $\gamma \in \left[0, \frac{1}{2}\right], \delta \in [0, 1]$ be parameters. Let $\mathbf{x} = (\mathbf{x}_1, \ldots, \mathbf{x}_k)$ be a distribution over $\mathbb{F}^k$ and assume that there exist k' values $\mathbf{x}_{i_1}, \ldots, \mathbf{x}_{i'_k}$ that are γ-close to uniform and that all the other $k - k'$ values $\mathbf{x}_i$ are uniform. Finally, let $\boldsymbol{\alpha}$ be any δ-average-probing function. Then,*

$$\Pr\left[\boldsymbol{\alpha}(\mathbf{x}) = \perp\right] \geq 1 - \left(k + k'\gamma|\mathbb{F}|\right)\delta$$

The proof of the above facts can be found in the full version [9].

3 Composable Gadgets Against Average Probing

In this section, we design the gadgets that we are using in our circuit compiler. In Sect. 4 we will define a circuit simulator to prove that, intuitively, our compiler transforms random-probing-resilient circuits into average-probing-resilient circuits. To do so, the simulator only receives as input the random probing leakage $\rho(\mathbf{W}(x))$ from the original circuit $\mathcal{C}$. Our strategy is to construct gadgets in a composable way so that we can reduce the simulatability of the circuit to the simulatability of every gadget. In particular, the circuit simulator will forward the random probing leakage (or part of it) to the gadget simulator, which will then produce leakage from the wires of the gadgets. The main difficulty here is that, for every gadget, the distribution of the values on the wires depends on the distribution of the input values, and such distribution is not always the same if we condition on all the leakage that happened before the gadget. However, if we allow the gadget simulator to also receive, when available, the encoding of the input, then the simulation can be accurate. Intuitively, the notion of simulatabilty should look like

$$\forall \widehat{x} \in \mathbb{F}^{\ell m} : \Lambda \equiv \mathsf{Sim}_{\widehat{g}}\left(\mathsf{Blind}^*_{\rho(x)}(\widehat{x})\right),$$

where Λ is the leakage from the wires of the real gadget and $x = \mathsf{Dec}(\widehat{x})$. Looking forward, when simulating two consecutive gadgets, the circuit simulator has no way to generate the input to the second gadget simulator, since it does not come from the real circuit. This means that every simulator is required to simulate the output of the gadget as well, unless it is not needed (i.e., when the random probing $\rho(y)$ of the output value y results in $\bot$). The following definition captures exactly this property.

Definition 1 (Gadget simulatability). *Let $\varepsilon, \delta \in [0,1], \ell \in \mathbb{N}$ be parameters. Let g be a functional gate with fan-in m and fan-out n. Let $\widehat{g}$ be the corresponding gadget for an encoding of size ℓ. We say that $\widehat{g}$ is ε-random to δ-average leakage-simulatable if for every δ-average probing function $\boldsymbol{\alpha}$ there exists a simulator $\mathsf{Sim}_{\widehat{g}}$ such that*

$$\forall \widehat{x} \in \mathbb{F}^{\ell m} : \mathsf{Real}_{\widehat{g}}(\widehat{x}) \equiv \mathsf{Sim}_{\widehat{g}}\left(\mathsf{Blind}^*_{\rho(x)}(\widehat{x}), y\right)$$

and

$$\forall \widehat{x} \in \mathbb{F}^{\ell m} : (\Lambda, \bot) \equiv \mathsf{Sim}_{\widehat{g}}\left(\mathsf{Blind}^*_{\rho(x)}(\widehat{x}), \bot\right).$$

In the above, $x = \mathsf{Dec}(\widehat{x}), y = g(x)$, $\boldsymbol{\rho}$ is the ε-random probing function and $(\Lambda, \widehat{y}) = \mathsf{Real}_{\widehat{g}}$ is a sample from the real experiment, which computes $\widehat{y} \equiv \widehat{g}(\widehat{x})$, obtains the average-probing leakage Λ from the wires and then outputs $(\Lambda, \widehat{y})$.

Additional Properties. Now that we established the notion, we want to show that we are actually able to achieve it. Intuitively, we should construct every gadget and then prove that they meet the above definitions; however, the proofs are quite long and very similar. Instead, we proceed the other way around: first, we show a general technique to construct a simulator, and then we show that such general technique can be applied to simulate all the gadgets that we construct. In this way, we only have a general proof for the simulator and then one corollary for every gadget. However, to proceed in this way, we need two additional properties from the gadgets.

The first property states, informally, that every wire on the gadget carries a close-to-uniform value when considered independently of the rest of the gadget.

Definition 2 (Close-to-uniform gadget). *Let g be any gate and let $\widehat{g}$ be the corresponding gadget. Let k be the number of wires in $\widehat{g}$ and let $\gamma \in \left[0, \frac{1}{2}\right], k' \in \mathbb{N}$ be parameters such that $k' \leq k$. Furthermore, let $(\mathbf{w}_1, \ldots, \mathbf{w}_k)$ be the random variable of the values on the wires of $\widehat{g}$. We say that $\widehat{g}$ is a (k, k', γ)-close-to-uniform gadget if $\mathbf{w}_1, \ldots, \mathbf{w}_k$ are all γ-close-to-uniform and, additionally, there are $k - k'$ indices $i \in [k]$ such that $\mathbf{w}_i$ is uniform. If $k' = 0$ (i.e., the gadget does not contain non-uniform wires), we simply say that the gadget is k-uniform.*

In the following corollary, which is a direct consequence of Lemma 4, we show that, intuitively, close-to-uniform gadgets have nice "hiding" properties.

Corollary 1. *Let* $\delta \in (0,1), \gamma \in \left[0, \frac{1}{2}\right], k, k', \ell, m \in \mathbb{N}$ *be parameters such that* $k' \leq k$ *and* ℓ *is the size of the encoding. Let* g *be a functional gate with fan-in* m, *and let* $\widehat{g}$ *be the corresponding gadget for an encoding of size* ℓ. *Assume that* $\widehat{g}$ *is* (k, k', γ)-*close-to-uniform. Then, for all* $\widehat{x} \in \mathbb{F}^{\ell m}$ *and all* δ-*average probing functions* α,

$$\Pr\left[\Lambda = \perp\right] \geq 1 - k\delta - k'\gamma\delta|\mathbb{F}|,$$

where $\Lambda := \mathsf{Leak}_{\widehat{g}}(\alpha, \widehat{x})$ *is the distribution of the leakage from the wires of* $\widehat{g}$ *upon input* $\widehat{x}$.

The second property states, informally, that every *internal* wire of the gadget carries a value that, when considered independently of the other internal wires, is also independent of the output of the gadget.

Definition 3 (Output independence). *Let* g *be any gate with fan-out* n *and let* $\widehat{g}$ *be the corresponding gadget for an encoding of size* $\ell \in \mathbb{N}$. *Let* $k \in \mathbb{N}$ *be the number of wires in* $\widehat{g}$ *and let* $n \in \mathbb{N}$ *be the fan-out of* g. *Furthermore, let* $(\mathbf{w}_1, \dots, \mathbf{w}_{k-\ell n})$ *be the random variable of the values on the* internal *wires of* $\widehat{g}$ *and let* $\widehat{\mathbf{y}}$ *be the random variable of the values on the* output *wires. We say that* $\widehat{g}$ *is* output-independent *if*

$$\forall i \in [k - \ell n], \forall w \in \mathbb{F} : \Pr\left[\mathbf{w}_i = w \,|\, \widehat{\mathbf{y}} = \widehat{y}\right] = \Pr\left[\mathbf{w}_i = w\right]$$

and, additionally,

$$\widehat{\mathbf{y}} \equiv \mathsf{Enc}(\mathsf{Dec}(\widehat{\mathbf{y}})).$$

The following lemma shows a useful lower bound on the distribution of any non-leaking output of close-to-uniform gadgets with output-independence. Roughly speaking, this means that, when the gadget does not leak anything (i.e., $\Lambda = \perp$), it is still possible to approximate from below the output distribution of the gadget with a distribution that does not depend on the input value $\widehat{x}$, namely, the distribution $\mathsf{Enc}(y) | \alpha(\mathsf{Enc}(y)) = \perp$.

Lemma 5. *Let* $\gamma \in \left[0, \frac{1}{2}\right], \delta \in (0,1), k, k', \ell, m, n \in \mathbb{N}$ *be parameters such that* $k' \leq k$ *and* $(k + k'\gamma|\mathbb{F}|)\delta < 1$. *Let* g *be any gate with fan-in* m *and fan-out* n *and let* $\widehat{g}$ *be the corresponding gadget for an encoding of size* ℓ. *Assume that* $\widehat{g}$ *is* (k, k', γ)-*close-to-uniform and output-independent. Then, for all* $\widehat{x} \in \mathbb{F}^{\ell m}$ *and all* $\widehat{y} \in \mathcal{Out}_{\widehat{g}}(\widehat{x})$,

$$\Pr\left[\mathsf{Enc}(y) = \widehat{y} \,|\, \alpha(\mathsf{Enc}(y)) = \perp\right] \leq \frac{\Pr\left[\mathsf{Real}_g(\widehat{x}) = (\perp, \widehat{y})\right]}{1 - (k + k'\gamma|\mathbb{F}|)\delta}, \tag{1}$$

where $y = \mathsf{Dec}(\widehat{y})$.

The proof of this fact can be found in the full version [9].

The Gadget Simulator. Now we are ready to define the actual gadget simulator. Recall that the simulator receives two inputs which are possibly "blinded", namely the input of the gadget $\widehat{x}$ and the output of the original gate y. In what follows, we assume that, whenever $y \neq \perp$, $y \in \mathbb{F}^n$ or, in other words, y is given in full to the simulator;[4] it is easy to extend the simulator and the analysis to the general case.

For a gate g with fan-in m and fan-out n and its respective gadget $\widehat{g}$ for an encoding of size ℓ, we consider the following simulator $\mathsf{Sim}_{\widehat{g}}$.

- Upon input $(\perp, \perp)$, simply output $(\perp, \perp)$.
- Upon input $(\perp, y)$, sample $\widehat{y}$ with probability

$$\Pr\left[\mathsf{Enc}(y) = \widehat{y} \mid \alpha(\mathsf{Enc}(y)) = \perp\right]$$

  and output $(\perp, \widehat{y})$.
- Upon input $(\widehat{x}, \perp)$, sample $\Lambda \neq \perp$ with probability

$$\frac{1}{\varepsilon^m} \Pr\left[\Lambda = \Lambda\right],$$

  where Λ is the leakage performed by the real experiment $\mathsf{Real}_{\widehat{g}}$, or set $\Lambda = \perp$ with probability

$$\frac{1}{\varepsilon^m} \Pr\left[\Lambda = \perp\right] - \frac{1 - \varepsilon^m}{\varepsilon^m}.$$

  Then, output $(\Lambda, \perp)$.
- Upon input $(\widehat{x}, y)$, sample $(\Lambda, \widehat{y})$ for $\Lambda \neq \perp$ with probability

$$\frac{1}{\varepsilon^m} \Pr\left[\mathsf{Real}_{\widehat{g}}(\widehat{x}) = (\Lambda, \widehat{y})\right]$$

  and sample $(\perp, \widehat{y})$ with probability

$$\frac{1}{\varepsilon^m} \Pr\left[\mathsf{Real}_{\widehat{g}}(\widehat{x}) = (\perp, \widehat{y})\right] - \frac{1 - \varepsilon^m}{\varepsilon^m} \Pr\left[\mathsf{Enc}(y) = \widehat{y} \mid \alpha(\mathsf{Enc}(y)) = \perp\right].$$

  Finally, output the sampled values.

The remainder of the section is dedicated to the proof of the following theorem stating that, informally, the output of the simulator is identically distributed to the output of the real experiment.

Theorem 1. *Let $\gamma \in \left[0, \frac{1}{2}\right], \varepsilon, \delta \in (0, 1), k, k', \ell, m, n \in \mathbb{N}$ be parameters such that $k' \leq k$ and*

$$(k + k'\gamma|\mathbb{F}|)\delta < \varepsilon^m.$$

Let g be a functional gate with fan-in m and fan-out n and let $\widehat{g}$ be the corresponding gadget for an encoding of size ℓ. Assume that $\widehat{g}$ is (k, k', γ)-close-to-uniform and output-independent. Then, the above simulator is such that

$$\forall \widehat{x} \in \mathbb{F}^{\ell m} : \mathsf{Real}_{\widehat{g}}(\widehat{x}) \equiv \mathsf{Sim}_{\widehat{g}}\left(\mathsf{Blind}^*_{\rho(x)}(\widehat{x}), y\right)$$

---

[4] Notice that the only gate with $n > 1$ is the copy gate, for which all the components of y are the same.

and

$$\forall \widehat{x} \in \mathbb{F}^{\ell m} : (\Lambda, \perp) \equiv \mathsf{Sim}_{\widehat{g}}\left(\mathsf{Blind}^*_{\rho(x)}(\widehat{x}), \perp\right).$$

In the above, $x = \mathsf{Dec}(\widehat{x}), y = g(x)$, ρ *is the* ε-*random probing function and* $(\Lambda, \widehat{y}) = \mathsf{Real}_{\widehat{g}}$ *is a sample from the real experiment, which computes* $\widehat{y} \equiv \widehat{g}(\widehat{x})$, *obtains the average-probing leakage* Λ *from the wires and then outputs* $(\Lambda, \widehat{y})$.

Proof. First of all, we need to show that the simulator is well-defined. Namely, we need to show that the output of the simulator is actually a distribution, meaning that all the probabilities are non-negative and sum up to 1. This is trivial when the simulator receives $(\perp, \perp)$ or $(\perp, y)$ as input, therefore, in what follows, we focus on the case in which the simulator actually receives $\widehat{x}$.

– When the simulator receives $(\widehat{x}, \perp)$ as input, it samples Λ and outputs $(\Lambda, \perp)$. All the probabilities of the simulator outputting $\Lambda \neq \perp$ are trivially non-negative. When summing all of them, we get that the probability of outputting any $\Lambda \neq \perp$ is

$$\frac{1}{\varepsilon^m} \Pr\left[\Lambda \neq \perp\right].$$

Since $\widehat{g}$ is close-to-uniform, we can apply Corollary 1 to obtain that

$$\frac{1}{\varepsilon^m} \Pr\left[\Lambda \neq \perp\right] \leq \frac{1}{\varepsilon^m}(k + k'\gamma|\mathbb{F}|)\delta < 1, \tag{2}$$

where the last inequality holds by the hypothesis on the parameters. On the other side, the simulator outputs $\Lambda = \perp$ with probability

$$\frac{1}{\varepsilon^m} \Pr\left[\Lambda = \perp\right] - \frac{1 - \varepsilon^m}{\varepsilon^m} = 1 - \frac{1}{\varepsilon^m} \Pr\left[\Lambda \neq \perp\right] > 0,$$

where the last inequality follows from Eq. (2). It follows that the probabilities are non-negative and that they sum up to 1.

– When the simulator receives $(\widehat{x}, y)$ as input, the proof is very similar to the above. Indeed, the simulator samples $(\Lambda, \widehat{y})$ for $\Lambda \neq \perp$ always with non-negative probability; on the other side, the probability of sampling $(\perp, \widehat{y})$ is non-negative if and only if

$$\Pr\left[\mathsf{Real}_{\widehat{g}}(\widehat{x}) = (\perp, \widehat{y})\right] - (1 - \varepsilon^m)\Pr\left[\mathsf{Enc}(y) = \widehat{y} \mid \alpha(\mathsf{Enc}(y)) = \perp\right] \geq 0$$

or, by rearranging the terms, if and only if

$$\Pr\left[\mathsf{Enc}(y) = \widehat{y} \mid \alpha(\mathsf{Enc}(y)) = \perp\right] \leq \frac{\Pr\left[\mathsf{Real}_{\widehat{g}}(\widehat{x}) = (\perp, \widehat{y})\right]}{1 - \varepsilon^m}. \tag{3}$$

However, since $\widehat{g}$ is close-to-uniform and output-independent by hypothesis, we can apply Lemma 5, which gives

$$\Pr\left[\mathsf{Enc}(y) = \widehat{y} \mid \alpha(\mathsf{Enc}(y)) = \perp\right] \leq \frac{\Pr\left[\mathsf{Real}_g(\widehat{x}) = (\perp, \widehat{y})\right]}{1 - (k + k'\gamma|\mathbb{F}|)\delta}.$$

Then, Eq. (3) follows from the hypothesis $(k + k'\gamma|\mathbb{F}|)\delta < \varepsilon^m$. Finally, it is easy to see that all the terms sum up to 1.

Now it remains to show that the simulator perfectly simulates the real distribution. We start the analysis of the simulator from the simple case of $\Lambda \neq \bot$. Notice that $\mathsf{Sim}_{\widehat{g}}$ only outputs $\Lambda \neq \bot$ if it receives $\widehat{x}$ as input (otherwise, the simulator plays safe and outputs $\bot$). Therefore,

$$\Pr\left[\mathsf{Sim}_{\widehat{g}}\left(\mathsf{Blind}^*_{\rho(x)}(\widehat{x}), y\right) = (\Lambda, \widehat{y})\right]$$

$$= \Pr\left[\mathsf{Blind}^*_{\rho(x)}(\widehat{x}) = \widehat{x}\right]\Pr\left[\mathsf{Sim}_{\widehat{g}}(\widehat{x}, y) = (\Lambda, \widehat{y})\right] \tag{4}$$

$$= \Pr\left[\rho(x) = x\right]\Pr\left[\mathsf{Sim}_{\widehat{g}}(\widehat{x}, y) = (\Lambda, \widehat{y})\right] \tag{5}$$

$$= \varepsilon^m \Pr\left[\mathsf{Sim}_{\widehat{g}}(\widehat{x}, y) = (\Lambda, \widehat{y})\right] \tag{6}$$

$$= \Pr\left[\mathsf{Real}_{\widehat{g}}(\widehat{x}) = (\Lambda, \widehat{y})\right], \tag{7}$$

where Λ is the leakage produced by the real experiment $\mathsf{Real}_{\widehat{g}}$. In the above derivation,

- Equation (4) follows by definition of conditional probability;
- Equation (5) holds because $\mathsf{Blind}^*_{\rho(x)}(\widehat{x}) = \widehat{x}$ if and only if $\rho(x) = x$;
- Equation (6) follows by definition of random probing and from the fact that $x \in \mathbb{F}^m$;
- and finally, Eq. (7) follows by how we defined the simulator to behave upon input $(\widehat{x}, y)$.

The proof for the case in which the simulator does not get y is analogous, therefore we now only focus on the case $\Lambda = \bot$. This case is a bit more involved, because $\mathsf{Sim}_{\widehat{g}}$ may output $\Lambda = \bot$ both when the input $\widehat{x}$ is given and when the simulator receives $\bot$. Namely,

$$\Pr\left[\mathsf{Sim}_{\widehat{g}}\left(\mathsf{Blind}^*_{\rho(x)}(\widehat{x}), y\right) = (\Lambda, \widehat{y})\right]$$

$$= \Pr\left[\mathsf{Blind}^*_{\rho(x)}(\widehat{x}) = \widehat{x}\right]\Pr\left[\mathsf{Sim}_{\widehat{g}}(\widehat{x}, y) = (\bot, \widehat{y})\right]$$

$$\quad + \Pr\left[\mathsf{Blind}^*_{\rho(x)}(\widehat{x}) = \bot\right]\Pr\left[\mathsf{Sim}_{\widehat{g}}(\bot, y) = (\bot, \widehat{y})\right] \tag{8}$$

$$= \Pr\left[\rho(x) = x\right]\Pr\left[\mathsf{Sim}_{\widehat{g}}(\widehat{x}, y) = (\bot, \widehat{y})\right]$$

$$\quad + \Pr\left[\rho(x) = \bot\right]\Pr\left[\mathsf{Sim}_{\widehat{g}}(\bot, y) = (\bot, \widehat{y})\right] \tag{9}$$

$$= \varepsilon^m \Pr\left[\mathsf{Sim}_{\widehat{g}}(\widehat{x}, y) = (\bot, \widehat{y})\right]$$

$$\quad + (1 - \varepsilon^m)\Pr\left[\mathsf{Sim}_{\widehat{g}}(\bot, y) = (\bot, \widehat{y})\right] \tag{10}$$

$$= \Pr\left[\mathsf{Real}_{\widehat{g}}(\widehat{x}) = (\bot, \widehat{y})\right] - (1 - \varepsilon^m)\Pr\left[\mathsf{Enc}(y) = \widehat{y} \mid \alpha(\mathsf{Enc}(y)) = \bot\right]$$

$$\quad + (1 - \varepsilon^m)\Pr\left[\mathsf{Enc}(y) = \widehat{y} \mid \alpha(\mathsf{Enc}(y)) = \bot\right] \tag{11}$$

$$= \Pr\left[\mathsf{Real}_{\widehat{g}}(\widehat{x}) = (\bot, \widehat{y})\right]. \tag{12}$$

In the above derivation,

- Equations (8) to (10) follow for the same reasoning as in Eqs. (4) to (6);
- Equation (11) follows by how we defined the simulator to behave upon input $(\widehat{x}, y)$;

– and finally, Eq. (12) follows by simplifying the sum and subtraction of the same term.

This concludes the proof.   □

Now that we proved the main result of this section, we define the gadgets that we are going to use in the final construction.

3.1 Basic Arithmetic Gadgets

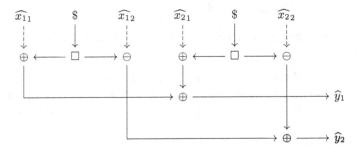

Fig. 1. Scheme for the $\widehat{\mathrm{ADD}}$ gadget.

We start by constructing the $\widehat{\mathrm{ADD}}$ gadget, depicted in Fig. 1 and consisting of 2 RND gates, 2 CPY gates, 4 ADD gates and 2 SUB gates, for a total of 10 gates. Furthermore, the $\widehat{\mathrm{ADD}}$ gadget consists of 12 wires. The random gates output uniform random values $\mathbf{r}_1$ and $\mathbf{r}_2$, which are then copied and used to refresh the input values. Then, the refreshed values are summed component-wise in order to obtain $\widehat{y}_1, \widehat{y}_2$. Overall, without taking into account wires carrying the same value, the wires in the gadget carry the following values:

$\mathbf{r}_1, \mathbf{r}_2,$	(From the random gates)
$\widehat{x_{11}} + \mathbf{r}_1, \widehat{x_{12}} - \mathbf{r}_1,$	(Refreshing of the first input)
$\widehat{x_{21}} + \mathbf{r}_2, \widehat{x_{22}} - \mathbf{r}_2,$	(Refreshing of the second input)
$\widehat{x_{11}} + \mathbf{r}_1 + \widehat{x_{21}} + \mathbf{r}_2, \widehat{x_{12}} - \mathbf{r}_1 + \widehat{x_{22}} - \mathbf{r}_2$	(Output encoding)

It is easy to see that every one of the above values is uniformly distributed when taken independently. Finally, ADD is a deterministic gate with fan-in 2 and fan-out 1, therefore it is a functional gate.

From the above, $\widehat{\mathrm{ADD}}$ is a 12-uniform gadget for a deterministic functional gate. We now show that the gadget is output-independent. Indeed, we have that

$$\widehat{y}_1 = \widehat{x_{11}} + \mathbf{r}_1 + \widehat{x_{21}} + \mathbf{r}_2 \quad \text{and} \quad \widehat{y}_2 = \widehat{x_{12}} - \mathbf{r}_1 + \widehat{x_{22}} - \mathbf{r}_2,$$

which means that, by uniformity of $\mathbf{r}_1$ and $\mathbf{r}_2$, the output is identically distributed to a fresh encoding. Furthermore, for the internal wires we have that, for every $r \in \mathbb{F}$, every $\widehat{x} \in \mathbb{F}^4$, and every $\widehat{y} \in \mathcal{O}ut_{\widehat{\mathrm{ADD}}}(\widehat{x})$,

$$
\begin{aligned}
\Pr\left[\mathbf{r}_1 = r \mid \widehat{\mathbf{y}} = \widehat{y}\right] &= \Pr\left[\mathbf{r}_1 = r \;\middle|\; \begin{array}{l} \widehat{x_{11}} + \mathbf{r}_1 + \widehat{x_{21}} + \mathbf{r}_2 = \widehat{y_1} \\ \widehat{x_{12}} - \mathbf{r}_1 + \widehat{x_{22}} - \mathbf{r}_2 = \widehat{y_2} \end{array}\right] \\
&= \Pr\left[\mathbf{r}_1 = r \mid \mathbf{r}_1 = c_1 - \mathbf{r}_2\right] \\
&= \Pr\left[\mathbf{r}_2 = c_1 - r\right] \\
&= \Pr\left[\mathbf{r}_1 = r\right],
\end{aligned}
$$

where $c_1 = \widehat{y_1} - \widehat{x_{11}} - \widehat{x_{21}}$, the first equality follows from making $\widehat{y}$ explicit, the second equality follows by rearranging the terms and the fact that $\widehat{y} \in \mathcal{O}ut_{\widehat{\mathrm{ADD}}}(\widehat{x})$, the third equality follows by replacing $\mathbf{r}_1$ with its value given by the condition, and the last equality follows because both $\mathbf{r}_1, \mathbf{r}_2$ are uniform samples from $\mathbb{F}$. A similar reasoning can be applied to the values carried by all the other internal wires, thus proving output-independence.

Now that we proved that the gadget is 12-uniform and output-independent, we can apply Theorem 1 to obtain the following.

Corollary 2. *Let $\varepsilon, \delta \in (0,1)$ be parameters such that*

$$12\delta < \varepsilon^2.$$

Then, $\widehat{\mathrm{ADD}}$ is ε-random to δ-average simulatable.

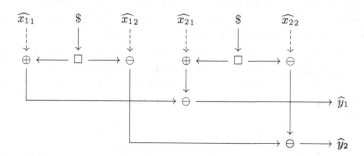

Fig. 2. Scheme for the $\widehat{\mathrm{SUB}}$ gadget.

By replacing the last two ADD gates with SUB gates in $\widehat{\mathrm{ADD}}$, we obtain the new gadget $\widehat{\mathrm{SUB}}$, depicted in Fig. 2, which computes SUB. The analysis is completely analogous to the one for $\widehat{\mathrm{SUB}}$, hence we have the following.

Corollary 3. *Let $\varepsilon, \delta \in (0,1)$ be parameters such that*

$$12\delta < \varepsilon^2.$$

Then, $\widehat{\mathrm{SUB}}$ is ε-random to δ-average simulatable.

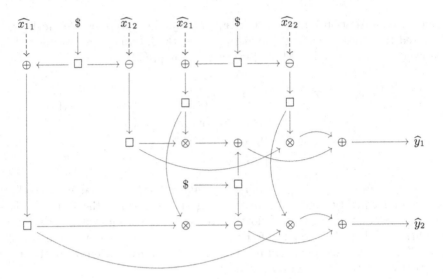

Fig. 3. Scheme for the $\widehat{\text{MUL}}$ gadget. To make the diagram easier to understand, the wires carrying an encoding of x_1 are marked in red, the wires carrying an encoding of x_2 are marked in green, and the wires after the multiplication are marked in blue. (Color figure online)

3.2 Multiplication Gadget

The $\widehat{\text{MUL}}$ gadget, depicted in Fig. 3, is probably the most complex gadget due to the properties of multiplication. Indeed, it is the only non-uniform gadget, consisting of 3 RND gates, 7 CPY gates, 5 ADD gates, 3 SUB gates, and 4 MUL gates, for a total of 22 gates. Furthermore, the $\widehat{\text{MUL}}$ gadget consists of 29 wires. The first two random gates output uniform random values r_1 and r_2, which are then copied and used to refresh the input values. Then, the refreshed values are (copied and) multiplied so to obtain the four terms of the product of two binomials:

$$(a_1 + a_2)(b_1 + b_2) = a_1 b_1 + a_1 b_2 + a_2 b_1 + a_2 b_2.$$

Finally, the partial sums are computed, in order to have encodings of only two elements, and then a third random gate is used to refresh the output encoding. Overall, without taking into account wires carrying the same value, the wires in the gadget carry the following values:

r_1, r_2, r_3 (From the random gates)

$\widehat{x_{11}} + r_1, \widehat{x_{12}} - r_1,$ (Refreshing of the first input)

$\widehat{x_{21}} + r_2, \widehat{x_{22}} - r_2,$ (Refreshing of the second input)

$(\widehat{x_{12}} - r_1)(\widehat{x_{21}} + r_2),$ (First column of multiplications)

$\quad (\widehat{x_{11}} + r_1)(\widehat{x_{21}} + r_2)$

$(\widehat{x_{12}} - r_1)(\widehat{x_{22}} - r_2),$ (Second column of multiplications)

$\quad (\widehat{x_{11}} + r_1)(\widehat{x_{22}} - r_2)$

$(\widehat{x_{12}} - r_1)(\widehat{x_{21}} + r_2) + r_3,$ (First column rerandomized)

$\quad (\widehat{x_{11}} + r_1)(\widehat{x_{21}} + r_2) - r_3$

$(\widehat{x_{12}} - r_1)(\widehat{x_{21}} + r_2) + r_3$ (First output component)

$\quad + (\widehat{x_{12}} - r_1)(\widehat{x_{22}} - r_2)$

$(\widehat{x_{11}} + r_1)(\widehat{x_{21}} + r_2) - r_3$ (Second output component)

$\quad + (\widehat{x_{11}} + r_1)(\widehat{x_{22}} - r_2).$

It is easy to see that all the values on the red and green wires are uniform when considered independently, and so are the output wires and the wires carrying r_3. The only wires that are not uniform are the outputs of the four MUL gates. However, by Lemma 1, the outputs of the MUL gates are $\frac{1}{|\mathbb{F}|}$-close-to-uniform. Finally, a reasoning similar to the one in Sect. 3.1 shows that multiplication gadgets are also output-independent. This suffices to apply Theorem 1 with parameters $k = 29$, $k' = 6$ and $\gamma = \frac{1}{|\mathbb{F}|}$, and obtain the following result.

Corollary 4. *Let $\varepsilon, \delta \in (0,1)$ be parameters such that*

$$\left(29 + 6 \cdot \frac{1}{|\mathbb{F}|} \cdot |\mathbb{F}|\right) \delta = 35\delta < \varepsilon^2.$$

Then, $\widehat{\mathsf{MUL}}$ is ε-random to δ-average simulatable.

3.3 Copy Gadget

The last functional gadget is the $\widehat{\mathsf{CPY}}$ gadget, depicted in Fig. 4, which is fairly simple. It consists of 3 RND gates, 5 CPY gates, 3 ADD gates and 3 SUB gates, for a total of 14 gates. Furthermore, the $\widehat{\mathsf{CPY}}$ gadget consists of 19 wires. There are no arithmetic operations except for the ones needed to refresh the encodings; on the other hand, the encodings are refreshed both on the input side, to ensure that the gadget is uniform, and on the output side, to ensure that the gadget is output-independent.

By applying Theorem 1, we obtain the following.

Corollary 5. *Let $\varepsilon, \delta \in (0,1)$ be parameters such that*

$$19\delta < \varepsilon^2.$$

Then, $\widehat{\mathsf{CPY}}$ is ε-random to δ-average simulatable.

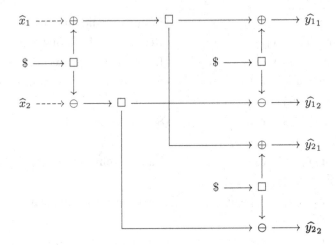

Fig. 4. Scheme for the $\widehat{\mathsf{CPY}}$ gadget.

3.4   Putting Everything Together

The only missing gadgets are the ones for IN, OUT, RND. However, OUT only has input wires, therefore the corresponding gadget would be empty. On the other hand, IN and RND are very similar, therefore we focus on IN and then explain later the differences with RND.

Let g_0 be any input gate and let g_1 be the gate that receives the input from g_0; finally, let $w = (g_0, g_1)$ be the wire connecting the two gates. By assuming a leak-free encoder before the circuit, the encoding that we would place on the wire bundle $\widehat{w}$ is already a fresh encoding or, in other words, the value on every wire of the bundle is uniformly distributed when considered independently. This actually means two things:

– there is no need to re-randomize the values directly coming from the input in gadget $\widehat{g_1}$;
– if we consider $\widehat{g_0} \cup \widehat{w} \cup \widehat{g_1}$, we are only adding two uniform wires.

By applying the above, we can remove the re-randomization component (thus removing 3 wires) and consider the input wires as part of the gadget instead (thus adding 2 wires). As an example, Fig. 5 is what the $\widehat{\mathsf{ADD}}$ gadget looks like when we apply the above strategy.

Corollary 6. *Let $k, k' \in \mathbb{N}$, $\gamma \in \left[0, \frac{1}{2}\right]$, $\varepsilon, \delta \in (0, 1)$ be parameters such that*

$$(k + k'\gamma|\mathbb{F}|)\,\delta \le \varepsilon^2$$

and assume that $\widehat{g}$ is a (k, k', γ)-close-to-uniform and output-independent gadget. Then, the above operation of merging the input wires and removing the re-randomization component produces a new gadget $\widehat{g}'$ that is $(k-1, k', \gamma)$-close-to-uniform and output-independent.

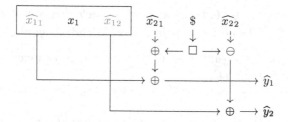

Fig. 5. Scheme for the $\widehat{\text{ADD}}$ gadget, in which we replaced the rerandomizing component with the input wires; the box represents the leak-free encoding circuit that takes as input x_1 and outputs the fresh encoding $(\widehat{x_{11}}, \widehat{x_{12}})$.

Proof. Notice that the above operation removes three uniform wires (namely, the ones from the random gate that are used to re-randomize the encoding) and adds two uniform wires (namely, the ones carrying the fresh encoding). Hence, this operation converts a (k, k', γ)-close-to-uniform gadget into a $(k - 1, k', \gamma)$-close-to-uniform gadget. Finally, this operation does not modify any other wire, and it is easy to see that the output-independence property is preserved.   □

Since we addressed all gadgets, we can have the following general corollary that handles all of them.

Corollary 7. *Let $\varepsilon, \delta \in (0, 1)$ be parameters such that*

$$35\delta \leq \varepsilon^2.$$

Then, all the gadgets defined so far are ε-random to δ-average simulatable.

4   The Circuit Compiler

The circuit compiler simply replaces every wire with the respective wire bundle and every gate with the respective gadget. Our goal is to achieve the following definition.

Definition 4 (Simulatability of circuits). *Let C be a circuit with fan-in m^* and fan-out n^*. Let $\widehat{C}$ be the corresponding transformed circuit. Let Φ, Ψ be two families of (possibly randomized) functions. Finally, let $\ell \in \mathbb{N}$ be the size of the encoding. We say that $\widehat{C}$ is Φ-to-Ψ-simulatable (from C) if there exists a simulator Sim_C such that for every $x^* \in \mathbb{F}^{m^*}$ input to C and every function $\psi \in \Psi$ there exists a function $\varphi \in \Phi$:*

$$\text{Leak}_C\left(\text{Enc}(x^*)\right) \equiv \text{Sim}_C\left(\varphi\left(\mathbf{W}(x^*)\right)\right). \tag{13}$$

In the above, $\mathbf{W}(x^*)$ is the distribution of the values on the wires of the original circuit C upon input x^*.

In what follows, we show the following.

Theorem 2. *Let $\varepsilon, \delta \in (0,1)$ be parameters such that $35\delta < \varepsilon^2$. Let $\mathcal{C}$ be a circuit and let $\widehat{\mathcal{C}}$ be the circuit transformed in the following way:*

- *for every functional gate $g \in \mathcal{C}$, we place the corresponding gadget, as described in Sect. 3, in $\widehat{\mathcal{C}}$;*
- *for every wire $w \in \mathcal{C}$, we place the corresponding wire bundle in $\widehat{\mathcal{C}}$, consisting of 2 wires;*
- *if $w = (g_1, g_2)$, the corresponding wire bundle $\widehat{w}$ will connect $\widehat{g_1}$ to $\widehat{g_2}$.*

Then, the transformed circuit $\widehat{\mathcal{C}}$ is ε-random to δ-average simulatable.

The proof proceeds by hybrid argument. Namely, let k^* be the number of functional gates in $\mathcal{C}$. Then, the real experiment $\mathsf{Leak}_{\mathcal{C}}(\mathsf{Enc}(x^*))$ can be rewritten as follows.

1. Sample $\widehat{x^*} = \mathsf{Enc}(x^*)$.
2. For every $j \in [k^*]$, compute $\Lambda_j, \widehat{y}_j$ as follows.
   (a) For every input bundle of gadget $\widehat{g}_j$ that comes from an input of the circuit, place the corresponding value taken from the vector $\widehat{x^*}$.
   (b) For every input bundle of gadget $\widehat{g}_j$ that comes from a random gate of the circuit, sample uniform $r \in \mathbb{F}$ and place $\mathsf{Enc}(r)$ on the wires.
   (c) Since $\mathcal{C}$ is topologically sorted, every other input bundle of gadget $\widehat{g}_j$ already has a value, which has been computed in a previous iteration as $\widehat{y}_{j'}$ for some $j' < j$.
   (d) Let $\widehat{W}_j \in \mathbb{F}^{k_j}$ be the list of values on all the k_j wires of $\widehat{g}_j$.
   (e) The leakage Λ_j is set to be $\Lambda_j := \alpha(\widehat{W}_j)$, while the output $\widehat{y}_j$ is taken from the output values stored in $\widehat{W}_j$.
3. Output $\Lambda = \Lambda_1 || \ldots || \Lambda_{k^*}$.

The above experiment, which we denote as $\mathsf{Hyb}_{k^*+1}(x^*)$, only differs from the original experiment $\mathsf{Leak}_{\mathcal{C}}(\mathsf{Enc}(x^*))$ in when the leakage occurs. Namely, in $\mathsf{Leak}_{\mathcal{C}}$ first the circuit is computed entirely and then the leakage is computed, while Hyb_{k^*+1} computes the leakage immediately after the values on the wires are available. Therefore,

$$\mathsf{Leak}_{\mathcal{C}}(\mathsf{Enc}(x^*)) \equiv \mathsf{Hyb}_{k^*+1}(x^*).$$

Now we define, for $i \in [k^*]$, the following hybrid experiment $\mathsf{Hyb}_i(x^*)$.

1. Sample $\widehat{x^*} = \mathsf{Enc}(x^*)$ and $\widehat{x^*_?} = \mathsf{Blind}_{\rho(x^*)}(\widehat{x^*})$.
2. For every $j \in [k^*]$, compute $\Lambda_j, \widehat{y}_j$ as follows.
   - If $j < i$, do the following.
     (a) For every input bundle of gadget $\widehat{g}_j$ that comes from an input of the circuit, place the corresponding value taken from the vector $\widehat{x^*}$.
     (b) For every input bundle of gadget $\widehat{g}_j$ that comes from a random gate of the circuit, sample uniform $r \in \mathbb{F}$ and place $\mathsf{Enc}(r)$ on the wires.

(c) Since $\mathcal{C}$ is topologically sorted, every other input bundle of gadget $\widehat{g}_j$ already has a value, which has been computed in a previous iteration as $\widehat{y}_{j'}$ for some $j' < j$.

(d) Let $\widehat{W}_j \in \mathbb{F}^{k_j}$ be the list of values on all the k_j wires of $\widehat{g}_j$.

(e) The leakage Λ_j is set to be $\Lambda_j := \alpha(\widehat{W}_j)$, while the output $\widehat{y}_j$ is taken from the output values stored in $\widehat{W}_j$.

(f) Compute $y_j = \mathsf{Dec}(\widehat{g}_j)$ and sample $\widehat{y}_{j?} = \mathsf{Blind}_{\rho(y_j)}(\widehat{g}_j)$.

If $j \geq i$, the leakage and the output will be generated by the corresponding simulator $\mathsf{Sim}_{\widehat{g}_j}$. Namely, do the following.

(a) Let $\widehat{x}_?$ be possibly blinded the values on the input bundles of gadget $\widehat{g}_j$. Notice that, for every input bundle, there are only four possibilities:

- the input bundle comes from input gates, in which case $\widehat{x}_?$ has already been computed among the circuit inputs $\widehat{x}^*_? = \mathsf{Blind}_{\rho(x^*)}(\widehat{x}^*)$;
- the input bundle comes from random gates, in which case just sample uniform $r \in \mathbb{F}$ and sample $\widehat{x}_? = \mathsf{Blind}_{\rho(r)}(\mathsf{Enc}(r))$;
- the input bundle is an output bundle of a functional gadget $\widehat{g}_{j'}$ for $j' < i$, in which case we already computed $\widehat{x}_?$ as $\widehat{y}_{j?} = \mathsf{Blind}_{\rho(y_j)}(\widehat{g}_j)$ in a previous step;
- the input bundle is an output bundle of a functional gadget $\widehat{g}_{j'}$ for $j' \geq i$ and $j' < j$, in which case $\widehat{x}_?$ has already been output by a previous simulator as $\widehat{y}_{j?}$.

In any case, $\widehat{x}_?$ is always available.

(b) If some of the values of $\widehat{x}_?$ are $\bot$, set $\widehat{x}_? \leftarrow \bot$; otherwise, leave it unchanged. This is equivalent to convert the output of Blind into the output of Blind^*.

(c) Let $y = g(x)$, where $x = \mathsf{Dec}(\widehat{x})$ and $\widehat{x}$ is the collection of the input values computed as above. Notice that, even if $\widehat{x}$ is not available to the experiment, x is always available: indeed, the experiment knows the input x^* and the random coins sampled so far, therefore is able to deterministically reconstruct x.

(d) Probe $y_? \leftarrow \rho(y)$.

(e) Run the simulator $(\Lambda_j, \widehat{y}_?) \leftarrow \mathsf{Sim}_{\widehat{g}_i}(\widehat{x}_?, y_?)$.

3. Output $\Lambda = \Lambda_1 || \ldots || \Lambda_{k^*}$.

Notice that, if we instantiate the above algorithm with $i = k^* + 1$, the part $j \geq i$ is never executed, and the part $j < i$ is exactly the same as in $\mathsf{Hyb}_{k^*+1}(x^*)$.

The following lemma says that the changes that we are introducing do not affect the final distribution of the leakage.

Lemma 6. *Let x^* be any input to $\mathcal{C}$. Then, for every $i \in [k^*]$,*

$$\mathsf{Hyb}_i(x^*) \equiv \mathsf{Hyb}_{i+1}(x^*)$$

The proof of this fact is a simple but long reduction, which can be found in the full version of the paper [9].

For the next step of the proof, we take a closer look at $\mathsf{Hyb}_1(x^*)$. Namely, since the branch $j < 1$ is never executed and all the real functional gadgets have been replaced with the respective simulators, the description of $\mathsf{Hyb}_1(x^*)$ looks as follows.

1. Sample $\widehat{x}^* = \mathsf{Enc}(x^*)$ and $\widehat{x^*_?} = \mathsf{Blind}_{\rho(x^*)}(\widehat{x}^*)$.
2. For every $j \in [k^*]$, compute $\Lambda_j, \widehat{y}_j$ as follows.
   (a) Let $\widehat{x}_?$ be the possibly blinded values on the input bundles of gadget $\widehat{g}_j$. Notice that, for every input bundle, there are only three possibilities:
   - the input bundle comes from input gates, in which case $\widehat{x}_?$ has already been computed among the circuit inputs $\widehat{x^*_?} = \mathsf{Blind}_{\rho(x^*)}(\widehat{x}^*)$;
   - the input bundle comes from random gates, in which case just sample uniform $r \in \mathbb{F}$ and sample $\widehat{x}_? = \mathsf{Blind}_{\rho(r)}(\mathsf{Enc}(r))$;
   - the input bundle is an output bundle of a functional gadget $\widehat{g}_{j'}$ for $j' < j$, in which case $\widehat{x}_?$ has already been output by a previous simulator as $\widehat{y_{j?}}$.
   In any case, $\widehat{x}_?$ is always available.
   (b) If some of the values of $\widehat{x}_?$ are $\bot$, set $\widehat{x}_? \leftarrow \bot$; otherwise, leave it unchanged. This is equivalent to convert the output of Blind into the output of Blind^*.
   (c) Let $y = g(x)$, where $x = \mathsf{Dec}(\widehat{x})$ and $\widehat{x}$ is the collection of the input values computed as above. Notice that, even if $\widehat{x}$ is not available to the experiment, x is always available: indeed, the experiment knows the input x^* and the random coins sampled so far, therefore is able to deterministically reconstruct x.
   (d) Probe $y_? \leftarrow \rho(y)$.
   (e) Run the simulator $(\Lambda_j, \widehat{y}_?) \leftarrow \mathsf{Sim}_{\widehat{g}_i}(\widehat{x}_?, y_?)$.
3. Output $\Lambda = \Lambda_1 || \ldots || \Lambda_{k^*}$.

We define the last hybrid experiment $\mathsf{Hyb}_0(x^*)$ as follows. Here we underline the differences between Hyb_1 and Hyb_0.

1. Run $\mathcal{C}(x^*)$ and sample $W_? := \rho(\mathbf{W}(x^*))$.
2. For every $j \in [k^*]$, compute $\Lambda_j, \widehat{y}_j$ as follows.
   (a) Let $\widehat{x}_?$ be possibly blinded the values on the input bundles of gadget $\widehat{g}_j$. Notice that, for every input bundle, there are only three possibilities:
   - the input bundle comes from input gates, in which case we set $\widehat{x}_? = \mathsf{Enc}(x)$ if the random probing on the original input x was successful and $\widehat{x}_? = \bot$ otherwise.
   - the input bundle comes from random gates, in which case just sample uniform $r \in \mathbb{F}$ and sample $\widehat{x}_? = \mathsf{Blind}_{\rho(r)}(\mathsf{Enc}(r))$;
   - the input bundle is an output bundle of a functional gadget $\widehat{g}_{j'}$ for $j' < j$, in which case $\widehat{x}_?$ has already been output by a previous simulator as $\widehat{y_{j?}}$.
   In any case, $\widehat{x}_?$ is always available.
   (b) If some of the values of $\widehat{x}_?$ are $\bot$, set $\widehat{x}_? \leftarrow \bot$; otherwise, leave it unchanged. This is equivalent to convert the output of Blind into the output of Blind^*.

(c) Let $y_?$ be the random probing of the output y of the original gate g_j, as already sampled in $W_?$.

(d) Run the simulator $(\Lambda_j, \widehat{y_?}) \leftarrow \mathsf{Sim}_{\widehat{g_j}}(\widehat{x_?}, y_?)$.

3. Output $\Lambda = \Lambda_1 || \ldots || \Lambda_{k^*}$.

Lemma 7. *Let x^* be any input to $\mathcal{C}$. Then, for every $i \in [k^*]$,*

$$\mathsf{Hyb}_0(x^*) \equiv \mathsf{Hyb}_1(x^*)$$

Proof. The only differences between the two hybrid experiments are when and how the random probing is sampled. In particular, Hyb_1 runs the transformed circuit $\widehat{\mathcal{C}}$, decodes the values on the wires and then samples random and average probing leakage. On the other hand, Hyb_0 runs the original circuit $\mathcal{C}$, computes the random probing and then only samples the average probing when needed, i.e., for the input bundles that are part of the input of the circuit or for the input bundles that come from random gates. Finally, the average probing samples in Hyb_0 are identically distributed to the ones of Hyb_1, since both are identically distributed to the samples in the real case. The lemma follows. □

Finally, notice that the only use that $\mathsf{Hyb}_0(x^*)$ makes of x^* is to compute the values on the wires of the original circuit, which is then only used to sample the random probing $W_? := \rho(\mathbf{W}(x^*))$. We can now extract this procedure outside the hybrid experiment and directly give the value $W_?$ to the experiment; the simulator is then defined as receiving the random probing $W_?$ from the wires and then running exactly as $\mathsf{Hyb}_0(x^*)$ from the second step on. Therefore, the following holds.

Corollary 8. *Let x^* be any input to $\mathcal{C}$. Then, for every $i \in [k^*]$,*

$$\mathsf{Hyb}_0(x^*) \equiv \mathsf{Sim}_{\mathcal{C}}(\rho(\mathbf{W}(x^*))).$$

By putting everything together, we are finally able to prove Theorem 2.

Proof. As observed at the beginning, $\mathsf{Hyb}_{k^*+1}(x^*)$ is just a syntactic change from $\mathsf{Leak}_{\mathcal{C}}(\mathsf{Enc}(x^*))$ and is, otherwise, identical. Hence:

$$
\begin{aligned}
\mathsf{Leak}_{\mathcal{C}}(\mathsf{Enc}(x^*)) &\equiv \mathsf{Hyb}_{k^*+1}(x^*) \\
&\equiv \mathsf{Hyb}_{k^*}(x^*) && \text{(By applying Lemma 6)} \\
&\equiv \mathsf{Hyb}_1(x^*) && \text{(By repeatedly applying Lemma 6)} \\
&\equiv \mathsf{Hyb}_0(x^*) && \text{(By applying Lemma 7)} \\
&\equiv \mathsf{Sim}_{\mathcal{C}}(\rho(\mathbf{W}(x^*))). && \text{(By applying Corollary 8)}
\end{aligned}
$$

This concludes the proof.

5 Conclusions and Open Problems

In this work, we presented the first generic compiler that compiles any ε-random probing resilient circuit $\mathcal{C}$ into a δ-average probing resilient circuit $\widehat{\mathcal{C}}$, as long as

$$35\delta < \varepsilon^2.$$

Our compiler takes a circuit $\mathcal{C}$ with W wires and G gates and produces a new circuit $\widehat{\mathcal{C}}$ with $W' \leq 2W + 27G$ wires and $G' \leq 22G$ gates. Notice that W' and G' are maximum when $\mathcal{C}$ only contains multiplication gates, and in practical settings, we will usually be below such bounds.

As an immediate application, we are able to achieve the first random-probing to noisy-leakage compiler where the loss in the noise parameter does not depend on the size of the underlying field. We briefly recall below the definition of noisy-leakage from [24] and the main result of [17].

Definition 5 ([24]). *Let $\varepsilon \in (0,1)$ be a parameter. A (randomized) function $\nu : \mathbb{F} \to \Omega$ is ε-noisy leakage if*

$$\Delta\left((\nu(\mathbf{x}), \mathbf{x}), (\nu(\mathbf{x}), \mathbf{x}')\right) \leq \varepsilon,$$

where $\mathbf{x}, \mathbf{x}'$ are uniform over $\mathbb{F}$.

Theorem 3 ([17]). *For every $\varepsilon \in (0,1)$, and every circuit $\mathcal{C}$, $\mathcal{C}$ is ε-average-probing to ε-noisy-leakage simulatable.*

In the above, we formalized the result of [17] using Definition 4. Notice that [17] does not use a compiler to transform the circuit $\mathcal{C}$, therefore the circuit is simulatable from $\mathcal{C}$ itself. The following corollary is an immediate consequence of the above and Theorem 2. It implies that circuits transformed by our compiler from Sect. 4 are δ-noisy secure, if the original circuit is secure against ϵ-random probing leakage for parameters ϵ and δ as given in the corollary below.

Corollary 9. *Let $\varepsilon, \delta \in (0,1)$ be parameters such that*

$$35\delta < \varepsilon^2.$$

Let $\mathcal{C}$ be any circuit and let $\widehat{\mathcal{C}}$ be the circuit transformed according to the compiler in Sect. 4. If $\mathcal{C}$ is ε-random-probing resilient, then $\widehat{\mathcal{C}}$ is δ-average-probing to δ-noisy-leakage simulatable.

One limitation of our current analysis is a tightness loss in the noise parameters. Concretely, if the circuit $\mathcal{C}$ is ϵ-random probing secure, then $\widehat{\mathcal{C}}$ is δ-noisy leakage resilient where $35\delta < \varepsilon^2$. The quadratic loss is a consequence of the fact that our gadget simulator in Sect. 3 only simulates the leakage when random-probing is successful on *all* the inputs of the gate in the original circuit. This happens with probability ε^2 for gates with 2 inputs. With our current techniques, this is somewhat inherent due to the nature of average-probing. In particular, the simulator cannot simulate the leakage in a consistent way by just receiving partial leakage from one of the inputs (e.g., because the simulator may incorrectly assume some values being on the wires that contradict previous leakage from the circuit). We leave it as an important open problem to further improve our result and eliminate the quadratic loss.

Acknowledgements. Stefan Dziembowski and Gianluca Brian were supported by an NCN Grant 2019/35/B/ST6/04138 and by the Copernicus Awards (agreement no. COP/01/ 2020). This work has been partially funded by the German Research Foundation (DFG) CRC 1119 CROSSING (project S7), the German Federal Ministry of Education and Research and the Hessen State Ministry for Higher Education, Research and the Arts within their joint support of the National Research Center for Applied Cybersecurity ATHENE, by the ERC Grant 101044770 (CRYPTOLAYER) and the Copernicus Award (INST 18989/419-1).

References

1. Ajtai, M.: Secure computation with information leaking to an adversary, pp. 715–724 (2011)
2. Ananth, P., Ishai, Y., Sahai, A.: Private circuits: a modular approach. In: Shacham, H., Boldyreva, A. (eds.) CRYPTO 2018. LNCS, vol. 10993, pp. 427–455. Springer, Cham (2018). https://doi.org/10.1007/978-3-319-96878-0_15
3. Andrychowicz, M., Dziembowski, S., Faust, S.: Circuit compilers with $O(1/\log(n))$ leakage rate. In: Fischlin, M., Coron, J.-S. (eds.) EUROCRYPT 2016. LNCS, vol. 9666, pp. 586–615. Springer, Heidelberg (2016). https://doi.org/10.1007/978-3-662-49896-5_21
4. Battistello, A., Coron, J.-S., Prouff, E., Zeitoun, R.: Horizontal side-channel attacks and countermeasures on the ISW masking scheme. In: Gierlichs, B., Poschmann, A.Y. (eds.) CHES 2016. LNCS, vol. 9813, pp. 23–39. Springer, Heidelberg (2016). https://doi.org/10.1007/978-3-662-53140-2_2
5. Béguinot, J., et al.: Removing the field size loss from Duc et al.'s conjectured bound for masked encodings. Cryptology ePrint Archive, Report 2022/1738 (2022). https://eprint.iacr.org/2022/1738
6. Belaïd, S., Mercadier, D., Rivain, M., Taleb, A.R.: IronMask: versatile verification of masking security, pp. 142–160 (2022)
7. Belaïd, S., Rivain, M., Taleb, A.R.: On the power of expansion: more efficient constructions in the random probing model. In: Canteaut, A., Standaert, F.-X. (eds.) EUROCRYPT 2021. LNCS, vol. 12697, pp. 313–343. Springer, Cham (2021). https://doi.org/10.1007/978-3-030-77886-6_11
8. Belaïd, S., Rivain, M., Taleb, A.R., Vergnaud, D.: Dynamic random probing expansion with quasi linear asymptotic complexity. In: Tibouchi, M., Wang, H. (eds.) ASIACRYPT 2021. LNCS, vol. 13091, pp. 157–188. Springer, Cham (2021). https://doi.org/10.1007/978-3-030-92075-3_6
9. Brian, G., Dziembowski, S., Faust, S.: From random probing to noisy leakages without field-size dependence. Cryptology ePrint Archive, Paper 2024/339 (2024). https://eprint.iacr.org/2024/339
10. Cassiers, G., Faust, S., Orlt, M., Standaert, F.-X.: Towards tight random probing security. In: Malkin, T., Peikert, C. (eds.) CRYPTO 2021. LNCS, vol. 12827, pp. 185–214. Springer, Cham (2021). https://doi.org/10.1007/978-3-030-84252-9_7

11. Cassiers, G., Standaert, F.-X.: Towards globally optimized masking: from low randomness to low noise rate **2019**(2), 162–198 (2019). https://tches.iacr.org/index.php/TCHES/article/view/7389

12. Chari, S., Jutla, C.S., Rao, J.R., Rohatgi, P.: Towards sound approaches to counteract power-analysis attacks. In: Wiener, M. (ed.) CRYPTO 1999. LNCS, vol. 1666, pp. 398–412. Springer, Heidelberg (1999). https://doi.org/10.1007/3-540-48405-1_26

13. Coron, J.-S., Greuet, A., Zeitoun, R.: Side-channel masking with pseudo-random generator. In: Canteaut, A., Ishai, Y. (eds.) EUROCRYPT 2020. LNCS, vol. 12107, pp. 342–375. Springer, Cham (2020). https://doi.org/10.1007/978-3-030-45727-3_12

14. Coron, J.-S., Rondepierre, F., Zeitoun, R.: High order masking of look-up tables with common shares **2018**(1):40–72 (2018). https://tches.iacr.org/index.php/TCHES/article/view/832

15. Duc, A., Dziembowski, S., Faust, S.: Unifying leakage models: from probing attacks to noisy leakage. In: Nguyen, P.Q., Oswald, E. (eds.) EUROCRYPT 2014. LNCS, vol. 8441, pp. 423–440. Springer, Heidelberg (2014). https://doi.org/10.1007/978-3-642-55220-5_24

16. Duc, A., Faust, S., Standaert, F.-X.: Making masking security proofs concrete (or how to evaluate the security of any leaking device), extended version **32**(4), 1263–1297 (2019)

17. Dziembowski, S., Faust, S., Skorski, M.: Noisy leakage revisited. In: Oswald, E., Fischlin, M. (eds.) EUROCRYPT 2015. LNCS, vol. 9057, pp. 159–188. Springer, Heidelberg (2015). https://doi.org/10.1007/978-3-662-46803-6_6

18. Goudarzi, D., Joux, A., Rivain, M.: How to securely compute with noisy leakage in quasilinear complexity. In: Peyrin, T., Galbraith, S. (eds.) ASIACRYPT 2018. LNCS, vol. 11273, pp. 547–574. Springer, Cham (2018). https://doi.org/10.1007/978-3-030-03329-3_19

19. Ishai, Y., Sahai, A., Wagner, D.: Private circuits: securing hardware against probing attacks. In: Boneh, D. (ed.) CRYPTO 2003. LNCS, vol. 2729, pp. 463–481. Springer, Heidelberg (2003). https://doi.org/10.1007/978-3-540-45146-4_27

20. Kocher, P.C.: Timing attacks on implementations of Diffie-Hellman, RSA, DSS, and other systems. In: Koblitz, N. (ed.) CRYPTO 1996. LNCS, vol. 1109, pp. 104–113. Springer, Heidelberg (1996). https://doi.org/10.1007/3-540-68697-5_9

21. Kocher, P.C., Jaffe, J., Jun, B.: Differential power analysis, pp. 388–397 (1999)

22. Maurer, U., Pietrzak, K., Renner, R.: Indistinguishability amplification. In: Menezes, A. (ed.) CRYPTO 2007. LNCS, vol. 4622, pp. 130–149. Springer, Heidelberg (2007). https://doi.org/10.1007/978-3-540-74143-5_8

23. Prest, T., Goudarzi, D., Martinelli, A., Passelègue, A.: Unifying leakage models on a Rényi Day. In: Boldyreva, A., Micciancio, D. (eds.) CRYPTO 2019. LNCS, vol. 11692, pp. 683–712. Springer, Cham (2019). https://doi.org/10.1007/978-3-030-26948-7_24

24. Prouff, E., Rivain, M.: Masking against side-channel attacks: a formal security proof. In: Johansson, T., Nguyen, P.Q. (eds.) EUROCRYPT 2013. LNCS, vol. 7881, pp. 142–159. Springer, Heidelberg (2013). https://doi.org/10.1007/978-3-642-38348-9_9

A Direct PRF Construction
from Kolmogorov Complexity

Yanyi Liu[1(✉)] and Rafael Pass[1,2]

[1] Cornell Tech, New York, USA
yl2866@cornell.edu
[2] Tel-Aviv University, Tel Aviv, Israel
rafaelp@tau.ac.il

Abstract. While classic results in the 1980s establish that one-way functions (OWF) imply the existence of pseudorandom generators (PRG) which in turn imply pseudorandom functions (PRF), the constructions (most notably the one from OWFs to PRGs) is complicated and inefficient.

Consequently, researchers have developed alternative *direct* constructions of PRFs from various different concrete hardness assumptions. In this work, we continue this thread of work and demonstrate the first direct construction of PRFs from average-case hardness of the time-bounded Kolmogorov complexity problem $MK^tP[s]$, where given a threshold, $s(\cdot)$, and a polynomial time-bound, $t(\cdot)$, $MK^tP[s]$ denotes the language consisting of strings x with t-bounded Kolmogorov complexity, $K^t(x)$, bounded by $s(|x|)$.

In more detail, we demonstrate a direct PRF construction with quasi-polynomial security from mild avg-case of hardness of $MK^tP[2^{O(\sqrt{\log n})}]$ w.r.t the uniform distribution. We note that by earlier results, this assumption is known to be equivalent to the existence of quasi-polynomially secure OWFs; as such, our results yield the first direct (quasi-polynomially secure) PRF construction from a natural hardness assumptions that also is known to be implied by (quasi-polynomially secure) PRFs.

Perhaps surprisingly, we show how to make use of the Nisan-Wigderson PRG construction to get a cryptographic, as opposed to a complexity-theoretic, PRG.

1 Introduction

Pseudorandom functions (PRFs), introduced by Goldwasser, Goldreich, and Micali [14] in the 1980s are one of the most important cryptographic primitives. Roughly speaking, a PRF is a family of efficiently computable functions

Y. Liu—Work done while visiting the Simons Institute (during the Meta-complexity program) and visiting University of Washington. Supported by a JP Morgan fellowship.
R. Pass—Supported in part by NSF Award CNS 2149305, AFOSR Award FA9550-18-1-0267, AFOSR Award FA9550-23-1-0387, ISF Grant No. 2338/23 and an Algorand Foundation award. This material is based upon work supported by DARPA under Agreement No. HR00110C0086. Any opinions, findings and conclusions or recommendations expressed in this material are those of the author(s) and do not necessarily reflect the views of the United States Government, DARPA, AFOSR or the Algorand Foundation.

M. Joye and G. Leander (Eds.): EUROCRYPT 2024, LNCS 14654, pp. 375–406, 2024.
https://doi.org/10.1007/978-3-031-58737-5_14

$\{f_z\}_{z\in\{0,1\}^*}$, where given a randomly sampled seed z, the outputs of $f_z(x)$ on (adversarially-selected) inputs x is indistinguishable from the outputs of a truly random function $F(x)$ (with respect to a computationally bounded machine). Most notably they are a central object in private-key cryptography: they give simple and direct constructions of private-key encryption, message authentication, and identification (between parties with shared keys) [13,15,34]. In addition, they have also found many other applications in cryptography, including resettable security [5], oblivious RAM [17] (and more), and also in computational complexity [45] and computational learning theory [51]; the reader is referred to a nice survey by Bogdanov and Rosen [4].

While classic results in the 1980s by Hastad, Impagliazzo, Levin and Luby [23] and Goldreich, Goldwasser and Micali [14] established that one-way functions (OWFs) imply the existence of pseudorandom generators (PRGs) [23] which in turn imply pseudorandom functions (PRFs) [14], the constructions (most notably the one from OWFs to PRGs) is complicated and inefficient. Although there has been great progress over the last decades in improving the construction of PRGs [19,20,25,50], the currently best constructions of [36] has a seed length $\omega(n^3/\log n)$ and requires calling the underlying OWFs $\omega(n^3/\log^2 n)$ times.

Direct Constructions of PRFs. Consequently, towards the goal of developing practical and provably secure PRF constructions, researchers have developed alternative *direct* constructions of PRFs from various different concrete hardness assumptions—most notably based on the Decisional Diffie-Hellman (DDH) assumption [38,39], the hardness of factoring Blum-integers [40], and the hardness of lattice problems [3].

In this work, we continue this thread of work and demonstrate the first direct constructions of PRFs from average-case hardness of the standard time-bounded Kolmogorov complexity problem $\mathsf{MK}^t\mathsf{P}[s]$ [1,2,22,28,29,46], where given a threshold, $s(\cdot)$, and a polynomial time-bound, $t(\cdot)$, $\mathsf{MK}^t\mathsf{P}[s]$ denotes the language consisting of strings x with t-bounded Kolmogorov complexity, $K^t(x)$, bounded by $s(|x|)$. In more detail, we demonstrate a direct PRF construction with *quasi-polynomial security* from mild average-case of hardness of $\mathsf{MK}^t\mathsf{P}[2^{\sqrt{\log n}}]$ w.r.t the uniform distribution.[1] We note that by earlier results, this assumption is known to be equivalent to the existence of quasi-polynomially secure OWFs; as such, our results yield the first direct (quasi-polynomially secure) PRF construction from a natural hardness assumption that also is known to be implied by PRFs.

To explain this result in more detail, let us first recall the notion of (time-bounded) Kolmogorov complexity, and the notion of (mild) average-case hardness that we rely on.

The $\mathsf{MK}^t\mathsf{P}$ Problem. Given a truth table $x \in \{0,1\}^n$ of a Boolean function, what is the size of the smallest "program" that computes x? This problem has fascinated researchers since the 1950 [48,52,53], and various variants of it have been considered depending on how the notion of a program is formalized.

---

[1] The threshold $2^{\sqrt{\log n}}$ is the inverse of $2^{\log^2 n} = n^{\log n}$.

For instance, when the notion of a program is taken to be circuits (e.g., with AND,OR,NOT gates), then it corresponds to the Minimum Circuit Size problem (MCSP) [27,48], and when the notion of a program is taken to be a time-bounded Turing machine, then it corresponds to the Minimum Time-Bounded Kolmogorov complexity problem (MK^{t}P) [1,2,22,28,29,46]. Our focus here is on the latter scenario. Given a string x describing a truth table, let $K^t(x)$ denote the t-bounded Kolmogorov complexity of x—that is, the length of the shortest string Π such that for every $i \in [n]$, $U(\Pi, i) = x_i$ within time $t(|\Pi|)$, where U is a fixed Universal Turing machine.[2]

Given a threshold, $s(\cdot)$, and a polynomial time-bound, $t(\cdot)$, let MK^{t}P$[s]$ denote the language consisting of strings x such that $K^t(x) \leq s(|x|)$; MK^{t}P$[s]$ is clearly in NP, but it is unknown whether it is NP-complete. In [30], Liu and Pass recently showed that when the threshold $s(\cdot)$ is "large" (more precisely, when $s(n) = n - c \log n$, for some constant c), then mild *average-case hardness* of this language w.r.t. the uniform distribution of instances is equivalent to the existence of one-way functions (OWF).[3]

Even more recently, a different work by Liu and Pass [31] demonstrated that when the threshold is smaller then an appropriate notion of average-case hardness of the problem characterizes quasi-polynomial or sub-exponential one-way functions (depending on the threshold). In more detail, when the threshold s is small, MK^{t}P$[s]$ is a sparse language so it can never the average-case hard w.r.t. the uniform distribution (simply saying NO succeeds with overwhelming probability). To deal with this issue, [31] thus argued that the right notion of average-case case hardness of a sparse language ought to *condition* on both YES and NO instances. In more detail, we refer to a language $L \subset \{0,1\}^*$ as $D(\cdot)$-dense if for all $n \in \mathbb{N}$, $|L_n| = D(n)$, where $L_n = L \cap \{0,1\}^n$. We say that a $D(\cdot)$-dense language L is $\alpha(\cdot)$ *hard-on-average* with respect to* $T(\cdot)$-*time attackers* ((T, α)-*HoA**) if for all probabilistic T-time heuristics $\mathcal{H}$, for all sufficiently large n, there exist $\mu \in \{0,1\}$ such that,

$$\Pr[x \leftarrow \{0,1\}^n : \mathcal{H}(x) = \mu \mid L(x) = \mu] < 1 - \alpha(n^*),$$

---

[2] There are many ways to define time-bounded Kolmogorov complexity. We here consider the "local compression" version—which corresponds to the above truth table compression problem—and where the running-time bound is a function of the length of the program. A different version of (time-bounded) Kolmogorov complexity instead considers the size of the shortest program that outputs the *whole* string x. This other notion refers to a "global compression" notion, but is less appealing from the point of view of truth table compression, as the running-time of the program can never be smaller than the length of the truth table x.

[3] Strictly speaking, [30] considered the "global compression" version of Kolmogorov complexity, but when the threshold is large, these notions are essentially equivalent, and the result from [30] directly applies also the "local compression" notion of Kolmogorov complexity considered here.

where $n^* = \log D(n)$. n^* is referred to as the *normalized input length*. In other words, there does not exist a T-time "heuristic" that decides L with probability $1 - \alpha(n^*)$ *conditioned* on YES (and NO) instances.[4]

[31] showed that for any $\delta > 0$, quasi-polynomially secure and subexponentially secure OWFs are characterized by $(n^\delta, O(1/n^3))$-average-case* hardness of $\mathsf{MK}^t\mathsf{P}[s]$ where the threshold are $s(n) = 2^{O(\sqrt{\log n})}$ and $s(n) = \text{poly} \log n$ respectively. Intriguingly, their result—following a literature on so-called *hardness magnification* [7–10,37,42–44] shows that it suffices to assume *sublinear* hardness of these problems to provide those characterizations (when the threshold is sublinear). While the original result of [31] only showed equivalence in the non-uniform regime, it was recently shown how to also establish an equivalence also in the uniform regime [33]; additionally, [33] also (implicitly) show that the equivalence still holds if the error parameter becomes larger—it is (sufficient and) also necessary to assume $(n^\delta, \frac{1}{n^\beta})$-average-case* hardness of $\mathsf{MK}^t\mathsf{P}[s]$ for any $\beta > 0$.

In more detail, focusing on quasi-polynomially secure OWFs, we have the following. We say that a function f is a *quasi-polynomially secure* OWF if there exists a constant $c > 0$ such that f is $(T, 1/T)$-one-way for $T(n) = 2^{c \log^2 n}$.

Theorem 1 ([31,33]). *For any polynomial $t(n) \geq (1 + \varepsilon)n, \varepsilon > 0$, any $\beta > 0$, $\delta > 0$, the following are equivalent:*

- *Quasi-polynomially secure (resp non-uniformly quasi-polynomially secure) OWFs exist.*
- *There exists a constant $c > 0$, $s(n) = 2^{c\sqrt{\log n}}$, such that $\mathsf{MK}^t\mathsf{P}[s]$ is $(n^\delta, \frac{1}{n^\beta})$-HoA* (resp non-uniformly HoA*).*

Our Main Result. Our main result is a direct construction of quasi-polynomially secure PRFs (with input domain $\{0,1\}^{\Omega(\log^2 k)}$ where k is the seed length) from the average-case* of hardness of $\mathsf{MK}^t\mathsf{P}[2^{O(\sqrt{\log n})}]$ w.r.t the uniform distribution and with respect to attackers of size n^3. (Formally proved in Sect. 5.3.)

Theorem 2 (Main Theorem). *Consider some threshold $s(n) = 2^{c\sqrt{\log n}}$, $c > 0$, polynomial $t(n) \geq (1 + \varepsilon)n, \varepsilon > 0$, and any $\beta > 0$. Assume that $\mathsf{MK}^t\mathsf{P}[s]$ is $(n^3, \frac{1}{n^\beta})$-HoA* (resp. non-uniformly $(n^3, \frac{1}{n^\beta})$-HoA*). Then, there exists a quasi-polynomially secure (resp. non-uniformly quasi-polynomially secure) PRF $h : 1^\lambda \times \{0,1\}^{\tilde{O}(\lambda^{1+\beta})} \times \{0,1\}^{\Omega(\log^2 \lambda)} \rightarrow \{0,1\}$.*

---

[4] The reason the error probability, α is a function of the logarithm of the number of YES-instances (i.e., the "normalized" input length, n^*, as opposed to just n (i.e., the logarithm of the number of instances) is to ensure that this notion meaningfully relaxes the notion of a one-sided heuristic, also for very sparse languages. If it wasn't, then a $1/n$-heuristic* could not make *any* mistakes on YES instances when the languages contains less than n YES-instances.

As noted above (see Theorem 1), the above assumption is equivalent to the existence of quasi-polynomially secure OWFs. Thus, Theorem 2 follows from Theorem 1 and the results of [14,23] (which show how to get a quasi-polynomially secure PRF from any quasi-polynomially secure PRG, with an explicit reduction). The point here is that we present a *direct* proof of this result, without passing through the result of [23], and thus as a result the construction becomes much simpler and more efficient. See the paragraph below discussing the efficiency of the construction.

As far as we know, our results thus yield the first direct PRF construction from a natural hardness assumption that also is known to be implied by PRFs.

A Non-Black-Box Security Reduction. We highlight that whereas we provide an explicit security reduction when proving the security of our PRF, the reduction is *non-black box*. In particular, we are relying on the fact that the PRF attacker is computationally bounded and has a small description. For this reason, the proof for the uniform case does not directly imply security in the non-uniform setting and we need to work a bit harder to demonstrate security also in the non-uniform setting. Roughly speaking, the non-black box nature of the reduction stems from the fact that we will use the attacker to "compress" the instance string x (in order to determine if its K^t complexity is small).

On the PRF Domain Size. We highlight that our PRF only has a $O(\log^2 \lambda)$ bit input domain where λ is the security parameter. Such (small domain) PRFs suffices for typical applications of PRFs [13] (e.g., to CPA-secure private-key encryption [18]). Of course we can always extend the domain using the standard tree construction [13] (but at a loss in efficiency). Alternatively, we note that if we consider hardness of $\mathsf{MK}^t\mathsf{P}[s]$ with an even smaller threshold $s(n) = \mathsf{poly}\log(n)$ (which is equivalent to subexponentially secure OWFs), then the construction directly extends to give a PRF with a λ^ϵ-bit input domain; see Theorem 18 for a generalized version of Theorem 2, Corollary 19, and Corollary 20.

On the Efficiency on the PRFs. We present an explicit reduction from an attacker that breaks the security of our PRF to breaking $\mathsf{MK}^t\mathsf{P}[s]$ on a particular instance $x \in \{0,1\}^n$. The efficiency of the PRF is a function of the time-bound t and the length of the threshold $\lambda = s(n)$ (which roughly equals the "normalized input length" of $\mathsf{MK}^t\mathsf{P}[s]$). In particular, its running time is $\tilde{O}(\lambda^\beta) \cdot t(\lambda)$ where β is any constant > 0, and the seed length is $\tilde{O}(\lambda^{1+\beta})$. At first it would seem that the efficiency of the construction is "too good to be true"—since $\lambda = s(n)$ is *sublinear* in the length n of the instance $x \in \{0,1\}^n$ we reduce security from. The point, however, is that the $\mathsf{MK}^t\mathsf{P}[s]$ problem can be trivially decided in time $2^{s(n)}$ (and is generally conjectured to be hard for time $2^{\Omega(s(n))}$—this is referred to as the *Perebor Conjecture* [48])—so the "fair" way to measure efficiency is in terms of the threshold s (and not the instance length n), and this is why we let the security parameter be defined as $\lambda = s(n)$ (instead of defining it as n).

Comparisons with Existing PRFs. Let us briefly compare our PRF with existing constructions. We first focus our attention on a "baseline" PRF, in which we apply the generic transformation of [14,23] (from OWFs to PRFs) to the

OWF construction of [31]. Given that both (our and the baseline) constructions base their security on the hardness of $\mathsf{MK}^t\mathsf{P}[s]$, we here consider a linear running time bound $t(n) = O(n)$, and $(n^3, \frac{1}{n^\beta})$-average-case* hardness of $\mathsf{MK}^t\mathsf{P}[s]$ for some arbitrarily small constant $\beta > 0$. In this setting, the [31] OWF has both the running time and the seed length of $\tilde{O}(\lambda^{1+\beta})$. However, recall that even the start-of-the-art OWF-to-PRG construction [36] incurs a $\tilde{O}(\lambda^3)$ blow up in both the seed length and the running time, whereas our PRF construction achieves runtime $\tilde{O}(\lambda^{1+\beta})$ and seed length $\tilde{O}(\lambda^{1+\beta})$.

We also provide comparisons with the PRFs constructed in [3,38], and [40]. We highlight that these constructions are based on hardness assumptions that are not known to be also implied by PRFs. Nevertheless, we still give an efficiency comparison, the results of which are summarized in Table 1.

Table 1. Efficiency comparisons with existing PRFs. (All assumptions are quasi-polynomially hard, $\beta > 0$ is an arbitrarily small constant.)

	Seed Length	Runtime	Input Length
LWE [3]	$\tilde{O}(\lambda^2)$	$\tilde{O}(\lambda^2)$	$\log^2 \lambda$
R-LWE [3]	$\tilde{O}(\lambda)$	$\tilde{O}(\lambda)$	$\log^2 \lambda$
DDH [38], Factoring [40]	$O(\lambda)$	$\tilde{O}(\lambda)$	$\log^2 \lambda$
DDH [38], Factoring [38]	$O(\lambda)$	$\tilde{O}(\lambda^2)$	λ
Ours	$\tilde{O}(\lambda^{1+\beta})$	$\tilde{O}(\lambda^{1+\beta})$	$\log^2 \lambda$

Notice that [3] only gets PRF with input length $\log^2 \lambda$ (rather than λ), just as we do, from quasi-poly assumptions.

We, as well as [3], can always use standard domain extension (incurring an overhead of λ in terms of running time) to extend the domain to λ bits. In essence, all of the constructions (except for the LWE one) have the same efficiency. Ours is β worse in the exponent for any arbitrary small $\beta > 0$, and the LWE based construction is strictly worse, losing a factor of λ.

1.1   Construction Overview

We here provide a brief outline of the construction. Towards this, let us first briefly review the Nisan-Wigderson PRG [41].

The NW Construction. The construction NW starts off with a function f that is assumed to be average-case hard to compute (with probability better than $1/2 + \delta$) over random inputs $\in \{0,1\}^\ell$, and is parameterized by a collection of sets of indexes $\mathcal{I} = \{I_i\}_{i\in[m]}$ referred to as the *designs*; these design sets I_i, $|I_i| = \ell$ are efficiently computable given i and in their simplest implementation involve evaluating a polynomial "indexed" by i—more details on this construction below.[5]

---

[5] This polynomial-based design construction appeared in [41], and is used to obtain the so-called "low-end" derandomization. There are many other constructions of

Next, given a seed y, to compute the bit i of output of the PRG NW, we simply apply f to the "projected" input y_{I_i} defined as y restricted to the indexes in I_i:

$$\mathrm{NW}^f_{\mathcal{I}}(y) = f(y_{I_1}) \ldots f(y_{I_m})$$

See Fig. 1 for an illustrative example of the NW construction (in which we will employ the design construction that we describe in the next paragraph).

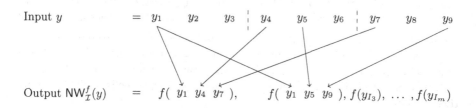

Fig. 1. An illustrative example of the NW construction with function $f : \{0,1\}^\ell \to \{0,1\}$ and designs $\mathcal{I}$. In this example, $\ell = q = 3$. The design construction is based on polynomials, where $I_1 = \{1,4,7\}$ corresponds to the polynomial $p_1(x) = 0$, and $I_2 = \{1,5,9\}$ corresponds to the polynomial $p_2(x) = x$.

For concreteness, let us recall the design construction of [41] that we will rely on. Let ℓ denote the input length to f, and let q denote a prime (or the smallest power of 2) such that $q \geq \ell$. We consider designs with universe $[d]$ where $d = \ell q$. The seed length of the NW generator, $|y|$, will also be picked to be d. We interpret each number $j \in [d]$ as a tuple in $[\ell] \times [q]$. Each set $I_i \subseteq [d]$ is defined to be the set $\{j_k = (k, p(k))\}_{k \in [\ell]}$ where p is the i-th polynomial of $\mathbf{F}_q$ (according to some canonical enumeration of all polynomials in $\mathbf{F}_q$, in a degree increasing order). Notice that each I_i contains ℓ elements, and thus the length of the projected seed y_{I_i} is equal to the input length of f.

The NW Reconstruction Procedure. It will be useful to review the security reduction of the NW PRG. Roughly speaking, [41] show that any distinguisher D (of the output of the PRG and a random string) with advantage ε, can be used to approximate f with probability $1/2 + O(\varepsilon/m)$ using a small (but larger than $m \cdot m^{1/\log \ell}$) bits of non-uniform advice z. This is referred to as the NW reconstruction procedure. (In particular, if f cannot be approximated by programs of size $|D| + |z|$ this yields a contradiction.)

The NW Construction as a PRF. Let us highlight one particular feature of the NW PRG when using the *above* design construction (based on polynomials). Given the seed y and the output index i, we can efficiently—i.e., in time polynomial in $(|i|, \ell)$ rather than in (i, ℓ)—compute the set I_i. Besides this, computing the ith output bit of the generator only needs one call to the underlying

---

designs, but, for our purposes, the polynomial-based one is useful as it is efficient in $|i|$.

hard function f. In other words, the output bits of the NW PRG are *locally computable*. As a consequence, if we are able to show that the above generator actually is a PRG with superpolynomial stretch (and f is efficient), then it actually also yields a PRF; this will be the approach that we will rely on.

Our PRF. Consider some running time bound $t(n) \geq (1+\varepsilon')n$, $\varepsilon' > 0$, threshold function $s(n) = 2^{\sqrt{\log n}}$, and hardness parameter $\alpha(\lambda) = 1/\lambda^\beta$. We construct a PRF $h : \{0,1\}^{\tilde{O}(\lambda^{1+\beta})} \times \{0,1\}^{\Omega(\log^2 \lambda)} \to \{0,1\}$ whose security can be based on α-average-case* hardness of $\mathsf{MK}^t\mathsf{P}[s]$ of input length n such that $s(n) = \lambda$.[6] To simplify notation, we here abuse the notation and specify h rather as a PRG of the form $h : \{0,1\}^{\tilde{O}(\lambda^{1+\beta})} \to \{0,1\}^{n=2^{\log^2 \lambda}}$, but note that due to our use of the NW PRG, each bit of the output h is locally computable (i.e., efficiently as a function of the seed and the index i) so this actually yields the desired PRF.

The construction of the (PRG-representation of) h proceeds in the following three steps.

- We start by appealing to the [30,31] OWF construction. Given a seed $\Pi' \in \{0,1\}^{\lambda+1}$, and an input $i \in \{0,1\}^{\log n}$, the function f removes all '0' from the end of Π' (if any), and removes an extra '1' from the end.[7] Let Π denote the remaining string. f simply outputs the bit produced by Π after running on input i for $t(|\Pi|)$ steps. In more detail,

$$f(\Pi', i) = U(\Pi(i), 1^{t(|\Pi|)})$$

  where U is the universal Turing machine fixed in the definition of K^t.
- Next, relying on the Nisan-Wigderson generator, we define the function $g(\Pi', y)$ as

$$g(\Pi', y) = \mathsf{NW}_\mathcal{I}^{f(\Pi', \cdot)}(y)$$

  where $\Pi' \in \{0,1\}^{\lambda+1}$, $f(\Pi', \cdot)$ is a function $\{0,1\}^{\log n} \to \{0,1\}$, $y \in \{0,1\}^d$, $d = O(\log^2 n) = O(\log^4 \lambda)$, and $\mathcal{I}$ is the polynomial-based design as introduced above.[8] The output size of the NW generator is set to be $m = n^\varepsilon = 2^{\varepsilon \log^2 \lambda}$ (where $\varepsilon = 1/8$).

  In more detail, g divides its seed into Π' and y, instantiates the NW generator with hard function $f(\Pi', \cdot)$, and simply computes the NW generator on seed y. The seed length of g is $|\Pi'| + |y| = (\lambda + 1) + O(\log^4 \lambda) = O(\lambda)$.
- Finally, we amplify the security of g, by considering the function h that takes the XOR of g on many independent seed. In more detail, h is defined as

$$h(\Pi_1', y_1, \ldots, \Pi_\gamma', y_\gamma) = g(\Pi_1', y_1) \oplus \ldots \oplus g(\Pi_\gamma', y_\gamma)$$

---

[6] In this proof overview, we assume that n is a power of 2 for simplicity.

[7] The [30] construction was slightly different; the above modified version has a slightly tighter analysis and shaves $\log \lambda$ bits in the input length.

[8] The $O(\log^2 n) = O(\log^4 \lambda)$ seed length of the PRG comes from our choice of designs. We note that there are explicitly computable designs that support our use of the NW PRG with only $O(\log n)$ seed length. See [21] and [11, Lemma A.2]. It may be that those designs lead to a more practical construction.

where $\gamma = \log n/\alpha = \lambda^\beta \log^2 \lambda$.

Note that the seed length of h is $O(\lambda)\cdot\gamma \leq O(\lambda^{1+\beta} \log^2 \lambda)$, and the output size will be $n^\varepsilon = 2^{\varepsilon \log^2 \lambda}$ (so its corresponding PRF has input domain $\{0,1\}^{\Omega(\log^2 \lambda)}$). Also notice that the running time of our PRF is $O(t(\lambda) \cdot \lambda^\beta \log^2 \lambda)$. (The reader is refer to Sect. 5.2 for a more detailed presentation of our PRF.)

We remark that there are two aspects of the construction that a-priori seem strange:

- In the derandomization literature, NW generators are used to fool attackers with smaller running time than the time needed to compute the hard function, whereas we are dealing with attackers that are more powerful than what is required to run the construction;
- The above PRG construction (without the amplification step), is very similar to the derandom-ization-style PRG[9] constructions based on the hardness of time-bounded Kolmogorov complexity problems appearing in [32]. These constructions, however, just as most more recent NW generators [26,47] are instantiated with a hard function encoded by error-correcting codes (ECCs) in order to make sure the reconstruction procedure is able to actually compress the input (since the "plain" NW reconstruction procedure only shows how the function can be computed with non-trivial probability). Note that using ECCs would not work in our setting as to get a PRF—we would need the ECC to be locally encodable, and such ECC cannot exist.

Both of the above differences mean that we cannot rely on simply the "standard" NW proof. However, we shall show that since we are starting off with average-case hardness of a *particular* hard function (i.e., based on $\mathsf{MK}^t\mathsf{P}[s]$), we are able to overcome these issues.

1.2 Proof Overview

We briefly explain why the above construction is secure, assuming α-average-case* hardness of $\mathsf{MK}^t\mathsf{P}[s]$ where $\alpha(\lambda) = 1/\lambda^\beta$ and $s(n) = 2^{\sqrt{\log n}}$. The proof will proceed in two steps. First, we will show that the function g above (i.e., applying just the plain NW generator on the sampled function) satisfies a weak PRG property. Next, we show that the general XOR construction used in the final PRG h amplifies such a weak PRG into a standard one. Finally, as noted above, since each bit is locally computable, the PRG actually yields a PRF.

Let us start by describing the notion of a weak family of PRGs and how they can be amplified into a standard PRG using the construction employed in function h.

Weak Families of PRGs. We refer to a family of functions $\{g_j\}_{j\in\{0,1\}^\lambda}$ as a α-*weak family of PRGs* if for every efficient distinguisher D, it holds that with probability $\alpha(\lambda)$ over $j \leftarrow \mathcal{U}_\lambda$, D distinguishes $g_j(\mathcal{U}_d)$ from uniform with at most negligible probability.

---

[9] In fact, hitting set generators.

In essence, with reasonable probability over the index, we get a full-fledged (strong) PRG. We remark that this notion is different from previous notions of weak PRGs [12,35] in the aspect that we consider a family of functions, whereas these other definitions consider a single PRG whose output is only weakly indistinguishable from random. A weak family of PRGs also yields such a weak PRG when the expansion is long enough so as to recover the index (which indeed will be the case for us). The issue is that the weak PRG it gives has indistinguishability gap of $1 - \alpha$, but the results of [12,35] only apply when the indistinguishability gap is smaller than $1/2$. Consequently, we directly leverage the fact that the once a "good" index of the family has been sampled, the PRG is actually fully indistinguishable from random. Relying on this, we next present a general proof that such weak families of PRGs can be amplified into a standard PRG[10] using the XOR construction and while relying on proof techniques similar to those used in Yao's classic hardness amplification theorem [16,54].

Showing that g is a Weak Family of PRGs. The central part of our paper is demonstrating that the function g can be viewed as a $\Omega(\alpha)$-weak family of PRGs assuming α-average-case* hardness of $\mathsf{MK}^t\mathsf{P}[s]$. In more detail, we define a weak family of PRGs $g'_{\Pi'}(y) = g(\Pi', y)$, and assume for contradiction that there exists a distinguisher that breaks its security for $1 - \alpha/O(1)$ fraction of index Π' of the family. We aim to use this distinguisher to decide $\mathsf{MK}^t\mathsf{P}[s]$ on average (conditioned on both YES- and NO-instances). The general approach will combine ideas from [6,24,30–32]. Roughly speaking, to decide an instance x, we view x as a hard function to use in the NW generator (as in [24,32], following [6]), except that we do not rely on an ECC as done by [24,32]), and feed the output of this generator to the attacker. If the attacker succeeds in distinguishing, we answer YES and otherwise NO. The key point is that, intuitively, if the distinguisher succeeds, then by the NW reconstruction argument, we can get a short description of program that approximates x with non-trivial probability, and intuitively, most NO instances do not have such short approximate description. Let us make two observations here: (1) the reason we do not need to rely on an ECC is exactly the fact that NO instances do not have even short *approximate* descriptions (as we shall soon argue), (2) the use of the NW reconstruction algorithm (similar to its use in [6,24,32]) is what makes the reduction non-black box since we are relying on the fact that the distinguisher has a small description.

We next need to argue that on random YES instances, the distinguisher actually works; this will rely on a probabilistic domination argument from [30,31] and it is here that we require the original distinguisher (breaking the PRGs g') to succeed for a large fraction of indices.

In more detail, assume for contradiction that there exists a distinguisher D that breaks the $(\alpha/O(1))$-weak family of PRGs g'; that is, over at least a $1 - \alpha/O(1)$ fraction of the indices Π', D breaks $g_{\Pi'}$ with a non-negligible advantage.

---

[10] For the ease of presentation, we only consider standard (polynomially secure) PRGs and negligible distinguishing advantage. Our proof will also show that the PRG (after amplification) is quasi-polynomially secure, as desired.

Notice that we can assume D breaks each such $g_{\Pi'}$ with advantage at least $\frac{1}{2^{\varepsilon \log^2 \lambda}}$ (which is negligible in λ) and also notice that $\frac{1}{2^{\varepsilon \log^2 \lambda}} = \frac{1}{n^\varepsilon}$. We will use D to decide $\mathsf{MK}^t\mathsf{P}[s]$ with probability at least $1 - \alpha$ conditioned on both YES instances and NO instances. Let us assume for simplicity in this proof overview that D is a deterministic uniform distinguisher. (In the actual proof, we will deal with probabilistic distinguishers, or even non-uniform algorithms.)

First note that by the security (of the reconstruction procedure) of the Nisan-Wigderson generator [41] (see also [6,24,32]), if x is a random NO instance, then with very high probability (much larger than $1 - \alpha$) over x, D cannot succeed in distinguishing between $\mathcal{U}_{n^\varepsilon}$ and $\mathsf{NW}^x(\mathcal{U}_d)$—the reason for this is that if D could do so, then the Nisan-Wigderson reconstruction procedure would approximate x over at least a $1/2 + 1/n^{2\varepsilon}$ fraction of coordinates (but in a randomized local fashion). In addition, the reconstruction procedure only requires $O(n^{2\varepsilon})$ bits as advice, so we have managed to approximately compress x. Observe that the distribution of a random NO instance is statistically close to the uniform distribution, so it remains to show that such an approximate local compression is impossible for almost all of random strings $x \in \{0,1\}^n$.

Random Strings Cannot be Approximately Compressed. It is well-known that by a standard counting argument, most of random strings cannot be exactly compressed (and thus have high Kolmogorov-complexity). Proving that they cannot be locally $(1/2 + 1/n^{2\varepsilon})$-approximated (by randomized programs of size $n^{2\varepsilon}$) requires a slightly more delicate argument. We will show that a (fixed) randomized program Π can only $(1/2 + 1/n^{2\varepsilon})$-approximate a uniform random string x with very small probability; the proof is then concluded using a union bound over all programs (of size $n^{2\varepsilon}$).

Let P denote the set of strings $x \in \{0,1\}^n$ such that given x, the randomized program Π on input a random index $i \in [n]$ (with fresh randomness) computes x_i with probability $\geq 1/2 + 1/n^{2\varepsilon}$. Our goal is to show that $|P|$ is very small.

Towards this, the key idea is to derandomize Π, and next simply argue that most random string will be far from the output of the deterministic version of Π. At first it would seem that we can simply fix the best random tape for Π; the issue, however, is that Π may succeed to compute different bits i with different random tapes. To overcome this issue, we use an averaging argument to show that for each $x \in P$, there exists at least a $\frac{1}{2n^{2\varepsilon}}$ fraction of random tapes r such that the output of the deterministic machine Π_r (the program Π with its random tape fixed to r) is $(1/2 + 1/(2n^{2\varepsilon}))$-close to x. From this it follows that over random x, r, the probability that Π_r produces a string that is $(1/2 + 1/(2n^{2\varepsilon}))$-close to x is at least

$$\frac{1}{2n^{2\varepsilon}} \cdot \frac{|P|}{2^n}$$

We are now ready to derandomize Π. Observe that if we fix the random tape of Π to a string r^* that maximizes the above probability (over a random x), we have that the output of Π_{r^*} is $(1/2 + 1/(2n^{2\varepsilon}))$-close to x is at least

$$\frac{1}{2n^{2\varepsilon}} \cdot \frac{|P|}{2^n}$$

over random $x \in \{0, 1\}^n$.

Next, notice that the deterministic program Π_{r^*} will output a fixed string, but by a Chernoff bound, it follows that a *random* string is $(1/2 + 1/n^{2\varepsilon})$-close to it with probability at most

$$e^{-\Omega(n^{1-4\varepsilon})}$$

(To see this, note that each bit of the random string matches the fixed string independently with probability $1/2$, so the distance between them is simply the sum of n independent random variables with expectation $1/2$.) Therefore, we have that

$$\frac{|P|}{2^n} \leq 2n^{2\varepsilon} e^{-\Omega(n^{1-4\varepsilon})}$$

Finally, by taking a Union bound over all randomized program of size at most $n^{2\varepsilon}$, we conclude that the probability that a random string x can be approximately compressed is at most

$$2^{n^{2\varepsilon}} \cdot 2n^{2\varepsilon} e^{-\Omega(n^{1-4\varepsilon})} = 2n^{2\varepsilon} \cdot 2^{-\Omega(n^{1-4\varepsilon})+n^{2\varepsilon}}$$

In addition, the above probability will be negligible when $2\varepsilon < 1 - 4\varepsilon$ (which will hold since $\varepsilon = 1/8$).

Why the Distinguisher D Works on YES Instances. On the other hand, when x is a random YES instance of $\mathsf{MK}^t\mathsf{P}[s]$, we claim that D will manage to distinguish between $\mathsf{NW}^x(\mathcal{U}_d)$ and $\mathcal{U}_{n^\varepsilon}$, for at least a $1 - \alpha$ faction of x. Observe that if x is a YES instance, then x will appear as the truth table of the function $f(\Pi', \cdot)$ for some $\Pi' \in \{0, 1\}^{\leq \lambda}$ (e.g., the K^t-witness of x), and thus $\mathsf{NW}^x(\mathcal{U}_d)$ will always be one PRG inside the family of PRGs that g' defines. Since D has to break a $1 - \alpha/O(1)$ fraction of PRGs in the family, it would seem that D has to distinguish between $\mathsf{NW}^x(\mathcal{U}_d)$ and $\mathcal{U}_{n^\varepsilon}$ for at least a $1 - \alpha$ fraction of x. However, the distribution of a random YES instance is very different from how the truth table of $f(\Pi', \cdot)$ is distributed in our construction of g. So we have no guarantee how the distinguisher D performs if we sample x from the random-YES distribution. To deal with this issue, we rely on an argument in [30, 31] to show that the $f(\Pi', \cdot)$-truth-table distribution "dominates" the random-YES distribution, and therefore if D succeeds with probability $1 - \alpha/O(1)$ over the $f(\Pi', \cdot)$-truth-table distribution, D must succeed also with probability $1 - (\alpha/O(1)) \cdot O(1) \geq 1 - \alpha$ over the random-YES distribution. This concludes that we can always decide $\mathsf{MK}^t\mathsf{P}[s]$ with probability $\geq 1 - \alpha$ conditioned on both YES and NO instances, and concludes the construction of a $(\alpha/O(1))$-weak family of PRGs.

2   Preliminaries

For any two random variables X and Y defined over some set $\mathcal{V}$, we let $\mathsf{SD}(X, Y) = \max_{T \subseteq \mathcal{V}} |\Pr[X \in T] - \Pr[Y \in T]| = \frac{1}{2} \sum_{v \in \mathcal{V}} |\Pr[X = v] - \Pr[Y = v]|$ denote the *statistical distance* between X and Y. It will be helpful to note that the expression is maximixed when the "distinguisher" $T = \{v : \Pr[X = v] > \Pr[Y = v]\}$.

Let $\mathcal{U}_n$ denote the uniform distribution over $\{0,1\}^n$, for any $n \in \mathbb{N}$.

2.1 Time-Bounded Kolmogorov Complexity

We define the notion of t-time-bounded Kolmogorov complexity that we rely on. We consider some universal Turing machine U that can emulate any Turing machine M with polynomial overhead. The universal Turing machine U receives as input a description/program $\Pi \in \{0,1\}^* = (M, w)$ where M is a Turing machine and $w \in \{0,1\}^*$ is an input to M; we let $U(\Pi(i), 1^{t(|\Pi|)})$ denote the output of $M(w,i)$ when emulated on U for $t(|\Pi|)$ steps.

Definition 3. *Let U be a universal Turing machine and $t(\cdot)$ be a polynomial. Define*

$$K^t(x) = \min_{\Pi \in \{0,1\}^*} \{|\Pi| : \forall i \in [|x|], U(\Pi(i), 1^{t(|\Pi|)}) = x_i\}.$$

We remark that the notion of time-bounded Kolmogorov complexity has been defined in a lot of different ways [2,28,29,46,48]; the definition we consider here is the "local compression" version [31] where the program Π is required to efficiently output each individual bit x_i of the string x, given i as input.

Let $\mathsf{MK}^t\mathsf{P}[s(n)]$ be a language consisting of strings x with K^t-complexity at most $s(|x|)$. We recall the following fact about (time-bounded) Kolmogorov complexity.

Fact 4 ([31]) *There exists a constant c such that for every polynomial $t(n) \geq (1+\varepsilon)n, \varepsilon > 0$, the following holds:*

(1) For every $x \in \{0,1\}^*$, $K^t(x) \leq |x| + c$;
(2) For every $n \in \mathbb{N}$, every function $0 < s(n) < n$, $2^{\lfloor s(n) \rfloor - c} \leq |\mathsf{MK}^t\mathsf{P}[s(n)] \cap \{0,1\}^n| \leq 2^{\lfloor s(n) \rfloor + 1}$.

2.2 Average-Case* Hardness

We introduce the notion of average-case* hardness, defined in [31]. On a high-level, average-case* hardness provides a meaningful notion of average-case hardness w.r.t. two-sided error heuristics for *sparse* languages. Before describing the definition, let us first define the density of a language: We say that a language $L \subset \{0,1\}^*$ is $D(\cdot)$-dense if for all $n \in \mathbb{N}$, $|L_n| = D(n)$, where $L_n = L \cap \{0,1\}^n$. Now we are ready to define the notion of average-case* hardness.

Definition 5 (Average-case* Hardness). *We say that a $D(\cdot)$-dense language L is $\alpha(\cdot)$ hard-on-average* (resp non-uniformly $\alpha(\cdot)$ hard-on-average*) with respect to $T(\cdot)$-time attackers ((T, α)-HoA* (resp non-uniformly (T, α)-HoA*)) if for all probabilistic T-time (resp non-uniform T-time) heuristics $\mathcal{H}$, for all sufficiently large n, there exist $\mu \in \{0,1\}$ such that,*

$$\Pr[x \leftarrow \{0,1\}^n : \mathcal{H}(x) = \mu \mid L(x) = \mu] < 1 - \alpha(n^*),$$

where $n^* = \log D(n)$. n^* is referred to as the normalized input length.

In other words, there does not exist a T-time "heuristic*" that decides L with probability $1 - \alpha(n^*)$ *conditioned* on YES (and NO) instances. We refer the reader to [31] for how average-case* hardness meaningfully generalizes (and lies between) the two standard notions of average-case hardness (errorless and 2-sided error average-case hardness).

In this work, we are interested in the average-case* hardness of $\mathsf{MK}^t\mathsf{P}[s]$. We note that the normalized input length n^* of $\mathsf{MK}^t\mathsf{P}[s]$ on input length n is roughly as large as the threshold $s(n)$.

Claim 1. *Let c be the constant as in Fact 4. For any polynomial $t(\cdot)$, any function $0 < s(n) < n$, for any input length n, it follows that $s(n) - c \leq n^* \leq s(n) + 1$.*

Proof: This claim immediately follows from Fact 4.   ∎

2.3   One-Way Functions and $\mathsf{MK}^t\mathsf{P}[s]$

We recall the standard definitions of one-way functions.

Definition 6. *Let $f : \{0,1\}^* \to \{0,1\}^*$ be a polynomial-time computable function. f is said to be a (T, ε)-one-way function $((T, \varepsilon)$-OWF) (resp non-uniformly secure (T, ε)-OWF) if for any probabilistic $T(n)$-time (resp non-uniform $T(n)$-time) algorithm $\mathcal{A}$, for all sufficiently large $n \in \mathbb{N}$,*

$$\Pr[x \leftarrow \{0,1\}^n; y = f(x) : \mathcal{A}(1^n, y) \in f^{-1}(f(x))] < \varepsilon(n)$$

In addition, we say that f is *quasi-polynomially secure* if it is $(T, 1/T)$-one-way for some constant $c > 0$ and some function $T(n) = 2^{c \log^2 n}$. We say that f is *subexponentially secure* if it is $(T, 1/T)$-one-way for some constant $\varepsilon > 0$ and some function $T(n) = 2^{n^\varepsilon}$.

As mentioned in the introduction, [31] showed that OWFs are characterized by average-case* hardness of $\mathsf{MK}^t\mathsf{P}[s]$ and how small the threshold is determines how hard (or secure) the OWF we obtain. As also mentioned, while the original result of [31] only showed equivalence in the non-uniform regime, it was recently shown how to also establish an equivalence also in the uniform regime [33]; additionally, [33] also (implicitly) show that the equivalence still holds if the error parameter becomes larger—it is (sufficient and) also necessary to assume $(n^\delta, \frac{1}{n^\beta})$-average-case* hardness of $\mathsf{MK}^t\mathsf{P}[s]$ for any $\beta > 0$. We here formally state their results.

Theorem 7 ([31,33]) *For any polynomial $t(n) \geq (1 + \varepsilon)n, \varepsilon > 0$, any $\beta > 0$, any $\delta > 0$, the following statements hold:*

- *Quasi-polynomially secure (resp non-uniformly quasi-polynomially secure) OWFs exist iff there exists a constant $c > 0$, $s(n) = 2^{c\sqrt{\log n}}$, such that $\mathsf{MK}^t\mathsf{P}[s]$ is $(n^\delta, \frac{1}{n^\beta})$-HoA* (resp non-uniformly HoA*).*
- *Subexponentially secure (resp non-uniformly subexponentially secure) OWFs exist iff there exists a constant $c > 0$, $s(n) = \log^c(n)$, such that $\mathsf{MK}^t\mathsf{P}[s]$ is $(n^\delta, \frac{1}{n^\beta})$-HoA* (resp non-uniformly HoA*).*

2.4   Pseudorandom Generators and Pseudorandom Functions

We recall the standard definitions of pseudorandom generators (PRGs).

Definition 8. *Let* $g : 1^\lambda \times \{0,1\}^{d(\lambda)} \rightarrow \{0,1\}^{m(\lambda)}$ *be a function. g is said to be a $(T(\cdot), \varepsilon(\cdot))$-pseudorandom generator $((T, \varepsilon)$-PRG) (resp non-uniformly secure (T, ε)-PRG) if for any probabilistic $T(\cdot)$-time (resp non-uniform $T(\cdot)$-time) algorithm $\mathcal{A}$ (whose running time is $T(\cdot)$ in the length of its first input), for all sufficiently large λ,*

$$|\Pr[x \leftarrow \{0,1\}^{d(\lambda)} : \mathcal{A}(1^\lambda, g(x)) = 1] - \Pr[y \leftarrow \{0,1\}^{m(\lambda)} : \mathcal{A}(1^\lambda, y) = 1]| \leq \varepsilon(\lambda).$$

In addition, we say that g is locally-computable if each bit of the output of g can be computed in time $\mathsf{poly}(d(\lambda), \log m(\lambda))$.

We note that to simplify notations, we relax the efficiency requirement on g, since we also consider locally computable PRGs that output quasi-polynomially (or sub-exponentially) many bits (where it will be guaranteed that each bit of the output can be computed efficiently) (and such functions are inherently inefficient due to its output length).

We turn to introducing pseudorandom functions.

Definition 9. *Let* $f : 1^\lambda \times \{0,1\}^{d(\lambda)} \times \{0,1\}^{k(\lambda)} \rightarrow \{0,1\}$ *be a polynomial-time computable function. f is said to be a $(T(\cdot), \varepsilon(\cdot))$-pseudorandom function (T, ε)-PRF (resp non-uniformly secure (T, ε)-PRF) if for any probabilistic $T(\cdot)$-time (resp non-uniform T-time) algorithm $\mathcal{A}$, for all sufficiently large n,*

$$|\Pr[x \leftarrow \{0,1\}^{d(\lambda)} : \mathcal{A}^{f(x, \cdot)}(1^\lambda) = 1] - \Pr[f' \leftarrow \mathcal{F} : \mathcal{A}^{f'}(1^\lambda) = 1]| \leq \varepsilon(n)$$

where $\mathcal{F} = \{f' : \{0,1\}^{k(\lambda)} \rightarrow \{0,1\}\}$.

In addition, we say that f is *quasi-polynomially secure* if there exists a constant $c > 0$, $T(\lambda) = 2^{c \log^2 \lambda}$, f is a $(T, 1/T)$-PRF. We say that f is *subexponentially secure* if there exists a constant $\varepsilon > 0$, $T(\lambda) = 2^{\lambda^\varepsilon}$, f is a $(T, 1/T)$-PRF.

3   Weak Family of PRGs and Security Amplification

In this section, we introduce the notion of weak family of PRGs and prove a security amplification lemma for such PRGs.

Roughly speaking, a weak family of PRGs $\{g'_j(1^\lambda)\}_{j \in \{0,1\}^{d_1(\lambda)}}$ is a family of functions such that for any distinguisher D, there is at least some fraction of functions in the family whose output is pseudorandom. In addition, we say that the weak family has *running time* $t(\lambda)$ if there exists a function g such that $g(1^\lambda, j, y) = g'_j(1^\lambda, y)$ and $g(1^\lambda, j, y)$ runs in time $t(\lambda)$.

Definition 10. *We say that a family of functions* $g' : \{g'_j(1^\lambda) : \{0,1\}^{d_2(\lambda)} \rightarrow \{0,1\}^{m(\lambda)}\}_{j \in \{0,1\}^{d_1(\lambda)}}$ *is a α-weak family of (T, ε)-pseudorandom generator (α-weak family of (T, ε)-PRGs) if for all $T(\lambda)$-time distinguisher D (such that D*

runs in time $T(\lambda)$ when its first input is 1^λ), for all sufficiently large $n \in \mathbb{N}$, it holds that

$$\Pr[j \leftarrow \{0,1\}^{d_1(\lambda)} : \mathsf{Adv}_{D,\lambda}(g'_j(\mathcal{U}_{d_2(\lambda)}), \mathcal{U}_{m(\lambda)}) \le \varepsilon(\lambda)] \ge \alpha(\lambda)$$

where for any random variables X, Y, $\mathsf{Adv}_{D,\lambda}(X,Y)$ is defined to be

$$\mathsf{Adv}_{D,\lambda}(X,Y) \overset{\mathrm{def}}{=} |\Pr[r_1 \leftarrow X : D(1^\lambda, r_1) = 1] - \Pr[r_2 \leftarrow Y : D(1^\lambda, r_2) = 1]|$$

We refer to j as the index *and y as the* seed.

We say that g' is non-uniformly secure if the above holds for all non-uniform $T(\lambda)$-time distinguisher.

Notice that we will also consider PRGs whose output length is super polynomial in its seed length. Although such PRGs are inherently not efficiently computable, we will require them to be locally computable.

We show that weak family of PRGs can be amplified to obtain a full-fledged PRG (as long as PRGs in the weak family are expanding enough).

Lemma 11. *Let $\{g'_j(1^\lambda) : \{0,1\}^{d_2(\lambda)} \to \{0,1\}^{m(\lambda)}\}_{j \in \{0,1\}^{d_1(\lambda)}}$ be a α-weak family of (T, ε)-PRG with running time $t(\lambda)$. Let $\gamma(\lambda)$ be a (time-constructible) parallel repetition parameter, and let $h : 1^\lambda \times \{0,1\}^{(d_1(\lambda)+d_2(\lambda))\gamma(\lambda)} \to \{0,1\}^{m(\lambda)}$ be the xor of γ-fold repetition of g':*

$$h(j_1, y_1, \ldots, j_\gamma, y_\gamma) = g'_{j_1}(y_1) \oplus \ldots \oplus g'_{j_\gamma}(y_\gamma)$$

It holds that h is a $(T'(\lambda), \varepsilon'(\lambda))$-PRG where $T'(\lambda) = T(\lambda) - \gamma(\lambda)t(\lambda)$, $\varepsilon'(\lambda) = 2\max\{(1-\alpha(\lambda))^{\gamma(\lambda)}, \varepsilon(\lambda) \cdot \gamma(\lambda)\}$. In addition, the lemma also holds in the non-uniform setting.

We defer the proof of Lemma 11 to the full version due to space limit.

4 Unapproximability of Random Strings for Small Programs

It is well known that most random strings cannot be (exactly) produced by small programs (and thus have high Kolmogorov complexity). In this section, we show that most random strings cannot even be approximated with slightly non-trivial probability by small programs. We say that a program approximates a string with probability $\frac{1}{2} + \delta$ if over a random index i (and randomness of the program), the program on input i outputs the bit on the i-th coordinate of the string with probability $\frac{1}{2} + \delta$.

We are going to prove that most random strings of length n cannot be approximated with probability $\ge 1/2 + 1/n^\varepsilon$ by programs of size n^δ.

Lemma 12. *For any constants $\varepsilon, \delta > 0$, $\delta < 1 - 2\varepsilon$, there exists constants n_0 such that for all $n \ge n_0$, with probability at least*

$$1 - n^\varepsilon \cdot 2^{-n^{1-2\varepsilon}/2 + n^\delta + 2}$$

over a uniform random string $x \in \{0,1\}^n$, it holds that no (probabilistic) program Π (that always terminates on every random tape) of description length $\leq n^\delta$ can approximate the string x with probability $1/2 + 1/n^\varepsilon$; that is

$$\Pr[i \leftarrow [n] : \Pi(i) = x_i] \geq \frac{1}{2} + \frac{1}{n^\varepsilon}$$

where the probability is also taken over the internal randomness of Π.

Proof: Let Π_r denote the deterministic machine of Π with random tape fixed to be r. Since Π always terminates, let t_Π denote the running time of the program Π. Fix any such program $\Pi \in \{0,1\}^*$, $|\Pi| \leq n^\delta$, we claim that there is no more than a $n^\varepsilon 2^{-n^{1-2\varepsilon}/2+1}$ fraction of strings $x \in \{0,1\}^n$ such that Π approximates x with probability $\frac{1}{2} + \frac{1}{n^\varepsilon}$. Formally, we claim that

$$\Pr\left[x \leftarrow \{0,1\}^n : \Pr_{r \leftarrow \{0,1\}^{t_\Pi}, i \leftarrow [n]}[\Pi_r(i) = x_i] \geq \frac{1}{2} + \frac{1}{n^\varepsilon}\right] \leq n^\varepsilon 2^{-n^{1-2\varepsilon}/2+1} \quad (1)$$

If this holds, by taking a union bound over all Π, we have that

$$\Pr\left[x \leftarrow \{0,1\}^n : \exists \Pi, |\Pi| \leq n^\delta,\right.$$

$$\left.\Pr_{r \leftarrow \{0,1\}^{t_\Pi}, i \leftarrow [n]}[\Pi_r(i) = x_i] \geq \frac{1}{2} + \frac{1}{n^\varepsilon}\right] \leq n^\varepsilon 2^{-n^{1-2\varepsilon}/2+n^\delta+2}$$

since (by a standard counting argument) there are at most $2^{n^\delta+1}$ such programs Π, which proves the lemma.

We proceed to proving Inequality 1. Notice that if Π approximates x with probability $\frac{1}{2} + \frac{1}{n^\varepsilon}$, by a standard averaging argument, there are at least a $\frac{1}{2n^\varepsilon}$ fraction of r such that the deterministic machine Π_r approximate x with probability $\frac{1}{2} + \frac{1}{2n^\varepsilon}$. Thus, the LHS of Inequality 1 is at most

$$\Pr\left[x \leftarrow \{0,1\}^n : \Pr_{r \leftarrow \{0,1\}^{t_\Pi}}\left[\Pr_{i \leftarrow [n]}[\Pi_r(i) = x_i] \geq \frac{1}{2} + \frac{1}{2n^\varepsilon}\right] \geq \frac{1}{2n^\varepsilon}\right]$$

$$\leq 2n^\varepsilon \Pr\left[x \leftarrow \{0,1\}^n, r \leftarrow \{0,1\}^{t_\Pi} : \Pr_{i \leftarrow [n]}[\Pi_r(i) = x_i] \geq \frac{1}{2} + \frac{1}{2n^\varepsilon}\right]$$

$$\leq 2n^\varepsilon \Pr\left[x \leftarrow \{0,1\}^n : \Pr_{i \leftarrow [n]}[\Pi_{r^*}(i) = x_i] \geq \frac{1}{2} + \frac{1}{2n^\varepsilon}\right] \quad (2)$$

where r^* is picked to be the random tape that maximizes the probability. Notice that the deterministic program Π_{r^*} can output only a single string. Let z_i be the random variable such that $z_i = 1$ iff $\Pi_{r^*}(i) = x_i$. Since x is a random string, the random variables z_i are independently distributed with mean $1/2$. It follows that

$$\Pr\left[x \leftarrow \{0,1\}^n : \Pr_{i \leftarrow [n]}[\Pi_{r^*}(i) = x_i] \geq \frac{1}{2} + \frac{1}{2n^\varepsilon}\right]$$

$$= \Pr\left[x \leftarrow \{0,1\}^n : \sum_{i \in [n]} z_i \geq \frac{n}{2} + \frac{n}{2n^\varepsilon}\right]$$

$$\leq e^{-n^{1-2\varepsilon}/2} \leq 2^{-n^{1-2\varepsilon}/2}$$

where the (second) last step follows from the Chernoff bound. Plugging this into the Inequality 2, the claim follows. ∎

5   PRF Construction from $\mathsf{MK}^t\mathsf{P}$

In this section, we show how to construct a PRF from hardness of $\mathsf{MK}^t\mathsf{P}[s]$.

5.1   Tools

Let us briefly introduce the technical tools needed in our construction. We start by recalling the construction of the Nisan-Wigderson (NW) PRG [41].

Definition 13 (NW generator [41]). *Let $\mathcal{I} = (I_1, \ldots, I_m)$ be a family of subsets of $[d]$ with each $|I_j| = \ell$ and let $f : \{0,1\}^\ell \to \{0,1\}$ be a function. The $(\mathcal{I}, f)$-NW generator is the function $\mathsf{NW}_{\mathcal{I}}^f : \{0,1\}^d \to \{0,1\}^m$ that takes any string $y \in \{0,1\}^d$ as a seed and outputs*

$$\mathsf{NW}_{\mathcal{I}}^f(y) = f(y_{I_1}) \ldots f(y_{I_m})$$

where for any set $I_j = \{i_1, \ldots, i_\ell\} \subseteq [d]$, any $y = y_1 y_2 \ldots y_d$, $y_{I_j} \overset{\text{def}}{=} y_{i_1} y_{i_2} \ldots y_{i_\ell}$ denotes the "projection" of string y onto coordinates in I_j.

The core ingredient of the Nisan-Wigderson construction is a combinatorial design which will be used as the family of subsets in a NW generator.

Definition 14 (Combinatorial designs [41]). *A family of sets $\mathcal{I} = \{I_1, \ldots, I_m\} \subseteq [d]$ is said to be a (d, ℓ, κ)-design if for every $i \in [m]$, $|I_i| = \ell$, and for every $j \in [m], j \neq i, |I_i \cap I_j| \leq \kappa$.*

We rely on the following explicit design generation algorithm.

Definition 15 (Explicit design generation [41]). *Let DesignNWGen be the following algorithms. On input $\ell, \kappa, i \in \mathbb{N}$ such that $\kappa < \ell, 1 \leq i \leq \ell^\kappa$, let q be the smallest power of 2 such that $q \geq \ell$. The algorithm DesignNWGen will output a set $I \subseteq [d]$ such that $|I| = \ell$, where $d = \ell q$. The algorithm proceeds as follows:*

- *Let $p(\cdot)$ be the i-th polynomial on $\mathbf{F}_q$ of degree κ (with respect to the canonical enumeration of all polynomials of degree κ on $\mathbf{F}_q$).*

– *Consider each number in $[d] = [\ell \times q]$ as a pair of numbers in $[\ell] \times [q]$. The set I will be defined to be*

$$I = \{(a, p(a)) \mid a \in [\ell]\}$$

where we abuse the notation and view a as also a field element in $\mathbf{F}_q$.

Recall that the above construction gives us a good combinatorial design.

Lemma 16 ([41]). *For any $\ell, \kappa, m \in \mathbb{N}$, $m \leq \ell^\kappa$, let $\mathsf{DesignNWGen}$ be the algorithm and $d \in \mathbb{N}$ as in Definition 15. Let $\mathcal{I} = \{I_i = \mathsf{DesignNWGen}(\ell, \kappa, i)\}_{i \in [m]}$. It holds that $\mathcal{I}$ is a (d, ℓ, κ)-design.*

The following version of the reconstruction theorem will be useful for us.

Lemma 17 (Implicit in [26,41], explicit in [32]; see also [49]). *There exists a PPT algorithm $\mathsf{NWRecon}$ such that the following conditions hold.*

– *Input: the truth table of a function $f : \{0,1\}^\ell \to \{0,1\}$, a (d, ℓ, κ)-design $\mathcal{I} = \{I_1, \dots, I_m\}$, and a distinguishing gap parameter $1^{\varepsilon^{-1}}$.*
– *Given oracle access to a (probabilistic) oracle $D \subseteq \{0,1\}^m$ such that*

$$\left| \Pr[y \leftarrow \{0,1\}^d : D(\mathsf{NW}^f_\mathcal{I}(y)) = 1] - \Pr[w \leftarrow \{0,1\}^m : D(w) = 1] \right| \geq \varepsilon.$$

– *Output: a (deterministic) program M of description length $\leq m \cdot 2^\kappa + m + d + O(\log d)$ such that*

$$\Pr[p \leftarrow [2^\ell] : \Pi(p) = f(p)] \geq \frac{1}{2} + \frac{\varepsilon}{2m}$$

where $\Pi = M^D(\mathcal{I})$ and the probability is also taken over the internal randomness of D.

5.2   The PRF Construction

We present our PRF construction from the average-case* hardness of $\mathsf{MK}^t\mathsf{P}$. Consider any (monotonically increasing) polynomial $t(\cdot)$, $t(n) \geq (1 + \varepsilon)n$, $\varepsilon > 0$.

Let λ be a program size parameter (which will also serve as a security parameter in the construction), $k = k(\lambda)$ denote the PRF input length parameter, and let $\gamma = \gamma(\lambda)$ be a parallel repetition parameter. To base the security of our construction on the $\alpha(\cdot)$-average-case* hardness of $\mathsf{MK}^t\mathsf{P}[s]$, we state the concrete choices of the parameters: We consider input length n such that $s(n) = \lambda$, and we pick $k = 1/8 \log n$, $\gamma = O(\log n / \alpha(\lambda))$.

Our goal is to construct a PRF with input domain $\{0,1\}^k$. (Towards this, we will be needing a Nisan-Widgerson PRG of output length $m = 2^k$.) The construction relies on the following ingredients. (We refer the reader to Sect. 5.1 for definitions of the technical tools used in this construction.)

- We will rely on the following decoding procedure Dec that maps any string $\Pi' \in \{0,1\}^*$ to a string $\Pi \in \{0,1\}^{<|\Pi'|}$. Π is obtained by removing all '0' in the end of Π' (if any), and then removing an additional '1'.
- We define a function f that receives a seed $\Pi' \in \{0,1\}^{\lambda+1}$ and an input $i \in \{0,1\}^{k'}$, computes $\Pi = \text{Dec}(\Pi')$ and interprets it as a program, runs the program Π on input i for $t(|\Pi|)$ steps, and outputs what the program outputs, where k' is picked to be $8k$. Formally,

$$f(\Pi', i) = U(\Pi(i), 1^{t(|\Pi|)})$$

where U is the universal Turing machine we fixed in the definition of K^t.
- We will be needing a combinatorial design to instantiate a Nisan-Wigderson PRG. Let $\ell = k'$, $\kappa = k$, $m = 2^k$. For each $i \in [2^k]$, let I_i be the set generated by DesignNWGen on input ℓ, κ, i. Let

$$\mathcal{I} = (I_1, I_2, \dots, I_m)$$

And note that $\mathcal{I}$ will be a (d, ℓ, κ)-design (by Lemma 16) where $d = \ell q$ and q is the smallest power of 2 such that $q \geq \ell$. Also notice that DesignNWGen on input ℓ, κ will be able to generate at most ℓ^κ sets, and we here need 2^k sets. Due to our choice of parameters, it holds that $\ell^\kappa \geq 2^\kappa = 2^k = m$.
- Define $g(\Pi', y)$ as the Nisan-Wigderson generator instantiated with the function $f(\Pi', \cdot)$ and the design $\mathcal{I}$. In more detail, for any seed $\Pi' \in \{0,1\}^{\lambda+1}$, $y \in \{0,1\}^d$, $g(\Pi', y)$ is defined as

$$g(\Pi', y) = \text{NW}_{\mathcal{I}}^{f(\Pi', \cdot)}(y)$$

And note that the output size is m. Moreover, we define a family of function $\{g'_{\Pi'} \stackrel{\text{def}}{=} g(\Pi', \cdot)\}_{\Pi' \in \{0,1\}^{\lambda+1}}$ where we simply view Π' as an index (that indices a NW generator) and y as the seed of $g'_{\Pi'}$.

Now we are ready to describe our PRF construction.

- The PRF construction h is defined as a function $h : \{0,1\}^{(\lambda+1+d)\gamma} \times \{0,1\}^k \to \{0,1\}$.
- h receives as the seed a string $z = (\Pi'_1, y_1, \dots, \Pi'_\gamma, y_\gamma)$ of length $(\lambda+1+d)\gamma$, where for each $j \in [\gamma]$, Π'_j is of length $\lambda + 1$ and each y_j is of length d.
- On input $i \in \{0,1\}^k$, the output of h is defined to be

$$h(z, i) = g(\Pi'_1, y_1)[i] \oplus \dots \oplus g(\Pi'_\gamma, y_\gamma)[i]$$

where $g(\Pi'_j, y_j)[i]$ denote the i-th bit of $g(\Pi'_j, y_j)$, for any $j \in [\gamma]$.

The seed length of the construction is $(\lambda + 1 + d)\gamma \leq (\lambda + O(k^2)) \cdot \gamma$. We next analyze the running time of our construction. f_Π emulates the program Π for $t(|\Pi|)$ steps, so f_Π runs in time $O(t(|\Pi|)) \leq O(t(\lambda))$ (since t is monotonically increasing). To compute $g(\Pi', y)$, for each $i \in [2^k]$, we need to invoke DesignNWGen on input (ℓ, k, i), which runs in time $O(\ell^2) = O(k^2)$, and we also need to compute $f(\Pi', y_{I_i})$, which runs in time $O(t(\lambda))$. Thus, $g(\Pi', y)$ takes $O(2^k(t(\lambda) + \ell^2))$.

In order to analyze the running time of h, we notice that $g(\Pi', y)$ can be computed *locally* – on each index $i \in [2^k]$, $g(\Pi', y)[i]$ can be computed in time $O(t(\lambda) + \ell^2)$. $h(z, i)$ will take the xor of γ independent instances of $g(\Pi', y)[i]$. Thus, the running time of h is $O((t(\lambda) + \ell^2)\gamma)$.

5.3 Security of the PRF Construction

Theorem 18. *Consider any (monotonically increasing) polynomial $t(n) \geq (1 + \varepsilon)n$, $\varepsilon > 0$, any threshold function $s(n) = n^{o(1)}$, and its inverse $n_s(\cdot) = s^{-1}(\cdot)$, and any hardness parameter $\alpha(n) = \frac{1}{n^\beta}$, $\beta > 0$. Assume $\mathsf{MK}^t\mathsf{P}[s(n)]$ is (n^3, α)-HoA* (resp non-uniformly (n^3, α)-HoA*).*

Then, there exist constants $\gamma_0 > 0, \delta > 0$ such that for parameters $n' = n_s(\lambda)$, $k(\lambda) = 1/8 \log n'$, $\gamma(\lambda) = \gamma_0 \cdot \log n'/\alpha(\lambda)$, it holds that the function $h : 1^\lambda \times \{0,1\}^{(\lambda+1+2\log^2 n')\gamma} \times \{0,1\}^{k(\lambda)} \rightarrow \{0,1\}$ (constructed in Sect. 5.2) is a $(n'^\delta, \frac{1}{n'^\delta})$-PRF (resp non-uniformly secure $(n'^\delta, \frac{1}{n'^\delta})$-PRF).

Notice that there are two immediate corollaries of Theorem 18, by considering threshold $s(n) = 2^{O(\sqrt{\log n})}$ (from which we obtain Corollary 19, where $n' = 2^{\Omega(\log^2 \lambda)}$, and the assumption is equivalent to quasi-polynomially secure OWFs; the PRF domain is $\{0,1\}^{\Omega(\log^2 \lambda)}$) and threshold $s(n) = \text{poly}\log(n)$ (from which we obtain Corollary 20, where $n' = 2^{\lambda^{1/c}}$, and the assumption is equivalent to subexponentially secure OWFs; the PRF domain is $\{0,1\}^{\lambda^{1/c}}$). The reader is referred to Sect. 2.3 for equivalence between OWFs and average-case hardness of $\mathsf{MK}^t\mathsf{P}[s]$.

Corollary 19 (PRF with input length $\Omega(\log^2 \lambda)$). *Consider a threshold function $s(n) = 2^{\delta\sqrt{\log n}}$, $\delta > 0$, polynomial $t(n) \geq (1 + \varepsilon)n$, $\varepsilon > 0$, and any $\beta > 0$. Assume that $\mathsf{MK}^t\mathsf{P}[s]$ is $(n^3, \frac{1}{n^\beta})$-HoA* (resp. non-uniformly $(n^3, \frac{1}{n^\beta})$-HoA*).*

Then, the function $h : 1^\lambda \times \{0,1\}^{\tilde{O}(\lambda^{1+\beta})} \times \{0,1\}^{\log^2 \lambda/(8\delta)} \rightarrow \{0,1\}$ (constructed in Sect. 5.2) is a quasi-polynomially secure (resp. non-uniformly quasi-polynomially secure) PRF.

Corollary 20 (PRF with input length $\Omega(\lambda^{1/c})$). *Consider a threshold function $s(n) = \log^c n$, $c > 2$, polynomial $t(n) \geq (1 + \varepsilon)n$, $\varepsilon > 0$, and any $\beta > 0$. Assume that $\mathsf{MK}^t\mathsf{P}[s]$ is $(n^3, \frac{1}{n^\beta})$-HoA* (resp. non-uniformly $(n^3, \frac{1}{n^\beta})$-HoA*).*

Then, the function $h : 1^\lambda \times \{0,1\}^{\tilde{O}(\lambda^{1+\beta+1/c})} \times \{0,1\}^{\lambda^{1/c}/8} \rightarrow \{0,1\}$ (constructed in Sect. 5.2) is a sub-exponentially secure (resp. non-uniformly subexponentially secure) PRF.

We proceed to proving the Theorem 18. In what follows, we consider any polynomial $t(n) \geq (1 + \varepsilon)n$, $\varepsilon > 0$, any threshold function $s(\cdot)$ (with its inverse denoted by $n_s(\cdot) = s^{-1}(\cdot)$) such that $s(n) = n^{o(1)}$, and any hardness parameter $\alpha(n) = \frac{1}{n^\beta}$, $\beta > 0$. We will show that h is a PRF assuming hardness of $\mathsf{MK}^t\mathsf{P}[s]$.

Switching Distributions. Recall that the α-average-case* hardness of $\mathsf{MK}^t\mathsf{P}[s]$ considers hardness of $\mathsf{MK}^t\mathsf{P}[s]$ over the uniform distribution (conditioned on both YES and NO instances), whereas our PRF security game concerns the performance of the distinguisher over the pseudorandom function distribution vs. its performance over the random function distribution. We start by showing that our hardness assumption implies hardness of $\mathsf{MK}^t\mathsf{P}[s]$ over distributions that are easier to work with.

Let us first introduce the distributions that are needed in our proof. We will be needing the notion of (t, s)-universal distribution (ensemble) $\{D_{\mathsf{univ},n}\}_{n \in \mathbb{N}}$, defined as follows.[11] $D_{\mathsf{univ},n}$ will pick a uniform random string $\Pi \in \{\{0, 1\}^{\leq s(n)} \cup \epsilon\}$[12], and interprets it as a program. $D_{\mathsf{univ},n}$ will output $x \in \{0, 1\}^n$, where each x_i, $i \in [n]$, is the bit produced by running the program Π on input i after $t(|\Pi|)$ steps. Formally, $x_i = U(\Pi(i), 1^{t(|\Pi|)})$ where U is the universal Turing machine we consider. The other distribution we need is the uniform distribution.

We proceed to introducing the notion of average-case* hardness with respect to two distributions, $\mathcal{D}_Y$ and $\mathcal{D}_N$, defined similarly to Definition 5 but considering more general distributions. Roughly speaking, this requires no attacker can simultaneously output 1 with high probability over $\mathcal{D}_Y$ and output 0 over $\mathcal{D}_N$.

Definition 21 (Average-case* Hardness w.r.t. $\mathcal{D}_Y$ and $\mathcal{D}_N$). *We say that a $D(\cdot)$-dense language L is $\alpha(\cdot)$ hard-on-average* for T-time attackers with respect to $\mathcal{D}_Y = \{D_{Y,n}\}_{n \in \mathbb{N}}$ and $\mathcal{D}_N = \{D_{N,n}\}_{n \in \mathbb{N}}$ ((T, α)-HoA* w.r.t. $\mathcal{D}_Y$ and $\mathcal{D}_N$) (resp non-uniformly (T, α)-HoA* w.r.t. $\mathcal{D}_Y$ and $\mathcal{D}_N$) if for all probabilistic T-time (resp non-uniform T-time) heuristics $\mathcal{H}$, for all sufficiently large n, it holds that either*

$$\Pr[x \leftarrow D_{Y,n} : \mathcal{H}(x) = 1] < 1 - \alpha(n^*),$$

or

$$\Pr[x \leftarrow D_{N,n} : \mathcal{H}(x) = 0] < 1 - \alpha(n^*).$$

where $n^* = \log D(n)$. n^* is referred to as the normalized input length.

We will show that average-case* hardness of $\mathsf{MK}^t\mathsf{P}[s]$ over uniform distribution implies average-case* hardness of $\mathsf{MK}^t\mathsf{P}[s]$ over the distributions that we are interested in.

Lemma 22. *There exists a constant $c' > 0$ such that for any threshold function $s(n) \leq n/10$, any polynomial $t(n) \geq (1 + \varepsilon)n$, $\varepsilon > 0$, any hardness parameter $\alpha(\lambda) = \frac{1}{\lambda^\beta}$, $\beta > 0$, the following holds.*

Assume that $\mathsf{MK}^t\mathsf{P}[s]$ is (T, α)-HoA. Then, $\mathsf{MK}^t\mathsf{P}[s]$ is (T, α')-HoA* w.r.t. the (t, s)-universal distribution and the uniform distribution where $\alpha' = \alpha/c'$. Moreover, the lemma also holds in the non-uniform setting.*

---

[11] Note that there are many ways of defining the universal distribution, and we here consider the definition that is most relevant to us.

[12] For technical reason, we also consider the empty string ϵ.

Proof: Let $c' = 2^{c+1}$ be a constant where c is the constant as in Fact 4. Let $\alpha'(n) = \alpha(n)/c'$. For any input length n of $\mathsf{MK}^t\mathsf{P}[s]$, let n^* be the "normalized input length". Assume for contradiction that there exists a T-time heuristic* H such that H breaks the $(T, \alpha/c')$-HoA* of $\mathsf{MK}^t\mathsf{P}[s]$ w.r.t. the universal distribution and the uniform distribution; that is, for infinitely many $n \in \mathbb{N}$, the following two conditions hold simultaneously: (1) H will output 1 with probability at least $1 - \alpha'(n^*)$ over $D_{\mathsf{univ},n}$ and (2) H will output 0 with probability at least $1 - \alpha'(n^*)$ over $\mathcal{U}_n$. We will show that the attacker H will also break the (T, α) average-case* hardness of $\mathsf{MK}^t\mathsf{P}[s]$. Fix some sufficiently large $n \in \mathbb{N}$ such that our heuristic* H succeeds on inputs of length n.

We first show that H will output 1 with probability at least $1 - \alpha(n^*)$ over a uniform random YES instance $\in \mathsf{MK}^t\mathsf{P}[s]$. Suppose not, and we have that H fails (to output 1) with probability $> \alpha(n^*)$. By Fact 4, there are at least $2^{s(n)-c}$ YES instances in $\mathsf{MK}^t\mathsf{P}[s]$. Therefore, for any $x \in \mathsf{MK}^t\mathsf{P}[s] \cap \{0,1\}^n$, with probability at most

$$\frac{1}{2^{s(n)-c}}$$

a random YES instance will hit x. On the other hand, since $x \in \mathsf{MK}^t\mathsf{P}[s]$, there exists a program Π, $|\Pi| \leq s(n)$, such that on input i, Π will output x_i within time $t(|\Pi|)$, for each $i \in [n]$. It follows that x will be sampled with probability at least

$$\frac{1}{2^{s(n)+1}}$$

in the universal distribution (since the universal distribution will pick a random program of length $\leq s(n)$ and there are $2^{s(n)+1}$ such programs (including the empty string); x will be sampled from the distribution when the program Π is picked). Thus, H must also fail over the universal distribution with probability at least

$$\Pr[x \leftarrow D_{\mathsf{univ},n} : H(x) \neq 1]$$
$$= \sum_{x \in \mathsf{MK}^t\mathsf{P}[s]} \Pr[D_{\mathsf{univ},n} = x] \cdot \Pr[H(x) \neq 1]$$
$$\geq \sum_{x \in \mathsf{MK}^t\mathsf{P}[s]} \frac{1}{2^{c+1}} \frac{1}{2^{s(n)-c}} \Pr[H(x) \neq 1]$$
$$\geq \sum_{x \in \mathsf{MK}^t\mathsf{P}[s]} \frac{1}{2^{c+1}} \Pr[x' \leftarrow \{0,1\}^n \cap \mathsf{MK}^t\mathsf{P}[s] : x' = x] \cdot \Pr[H(x) \neq 1]$$
$$> \frac{1}{2^{c+1}} \alpha(n^*)$$
$$= \alpha'(n^*)$$

which contradicts to the condition (1).

We turn to proving that, on input a random NO instance of $\mathsf{MK}^t\mathsf{P}[s]$, H will output 0 with probability at least $1 - \alpha(n^*)$. This follows from the fact that the random NO distribution is statistically close the uniform distribution. In more detail, let

$$Z_1 = \mathcal{U}_n$$

be the uniform distribution over n-bit strings. And let

$$Z_2 = \{x \leftarrow \{0,1\}^n : x \notin \mathsf{MK}^t\mathsf{P}[s]\}$$

be the distribution of a random NO instance. Recall that by condition (2), the probability that H outputs 1 over Z_1 is at least

$$\Pr[x \leftarrow Z_1 : H(x) = 1] \leq \frac{1}{\alpha'(n^*)} = \alpha(n^*)/c'$$

We then show that statistical distance between Z_1 and Z_2 is at most $2^{-n+s(n)+1}$. By Fact 4, there are at most $2^{s(n)+1}$ n-bit strings that are YES-instances of $\mathsf{MK}^t\mathsf{P}[s]$, thus there are at most $2^{s(n)+1}$ points that have higher probability mass in Z_1 than in Z_2, and the difference in probability mass for each such point is exactly 2^{-n}. By the observation noted after the definition of statistical distance[13], it follows that the statistical distance is upper bounded by

$$\frac{1}{2^{n-s(n)-1}} \leq \frac{1}{2^{n^*+1}} \leq \frac{\alpha(n^*)}{2}.$$

(The first inequality holds since (1) we are only considering threshold functions such that $s(n) \leq n/10$, and thus $n - s(n) + 1 \geq n - n/10 + 1$; (2) recall that $n^* \leq s(n) + 1$ by Claim 1. The second inequality holds since $\alpha(n) = \frac{1}{n^\beta}$ for any constant $\beta > 0$.) Thus, the probability that H outputs 1 over Z_2 is at most

$$\Pr[x \leftarrow Z_2 : H(x) = 1]$$
$$\leq \Pr[x \leftarrow Z_1 : H(x) = 1] + \mathsf{SD}(Z_1, Z_2)$$
$$\leq \alpha(n^*)/c' + \alpha(n^*)/2 < \alpha(n^*)$$

Finally, notice that there are infinitely many such input lengths n, and we conclude that H also breaks the (T, α) average-case* hardness of $\mathsf{MK}^t\mathsf{P}[s]$.

Note that our proof only makes black-box use of the heuristic* H, and we conclude that it also holds in the non-uniform setting. ∎

Constructing a Weak Family of PRGs. We turn to showing that the function $g(\Pi', y)$ (specifically, the family g') we construct in Sect. 5.2 will be a weak family of PRGs.

Let us briefly recall the construction and introduce the parameters. We consider any polynomial $t(n) \geq (1+\varepsilon)n, \varepsilon > 0$. Our security parameter is denoted by λ. (We will base the security of our construction on the hardness of $\mathsf{MK}^t\mathsf{P}[s]$ with respect to input length n such that $n = n_s(\lambda)$.) We will consider a PRF input length parameter k satisfying $k = k(\lambda) = 1/8 \log n_s(\lambda)$. Let f be the function, g' be the family, $k' = k'(\lambda), \ell = \ell(\lambda), d = d(\lambda), m = m(\lambda)$ be the parameters as defined in Sect. 5.2. We are going to show that g' is a weak family of PRGs.

---

[13] That is, that the optimal distinguisher is $T = \{\omega : \Pr[Z_1 = \omega] > \Pr[Z_2 = \omega]\}$.

Lemma 23 *Let $t, s, s_n, k, k', \ell, d, m, f, g$ be as above, $s(n) \le n/2$. Let $\alpha'(\lambda) = \frac{1}{c'\lambda^\beta}$ be a hardness parameter (for some constant $\beta > 0, c' > 0$).*

Assume $\mathsf{MK}^t\mathsf{P}[s]$ is (n^3, α')-HoA^* w.r.t. the (t, s)-universal distribution and the uniform distribution. Then, $\{g'_{\Pi'}(1^\lambda) : \{0,1\}^{d(\lambda)} \to \{0,1\}^{m(\lambda)}\}_{\Pi' \in \{0,1\}^{\lambda+1}}$ is a $(\alpha'(\lambda)/4)$-weak family of $(T'(\lambda), \varepsilon'(\lambda))$-PRGs where $T'(\lambda) = 2^{2k(\lambda)}$, $\varepsilon'(\lambda) = \frac{1}{2^{k(\lambda)}}$.

In addition, the lemma also holds in the non-uniform setting.

Proof: We suppose for contradiction that there exists a distinguisher D that breaks the weak family of PRGs g'. Since D is a good distinguisher, it follows that there exist infinitely many $\lambda \in \mathbb{N}$ such that for at least a $1 - \alpha'(\lambda)/4$ fraction of its index $\Pi' \in \{0,1\}^{\lambda+1}$,

$$| \Pr[D(1^\lambda, g'_{\Pi'}(\mathcal{U}_d)) = 1] - \Pr[D(1^\lambda, \mathcal{U}_m) = 1]| \ge \varepsilon'(\lambda)$$

We will use this distinguisher D to construct an heuristic* H breaking the average-case* hardness of $\mathsf{MK}^t\mathsf{P}[s]$.

Our heuristic* H, on input a string $x \in \{0,1\}^n$, will proceed as follows.

- H first computes the security parameter $\lambda = s(n)$, the input length parameters $k = k(\lambda)$ and $k' = 8k$, and the other parameters needed in the construction of g.
- Let x' be the first $2^{k'}$ bits of x, and H will view x' as the truth table of a function $f_{x'}$ $\{0,1\}^{k'} \to \{0,1\}$.
- H will instantiate the NW generator NW with the function $f_{x'}$ (and the design $\mathcal{I}$ as in Sect. 5.2), and check whether the distinguisher D (on input the security parameter λ) will distinguish $\mathsf{NW}^{x'}_{\mathcal{I}}(\mathcal{U}_d)$ from random with advantage at least $\varepsilon'(\lambda)/2$.
- In more detail, let ρ_x denote the random variable $D(1^\lambda, \mathsf{NW}^{x'}_{\mathcal{I}}(\mathcal{U}_d))$ and θ denote the random variable $D(1^\lambda, \mathcal{U}_m)$. H will estimate $\mathbb{E}[\rho_x]$ by drawing $4\frac{1}{(\varepsilon'(\lambda)/8)^2} \log(\frac{1}{\alpha'(\lambda)/8})$ samples from ρ_x and take the average. Let ρ^* be the random variable of the average value. (Note that by the Hoeffding's Inequality, ρ^* is guaranteed to be (additively) $(\varepsilon'(\lambda)/8)$-close to $\mathbb{E}[\rho_x]$ with probability $\ge 1 - \alpha'(\lambda)/8$.) We repeat the above procedure to also estimate $\mathbb{E}[\theta]$ and denote the average by θ^*.
- Finally, H will output 1 if $|\rho^* - \theta^*| \ge \varepsilon'(\lambda)/2$.

We turn to analyzing the running time of H. Drawing a sample from ρ_x requires to run $\mathsf{NW}^{x'}_{\mathcal{I}}(\mathcal{U}_d)$. Using the same analysis as in Sect. 5.2 for $g(\Pi', y)$, we conclude that $\mathsf{NW}^{x'}_{\mathcal{I}}(\mathcal{U}_d)$ runs in time $O(2^k \cdot (n + \ell^2)) \le O(n^2)$. In addition, we need to evaluate the distinguisher D, which takes time $T'(\lambda)$. Note that drawing a sample from θ takes at most as much time as sampling from ρ_x, we conclude that H runs in time $4\frac{1}{(\varepsilon'(\lambda)/8)^2} \log(\frac{1}{\alpha'(\lambda)/8}) \cdot 2(O(n^2) + T'(\lambda)) \le O(2^{2k} \log \frac{1}{\alpha'(\lambda)}) \cdot O(2^{2k} + n^2) \le n^3$.

We proceed to showing that H is a good heuristic*: H will output 1 with probability at least $1 - \alpha'(n^*)$ over the distribution for YES instances, H will output 0 also with probability at least $1 - \alpha'(n^*)$ over the distribution for NO instances, and this holds for infinitely many input lengths n (where n^* is the "normalized" input length as in Definition 21). Fix some sufficiently large security parameter λ on which the distinguisher D breaks the weak family of PRGs g', and consider an input length n such that $n = n_s(\lambda)$.

We first analyze how our algorithm performs over the (t, s)-universal distribution $D_{\mathsf{univ},n}$ on input length n. It is helpful here to introduce a new notation $\mathsf{tt}(\cdot)$: For any binary function f, let $\mathsf{tt}(f)$ denote its truth table, and let $\mathsf{tt}_n(f)$ denote the n-bit prefix of the truth table. Consider the following two distribution:

- $\{x' = [x]_{2^{k'}} : x \leftarrow D_{\mathsf{univ},n}\}$, and
- $\{\mathsf{tt}_{2^{k'}}(f(\Pi', \cdot)) : \Pi' \leftarrow \{0,1\}^{\lambda+1}\}$

where $[x]_{2^{k'}}$ denotes the $(2^{k'})$-bit of x. Observe that (1) the above two distributions are identically distributed, (2) $g'_{\Pi'}(\mathcal{U}_d)$ will be identical to $\mathsf{NW}_{\mathcal{I}}^{x'}(\mathcal{U}_d)$ as long as $\mathsf{tt}_{2^{k'}}(f(\Pi, \cdot)) = x'$, and (3) over a random program Π' sampled from the second distribution, with probability at least $1 - \alpha'(\lambda)/4$, the distinguisher will distinguish $g'_{\Pi'}(\mathcal{U}_d)$ from random with advantage at least $\varepsilon'(\lambda)$ (which follows from the fact that D is a good distinguisher breaking g'). We conclude that (3) will still hold if we replace $f(\Pi', \cdot)$ by $f_{x'}$, and thus with probability at least $1 - \alpha'(\lambda)/4$ over $x \leftarrow D_{\mathsf{univ},n}$, D will distinguish $\mathsf{NW}_{\mathcal{I}}^{x'}(\mathcal{U}_d)$ from random and it holds that

$$|\mathsf{E}[\rho_x] - \mathsf{E}[\theta]| \geq \varepsilon'(\lambda) \tag{3}$$

Recall that ρ^* (resp θ^*) is our empirical estimation of $E[\rho_x]$ (resp $\mathsf{E}[\theta]$). As argued before, using Hoeffding's Inequality (and taking a Union Bound), we can show that except for probability $\alpha'(\lambda)/4$, the two estimations will be close to their expectations with difference $\leq \varepsilon'(\lambda)/8$. If so, it follows from Eq. 3 that the difference between their estimations should be at least

$$|\rho^* - \theta^*| \geq |\mathsf{E}[\rho_x] - \mathsf{E}[\theta]| - \varepsilon'(\lambda)/4 \geq \varepsilon'(\lambda)/2 \tag{4}$$

By applying the Union Bound again (taking into account that Eq. 3 holds with high probability and our estimations are accurate with high probability), it follows Eq. 4 holds with probability at least

$$1 - \alpha'(\lambda)/4 - \alpha'(\lambda)/4 = 1 - \frac{1}{2\lambda^\beta c'} \geq 1 - \frac{1}{(n^*)^\beta c'} = 1 - \alpha(n^*)$$

where the first inequality holds since recall that $\alpha'(\lambda) = \frac{1}{\lambda^\beta c'}$ for some constants β, c', and the second inequality holds since, by Claim 1, $\lambda = s(n) \leq n^* - 1$. Finally, note that if Eq. 4 holds, our algorithm H will output 1, which concludes that H outputs 1 with probability $\geq 1 - \alpha(n^*)$ over the YES distribution.

We move on to proving that our algorithm H will output 0 with probability at least $1 - \alpha'(n^*)$ over the uniform distribution over $x \in \{0,1\}^n$. We refer to a string $x \in \{0,1\}^n$ as being *bad* if our distinguisher D distinguishes $\mathsf{NW}_{\mathcal{I}}^{x'}(\mathcal{U}_d)$ (where x' is the first $2^{k'}$ bits of x) from random with at least $\varepsilon'(\lambda)/4$; that is,

$$|\mathsf{E}[\rho_x] - \mathsf{E}[\theta]| \geq \varepsilon'(\lambda)/4 \tag{5}$$

Notice that if a string x is *not* bad, using the same Chernoff/Hoeffding-type argument we did for YES instances, it follows that $H(x)$ will output 0 with probability at least $1 - \alpha'(\lambda)/4 = 1 - \alpha'(s(n))/4 \geq 1 - \alpha'(n^*)/2$, as desired. Thus, we will show that the faction of bad strings over $\{0,1\}^n$ is very small. We consider any bad string $x \in \{0,1\}^n$. It follows from Eq. 5 that $D(1^\lambda)$ will distinguish $\mathsf{NW}_{\mathcal{I}}^{x'}(\mathcal{U}_d)$ from random with advantage

$$|\Pr[D(1^\lambda, \mathsf{NW}_{\mathcal{I}}^{x'}(\mathcal{U}_d)) = 1] - \Pr[D(1^\lambda, \mathcal{U}_m) = 1]| \geq \varepsilon'(\lambda)/4$$

Recall from Lemma 16 that $\mathcal{I}$ is a (d, ℓ, κ)-design. By Lemma 17, the Nisan-Wigderson reconstruction algorithm $\mathsf{NWRecon}^{D(1^\lambda, \cdot)}(x')$ will output (with high probability) a program M that given oracle access to D approximates the function $f_{x'}$ where $\mathsf{tt}(f_{x'}) = x'$ (and therefore, approximates the prefix of the string x). In more detail, the program M is of description length $\leq m 2^\kappa + m + d + O(\log d)$, and the oracle-aided program $M' = M^{D(1^\lambda, \cdot)}(\mathcal{I})$ will satisfy that

$$\Pr[p \leftarrow [2^{k'}] : M'(p) = x_p]$$
$$= \Pr[p \leftarrow [2^{k'}] : M'(p) = f_{x'}(p)]$$
$$\geq \frac{1}{2} + \frac{\varepsilon'(\lambda)}{8m} = \frac{1}{2} + \frac{1}{8 \cdot 2^k \cdot 2^k} \geq \frac{1}{2} + \frac{1}{2^{(5/16)k'}}$$

where the last inequality holds when $k' = 8k, k = 1/8 \log n$ is sufficiently large. We will further argue that M' has a small description length: Consider an implementation of M' with the program M, the code of D, parameters λ, ℓ, k hardwired in it. It first invokes the design generation algorithm to generate the design $\mathcal{I}$. It will then simulate $M^{D(1^\lambda, \cdot)}(\mathcal{I})$ and will output whatever M outputs. Notice that hardwiring the code of D takes either $O(1)$ bits (when D is a uniform attacker), or $O(2^{2k})$ bits (when D is a non-uniform attacker since D runs in time 2^{2k}), and storing the parameters takes $O(\log \lambda) + O(\log d)$ bits. So when k is sufficiently large, the description length of M' is at most

$$m 2^\kappa + m + d + O(2^{2k}) + O(\log d) + O(\log \lambda)$$
$$= 2^k \cdot 2^k + 2^k + O(k^2) + O(2^{2k}) + O(\log k^2) + O(\log s(n))$$
$$\leq O(2^{2k}) + 2^k + O(k^2) \leq 2^{(5/16)k'}$$

due to our choice of parameters (where $d = O(\ell^2) = O(k^2)$ and $k' = 8k$). Thus, we conclude that for any bad $x \in \{0,1\}^n$, its $(2^{k'})$-bit prefix can be approximated by a program (i.e., M') of description length $\leq 2^{(5/16)k'}$ with probability at least $\frac{1}{2} + \frac{1}{2^{(5/16)k'}}$. By Lemma 12, a random string x is bad with probability at most

$$2^{(5/16)k'} \cdot \exp(-2^{(1-2(5/16))k'}/2 + 2^{(5/16)k'} + 2)$$
$$= 2^{(5/16)k'} \cdot \exp(-2^{(6/16)k'}/2 + 2^{(5/16)k'} + 2)$$
$$= n^{5/16} \cdot \exp(-n^{6/16}/2 + n^{5/16} + 2)$$
$$\leq 2^{-n^{5/16}} \leq \alpha'(n^*)/2$$

where $\exp(\cdot)$ denotes $2^{(\cdot)}$ and the last inequality holds when n is sufficiently large since $n^* \leq n$ and $\alpha'(n^*) = \frac{1}{(n^*)^{\beta}c'}$ for some constants $\beta, c' > 0$. Taken this together with the fact that H will output 0 with probability at least $1 - \alpha'(n^*)/2$ when the input string x is not bad, we conclude that $H(x)$ outputs 0 over the uniform distribution with probability at least $1 - \alpha'(n^*)$, which finishes the proof for the NO instances. ■

Remark 1 (A note on non-black box nature of the reduction). We remark that the proof of Lemma 23 implicitly defines a reduction R that breaks the average-case* hardness of $\mathsf{MK}^t\mathsf{P}[s]$ given any *"efficient"* machine D that breaks the weak family of PRGs. Although the reduction only accesses D as a black-box, the reduction is actually *non-black box* because in the analysis of the reduction, we are relying on the fact that D has a relatively short description—this is instrumental on argue that we succeed on NO instances (where D is used to approximately compress the instance x).

Amplifying Weak Families of PRGs. We proceed to proving that the construction h in Sect. 5.2 will be a PRF assuming that g' is a weak family of PRGs. In Sect. 3, we have shown that weak families of PRGs can be amplified by taking the xor of the independent outputs. Notice that if we consider the function h' that takes as input a seed z and outputs the truth table of $h(z, \cdot)$, this function is the xor of the function g'. By Lemma 11, we conclude that h' is a PRG, and it follows that h will be a PRF since each bit on the truth table of $h(z, \cdot)$ can be computed explicitly (as argued in Sect. 5.2).

Returning to Proving Theorem 18. We here present a formal proof of Theorem 18.

Proof: [of Theorem 18] Let t, s, n_s, k, γ as in the theorem statement. Let c' be the constant as in Lemma 22. We first show that h will be a PRF with desired security if we assume $\mathsf{MK}^t\mathsf{P}[s]$ is (n^3, α)-HoA*, and we will argue that this proof implicitly defines a security reduction we need.

We pick the constant γ_0 to be $4c'$ and the constant $\delta = 1/16$. It follows (from Lemma 22) that $\mathsf{MK}^t\mathsf{P}[s]$ is $(n^3, \alpha/c')$-HoA* w.r.t. the (t, s)-universal distribution and the uniform distribution. Let $n' = n_s(\lambda)$. Then by Lemma 23, g' is a $(\alpha(\lambda)/(4c'))$-weak family of $(T'(\lambda), \varepsilon'(\lambda))$-PRG where $T'(\lambda) = 2^{2k} = n'^{1/4}$ and $\varepsilon'(\lambda) = \frac{1}{2^k} = \frac{1}{n'^{1/8}}$. Recall that g' runs in time $t'(\lambda) \stackrel{\text{def}}{=} 2^k(t(\lambda) + O(\ell^2)) = O(2^k t(\lambda))$.

We will rely on Lemma 11 to show that h is a PRF. However, Lemma 11 is only stated with respect to PRGs (instead of PRFs). As mentioned before, it suffices to show that h, being viewed as a PRG (by considering the function outputting the truth table of h on each seed as a pseudorandom string), is a PRG. If so, it follows that h will be a PRF since the pseudorandom string can be computed locally (as argued in Sect. 5.2). By Lemma 11, we have that h is a $(T''(\lambda), \varepsilon''(\lambda))$-PRG (when being viewed as a PRG) where $T''(\lambda) = T'(\lambda) - \gamma t'(\lambda)$

and $\varepsilon''(\lambda) = 2\max\{(1 - \alpha(\lambda)/(4c'))^\gamma, \gamma\varepsilon'(\lambda)\}$. Notice that

$$T''(\lambda) \geq n'^{1/4} - \gamma O(2^k t(\lambda)) \geq n'^{1/4} - \gamma_0 \log n'/\alpha(\lambda) \cdot O(2^k t(\lambda)) \geq n'^\delta$$

since (1) we only consider $\alpha(\lambda) = 1/\lambda^\beta$, $\beta > 0$, and $\lambda = s(n') = n'^{o(1)}$ (taken together, this implies that $1/\alpha(\lambda) = n'^{o(1)}$), and (2) $t(\lambda) = n'^{o(1)}$ since t is a polynomial. We turn to prove that $\varepsilon''(\lambda)$ is also small. $\varepsilon''(\lambda)$ is the maximal of the two values, and we will prove that each of the values will be upper bounded by $\frac{1}{n'^{1/16}} = \frac{1}{n'^\delta}$. Observe that on one hand,

$$2(1 - \alpha(\lambda)/(4c'))^\gamma = 2(1 - \alpha(\lambda)/(4c'))^{4c'/\alpha(\lambda)\cdot\log n'} \leq 2(1/e)^{\log n'} \leq \frac{1}{n'^{1/16}}$$

And on the other hand,

$$2\gamma\frac{1}{n'^{1/8}} = 2(4c'/\alpha(\lambda)\log n')\frac{1}{n'^{1/8}} \leq \frac{1}{n'^{1/16}}$$

since as argued above, $1/\alpha(\lambda) = n^{o(1)}$. This concludes that h is a $(n'^\delta, \frac{1}{n'^\delta})$-PRG.

Notice that our security proof (presented above, going through Lemma 22, Lemma 23, and Lemma 11) defines a security reduction that, given an attacker A that breaks the PRF h on security parameter 1^λ, breaks the hardness of $\mathsf{MK}^t\mathsf{P}[s]$ on input length $\lambda = s(n)$.

Also notice that the proof also works in the non-uniform setting since the lemmas needed in the proof all hold in the non-uniform setting. ∎

References

1. Allender, E.: When worlds collide: Derandomization, lower bounds, and kolmogorov complexity. In: International Conference on Foundations of Software Technology and Theoretical Computer Science, pp. 1–15. Springer (2001)
2. Allender, E., Buhrman, H., Koucký, M., Van Melkebeek, D., Ronneburger, D.: Power from random strings. SIAM J. Comput. **35**(6), 1467–1493 (2006)
3. Banerjee, A., Peikert, C., Rosen, A.: Pseudorandom functions and lattices. In: Annual International Conference on the Theory and Applications of Cryptographic Techniques, pp. 719–737. Springer (2012)
4. Bogdanov, Andrej, Rosen, Alon: Pseudorandom functions: three decades later. In: Tutorials on the Foundations of Cryptography. ISC, pp. 79–158. Springer, Cham (2017). https://doi.org/10.1007/978-3-319-57048-8_3
5. Canetti, R., Goldreich, O., Goldwasser, S., Micali, S.: Resettable zero-knowledge (extended abstract). In: STOC 2000, pp. 235–244 (2000). https://doi.org/10.1145/335305.335334
6. Carmosino, M.L., Impagliazzo, R., Kabanets, V., Kolokolova, A.: Learning algorithms from natural proofs. In: 31st Conference on Computational Complexity (CCC 2016). Schloss Dagstuhl-Leibniz-Zentrum fuer Informatik (2016)
7. Chen, L., Hirahara, S., Oliveira, I.C., Pich, J., Rajgopal, N., Santhanam, R.: Beyond natural proofs: Hardness magnification and locality. In: 11th Innovations in Theoretical Computer Science Conference (ITCS 2020). Schloss Dagstuhl-Leibniz-Zentrum für Informatik (2020)

8. Chen, L., Jin, C., Williams, R.R.: Hardness magnification for all sparse np languages. In: 2019 IEEE 60th Annual Symposium on Foundations of Computer Science (FOCS), pp. 1240–1255. IEEE (2019)

9. Chen, L., McKay, D.M., Murray, C.D., Williams, R.R.: Relations and equivalences between circuit lower bounds and karp-lipton theorems. In: 34th Computational Complexity Conference (CCC 2019). Schloss Dagstuhl-Leibniz-Zentrum fuer Informatik (2019)

10. Chen, L., Tell, R.: Bootstrapping results for threshold circuits "just beyond" known lower bounds. In: Proceedings of the 51st Annual ACM SIGACT Symposium on Theory of Computing, pp. 34–41 (2019)

11. Chen, L., Tell, R.: Hardness vs randomness, revised: uniform, non-black-box, and instance-wise. Electronic Colloquium on Computational Complexity (2021). https://eccc.weizmann.ac.il/report/2021/080/l

12. Dodis, Y., Impagliazzo, R., Jaiswal, R., Kabanets, V.: Security amplification for interactive cryptographic primitives. In: Theory of Cryptography: 6th Theory of Cryptography Conference, TCC 2009, San Francisco, CA, USA, March 15-17, 2009. Proceedings 6, pp. 128–145. Springer (2009)

13. Goldreich, O.: Foundations of Cryptography — Basic Tools. Cambridge University Press (2001)

14. Goldreich, O., Goldwasser, S., Micali, S.: How to construct random functions. In: FOCS (1984)

15. Goldreich, O., Goldwasser, S., Micali, S.: On the cryptographic applications of random functions. In: Advances in Cryptology: Proceedings of CRYPTO 84 4, pp. 276–288. Springer (1985)

16. Goldreich, O., Nisan, N., Wigderson, A.: On yao's xor lemma. Technical Report TR95–050, Electronic Colloquium on Computational Complexity (1995)

17. Goldreich, O., Ostrovsky, R.: Software protection and simulation on oblivious rams. J. ACM **43**(3), 431–473 (1996)

18. Goldwasser, S., Micali, S.: Probabilistic encryption. J. Comput. Syst. Sci. **28**(2), 270–299 (1984)

19. Haitner, I., Harnik, D., Reingold, O.: On the power of the randomized iterate. In: CRYPTO, pp. 22–40 (2006)

20. Haitner, I., Reingold, O., Vadhan, S.: Efficiency improvements in constructing pseudorandom generators from one-way functions. In: Proceedings of the Forty-Second ACM Symposium on Theory of Computing, pp. 437–446 (2010)

21. Hartman, T., Raz, R.: On the distribution of the number of roots of polynomials and explicit weak designs. Random Struct. Algorithms **23**(3), 235–263 (2003)

22. Hartmanis, J.: Generalized kolmogorov complexity and the structure of feasible computations. In: 24th Annual Symposium on Foundations of Computer Science (sfcs 1983). pp. 439–445, November 1983. https://doi.org/10.1109/SFCS.1983.21

23. Håstad, J., Impagliazzo, R., Levin, L.A., Luby, M.: A pseudorandom generator from any one-way function. SIAM J. Comput. **28**(4), 1364–1396 (1999)

24. Hirahara, S.: Non-black-box worst-case to average-case reductions within NP. In: 59th IEEE Annual Symposium on Foundations of Computer Science, FOCS 2018, pp. 247–258 (2018)

25. Holenstein, T.: Pseudorandom generators from one-way functions: a simple construction for any hardness. In: TCC, pp. 443–461 (2006)

26. Impagliazzo, R., Wigderson, A.: $P = BPP$ if e requires exponential circuits: Derandomizing the xor lemma. In: STOC 1997, pp. 220–229 (1997)

27. Kabanets, V., Cai, J.: Circuit minimization problem. In: Proceedings of the Thirty-Second Annual ACM Symposium on Theory of Computing, May 21-23, 2000, Portland, OR, USA, pp. 73–79 (2000)
28. Ko, K.: On the notion of infinite pseudorandom sequences. Theor. Comput. Sci. 48(3), 9–33 (1986)
29. Kolmogorov, A.N.: Three approaches to the quantitative definition of information. Int. J. Comput. Math. 2(1–4), 157–168 (1968)
30. Liu, Y., Pass, R.: On one-way functions and Kolmogorov complexity. In: 61st IEEE Annual Symposium on Foundations of Computer Science, FOCS 2020, Durham, NC, USA, November 16-19, 2020, pp. 1243–1254. IEEE (2020)
31. Liu, Y., Pass, R.: Cryptography from sublinear time hardness of time-bounded kolmogorov complexity. In: STOC (2021)
32. Liu, Y., Pass, R.: Characterizing derandomization through hardness of levin-kolmogorov complexity. In CCC (2022)
33. Liu, Y., Pass, R.: On one-way functions and the worst-case hardness of time-bounded kolmogorov complexity. Cryptology ePrint Archive p. 1086 (2023)
34. Luby, M.G.: Pseudorandomness and cryptographic applications, vol. 1. Princeton University Press (1996)
35. Maurer, U., Tessaro, S.: Computational indistinguishability amplification: tight product theorems for system composition. In: Halevi, S. (ed.) CRYPTO 2009. LNCS, vol. 5677, pp. 355–373. Springer, Heidelberg (2009). https://doi.org/10.1007/978-3-642-03356-8_21
36. Mazor, N., Pass, R.: Counting unpredictable bits: A simple prg from one-way functions. Cryptology ePrint Archive (2023)
37. McKay, D.M., Murray, C.D., Williams, R.R.: Weak lower bounds on resource-bounded compression imply strong separations of complexity classes. In: Proceedings of the 51st Annual ACM SIGACT Symposium on Theory of Computing, pp. 1215–1225 (2019)
38. Naor, M., Reingold, O.: Synthesizers and their application to the parallel construction of pseudo-random functions. J. Comput. Syst. Sci. 58(2), 336–375 (1999)
39. Naor, M., Reingold, O.: Number-theoretic constructions of efficient pseudo-random functions. J. ACM (JACM) 51(2), 231–262 (2004)
40. Naor, M., Reingold, O., Rosen, A.: Pseudo-random functions and factoring. In: Proceedings of the Thirty-Second Annual ACM Symposium on Theory of Computing, pp. 11–20 (2000)
41. Nisan, N., Wigderson, A.: Hardness vs randomness. J. Comput. Syst. Sci. 49(2), 149–167 (1994)
42. Oliveira, I., Pich, J., Santhanam, R.: Hardness magnification near state-of-the-art lower bounds (2019)
43. Oliveira, I.C.: Randomness and intractability in kolmogorov complexity. In: 46th International Colloquium on Automata, Languages, and Programming (ICALP 2019). Schloss Dagstuhl-Leibniz-Zentrum fuer Informatik (2019)
44. Oliveira, I.C., Santhanam, R.: Hardness magnification for natural problems. In: 2018 IEEE 59th Annual Symposium on Foundations of Computer Science (FOCS), pp. 65–76. IEEE (2018)
45. Razborov, A.A., Rudich, S.: Natural proofs. J. Comput. Syst. Sci. 55(1), 24–35 (1997)
46. Sipser, M.: A complexity theoretic approach to randomness. In: Proceedings of the 15th Annual ACM Symposium on Theory of Computing, 25–27 April, 1983, Boston, Massachusetts, USA, pp. 330–335. ACM (1983)

47. Sudan, M., Trevisan, L., Vadhan, S.: Pseudorandom generators without the xor lemma. J. Comput. Syst. Sci. **62**(2), 236–266 (2001)
48. Trakhtenbrot, B.A.: A survey of Russian approaches to perebor (brute-force searches) algorithms. Annal. History Comput. **6**(4), 384–400 (1984)
49. Vadhan, S.P.: Pseudorandomness. Foundations and Trends® in Theoretical Comput. Sci. **7**(1–3), 1–336 (2012)
50. Vadhan, S.P., Zheng, C.J.: Characterizing pseudoentropy and simplifying pseudorandom generator constructions. In: STOC, pp. 817–836 (2012)
51. Valiant, L.G.: A theory of the learnable. Commun. ACM **27**(11), 1134–1142 (1984)
52. Yablonski, S.: The algorithmic difficulties of synthesizing minimal switching circuits. Problemy Kibernetiki **2**(1), 75–121 (1959)
53. Yablonski, S.V.: On the impossibility of eliminating perebor in solving some problems of circuit theory. Dokl. Akad. Nauk SSSR **124**(1), 44–47 (1959)
54. Yao, A.C.: Theory and applications of trapdoor functions (extended abstract). In: 23rd Annual Symposium on Foundations of Computer Science, Chicago, Illinois, USA, 3–5 November 1982, pp. 80–91 (1982)

Author Index

© International Association for Cryptologic Research 2024
M. Joye and G. Leander (Eds.): EUROCRYPT 2024, LNCS 14654, p. 407, 2024.
https://doi.org/10.1007/978-3-031-58737-5

Printed in the United States
by Baker & Taylor Publisher Services